STUDIES OF CONGRESS

STUDIES OF CONGRESS

edited by
Glenn R. Parker
Florida State University

a division of
Congressional Quarterly Inc.
1414 22nd Street N.W., Washington, D.C. 20037

Printed in the United States of America

Library of Congress Cataloging in Publication Data
    Main entry under title:

Studies of Congress

    Bibliography: p.
    Includes index.
    1. United States. Congress — Addresses, essays, lectures. I. Parker, Glenn R. II. Congressional Quarterly, inc.
JK1061.S78 1985   328.73   84-16993
ISBN 0-87187-333-8

To those who have stimulated my interest in the study of Congress:
Marv, Roger, and Dick

TABLE OF CONTENTS

PREFACE

This text is designed to address two traditionally important questions in political science: How are decisions made within the political system? How and why do institutions change? These questions underlie most of the research in a variety of areas in political science, from political theory to mathematical modeling, and serve as important guides to inquiry because they shed light on the operations of institutions and the behavior of political elites. They are especially valuable in the study of Congress and the behavior of its members. The question of how decisions are made within the political system directs our attention to the behavior of party leaders in Congress and the voting behavior of members on the floor and within committees; the question of institutional change provides the rationale for examining the decline of competition in congressional elections and how congressional norms and structures change over time.

With these questions in mind, I have selected 21 articles that explore central topics in the study of Congress from the perspective of both the House of Representatives and the Senate. This bicameral approach should broaden our understanding of how decisions are made within Congress, why Congress has changed in the ways that it has, and how the House and Senate differ.

My personal objective in organizing this reader was to encourage student interest in and research on the U.S. Congress. Course lectures and text-books provide students with only indirect contact with congressional research; rarely do they familiarize them with the elements of research design or the logic of inquiry. As a result, students often have little awareness of how questions about Congress have been formulated and analyzed. Direct exposure to the types of congressional research presented here should enhance student interest in the study of Congress and, I hope, stimulate further empirical research on congressional politics.

The book is divided into six research areas that span the study of Congress: the competition in congressional elections; the development and modification of House and Senate norms; the effects of conflict and consensus in congressional committee decision making; the strategies and tactics of legislative leaders and the constraints placed upon leadership influence; the major determinants of voting in the House and Senate; and the nature of congressional change. Each of these sections begins with a short essay that summarizes the basic literature on that topic and introduces the reader to the themes that are reflected in the articles that follow. At times, these essays fill gaps in the research and conclusions presented in the readings by supplying additional information. Thus, the essays complement and supplement the articles included in each section.

Preface

This book reflects my own biases concerning the major themes in the study of Congress and the best articles on these topics. Several criteria influenced my decisions on what to include. First, I chose to concentrate on those areas of legislative research where empirical findings and generalizations have begun to accumulate because research topics that are dominated by ambiguity and unbounded speculation are often as confusing to the congressional scholar as they are to the student. The book is organized around topics that are central to the study of Congress and also are capable of engaging and holding the interest of students.

Second, I tried to appeal to as wide a spectrum of students and legislative scholars as possible. I expect that what the reader will gain from exposure to these articles will vary according to his or her sophistication and level of education. Undergraduates will be able to understand the basic ideas and themes that are presented in the articles, but they may be unable to fully appreciate the finer aspects of the research question and its analysis. Graduate students, on the other hand, will find the research design and the logic of the analysis reported in the articles to be as invaluable as the substantive conclusions and generalizations that are drawn from that research.

Third, I have included articles that span several years so that the findings reported in them would not be time bound. Finally, articles that build upon the work of others were included because they provide continuity with the past research on Congress and suggest useful avenues for further study. In sum, centrality of the research question, breadth of the analysis, simplicity of presentation, and continuity in the research were my criteria for selecting the articles.

My choices may differ in some ways from those that other scholars might make using these criteria, but that, I suggest, is a reflection of the wealth of good congressional research rather than any real differences of opinion.

Glenn R. Parker

ACKNOWLEDGMENTS

I would like to express my appreciation to those who have made this volume possible: To Joanne Daniels, Nancy Blanpied, Mary Ames Booker, Barbara de Boinville, and Margaret Thompson at Congressional Quarterly for the editorial guidance that they provided throughout the course of this project; to Susanne Miles, Betty Messer, and Mary Schneider for their cooperation in preparing the manuscript; and to Chuck Bullock, Larry Dodd, and Suzanne Parker for their advice as critical consumers of congressional research.

CONTRIBUTORS

Herbert B. Asher, *Ohio State University*
David W. Brady, *Rice University*
Charles S. Bullock III, *University of Georgia*
Joseph Cooper, *Rice University*
Lawrence C. Dodd, *Indiana University*
Richard F. Fenno, Jr., *University of Rochester*
John A. Ferejohn, *Stanford University*
Morris P. Fiorina, *Harvard University*
Barbara Hinckley, *University of Wisconsin, Madison*
Charles O. Jones, *University of Virginia*
John W. Kingdon, *University of Michigan*
David R. Mayhew, *Yale University*
Warren E. Miller, *Arizona State University*
James T. Murphy, *St. Johns University, Minnesota*
Norman J. Ornstein, *Catholic University*
Glenn R. Parker, *Florida State University*
Suzanne L. Parker, *Florida State University*
Robert L. Peabody, *Johns Hopkins University*
Nelson W. Polsby, *University of California, Berkeley*
Randall B. Ripley, *Ohio State University*
David W. Rohde, *Michigan State University*
Michael J. Scicchitano, *University of Georgia*
Barbara Sinclair, *University of California, Riverside*
Donald E. Stokes, *Princeton University*
Herbert F. Weisberg, *Ohio State University*

I

COMPETITION IN CONGRESSIONAL ELECTIONS

O ne of the most enduring features of congressional elections is the general lack of electoral competition. Whether measured in terms of interparty competition (Jones, 1964) or the election margins of incumbents (Mayhew, 1974), the picture remains the same: electoral competition in House elections is virtually nonexistent. Furthermore, the trend appears toward less rather than greater competition in House elections. This has led scholars to attribute the decline in competition to the electoral advantages that incumbents enjoy. The lack of electoral competition also has been evident in the split-ticket voting during presidential election years and the diminished effects of presidential "coattails" (Kritzer and Eubank, 1979; Calvert and Ferejohn, 1983). These findings suggest that House elections are relatively insulated from waves of national sentiment and generally immune to the effects of national events. The incumbency advantage serves as the focus for the discussion of congressional elections.

Early research on congressional elections suggested that the outcomes of House elections reflected "the underlying division of party loyalties" (Campbell, 1966, p. 457). The relationship was especially noticeable in midterm election results: "the low frequency of deviation from party, together with the low frequency of independent voting, indicates that the meaning of the midterm vote depends in large part on the nature of party voting" (Stokes and Miller, 1966, p. 198). This characterization of congressional elections is no longer valid because partisan defections in congressional elections have increased along with split-ticket voting. Previous findings about the importance of party in congressional voting were based on elections where party loyalty was, indeed, an important deterrent to partisan defection. But since the mid-1960s partisan defections have increased (Bullock and Scicchitano, 1982). In fact, the percentage of defectors has doubled between the first national studies of congressional elections in 1958 and those in 1982. Clearly, party loyalty no longer pays the high dividends of the past; incumbency appears to have replaced the party as the dominant influence on congressional voting.

Without doubt, House incumbents have been remarkably successful in taking advantage of their status: about 90 percent of incumbents seeking reelection have been victorious during the last few decades. Not only are House

3

incumbents frequently returned to office, but their congressional districts are becoming increasingly safe. Since the mid-1960s House incumbents have been able to manufacture large and relatively constant election margins for themselves (Erikson, 1972; Mayhew, 1974; Fiorina, 1977a).

In the past, marginal districts have accounted for the vast change in the composition of Congress; national swings, such as occurred in 1964, can exact a high toll in representatives from such districts. Marginal districts normally are defined by congressional victories within the 50-55 percent range. These slim margins make such districts especially susceptible to volatile national forces and to stiff electoral challenges. The decline in the number of these districts enhances the stability of Congress and reduces the policy changes that often occur with congressional turnover. House incumbents are the causes, as well as the beneficiaries, of the decline in marginal districts. The benefits that accrue to incumbents provide some explanation of their ability to eliminate sources of potential electoral threat.

Visibility

House elections are low-information affairs. It is a struggle for even the most dedicated and avid followers of congressional politics to obtain news about the ongoing House elections (Stokes and Miller, 1966). The incumbent's advantage here is clear: repeated exposure through trips to the district (Fenno, 1978; Parker, 1980b) and mass mailings (Cover, 1977) ensures greater voter recognition. And candidate visibility is essential to attract support from the opposition party: "However little the public may know of those seeking office, any information at all about the rival party's candidate creates the possibility of a choice deviating from party" (Stokes and Miller, 1966, p. 204). "To be perceived at all is to be perceived favorably" (Stokes and Miller, 1966, p. 205) is an advantage that largely falls to incumbents and contrasts sharply with the invisibility of challengers (Hinckley, 1980; Mann and Wolfinger, 1980; Jacobson, 1983). Fewer voters know, or can recognize, the name of the challenger compared to the name of the incumbent, and the differential is quite large.

House incumbents have an assortment of resources for promoting their visibility within their districts. The perquisites of office (Cover, 1977) provide a member with funds to operate district offices and/or mobile vans that keep the incumbent's name prominent within the district and the local press; these incumbent "enterprises" (Salisbury and Shepsle, 1981) are staffed and operated at public expense. In addition, House incumbents have use of the congressional frank that permits them to send mail to their constituents also free of charge. The electoral relevance of such mass mailings is evident by the cycles in their distribution:

> Relatively quiet in nonelection years, the folding room moves into a higher gear as elections approach. Immediately before an election the folding room is pressed still further as a last minute surge of material is sent down from congressional offices. There follows a brief, tranquil period before Congress gets back to business again (Cover, 1977, p. 538).

To curb the obvious electoral exploitation of the franking privilege, Congress has prohibited franked mail from being distributed less than 60 days before an election. Nonetheless, mass mailings retain their electoral value. They often elicit constituent opinion and in the process give voters a feeling that their representative is interested in their opinions. And it may behoove members of Congress to follow the results of their constituent polls despite the potential bias in the return rate of the questionnaires: the opinion surveys that are returned tend to come from those who are potential supporters of the incumbent (Stolarek, Rood, and Taylor, 1981). Therefore, if there is a bias, it works in the incumbent's favor — he or she is apt to hear from likely supporters. Clearly, keeping this segment of the constituency happy makes good electoral sense.

Mass mailings also serve to "advertise" the incumbent's service to the district and to generate favorable images and electoral support among constituents (Mayhew, 1974). The message contained in these mailings may be just as important as the volume of mail reaching citizens. In these mailings members emphasize the ways in which they are helping constituents by gaining influence within the federal government and Congress, bringing federal money to the region, and representing district sentiment within Congress. As members advertise their service to the district, they implicitly (and, in many instances, explicitly) encourage their constituents to seek assistance from them. This provides representatives with greater contact with their constituents and increases opportunities for cultivating a favorable image among potential voters (Parker, 1980a).

Finally, mass mailings also provide incumbents with opportunities to "claim credit" for whatever benefits the district may be gaining from federal programs. Each member of Congress tries "to peel off pieces of governmental accomplishment for which he can believably generate a sense of responsibility" (Mayhew, 1974, p. 53). Members can claim credit for resolving constituent problems and grievances and providing pork-barrel projects for the district such as federal contracts and buildings. Credit-claiming, like advertising, is a useful way of cultivating a favorable image. Each activity keeps the incumbent's name noticeable to constituents. The ubiquitous nature of representative-constituent contacts and the information obtained from them provide effective channels for disseminating the incumbent's name.

The increase in the electoral safety of House incumbents that began in the mid-1960s, however, cannot be attributed to visibility alone because there has not been a corresponding growth in that visibility (Ferejohn, 1977). House incumbents may maintain an edge over their challengers in terms of visibility, but that advantage does not easily translate into safe electoral margins. It seems that candidate awareness is a function of how much constituents know about the incumbents and challengers (Parker, 1981b): the greater availability of information about incumbents creates a greater awareness of them; the scarcity of information available about most congressional challengers, as well as the greater costs of obtaining that information, account for their relative invisibility. The greater ease with which voters can obtain information about incumbents, therefore, may explain their higher profile within the electorate. Nonetheless, it

5

fails to account for the gradual disappearance of the marginal congressional district.

Campaign Spending

House incumbents have another advantage over their challengers: the ability to generate large campaign contributions. Regardless of ideological and policy differences, most interest groups channel their contributions to elected representatives. Such funds enable incumbents to purchase television and radio time, to support campaign staffs, and to design and circulate a variety of campaign materials. Ironically, the fact is that House incumbents rarely need to spend much money to defeat their normally underfinanced opponents because the "perks" of office provide a sizable financial advantage, perhaps as much as $400,000. House incumbents have a full-time staff that functions as a campaign organization both at and between elections. Mass mailings, telephone, and stationery allowances also ease the financial burden on the representatives' campaign funds. Because the resources at the command of incumbents are extensive and electorally useful, they appear to spend in response to the electoral threat:

> Incumbents, then, acquire and spend funds only in proportion to the perceived necessity to do so. And they can usually get all they feel they need, although they may not enjoy doing it (Jacobson, 1980, p. 139).

House incumbents who are facing a severe electoral threat may find it necessary to spend large sums of money on their campaigns, but most members avoid doing so. In fact, if an incumbent is forced to compete with a challenger in terms of campaign expenditures, he or she is in real trouble and is likely to lose the congressional race. For most incumbents, campaign spending is of marginal value because of the vast campaign resources supplied and subsidized by the government and the weak financial position of most congressional challengers. Challengers, however, appear to benefit from campaign spending, perhaps because it purchases the visibility and campaign materials necessary to wage a serious race.

In addition to reactive spending, incumbents also engage in preemptive spending. A major advantage incumbents have over their challengers is the ability to spend campaign funds early in the campaign:

> With surpluses from the previous race and early contributions to the current one, they can pace themselves better across the campaign and exert an influence on the nature of the opposition they eventually will face (Goldenberg and Traugott, 1984, p. 95).

Preemptive spending involves accumulating large campaign "war chests" through fund-raising activities and spending these funds well in advance of the general election in an effort to deter serious electoral opposition. If successful, reactive spending may be unnecessary because "potentially strong opponents have dropped out of the primary race in the face of large sums of money stockpiled by an apparently invincible incumbent" (Goldenberg and Traugott, 1984, p. 94).

Redistricting

Media reports, anecdotes, and judicial rulings have convinced some that redistricting by state legislatures has contributed to the remarkable survival of House incumbents. Congressional districts normally are drawn with an eye to protecting as many incumbents as possible. The mix of "safe" Republican and Democratic congressional districts may depend upon which party controls the state legislature and governorship. Only judicial interference and pressure can normally prevent partisan manipulation of congressional district boundaries. Incumbents, therefore, can use their influence in the state legislature and party organization to ensure that whenever district lines are redrawn, the final configuration promotes their electoral security. The decline of the marginal congressional district may be a result of redistricting practices that favor established House incumbents:

> A major element in the job security of incumbents is their ability to exert significant control over the drawing of district boundaries; indeed, some recent redistricting laws have been described as the Incumbent Survival Acts of 1972 (Tufte, 1973, p. 551).

This explanation for the decline of the marginal district seems quite plausible. The Supreme Court's 1962 decision (*Baker v. Carr*) affirming the authority of the courts to consider redistricting cases, increased the opportunities for entrenching House incumbents by permitting the intrusion of political considerations in the redistricting process. Territorial swaps were a major way in which redistricting plans gained legislative and executive approval. Disregarding county lines in drawing congressional district lines to equalize populations created flexibility and even may have facilitated politically motivated territorial swaps.

Nonetheless, there is little evidence to support the redistricting explanation for the decline in the marginal district. The number of marginal congressional seats following state reapportionments has been reduced, but the decline also has occurred in constituencies that have escaped redistricting (Ferejohn, 1977). The redistricting process may have promoted the electoral safety of some House incumbents, but it cannot account for the increased security of others who avoided the process.

Weak Challengers

In light of the electoral strength of most House incumbents, it is not really too surprising that few relish the opportunity to challenge them (Kazee, 1983). Recruiting challengers is akin to asking someone not just to support a losing cause, but also to lead one. As a result, it is extremely difficult to find able politicians willing to challenge entrenched congressional incumbents. The poor quality of most challengers often produces even more lopsided incumbent victories (Jacobson and Kernell, 1981). Although poorly financed and less visible in comparison to House incumbents, the weakness of challengers also may be magnified by the popularity of incumbents.

7

Qualified candidates who could pose an effective challenge may avoid doing so if the incumbent is extremely popular within the district. If an incumbent has been weakened by political or ethical transgressions, the number and quality of challenges will increase. In that case, members from the incumbent's own party may even line up months before the primary election for a chance to run.

Incumbent Popularity

Perhaps the most obvious reason that House incumbents win so frequently and by such safe margins is that they are extremely popular among their constituents. The fact that the performance of House incumbents normally receives high marks from constituents has led Richard Fenno (1975) to ask, "if we love our Congressman, why not the Congress?" Historically, citizens have been critical of Congress as an institution but favorably disposed toward their own representatives (Parker, 1981a). To most constituents, their own representative is unique among legislators: he or she is more attentive to constituent interests, more honest, and generally "better" than most other members of Congress (Parker, 1981a). House incumbents are popular because they are able easily to satisfy the criteria that constituents use to evaluate their performance in office (Parker and Davidson, 1979).

Congress as a whole, however, is expected to meet far more exacting standards: the resolution of major social problems. That task is far more demanding than serving a single district (Parker and Davidson, 1979). Moreover, Congress does not enhance its public standing when it attempts to deal with pressing national issues. First, the legislative process is perceived as cumbersome and slow — two characterizations that generate negative attitudes. (Parker, 1981a). Second, any major policy resolution is almost certain to alienate significant segments of society. For example, Arthur Miller (1974) has shown that attempts by the federal government to pursue a "middle course" in terms of policy alternatives have served to alienate citizens on both the liberal and conservative ends of the ideological spectrum. And trust in government is an important component in popular evaluations of congressional performance. When individuals become disenchanted with government and lose faith in those that run it, they are unlikely to harbor positive feelings toward the institutions within that political system (Parker, 1981a). In light of these considerations, it is easy to understand why Congress throughout history has borne the brunt of popular criticism.

Individual members of Congress, in contrast to the institution of Congress, have little difficulty in satisfying constituent expectations that he or she will look after district interests while in Washington. One reason incumbents appear to be so successful in satisfying these expectations is because they engage in member-promotion activities on a rather continuous basis:

> Much of the member-promotion is done by the personal staff, of course, and as every member has such a staff regardless of seniority, committee assignment, or leadership responsibility, it may be regarded as the core of the member

enterprise. The sine qua non of the other functions (Salisbury and Shepsle, 1981, p. 564).

These promotional activities (for example, media attention, casework, and newsletter production) are designed to foster favorable images of representatives and senators within their constituencies. Moreover, some of the differences in the content of popular evaluations of members of Congress and Congress itself may be due to varied expectations. Nonetheless, incumbents play a major role in promoting standards of evaluation that reflect favorably upon them. In this way, incumbents take an active role in maintaining their own popularity among constituents (Parker, 1981a).

House incumbents are popular because they are able to focus constituent attention on aspects of their job performance, or on characteristics related to that performance, that produce favorable impressions of their overall accomplishments (Parker, 1980a). Incumbents are able to capture constituent attention because they exercise a virtual monopoly over the dissemination of information about themselves. Because few district newspapers can afford a Washington correspondent, most information about a House member originates in his or her own congressional office. The "advertising" and "credit-claiming" resources of incumbents (Mayhew, 1974) can be viewed as continuing efforts to focus constituent attention; the "home-style" behaviors of House members described by Richard Fenno (1978) serve a similar function.

Constituency Attention

Attention to constituency affairs can be an asset for House and Senate members because it demonstrates that they are looking after the interests of the district or state. Constituency attentiveness includes all of those activities that incumbents perform on behalf of their constituents, such as handling constituent inquiries and bringing federal money and projects to the district or state.[1] Douglas Arnold (1979) cites three ways in which the allocation of federal expenditures to a member's district or state can aid in reelection. First, if the beneficiaries of a particular program can be led to believe that the benefits they are receiving are the result of their member's efforts, they have good reason to support the incumbent in subsequent elections. Second, the allocation of funds to a representative's district or a senator's state provides a number of opportunities to create favorable publicity: "Since the announcement of federal money for even the smallest project is usually considered newsworthy in all but the largest American cities, it is not surprising that congressmen are eager to make such announcements themselves" (Arnold, 1979, p. 29). Finally, federal expenditures can affect the prosperity of the local economy; such prosperity may be exploited by incumbents to demonstrate their interest in and concern for the constituents' well being.

House incumbents reap at least three benefits from attentiveness: constituents are very much aware of it (Parker and Davidson, 1979; Parker, 1980a); there is a positive value attached to it — rarely is attentiveness mentioned by constituents as something they dislike about their representatives; and attentiveness is unlikely to be mentioned in positive evaluations of challengers to House incumbents. In fact, attentiveness is one area in which constituents display no ambivalence between what is liked about the incumbent and what is liked about the challenger.

In a sense, attentiveness distinguishes the incumbent from other members of Congress, as well as from the challenger, in the eyes of constituents. This is evident in the fact that people who mention attentiveness in evaluating their representative's job performance perceive their representative as devoting more time than other members of Congress to district concerns.[2] Furthermore, more than one-third of the reasons cited by respondents for believing their representatives to be "better than most other congressmen" made reference to the attentiveness of the incumbent (Commission on Administrative Review, 1977, p. 820).[3] Therefore, constituents may be unwilling to vote against incumbents because of the fear that his or her replacement may be as inattentive to constituent interests as they perceive other House members to be.

It also may be more rational for constituents to base their voting decisions on the incumbent's service to the district or state than his or her policy stands and votes. The lack of information about the voting record of most incumbents minimizes any meaningful use of it as a means of evaluating performance. Even where it might be useful, the members' ability to "explain their votes" (Kingdon, 1975; Fenno, 1978) is apt to limit the impact of the voting record on electoral support. There is yet another reason why voters might rationally pay less attention to the policy positions of incumbents:

> In legislative elections citizens are choosing between platforms which will be realized only probabilistically. And in very large legislatures (especially in systems with independent executives) these probabilities will generally be very small (Fiorina and Noll, 1979, p. 1093).

Thus, attention to district and state affairs provides constituents with explicit and predictable benefits, while the implementation of policy preferences is far more uncertain.

A variety of longitudinal information exists to support the proposition that the withering away of the marginal district is due to the greater opportunities afforded to incumbents for demonstrating (and publicizing) their attentiveness to district affairs. Fiorina (1977a) presents data demonstrating that members today are placing greater emphasis on constituency services than they did in the past. In addition, House members are spending more time in their congressional districts than previously.[4] The increase is due both to the growth in travel allowances and to electoral turnover; members elected before 1965 spend less time in their districts than those elected after that date (Parker, 1980b). Time spent at home base is direct evidence that an incumbent is attentive to district affairs; it also provides an unobtrusive channel for disseminating favorable impressions of record and service.

The proportion of citizens who have written to their members of Congress also has increased substantially. This influx of mail has increased the opportunities for members to serve their constituents and to publicize their concern, thereby capitalizing on the positive effect that accompanies attention to district matters. It also means that incumbents are better able to reach their constituents in a personal way (for example, letters addressed to a specific individual rather than to "occupant"). Finally, the growth in office perquisites has increased the opportunities for incumbents to advertise their service to the district and to claim credit for the benefits that have accrued to it.

Indeed, incumbents may even have overstimulated constituent needs for legislative services because such activities seem certain to escalate the costs of constituency attention. While some of the costs can be transferred to the staff, other responsibilities, such as personal attention to constituents, are clearly nontransferable and directly increase the costs of constituency attention for most incumbents.

The four articles in this section represent attempts to examine and explain the levels of competition in congressional elections. One of the major questions that provoked these analyses was the contemporary decline in congressional turnover. David Mayhew's study of the electoral competitiveness of congressional districts (1974) provided a valuable key to the mystery surrounding the decline in congressional turnover. Mayhew examined the shapes of the vote distributions for incumbents in congressional races (histograms) between 1956 and 1972; he was interested in the percentage of congressional districts in which the vote outcomes indicated that the district was marginal (winning incumbent elected by less than 55 percent of the vote). Mayhew's analysis of these histograms revealed that more and more congressional districts were becoming electorally safe for House incumbents. In short, the decline in congressional turnover could be attributed to the disappearance of the types of congressional districts that normally produced heavy turnover — the marginal district.

Electoral safety also appears to have been on the rise in Senate elections. At about the same time that the marginal congressional district was beginning to decline, the electoral safety of senators also was increasing. Warren Kostroski (1973) presents data demonstrating that senators were indeed being reelected at rates that differed significantly from the past: "each election year sitting senators have become, on the average, almost 'two percent safer'." Kostroski concluded that while the importance of party in terms of electoral influence has declined, incumbency has assumed greater significance in Senate elections. The article by Charles Bullock and Michael Scicchitano (1982, p. 486) finds support for Kostroski's conclusion.[5]

Despite the importance of incumbency in Senate elections, House members are far more electorally secure than their Senate counterparts. One hypothesis that seeks to explain this interchamber difference in electoral safety is the differential in the visibility of House and Senate challengers, which accounts for the greater electoral security of representatives. The "invisibility" of most House challengers enables House incumbents to create defections among the ranks of the challengers' supporters. This provides representatives with an electoral edge that Senate incumbents do not possess. The higher visibility of Senate challengers prevents Senate incumbents from inducing rates of defection that are comparable

11

to those produced by representatives. Bullock and Scicchitano (1982) examine the "defection hypothesis" by comparing the rates of defections among voters who identified with the incumbent's or challenger's political party in both House and Senate elections during the last three decades. Their analysis suggests that differing levels of partisan defections cannot explain the interchamber differences in electoral safety.

John Ferejohn and Morris Fiorina analyze the emergence of the electoral advantage of incumbency. Ferejohn (1977, p. 174) suggests that change in voting behavior is the principal cause of declining competitiveness in congressional elections: "voters seem to be shifting away from the use of party affiliation as a decision rule and toward increased utilization of incumbency." Fiorina (1977b, p. 181) proposes a different reason for the increased safety of House incumbents: "To explain the vanishing marginals one need only argue that over the past thirty years, expanded constituency service opportunities have given the marginal congressmen the ability to capture 5-10 percent of his district's voters who might otherwise oppose him on party or policy grounds." According to Fiorina, more and more House incumbents are operating as ombudsmen devoted to expediting bureaucratic activity and serving district interests. This behavioral change has promoted the electoral safety of House members and produced the decline in the marginal congressional district.

Although these four studies represent only a small portion of all the articles published on competition in congressional elections, they have served to stimulate considerable research in this area.

Notes

1. For research purposes, constituency attentiveness can be described as a category for classifying respondent "likes" and "dislikes" about their incumbent representative. As evidence of the perceived attentiveness of congressional incumbents, mass opinion studies that use this concept normally specify activities such as personally assisting people in the district, soliciting district opinion and representing those views within Congress, keeping people informed about the operations of government, and helping the district's economy.
2. For example, those individuals who base their evaluations on district service criteria perceive that their representative places greater emphasis on district-related activities such as securing federal funds for the district ($r = .19$), spending time in the district ($r = .22$), helping constituents with government- related problems ($r = .23$), explaining the functioning of government to constituents ($r = .23$), and informing constituents about congressional activity ($r = .18$). For a further discussion of these data, see Parker (1981a).
3. The responses that were considered to reference the incumbent's attentiveness to the district were: 1) He cares about, has feelings for, is concerned about people, his constituents; (2) He's concerned about representing his people, visits them, tries to help solve their problems; (3) He mails out newsletters, bulletins, communicates through the media, tries to keep people informed of what he's doing; (4) He has accomplished a lot for the people in his state (for example, obtained federal funds for housing, sewer, water

system, business loans, etc.). For a description of all of the response categories, see Commission on Administrative Review *(1977, pp. 820-821)*.

4. These data are based on the travel vouchers filed by House members with the Clerk of the House of Representatives between 1970 and 1976. For a more elaborate discussion of these data, see Parker (1980b).

5. This electoral advantage for Senate incumbents persisted throughout the 1962-1972 period, but in the elections between 1974 and 1980 the influence of Senate incumbency declined.

1. CONGRESSIONAL ELECTIONS: THE CASE OF THE VANISHING MARGINALS

David R. Mayhew

Of the electoral instruments voters have used to influence American national government few have been more important than the biennial "net partisan swing" in United States House membership. Since Jacksonian times ups and downs in party seat holdings in the House have supplied an important form of party linkage.

The seat swing is, in practice, a two-step phenomenon. For a party to register a net gain in House seats there must occur (a) a gain (over the last election) in the national proportion of popular votes cast for House candidates of the party in question. That is, the party must be the beneficiary of a national trend in popular voting for the House.[1] But there must also occur (b) a translation of popular vote gains into seat gains.[2] Having the former without the latter might be interesting but it would not be very important.

The causes of popular vote swings have only recently been traced with any precision. There is voter behavior that produces the familiar mid-term sag for parties in control of the presidency.[3] There is the long-run close relation between changes in economic indices and changes in the House popular vote.[4] There are doubtless other matters that can give a national cast to House voting, including wars.[5]

The consequences of partisan seat swings (built on popular vote swings) have been more elusive but no less arresting. As in the case of the Great Society Congress (1965-1966), House newcomers can supply the votes to pass bills that could not have been passed without them. Presidents with ambitious domestic programs (Woodrow Wilson, Franklin Roosevelt, Lyndon Johnson) have relied heavily on the votes of temporarily augmented Democratic House majorities. No clear argument can be made, of course, that a bill-passing binge like that of 1965-1966 offers a direct conversion of popular wishes into laws. The evidence is more ambiguous. At the least a House election like the one of 1964 produces a rotation of government elites that has policy consequences; at the most there is some detectable relation between what such temporarily empowered elites do and what popular wishes are. Over time the working of the seat swing has sometimes given a dialectical cast to national policy-making, with successive elites making

Source: *Polity* (1974) vol. 6, no. 3. Reprinted with permission of the publisher.

successive policy approximations. A case in point is the enactment of the Wagner Act in the Democratic Seventy-fourth Congress followed by its Taft-Hartley revision in the Republican Eightieth. Because of all the translation uncertainties the House seat swing has been a decidedly blunt voter instrument, but it has been a noteworthy instrument nonetheless.

The foregoing is a preface to a discussion of some recent election data. The data, for the years 1956-1972, suggest strongly that the House seat swing is a phenomenon of fast declining amplitude and therefore of fast declining significance. The first task here will be to lay out the data — in nearly raw form — in order to give a sense of their shape and flow. The second task will be to speculate about causes of the pattern in the data, the third to ponder the implications of this pattern.

I.

The data are presented in Figure 1-1, an array of 22 bar graphs that runs on for five pages. If the pages are turned sideways and read as if they were one long multi-page display, the graphs appear in three columns of nine, nine, and four. It will be useful to begin with an examination of the four graphs in the right-hand column.

Each of the four right-hand graphs is a frequency distribution in which congressional districts are sorted according to percentages of the major-party presidential vote cast in them in one of the four presidential elections of the years 1956-1968.[6] The districts are cumulated vertically in percentages of the total district set of 435 rather than in absolute numbers. The horizontal axis has column intervals of five percent, ranging from a far-left interval for districts where the Democratic presidential percentage was 0-4.9 to a far-right interval where the percentage was 95-100. Thus the 1956 graph shows that the Stevenson-Kefauver ticket won 50 to 54.9 percent of the major-party vote in about 7 percent of the districts (actual district $N = 30$) and a modal 40 to 44.9 percent of the vote in about 20 percent of the districts (actual $N = 87$).

In themselves these presidential graphs hold no surprises; they are presented for the purpose of visual comparison with the other data. The presidential mode travels well to the left of the 50 percent mark in 1956 and well to the right in 1964, but the four distributions are fundamentally alike in shape — highly peaked, unimodal, not far from normal.

The center and left columns give frequency distributions, organized on the same principles as the four presidential graphs, in which House districts are sorted according to percentages of the major-party House vote cast in them in each of the nine congressional elections in the years 1956-1972. But for each House election there are two graphs side by side. For each year the graph in the left column gives a distribution of returns for all districts in which an incumbent congressman was running, the center column a set of returns for districts with no incumbents running.[7]

The center graphs, the "open seat" distributions, are erratically shaped because the N's are small. The number of House districts without incumbents

Figure 1-1 Frequency Distributions of Democratic Percentages of the Two-Party Vote in House Districts

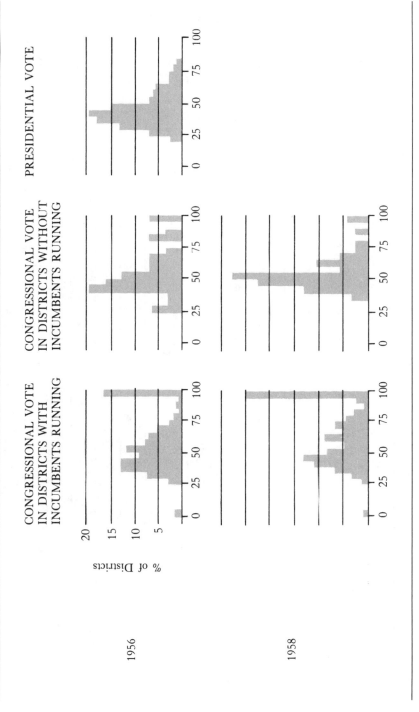

Figure 1-1 (Continued)

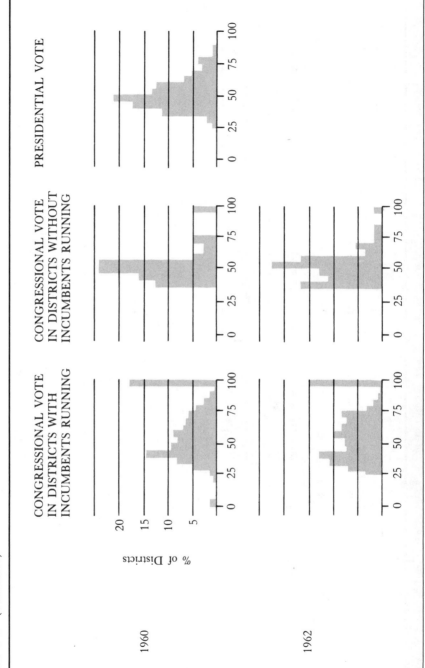

Figure 1-1 (Continued)

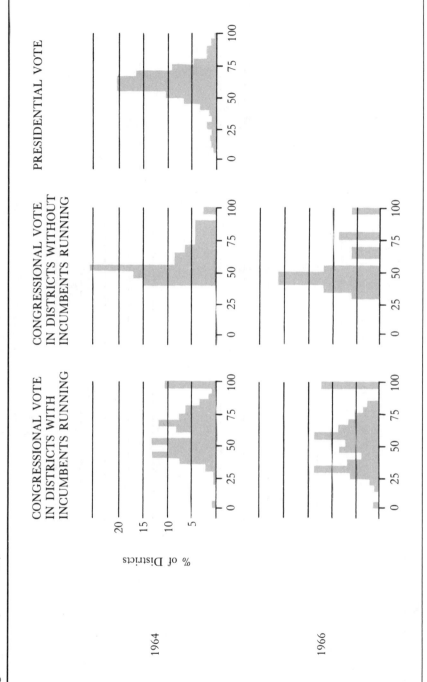

Figure 1-1 (Continued)

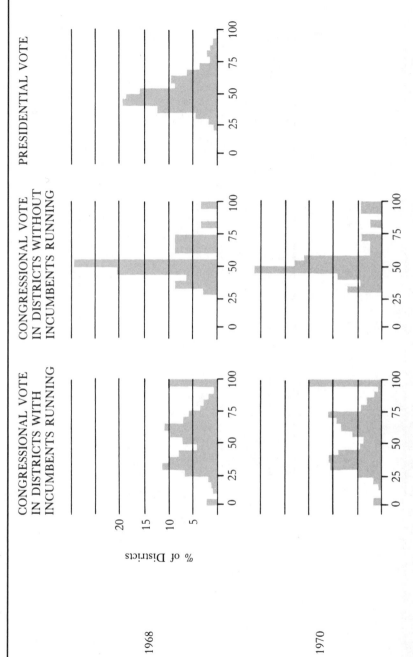

Figure 1-1 (Continued)

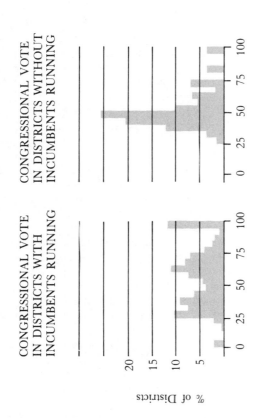

CONGRESSIONAL VOTE
IN DISTRICTS WITH
INCUMBENTS RUNNING

CONGRESSIONAL VOTE
IN DISTRICTS WITHOUT
INCUMBENTS RUNNING

% of Districts

1972

running averages 43 (about a tenth of the membership) and ranges from 31 (in 1956) to 59 (in 1972); there is no discernible upward or downward trend in the series. With allowances made for erratic shape these nine "open seat" distributions are much alike. All are highly peaked and centrally clustered. In 1958 and 1968 nearly 30 percent of the readings appear in the modal interval (in both cases the 50-54.9 percent Democratic interval). Over the set of nine elections the proportion of "open seat" outcomes falling in the 40-59.9 percent area ranges from 54.8 percent to 70.2 percent, the proportion in the 45-54.9 percent area from 29.0 percent to 50.1 percent. All of which imparts the simple and obvious message that House elections without incumbents running tend to be closely contested.

The nine graphs in the left-hand column give distributions for districts with incumbents running.[8] Thus in 1956 about 9 percent of districts with incumbents running yielded returns in the 45-49.9 percent Democratic interval. In some of these cases the incumbents were Democrats who thereby lost their seats; in any of these nine graphs the election reading for a losing incumbent will appear on what was, from his standpoint, the unfortunate side of the 50 percent line. In an Appendix the nine data sets are disaggregated to show where in fact incumbents lost.

Immediately visible on each of the incumbency graphs is the isolated mode in the 95-100 percent interval, recording the familiar phenomenon of uncontested Democratic victories — mostly in the South. But, if these right-flush modes can be ignored for a moment, what has recently been happening in the contested range is far more interesting. In 1956 and 1960 the distributions in the contested range are skewed a little to the right, but still not far from normal in shape. In the 1958 and 1962 midterm years the distributions are somewhat flatter and more jagged.[9] In 1964 and 1966 they appear only tenuously normal. In 1968, 1970, and 1972 they have become emphatically bimodal in shape. Or, to ring in the uncontested Democratic seats again, the shape of incumbency distributions has now become strikingly trimodal. Thus in the 1972 election there was a range of reasonably safe Republican seats (with the 25-29.9 percent and 35-39.5 percent intervals most heavily populated), a range of reasonably safe Democratic seats (peaked in the 60-64.9 percent interval), and a set of 44 uncontested Democratic seats.

The title of this paper includes the phrase, "The Case of the Vanishing Marginals." The "vanishing marginals" are all those congressmen whose election percentages could, but now do not, earn them places in the central range of these incumbency distributions. In the graphs for the most recent elections the trough between the "reasonably safe" Republican and Democratic modes appears in the percentage range that we are accustomed to calling "marginal." Figure 1-2 captures the point, with time series showing how many incumbent congressmen have recorded percentages in the "marginal" range in each election from 1956 through 1972.[10] The lower series on the two Figure 1-2 graphs show, for comparative purposes, the number of "open seat" outcomes in the marginal range. In one graph marginality is defined narrowly (45-54.9 Democratic percentage of the major-party vote), in the other broadly (40-59.9 percent). By either definition the number of incumbents running in the marginal zone has

Figure 1-2 Numbers of House Elections Won in the "Marginal" Range, 1956-1972, in Districts With and Without Incumbents Running

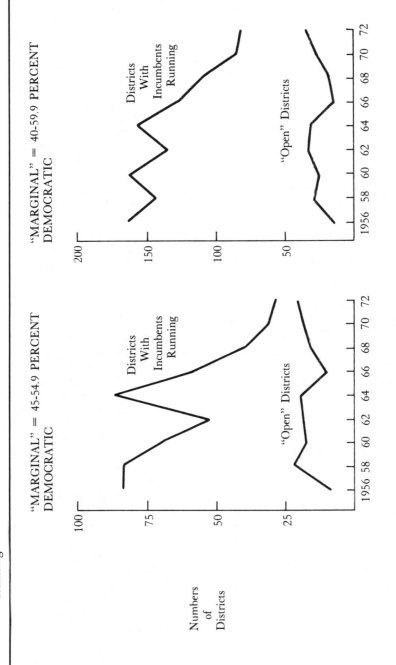

roughly halved over the sixteen-year period.[11] For some reason, or reasons, it seems to be a lot easier now than it used to be for a sitting congressman to win three-fifths of the November vote.

II.

Why the decline in incumbent marginality? No clear answer is available.[12] Adding complexity to the problem is the fact that the proportion of House seats won in the marginal range has been slowly declining for over a century.[13] Whatever mix of causes underlies the long-run change could account for much of the rapid current change as well. On the assumption that the contemporary decline is not ephemeral, perhaps the most useful thing to do here is to set out some hypotheses which may singly or in combination account for it. Five hypotheses are offered below. Some have a more persuasive ring than others; none is wholly implausible. The first has to do with district line-drawing, the next three with congressmen's actions designed to attract votes, the last with voter behavior not inspired by congressmen's actions.

(1) The line-drawing explanation is easy to reach for. In the last decade of chronic redistricting the possibility of building districts to profit incumbents has not been lost on House members or others acting in their interest. With county lines less sacred than they once were, ingenious districts can be and have been drawn. And there are good examples of cross-party districting deals among congressmen of large state delegations.[14] But the problem with the line-drawing hypothesis is that it seems not to explain very much. Manipulation of the aggregate national data does not yield an impressive relation between redistricting and electoral benefit.[15] Moreover, if voters are being partitioned into safe House districts it can be argued that bimodal patterns ought to appear sooner or later in presidential and "open seat" distributions of the sort displayed in Figure 1-1. Of bimodalism the relevant Figure 1-1 graphs give no trace, although it must be said that the evidence is inconclusive. The evidence on redistricting generally is incomplete and inconclusive. But the odds are that it will not explain very much. If all 435 congressmen were suddenly to retire in 1974, and if elections to replace them were conducted in the 1972 district set, the odds are that a distribution of new member percentages would look like a presidential or an evened out "open seat" distribution — unimodal and roughly normal, though perhaps still with a modest isolated mode for uncontested Southerners.

The next four hypotheses hinge on the assumption that House incumbency now carries with it greater electoral advantages than it has in the past. There is evidence that it does.[16] One way to try to find out is to look at what happens to party fortunes in districts where congressmen die, retire, or lose primaries — to compare the last November percentages of veteran incumbents with the percentages of their successor nominees. Table 1-1 does this for the six elections in the years 1962-1972. Figures are given for transitions in which the retirees were at least two-term veterans and where the bracketing elections were both contested by both parties. It is hard to tease conclusions out of these data; the universes for the six elections are small, the districts in each inter-election set vary widely in their change percentages, national trends affect Democrats and Republicans differently, and there is the redistricting problem throughout. But these are all of the data there are on the point. Most of the columns in the table include figures on districts with line changes. Including these raises the obvious problems that redistricting itself can affect party percentages. But there is some justification for the inclusion. For one thing, no systematic difference appears here between what happens electorally in redrawn and untouched districts. For another, it is impossible to get any reading at all on the 1972 election without inspecting the redrawn districts; 25 of the 27 "succession nominations" occurred in 1972 in districts with line changes. If handled carefully the altered districts can yield information. Redrawn districts are covered here if they were treated in the press as being more or less "the same" as districts preceding them; thus, for example, Paul Cronin is commonly regarded as Bradford Morse's successor in the fifth Massachusetts district although Cronin's 1972 boundaries are somewhat different from Morse's old ones.

What to look for in Table 1-1 is whether switches in party nominees bring about drops in party percentages. The bigger the drop the higher the putative value of incumbency. Inter-election changes in party percentage are calculated here by comparing party shares of the total congressional district vote in the bracketing elections.[17] The first three columns in the table give data only on districts without line changes. Thus in 1962 there were four Democratic retirements (or deaths, etc.) in districts with 1960 lines intact; the Democratic share of the total vote fell an average of 5.2 percent in these four districts between 1960 and 1962. In the four Republican retirement districts in 1962 the Republican share of the total vote fell an average of 0.2 percent. In 1964 there was an understandable party gain in the Democratic retirement districts, and an especially heavy mean loss in the Republican set. Fortuitously the numbers of retirement districts for the two parties are almost identical in each of the five elections in 1962 through 1970, so it makes sense to calculate mean change values for all retirement districts regardless of party in each year in order to try to cancel out the effects of election-specific national trends. This is done in the third column, a list of cross-party percentage change means for the six elections. (Thus in 1964 the average change in the 25 retirement seats was a negative 1.6 percent even though the average party values were far apart; Republicans generally lost more in their transitions that Democrats gained in theirs.) Here there emerges some fairly solid evidence. Mean drops in percentage were higher in 1966, 1968, and 1970 than in 1962 and 1964. (1972, with its N of 2, can be ignored.) The best evidence is for 1964 and 1970, with their large N's. Loss of incumbents cost the parties a mean of 1.6 percent in 1964, a mean of 6.5 percent in 1970.

In the fourth column figures on transitions in redrawn districts are introduced. The values are mean changes for redrawn retirement districts by year regardless of party. It will be seen that these values differ in no systematic way from the values for undisturbed districts in the third column. There is the same general trend toward bigger drops in percentage. Especially striking is the 1972 value of minus 9.5 percent, lower than any other reading in the list of values for redrawn districts. The fifth, sixth, and seventh columns of the table give mean

Table 1-1 Change in Party Percentage in House Districts Where Incumbents Have Retired, Died, or Lost Primaries

| | Transitions in Districts Without Line Changes | | | | | | Transitions in Districts With Line Changes | |
| | Democratic Districts | | Republican Districts | | All Districts | | All Districts | |
	N	MEAN	N	MEAN	N	MEAN	N	MEAN
1962	(4)	−5.2	(4)	−0.2	(8)	−2.7	(9)	+1.3
1964	(12)	+5.5	(13)	−8.2	(25)	−1.6	*	*
1966	(3)	−6.2	(3)	−2.5	(6)	−4.3	(7)	−7.7
1968	(4)	+1.1	(3)	−14.9	(7)	−5.8	(12)	−8.6
1970	(15)	−4.9	(17)	−7.9	(32)	−6.5	(4)	−5.7
1972	(2)	−26.7		*	(2)	−26.7	(25)	−9.5

	Democratic Districts		Republican Districts		All Districts		WGHTD All Districts		All Districts	
	N	MEAN	N	MEAN	N	MEAN	N	MEAN	N	MEDIAN
1962	(5)	−6.0	(12)	+1.8	(17)	−0.5	(17)	−2.1	(17)	−3.1
1964	(12)	+5.5	(13)	−8.2	(25)	−1.6	(25)	−1.3	(25)	−3.1
1966	(8)	−8.9	(5)	−1.8	(13)	−6.2	(13)	−5.4	(13)	−8.2
1968	(10)	−1.4	(9)	−14.5	(19)	−7.6	(19)	−8.0	(19)	−4.7
1970	(19)	−5.1	(17)	−7.9	(36)	−6.4	(36)	−6.0	(36)	−5.6
1972	(12)	−13.1	(15)	−9.0	(27)	−10.8	(27)	−11.1	(27)	−10.2

values by year, respectively, for Democratic, Republican, and all retirement districts, with no distinctions being made between altered and unaltered districts. The eighth column gives a weighted mean for each year, a simple average of the party averages. Finally the ninth column gives a median value for the seat of all readings in each year.

These readings, tenuous as they are, all point in the same direction. Incumbency does seem to have increased in electoral value, and it is reasonable to suppose that one effect of this increase has been to boost House members of both parties out of the marginal electoral range. If incumbency has risen in value, what accounts for the rise? The second, third, and fourth hypotheses below focus on electorally useful activities that House members may now be engaging in more effectively than their predecessors did ten or twenty years ago.

(2) House members may now be advertising themselves better. Simple name recognition counts for a lot in House elections, as the Survey Research Center data shows.[18] A name perceived with a halo of good will around it probably counts for more. If House members have not profited from accelerated advertising in the last decade, it is not from want of trying. The time series in Figure 1-3 shows, in millions of pieces, how much mail was sent out from the Capitol (by both House and Senate members) in each year from 1954 through 1970.[19] The mail includes letters, newsletters, questionnaires, child-care pamphlets, etc., some of them mailed to all district box-holders. Peak mailing months are the Octobers of even-numbered years. Mail flow more than sextupled over the sixteen-year period, with an especially steep increase between 1965 and 1966. In fact the mail-flow curve matches well any incumbency-advantage curve derivable from the data in Table 1-1. There is no let-up in sight; one recent estimate has it that House members will send out about 900,000 pieces of mail per member in 1974, at a total public cost of $38.1 million.[20] So the answer to the incumbency advantage question could be a remarkably simple one: the more hundreds of thousands of messages congressmen rain down on constituents the more votes they get. Whether all this activity has significantly raised the proportion of citizens who know their congressmen's names is uncertain. There are some Gallup readings showing that the share of adults who could name their congressmen rose from 46 to 53 percent between 1966 and 1970.[21]

(3) Another possibility is that House members may be getting more political mileage out of federal programs. The number of grant-in-aid programs has risen in the last decade at something like the rate of Capitol mail flow. The more programs there are, the more chances House members have to claim credit ostentatiously for the local manifestations of them — housing grants, education grants, anti-pollution grants, etc.

(4) Yet another possibility is that House members have become more skilled at public position-taking on "issues." The point is a technological one. If more congressmen are commissioning and using scientific opinion polls to plumb district sentiment, then House members may have become, on balance, more practiced at attuning themselves to district opinion.[22] There is a possibility here, however hard it is to try to measure. There may be a greater general sophistication today about polling and its uses. In 1964, forty-nine Republican

Figure 1-3 Franked Mail Sent out by House and Senate Members, in Millions of Pieces, 1954-1970

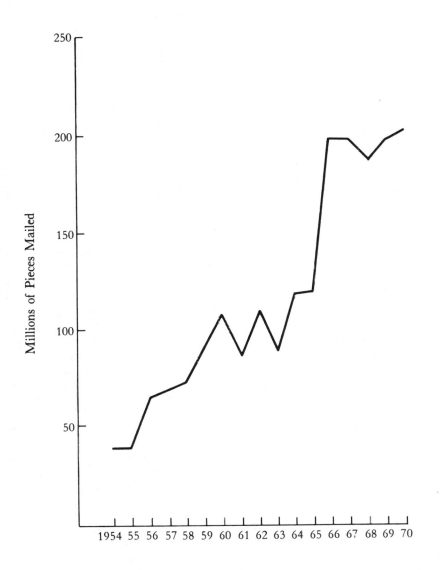

Source: U.S. Congress, House, Committee on Appropriations, *Hearings Before a Subcommittee of the Committee on Appropriations, Legislative Branch Appropriations for 1970,* 91st Cong., 1st sess., 1969, p. 501 has 1954-1968 data. Subsequent annual hearings update estimated franking use.

House members running for re-election signed a pre-convention statement endorsing Senator Goldwater. It was claimed that Goldwater's nomination would help the party ticket. The forty-nine suffered disproportionately in November.[23] In 1972 there was no comparable rush among House Democrats to identify themselves with Senator McGovern.

(5) The fifth and last hypothesis has to do with changes in voter behavior not inspired by changes in incumbent activities. It is possible that incumbents have been profiting not from any exertions of their own but from changes in voter attitudes. A logic suggests itself. Voters dissatisfied with party cues could be reaching for any other cues that are available in deciding how to vote. The incumbency cue is readily at hand. This hypothesis assumes a current rise in discontent with parties; it assumes nothing about changes in the cues voters have been receiving from congressmen.

There is no point in speculating further here about causes. But it is important that the subject be given further treatment, if for no other reason than that some of the variables can be legally manipulated. The congressional franking privilege comes first to mind.

III

If fewer House members are winning elections narrowly, and if the proportion of "open seats" per election is not rising, it ought to follow that congressional seat swings are declining in amplitude. The argument requires no assumption that national swings in the House popular vote are changing in amplitude — and indeed there is no evidence in the contemporary data that they are. It does require the assumption that a congressman's percentage showing in one election supplies information on his strength as he goes into the next. That is, a House member running at the 60 percent level is less likely to be unseated by an adverse 5 percent party trend next time around than one running at the 54 percent level. It is easy to predict that a popular voting trend will cut less of a swath through a set of congressmen whose last-election percentages are arrayed like those in the 1968, 1970, and 1972 incumbency graphs of Figure 1-1 than through a set whose percentages are centrally and normally distributed.

There is evidence suggesting that the flight from marginality is having its posited effect. Edward Tufte has found that a "swing ratio" — a rate of translation of votes into seats — built on data from the 1966, 1968, and 1970 elections yields an exceptionally low value when compared with ratios for other election triplets over the last century.[24] The figures in Table 1-2 point in the same direction. Supplied here are data on popular vote swings, net partisan seat swings, and incumbent defeats for each and both parties in the election years from 1956 through 1972.[25] It is worth noting that the large seat swings of 1958, 1964, and 1966 were heavily dependent upon defeats of incumbents. Very few incumbents have lost since 1966. (Almost all the 1972 losers were victims of line changes.) Especially interesting are the figures for 1970, a year in which the popular vote swing was a fairly sizable 3.3 percent. Yet only nine incumbents of the disfavored party lost and the net swing over 1968 was only twelve — of which three changed

Table 1-2 House Vote Swings and Seat Swings, 1956-1972

	Change in National Popular Vote Over Last Election	Net Partisan Seat Swing Over Last Election	Incumbent Losses to Opposite Party Challengers		
			D	R	Total
1956	1.5% D	2 D	8	7	15
1958	5.1% D	49 D	1	34	35
1960	1.1% R	20 R	22	3	25
1962	2.2% R	2 R	9	5	14
1964	4.7% D	36 D	5	39	44
1966	6.2% R	47 R	39	1	40
1968	0.4% R	5 R	5	0	5
1970	3.3% D	12 D	2	9	11
1972	1.4% R	12 R	6	3	9

over in 1969 by elections. Part of the explanation here is doubtless that the disfavored party had relatively few incumbents in the vulnerable range to protect. Only 47 Republicans running in 1970 had won under the 60 percent mark in 1968, whereas there had been 82 comparably exposed Republicans running in 1958, 76 Republicans in 1964, and 79 Democrats in 1966.

What general conclusions can be drawn? If the trends hold we are witnesses to the blunting of a blunt instrument. It may be too soon to say that seat swings of the 1958 or 1964 variety can be consigned to the history books, but it is hard to see how they could be equaled in the newer electoral circumstances. There is probably another manifestation here of what Walter Dean Burnham calls "electoral disaggregation" — a weakening of the peculiar links that party has supplied between electorate and government.[26] There is a concomitant triumph for the Madisonian vision; a Congress less affected by electoral tides is, on balance, one less susceptible to presidential wiles. But there is a long-run danger that a Congress that cannot supply quick electoral change is no match for a presidency that can.

Appendix

The columns of figures below are frequency distributions of Democratic percentages of the November two-party House vote recorded in districts with incumbents of either (but not both) of the parties running, in biennial elections from 1956 through 1972, with separate columns for each year for districts harboring Democratic and Republican incumbents. Thus in 1956 there were twenty-eight districts with Republican incumbents running in which Democratic percentages were in the 45-49.9 percent range. There were also eight districts with Democratic incumbents running in which Democratic percentages were in the 45-49.9 percent range; these eight Democrats thereby lost their seats. Squares or rectangles are drawn around cells below which contain values for incumbents who lost seats to opposite-party challengers.

Numbers of Districts, by Year and by Party of Incumbent

Democratic % of the Two-Party Vote	1956 D	1956 R	1958 D	1958 R	1960 D	1960 R	1962 D	1962 R	1964 D	1964 R	1966 D	1966 R	1968 D	1968 R	1970 D	1970 R	1972 D	1972 R
0- 4.9		3		1		3		1		1		4		9		5		7
5- 9.9																		
10- 14.9																		
15- 19.9														1				
20- 24.9				1		1						3		3		2		2
25- 29.9		13		11		3		11		1		8		6		5		7
30- 34.9		28		27		16		24		7		24		25		15		38
35- 39.9		54		44		33		39	2	25	1	53		47		40		27
40- 44.9		54		50	3	56	2	45	2	47	8	26		39		41	2	36
45- 49.9	8	28	1	27	19	19	7	19	1	38	30	6	5	31	2	34	4	22
50- 54.9	40	6	4	7	28	3	23	4	14	35	28	3	26	10	8	15	15	10
55- 59.9	28	1	11		36		36	1	18	4	53	1	38		20	7	27	2
60- 64.9	28		33		27		32		35		34		43		28	1	40	1
65- 69.9	21		19		26		27		45		26		24		35	1	30	
70- 74.9	10		26		21		31		29		20		22		42		26	
75- 79.9	7		17		16		11		24		13		12		15		16	
80- 84.9	2		10		11		4		13		9		10		12		9	
85- 89.9	4		1		4		2		4				4		9		7	
90- 94.9	1		5		3		1		2				1		4		1	
95-100.0	68		95		72		56		40		51		41		56		44	

Notes

1. To put it yet another way, a voting for House candidates must have a "national component" to it. See Donald E. Stokes, "Parties and the Nationalization of Electoral Forces," ch. 7 in William N. Chambers and Walter D. Burnham, *The American Party Systems* (New York: Oxford University Press, 1967).
2. The best analysis of translation formulas is in Edward R. Tufte, "The Relation Between Seats and Votes in Two Party Systems," *American Political Science Review*, 67 (June 1973), 540-554.
3. Angus Campbell, "Surge and Decline: A Study in Electoral Change," ch. 3 in Campbell et al., *Elections and the Political Order* (New York: Wiley, 1966).
4. Gerald H. Kramer, "Short-Term Fluctuations in U.S. Voting Behavior, 1896-1964," *American Political Science Review*, 65 (1971), 131-143.
5. Ibid., p. 140.
6. At the time of writing no comparable figures were yet available for the 1972 election. Dealing with the 1968 returns by calculating percentages of the major-party vote poses obvious problems — especially in the South — but so does any alternative way of dealing with them. Congressional district data used in Figure 1-1 and following tables and figures were taken from *Congressional Quarterly* compilations.
7. An incumbent is defined here as a congressman who held a seat at the time he was running in a November election, even if he had first taken the seat in a recent by-election.
8. The center graphs cover districts with no incumbents, the left-hand graphs districts with one incumbent. This leaves no place in the diagram for districts with two opposite-party incumbents running against each other. There were 16 of these throw-in cases over the period: 7 in 1962, 1 in 1966, 4 in 1968, 1 in 1970, 3 in 1972. Republicans won in 10 of them.
9. On balance it can be expected that distributions will be more centrally clustered in presidential than in midterm years, for the reason that presidential elections enroll expanded electorates in which disproportionate numbers of voters violate district partisan habits in their congressional voting. See Harvey Kabaker, "Estimating the Normal Vote in Congressional Elections," *Midwest Journal of Political Science*, 13 (1969), 58-83.
10. Again, the 16 throw-in cases are not included. It should be recalled here that some of these incumbents in the marginal range moved across the 50 percent mark and lost their seats. (See the Appendix.) Of the 198 incumbents who lost elections to opposite-party challengers in the 1956-1972 period, only 4 plummeted far enough to fall outside the broadly defined (40-59.9 percent) marginal range.
11. The decline has come in spite of Republican inroads in Southern House districts. One reason here is that, once they have gotten their seats, Southern Republican incumbents tend to win elections handily; 16 of 22 of them won with over 60 percent of the major-party vote in 1970, 18 of 22 in 1972.
12. Albert D. Cover is conducting research at Yale on incumbency and marginality in the 1960s.
13. I owe this point to Walter D. Burnham. On long-run decline in House turnover see Charles O. Jones, "Inter-Party Competition for Congressional Seats," *Western Political Quarterly*, 17 (1964), 461-476.
14. Some strategies and examples are discussed in David R. Mayhew, "Congressional Representation: Theory and Practice in Drawing the Districts," ch. 7 in Nelson W. Polsby, ed. *Reapportionment in the 1970's* (Berkeley: University of California Press, 1971), pp. 274-284.

15. On the 1966 election see Robert J. Erikson, "Malapportionment, Gerrymandering, and Party Fortunes in Congressional Elections," *American Political Science Review*, 66 (1972), 1238.
16. Robert Erikson estimates that incumbency status was worth about 2 percent of the vote in the 1950s and early 1960s, but about 5 percent in 1966 and thereafter. Erikson, "The Advantage of Incumbency in Congressional Elections," *Polity*, 3 (1971), 395-405. Erikson, "Malapportionment, Gerrymandering, and Party Fortunes in Congressional Elections," op. cit., 1240.
17. Figures 1-1 and 1-2 are built on candidate percentage of the majority-party vote, Table 1-1 on percentages of the total vote.
18. Donald E. Stokes and Warren E. Miller, "Party Government and the Saliency of Congress," ch. 11 in Angus Campbell, et al., *Elections and the Political Order* (New York: Wiley, 1966), pp. 204-209.
19. Data supplied by Albert D. Cover.
20. Norman C. Miller, "Yes, You Are Getting More Politico Mail; And It Will Get Worse," *Wall Street Journal*, March 6, 1973.
21. Gallup survey in *Washington Post*, September 20, 1970.
22. There is a discussion of roll-call position-taking and its electoral effects in Robert Erikson, "The Electoral Impact of Congressional Roll Call Voting," *American Political Science Review*, 65 (1971), 1018-1032.
23. Robert A. Schoenberger, "Campaign Strategy and Party Loyalty: the Electoral Relevance of Candidate Decision-Making in the 1964 Congressional Elections," *American Political Science Review*, 63 (1969), 515-520.
24. Op. cit., pp. 549-550.
25. The incumbency defeat figures cover only losses to opposite-party challengers. Thus once again the 16 throw-in cases are disregarded. Also ignored are the November losses of two highly visible Democrats — Brooks Hays (1958) and Louise Day Hicks (1972) — to independents who thereupon enrolled as Democrats themselves in Washington. It might be added here that some incumbents do after all lose their primaries. The figures for losses to primary challengers are: 6 in 1956, 4 in 1958, 5 in 1960, 8 in 1962, 5 in 1964, 5 in 1966, 3 in 1968, 9 in 1970, 8 in 1972. The figures for losses where redistricting has thrown incumbents into the same primary: 5 in 1962, 3 in 1964, 3 in 1966, 1 in 1968, 1 in 1970, 6 in 1972. Whatever their qualitative effects, primaries have not rivaled the larger November swings in turnover leverage.
26. "The End of American Party Politics," *Trans-Action*, 7 (December 1969), 18-20.

2. PARTISAN DEFECTIONS AND SENATE INCUMBENT ELECTIONS

Charles S. Bullock III
and
Michael J. Scicchitano

An intriguing facet of congressional election research is the greater security of House than Senate incumbents. Analysts of the 1978 election survey data have concluded that Senate incumbents have suffered because their opponents are well-known while House members run against frequently invisible challengers (Hinckley, 1980b; Mann and Wolfinger, 1980). For incumbents and challengers, visibility is linked to voter approval. Since few candidates are perceived negatively, "in both the Senate and House, the choice involves either two positive or one positive and one neutral perception" (Hinckley, 1980a: 645). Where only one candidate is known to the voter, the tendency is to prefer the known to the unknown (Abramowitz, 1980: 636).

Mann and Wolfinger have suggested that the greater visibility of House incumbents enables them to win the support of voters who identify with the challenger's party but forsake their party's unknown nominee. From this comes the defection hypothesis as a potential explanation for differences in Senate and House reelection rates. Specifically, Senate incumbents should have a smaller net gain from partisan defectors than do House incumbents since senators face more widely recognized challengers. Differences in partisan defection rates, according to the defection hypothesis, would account for inter-chamber differences in incumbent reelections. Another expectation derived from the defection hypothesis is that variations in reelection rates within a chamber should be related to changes in defection patterns.

Differences in the rates at which House and Senate incumbents are reelected have increased since the late 1950s. From 1956-1966, House incumbents were reelected at a rate 5.4 percentage points higher than senators. The average difference grew to 11.4 points for 1968-1974 and 21.7 points since 1976. If partisan defections are linked to electoral competitiveness, then as larger numbers

Authors' Note: This paper updates and revises an earlier work of the authors that was published as "Partisan Defections and Senate Reelections." *American Politics Quarterly*, 10 (October 1982), 477-488. We appreciate the suggestions of Bob Eubank and Glenn Parker that contributed to this revision.

of senators have been defeated, defections should be less concentrated among Senate challengers' partisans. Specifically, senators running in 1976 through 1980 should have attracted relatively few defectors since Senate challengers won a third of the seats in those years. This contrasts with the 94 percent reelection rate for House incumbents who have attracted increasing numbers of defectors (Cover, 1977: 535; Mann and Wolfinger, 1980: 620).

In this article, survey data on voter preferences in Senate elections collected by the Center for Political Studies are analyzed. Questions which allow a determination of whether voters bolted from their party have been asked for each election since 1956 except for 1962.[1]

The analysis will begin with longitudinal data on partisan voting in Senate elections comparable to figures Mann and Wolfinger (1980: 620) present for House elections. The Senate data will reveal whether the pattern of increased defections found for House and presidential elections occurs for the Senate. Table 2-2 looks only at defection rates in races featuring an incumbent.

In order to facilitate comparisons with the House, data for both chambers are presented in Tables 2-2 and 2-3. In Table 2-3 we explore the inter-chamber pattern for defections and reelections. Finally, we look at defection patterns controlling for whether the incumbent senator won or lost.

Analysis

Data in Table 2-1 show that partisan defections in Senate elections have increased. From 1956 to 1960 the average proportion of the vote cast by defectors was 12 percent. This is similar to the 11 percent defection rate in House races and 14 percent in presidential elections.[2] From 1972 through 1982 Senate defections averaged 20 percent, compared with 19 percent and 20 percent for House and presidential elections respectively. Thus at the least refined level, there is no evidence of differences in Senate and House defection rates.

The increased defections have not been distributed evenly between incumbents and challengers. As reported in Table 2-2, defections have increased slightly among senators' partisans, but defections from the challengers' ranks have risen substantially, reaching more than a third of all voters in the challengers' party in 1968 and 1974.[3] For the last four elections, defections have averaged 30.8 percent among challengers' partisans. Despite the current frequent defections from challengers, incumbents are now returned at lower rates, which is not what one would expect if challengers' recent successes were due to an ability to retain the support of their partisans.

Inter-chamber comparisons in Table 2-2 reveals that prior to 1970 the defection patterns were similar for the two chambers; only in 1966 did the inter-chamber difference reach five percentage points. Since 1970, there has been at least a five point difference between House and Senate defections in every year except 1974. Over the last seven elections, defection rates have been higher among challengers' partisans in House than Senate elections. Also, during the last seven elections, defections among incumbents' challengers have been less common in House than Senate contests. The 1974 election is the only exception to these two patterns.

Table 2-1 Partisan Defections in Incumbent and Open Seat Senate Elections

	Party Voters % (n)		Defectors % (n)		Independents % (n)	
1956	79.7	(656)	11.5	(95)	8.7	(72)
1958	83.3	(415)	12.5	(62)	4.2	(21)
1960*	78.3	(342)	11.0	(48)	10.7	(47)
1964	79.2	(679)	15.1	(129)	5.7	(49)
1966	73.9	(192)	19.6	(51)	6.5	(17)
1968	74.5	(455)	19.0	(116)	6.5	(40)
1970	79.2	(370)	12.2	(57)	8.6	(40)
1972	69.2	(504)	22.1	(161)	8.7	(63)
1974	70.3	(396)	21.3	(120)	8.4	(47)
1976	69.0	(490)	20.0	(142)	11.0	(78)
1978	71.5	(397)	20.0	(111)	8.6	(48)
1980	70.5	(422)	21.4	(128)	8.1	(49)
1982	77.4	(415)	16.8	(90)	5.8	(31)

* No survey of Senate voters was conducted in 1962.

Table 2-2 Proportion of Voters Who Defected from Their Party's Candidate in Incumbent Senatorial and House Elections*

	Defected From				Total %	Defections n
	Incumbent		Challenger			
	S	H	S	H		
1956	10.5	(6.4)	17.9	(15.1)	13.8	77
1958	8.5	(7.0)	20.2	(16.1)	13.9	33
1960	8.8	(8.4)	21.3	(18.6)	14.0	41
1964	10.0	(10.8)	21.4	(24.8)	15.2	102
1966	10.2	(9.8)	26.0	(33.7)	17.4	28
1968	13.8	(13.0)	34.6	(32.3)	22.3	71
1970	10.6	(5.8)	20.3	(32.9)	15.1	48
1972	16.3	(10.0)	30.2	(37.2)	25.8	144
1974	13.0	(11.9)	34.5	(32.0)	22.1	76
1976	17.7	(8.1)	29.3	(40.7)	22.8	117
1978	11.2	(4.4)	31.3	(53.5)	21.2	76
1980	14.5	(9.5)	31.1	(48.3)	22.1	77
1982	8.1	5.4	31.3	36.9	18.7	73

House figures given in parentheses are from Eubank and Gow (1983: 124).

* The Senate figures for the years 1972-1976 differ from an earlier study (Bullock and Scicchitano, 1982) because of a revised method of coding vote for Senate incumbent elections suggested by Eubank (1984: 5).

It will be easier to compare defection patterns if a single figure is used for each chamber. To this end, Table 2-3 reports the share of all defections which came from challengers' partisans.[4] Since Senate challengers are better known than their House counterparts and candidate recognition leads to greater ability to retain the support of one's own partisans (Mann and Wolfinger, 1980), the defection hypothesis predicts that defections should be less concentrated among Senate than House challengers. This should be especially true for 1976-1980, the period during which House incumbents were far more likely to win reelection than were senators. According to Table 2-3, challenger defections were indeed more concentrated among House than Senate challengers' partisans after 1974. In the preceding elections, challenger defections were either greater in Senate contests or quite similar for the two chambers, except in 1970. These patterns seem to support the defection hypothesis.

Before wholeheartedly embracing the defection hypothesis however, let us consider, first, the consistency with which defection patterns are related to inter-chamber differences in return rates and, second, patterns within the Senate alone. In pursuing inter-chamber comparisons, note such inconsistencies as (1) differences in reelection rates were almost identical for 1970 and 1972 but House

Table 2-3   Challenger Defections and Reelection Rates for Senate and House

	Challenger Defections as % of All Defections			Reelected as a % of Those seeking Reelection In General Election		
	Senate (1)	*House** (2)	*House Minus Senate* (3)	*Senate* (4)	*House* (5)	*House Minus Senate* (6)
1956	58.4	61.1	2.7	86.2	96.0	9.8
1958	66.6	63.2	−3.4	64.3	90.6	26.3
1960	63.4	61.7	−1.7	96.6	93.4	−3.2
1964	62.7	62.4	−0.3	87.5	88.4	0.9
1966	67.9	72.6	4.7	96.6	89.8	−6.8
1968	63.4	67.1	3.7	83.3	97.8	14.5
1970	62.5	81.6	19.1	80.0	96.9	16.9
1972	68.1	70.5	2.4	80.0	96.6	16.6
1974	65.6	69.6	4.0	92.0	89.6	−2.4
1976	56.4	80.1	24.3	64.0	96.6	32.6
1978	73.7	89.1	15.4	68.1	95.0	26.9
1980	64.4	78.8	14.4	64.0	92.1	28.1
1982	76.7	82.1	5.4	93.1	92.4	0.7

* Figures for years 1956-1980 in column two are from same source used in Table 1-2.

incumbents were much more advantaged in defections than were senators in 1970 (19.1 points) than in 1972 (2.4 points), and (21) in 1968 a 3.7 point House advantage in defections coincided with a 14.4 point higher incumbent return rate while a 5.4 House advantage in 1982 coincided with reelection rates which were almost equal for the two chambers. When the figures in columns 3 and 6 are correlated, an R^2 of .34 is produced. Clearly, then, chamber differences in defection patterns leave much of the variance in incumbent reelection rates unexplained.

When results for the Senate are analyzed alone, if the defection hypothesis is correct, then the proportion of defections coming from challengers should vary positively with incumbent reelection rates. In 1978 defections favored incumbents more than at anytime in the previous 22 years, yet incumbent reelection rates (68 percent) were well below average. Four years earlier incumbents had been less successful in terms of the net shift of partisans (65.6 percent of the defections were pro-incumbent in 1974 compared with 73.7 percent in 1978), but incumbents were returned at one of the highest rates (92 percent). The Senate reelection rates for 1976 and 1980 were similar to 1978, but with a defection pattern that was much less favorable to incumbents. The incumbents' relative disadvantage in defections for 1980 cannot fully account for the large numbers of defeats. In 1960, when the defection ratio was similar to 1980, Senate incumbents were more successful than at any other time since 1956. Given these examples, it is not surprising that the Pearson correlation coefficient between Senate defection patterns and incumbent reelection (columns 1 and 4) is only .16.

These inconsistent results prompted us to analyze separately races in which Senate incumbents won and those in which they lost. Table 2-4 shows that when an incumbent is victorious, the rate of defections from challengers is many times greater than the defection rate in the incumbents' party. The average successful incumbent lost less than 9 percent of his/her partisans while attracting over a third of the voters who identified with the opposition party. In contrast, when the incumbent is rejected, the defection rate among challengers' partisans is less than that among the incumbents' partisans, except in 1978. There are quite different patterns depending on who wins, even though the overall mean defection rates for the two types of election outcomes are almost identical. While it would be remiss not to caution that the number of respondents in races won by challengers is small and the number of partisan defectors smaller yet, the results are so dissimilar from those for races won by incumbents that they deserve some attention.

Conclusions

Overall defection rates have increased at about the same pace for Senate and House elections since the late 1950s. Moreover, in both chambers defections among incumbents' partisans have stayed relatively constant while among challengers' partisans, defections have risen sharply. Despite these similarities, since 1970 there have been sizable inter-chamber differences in defection rates in races in which an incumbent sought reelection. Except for 1974, Senate incumbents have suffered substantially higher rates of defections and Senate challengers have experienced lower rates of defections than have comparable sets of House candidates. During the last four elections, defections have been much more concentrated among House than Senate challengers. The inter-chamber differences are, however, matters of degree within a shared pattern.

At first glance the results, particularly if one focuses exclusively on the recent data in Table 2-3, appear to support the defection hypothesis for House-Senate differences in incumbent reelection rates. Closer inspection reveals disconcerting items which show the defection hypothesis to be inadequate.

Senate defection patterns in Table 2-3 for 1976 and 1978 do not differ substantially from 1956 and 1982, respectively, years in which sitting senators fared well. Focusing on defections in races won by challengers (Table 2-4), 1978 was the only election in which successful challengers suffered higher defections than did the defeated incumbents — a counter-intuitive finding. Lest we make too much of these findings, let us reiterate the warnings about the nature and size of the sample.

The linkage between defections and return rates is ambiguous for both chambers when they are analyzed separately. In the Senate, the proportion of *defections going to incumbents* from 1974-1978 was appreciably below the mean for the 13 elections (x = 65.4) only in 1976. Thus the high incidence of defeats in recent years is not linked to an inability of incumbents to seduce adherents to the challengers' party. As another perspective on the lack of connection between defections and incumbent defeats, consider that although about a third of the incumbents were defeated in each election from 1976 to 1980, the incidence of the defections won by the incumbent varied from 56.4 to 73.7 percent of all defections. In 1978 senators benefitted more from defections than in any other year, except 1982, yet suffered heavy losses. Thus, senators' defeats are *not* due to their inability to attract substantially more of their opponent's partisans than they lose among their own.

In the House where pro-incumbent defections are even more pronounced, rising to 89.1 percent in 1978, return rates for incumbents have varied over a narrow ten percentage point range. Defections among challengers' partisans may account for what Mayhew (1974) identified as the decline in marginal House seats, but this has not affected the small number of incumbents who failed at the polls. For example, 96 percent of the House incumbents who sought reelection succeeded in 1956, as did 95 percent in 1978. However in the first year incumbents won only 61 percent of the defectors as opposed to 89 percent in 1978.[5]

Finally, while post-1970 data in Table 2-3 indicate that senators' vulnerability relative to representatives is greater when senators win a smaller share of the defectors, a major question remains unanswered. Since senators did at least as well during 1976-1980 in attracting their opponent's partisans as they did in earlier years, why were they so defeat-prone in those three recent elections?

The answer involves something more than the nature of the samples. States in which incumbent senators have been defeated have *not* been consistently undersampled. In the last seven elections, states in which incumbents lost were undersampled only in 1980 and 1982, and they were over-sampled in 1970, 1976, and 1978. States in which incumbents lost were represented proportionally in the two remaining elections.

Table 2-4 Proportion of Voters Who Defected from Their Party's Senatorial Candidate, Controlling for Election Outcome

	INCUMBENT WINS				INCUMBENT LOSES			
	Defected from		Total Defections		Defected from		Total Defections	
	Incumbent	Challenger	%	n	Incumbent	Challenger	%	n
1956	6.9%	20.0%	10.2%	50	19.5%	13.0%	16.5%	27
1958	3.7	51.9	15.6	17	17.7	9.8	12.4	16
1960	8.8	21.3	14.0	41	No incumbents defeated in the states sampled			
1964	9.1	23.7	15.1	82	17.1	15.5	16.0	20
1966	4.5	27.9	15.6	20	28.6	20.0	24.5	8
1968	8.7	44.2	22.3	50	28.0	15.9	22.3	21
1970	5.8	24.5	14.7	30	22.0	10.9	15.8	18
1972	12.9	39.5	25.8	119	22.6	22.4	22.5	25
1974	12.9	37.7	22.9	73	14.3	12.5	13.0	3
1976	11.2	48.5	26.2	64	24.5	16.0	20.5	23
1978	9.9	38.8	24.5	50	12.8	21.1	16.8	26
1980	8.7	40.0	22.8	53	33.3	10.4	22.9	24
1982	8.1	31.3	18.7	73	No incumbents defeated in the states sampled			
Mean	8.6%	34.6%	19.1%		21.8%	15.2%	18.5%	

The wider recognition enjoyed by Senate challengers may account for the lower proportion of all defections from among those who profess loyalty to the challenger's party in the Senate than the House. Thus, although the incumbency effect may be less in the Senate, it has continued the post-war trend of eroding party ties which Kostroski (1973) noted.

Doubts about the adequacy of the defection hypothesis lead us to speculate further about the way in which the greater visibility of Senate challengers may inspire higher turnout among their partisans than do House challengers, a number of whose partisans may be cross-pressured between party ties and a hesitancy to vote for their party's unknown nominee. Among Senate incumbents' partisans, the situation may be just the opposite since senators' ideologies are more widely known (Abramowitz, 1980: 638-639), some of their partisans who disagree with the incumbent may experience cross-pressure which, if unresolved, will cause them not to vote.

Another possible explanation involves independents. The more extensive information readily available on Senate challengers may account for the lower rates at which independents support senators than representatives (Abramowitz, 1980: 638).

The defection hypothesis alone can only partially account for chamber differences in defection rates. Partisan defections in combination with different turnout rates and the behavior of independents may account for enough voters to explain the higher level of Senate than House incumbent losses. In the absence of evidence to sustain some of these speculations, it would be best if not too much were attributed to defections. Defection rates are even less successful in accounting for differences or variations in incumbent reelection rates within chambers.

Notes

1. Use of these data should be accompanied by a caveat. The CPS data for Senate elections are less than ideal. In most years very little information about voter preferences in Senate elections was gathered. Also, the samples were not drawn for the purpose of analyzing Senate elections. Prior to 1978, CPS used what it defined as primary sampling units; since then the congressional district has been the sampling unit. As Mann and Wolfinger (1980: 618), and Jacobson (1981: 185), have pointed out, there are limitations in these samples. Respondents are not interviewed in all states having contested Senate races. However, the surveys include respondents from, on average, 64 percent of the states in which incumbent senators faced challengers which is a far more comprehensive sampling than for House contests. Unequal numbers of voters per state and district have been a perennial problem (Erikson, 1978: 512-513). Caution is therefore dictated when interpreting the results, especially when the number of cases is small.
2. Figures for House and presidential elections are from Mann and Wolfinger (1980: 620) prior to 1980.

3. The difference in the number of defections between Tables 2-1 and 2-2 is explained by the types of Senate races examined in each. Table 2-1 includes all Senate races, incumbent and open seat, sampled by the CPS surveys. The number of defections in Table 2-2 is smaller because only Senate races in which there was an incumbent were included.

4. This measure is used since it is preferable to several alternatives. It introduces standardization across the uneven number of defections for individual years. Also it is a measure of net gain or loss to incumbents.

5. The correlation between the share of partisan defections won by House incumbents and the reelection rates of House incumbents is $r = .26$.

3. ON THE DECLINE OF COMPETITION
IN CONGRESSIONAL ELECTIONS

John A. Ferejohn

In a recent article, Mayhew discovered that since the middle of the 1950s there has been a steady decline in the proportion of "competitive" congressional districts.[1] In related work, Erikson found that the incumbency advantage more than doubled between the late 1950s and 1966.[2] For the same period Tufte showed that a substantial drop in the "swing ratio" (the percentage increase in House seats a party obtains when it received a one percent increase in popular vote) had taken place.[3] Finally, Kostroski also discovered a substantial increase in the incumbency advantage in postwar Senate elections.[4]

Not surprisingly, scholars differ in their explanations of these findings. Without doing violence to anyone's position, one can enunciate three proposed explanations. Some authors argue that changes in the institutional setting of congressional elections have worked to alter the outcomes of these elections. For example, Tufte attributes the decline in the swing ratio to the control incumbents have over redistricting:

> Our data indicate that a major element in the job security of incumbents is their ability to exert significant control over the drawings of district boundaries. . . . Ironically, reapportionment rulings have given incumbents new opportunities to construct secure districts for themselves, leading to a reduction in turnover that is in turn reflected in the sharply reduced swing ratio of the last few elections.[5]

Tufte argues further that in Senate districts (states, to institutionalists) there has been no reapportionment and no decline in the proportion of marginal seats. Finally, he notes that if House elections are examined in states that have reapportioned "there is an immediate decline in the competitiveness of the races in the first election after the new districting."[6]

Author's Note: This paper has benefited greatly from the assistance of John Land, my research assistant, and from the detailed critical comments of Morris Fiorina, Sam Kernell, Robert Erikson, John Kingdon, Ben Page, Gary Jacobson, Michael Cohen, J. Vincent Buck, Robert Bates, and Lance Davis. I could not take all their criticisms into account, but I am deeply grateful for their generous donations of time. Some of the data employed in this study were made available by the Inter-University Consortium for Political Research at the University of Michigan. I alone am responsible for the analysis and conclusions.

Source: *American Political Science Review* 71 (March 1977): 166-176. Reprinted with permission of the author.

A second position attributes the changing nature of congressional elections to a shift in the behavior of the electorate. Perhaps the most explicit statement of this position is advanced by Burnham:

> Tufte's argument about the effects of bipartisan gerrymandering of districts is ingenious but not ultimately convincing. For there is a host of evidence . . . to support the view that *the most important single factor has been systematic change in mass voting behavior since 1960.*[7]

Burnham argues that "the very high . . . swing ratios of the late nineteenth century were associated with a period in which party identification and party voting were extremely salient, by all aggregate indicators."[8] In a somewhat earlier contribution, Erikson anticipated Burnham's point:

> An increased incumbency advantage in 1966 is not so mysterious as it may seem, since the timing of its occurrence coincides with that of the reported erosion of party identification as an electoral force in the late sixties. Possibly the electorate's decreasing partisan loyalty, signaled by such indicators as the post-1964 surge in the number of independent voters, is the cause of the apparent boost in the incumbency advantage.[9]

A third, intermediate, possibility is that institutional change has modified voter behavior. For example, Mayhew argues that people in the same situation (in terms of information about the candidates) behaved in the same way in 1966 as they did in 1958 but that incumbents had more of an advantage in promulgating information than they did in the earlier period. According to this view there is aggregate behavioral change, but it is caused by a shift in the marginal distributions of people across the various informational categories. Mayhew hypothesizes that these shifts stem from the increasing use of the institutional advantages of incumbency such as the franking privilege, or from increasing skill in using polls and publicity. Mayhew writes, "The answer to the incumbency advantage question could be a remarkably simple one: the more hundreds of thousands of messages congressmen rain down on constituents the more votes they get."[10]

In this paper some data are presented which will help to clarify some of the issues in this debate. I argue that both Tufte's pure institutional change theory and Mayhew's argument that the informational advantage of incumbents has increased, are inadequate to account for the observed phenomena. Thus any acceptable explanation of why the incumbency advantage has increased must be based on a basic shift in the behavior of the electorate. Of course, a shift in electoral behavior may be of two basic sorts. What might be called the *distribution* theory holds that different kinds of party identifiers (strong Democrats, weak Democrats, etc.) are acting the same as always but the distribution of people into these categories has shifted. The *behavioral change* theory holds that within each party-identification category there has been a change in behavior. The data I present will provide some evidence that at least part of the change occurring is of the latter sort.

The plan of the paper is as follows. First, by presenting data on redistricting, I show why Tufte's explanation fails. Second, I analyze survey data which indicate an increase in incumbency voting at the level of the individual voter.

Third, I show that increased incumbency voting results only partly from the increased informational advantage of incumbents over nonincumbents *and* the propensity of voters to cast their ballots in favor of candidates who are known to them. Both of these factors have undergone some change between 1958 and 1970, but the change in the informational advantage is not adequate to account for the change in incumbency voting. Finally, data are presented which suggest that the inclination of voters to vote for candidates they know has increased over the period under study at all levels of party identification.

Redistributing and Competition

In his reply to Burnham's comment on his 1973 article, Tufte remarks that more important than ascertaining whether or not there has been an underlying shift in voter behavior that would account for the shift in the swing ratio is "allocating the effects on political competition of redistricting on the one hand and the increase in incumbent resources on the other." [11] This prescription is sensible as long as there is some reason to believe that these two effects capture a substantial fraction of the variance in the dependent variable. In this section I argue that there is no reason to expect that redistricting has much influence on the variables of interest.

In two papers and a reply to a comment, Tufte has advanced several pieces of evidence indicating that redistricting has a major effect on the decline of the swing ratio. In his first paper (1973), Tufte notes that the proportion of competitive seats in the House has declined from about .20 in 1958 to .13 in 1970, while in the Senate (where no redistricting ever takes place), there has been no decline. He then says that "some recent redistricting laws have been described as the Incumbent Survival Acts of 1972." [12] He claims that "reapportionment rulings have given incumbents new opportunities to construct secure districts for themselves. . . ." [13] Tufte goes on to present data on the number of marginal seats in Michigan, Illinois, Pennsylvania, and Ohio for the 1970 elections (all these states had been redistricted during the decade). Finally he claims that "the independent contribution of reapportionment to the job security of incumbents can also be seen in the elections immediately following reapportionment in a state: there is an immediate decline in the competitiveness of the races in the first election after the new districting." [14]

In his rejoinder to Burnham's communication, Tufte presents what he calls the *"seats-votes" curves* for California in 1966 (before redistricting) and 1968 (after redistricting). These curves indicate a substantial decline in the number of competitive districts in the state following the redistricting.

Finally, in his article,[15] Tufte presents the seats/votes curves for Illinois, Michigan, Pennsylvania, and Ohio for 1950 and 1970. In each case there is a substantial decline in the swing ratio (and of course in the number of competitive districts). As far as I know, this is all the evidence that Tufte has presented in support of the redistricting explanation.

As the reader may suspect, I have several objections to this explanation. First, it is highly implausible *a priori*. Before the Court rulings on reapportionment, there were fewer legal restrictions on the amount of gerrymandering that could be done than there are now. Aside from some anecdotal remarks, Tufte has presented no evidence that incumbents have more control over redistricting now than they ever did. It appears to me that he must bear the burden of proof on this point and establish the plausibility of his contention.

Second, while Tufte presents some data on the number of competitive districts in certain states before and after redistricting, he fails to look at changes in the number of competitive districts in states where no reapportionment has occurred. If *any* of the opposing explanations are correct he would find that there has been a decline in the number of competitive seats after reapportionment but that decline need have nothing to do with the reapportionment itself. In those states which underwent it, reapportionment is simply correlated perfectly with the change in voting behavior (if Burnham and Erikson are right) or with the increase in resources held by the incumbent (if Mayhew is correct). This problem seems to be easily remedied by comparing the number of marginal districts over time in states which redistricted with those which did not. In Tables 3-1 and 3-2 any district in which the winner received no more than 60 percent of the vote is called competitive, while all others are called noncompetitive.

These tables indicate that the drop in the percentage of competitive seats that Tufte found following reapportionments is not due to redistricting, since the decline occurred in unredistricted areas as well. These data suggest that redistricting has no influence at all on the swing ratio. The decline in the number of marginal districts is a general one which must be accounted for by a theory of the sort advanced by either Mayhew or Burnham.

Before proceeding with a somewhat more detailed consideration of the explanations of Mayhew, Burnham and Erikson, I shall present one more piece of evidence which seems to bear on the problem. In an article on postwar Senate elections, Kostroski found that when the percentage of a senatorial candidate's popular vote is regressed on measures of "base party vote," "national tides," and "incumbency" within party, there has been a substantial increase in the effect of incumbency on vote percentage.[16] For the present purposes it is significant that this increase has occurred in "districts" in which no redistricting took place. In my view, Kostroski's results fit quite well with the observed drop in the swing ratio in House districts, since this drop might well be due to an increase in incumbency voting in House elections. Kostroski's research indicates that incumbency voting has in fact increased during the postwar period and that this increase occurred in areas which have not been redistricted.

On the Incumbent's Increasing Control of Resources

Mayhew suggests that a principal source of the change in the number of competitive seats may be found in the "greater electoral advantage" that incumbents hold over their opponents. He cites two pieces of evidence that this advantage has increased. First he remarked that Erikson found that the incumbency advantage more than doubled between the 1950s and 1966.[17] Second, Mayhew computed the drops in the percentage of the vote that a party suffers in a district when an incumbent retires. He found that these drops were larger in 1966, 1968, and 1970 than in 1962 and 1964. He concluded that "Incumbency

Table 3-1   Decline in Percentage of Competitive Seats in Non-Southern States That Have and Have Not Been Redistricted, 1962-1966[a]

	Redistricted	Not Redistricted
1962	51	51
1966	40	28
Number of districts	182	132

[a] The data are from *America Votes*, Vol. 9, ed. Richard Scammon, *Congressional Quarterly*, 1972. Entries are the percentage of competitive districts.

Table 3-2   Decline in Percentage of Competitive Seats in Non-Southern States That Have and Have Not Been Redistricted, 1966-1970[a]

	Redistricted	Not Redistricted
1966	35	39
1970	27	33
Number of districts	177	153

[a] The data are from Scammon. Entries are the percentage of competitive districts.

does seem to have increased in electoral value, and it is reasonable to suppose that one effect of this increase has been to boost House members of both parties out of the marginal electoral range." [18]

Mayhew attempted to trace the decline in the number of marginal districts and the concomitant apparent increase in the advantage of incumbency to real changes in the quantity of resources held and employed by incumbents. He argued that incumbent congressmen currently make substantially greater use of the franking privilege than did incumbents in the 1950s. Indeed the quantity of junk mail quadrupled between 1954 and 1970. Further, this increase in the control and utilization of tangible resources has allegedly translated into an increase in the level of recognition enjoyed by incumbents. Mayhew cites Gallup poll data which indicate that there was a seven percent increase in the precentage of people who knew their congressman between 1966 and 1970.

While I do not have data that bear directly on whether incumbent congressmen enjoy more of an advantage over their opponents in the control of campaign resources than did the incumbents of the 1950s, it is possible to utilize data collected by the SRC to question whether any effects on voting behavior may be imputed to this alleged change. If Mayhew's argument is correct, one should be able to observe, first of all, an overall increase in the level of recognition of the incumbent. Second, the relative level of recognition of incumbents versus challengers should also show an increase. Additionally one ought to find that the increased level (or relative level) of recognition translates behaviorally into an increased level of incumbency voting.

The data I present below indicate the following: (1) a substantial increase in incumbency voting on the level of the individual voter; (2) no increase in the level of recognition of incumbents; and (3) little if any increase in the gap between recognition levels of incumbents and challengers. I reserve treatment of the behavioral linkage between candidate recognition and voting until the next section of the paper.

The data utilized here are from the SRC election surveys for 1956, 1958, 1960, 1964, 1966, 1968 and 1970. These are all of the years in which information on incumbency was collected by SRC or in which congressional districts identification was provided so that incumbency status could be supplied by the author. Unfortunately, only three off-year elections are available for these purposes, and so some of the results are advanced here only tentatively.

Has there been a change in the frequency of incumbency voting during this period? To answer this question for each year and for Democrats, Republicans and Independents, the percentage of voters in each partisan category in districts with Democratic incumbents who voted for the Republican candidate was subtracted from the percentage of voters (in the same category) in districts with Democratic incumbents who cast their ballots for the Democratic candidate. Figure 3-1 reports these data during the period.

First notice that for Independents the tendency to vote for the incumbent is substantially greater in off years than in years of presidential elections. Further, while there is some discernible long-term shift in the behavior of the Independents, it is particularly interesting that partisan identifiers (especially the Democrats) became more likely to respond to incumbency later in the period of observation than they had been earlier. One may conjecture that their behavior has become more like that of the Independents over time. Of course, until more data are available, this possibility is only speculative.

We now examine an important intervening step in Mayhew's argument. Has the informational advantage held by incumbents increased during the period? To answer this question, each respondent was asked to name the candidates for the House in his district. If the respondent could provide the name of a candidate, then he was considered to be "aware" of the candidate, otherwise not. Among the surveys for which we had incumbency information, this question was asked only in 1958, 1964, 1966, 1968 and 1970 so that the data are a bit more limited than those reported earlier.

Figure 3-1   Change in Incumbency Voting, 1956-1970, for Republicans (SR & WR), Democrats (WD & SD) and Independents (ID & I & IR) in All Contested Districts

Percentage difference in voting Democratic due to voting in a district with a Democratic incumbent rather than a Republican

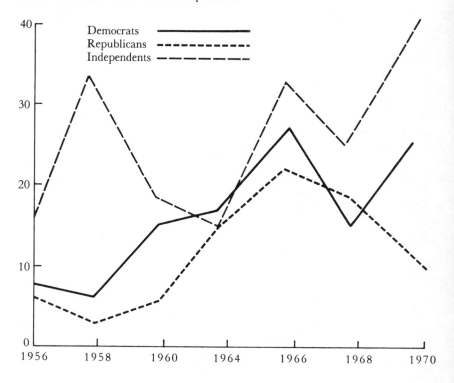

If Mayhew's theory is correct, these data should show that incumbents are more likely to be known to voters after 1964 than in 1958. Further, the advantage which incumbents enjoy in this respect ought to have increased over the three elections. Table 3-3 gives the percentage who know a candidate given that this candidate is or is not an incumbent in all three years. This table indicates that among voters in contested districts with incumbents running *there has been no increase in awareness of the incumbent.* Rather, in years of presidential elections among voters in contested elections who live in districts with an incumbent running, the percentage who know the incumbent's name is constant at 63 percent. In off years the figure remains constant at about 55 percent. On the other hand, the corresponding variable for nonincumbents displays no clear trend. During the off years, recognition of nonincumbents has declined, while during presidential election years, it seems to have increased somewhat. These data suggest that the increasing control of resources by incumbents, if it has any effect at all in incumbency voting, does not directly impinge on voter awareness of congressional candidates. In my view this result casts serious doubts on Mayhew's explanation of the declining number of competitive seats.

Incumbency and Salience of Congressional Candidates

A critical component of Mayhew's argument is that an increase in the salience of a candidate will have the effect of increasing his vote. No doubt the source of this assumption is to be found in Stokes and Miller's classic article demonstrating that candidate salience has an effect on congressional vote. Mayhew drew the following policy conclusion from this study: if a candidate is able through the expenditure of campaign resources to increase his level of recognition, his vote will increase. This proposition, although never directly examined, seems to play a large part in popular reasoning about congressional elections. The following analysis is designed to illustrate whether or not this policy conclusion may be safely drawn from the Stokes-Miller data.

Under the assumption that the effects of salience would not interact with the effects of party identification or of incumbency status, the following regression equation was estimated utilizing an iterative generalized least-squares procedure described in Goldberger.[19]

Table 3-3　Percentage of Voters Who Are Aware of House Candidates in Contested Districts

	Incumbent	Nonincumbent
1958	57.6 (738)[a]	38.0 (947)
1964	63.0 (856)	39.8 (920)
1966	55.9 (583)	37.6 (703)
1968	63.7 (703)	46.5 (861)
1970	54.7 (548)	31.3 (630)

[a] The number in parentheses is the number of voters in districts with an incumbent running (column 1) or a nonincumbent running (column 2).

$$Y = \alpha + \beta_1 X_1 + \beta_2 X_2 + \ldots + \beta_6 X_6 + \epsilon, \qquad (1)$$

where $Y = 1$ if respondent voted Democratic,
　　　　0 otherwise;

$X_1 = 1$ if respondent resided in a district with Republican incumbent,
　　　　0 otherwise;

$X_2 = 1$ if respondent was aware of the Democratic candidate,
　　　　0 otherwise;

$X_3 = 1$ if respondent was aware of the Republican candidate,
　　　　0 otherwise;

$X_4 = 1$ if respondent was aware of both candidates,
　　　　0 otherwise;

$X_5 = 1$ if respondent was a Democrat (SD or WD),
　　　　0 otherwise;

$X_6 = 1$ if respondent was a Republican (SR or WD),
　　　　0 otherwise;

　　　The samples of observations on which the equation was estimated consisted of all contested districts in which an incumbent was running during 1958, 1964, 1966, 1968 and 1970 taken separately.

　　　The question at issue was whether or not, when incumbency status and party ID were fixed, changes in candidate salience had an intuitively predictable effect on the vote. In particular, if a citizen learned of the Democratic candidate, having previously known neither candidate, or, alternatively, known only the Republican, would that citizen's probability of voting Democratic increase significantly? Table 3-4 gives the regression results.

　　　The estimates reported in Table 3-4 indicate that, except for 1966 when a voter who knew the Republican candidate was more likely to vote Democratic than one who knew both candidates, the effect of salience was in the predicted direction. Further, the data in Table 3-4 indicate that in 1958, incumbency had no independent effect on voting (at the .05 level) once the effect of awareness is taken into account. On the other hand, these data suggest that in 1964, 1966, 1968, and 1970 incumbency had a significant effect on the voting decision, once salience is controlled. Voters were apparently using incumbency as a voting cue whether or not they could recall the names of the incumbent candidate in the interview situation.

　　　The model estimated here is obviously extremely simpleminded and, in light of Tufte's results on the causes of voting decisions in congressional elections, using more aggregated data, unsatisfactory as an explanatory model of congressional voting behavior. It was employed here to learn if the widely held belief that the incumbency effect in voting works through candidate salience had any validity. Based on these data it appears that the popular view cannot be rejected for the 1958 data but that in 1964, 1966, 1968 and 1970 there was evidently an

Table 3-4 Regression Estimates for Equation (1)

	1958	1964	1966	1968	1970
β_1 (R Increase)	−.023 (.026)[a]	−.082 (.034)	−.228 (.040)	−.067 (.028)	−.099 (.03)
β_2 (Aware Democrat)	+.073 (.028)	.148 (.037)	.123 (.032)	.177 (.048)	.301 (.04)
β_3 (Aware Republican)	−.089 (.030)	−.092(.040)	.041 (.039)	−.110 (.033)	−.033 (.03)
β_4 (Aware Both)	+.032 (.036)	.012 (.047)	−.176 (.046)	.011 (.053)	−.147 (.05)
β_5 (Democrat)	.465 (.050)	.213 (.044)	.373 (.049)	.375 (.039)	.283 (.05)
β_6 (Republican)	−.321 (.051)	−.345 (.047)	−.249 (.052)	−.170 (.036)	−.250 (.05)
α	.446 (.051)	.558 (.045)	.509 (.050)	.331 (.041)	.366 (.05)
R^2	.583	.305	.455	.304	.380
N	720	920	555	723	592

[a] Standard errors are in parentheses.

independent incumbency effect. In the later period perhaps many voters who were not able to identify the candidate for the interviewer were able nevertheless to distinguish incumbent from nonincumbent in the voting booth and use that information in making their voting decision.

Analysis of the residuals from the regression equations indicated that a number of cases produced estimates for the probability of voting Democratic outside the range between zero and one. This finding indicates interactions between the independent variables in their effects on the dependent variable; that is, the effect of salience on the conditional probability of voting Democratic apparently varies according to incumbency status or party identification.

In order to examine this phenomenon the following table was examined utilizing essentially the same information that was contained in the regression equations but allowing for the interactions between salience and incumbency.

The striking thing about Table 3-5 is that controlling for incumbency status, in four of ten comparisons increased awareness of own party candidate actually *decreased* the probability of voting for him. In two other comparisons there was essentially no difference at all. These data must cause scholars to reconsider very carefully the maxim advanced by Stokes and Miller "to be perceived at all is to be perceived favorably." [20] A candidate of the same party as a given voter may be more likely to receive his vote if the voter does not recognize him than if he does. On the other hand, if a similar set of tables was displayed with a variable indicating whether or not the voter is aware of the other party's candidate, the effects of salience appear to be much more intuitive. One may only conclude that the effects of name recognition seem to be quite complex and that more investigation is required before one can conclude that increased name recognition will increase a candidate's vote.

Behavioral Change Theories

The arguments in the first three sections of this paper provide strong *prima facie* evidence to believe that neither Tufte's nor Mayhew's theories can adequately explain the decline in the number of marginal districts. In this section I wish to turn from the gleeful enterprise of attacking existing theories to the more difficult and thankless one of constructing part of a new one. Unfortunately, while I cannot claim the credit for inventing the new theory — that must be divided between Burnham and Erikson — I would hold myself partly responsible if it too should turn out to be invalid.

The data in Figure 3-1 suggest that the principal change in incumbency voting between 1956 and 1970 occurred primarily among the partisan identifiers rather than among Independents. Thus, this section focuses mainly on examining the behavior of the partisans rather than that of the Independents. The major question is this: Is the changing level of incumbency voting due to the changing distribution of partisan identifiers or to changes in behavior within the various party identification categories? Of course one cannot expect a simple answer to

Table 3-5 Percentage Voting for Own Party by Awareness and Incumbency

	1958		1964		1966		1968		1970	
	Own Party Candidate Incumbent	*Other Party Candidate Incumbent*	*Own Party Candidate Incumbent*	*Other Party Candidate Incumbent*	*Own Party Candidate Incumbent*	*Other Party Candidate Incumbent*	*Own Party Candidate Incumbent*	*Other Party Candidate Incumbent*	*Own Party Candidate Incumbent*	*Other Party Candidate Incumbent*
Aware of Own Party Candidate	91.3 (206)[a]	85.2 (115)	92.0 (264)	71.3 (136)	95.4 (152)	72.6 (73)	85.6 (174)	70.8 (113)	92.5 (133)	79.2 (72)
Not Aware of Own Party Candidate	95.7 (140)	91.2 (137)	90.3 (145)	79.3 (140)	91.4 (116)	68.4 (95)	89.2 (102)	70.1 (117)	92.2 (103)	68.4 (114)

[a] Entries in parentheses are the number of cases on which the percentages are based.

such a question, and it seems likely that both kinds of change will be found. Nevertheless, I would think it significant and interesting if the hypothesis of behavioral change within party identification categories could not be rejected.

In their paper on congressional elections, Stokes and Miller showed that "the saliency of the candidate is of critical importance if he is to attract support from the opposite party." [21] They produced the following table [Table 3-6] based on survey data from the 1958 elections. These data suggest that while party is a fairly good indicator of how a party identifier will cast his vote, the various categories of knowledge of the candidates have some effect on this relationship.

In Table 3-7, data are presented from the 1958, 1965, 1966, 1968 and 1970 SRC surveys which correspond roughly to the 1958 data presented by Stokes and Miller. The number on which the 1958 percentages are based do not quite agree with those presented by the earlier authors, but the percentages are fairly close to theirs.

The first thing to notice in Table 3-7 is that in every information category a smaller fraction of people voted for the candidate of their own party in 1964, 1966, 1968 and 1970 than in 1958. This difference is most pronounced in the category of people who could mention only the candidate of the other party. Chi-square tests for homogeneity between 1958 and each of the ensuing years were computed under the null hypothesis that the observations were drawn from the same populations. In each case this hypothesis was rejected at the .05 level.

To construct Table 3-7, all party identifiers were aggregated (weak, strong, and Independent-leaners). Perhaps a shift in the distribution of the electorate across the various categories in the seven-point SRC party identification scale accounts for this apparent change in behavior. If so, then one may hope to explain the apparent change in voting behavior by explaining why this distribution has shifted. Indeed, if the percentage of strong identifiers who resided in districts in which an incumbent was running in 1956 and 1958 is compared with the same percentages in 1966 and 1968, there was a decline from approximately 43 percent to about 36 percent. There was an increase in weak and Independent-leaning identifiers over the same period of about 6 percent. Since party is less of an anchor for weak and Independent-leaning identifiers than for strong identifiers, the observed change in Table 3-7 may be due to the changing proportion of the electorate in various party identification categories.

In order to test whether this distributional shift accounts for these changes, a regression model was constructed in which the dependent variable was 1 if the respondent voted for the Democratic candidate and 0 if he or she voted for the Republican. The independent variables were constructed to yield a two-way layout with six party identification categories (excluding Independents) and the four informational categories with all interaction terms included. If the changes in

Table 3-6 Effect of Information on Congressional Voting in Contested Districts in 1958

Percentage Who Voted for Candidate	Voter Was Aware of:			
	Both Candidate	Own Party Candidate	Other Party Candidate	Neither Candidate
Of Own Party	83	98	60	92
Of Other Party	17	2	40	9
N =	196	166	68	368

Table 3-7 are due to a changing propensity of citizens in a given category of information and party affiliation to vote Democratic, there should be a change in the parameters between 1958 and each of the four following elections — 1964, 1966, 1968, and 1970.

The statistical model and estimation procedures are given in the Appendix as are the coefficient estimates for each of the equations. Of particular interest

Table 3-7 Effect of Information on the Congressional Vote in Contested Districts[a]

Percentage Who Voted for Own Party in	Voter Was Aware of:			
	Both Candidates	Own Party Candidates	Other Party Candidates	Neither Candidates
1958	81.0 (221)	99.3 (134)	66.7 (30)	95.1 (290)
1964	78.8 (245)	94.8 (164)	59.6 (34)	85.6 (250)
1966	80.7 (163)	96.0 (96)	34.9 (15)	86.5 (193)
1968	77.0 (235)	94.9 (94)	48.3 (28)	81.7 (192)
1970	75.9 (107)	99.1 (110)	36.4 (16)	89.8 (185)

[a] Number of cases in each awareness category are in parentheses.

was the null hypothesis, i.e., that no parametric change had occurred between 1958 and each of the four later elections. This hypothesis was rejected at the .01 level in every case. Thus, the present evidence indicates that not all of the changes from 1958 can be accounted for by the changing distribution of party identifiers. At least some of the change in voting behavior has occurred *within* party identification levels.

This finding suggests that while political observers have been lamenting or celebrating, depending on their inclinations, the decline in the number of partisan identifiers, a related sort of change has been occurring. Those people who still identify with one of the parties seem to be using it less and less as a cue in making their voting decisions in congressional elections.

Discussion

The main purpose of this paper is to elucidate and examine critically the principal explanations proffered by scholars for the widely observed decline in the number of marginal seats. By and large the view advanced by Burnham and Erikson, that a behavioral change accounts for the decline, has received the greatest support. Voters are different than they used to be, and not merely because there are more Independents. The party identifiers seem recently to be more responsive in House elections than they have been in the past, and in that sense they are behaving more like the Independents.

As Tufte pointed out, the decline in the number of marginal seats may have the effect of mediating the responsiveness of House elections to national tides. The claim here is that the cause of this phenomenon is to be found in a shift in the behavior of the electorate. Perhaps, as some analysts suggest, the change in electoral behavior is rooted in an increased unwillingness of voters to utilize party identification as a voting cue. This possibility is certainly consistent with many other findings. For example, Tufte, and Arseneau and Wolfinger report that party identification accounts for a decreasing proportion of the congressional vote over time.[22] At the level of congressional voting the decreasing reliance on party as a "shorthand" cue may not turn voters toward issue voting but may simply increase their reliance on other rules of thumb such as incumbency or satisfaction with presidential performance. This would be a curious consequence, since it would suggest that increased issue voting in presidential elections and the declining number of competitive House districts have essentially the same causes. As the voters come to approximate more closely the "ideal citizens" of certain democratic theories, they may (inadvertently) end up insulating their congressmen from defeat and hence to some extent reduce their representatives' incentive to respond to constituent desires.

Indeed, recent research reported by Kernell indicates that the perceived performance of the President in office has a pronounced effect on individual citizens in deciding whether and how to vote in off-year elections.[23] Tufte found that at the aggregate level, presidential performance was an important variable in accounting for the midterm votes. Such findings suggest that the scarcity and resulting costliness of information in congressional elections forces most citizens to rely on simple decision rules in deciding how to cast their votes. The decision rules that currently seem to be operating in the electorate are based on party affiliation, presidential performance, and incumbency. The findings in this paper suggest that voters seem to be shifting away from the use of party affiliation as a decision rule and toward increased utilization of incumbency. I have had nothing at all to say about the fact that voters apparently also respond to presidential performance in deciding how to cast their vote. If the importance of this explanatory component is increasing, then at least the partisan makeup of Congress may end up being quite responsive to national forces.

Given the limited quantity of data presented here and the difficulty of ascertaining voter responsiveness to national forces in the SRC data, only guesses and speculations can be advanced about the significance of the results reported here. One effect of the apparent increase in the electorate's use of incumbency as a voting cue has been to decrease the proportion of competitive seats. We might conjecture that a congressman with a safe seat would be less concerned with responding to constituency demands. I hesitate to endorse this conclusion since part of the explanation of the increased incumbency effect may be found in the increased ability of sitting congressmen to satisfy constituency requests. Indeed, the increasing decentralization of the policymaking process in the Congress would seem to point in this direction. It may still be true that if a congressman decides not to make use of his many opportunities to assist his constituents, he would not benefit from any incumbency advantage. Indeed, congressmen and congressional scholars are able to recount many stories illustrating this very point. Obviously much more research is needed to settle these questions.

Appendix: Procedures

The following regression equation formed the basis for the analysis in the discussion of Behavioral Change Theories in this paper:

The regression equation that was estimated was

$$Y_K = \alpha + \sum_{i=1}^{5} \beta_i X_{iK} + \sum_{i=1}^{3} \gamma_i Z_{iK} + \sum_{i=1}^{5} \sum_{j=1}^{3} \delta_{ij} X_{iK} Z_{jK} + \\ + \epsilon_{iK}, \tag{A.1}$$

where Y_K = 1 if respondent voted for Democratic candidate
          0 if respondent voted for Republican candidate

X_{1K} = 1 if respondent is a strong Democrat
          0 otherwise

X_{2K} = 1 if respondent is a weak Democrat
          0 otherwise

X_{3K} = 1 if respondent is independent-leaning Democrat
          0 otherwise

X_{4K} = 1 if respondent is independent-leaning Republican
          0 otherwise

X_{5K} = 1 if respondent is weak Republican

Table 3-8 Generalized Least-Squares Estimates of Equation A.1

	1958		1964		1966		1968	
	Coeff.	Std. errors	Coeff.	Std. errors	Coeff.	Std. errors	Coeff.	Std. errors
$\tilde{\alpha}$	.085	.04	.133	.04	.050	.03	.119	.05
β_1	.878	.04	.748	.05	.814	.06	.738	.06
β_2	.712	.06	.648	.07	.634	.08	.523	.08
β_3	.524	.10	.597	.09	.617	.13	.714	.08
β_4	.248	.11	.158	.10	.283	.12	.068	.08
β_5	.242	.07	.229	.07	.220	.08	.209	.08
γ_1	−.085	.04	−.133	.04	.013	.07	−.119	.04
γ_2	.486	.18	−.133	.04	.700	.21	−.119	.04
γ_3	−.069	.04	−.133	.04	.050	.06	−.070	.05
δ_{11}	.122	.04	.239	.06	.124	.08	.208	.07
δ_{21}	.257	.07	.216	.08	.303	.10	.432	.09
δ_{31}	.476	.10	.403	.09	.121	.19	.063	.16
δ_{41}	−.248	.11	−.158	.10	−.346	.13	−.068	.08
δ_{51}	−.214	.08	−.047	.13	−.211	.12	−.209	.08
δ_{12}	−.825	.22	−.248	.20	−.939	.27	−.147	.16
δ_{22}	−.394	.21	−.016	.12	−1.241	.26	−.142	.16
δ_{32}	−.595	.28	.003	.23	−1.167	.30	−.521	.14
δ_{42}	.180	.21	.342	.26	−.478	.29	.333	.16
δ_{52}	−.225	.22	.464	.14	−.278	.25	.422	.19
δ_{13}	.087	.05	.208	.06	.066	.08	.020	.09
δ_{23}	.191	.07	.242	.07	.125	.10	.137	.10
δ_{33}	.243	.13	.153	.12	−.190	.18	−.404	.13
δ_{43}	−.077	.15	.231	.15	−.071	.17	.130	.12
δ_{53}	−.165	.08	.073	.10	−.247	.10	−.176	.09
N	853		845		565		755	
R^2	.653		.488		.530		.464	

Table 3-8 (Continued)

1970		1958-1964		1958-1966		1958-1968		1958-1970	
Coeff.	Std. errors	Coeff.	Std. errors	Coeff.	Std. errors	Coeff.	Std. errors	Coeff.	Std. errors
.038	.05	.112	.03	.069	.03	.098	.03	.066	.03
.787	.07	.810	.04	.860	.03	.795	.04	.830	.04
.586	.08	.677	.05	.680	.05	.579	.05	.647	.05
.337	.16	.561	.07	.560	.08	.574	.07	.402	.09
.362	.15	.197	.07	.264	.08	.109	.06	.291	.09
.179	.09	.233	.05	.234	.05	.211	.05	.204	.06
−.038	.04	−.112	.03	−.046	.03	−.098	.03	−.066	.03
−.038	.07	.123	.09	.567	.14	.045	.09	.184	.15
−.008	.05	−.102	.03	−.025	.03	−.068	.03	−.045	.03
.163	.09	.183	.04	.117	.04	.147	.05	.152	.05
.368	.09	.231	.06	.275	.06	.302	.07	.264	.07
.663	.17	.439	.07	.299	.11	.292	.11	.597	.10
−.218	.20	−.197	.07	−.288	.08	−.109	.07	−.224	.11
−.179	.09	−.169	.06	−.218	.06	−.194	.06	−.190	.06
−.429	.15	−.454	.13	−.871	.17	−.331	.14	−.581	.18
−.433	.14	−.198	.12	−.760	.19	−.198	.15	−.488	.19
.163	.26	−.251	.18	−.832	.21	−.440	.16	−.153	.22
.210	.24	.234	.22	−.264	.22	.081	.18	−.041	.25
.266	.19	.165	.13	−.237	.17	.090	.16	−.086	.19
−.082	.09	.150	.04	.078	.04	.026	.05	−.030	.05
.004	.10	.218	.05	.159	.06	.141	.06	.071	.07
.133	.19	.193	.09	.064	.11	−.124	.10	.135	.11
−.342	.16	.086	.11	−.058	.11	.028	.09	−.232	.10
−.118	.11	−.047	.06	−.194	.06	−.178	.06	−.156	.06
585		1698		1418		1561		1391	
.558		.560		.589		.530		.599	

$$Z_{1K} = \begin{matrix} 0 \text{ otherwise} \\ 1 \text{ if respondent is aware of neither candidate} \end{matrix}$$

0 otherwise

Z_{1K} =1 if respondent is aware of neither candidate

0 otherwise

Z_{2K} =1 if respondent is aware of his own party's candidate

0 otherwise

Z_{3K} =1 if respondent is aware of other party's candidate

0 otherwise

The initial least-squares estimates $(\hat{\alpha},\beta,\hat{\gamma},\delta)$ were employed to estimate the conditional probability that the kth respondent would vote Democratic as follows.

$$P(k \text{ votes Democratic } | X_1 = \chi_{iK}, X_2 = \chi_{2K}$$

$$\ldots X_5 = , \chi_{5K}, Z_1 = z_{1K}, Z_2 =$$

$$Y_K = \alpha + \sum_{i=1}^{5} \beta_i \chi_{iK} + \sum_{i=1}^{3} \gamma_i Z_{iK} + \sum_{i=1}^{5} \sum_{j=1}^{3} \delta_{ij} \chi_{iK} Z_{iK}.$$

Thus since $(\hat{\alpha},\beta,\hat{\gamma},\delta)$ are consistent estimates of the parameters Y_K is also a consistent estimate and so one can obtain a consistent estimate of the variance of ϵ_K as $Y_K (1 - Y_K)$. We employed these estimates to generate an estimated variance-covariance matrix and then to form, the generalized least squares estimates $(\hat{\alpha},\beta,\hat{\gamma},\delta)$. These are reported in Table 3-8.

Notes

1. David Mayhew, "Congressional Elections: The Case of the Vanishing Marginals," *Polity*, 6 (Spring 1974), 295-317. Throughout this paper I define a competitive seat as one in which the margin of victory does not exceed 20 percent. This definition is not only arbitrary but it also has the defect of suggesting that what might be called the vulnerability of a seat is related in some simple way to vote margin. While it is possible that the connection between vulnerability and vote margin is not only complicated but is also unstable in time, I cannot investigate this question in the present paper. The reader is therefore asked to keep in mind the provisional nature of this definition in interpreting the results reported here.
2. Robert S. Erikson, "The Advantage of Incumbency in Congressional Elections," *Polity*, 3 (Spring 1971), 395-405; and "Malapportionment, Gerrymandering, and Party Fortunes in Congressional Elections," *American Political Science Review*, 66 (December 1972), 1234-1335.
3. Edward R. Tufte, "The Relationship Between Seats and Votes in Two-Party Systems," *American Political Science Review*, 67 (June 1973), 540-554.
4. Warren Lee Kostroski, "Party and Incumbency in Postwar Senate Elections," *American Political Science Review*, 67 (December 1973), 1213-1234.
5. Tufte, "Relationship Between Seats and Votes," p. 551.
6. Ibid., p. 553.
7. Walter Dean Burnham, "Communications," *American Political Science Review*, 68 (March 1974), 210.

8. Ibid.
9. Erikson, "Malapportionment," p. 1240.
10. Mayhew, "Congressional Elections," p. 311.
11. Edward R. Tufte, "Communications," *American Political Science Review,* 68 (March 1974), 212.
12. Tufte, "Relationship Between Seats and Votes," p. 551.
13. Ibid.
14. Ibid., p. 553.
15. Edward R. Tufte, "Determinants of the Outcome of Midterm Congressional Elections," *American Political Science Review,* (September 1975), 812-826.
16. Kostroski, "Party and Incumbency in Postwar Senate Elections."
17. Erikson, "Malapportionment."
18. Mayhew, "Congressional Elections," p. 310.
19. Arthur S. Goldberger, *Econometric Theory* (New York: John Wiley, 1964).
20. Donald E. Stokes and Warren E. Miller, "Party Government and the Saliency of Congress," in *Elections and the Political Order,* ed. Angus Campbell, Philip E. Converse, Warren E. Miller and Donald E. Stokes (New York: John Wiley, 1966).
21. Stokes and Miller, "Party Government and the Saliency of Congress," p. 204.
22. Tufte, "Communications"; and Robert B. Arseneau and Raymond E. Wolfinger, "Voting Behavior in Congressional Elections," paper presented at the meeting of the American Political Science Association, New Orleans, September 1973.
23. Samuel Kernell, "Presidential Popularity and Negative Voting," paper presented at the meeting of the American Political Science Association, Chicago, September 1974.

4. THE CASE OF THE VANISHING MARGINALS: THE BUREAUCRACY DID IT

Morris P. Fiorina

Introduction

The ongoing Erikson-Mayhew-Tufte-Burnham-Ferejohn exchange illustrates once again that political events and processes are easier to describe than to explain. We now are aware of a clear political trend: the decline of competition for House seats. The significance of this trend becomes apparent when coupled with evidence that policy change in the Congress results more from the replacement of incumbents than from changes in their behavior.[1] Seemingly, the primary determinants of change in national policies will soon be individual deaths and retirements rather than elections.

But what are we to do? Any attempt to stimulate competition in congressional elections presupposes an understanding of the factors which foster and inhibit it. And here E-M-T-B-F come to a parting of the ways. Somewhat casually, Tufte suggests that institutional change, namely redistricting, has put marginal districts on the endangered list. Ferejohn rejects Tufte's suggestion, as does Bullock in another contribution.[2] Among other possibilities, Mayhew recalls the venerable Stokes-Miller dictum that "to be known at all is to be known favorably" and exhibits evidence that now, more than ever, congressmen follow the sage advice, "use the frank, use the frank, use the frank." But here too, Ferejohn raises questions. Neither in absolute nor in relative terms do the incumbents of today enjoy a greater informational advantage than those of yesteryear.

Having discarded two potential explanations Ferejohn next offers his own. Following Erikson and Burnham, Ferejohn argues that changes in electoral behavior underlie the vanishing marginals. Perhaps many citizens use simple rules of thumb when voting in low information elections such as those for the House. According to proponents of the behavioral change view, party identification probably serves as the most common rule of thumb. But in recent years the

Author's Note: Without implicating any of them, I wish to thank Richard Fenno, John Kingdon, Charles Bullock, David Mayhew, Douglas Price, and Glenn Parker for their thoughtful comments and criticisms.

Source: *American Political Science Review* 71 (March 1977): 177-181. Reprinted with permission of the author.

citizenry has apparently become more informed, issue conscious, and ideological. And as this changing electorate monitored the divisive, highly charged politics of the 'sixties, increasing numbers of citizens grew suspicious of their traditional rule of thumb. Ferejohn and others suggest that incumbency voting has filled the void left by weakening party identification: for a significant number of citizens voting for the incumbent has replaced voting for their party.

The preceding argument has a curious ring to it. On the one hand we are to believe that party identification has declined in importance because citizens are increasingly aware and informed. But on the other hand we are to believe that these same citizens increasingly rely on the seemingly simpleminded rule of voting for incumbents. In a nutshell, voters are getting smarter, while voting behavior (other than presidential) is getting dumber. Moreover, consider the data analyzed by Arthur Miller.[3] With citizens increasingly dubious about government competence, intentions, and efficiency, is it plausible to argue that they increasingly support the objects of their cynicism?

Marginal districts are on the wane. Why? Some kind of incumbency effect exists, and apparently has come to exert an increasingly strong influence on congressional elections. But what is the nature of the incumbency effect, and why has it become more important over time? In this comment I propose another possible answer to the preceding questions. My thesis emerged during explorations of two congressional districts relatively alike in their demographic profiles but strikingly different in their electoral history. Basically, I will argue the following.

In the postwar period we have seen both the decline of the marginal district and the expansion of the federal role and its attendant bureaucracy. I believe that these two trends are more than statistically related, that they are in fact causally related. An institutional change — the growth of the bureaucracy — has encouraged behavioral change *among congressmen,* which in turn has encouraged behavioral change among some voters.

The Two Districts

The two congressional districts studied are reasonably similar in their demographic profiles. Both are in the same region of the country. Neither is metropolitan nor rural — each contains more than two counties, one medium-size city, and an important agricultural sector. Politically, however, the two districts present a striking contrast. District A is the quintessential marginal district. Since its creation in 1952 no election has produced a victory percentage as high as 58 percent; the average winning percentage is 53. Both parties have won the seat with at least two different candidates during the 1952-1974 period. In contrast, the political history of district B illustrates Burnham's "triumph of incumbency."[4] Until 1964, Republicans won the district with margins around 55 percent. But in 1964 a Democrat squeaked through, held on in 1966, and from the statistical record now appears safe.

Are there important differences between the two districts? Why did the Democrat who captured district A in 1964 not duplicate the feat of his counterpart in district B? Why has district A not experienced the triumph of incumbency on the Republican side? One explanation we can eliminate is redistricting. District A underwent no boundary change between 1952 and 1972, and then underwent a change amounting to less than 5 percent of the district population. District B has remained unchanged since World War II. What then, explains the political differences between districts A and B?

Consider district A. During the 1950s both national and state races activated local ties, to Republican advantage in the former case and Democratic advantage in the latter. Congressmen rose and fell partially for reasons beyond their control. The Republican congressman who followed the Eisenhower era was a rural conservative, a crusty personality of unquestioned integrity, who took pride in his attendance record, perceived his job as the making (and obstructing) of national policy, and in general operated rather independently of his district. In 1964 he refused to separate himself from Goldwater and followed his leader into enforced retirement. Unlike the beneficiary of the Johnson landslide in district B, however, the Democrat in district A failed to retain his seat in 1966, losing it to the Republican he defeated two years earlier. In 1974, after more narrow victories, the conservative Republican retired, his party held the seat — by the narrowest of margins — but now Democrats and Republicans alike agree that after a year in office the freshman Republican successor is safe.

Why this turnabout, this triumph of incumbency? Several explanations are offered. The new Republican blankets his district with communications both greater in number and more "effective" than his predecessor's. District observers perceive that the freshman Republican's voting record is more closely attuned to his district than was his predecessor's conservative stands. "He throws a few votes our [opponents'] way now and then." And finally, the freshman Republican travels around his district from meeting to meeting saying, "I'm your man in Washington. What are your problems? How can I help you?" While generally favorable to his successor, the former Republican disapproves of the amount of time his successor spends in the district: "How can he do his job in Washington when he's back here so much? People shouldn't expect a Congressman to be running back home all the time."

In summary, district A was influenced by broader political forces during the 1950s. During the 1960s it elected congressmen who did not make all-out efforts to maximize their vote. Now that someone is doing so, local observers and participants are betting that another marginal has vanished.

Now consider district B which is simply ten years ahead of district A. Until 1964 district B was marginally Republican. The Representative for most of this period was involved in controversial legislation such as Taft-Hartley and Landrum-Griffin. He had a personal problem, and probably more important, a political problem: declining Republican registration. In 1948 Republicans had a comfortable registration edge, by 1964 this edge has dwindled, and today the parties are dead even. Some district politicians believe that the registration shift has little significance for national elections, that it is felt mostly on the local level. But it seems prudent to bear in mind that the triumph of incumbency in district B may reflect the changing political allegiances of the district. A defeated Republican congressman is partial to this view.

Still, the Democrat who barely won in 1964 bucked the tide in 1966 and has won by margins of 40,000 votes at times since. District observers agree that his strength is bipartisan; a county chairman contends that in only one instance has any other national, state, or local candidate of either party run ahead of the Democratic congressman in the district, or in the relevant common subarea of it. Equal registration does not explain such electoral one-sidedness.

But here again we find a behavioral difference between the pre-1964 Republican and the post-1964 Democratic congressmen. Although district B is not located in prime Tuesday-to-Thursday club area, the Democratic incumbent belongs to the club nonetheless. By general agreement he is a pervasive presence in the district. He relies on no campaign organization other than the formal party structure. But he personally works the district at a feverish pace. A party chairman from a Republican area commented: "Congressman _____ comes to see people. _____ [former Republican congressman] didn't. The people know _____. He's the first Congressman to take an active interest in them."

The Democratic incumbent maintains well-staffed offices in district B. In these offices secretaries busily work on social security and veterans' affairs matters. Here too we find a difference between the Democratic incumbent and his Republican predecessor. The latter commented: "When I was in office I had four staff members. Now they have a regiment, that's just not necessary. It's a waste of the taxpayer's money, a frivolous expense."

The matter of the congressional staff is especially interesting in that the retired Republican in district A spontaneously brought it up. In discussing examples of the "hypocrisy" of modern congressmen (one of which was the 1967 expansion of the staff) he said flatly: "No congressman could possibly use 16 staff members." The Democratic incumbent in district B is using them (ten in his district) and one can not dispute the results.

Clearly, the two districts show evidence that major changes in their congressional election patterns are associated with behavioral differences on the part of the congressmen they elected. What might produce such differences? Former Republican congressmen in the two districts lean toward the view that today's congressmen are not as good as the pre-1960 variety. Oversimplifying a bit, in olden days strong men walked the halls of the Capitol. They concentrated more heavily on affairs of state than do their successors. More than today's congressmen they believed that the public interest should take precedence over reelection.

Political scientists are justifiably skeptical of theories which postulate that human nature has changed for the worse, that yesterday's political giants have given way to today's political pigmies. Thus, I will not dwell on the notion that today's congressmen are more concerned with reelection than they were in the recent past. In all likelihood, since the New Deal era the average congressman's desire for reelection has remained constant. What has changed, however, is the set of resources he possesses to invest in his reelection effort. Today's congressmen have more productive reelection strategies than previously. And these strategies are an unforeseen by-product of the growth of an activist Federal government.

Morris P. Fiorina

Better to be Reelected as An Errand Boy Than Not to be Reelected at All

A plausible explanation of the differing political histories of the two cases I have studied would run something like this. The changing nature of congressional elections in these districts stems from the changing behavior of the congressmen who represented these districts. Both districts are heterogeneous in their socioeconomic characteristics, and in their political allegiances (e.g., registration). Thus, so long as these districts are represented by congressmen who function primarily as national policy makers (pre-1964 in district B, pre-1974 in district A) reasonably close congressional elections will naturally result. But given congressional incumbents who place heavy emphasis on nonpartisan constituency service, the districts will shift out of the marginal category. Can we expand this explanation, and use it to explain the vanishing marginals nationally?

A basic fact of life in post-New Deal America is the growth of the federal role and its instrument, the federal bureaucracy. Bureaucracy is the characteristic mode of delivering public goods and services. Ceteris paribus, the more the government attempts to do for people, the more extensive a bureaucracy the government will require.

While not malevolent, bureaucracies make mistakes (of commission and omission). Moreover, attempts at redress often meet with a characteristic unresponsiveness, inflexibility, and incorrigibility. Members of the U.S. Congress, however, hold an almost unique position vis-à-vis the bureaucracy: congressmen possess the power to expedite bureaucratic activity. This capability flows directly from congressional control over what bureaucrats value most — higher budgets and new program authorizations. In a very real sense congressmen are monopoly suppliers of bureaucratic "unsticking" services.

As the scope of government expands, more and more citizens and groups find themselves dealing with the federal bureaucracy. They may be seeking positive benefits such as social security checks and government grants or seeking to escape costs entailed by bureaucratic regulations. But in either case their congressman is a source of succor. And the greater the scope of government activity, the more often will his aid be requested. Moreover, unlike private monopolists, congressmen can not curtail the demand for their services by raising their price (at least legally). When the demand for his services rises, the congressman has no real choice except to meet that demand — to supply more — so long as he would rather be an elected official under any circumstances, than an unelected one. This vulnerability to constituency demands, however, is largely academic. Congressmen probably do not resist the gradual transformation from national legislator to errand person. They have not rushed to create a national ombudsman, for example, nor to establish Congressman Reuss's Administrative Counsel of the Congress. The nice thing about casework is that it is mostly profit; one makes many more friends than enemies. In fact, some congressmen undoubtedly stimulate the demand for their bureaucratic fixit services. Recall that the new Republican in district A says, "I'm your man in Washington. What are your problems? How can I help you?" And in district B the demand for the congressman's services presumably did not rise so much between 1962 and 1964 that a "regiment" of constituency staff become necessary. Rather, possessing the regiment, the new Democrat did his damndest to create the demand to which he could apply his regiment.[5]

In addition to profitable casework let us remember too that the expansion of the federal role has also produced a larger pork barrel. The pork barreler need not limit himself to dams and post offices. There is LEAA money for the local police; urban renewal and housing money for local officials; and educational program grants for the local education bureaucracy. The congressman can stimulate applications for federal assistance, put in a good word during consideration, and announce favorable decisions amid great fanfare. Bureaucratic decisions bestow benefits as well as create costs. By affecting either kind of decision, the congressman can accrue electoral credit.

Let us turn now to the matter of the incumbency effect. If, over time, an increasing number of U.S. representatives are devoting increasing resources to constituency service, then at the district level we would expect that increasing numbers of voters think of their congressman less as a policymaker than as an ombudsman. If so, other implications are immediate. First, party identification will be less influential in determining the congressional vote, not just because of the unusual presidential politics of the late 1960s, but because *objectively* the congressman is no longer considered so important for policymaking as he once was.[6] In legislative matters he holds one paltry vote out of 435. But in bureaucratic matters he is a benevolent, nonpartisan power. And if more and more citizens come to think of their congressmen in this manner, then the basis of the incumbency effect is obvious. *Experience in Washington and congressional seniority count when dealing with the bureaucracy.* Thus, so long as the incumbent can elude a personal morality rap, and refrain from casting outlandish votes, he is naturally preferred over a newcomer. *This incumbency effect is not only understandable, it is rational.* And it would grow over time as increasing numbers of citizens come to regard their congressman as a troubleshooter in the Washington bureaucracies.

The preceding argument provides a critical insight into Ferejohn's critique of Mayhew. Ferejohn concludes that the incumbency effect is not explained by the information that incumbents shower on constituents, because the informational advantage incumbents possess has not increased between 1958 and 1970, while the incumbency advantage apparently *has* increased during that period. But what if the *content* of the information has changed over time? What if in 1958 voters who have "heard or read something" about the incumbent have heard or read about a policy stand, whereas in 1970 they have heard or read about the good job the incumbent is doing to get Vietnam veterans' checks in the mail? Some voters will agree with a policy stand, some will disagree. But everyone will applaud the congressman's efforts in behalf of the veterans. Thus, a constant informational advantage may be quite consistent with an increasing incumbency advantage if information about the incumbent has become increasingly non-controversial in content. And, as suggested above, those voters who have "heard or read nothing" about either candidate act quite sensibly in voting for the incumbent to the extent that he is an ombudsman rather than a legislative giant.

For clarity's sake I have drawn the preceding argument in very bold strokes. Let me now fill in the picture a bit. In order to account for the vanishing marginals we do *not* need to argue that *all* congressmen have opted *exclusively* for an ombudsman role, and that *all* constituents now think of their congressmen in nonprogrammatic terms. The disappearance of a marginal requires only marginal change. To illustrate, if one deflates Mayhew's 1972 bimodal distribution by Erikson's 5 percent estimated incumbency effect, the trough in the marginal range disappears. To explain the vanishing marginals one need only argue that over the past thirty years, expanded constituency service opportunities have given the marginal congressman the ability to capture 5-10 percent of his district's voters who might otherwise oppose him on party or policy grounds.

One further question arises. The growth of the federal role has been continuous and reasonably gradual, although with definite jumps during the New Deal and World War II. The decline of congressional competition, however, has been more erratic. We would expect some lag between the onset of bureaucratic expansion and the decline of the marginals because congressmen presumably would not grasp the new opportunities immediately. But how would we explain the especially pronounced decline of congressional competition in the late 'sixties? It would be a bit much to contend that Great Society programs translated into casework and votes quite so quickly. One plausible explanation of the 'sixties decline lies in recent work by Richard Fenno.[7]

Fenno discusses the congressional "homestyle," a congressman's basic patterns of interaction with his district. According to Fenno, homestyles tend to persist once established. Now consider that between the 88th and 90th Congresses one-third the membership of the House changed. I think it is plausible to hypothesize that the homestyles of the new representatives placed relatively greater emphasis on constituency service than did the homestyles of the more senior congressmen they replaced.[8] The average freshman in 1965 for example, replaced a congressman elected in 1952 or 1954. Paradoxically, then, the electoral upheavals of the 1960s may have produced the electoral stability of the early 1970s. New congressmen chose homestyles best adapted to the changed congressional environment. Is it purely coincidence that these fresh Congresses raised staff allotments by almost 50 percent (eleven to sixteen) between 1967 and 1973?

Conclusion

Congressmen can earn electoral credit by taking positions on the issues, by bringing home the bacon, and by providing individual favors. The first option is inherently controversial. The latter two need not be. As the federal role has expanded, congressmen have shifted emphasis from the controversial to the noncontroversial, from the programmatic to the nonprogrammatic. Ferejohn no doubt is correct; electoral behavior has changed. But at least part of that change is endogenous to the system. Congressmen are not merely passive reactors to a changing electoral climate. In no small part they have helped to change that climate.[9]

Notes

1. Herbert Asher and Herbert Weisberg, "Congressional Voting Change: A Longitudinal Study of Voting on Selected Issues," paper presented at the *American Political Science Association Meeting*, San Francisco, 1975.
2. Charles S. Bullock III, "Redistricting and Congressional Stability, 1962-1972," *Journal of Politics* 37 (May 1975), 569-575.
3. Arthur H. Miller, "Political Issues and Trust in Government: 1964-1970," *American Political Science Review*, 68 (September 1974), 951-972.
4. Walter D. Burnham, "Party Systems and the Political Process," in *The American Party Systems*, ed. William Chambers and Walter Burnham, 2nd ed. (New York: Oxford, 1975), pp. 308-357.
5. The expansion of the congressional office cries out for further study. At the beginning of the 90th Congress in which the last major expansion took place *Congressional Staff Directory* listed 3,276 individuals of whom 26 per cent were in the districts. In 1974, 34 per cent of 5,109 were in the districts. What are these people doing?
6. Cf. Burnham, "Party Systems," p. 335. Burnham believes that the decline of party identification as an influence on congressional voting has increased the attractiveness of the ombudsman role. I am arguing that the causal influence is reciprocal if not the reverse.
7. Richard Fenno, "Congressmen in their Constituencies: An Exploration," *American Political Science Review* (September 1977), 883-917.
8. I should point out that the Democrat who won district A in 1964 and lost it in 1966 did *not* adopt an errand boy homestyle. According to local supporters he became totally engrossed in his Washington affairs.
9. Obviously, my argument suggests a variety of implications for the future operation of the American government. Space precludes me from entering upon such a discussion here. The interested reader should refer to my *Congress — Keystone of the Washington Establishment* (New Haven: Yale, 1977).

II

CONGRESSIONAL NORMS:
DEVELOPMENT AND CHANGE

Norms are standards that define the limits of acceptable behavior within Congress, prescribing the "rules of the game." They are "informal rules, frequently unspoken because they need not be spoken, which may govern conduct more effectively than any written rule." (Hinckley, 1983, p. 102). Although norms usually exhibit some stability over time, they are not immutable. The single most important cause of change in norms is the turnover of members of Congress. The greater the number of newcomers, the more susceptible norms are to modification.

In order for an institution to indoctrinate its members into accepted behavior, Irwin Gertzog suggests that there are three conditions that must be met:

> The ability of an organization adequately to indoctrinate new members to its rules, procedures and goals is affected by the extent to which the organization has the capacity to produce clear and unambiguous rules and norms for performance, the degree to which it has the capacity to provide opportunities for learning and practicing the required performance, and the extent to which it has the capacity selectively to reward or penalize the behavior of its recruits (Gertzog, 1970, p. 2).

Congress operates at a distinct disadvantage in its capacity to execute these three organizational tasks. It cannot control the selection of members and therefore has no voice in the kinds of individuals who arrive on Capitol Hill. In addition, Congress cannot deny a legislator membership in the institution except in the most unusual circumstances. The integration process is made all the more difficult because of the ambiguous nature of congressional conventions and the inability of the institution to provide sufficient opportunities for practicing the expected types of behaviors. These impediments to successful socialization are accentuated by the nature of legislative business: virtually all societal conflicts surface in legislative deliberations, and sharp value differences permeate legislative life. Thus, it is critical for representatives to abide by a set of rules that prevent conflicts from getting out of hand while they are engaged in legislative deliberations.

Norms vary in several ways. Some may be more pertinent than others, or their relevance may vary across time as the institution changes in composition, structure, and attractiveness. Adherence to norms also may vary. In some cases, they pay only lip service to the expectations dictated by certain norms, while in other instances, members are expected to strictly abide by the principles associated with a standard. Finally, the extent to which there is agreement about the utility of a norm also may vary. Some norms can be viewed as consensual, while others are supported only by a small number of members. Thus, as Congress has evolved, the prominence of and adherence to these norms have been modified. The purpose of this essay is to alert the reader to the variety of behavioral standards that exist within Congress and to show how institutional developments have altered these norms.

In this section we describe the types of norms that exist within the Congress and how and why they have changed over time. Two norms operate in similar ways in both chambers and appear to be quite stable over time: institutional loyalty and reciprocity. Two others differ between the chambers and appear to be undergoing considerable modification: specialization and apprenticeship.

Institutional Loyalty

Congressional insistence on institutional loyalty has two components. First, it requires that representatives and senators refrain from attacks on the institution. Members see Congress as something of a cultural monument that is worthy of praise and celebration. As Donald Matthews (1973, p. 101) points out, "Senators are expected to believe that they belong to the greatest legislative and deliberative body in the world." A similar feeling pervades the House of Representatives. Nonetheless, the violation of this norm when in the company of constituents is deviance that is tolerated, if not expected. Although senators and representatives pay Congress due respect while they are in Washington, they speak more critically of the institution when they are back home among their constituents.

Second, the norm of institutional loyalty implies that members are expected to defend Congress against encroachment on the legislature's prerogatives by presidents and federal agencies. Members also are expected to promote the interests of their chamber and to champion its causes in deliberations with members of the "other" body. Some of the most celebrated cases of congressional reprimand—the censure of Sen. Joseph McCarthy in 1954 and the refusal to seat Rep. Adam Clayton Powell in 1967— were justified on the grounds that these members had discredited the institution.

Reciprocity

Another stable norm is the expectation that senators and representatives will accommodate themselves to the needs of their colleagues. This is a reciprocal relationship in the sense that doing a favor for another member is expected to be repaid in something of equal value. A familiar lexicon has emerged to characterize such processes. Members are alerted to the fact that "if you scratch my back, I'll scratch yours" and that trading support or "logrolling" is a collective effort that produces particularized benefits. The sharp schisms among party members are reduced when this norm is adhered to in bargaining situations. Thus, reciprocity is a fundamental element of the legislative process that often involves a personal exchange of favors and assistance or the give-and-take that is the trademark of legislative negotiations. In many cases reciprocal behavior is both private and subtle; in other cases, such as congressional consideration of "porkbarrel" legislation, it is far more visible. Although journalists and others usually have viewed such bargaining techniques with contempt, Richard Fenno suggests that the reciprocity norm enables Congress to conduct its business amid the conflict that could paralyze the legislative process:

> Conflict is the very blood of a decision-making body in a free society. Yet it is amazing how much of the time and energy of House members is devoted to the business of avoiding conflict. The reason for this is simple. Excessive conflict will disrupt and disable the entire internal structure. In the interests of stability, therefore, a cluster of norms calling for negotiation and bargaining is operative at every point where conflict might destroy the institution. In view of the criticisms frequently pointed at bargaining techniques — "back scratching," "logrolling," "pork barrelling," "vote trading" — it should be noted that these techniques are designed to make majority building possible (Fenno, 1965, pp. 75-76).

This norm may be even more critical to the operations of the Senate because of the power individual senators wield over the flow of Senate business:

> A single senator, for example, can slow the Senate almost to a halt by systematically objecting to all unanimous consent requests. A few, by exercising their right to filibuster, can block the passage of all bills. Or a single senator could sneak almost any piece of legislation through the chamber by acting when floor attendance is sparse and by taking advantage of the looseness of the chamber rules (Matthews, 1973, pp. 100-101).

These observations indicate that the norm of reciprocity is necessary for the conduct of House and Senate business.

Specialization

Because specialization is necessary in a modern legislature where work is complex, technical, and voluminous, members are expected to concentrate on a narrow range of issues particularly important to their constituencies or immediately connected to their committee work. In this way, Congress maintains a level of expertise on far-ranging matters (weapons systems, tax provisions, health problems), while making the average member's workload more manageable. The application of this norm also may enable Congress to exercise some scrutiny over executive agencies and to counter the administration's expertise with its own.

The norm of specialization is not as confining for senators as it is for representatives. House members are called upon to develop expertise in a few narrow policy areas to maximize their effectiveness, but senators are expected to develop a broader range of national policy interests. Furthermore, the relatively large number of senators that harbor presidential aspirations (Polsby, 1969) precludes strict adherence to the specialization norm; presidential hopefuls are expected to espouse positions on a wide range of topics and issues. Finally, the relatively small size of the Senate makes the specialization norm less workable because each senator has more committee and subcommittee assignments than does each House member.

Apprenticeship

This norm encompasses the belief that a junior member should "observe an apprenticeship—to work hard, tend to his constituency, learn his committee work, specialize in an area of public policy, appear often but speak very seldom on the floor, and cooperate with the leaders of his committee and of his party" (Fenno, 1965, p. 71). Conformity with this norm has virtually vanished in the Senate, and it has been substantially diminished in the House. The election of younger and less conservative senators during the late 1950s and throughout the 1960s and 1970s has made the congressional environment more amenable to the activism of junior members. The dominance of small groups of older, conservative, and largely southern senior members has dissipated, and legislative leadership has fallen into the hands of members who are more receptive to the wishes of junior colleagues. In fact, by 1969, Herbert Asher (1973) reported that about two-thirds of the incumbent House members he had interviewed had rejected the norm of apprenticeship. And, in the Senate, some senior members have encouraged rather than discouraged the participation of their more junior colleagues in deliberations—a dramatic change from past practices (Rohde, Ornstein, and Peabody, 1974).

Other Norms

The behavior of House and Senate incumbents appears to be governed by a few additional conventions: seniority, legislative work, interpersonal courtesy, senatorial courtesy, and universalism. *Seniority* in the House and Senate confers status upon a member that affects much of his or her legislative life and the perquisites that are available. For instance, office space is assigned on a seniority basis, and committee assignments and transfers often give added weight to the seniority of the requesting member. The norm of *legislative work* prescribes that members devote their energies to many highly detailed, dull, and politically unrewarding legislative tasks. This emphasis on attention to the time-consuming business associated with legislative deliberations has created a dichotomy between "show horses" (those who seek publicity) and "work horses" (those who attend to the mundane but necessary tasks associated with legislating). Members who do not shoulder their share of the legislative burden, or who appear to subordinate their efforts in the quest for personal advancement, are scorned. This does not mean that the pursuit of publicity is unacceptable—after all, publicity is essential for reelection, especially for senators—but, rather, that it should never be a primary objective that interferes with the performance of legislative duties.

Interpersonal courtesy enables legislators to resolve their conflicts in an atmosphere that is relatively free from personal attacks. This norm is strengthened by the formal rules that forbid questioning the motives of another member, criticizing another state, or making derogatory references to members of the other chamber. In addition, an air of impersonality pervades parliamentary procedure to some extent: members of the House and Senate do not refer to each other by name; rather, they may address the "gentleman from South Dakota" or the "senior senator from Florida," for example. Such interpersonal courtesy enhances cooperation. As Donald Matthews (1973, p. 97) has observed, "conflict does exist, but its sharp edges are blunted by the felt need expressed in the Senate folkways-for courtesy."

Senatorial courtesy is a norm that applies to the Senate's constitutional role (Article II, section 2) of providing "advice and consent" to presidential nominations for federal appointments. The application of this norm requires that nominations be defeated if the senator from the same party as the president, and from the same state where the appointment is to take place, objects. Although the objecting senator may be expected to explain his opposition, that is not required. Senatorial courtesy is seldom invoked because senators invariably are consulted throughout the nominating process and have a critical voice in the making of federal appointments within their states.

A final tradition is *universalism,* the tendency of members of Congress to seek unanimous passage of wide-ranging programs by including projects for every member who wants one. According to Barry Weingast,

> . . . representatives pursuing their own interests will prefer institutional arrangements (or norms) which increase their chances of success in gaining benefits for their districts. Universalism is such an institution. Rational self-interested legislators have compelling reasons to prefer decision making by maximal rather than minimal winning coalitions (Weingast, 1979, p. 250).

One factor that facilitates the development of legislative norms is the institutionalization of Congress. Nelson Polsby (1968) suggests that the House of Representatives has become differentiated from its external environment, has grown internally complex, and has adopted standardized rather than discretionary procedures and automatic rather than discretionary methods for the conduct of its business. The differentiation of the House from its external environment is evident in the development of House leadership positions, the stability of membership, and the increases in the overall seniority of House members. Three institutional developments in the House exhibit its increasing internal complexity and consequent shift away from discretionary decision making toward automatic decision rules. First, the number of unspecialized appendages of party leadership has grown. Second, the perquisites of office and the auxiliary aids available to members have increased. Third, the seniority system has grown (Polsby et al, 1969c) as has the practice of deciding contested elections on their merits. Polsby suggests that such processes of institutionalization have provided favorable conditions for the growth and persistence of congressional norms.

In the introduction to Part VI we suggest that some of these institutional developments appear to have experienced a decline or reversal during the 1970s. As a consequence, major norms and institutional practices have been altered. For example, the breadth of influence previously exercized by the seniority system has been sharply curtailed.

Although it has generally been accepted that new members must be indoctrinated into legislative norms, Herbert Asher suggests that little learning of congressional norms actually occurs:

> ... it seems as if the traditional image of the freshman Congressman as ignorant and bewildered had mistakenly led us to expect substantial learning of norms on the part of supposedly ill-informed newcomers. This expectation was unwarranted on two counts: the general House norms were not so abstruse as to require formal learning, and the traditional image of the freshman Congressman was found to be out of date... (Asher, 1973, p. 513).

In fact, Asher found that there was actually some erosion in the conformity and adherence to congressional norms among freshman representatives. Thus, he suggests that little socialization is involved in the transmission of norms to newcomers: congressional standards require little formal learning because members already accept and value these norms, perhaps because they represent rational reactions to the legislative environment.

The dramatic changes within the Senate during past decades also have altered the nature of Senate norms. David Rohde, Norman Ornstein, and Robert Peabody (1974) examine the continuity and change in two general categories of Senate norms: norms that generally provide benefits for all senators (general benefit norms) and those that benefit only a small number of senators (limited benefit norms). The authors argue that the redistribution of power in the Senate during the last few decades has affected member adherence to certain norms. Limited benefit norms enhanced the power and influence of Senate conservatives who controlled positions of institutional power during the 1950s. After that time, however, Senate conservatives lost much of their influence. Consequently, adherence to limited benefit norms has declined while general benefit norms remain operative because of the "collective" benefits that they provide.

5. THE INSTITUTIONALIZATION OF THE U.S. HOUSE OF REPRESENTATIVES

Nelson W. Polsby

Most people who study politics are in general agreement, it seems to me, on at least two propositions. First, we agree that for a political system to be viable, for it to succeed in performing tasks of authoritative resource allocation, problem solving, conflict settlement, and so on, in behalf of a population of any substantial size, it must be institutionalized. That is to say, organizations must be created and sustained that are specialized to political activity.[1] Otherwise, the political system is likely to be unstable, weak, and incapable of servicing the demands or protecting the interests of its constituent groups. Secondly, it is generally agreed that for a political system to be in some sense free and democratic, means must be found for institutionalizing representativeness with all the diversity that this implies, and for legitimizing yet at the same time containing political opposition within the system.[2]

Our growing interest in both of these propositions, and in the problems to which they point, can begin to suggest the importance of studying one of the very few extant examples of a highly specialized political institution which over the long run has succeeded in representing a large number of diverse constituents, and in legitimizing, expressing, and containing political opposition within a complex political system — namely, the U.S. House of Representatives.

The focus of my attention here will be first of all descriptive, drawing together disparate strands — some of which already exist in the literature[3] — in

Author's Note: This paper was written while I was a Fellow at the Center for Advanced Study in the Behavioral Sciences. I want to thank the Center for its incomparable hospitality. In addition, the study of which this is a part has received support from The Rockefeller Foundation, the Social Science Research Council, Wesleyan University, and the Carnegie Corporation of New York, which granted funds to The American Political Science Association for the Study of Congress. H. Douglas Price has been a constant source of ideas, information, and criticism. I gratefully acknowledge also the assistance of Barry Rundquist, Edward Dreyfus, John Neff, Andrew Kleinfeld, and Miriam Gallaher, whose efforts contributed greatly to the assembly of a large number of the historical time series reported here. My colleague Paul Kay took time from his own work to suggest ways in which they could be presented. An earlier version was presented at the 1966 meetings of the American Political Science Association.

Source: *American Political Science Review* (March 1968): 144-168. Reprinted with permission of the author.

an attempt to show in what sense we may regard the House as an institutional-ized organ of government. Not all the necessary work has been done on this rather difficult descriptive problem, as I shall indicate. Secondly, I shall offer a number of speculative observations about causes, consequences, and possible lessons to be drawn from the institutionalization of the House.

The process of institutionalization is one of the grand themes in all of modern social science. It turns up in many guises and varieties: as Sir Henry Maine's discussion of the change from status to contract in the history of legal ob-ligations,[4] as Ferdinand Tönnies' treatment of the shift from *Gemeinschaft* to *Gesellschaft*,[5] as Max Weber's discussion of the development of "rational-legal" modes of legitimization as an alternative to "traditional" and "charismatic" modes,[6] as Durkheim's distinction between "mechanical" and "organic" solidar-ity in his treatment of the consequences of the division of labor[7] and finally — dare we say finally? — as the central process at work in the unfolding of organizations that are held to obey Parkinson's Law.[8]

Such theoretical riches are bound to prove an embarrassment to the empirical researcher, since, unavoidably, in order to do his work, he must pick and choose among a host of possibilities — not those that initially may be the most stimulating, but those that seem most likely to be reflected in his data, which, perforce, are limited.[9] Thus the operational indices I am about to suggest which purport to measure empirically the extent to which the U.S. House of Representatives has become institutionalized may strike the knowledgeable reader as exceedingly crude; I invite the ingenuity of my colleagues to the task of suggesting improvements.

For the purposes of this study, let us say that an institutionalized organization has three major characteristics: 1) it is relatively well-bounded, that is to say, differentiated from its environment. Its members are easily identifiable, it is relatively difficult to become a member, and its leaders are recruited principally from within the organization. 2) The organization is relatively complex, that is, its functions are internally separated on some regular and explicit basis, its parts are not wholly interchangeable, and for at least some important purposes, its parts are interdependent. There is a division of labor in which roles are specified, and there are widely shared expectations about the performance of roles. There are regularized patterns of recruitment to roles, and of movement from role to role. 3) Finally, the organization tends to use universalistic rather than particularistic criteria, and automatic rather than discretionary methods for conducting its internal business. Precedents and rules are followed; merit systems replace favoritism and nepotism; and impersonal codes supplant personal preferences as prescriptions for behavior.

Since we are studying a single institution, the repeated use of words like "relatively" and "tends" in the sentences above refers to a comparison of the House of Representatives with itself at different points in time. The descriptive statement: "The House of Representatives has become institutionalized over time" means then, that over the life span of this institution, it has become perceptibly more bounded, more complex, and more universalistic and automatic in its internal decision making. But can we find measures which will capture enough of the meaning of the term "institutionalization" to warrant their use in an investigation of the process at work in the U.S. House of Representatives?

I. The Establishment of Boundaries

One aspect of institutionalization is the differentiation of an organization from its environment. The establishment of boundaries in a political organization refers mostly to a channeling of career opportunities. In an undifferentiated organization, entry to and exit from membership is easy and frequent. Leaders emerge rapidly, lateral entry from outside to positions of leadership is quite common, and persistence of leadership over time is rare. As an organization institutionalizes, it stabilizes its membership, entry is more difficult, and turnover is less frequent. Its leadership professionalizes and persists. Recruitment to leadership is more likely to occur from within, and the apprenticeship period lengthens. Thus the organization establishes and "hardens" its outer boundaries.

Such measures as are available for the House of Representatives unmistakably show this process at work. In the 18th and 19th centuries, the turnover of Representatives at each election was enormous. Excluding the Congress of 1789, when of course everyone started new, turnover of House members exceeded fifty percent in fifteen elections — the last of which was held in 1882. In the 20th century, the highest incidence of turnover (37.2 percent — almost double the twentieth century median) occurred in the Roosevelt landslide of 1932 — a figure exceeded forty-seven times — in other words almost all the time — in the 18th and 19th centuries. As Table 5-1 and Figure 5-1 make clear, there has been a distinct decline in the rate at which new members are introduced into the House. Table 5-2 and Figure 5-2 make a similar point with data that are partially independent; they show that the overall stability of membership, as measured by the mean terms of members (total number of terms served divided by total number of Representatives) has been on the rise.

These two tables provide a fairly good indication of what has happened over the years to rank-and-file members of the House. Another method of investigating the extent to which an institution has established boundaries is to consider its leaders, how they are recruited, what happens to them, and most particularly the extent to which the institution permits lateral entry to and exit from positions of leadership.

The classic example of lateral movement — possibly the most impressive such record in American history — is of course contained in the kaleidoscopic career of Henry Clay, seventh Speaker of the House. Before his first election to the House, Clay had already served two terms in the Kentucky House of Representatives, and had been sent by the legislature to the U.S. Senate for two nonconsecutive short terms. Instead of returning to the Senate in 1811, he ran for the Lexington seat in the U.S. House and was elected. He took his seat on March 4, 1811, and eight months later was elected Speaker at the age of 34. Three years later, he resigned and was appointed a commissioner to negotiate the Treaty of Ghent with Great Britain. The next year, he returned to Congress, where he was again promptly elected Speaker. In 1820 he resigned once again and left public office for two years. But in 1823 he returned to the House, served as Speaker two

Table 5-1 The Establishment of Boundaries: Decline in Percentage of First Term Members, U.S. House of Representatives, 1789-1965

Congress	Year of 1st Term	% 1st Term Members	Congress	Year of 1st Term	% 1st Term Members
1	1789	100.0	45	1877	46.6
2	1791	46.5	46	1879	42.3
3	1793	56.5	47	1881	31.8
4	1795	38.9	48	1883	51.5
5	1797	43.1	49	1885	38.0
6	1799	36.0	50	1887	35.6
7	1801	42.5	51	1889	38.1
8	1803	46.9	52	1891	43.8
9	1805	39.9	53	1893	38.1
10	1807	36.2	54	1895	48.6
11	1809	35.9	55	1897	37.9
12	1811	38.5	56	1899	30.1
13	1813	52.6	57	1901	24.4
14	1815	42.9	58	1903	31.3
15	1817	59.2	59	1905	21.0
16	1819	40.8	60	1907	22.5
17	1821	45.2	61	1909	19.9
18	1823	43.2	62	1911	30.5
19	1825	39.4	63	1913	34.4
20	1827	33.2	64	1915	27.2
21	1829	41.0	65	1917	16.0
22	1831	38.0	66	1919	22.7
23	1833	53.7	67	1921	23.6
24	1835	40.0	68	1923	27.1
25	1837	48.6	69	1925	16.3
26	1839	46.3	70	1927	13.3
27	1841	37.7	71	1929	17.7
28	1843	66.7	72	1931	19.0
29	1845	49.0	73	1933	37.2
30	1847	50.4	74	1935	23.4
31	1849	53.1	75	1937	22.7
32	1851	53.3	76	1939	25.5
33	1853	60.5	77	1941	17.0
34	1855	57.5	78	1943	22.9
35	1857	40.2	79	1945	15.8
36	1859	45.1	80	1947	24.1
37	1861	53.9	81	1949	22.3
38	1863	58.1	82	1951	14.9
39	1865	44.3	83	1953	19.5
40	1867	46.0	84	1955	11.7
41	1869	49.2	85	1957	9.9
42	1871	46.5	86	1959	18.2
43	1873	52.0	87	1961	12.6
44	1875	58.0	88	1963	15.2
			89	1965	20.9

Data for 1st through 68th Congresses are from Stuart A. Rice, *Quantitative Methods in Politics* (New York: Knopf, 1928), pp. 296-297. Data for 69th through 89th Congresses are calculated from *Congressional Directories.*

Figure 5-1 The Establishment of Boundaries: Decline in Percentage of First Term Members, U.S. House of Representatives, 1789-1965.*

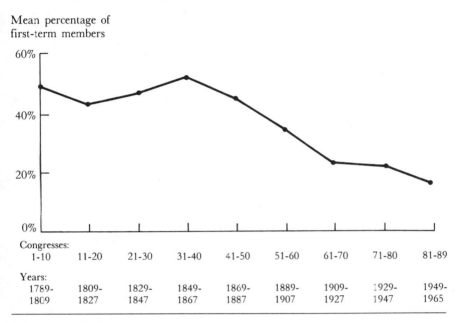

Mean percentage of
first-term members

Congresses:								
1-10	11-20	21-30	31-40	41-50	51-60	61-70	71-80	81-89
Years:								
1789- 1809	1809- 1827	1829- 1847	1849- 1867	1869- 1887	1889- 1907	1909- 1927	1929- 1947	1949- 1965

* Data from Table 5-1.

more terms, and then resigned again, to become Secretary of State in John Quincy Adams' cabinet. In 1831, Clay became a freshman Senator. He remained in the Senate until 1844, when he resigned his seat. Five years later he re-entered the Senate, this time remaining until his death in 1852. Three times (in 1824, 1832, 1844) he was a candidate for president.[10]

Clay's career was remarkable, no doubt, even in a day and age when the boundaries of the House of Representatives were only lightly guarded and leadership in the House was relatively open to lateral entry. But the point to be emphasized here is that Clay's swift rise to the Speakership is only slightly atypical for the period before the turn of the 20th century.

Table 5-3 demonstrates that there has been a change over time in the seniority of men selected for the Speakership. Before 1899, the mean years of service of members selected for the Speakership was six; after 1899, the mean rises steeply to twenty-six. Figure 5-3 and Table 5-4 summarize the gist of the finding in compact form.

Just as 19th-century Speakers arrived early at the pinnacle of House leadership, many left early as well and went on to other things: freshman Senators, state legislators, Cabinet members, and judges in the state courts. One became President of the U.S., one a Justice of the Supreme Court, one a Minister to Russia, one the Mayor of Auburn, New York, and one the Receiver-General

85

Table 5-2 The Establishment of Boundaries: Increase in Terms Served by Incumbent Members of the U.S. House of Representatives, 1789-1963

Congress	Beginning Term	Mean Terms of Service*	Congress	Beginning Term	Mean Terms of Service*
1	1789	1.00	45	1877	2.11
2	1791	1.54	46	1879	2.21
3	1793	1.64	47	1881	2.56
4	1795	2.00	48	1883	2.22
5	1797	2.03	49	1885	2.41
6	1799	2.23	50	1887	2.54
7	1801	2.25	51	1889	2.61
8	1803	2.14	52	1891	2.44
9	1805	2.36	53	1893	2.65
10	1807	2.54	54	1895	2.25
11	1809	2.71	55	1897	2.59
12	1811	2.83	56	1899	2.79
13	1813	2.31	57	1901	3.11
14	1815	2.48	58	1903	3.10
15	1817	1.93	59	1905	3.48
16	1819	2.15	60	1907	3.61
17	1821	2.23	61	1909	3.84
18	1823	2.29	62	1911	3.62
19	1825	2.42	63	1913	3.14
20	1827	2.68	64	1915	3.44
21	1829	2.55	65	1917	3.83
22	1831	2.59	66	1919	3.74
23	1833	2.15	67	1921	3.69
24	1835	2.23	68	1923	3.57
25	1837	2.13	69	1925	3.93
26	1839	2.17	70	1927	4.26
27	1841	2.30	71	1929	4.49
28	1843	1.76	72	1931	4.48
29	1845	1.90	73	1933	3.67
30	1847	2.00	74	1935	3.71
31	1849	1.92	75	1937	3.84
32	1851	1.84	76	1939	3.91
33	1853	1.69	77	1941	4.24
34	1855	1.81	78	1943	4.22
35	1857	2.04	79	1945	4.50
36	1859	2.02	80	1947	4.34
37	1861	1.83	81	1949	4.42
38	1863	1.75	82	1951	4.73
39	1865	2.00	83	1953	4.69
40	1867	2.12	84	1955	5.19
41	1869	2.04	85	1957	5.58
42	1871	2.11	86	1959	5.37
43	1873	2.07	87	1961	5.65
44	1875	1.92	88	1963	5.65

* Total number of terms served divided by total number of Representatives.

Figure 5-2   The Establishment of Boundaries: Increase in Terms Served by Incumbent Members of the U.S. House of Representatives, 1789-1963.*

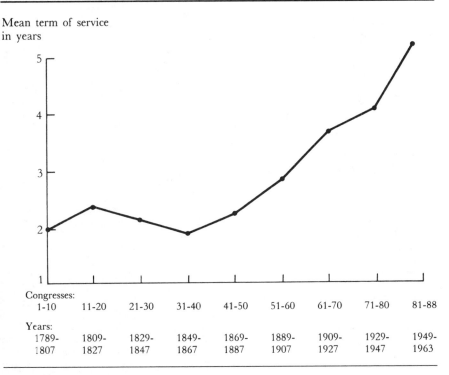

Mean term of service in years

Congresses:								
1-10	11-20	21-30	31-40	41-50	51-60	61-70	71-80	81-88
Years:								
1789-	1809-	1829-	1849-	1869-	1889-	1909-	1929-	1949-
1807	1827	1847	1867	1887	1907	1927	1947	1963

* Data from Table 5-2.

of the Pennsylvania land office. Indeed, of the first twenty-seven men to be Speaker, during the first eighty-six years of the Republic, *none* died while serving in the House of Representatives. In contrast, of the last Speakers, six died while serving, and of course one other sits in the House today. Table 5-5 and Figure 5-4 give the relevant information for all Speakers.

The importance of this information about Speakers' careers is that it gives a strong indication of the development of the Speakership as a singular occupational specialty. In earlier times, the Speakership seems to have been regarded as a position of political leadership capable of being interchanged with other, comparable positions of public responsibility — and indeed a high incidence of this sort of interchange is recorded in the careers of 19th century Speakers. That this sort of interchange is most unusual today suggests — as do the other data presented in this section — that one important feature in the development of the U.S. House of Representatives has been its differentiation from other organizations in the political system, a stabilization of its membership, and a growing specialization of its leaders to leadership of the House as a separate career.[11]

Table 5-3 The Establishment of Boundaries: Years Served in Congress Before First Selection as Speaker

Date of Selection	Speaker	Years	Date of Selection	Speaker	Years
1789	Muhlenberg	1 or less	1861	Grow	10
1791	Trumbull	3	1863	Colfax	8
1795	Dayton	4	1869	Pomeroy	8
1799	Sedgwick	11	1869	Blaine	6
1801	Macon	10	1875	Kerr	8
1807	Varnum	12	1876	Randall	13
1811	Clay	1 or less	1881	Keifer	4
1814	Cheves	5	1883	Carlisle	6
1820	Taylor	7	1889	Reed	12
1821	Barbour	6	1891	Crisp	8
1827	Stephenson	6	1899	Henderson	16
1834	Bell	7	1903	Cannon	28
1835	Polk	10	1911	Clark	26
1839	Hunter	2	1919	Gillett	26
1841	White	6	1925	Longworth	22
1843	Jones	8	1931	Garner	26
1845	Davis	6	1933	Rainey	28
1847	Winthrop	8	1935	Byrns	25
1849	Cobb	6	1936	Bankhead	15
1851	Boyd	14	1940	Rayburn	27
1855	Banks	2	1946	Martin	22
1857	Orr	7	1962	McCormack	34
1859	Pennington	1 or less			

The development of a specifically House leadership, the increase in the overall seniority of members, and the decrease in the influx of newcomers at any point in time have the effect not only of separating the House from other organizations in the political system, but also of facilitating the growth of stable ways of doing business within the institution, as we shall see shortly.

II. The Growth of Internal Complexity

Simple operational indices of institutional complexity and universalistic-automated decision making are less easy to produce in neat and comparable times series. As for the growth of internal complexity, this is easy enough to establish impressionistically, but the most obvious quantitative measure presents a drastic problem of interpretation. The temptation is great to measure internal differentiation by simply counting the number of standing committees in each Congress. This would produce a curiously curvilinear result, because in 1946 the number of standing committees was reduced from 48 to 19, and the number has since crept up only as far as 20.[12]

But the "streamlining," as it was called,[13] of 1946 can hardly be said to have reduced the internal differentiation of the House. On the contrary, by explicitly

Figure 5-3   The Establishment of Boundaries: Mean Years Served in Congress
Before First Becoming Speaker by 20-year Intervals.*

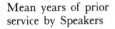

Mean years of prior
service by Speakers

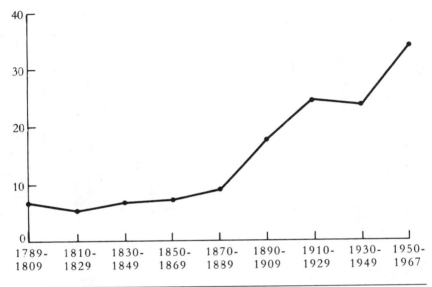

* Data from Table 5-3.

Table 5-4   The Establishment of Boundaries: Summary of Years Served in
Congress Before First Selection as Speaker

	Before 1899	1899 and after
8 years or less	25	0
9-14 years	8	0
15-20 years	0	2
21-28 years	0	10
	33 Speakers	12 Speakers

delineating the legislative jurisdictions of the committees, by consolidating
committees with parallel and overlapping functions, by assigning committees
exclusive oversight responsibilities over agencies of the executive branch, and by
providing committees with expanded staff aid, the 1946 reorganization contributed to, rather than detracted from, the reliance of the House upon committees in
the conduct of its business. Thus the mute testimony of the sheer numbers of com-

89

Table 5-5 The Establishment of Boundaries: Emergence of Careers Specialized to House Leadership

Speaker (term)	Elapsed years between last day of service as Representative and death	How Speakers finished their careers
1. Muhlenberg (1789-90, 1793-94)	6	Receiver-general of Pennsylvania Land Office
2. Trumbull (1791-92)	14	Governor of Connecticut
3. Dayton (1795-98)	25	Senator 1805; private life
4. Sedgwick (1799-1800)	12	Judge of Supreme Court of Massachusetts
5. Macon (1801-06)	17	Senate
6. Varnum (1807-10)	10	U.S. Senate and State Senate, Massachusetts
7. Clay (1811-13, 1815-19, 1823-24)	27	Senate
8. Cheves (1814)	42	President, Bank of U.S.; Chief Commissioner of Claims under Treaty of Ghent; private life
9. Taylor (1820, 1825-26)	21	State Senate, New York; private life
10. Barbour (1821-22)	11	Associate Justice, U.S. Supreme Court
11. Stevenson (1827-33)	23	Minister to Great Britain; Rector, University of Virginia
12. Bell (1834)	28	Senate; private life
13. Polk (1835-38)	10	President of U.S.
14. Hunter (1839-40)	40	State Treasurer, Virginia; Collector, Tappahannock, Virginia
15. White (1841-42)	1	Judge, 19th Judicial District, Virginia
16. Jones (1843-44)	3	Representative to Virginia State House of Delegates and Speaker
17. Davis (1845-46)	12	U.S. Commissioner to China, Governor of the Oregon Territory
18. Winthrop (1847-48)	44	Senator by appointment; unsuccessful candidate for Senate, Governor; private life
19. Cobb (1849-50)	11	Secretary of Treasury, Buchanan cabinet; Confederate major general; private life
20. Boyd (1851-54)	4	Lt. Governor of Kentucky
21. Banks (1855-56)	3	Served many nonconsecutive terms *after* Speakership; unsuccessful

22. Orr (1857-58)	14	Minister to Russia
23. Pennington (1859-60)	1	Failed of reelection; died soon after
24. Grow (1861-62)	4	Speaker in 37th; later private life; later still reelected to Congress; declined renomination; private life
25. Colfax (1863-68)	16	Private life; Vice-President
26. Pomeroy (1869)	36	Speaker 1 day; Mayor of Auburn, New York; private life
27. Blaine (1869-74)	17	Secretary of State; President, Pan-American Congress
28. Kerr (1875)	0	Speaker at his death, 1876
29. Randall (1876-80)	0	House of Representatives
30. Keifer (1881-82)	22	Not renominated to House after served as Speaker; Major General in Spanish American War; Returned later to House; private life
31. Carlisle (1883-88)	20	Senate, Secretary of Treasury; private life
32. Reed (1889-90, 1895-98)	3	Private life; law practice
33. Crisp (1891-94)	0	U.S. House of Representatives (nominated for Senate at time of death)
34. Henderson (1899-1902)	3	Private life; retired, House of Representatives
35. Cannon (1903-10)	3	Retired, House of Representatives
36. Clark (1911-18)	0	House of Representatives
37. Gillett (1919-24)	10	Senate; private life
38. Longworth (1925-30)	0	House of Representatives, Speaker
39. Garner (1931-32)	32+	Vice-President; private life
40. Rainey (1933-34)	0	House of Representatives, Speaker
41. Byrns (1935-36)	0	House of Representatives, Speaker
42. Bankhead (1936-39)	0	House of Representatives, Speaker
43. Rayburn (1940-45, 1947-52, 1955-61)	0	House of Representatives, Speaker
44. Martin (1946-47, 1953-54)	1+	Defeated for renomination, 1966, in his 82nd year and his 44th consecutive year of House service
45. McCormack (1962-67)	0+	House of Representatives, presently Speaker (1967)

Figure 5-4 The Establishment of Boundaries: Emergence of Careers Specialized to House Leadership.*

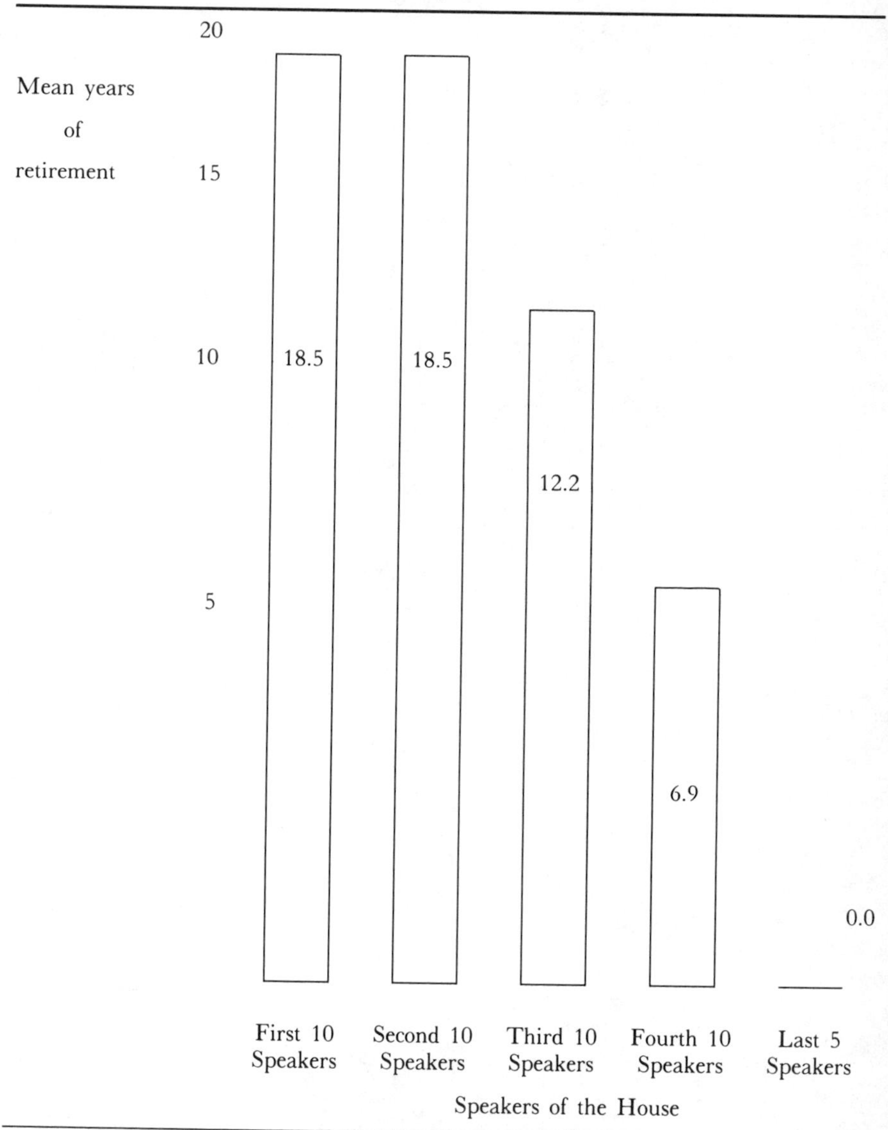

Mean years
of
retirement

	First 10 Speakers	Second 10 Speakers	Third 10 Speakers	Fourth 10 Speakers	Last 5 Speakers
	18.5	18.5	12.2	6.9	0.0

Speakers of the House

* Data from Table 5-5.

mittees cannot be accepted as an appropriate index of internal complexity. I shall therefore attempt a more anecdotal accounting procedure.

Briefly, the growth of internal complexity can be shown in three ways: in the growth in the autonomy and importance of committees, in the growth of specialized agencies of party leadership, and in the general increase in the provision of various emoluments and auxiliary aids to members in the form of office space, salaries, allowances, staff aid, and committee staffs.

A wholly satisfactory account of the historical development of the House committee system does not exist. But perhaps I can swiftly sketch in a number of plausible conclusions from the literature.

From the perspective of the present-day United States, the use of standing committees by Congress is scarcely a controversial issue.[14] Yet, in the beginning the House relied only very slightly upon standing committees. Instead of the present-day system, where bills are introduced in great profusion and automatically shunted to one or another of the committees whose jurisdictions are set forth in the rules, the practice in the first, and early Congresses was for subjects to be debated initially in the whole House and general principles settled upon, before they were parceled out for further action — fact-finding, detailed consideration or the proposal of a bill — to any one of four possible locations; an officer in the Executive Branch, a Committee of the Whole, a Select Committee formed *ad hoc* for the reception of a particular subject, or a standing committee. Generally, one of the alternatives to standing committees was used.

Of the First Congress, Harlow writes:

> The outstanding feature of procedure in the House was the important part played by the Committee of the Whole. Much of the business in the House of Delegates of Virginia was transacted in that way, and the Virginians were influential enough to impose their methods upon the federal House. . . . It was in Committee of the Whole that Congress worked out the first tarriff bill, and also the main outlines of such important measures as the laws organizing the executive departments. After the general principles were once determined, select committees would be appointed to work out the details, and to frame bills in accordance with the decision already agreed upon in Committee of the Whole. Considerable work was done by these select committees, especially after the first session.[15]

And Alexander says:

> In the early history of the House the select committee . . . was used exclusively for the consideration of bills, resolutions, and other legislative matters.[16] As business increased and kindred subjects became scattered, however, a tendency to concentrate inaugurated a system of standing committees. It rooted itself slowly. There was an evident distrust of the centralizing influence of permanent bodies. Besides, it took important business from the many and gave it to a few, one standing committee of three or five members often taking the place of half a dozen select committees.[17]

It is difficult to disentangle the early growth of the standing committee system from concurrent developments in the party system. For as Alexander Hamilton took control of the administration of George Washington, and extended his influence toward men of like mind in Congress, the third alternative to standing committees — reference to a member of the Executive Branch — became an important device of the Federalist majority in the House.

> By the winter of 1790 [Harlow writes] Hamilton was attracting attention because of his influence over Congress. . . . His ready intelligence grasped the

truth at once that Jefferson spent more than ten years learning: that not even the Constitution of the United States could keep apart two such inseparable factors in government as executive and legislature.[18]

In the first two Congresses Hamilton is said to have used the Federalist caucus to guide debate in the Committee of the Whole, and also to have arranged for key financial measures to be referred directly to himself for detailed drafting.[19] This practice led, in the Second Congress, to sharp clashes with followers of Jefferson, who

> made it perfectly clear that if they should ever get the upper hand in Congress, they would make short work of Hamilton, and restore to the House what they considered to be its constitutional authority over finance.[20]

The Republicans did in fact gain the upper hand in the Third Congress (elected in 1792) and they restored detailed power over finances to the Committee of the Whole. This did not work satisfactorily, however, and in the Fourth Congress a Committee on Ways and Means was formed. Harlow says:

> The appointment of . . . standing committees, particularly . . . Ways and Means, was in a way a manifestation of the Republican theory of government. From their point of view, the members of the House, as the direct representatives of the voters, ought to be the mainspring of the whole system. Hitherto, the Federalists had sold their birthright by permitting the executive to take a more active part in the government than was warranted by the Constitution. The Republicans now planned to bring about the proper balance between the different branches, by broadening at once the scope of the operations of the House, and restricting the executive. It was the better to enable the House to take its assigned part that the new type of organization was worked out. Just as the heads of departments were looked upon as agents of the executive, so the committees would be considered as the agents of the House.[21]

During the presidency of Thomas Jefferson, committees were constituted and employed as agents of the President's faction in Congress which was in most matters actively led by the President himself. Binkley says:

> . . . When the House of Representatives had elected its Speaker and the committee chairmen had been appointed it was apparent to the discerning that lieutenants of the President had not appointed them, but his wishes, confidentially expressed, had determined them just as surely as if he had formally and publicly nominated them. Here was the fulfillment of Marshall's prediction that Jefferson would "embody himself in the House of Representatives." [22]

There is, however, some doubt as to Jefferson's absolute mastery over committee appointments, since it is also reported that Speaker Macon was extremely important in constituting the committees, and, in particular, in keeping John Randolph on as chairman of the Ways and Means Committee for some time after Randolph had repeatedly and violently broken with the Jefferson administration.[23]

Recently the suggestion has been made that the direct evidence is slight and contradictory that political parties in Congress went through rapid organization and differentiation in the earliest years of the Republic. This revisionist interpretation lays greater stress upon boarding house cliques, more or less sectional and more or less ideologically factional in their composition, as the heretofore neglected building blocks out of which the more conventionally partisan Congressional politics of the Jacksonian era eventually grew.[24]

But even revisionists concede to Jefferson a large influence over Congressional politics; the conventional accounts of the growth of the committee system are pretty much undisturbed by their critique. In essence, by the early years of the 19th century, the House committee system had passed through two distinct phases: the no-committee, Hamiltonian era, in which little or no internal differentiation within the institution was visible; and a Jeffersonian phase, in which factional alignments had begun to develop — these were exploited by the brilliant and incessant maneuverings of the President himself, who selected his lieutenants and confidants from the ranks of Congress *ad hoc,* as political requirements and opportunities dictated. During this period a small number of standing committees existed, but were not heavily relied upon. Their jurisdictions were not so securely fixed that the Speaker could not instead appoint select committees to deal with business that ought to have been sent to them.[25]

The advent of Henry Clay and the victory of the War Hawk faction in the elections of 1810 brought the committee system to its third phase. Clay for the first time used the Speaker's prerogative of appointment of members to committees independently of Presidential designs. There is some question whether Clay's appointment policies were calculated to further his policy preferences or merely his popularity (and hence his Presidential ambitions) within the factionally divided house,[26] but there seems no reason to doubt that Clay won for the Speakership a new measure of independence as a power base in the American political system. Under Clay five House committees were constituted to oversee expenditures in executive departments, the first major institutionalization of the Congressional function of oversight. William N. Chambers writes:

> [By] 1814 the committee system had become the dominant force in the chamber. Thus effective power was exercised not by the President, as had been the case with Jefferson, but by factional Congressional leaders working through the speakership, the caucus, and the committees.[27]

For the next 100 years the committee system waxed and waned more or less according to the ways in which committees were employed by the party or faction that dominated the House and elected the Speaker. Figures from the latter decades of the 19th century testify amply to the leeway afforded Speakers — especially less of their prior composition.[28] In part, it was Speaker Cannon's increasing use of this prerogative in an attempt to keep control of his fragmenting party that triggered the revolt against his Speakership in 1910-11, and that led to the establishment of the committee system as we know it today.[29]

Under the fourth, decentralized, phase of the committee system, committees have won solid institutionalized independence from party leaders both inside and outside Congress. Their jurisdictions are fixed in the rules; their composition is

95

largely determined and their leadership entirely determined by the automatic operation of seniority. Their work is increasingly technical and specialized, and the way in which they organize internally to do their work is entirely at their own discretion. Committees nowadays have developed an independent sovereignty of their own, subject only to very infrequent reversals and modifications of their powers by House party leaders backed by large and insistent majorities.

To a degree, the development over the last sixty years of an increasingly complex machinery of party leadership within the House cross-cuts and attentuates the independent power of committees. Earlier, the leading faction in the House elected the Speaker and the Speaker in turn distributed the chairmanships of key committees to his principal allies and opponents. Thus the work of the House was centralized to the extent that the leading faction in the House was centralized. But differences of opinion are not uncommon among qualified observers. The Jeffersonian era, for example, is widely regarded as a high point of centralization during the 19th century. Harlow reports:

> From 1801 to 1808 the floor leader was distinctly the lieutenant of the executive. William B. Giles, who was actually referred to as "the premier, or prime minister," Caesar A. Rodney, John Randolph of Roanoke, and Wilson Cary Nicholas all held that honorable position at one time or another. It was their duty to look after party interests in the House, and in particular to carry out the commands of the President. The status of these men was different from that of the floor leader of today. . . . They were presidential agents, appointed by the executive, and dismissed at his pleasure.[30]

But another observer, a Federalist congressman quoted by Noble Cunningham, suggests that the Jeffersonian group was not at all times well organized:

> The ruling factions in the legislature have not yet been able to understand each other. . . . There evidently appears much rivalry and jealousy among the leaders. S[amuel] Smith thinks his experience and great address ought to give him a preponderance in all their measures, whilst Nicholson evidently looks upon these pretensions of his colleague with contempt, and Giles thinks the first representative of the Ancient Dominion ought certainly on all important occasions to take the lead, and Johnny Randolph is perfectly astonished that his great abilities should be overlooked. There is likewise a great number of other persons who are impatient of control and disposed to revolt at any attempts at discipline.[31]

This certainly squares with the reports of Jefferson's own continued attempts, also revealed in his letters, to recruit men to the House with whom he could work.[32]

Despite Jefferson's difficulties, he was the most consistently successful of all the 19th century Presidents in "embodying himself in the House of Representatives." After Jefferson, the Speaker became a power in his own right; not infrequently he was a candidate for the Presidency himself, and the House was more or less organized around his, rather than the President's, political interests. There was no formal position of majority leader; the leading spokesman for the majority party on the floor was identified by personal qualities of leadership and by the favor of the Speaker (or in the Jeffersonian era, of the President) rather than by his institutional position.[33]

Later, however, the chairman of the Ways and Means Committee — a key post reserved for the chief lieutenant of the Speaker — became *de facto* floor leader, a natural consequence of his responsibilities in managing the tariff bills that were so important in 19th century congressional politics. Occasionally the chairman of the Committee on Appropriations was the *de facto* leader, especially during periods of war mobilization, when the power of the House in the political system was coextensive with the power of the purse.[34] In the last part of the 19th century, however, the Committee on Appropriations was temporarily dismantled, and the chairman of Ways and Means Committee began to receive the formal designation as party leader.

The high point of the Ways and Means chairman's power came in the aftermath of the 1910 revolt against the Speaker. The power of committee appointments was for Democrats lodged in the Ways and Means Committee. Chairman Oscar Underwood, in cooperation with President Wilson, for a time (1911-1915) eclipsed the Speaker and the committee chairmen by operating the majority party by caucus.[35]

But Underwood's successor as Chairman of Ways and Means, Claude Kitchin (majority leader 1915-1919), disapproved of Wilson's war policies; this made it cumbersome and impractical for the leader of the majority on the floor and in caucus to hold this job by virtue of what was becoming an automatic succession through seniority to the chairmanship of Ways and Means. A separation of the two roles was effected after the Democrats became the minority in 1919.[36] Ever since then, the majority leader's job has existed as a full-time position; the incumbent now holds a nominal, junior committee post but he rarely attends committee meetings. At the same time, the majority leader has become less of a President's man, and the caucus is now dormant as an instrument of party leadership — although it now sometimes becomes a vehicle, especially at the opening of Congress, for the expression of widespread dissatisfaction by rank-and-file House members. Thus, while binding votes on policy matters have not been put through the caucus by party leaders, the Republican caucus has three times in recent years deposed party leaders and the Democratic caucus has deprived three of its members of their committee seniority.

Formally designated party whips are, like the differentiated post of majority leaders, an innovation principally of the twentieth century. The first whips date back to just before the turn of the century. In the early years, the designation seems to have been quite informal, and it is only recently that an elaborate whip system, with numerous deputies, a small staff, and formal procedures for canvassing members, has been established by both parties in the House.[37]

Thus, we can draw a contrast between the practices of recent and earlier years with respect to formal party leaders other than the Speaker:

(1) Floor leaders in the 20th century are officially designated; in the 19th, they were often informally designated, indefinite, shifting or even competitive, and based on such factors as personal prestige, speaking ability, or Presidential favor.[38]

(2) Floor leaders in recent years are separated from the committee system and elected by party members; earlier they were prominent committee chairmen who were given their posts by the Speaker, sometimes as a side-payment in the formation of a coalition to elect the Speaker.[39]

(3) Floor leaders today rely upon whip systems; before 1897 there were no formally designated whips.

A third indicator of the growth of internal organization is the growth of resources assigned to internal House management, measured in terms of personnel, facilities, and money. Visitors to Washington are not likely to forget the sight of the five large office buildings, three of them belonging to the House, that flank the Capitol. The oldest of these on the House side was built just after the turn of the century, in 1909, when a great many other of our indices show significant changes.

Reliable figures, past or present, on personnel assigned to the House are impossible to come by; but it is unlikely that a commentator today would agree with the observer early in this century who said:

> It is somewhat singular that Congress is one of the few legislative bodies that attempts to do its work almost entirely without expert assistance — without the aid of parliamentary counsel, without bill drafting and revising machinery and without legislative and reference agencies, and until now it has shown little inclination to regard with favor proposals looking toward the introduction of such agencies.[40]

Indeed, the only major contemporary study we have of congressional staff speaks of present "tendencies toward overexpansion of the congressional staff," and says that "Three-fourths of the committee aides interviewed" thought that professional staffs of committees were sufficiently large to handle their present work load.[41]

Needless to say, that work load has grown, and, though it is impossible to say precisely by how much, congressional staffs have grown as well. This is roughly reflected in figures that are more or less comparable over time on that portion of the legislative budget assigned to the House. These figures show the expected increases. However, except for the jump between 1945 and 1946, reflecting the new provisions for staff aid of the Legislative Reorganization Act, the changes in these figures over time are not as abrupt as is the case with other of our time series. Nor would changes over time be even as steep as they are in Table 5-6 if these figures were corrected for changes in the purchasing power of the dollar. So we must regard this indicator as weak, but nevertheless pointing in the expected direction.

III. From Particularistic and Discretionary to Universalistic and Automated Decision Making

The best evidence we have of a shift away from discretionary and toward automatic decision making is the growth of seniority as a criterion determining committee rank and the growth of the practice of deciding contested elections to the House strictly on the merits.

Table 5-6 The Growth of Internal Complexity: Expenditures Made by the House of Representatives*

Fiscal Year	Expenditures (1000s dollars)	Fiscal Year	Expenditures (1000s dollars)	Fiscal Year	Expenditures (1000s dollars)
1872	1,952	1905	3,367	1935	8,007
1873	3,340	1906	3,517	1936	8,377
1874	2,687	1907	3,907	1937	8,451
		1908	4,725	1938	8,139
1875	2,030	1909	5,005	1939	8,615
1876	2,201				
1877	2,232	1910	4,897	1940	9,375
1878	2,183	1911	5,066	1941	9,511
1879	2,230	1912	4,741	1942	9,678
		1913	5,148	1943	9,361
1880	2,137	1914	5,012	1944	10,944
1881	2,191				
1882	2,188	1915	5,081	1945	11,660
1883	2,339	1916	4,917	1946	14,243
1884	2,405	1917	5,400	1947	16,012
		1918	5,331	1948	18,096
1885	2,466	1919	5,304	1949	18,110
1886	2,379				
1887	2,232	1920	7,059	1950	20,330
1888	2,354	1921	6,510	1951	21,053
1889	2,416	1922	6,001	1952	23,474
		1923	6,588	1953	23,622
1890	2,567	1924	6,154	1954	23,660
1891	2,520				
1892	2,323	1925	7,761	1955	26,610
1893	2,478	1926	7,493	1956	34,587
1894	2,844	1927	7,526	1957	36,738
		1928	7,623	1958	39,524
1895	2,945	1929	7,813	1959	43,882
1896	2,843				
1897	3,108	1930	8,260	1960	44,207
1898	2,948	1931	8,269	1961	47,324
1899	3,063	1932	8,310	1962	50,295
1900	2,981	1933	7,598	1963	52,983
1901	3,066	1934	7,154	1964	55,654
1902	3,088				
1903	3,223			1965	58,212
1904	3,247				
				1966 (est.)	65,905
				1967 (est.)	70,883

* Source: U.S. Executive Office of President. Bureau of the Budget. *The Budget of United States Government*. Annual Volumes for 1921-1967. Washington, U.S. Government Printing Office.
U.S. Treasury Department. *Combined Statement of Receipts, Expenditures and Balances of the United States Government*. Annual volumes for 1872-1920. Washington, U.S. Government Printing Office.

The literature on seniority presents a welter of conflicting testimony. Some commentators date the seniority system from 1910;[42] others say that seniority as a criterion for determining the committee rank of members was in use well before.[43] Woodrow Wilson's classic account of *Congressional Government* in 1884 pays tribute both to the independence of the committees and their chairman and to the absolute discretion of the Speaker in the committee appointment process.[44] It is clear that the Speaker has no such power today. In another paper my colleagues and I present a detailed preliminary tabulation and discussion on the extent to which seniority in its contemporary meaning was followed in the selection of committee chairmen in the most recent 40 Congresses.[45] The central finding for our present purposes (summarized in Table 5-7 and Figure 5-5) is that the seniority system — an automatic, universally applied, nondiscretionary method of selection — is now always used, but that formerly the process by which chairmen were selected was highly and later partially discretionary.

The figures for before 1911 can be interpreted as indicating the use of the Speaker's discretion in the appointment of committee chairmen. After 1911, when committee appointment powers are vested in committees on committees, the figures principally reflect the growth of the norm that no one man should serve as chairman of more than one committee. Congressmen often sat on a large number of committees, and senior men rose to the top of more than one committee, but allowed less senior men to take the chair, much as the custom presently is in the U.S. Senate. After 1946, when the number of committees was drastically reduced, this practice died out, and a strictly automated system of seniority has asserted itself.

The settlement of contested elections on some basis other than the merits seems in earlier years to have been a common phenomenon. To this point, we can bring the testimony of a number of quotes and anecdotes, widely separated in time. Here are a few examples:

1795: A foreshadowing of future developments arose in the contested election of Joseph B. Varnum, of Massachusetts, in the Fourth Congress. This case became the focus of a struggle for power between the Federalists and the Anti-Federalists. It is an early instance of the triumph of the rule that all too often might makes right, at least in the settlement of election contests in the House of Representatives.

Varnum's election was contested on the principal ground that the Board of Selectmen of his home town (of which Board he was a member) had returned sixty votes more than there were qualified voters in the town. Since he had been elected with a certified overall plurality of eleven votes, investigation was warranted. Theodore Sedgwick, leader of the Federalists in the House, suggested that testimony be taken . . . inasmuch as the House alone had the power to compel the town clerk to produce the records containing the names of the illegal voters, if indeed any existed. Varnum, an Anti-Federalist, strongly protested against such a procedure. . . . He proposed . . . that petitions . . . should present the names of the illegal voters, if they could do so. . . . This was impossible, since only the town clerk had access to the voting records of the town. The Anti-Federalists, who controlled the House at the time, on a party-line vote

Table 5-7 The Growth of Universalism: Violations of Seniority in the Appointment of Committee Chairmen, U.S. House of Representatives, 1881-1963

	Percentage of Committees on which the Chairman was not selected by seniority, averaged by decades			
Congress:	47-51	52-56	57-61	62-66
Years:	1881-89	1891-99	1901-09	1911-19
Average:	60.4%	49.4%	19%	30.8%
Violations of Seniority				
Congress:	67-71	72-76	77-81	82-88
Years:	1921-29	1931-39	1941-49	1951-63
Average:	26%	23%	14%	.7%
Violations				

Figure 5-5 The Growth of Universalism; Decline in Violations of Seniority, Committee Chairmen, U.S. House of Representatives, 1881-1963.*

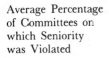

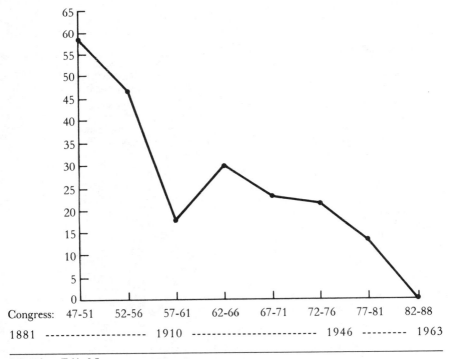

* Data from Table 5-7.

sustained Varnum's objections ... in fact, the controlling faction even went so far as to adopt a resolution, again by a partisan vote, declaring that "the charges against [Varnum] are wholly unfounded. ..." "Thus, amidst an outburst of derisive laughter, the incident closed like a harliquinade." [46]

1860: I served in my second term on the Committee on Elections. ... Election cases in the House up to that time were ... determined entirely by party feeling. Whenever there was a plausible reason for making a contest the dominant party in the House almost always awarded the seat to the man of its own side. There is a well-authorized story of Thaddeus Stevens, that going into the room of the Committee on Elections, of which he was a member, he found a hearing going on. He asked one of his Republican colleagues what was the point in the case. "There is not much point to it," was the answer. "They are both damned scoundrels." "Well," said Stevens, "which is the Republican damned scoundrel? I want to go for the Republican damned scoundrel." [47]

1869: All traces of a judicial character in these proceedings are fast fading away. ... Each case is coming to be a mere partisan struggle. At the dictate of party majorities, the Committee [on Elections] must fight, not follow, the law and the evidence. ... This tendency is so manifest ... that it has ceased to be questioned, and is now but little resisted. ... [E]fforts ... to hold the judgments of the Committee on Elections up above the dirty pool of party politics have encountered such bitter and unsparing denunciation, and such rebuke for treason to party fealty, that they are not likely often to be repeated. [48]

1890: The [elections] committee usually divides on the line of party ... and the House usually follows in the same way. ... The decision of election cases invariably increases the party which organized the House and ... appoints the majority of the Committee on Elections. Probably there is not an instance on record where the minority was increased by the decision of contested cases. ... It may be said that our present method of determining election cases is ... unjust to members and contestants and fails to secure the representation which the people have chosen. [49]

1895: A most casual inspection of the workings of the present system of deciding election contests will show that it barely maintains the form of a judicial inquiry and that it is thoroughly tainted with the grossest partisanship. ... When it is alleged that members of a minority do not generally contest seats, a striking tribute is paid to the partisanship of the present system. [50]

1899: The Republican majority in this House [56th Congress] was reduced about fifty from the previous Congress, but before the [first] session closed, a dozen or more Democrats lost their seats in election contests, which gave the Republicans a comfortable majority with which to do business. [51]

1905: Today it is simply a contest between two parties for political influence and the rewards of office, or sometimes a contest between the majority in the House and a constituency of the minority party. ... In the period [1865-1905, 39th through 58th Congresses] ... the majority deprived itself of seats only nine times, while it deprived the minority of seats eighty-two times. [52]

A journalist writing at the beginning of the twentieth century summarizes the situation as he had encountered it over a twenty-year period:

> It may be said . . . that there is no fairness whatever exercised in . . . contests for seats, especially where the majority needs the vote for party purposes. Hundreds of men have lost their seats in Congress, to which they were justly entitled upon all fair, reasonable, and legal grounds, and others put in their places for purely partisan reasons. This has always been so and doubtless will continue so. . . .[53]

In fact, it has not continued so; nowadays, contested elections are settled with much more regard to due process and the merits of the case than was true throughout the nineteenth century. By 1926, a minority member of the Committee on Elections No. 1 could say:

> In the eight years I have served on Elections Committees and six years upon this Committee, I have never seen partisanship creep into that Committee but one time. There has not been any partisanship in the Committee since the distinguished gentleman from Utah became Chairman of that Committee. A Democrat was seated the last time over a Republican by this Committee, and every member of the Committee voted to seat that Democrat.[54]

This quotation suggests a method by which the development of universalistic criteria for settling contested House elections can be monitored, namely, measuring the extent to which party lines are breached in committee reports and in voting on the floor in contest cases. I have made no such study, but on the basis of the accumulated weight of contemporary reports such as I have been quoting, I predict that a time series would show strict party voting in the 19th century, switching to unanimity or near-unanimity, in most cases, from the early years of the 20th century onward.

Attempts to establish legal precedents for the settlement of contested elections date from the recommendations of the Ames Committee in 1791. In 1798 a law was enacted prescribing a uniform mode of taking testimony and for compelling the attendance of witnesses. This law was required to be renewed in each Congress and was allowed to lapse in 1804. Bills embodying similar laws were proposed in 1805, 1806, 1810, 1813, and 1830. Not until 1851 was such a law passed, which provided for the gathering of testimony forming the bases of the proofs of each contestant's claim, but not for rules concerning other aspects of contested elections. More significant, however, was a clause permitting the House to set the law aside in whole or in part in specific cases, which apparently the House availed itself of with some regularity in the 19th century. With a few modifications this law is still in effect.[55]

The absolute number of contests shows a decrease in recent decades, as does the number of contests in relation to the number of seats. This suggests that the practice of instigating contests for frivolous reasons has passed into history; contemporary House procedures no longer hold out the hope of success for such contests.[56] Table 5-8 and Figure 5-6 give the figures, by decades.

There is today, certainly, no wholesale stealing of seats. If any bias exists in the system, it probably favors the protection of incumbents irrespective of party,[57]

Table 5-8 The Growth of Universalism: Contested Elections in the House by Decades, 1789-1964

Congress	Number of Contested Seats	Mean Seats in House for Decade	% Seats Contested Per Congress*
1- 5 (1789-1798)	16	89.8	3.56
6-10 (1799-1808)	12	126.6	1.90
11-15 (1809-1818)	16	166.4	1.92
16-20 (1819-1828)	12	202.6	1.18
21-25 (1829-1838)	11	230.0	.96
26-30 (1839-1848)	17	231.8	1.46
31-35 (1849-1858)	23	233.0	1.98
36-40 (1859-1868)	73	196.4	7.44
41-45 (1869-1878)	72	273.0	5.28
46-50 (1879-1888)	58	312.2	3.72
51-55 (1889-1898)	87	346.8	5.02
56-60 (1899-1908)	41	374.4	2.20
61-65 (1909-1918)	36	417.4	1.72
66-70 (1919-1928)	23	435.0	1.06
71-75 (1929-1938)	25	435.0	1.14
76-80 (1939-1948)	15	435.0	.68
81-85 (1949-1958)	12	435.0	.56
86-88 (1959-1964)	8	437.0	.90

* Column 2 divided by column 3, over the number of Congresses (5 except in last instance).

Sources: Dempsey *op. cit.*, Appendix I, and George B. Galloway, *History of the U.S. House of Representatives* (House Document 246, 87th Congress, 1st Session) (Washington: U.S. Government Printing Office, 1962), pp. 215-216.

Figure 5-6 The Growth of Universalism: Contested Elections in the House by Decades, 1789-1964.*

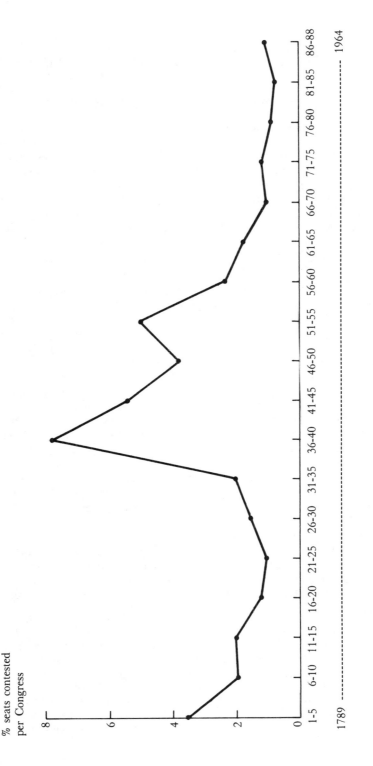

% seats contested
per Congress

* Data from Table 5-8.

and hence (we may surmise not incidentally) the protection of the boundaries of the organization.

IV. Causes, Consequences, Conclusions

It seems reasonable to conclude that one of the main long-run changes in the U.S. House of Representatives has been toward greater institutionalization. Knowing this, we may wish to ask, at a minimum, three questions: What caused it? What follows from it? What can this case tell us about the process in general? It is not from lack of space alone that our answers to each of three questions will be brief and highly speculative.

Not much, for example, is known about the causes of institutionalization. The best theoretical guess in the literature is probably Durkheim's: "The division of labor varies in direct ratio with the volume and density of societies, and, if it progresses in a continuous manner in the course of social development, it is because societies become regularly denser and generally more voluminous." [58] "Density" in at least some sense is capable of being operationalized and measured separately from its institutional consequences. For present purposes, the proposition can probably be rendered as follows: As the responsibilities of the national government grew, as a larger proportion of the national economy was affected by decisions taken at the center, the agencies of the national government institutionalized.[59] Another, complementary, translation of the density theorem would be that as organizations grow in size, they tend to develop internally in ways predicted by the theory of institutionalization. Size and increasing workload seem to me in principle measurable phenomena.[60] Size alone, in fact, seems almost too easy. Until a deliberative body has some minimum amount of work to do, the necessity for interaction among its members remains slight, and, having no purpose, coordination by means of a division of labor, rules and regulations, precedents and so on, seem unlikely to develop. So a somewhat more complicated formula has to be worked out, perhaps relating the size of an organization to the amount of work it performs (e.g., number of work-days per year, number of full-time as opposed to nominal members, number of items considered, number of reports rendered) before the strength of "density" and "volume" can be tested as causes of the process of institutionalization.

A discussion of the consequences of the House's institutionalization must be equally tentative. It is hard — indeed for the contemporary observer, impossible — to shake the conviction that the House's institutional structure does matter greatly in the production of political outcomes. A recent popular account begins:

> A United States Congressman has two principal functions: to make laws and to keep laws from being made. The first of these he and his colleagues perform only with sweat, patience and a remarkable skill in the handling of creaking machinery; but the second they perform daily, with ease and infinite variety.[61]

No observer who focuses upon policy results, or who cares about the outputs of the American legislative process, fails to note the "complicated forms and diversified structure" which "confuse the vision, and conceal the system which underlies its composition." [62] All this is such settled knowledge that it seems unnecessary to mention it here. Still, it is important to stress that the very features of the House which casual observers and freshman legislators find most obstructive are principal consequences of (among other things) the process we have been describing.[63]

It is, however, not merely the complexity or the venerability of the machinery that they notice. These, in our discussion so far, have been treated as defining characteristics rather than consequences of institutionalization. What puzzles and irks the outside observer is a partial displacement of goals, and a focus of resources upon internal processes at the expense of external demands, that come as a consequence of institutionalization. This process of displacement is, of course, well known by social theory in other settings.[64] A closer look at the general character of this displacement is bound to suggest a number of additional consequences.

For example, representatives may find that the process of institutionalization has increased their incentives to stay within the system. For them, the displacement of resources transforms the organization from a convenient instrument for the pursuit of social policies into an end value itself, a prime source of gratification, of status and power.[65]

The increasing complexity of the division of labor presents an opportunity for individual Representatives to specialize and thereby enormously increase their influence upon a narrow range of policy outcomes in the political system at large. Considered separately, the phenomenon of specialization may strike the superficial observer as productive of narrow-minded drones. But the total impact of a cadre of specialists operating over the entire spectrum of public policies is a formidable asset for a political institution; and it has undoubtedly enabled the House to retain a measure of autonomy and influence that is quite exceptional for a 20th century legislature.[66]

Institutionalization has, in the House, on the whole meant the decentralization of power. This has created a great many important and interesting jobs within the House, and thus increased the attractiveness of service therein as a career. Proposed reforms of Congress which seek to move toward a recentralization of Congressional power rarely consider this fact. But it is at least possible that some moves to restore discretion to the Speaker, or to centralized party agencies outside Congress, would reduce the effectiveness of Congress far below the level anticipated, because the House would come to be less valued in and of itself, its division of labor would provide less of a power base for subject matter specialists, and the incentives to stay within the organization would sharply decline.

Thus we can argue that, along with the more obvious effects of institutionalization, the process has also served to increase the power of the House within the political system and to spread somewhat more widely incentives for legislators to participate actively in policymaking.

A final possible consequence of institutionalization can be suggested: that the process tends to promote professional norms of conduct among participants. Indeed, something like these norms are built into the definition of institutionalization by some commentators.[67] But the built-in norms typically mentioned in discussions of "organization men" have to do with the segmental, ritualized interaction that characterizes organizations coordinated by hierarchical means; slightly different predictions about norms would have to be made for more decentralized, more egalitarian institutionalized legislative bodies.

In fact, there is coming to be a sizeable body of literature about the norms of professional legislative conduct. Time and again, the norms of predictability, courtesy, and reciprocity are offered by professional legislators as central to the rules of the legislative game.[68] Thus, we can suggest a hypothesis that the extent to which these norms are widely applied in a legislative body is a direct function of that body's structural institutionalization. Appropriate tests can be made cross-sectionally, by comparing contemporary legislatures that vary with respect to boundary-maintenance, internal complexity, and universalistic-automated internal decision making. Historically, less satisfactory tests are possible, since a number of vagaries enter into the determination of what is recorded and what is not, and since antecedent factors may account for both structural and normative institutionalization. This makes it hard to estimate the dispersion and importance of norms of conduct.

Nevertheless, the history of the House does suggest that there has been a growth in the rather tame virtue of reciprocity, courtesy, and predictability in legislative life since the turn of the century. Clem Miller describes human relations in the House of today:

> One's overwhelming first impression as a member of Congress is the aura of friendliness that surrounds the life of a congressman. No wonder that "few die and none resign." Almost everyone is unfailingly polite and courteous. Window washers, clerks, senators — it cuts all ways. We live in a cocoon of good feeling. . . .[69]

No doubt there are breaches in the fabric of good fellowship, mostly unpublicized, but the student of Congress cannot refrain even so from comparing this testimony with the following sampling of 19th century congressional conduct:

> Upon resuming his seat, after having replied to a severe personal arraignment of Henry Clay, former Speaker White, without the slightest warning, received a blow in the face. In the fight that followed a pistol was discharged wounding an officer of the police. John Bell, the distinguished Speaker and statesman, had a similar experience in Committee of the Whole (1838). The fisticuffs became so violent that even the Chair would not quell it. Later in the day both parties apologized and "made their submissions." On February 6, 1845, Edward J. Black, of Georgia, "crossed over from his seat, and coming within the bar behind Joshua R. Giddings as he was speaking, made a pass at the back of his head with a cane. William H. Hammett, of Mississippi, threw his arms round Black and bore him off as he would a woman from a fire. . . ."

> When Reuben M. Whitney was before a committee of investigation in 1837, Bailie Peyton, of Tennessee, taking offense at one of his answers, threatened him fiercely, and when he rose to claim the committee's protection, Mr. Peyton, with due and appropriate profanity, shouted: "You shan't say one word while you are in this room; if you do I will put you to death." The chairman, Henry A. Wise, added: "Yes; this insolence is insufferable." As both these gentlemen were armed

with deadly weapons, the witness could hardly be blamed for not wanting to testify before the committee again.

"These were not pleasant days," writes Thomas B. Reed. "Men were not nice in their treatment of each other." [70]

Indeed they were not: Nineteenth century accounts of Congressional behavior abound in passages like these. There is the consternation of members who put up with the presence on the floor of John Randolph's hunting dogs.[71] There is the famous scene on May 22, 1851, when Representative Preston Brooks of South Carolina entered the U.S. Senate and beat Senator Charles Sumner senseless with a cane,[72] and the record contains accounts of more than one such occasion:

> When Matthew Lyon, of Kentucky, spat in his face, [Roger] Griswold [of Connecticut, a member 1795-1805] stiffened his arm to strike, but remembering where he was, he cooly wiped his cheek. But after the House by its vote failed to expel Lyon, he "beat him with great violence," says a contemporary chronicle, "using a strong walking-stick." [73]

With all the ill will that the heat of battle sometimes generates currently, the House has long since left behind the era of guns and dogs, canings and fisticuffs, that occupied so much of the 19th century scene. No doubt this reflects general changes in manners and morals, but it also reflects a growth in the value of the House as an institution capable of claiming the loyalty and good behavior of its members.[74] The best test of the hypothesis, to be sure, remains the cross-sectional one. If American state legislatures, for example, can be found to differ significantly with respect to structural institutionalization, they may also be found to vary concomitantly with respect to the application of the norms of professional legislative life.[75]

Finally, the study of the institutionalization of the House affords us a perspective from which to comment upon the process in general. First, as to its reversibility. Many of our indicators show a substantial decay in the institutional structure of the House in the period surrounding the Civil War. In sheer numbers, the House declined from 237 members in the Congress of 1859 to 178 in the Congress of 1861; not until a decade later did the House regain its former strength. Frivolous contests for seats reached a height in this period, and our rank-and-file boundary measures reflect decay as well. It may be true, and it is is certainly amusing, that the strength of the British Admiralty grows as the number of ships declines;[76] but that this illustrates an inflexibly narcissistic law of institutional growth may be doubted. As institutions grow, our expectations about the displacement of resources inward do give us warrant to predict that they will resist decay, but the indications of curve-linearity in our present findings give us ample warning that institutions are also continuously subject to environmental influence and their power to modify and channel that influence is bound to be less than all-encompassing.

Some of our indicators give conditional support for a "take-off" theory of modernization. If one of the stigmata of the take-off to modernity is the rapid development of universalistic, bounded, complex institutional forms, the data presented here lend this theory some plausibility.[77] The "big bang" seems to come in the 1890-1910 period, on at least some of the measures.

In conclusion, these findings suggest that increasing hierarchical structure is not a necessary feature of the institutionalization process. Organizations other than bureaucracies, it seems clear, also are capable of having natural histories which increase their viability in the modern world without forcing them into uniformly centralized patterns of authority.

Notes

1. A good recent summary of literature bearing on this point as it applies to the study of political development may be found in Samuel P. Huntington, "Political Development and Political Decay," *World Politics,* 17 (April 1965), 386-430.
2. Robert A. Dahl speaks of "the three great milestones in the development of democratic institutions — the right to participate in governmental decisions by casting a vote, the right to be represented, and the right of an organized oppostion to appeal for votes against the government in elections and in parliament." In enumerating these three great achievements of democratic government, Dahl also implies that they are embodied principally in three main institutions: parties, elections, and legislatures: Robert A. Dahl (ed.), *Political Oppositions in Western Democracies* (New Haven and London: Yale University Press, 1966), p. xi. See also William Nisbet Chambers "Party Development and the American Mainstream," especially pp. 18-19, in Chambers and Walter Dean Burnham (eds.), *The American Party Systems: Stages of Political Development* (New York: Oxford, 1967).
3. See for example, Nelson W. Polsby, "Congressional Research and Congressional Data: A Preliminary Statement" (mimeo) delivered at the Conference on Congressional Research, sponsored by the Inter-university Consortium for Political Research and the Social Science Research Council at the Brookings Institution, Washington, D.C., April 3-4, 1964; H. Douglas Price, "The Congressman and the Electoral Arena" (mimeo, 1964); and T. Richard Witmer, "The Aging of the House," *Political Science Quarterly,* 79 (December 1964), 526-541.
4. Sir Henry Sumner Maine, *Ancient Law* (London: John Murray, 1908), pp. 220-325.
5. Ferdinand Tönnies, *Community and Society (Gemeinschaft und Gesellschaft)* (East Lansing: Michigan State University Press, 1957). See, in particular, the introductory commentary by Charles P. Loomis and John C. McKinney, "The Application of Gemeinschaft and Gesellschaft as Related to Other Typologies," *ibid.,* pp. 12-29.
6. Max Weber, *The Theory of Social and Economic Organization* (Glencoe: The Free Press, 1947), pp. 328ff.
7. Emile Durkheim, *The Division of Labor in Society* (Glencoe: The Free Press, 1947).
8. C. Northcote Parkinson, *Parkinson's Law* (Boston: Houghton Mifflin, 1957).
9. The only successful modern attempt I am aware of that employs a classical theory of institutionalization in an empirical study of something other than a bureaucracy is Harold W. Pfautz's "Christian Science: The Sociology of a Social Movement and Religious Group" (unpublished Ph.D. dissertation, Department of Sociology, University of Chicago, 1954). See also Harold W. Pfautz, "The Sociology of Secularization: Religious Groups," *The American Journal of Sociology,* 41 (September, 1955), 121-128, and Pfautz, "A Case Study of an Urban Religious Movement: Christian Science"

in E. W. Burgess and D. J. Bogue (eds.), *Contributions to Urban Sociology* (Chicago and London: University of Chicago Press, 1963), pp. 284-303.

10. On Clay, see Bernard Mayo, *Henry Clay: Spokesman of the New West* (Boston: Houghton Mifflin, 1937); Glyndon G. Van Deusen, *The Life of Henry Clay* (Boston: Little, Brown, 1937); Mary Parker Follett, *The Speaker of the House of Representatives* (New York: Longman's, Green, 1896), pp. 69-82; and Booth Mooney, *Mr. Speaker* (Chicago: Follett, 1964), pp. 21-48.

11. This pattern has been suggested before, by Douglas Price and myself, in unpublished papers (see Footnote 3). It is apparently not unique to the House. David Rothman, on what seem to me to be tenuous grounds, suggests something similar for the U.S. Senate in *Politics and Power: The U.S. Senate 1869-1901* (Cambridge: Harvard University Press, 1966). Consider, for a better example, where the United States gets its military leaders today and compare with this observation on the Mexican war period:

> The President [Polk] now undertook to offset this Whig advantage by making a number of Democratic generals.... He thereupon proceeded to name numerous Democrats to command the new divisions and brigades.... Even this flock of Democratic generals did not erase Polk's fears. After he had committed the command to Scott he considered giving the top authority to a civilian. He wanted to commission Senator Thomas Hart Benton a lieutenant general, and give him overall command....

(Roy F. Nichols, *The Stakes of Power: 1845-1877* New York: Hill and Wang, 1961, pp. 16,17.) One would expect civilians to serve high in the officer corps in wars of total mobilization, such as the Civil War and World War II, but not in a conflict involving only a partial mobilization, such as the Mexican War, Korea or Viet Nam. Nevertheless, the full professionalization of our army took place only in this century. During the Spanish-American War, another war of partial mobilization, the business of fighting was still carried on partially by militia and by federal volunteer regiments—irregulars—who fought side by side with, but independently of, regular troops. See Walter Millis, *Arms and Men* (New York: G. P. Putman's Sons, 1956), pp. 167-210. See also a contemporary Washington newsman's report: Arthur Wallace Dunn, *From Harrison to Harding* (New York: G. P. Putnam's Sons 1922), Vol. I, pp. 240ff, 272-274. Dunn says (Vol. I, pp. 240-41): "From the very beginning politics cut a leading part in the war. The appointments of generals and many other officers were due to influence rather than to merit or fitness.... One of these [appointments] was General Joe Wheeler, a member of Congress from Alabama. When he appeared with the twin stars of a major general on his shoulders, he joyously exclaimed: 'It is worth fifteen years of life to die on a battlefield'.... 'He will have twenty thousand men under him [remarked a critic] who do not share his opinion, and they will not care to lose fifteen years of their lives to give Joe Wheeler a glorious death.'" See also Samuel P. Huntington, *The Soldier and the State* (Cambridge: Harvard U. Press, 1957), esp. pp. 222-269. Huntington dates the rise of the American military as a profession from after the Civil War.

Consider also the following observation about the U.S. Supreme Court: "In the early years, resignations tended to occur for all sorts of reasons; Chief Justice Jay resigned to assume the governorship of New York, for example. But as the Court's prestige increased, justices found fewer reasons to step down from the bench": Samuel Krislov, *The Supreme Court in the Political Process* (New York: Macmillan, 1965), p. 9. David Danelski has suggested in a personal communication that while in its earliest years, the U.S. Supreme Court was neither a prestigious nor well-bounded institution, it became so more rapidly than the House, as the following table indicates:

Decade Appointed	Number of Justices Appointed	Average Tenure
1789-99	12 justices	10.3 years
1800-09	4	25.0
1810-19	2	29.0
1820-29	3	18.0
1830-39	6	20.3
1840-49	4	18.7
1850-59	3	12.3
1860-69	5	21.0
1870-79	5	18.0
1880-89	7	13.6
1890-99	6	16.1
1900-09	4	14.2
1910-19	7	15.0
1920-29	5	14.0
1930-39	6	20.0+ (Black and Douglas still on)
1940-49	8	9.4

It is, of course, not uncommon for students of the court to view the leadership of Chief Justice Marshall as highly significant in stabilizing the role of the Court in the political system and in enlarging its influence. Other indicators useful in tracing the institutionalization of the federal judiciary might be to study changes in the professional training of persons who have become federal judges, the increase in the number of judges on inferior federal courts, the codification of procedures for dealing with constitutional questions, the routinization of procedures for the granting of certiorari, and the growth of a bureaucracy to administer the federal court system. See, *inter alia*, Mr. Justice Brandeis' dissent in *Ashwander vs. T.V.A.* 297 U.S. 346-348; Edwin McElwain, "The Business of The Supreme Court as Conducted by Chief Justice Hughes," *Harvard Law Review*, 63 (November, 1949), 5-26; Merlo J. Pusey, *Charles Evans Hughes* (New York: Macmillan, 1951), Vol. II, pp. 603-690; Frederick Bernays Wiener, "The Supreme Court's New Rules," *Harvard Law Review*, 68 (November, 1954), 20-94; and Chief Justice Vinson's address before the American Bar Association, "The Work of the Federal Courts," September 7, 1949, reprinted in part in Walter F. Murphy and C. Herman Pritchett (eds.), *Courts, Judges and Politics* (N.Y.: Random House, 1961), pp. 54-58.

12. The combined totals of standing committees and subcommittees might be a better guide; but reliable information about subcommittees only exists for the most recent two decades.

13. I believe the word is George Galloway's. See *Congress at the Crossroads* (New York: Crowell, 1946), p. 340.

14. It certainly is, on the other hand, in the present-day United Kingdom, where purely legislative committees are regarded as a threat to the cohesion of the national political parties because they would give the parliamentary parties special instruments with which they could develop independent policy judgments and expertise and exercise oversight over an executive which is, after all, not formally constituted as an entity separate from Parliament. Thus committees can be construed as fundamentally inimical to unified Cabinet government. For an overview see Bernard Crick, *The Reform of Parliament* (Garden City: Doubleday Anchor, 1965); *The Political Quarterly*, 36 (July-September, 1965); and Andrew Hill and Anthony Whichelow, *What's Wrong with Parliament?* (Harmondsworth: Penguin, 1964), esp. pp. 64-82. See also a most illuminating essay by Robert C. Fried on the general conditions under which various political institutions (including legislatures) are strong or weak within their political systems: *Comparative Political Institutions* (New York: Macmillan, 1966), esp. p. 31.

15. Ralph V. Harlow, *The History of Legislative Methods in the Period Before 1825* (New Haven: Yale, 1917), pp. 127-128. See also Joseph Cooper, "Jeffersonian Attitudes Toward Executive Leadership and Committee Development in the House of Representatives 1789-1829," *Western Political Quarterly*, 18 (March, 1965), 45-63; and Cooper, "Congress and Its Committees in the Legislative Process" (unpublished Ph.D. dissertation, Department of Government, Harvard University, 1960), pp. 1-65.

16. On changes in the use of select committees, Lauros G. McConachie says: "Business of the earlier Houses went to hosts of select committees. At least three hundred and fifty were raised in the Third Congress. A special committee had to be formed for every petty claim. A bill founded on the report of one small committee had to be recommended to, or carefully drafted by, yet another committee. But the decline in the number of these select committees was strikingly rapid. In twenty years, at the Congress of 1813-1815 with its three war sessions, it had fallen to about seventy": *Congressional Committees* (New York: Crowell, 1898), p. 124. See also Galloway, *op. cit.*, p. 88.

17. DeAlva Stanwood Alexander, *History and Procedures of the House of Representatives* (Boston: Houghton-Mifflin, 1916), p. 228.

18. Harlow, *op. cit.*, p. 141.

19. *Ibid.*, pp. 120-150.

20. *Ibid.*, p. 151.

21. *Ibid.*, pp. 157-158.

22. Wilfred E. Binkley, *President and Congress* (New York: Vintage, 1962), p. 64.

23. Of Randolph's initial appointment as chairman of the Ways and Means Committee, in the Seventh Congress, Noble Cunningham writes: "in view of the close friendship of [Speaker] Macon and Randolph, it is unlikely that Jefferson had any influence in the choice of Randolph as Chairman of the Ways and Means Committee": *Jeffersonian Republicans in Power* (Chapel Hill: University of North Carolina Press, 1963), p. 73. See also Henry Adams, *John Randolph* (Boston: Houghton-Mifflin, 1886), pp. 54-55, 123-165ff; and Adams, *History of the United States of America During the Administrations of Thomas Jefferson and James Madison* (New York: Boni, 1930), Vol. III, p. 128.

24. This interpretation is the brilliant achievement of James S. Young in *The Washington Community: 1800-1828* (New York: Columbia University Press, 1966). It harmonizes with Richard P. McCormick's notion of a series of historically discrete American party systems. See McCormick, *The Second American Party System* (Chapel Hill: University of North Carolina Press, 1966).

25. See Wilfred Binkley, "The President and Congress," *Journal of Politics*, 11 (February, 1949), 65-79.

26. See Young, *op. cit.*, pp. 131-135.

27. William Nisbet Chambers, *Political Parties in a New Nation* (New York: Oxford, 1963), p. 194.

28. See Nelson W. Polsby, Miriam Gallaher and Barry Spencer Rundquist, "The Growth of the Seniority System in the Selection of Committee Chairman in the U.S. House of Representatives" (mimeo., October, 1967).

29. *Ibid.* Chang-wei Chiu says, "The power of appointing committees by the Speaker was a real issue in the attempts to reform the House. In the eyes of the insurgents no change would be of any real and permanent value to the country if that change did not take away from the Speaker the power of appointing standing committees": *The Speaker of the House of Representatives Since 1896* (New York: Columbia University Press, 1928), pp. 71-72.

30. Harlow, *op. cit.*, p. 176.

31. Cunningham, *op. cit.*, p. 74. The quotation is from a letter from Roger Griswold to John Rutledge, December 14, 1801.

32. See Jefferson's letters to Barnabas Bidwell and Wilson Cary Nicholas cited in *ibid.*, pp. 89-92. Also Henry Adams, *History, op. cit.*, Vol. III, pp. 166-171.

33. Randall Ripley, in his forthcoming Brookings study, *Party Leadership in the House of Representatives* (mimeo, 1966) says: "The Majority leader did not become a separate and consistently identifiable party figure until some time around the turn of the century." Ripley also discusses the indeterminancy of the minority leadership in the mid-19th century. Of an earlier period (1800-1828) Young *(op. cit.,* pp. 126-127) writes: "Party members elected no leaders, designated no functionaries to speak in their behalf or to carry out any legislative task assignments. The party had no whips, no seniority leaders. There were no committees on committees, no steering committees, no policy committees: none of the organizational apparatus that marks the twentieth-century congressional parties. . . ." On pp. 127-130 Young argues that although there were a number of party leaders in the House, there was no fixed majority leader. "[W]hile the names of Randolph, Giles, Nicholas and Rodney appear more frequently, at least twenty Republican legislators in the eight years of Jefferson's administration are either explicitly identified as leaders in the documentary record or are associated with activities strongly suggesting a role of presidential spokesmanship" (p. 130).

34. From 1865-1869, for example, Thaddeus Stevens left the chairmanship of Ways and Means (a post he had held from 1861-1865) to become chairman of the new Committee on Appropriations. See Samuel W. McCall, *Thaddeus Stevens* (Boston: Houghton-Mifflin, 1899), pp. 259-260. McCall says, oddly, that at the time the Appropriations Committee was not very important, but this is hard to credit. From 1895-1899, Joseph G. Cannon was floor leader and chairman of Appropriations. See Edward T. Taylor, *A History of the Committee on Appropriations* (House Document 299, 77th Congress, 1st Session) (Washington, Government Printing Office, 1941).

35. See George Rothwell Brown, *The Leadership of Congress* (Indianapolis: Bobbs Merrill, 1922), pp. 175-177, 183-184; Oscar King Davis, "Where Underwood Stands," *The Outlook* (December 23, 1911), 197-201. At p. 199: "Every move Mr. Underwood has made, every bill he has brought forward, he first submitted to a caucus. . . . Not until the last man had had his say was the vote taken that was to bind them all to united action in the House. Every time that vote has been either unanimous or nearly so, and invariably it has approved Mr. Underwood." See also Binkley, "The President and Congress," *op. cit.*, p. 72.

36. See Ripley, *op. cit.;* Hasbrouck, *op. cit.*, p. 94; and Alex M. Arnett, *Claude Kitchin*

and the Wilson War Policies (Boston: Little, Brown, 1937), pp. 42, 71-72, 75-76, 88-89 and passim.

37. See Randall B. Ripley, "The Party Whip Organization in the United States House of Representatives" this REVIEW, 58 (September, 1964), 561-576.
38. See, e.g., Alexander, *op. cit.*, pp. 111-114. "[W]ith very few exceptions, the really eminent debaters . . . were in the Senate: otherwise, MacDuffie [who served 1821-1834], Chief of the Hotspurs, could scarcely have justified his title to floor leader," p. 114.
39. *Ibid.*, p. 110: "In selecting a floor leader the Speaker often names his party opponent."
40. James W. Garner, "Executive Participation in Legislation as a Means of Increasing Legislative Efficiency," *Proceedings of the American Political Science Association at its Tenth Annual Meeting* (Baltimore: Waverly Press, 1914), p. 187.
41. Kenneth Kofmehl, *Professional Staffs of Congress* (Lafayette, Indiana: Purdue University Press, 1962), pp. 97-99. The quotation is at p. 99. Kofmehl presents a short, nonquantitative historical sketch of the growth of committee staffs on pp. 3-5. See also Samuel C. Patterson "Congressional Committee Professional Staffing: Capabilities and Constraints," a paper presented at the Planning Conference of the Comparative Administration Group, Legislative Services Project, Planting Fields, New York, December 8-10, 1967; and Lindsay Rogers "The Staffing of Congress" *Political Science Quarterly*, 56 (March, 1941), 1-22.
42. George B. Galloway, *op. cit.*, p. 187; George Goodwin, Jr., "The Seniority System in Congress" this REVIEW, 53 (June, 1959), p. 417.
43. Chiu, *op. cit.*, pp. 68-72; James K. Pollock, Jr., "The Seniority Rule in Congress," *The North American Review*, 222 (1925), 235, 236; Asher Hinds, "The Speaker of the House of Representatives," this REVIEW, 3 (May, 1909), 160-161.
44. Woodrow Wilson, *Congressional Government* (New York: Meridian Books, 1956) (First edition, 1884). See, for example, on pp. 85-86: "The Speaker is expected to constitute the Committees in accordance with his own political views . . . [and he] generally uses his powers as freely and imperatively as he is expected to use them. He unhesitatingly acts as the legislative chief of his party, organizing the Committees in the interest of this or that policy, not covertly or on the sly, as one who does something of which he is ashamed, but openly and confidently, as one who does his duty. . . ." Compare this with p. 82: "I know not how better to describe our form of government in a single phrase than by calling it a government by the chairmen of the Standing Committees of Congress. This disintegrate ministry, as it figures on the floor of the House of Representatives, has many peculiarities. In the first place, it is made up of the elders of the assembly; for, by custom, seniority in congressional service determines the bestowal of the principal chairmanships. . . ."
45. Polsby, Gallaher, and Rundquist, *op. cit.*
46. John Thomas Dempsey, "Control by Congress over the Seating and Disciplining of Members" (unpublished Ph.D. dissertation, The University of Michigan, 1956), pp. 50-51. The final quotation is from Alexander, *op. cit.*, p. 315.
47. George F. Hoar, *Autobiography of Seventy Years* (New York: Scribner, 1903), Vol. I, p. 268. Hoar claims that during the time he served on the Elections Committee in the Forty-second Congress (1871-73), contested elections were settled on the merits.
48. Henry L. Dawes, "The Mode of Procedure in Cases of Contested Elections," *Journal of Social Science* (No. 2, 1870), 56-68. Quoted passages are at p. 64. Dempsey, *op. cit.*, pp. 83-84, identifies Dawes as a one-time chairman of the House Committee on Elections. See also C. H. Rammelkamp, "Contested Congressional Elections," *Political Science Quarterly*, 20 (Sept. 1905), 434-435.
49. Thomas B. Reed, "Contested Elections," *North American Review*, 151 (July, 1890),

112-120. Quoted passages are at pp. 114 and 117. See also Alexander, *op. cit.,* p. 323.
50. Report from Elections Committee No. 3, Mr. McCall, chairman, quoted in Rammelkamp, *op. cit.,* p. 435.
51. O. O. Stealey, *Twenty Years in the Press Gallery* (New York: published by the author, 1906), p. 147.
52. Rammelkamp, *op. cit.,* pp. 421-442. Quoted passages are from pp. 423 and 434.
53. Stealey, *op. cit.,* p. 147.
54. Quoted in Paul De Witt Hasbrouck, *Party Government in the House of Representatives* (New York: Macmillan, 1927), p. 40.
55. See U.S., *Revised Statutes of the United States,* Title II, Ch. 8, Sections 105-130, and Dempsey, *op. cit.,* pp. 55-60. For indications of attempts to routinize the process of adjudication by setting up general criteria to govern House disposition of contested elections, see two 1933 cases: Gormley vs. Goss (House Report 893, 73rd Congress; see also 78 *Congressional Record,* pp. 4035, 7087, April 20, 1934) and Chandler vs. Burnham (House Report 1278, 73rd Congress; see also 78 *Congressional Record,* pp. 6971, 8921, May 15, 1934).
56. On the relatively scrupulous handling of a recent contest see Richard H. Rovere, "Letter from Washington," *The New Yorker* (October 16, 1965), 233-244. Rovere (at p. 243) identifies criteria governing the report on the 1965 challenge by the Mississippi Freedom Democratic Party to the entire Mississippi House delegation in the following passage: ". . . the majority could find no way to report favorably [on the challenge] without, as it seemed to them, abandoning due process and their constitutional responsibilities. Neither, for that matter, could the minority report, which went no further than to urge continued study."
57. See, e.g., the assignment of burden of proof in Gormley vs. Goss and Chandler vs. Burnham, *loc. cit.*
58. Durkheim, *op. cit.,* p. 262. Durkheim in turn cites Comte as describing this mechanism. Weber's notion, that the central precondition for the development of bureaucratic institutions is the money economy, strikes me as less interesting and less plausible. See H. H. Gerth and C. Wright Mills (eds.), *From Max Weber: Essays in Sociology* (New York: Oxford University Press, 1946), pp. 204-209. See, however, Weber's comment (p. 211): "It is obvious that technically the great modern state is absolutely dependent upon a bureaucratic basis. The larger the state, and the more it is or the more it becomes a great power state, the more unconditionally is this the case."
59. Cf. Young, *op. cit.,* pp. 252-253, who seems to put great stress on public attitudes and local political organization as causes of the growth in the influence of the central government.
60. George Galloway's *History of the U.S. House of Representatives,* 87th Congress, 1st Session, House Document No. 246 (Washington: U.S. Government Printing Office, 1962), pp. 215-216, has a convenient scorecard on the size and party composition of the House for the first 87 Congresses. Mere size has been found to be an indifferent predictor of the internal complexity of bureaucratic organizations. See Richard H. Hall, J. Eugene Haas and Norman J. Johnson, "Organizational Size, Complexity, and Formalization," *American Sociological Review,* 32 (December, 1967), 903-912.
61. Robert Bendiner, *Obstacle Course on Capitol Hill* (New York: McGraw-Hill, 1964), p. 15.
62. Woodrow Wilson, *op. cit.,* p. 57.
63. This is not to say, however, that the policy output of the House is exclusively determined by its level of institutionalization. The 88th, 89th and 90th Congresses all represent more or less equivalent levels of institutionalization, yet their policy outputs varied greatly. Nevertheless if the casual observer asked why it took thirty years, more

or less, to get the New Deal enacted in the House, and what sorts of strategies and circumstances made the legislative output of the 89th Congress possible, answers would have to refer quite extensively to structural properties of the institution.

64. See, e.g. Peter M. Blau, *The Dynamics of Bureaucracy* (Chicago: University of Chicago Press, 1955), *passim;* Philip Selznick, *TVA and the Grass Roots* (Berkeley: University of California Press, 1953), esp. pp. 250ff.

65. See Philip Selznick, *Leadership in Administration* (Evanston: Row, Peterson, 1957).

66. This position disagrees with Sidney Hyman, "Inquiry into the Decline of Congress," *New York Times Magazine,* January 31, 1960. For the argument that 20th century legislatures are on the whole weak see David B. Truman, "The Representative Function in Western Systems," in Edward H. Buehrig (ed.), *Essays in Political Science* (Bloomington: Indiana University Press, 1966), pp. 84-96; Truman, *The Congressional Party* (New York: Wiley, 1954), pp. 1-10; Truman, "Introduction: The Problem and Its Setting," in Truman (ed.), *The Congress and America's Future* (Englewood Cliffs: Prentice-Hall, 1965), pp. 1-4. For the beginning of an argument that the U.S. Congress may be an exception, see Nelson W. Polsby, *Congress and the Presidency* (New York: Prentice-Hall, 1964), pp. 2, 31-32, 47-115.

67. See Weber, *op. cit.,* p. 69, pp. 330-34; and Gerth and Mills, *op. cit.,* pp. 198-204.

68. See, for example, Donald Matthews, "The Folkways of the U.S. Senate," this REVIEW, 53 (December, 1959), 1064-1089; John C. Wahlke, Heinz Eulau, William Buchanan, and Leroy C. Ferguson, *The Legislative System* (New York: Wiley, 1962), pp. 141-169; Alan Kornberg, "The Rules of the Game in the Canadian House of Commons," *The Journal of Politics,* 26 (May, 1964), 358-380; Ralph K. Huitt, "The Outsider in The Senate," this REVIEW, 55 (September, 1961), 566-575; Nicholas A. Masters, "Committee Assignments in The House of Representatives," this REVIEW, 55 (June, 1961), 345-357; Richard F. Fenno, Jr., "The House Appropriations Committee as a Political System: The Problem of Integration," this REVIEW, 56 (June, 1962), 310-324.

69. Clem Miller, *Member of the House* (John W. Baker, ed.) (New York: Scribner, 1962), p. 93. See also pp. 80-81 and 119-122.

70. Alexander, *op. cit.,* pp. 115-116. The internal quotations are from John Quincy Adams' *Diary and from an article by Reed in the Saturday Evening Post,* December 9, 1899.

71. Mayo, *op, cit.,* p. 424; William Parkes Cutler and Julia Perkins Cutler (eds.), *Life, Journals and Correspondence of Reverend Manasseh Cutler* (Cincinnati: Robert Clark and Co., 1888), Vol. II, pp. 186-189.

72. A motion to expel Brooks from the House for this act was defeated; but soon thereafter Brooks resigned anyway. He was subsequently reelected to fill the vacancy caused by his resignation. See *Biographical Directory of The American Congress, 1774-1961* (Washington: Government Printing Office, 1961), p. 604.

73. Alexander, *op. cit.,* pp. 111-112. Other instances of flagrant misbehavior are chronicled in Ben Perley Poore, *Perley's Reminiscences of Sixty Years in the National Metropolis* (Philadelphia: Hubbard, 1886), Vol. I, pp. 394-395; and William Plumer, *Memorandum of Proceedings in the United States Senate* (Everett Somerville Brown, ed.) (New York: Macmillan, 1923), pp. 269-276.

74. A report on decorum in the 19th Century House of Commons suggests that a corresponding toning down has taken place although Commons was palpably a good bit less unruly to start with. Says an ecstatic commentator, "Like so much else that is good in the institutions of Parliament, the behaviour of the House has grown straight, or, like a river, purified itself as it flowed": Eric Taylor, *The House of Commons At Work* (Baltimore: Penguin, 1961), pp. 85-87. Anthony Barker says: "The close of the

19th Century has been described by Lord Campion as the ending of informality and the beginning of rigid government responsibility for policy in the procedures of the House of Commons": " 'The Most Important And Venerable Function': A Study of Commons Supply Procedure," *Political Studies,* 13 (February, 1965), p. 45.

75. Perhaps secondary analysis comparing the four states (California, New Jersey, Tennessee, Ohio) in the Wahlke, Eulau, Buchanan, and Ferguson study *(op. cit.)* will yield an acceptable test of the hypothesis. This study has good information on the diffusion of legislative norms; it is less strong on structural data, but these might be relatively easy to gather.

76. Parkinson, *op. cit.,* p. 39.

77. The growth of political institutions does not play a particularly important part in the interpretation offered by W. W. Rostow in *The Stages of Economic Growth* (Cambridge: Cambridge University Press, 1960), see, e.g., pp. 18-19, but these may afford at least as good support for his theory as some of the economic indicators he proposes.

6. THE LEARNING OF LEGISLATIVE NORMS

Herbert B. Asher

Studies of legislatures have uncovered the existence of informal norms or folkways or rules of the game that are presumed to be important for the maintenance of the legislative system.[1] It is often argued that the institution, be it the House or the Senate or a state legislature, must transmit its norms to legislative newcomers in order to insure the continued, unaltered operation of the institution, and that the member himself must learn these norms if he is to be an effective legislator. Whether or not this be necessary, it certainly is plausible to view freshman members of the legislative body as undergoing a socialization process which involves the learning of legislative norms. Yet previous studies have largely concentrated on the identification of legislative norms and have devoted little attention to their transmission to the newcomer. Is the freshman legislator aware of the expected types of behavior prior to taking his seat or does he learn them while in office? If he learns them in office, who actually are the agents of transmission? Or is the socialization process so informal that we cannot even speak of well-defined agents?

These questions and others have not been fully addressed, and thus the focus of this paper is on the learning of norms by freshman members of the United States House of Representatives.[2] My interest is in individual learning of legislative norms, regardless of whether the content learned is in conformity or opposition to the norms. Too often the emphasis in socialization research has been on system maintenance rather than individual adaptation, leading one to dismiss findings of deviance too readily. The data come from a broader panel study of the learning that freshman members elected to the House of Representatives in November, 1968, underwent with respect to perceptions of their job, legislative norms, and sources of voting cues.[3] Since a research interest in learning is a longitudinal concern, a two-wave panel design was employed, the first set of interviews conducted in late January and February of 1969, and the second set

Author's Note: I am grateful to John Kingdon, Herbert Weisberg, Richard Fenno, John Kessel, and Randall Ripley for their helpful comments and suggestions.

Source: *American Political Science Review* 67 (June 1973): 499-513. Reprinted with permission of the author.

119

the following May. The purpose of the panel was to capture the changes that the 91st class members underwent in the first few months of their legislative service, a period that seemed *a priori* to be crucial in talking about learning. Of the 37 freshmen in the 91st Congress, 30 were interviewed at t_1 (late January and February) and of these 30, 24 were reinterviewed at t_2.[4]

A norm has been defined herein as a rule or standard of conduct appropriate to a person in a specified situation within a group. The norm describes the type of behavior expected by almost all of the other members of the group and often, though not necessarily, has associated with it sanctions for deviance. Since concepts such as role and norm are useful because of their normative or mutual expectations component, and since a definitional attribute of a norm is that it be shared to a high degree by the members of the group, a sample of nonfreshman members of the House was also interviewed. Certainly if incumbent representatives agreed to the norms there would be an environment more supportive of freshmen learning them. Conversely, if there were marked disagreement about the norms on the part of nonfreshmen, we might then wish to reformulate or even reject these "norms." [5]

A variety of approaches can be used to ascertain information and attitudes about legislative norms. Wahlke and his colleagues employed an open-ended question that asked the respondents to identify the rules of the game in their respective state legislatures.[6] Such an approach is particularly valuable for identifying those norms most salient to the representative, but it may fail to elicit the nascent attitudes that freshmen early in their careers are likely to possess. Hence, freshmen and nonfreshmen were queried about specific norms, the determination of which was based upon a survey of the existing literature. The main norms investigated were specialization, reciprocity, legislative work, courtesy, and aspects of apprenticeship including learning the House rules, restrained participation, and attendance on the floor and in committee.[7] A focused interview approach was selected to collect information about these norms, although this procedure raises certain problems. For example, one cannot simply ask the representative whether a norm of reciprocity exists in the House, for such a label may be without meaning to the legislator. We must attach some behavioral tag to reciprocity, and in so doing we have a wide leeway. Thus, we might ask the representative whether he thought members should do favors for one another, but unless the representative was particularly misanthropic, we would expect unanimously affirmative responses to such an item, thereby reducing the discriminatory capacity of the question to zero. Therefore, reciprocity was operationalized in this study by placing it in the context of a voting situation, with all the attendant ambiguities and pressures. The actual question was: "Would you vote a certain way on a bill that you cared little about in order to gain the vote of a fellow representative on a bill that you did care about?" The general point to be made here is that questions seeking to uncover information about norms are best framed within a fairly specific behavioral situation. If we cannot observe behavior directly (and most often we cannot), then our questions should be as behaviorally oriented as possible.

Nonfreshmen and the Norms

Table 6-1 presents the level of agreement expressed by our sample of nonfreshman members of the 91st Congress to a series of items about House norms.[8] The highest level of agreement was reached on the importance of maintaining friendly relationships, with the importance of committee work running a close second, while the weakest consensus was found on the norm of apprenticeship. Some detailed analysis of the nonfreshman responses is very illuminating.

Specialization

Among the norms, specialization appeared to be adhered to largely because of certain properties of the House: Many members asserted that the heavy and varied workload of the House, as well as its large membership, made specialization mandatory. Of the eight incumbents who did not agree that Congressmen should specialize rather than generalize, six said that the member must do both because of the interdependence of issues, while two opted for being a generalist. The two representatives who cited a generalist orientation were both extreme liberals within their party and viewed the standing committees of the House as "the hand-maidens of special interest groups."

In an attempt to learn whether their attitudes toward specialization had changed since their first term, the nonfreshmen were asked whether they had felt the same way (about specialization) when they were freshmen, and, if not, what had led them to change their views. Twenty-six said yes, eleven said no, and two could not recall their earlier opinions. All eleven whose views about specialization had changed said that when they entered Congress, they did not realize how necessary specialization was, but that subsequent legislative and committee experience in the House had taught them differently. Two of the eleven said they initially thought it was possible to be knowledgeable on most important issues, but that the energy and time required for this was prohibitive.

Committee Work

While 38 of the 40 incumbents interviewed claimed that most of the important work of the House was done in committee rather than on the floor, the

Table 6-1   Nonfreshman Attitudes to the Norms

	% Agreeing	N
Friendly relationships important	97	40
Important work of House done in committee	95	40
House rules important	82	40
Would not personally criticize a fellow representative	82	40
Would be likely to trade votes	81	21
Congressman should be a specialist	80	40
Freshman should serve apprenticeship	38	65

remaining two representatives felt that neither place was crucial. Their responses revealed skepticism about the House's effectiveness as an arena for legislation.

> Most of the important work is done neither on the floor nor in committee. The most important work is done in the submission of bills to Congress by an administration when it has a majority in Congress. They get sorted and acted upon and we just screw around with them. Every time Congress tries to initiate legislation, it does a bad job — Smith Act, Taft-Hartley, Landrum-Griffin. Congress legislates in the heat of emotion as it is threatening to do now on campus unrest and did on draft resisters.

> If one means by the important work of the House constituent services and the like, which I do, then it is done neither on the floor nor in committee.

Six of the incumbents who asserted the preeminence of committee work stated that they had not held that point of view when they were freshmen. A midwestern Republican claimed that his previous state legislative experience had misled him, for he "came from a state Senate where the important work was done on the floor, where the substance of bills was often changed on the floor." This suggests that in some situations previous political experience may be dysfunctional and hence may have to be unlearned. Two representatives said that it was legislative experience in general that led them to recognize the primacy of committee work. Finally, a southern Republican gave a very interesting reply as to his perception of the importance of committees when he was a freshman.

> To some extent I felt that committees were most important. It became clear to me early that if you do not have the power, then you have to go to where the power is. It is difficult for a freshman to do much on the floor, but if he goes to his committee chairman or ranking minority member and has already proven his worth to him, if he makes a suggestion and leaves it at that and does not try to grandstand, he can influence legislation from the outset through the senior member of this committee.

Friendly Relationships

The level of agreement on the importance of friendly relationships was truly impressive. One reason cited for this attitude was instrumental: friendly relationships would presumably make one more effective in getting his ideas accepted and bills passed. The other reason was the vague belief that life in general was more pleasant when friendly relationships were the rule. Some responses exemplifying these reasons were:

> Friendly relationships are important because you never know when you'll need others' help or votes. For example, I've been working on a bill on the hijacking of airplanes and got a good reception from friends while testifying at the Interstate and Foreign Commerce committee hearings.

> Friendships are extremely important: that's why the gym is so valuable. You meet guys from the other side of the aisle, people you normally would not get intimate with.

But a number of representatives qualified what was meant by friendly relationships:

> It depends on what you mean by friendly. In terms of operating as a club, I'm not attracted by the sort of thing in which the gym is the key to friendship or advancement. But if by friendship, one means courtesy and respect, then, sure, it's important.

> Friendly relationships are important, but they do not require camaraderie. There's not too much of that that bears directly on getting things passed. One should be a person one feels he can deal with, one who will keep his word. But representatives recognize that one may have to violate this, that one may have to be a demagogue on an issue important to the district. Being buddy-buddy is not as important in the Congress as it is in the state legislature which is less sophisticated.

House Rules

A fairly high consensus was attained on the importance of learning the House rules. The few cases of disagreement, however, are quite interesting. One representative well known to his colleagues for his ambition and career plans beyond the House declared that the rules were not very important to learn. He said that he had not taken the time to learn them, that he worked around the system rather than within it, and that he had not been hurt by this approach so far. It may very well be that members who do not view the House in career terms will consider the rules to be less significant. This viewpoint was expressed by another representative, who said that the importance of the rules depended on what you wanted to do; if you wanted to get into the leadership, then they were "damned important." Another incumbent thought that the rules were not important for freshmen:

> The rules are important, but those used most often are those used in legislative action. If one is in a position of power, then the rules are important. Most members never come close to knowing the procedures at all, yet they can do a lot. Freshmen need know only the amenities and not the rules.

A northern Democrat thought that the rules were not all that important as the will of the majority usually prevailed; members did not use the rules against you. Another representative voiced a contrasting opinion; he said that the rules were unimportant because they were so often flouted.

Personal Criticism

While the level of agreement on the norm of refraining from personal criticism of fellow representatives was quite high, this item proved to be very difficult to answer for some members. Almost one-third of the responses were conditional or hypothetical: "I don't think I would," "I shouldn't," "It's not likely," "Not unless someone drove me to it." One representative admitted to having engaged in personal attacks, but vowed never to do it again because of the severe social consequences that he had suffered.

123

Herbert B. Asher

Reciprocity/Trading Votes

Most representatives were willing to trade votes, a manifestation of reciprocity, but many attached provisos to this type of action. Typical responses were:

> Yes, I'd trade votes, but this does not happen often. It is not a specific trade, but more a matter of good will. I never had a specific trade: this happens more in the Senate.

> It depends on the importance of the bill. On local bills, I think I would. For example, I am interested in a potato referendum bill in 48 states and I'm sure that my good friend _____ of New York couldn't care at all about the bill, but he'll probably support it because we're friends. And I'd do the same for him.

The negative responses to this item were usually spoken sharply and intensely, indicating an almost moral disapproval of this type of action. Unfortunately, the N involved here is only 21.

In summary, friendly relationships and the importance of committee work were the most commonly agreed upon norms. A somewhat lower level of consensus characterized attitudes toward specialization, reciprocity, restraint in personal criticism, and the importance of the House rules. The marked disagreement on apprenticeship calls into question the very existence of this norm.

Freshman Attitudes Toward the Norms at t₁

Table 6-2 presents the replies of the newcomers to the same norms questions asked of incumbents, as well as to some special freshman items; the nonfreshman figures are repeated as an aid to the reader.

The responses of the newcomers are quite similar to those of their more senior colleagues, suggesting a generally shared set of expectations. Both groups agree most strongly with the importance of friendly relationships; perhaps this implies that this norm, rather than being specific to the House, is carried over from general life experience. The freshmen also unanimously believed the rules to be important. The major difference between the newcomers' and incumbents' responses concerned the norm of apprenticeship; an additional 20 percent of the freshmen agreed that it is necessary. This may reflect a caution on the part of freshmen early in their incumbency.

Since the concept of norms involves shared expectations, the freshmen were queried about their perceptions of nonfreshman attitudes. They were asked whether they thought that more senior representatives favored the specialist or the generalist. All the newcomers who could answer said that senior members favored the specialist, which in effect confirmed their own earlier endorsement of specialization and committee work, but 29 percent (8 of 28) said that they did not know the preferences of senior members. And while the newcomers generally cited committee work over floor work, fully 73 percent thought it worthwhile, especially for freshmen, to spend time on the House floor. Attendance on the House floor was deemed important because it enabled the freshman represen-

Table 6-2 Freshman Attitudes to the Norms at t_1

	% Freshmen		% Nonfreshmen	
	Agreeing	N	Agreeing	N
Friendly relationships important	100	30	97	40
House rules important	100	30	82	40
Important work of House done in committee	90	30	95	40
Congressman should be a specialist	73	30	80	40
Worthwhile to spend time on House floor	73	30		
Would be likely to trade votes	72	29	81	21
Senior members favor the specialist	71	28		
Would not personally criticize a fellow representative	71	28	82	40
Freshman should serve apprenticeship	57	30	38	65

tative to learn the procedures and thereby complete his apprenticeship much sooner.

Deviant Responses of the Freshmen

One can conclude from this brief outline that freshmen shared to a similar degree the norms of nonfreshmen, a situation certainly conducive to the learning of norms, but not one that automatically implies that norms were formally transmitted from senior to freshman members. It is interesting to examine some of the deviant responses given by freshmen. Numerous hypotheses were entertained about the causes of noncompliance to the norms. For example, it was thought that freshmen with prior political experience, especially in the state legislature, would be more apt to give "correct" responses. It was also thought that freshmen with a strong dedication to a career in the House would be more sensitive to the norms. These hypotheses and others were neither confirmed nor refuted because of the very small number of cases involved. The most fruitful approach to the problem is a norm-by-norm analysis of the deviant responses.

Specialization

Eight of the thirty freshmen interviewed at t₁ did not unqualifiedly opt to be specialists. Two freshmen asserted that Congressmen should be generalists, five said that it depended on the individual or that a member must be both, and one did not know. One representative who chose to be a generalist cited the heterogeneous nature of his district as the determining factor in his decision. This representative had the most extensive state legislative experience of any freshman in the 91st Congress, thereby leading one to reject the too facile linkage of state legislative service with specialization. The other generalist appeared to be motivated by two forces: a suspicion of accepting others' advice and a recognition that congressmen had to vote on a wide range of issues and should therefore be broadly informed. The theme of distrust occurred throughout this interview; the representative was very much an ideologue with little confidence in the judgment and motives of his colleagues and with a very rigid view of his job. This suspiciousness was reflected in his responses to questions on voting cues; he was very wary of members giving him wrong information and was generally expecting his votes to be uninfluenced by his colleagues. Newcomers who said that a member had to be both a specialist and a generalist argued that assignment to a committee forced one to specialize, while floor voting on a wide variety of issues compelled one to be a generalist. Another representative rejected specialization partially because of the narrowness of his committee assignment. He said:

> One has to do both. I can tell you now that I will not spend the rest of my time becoming an expert on the price of hayseed oil.

An analysis of such background variables as prior political experience uncovered no systematic differences between specialists and nonspecialists.

Committee Work

Only three of thirty freshmen did not assert that most of the important work of the House was done in committee. One member, a southern Democrat with state legislative experience and highly directed toward a career in the House, said that he did not know where the work was done since the committees had only just organized. Another freshman, our distrustful ideologue mentioned above, said without qualification that most of the important work was done on the floor, since that was where the actual passage or defeat of a piece of legislation occurred. For him, voting was the crucial aspect of the job with the events preceding any vote being of only minor importance. The third freshman who failed to assert the primacy of committee work thought, in fact, that neither the committees nor the floor was the most significant arena:

> The important work is not done in either. It is too early to say where the important work is done, if, in fact, important work is done. The important work is to stir up public opinion about the important issues.

This representative more than any other freshman had an active national constituency. His energies were constantly spread thin over a number of liberal causes that were outside the immediate context of House legislative activity. He was one of the most active and reformist freshmen, yet his behavior very much followed the traditional, accepted patterns even though he denied the importance of committee and floor work. For example, in the interview, he coupled a stinging attack on the proceedings on the House floor with a statement and explanation as to why it is important to spend time there.

> Yes, it is worthwhile to spend time on the House floor. This is where the member lobbies, where he talks to others about bills, trades information, does logrolling. People will think you are arrogant if you don't spend much time there. Debate on the floor is a sham; it's dishonest. People get things in the *Record* without saying them in debate as happened in the HUAC controversy.

And his response to the item about the importance of friendly relationships probably best typifies the difference between the activist who is careful to observe the amenities and the would-be reformer who allows personal relationships to deteriorate.

> It's very important to maintain friendly relationships. I think a big mistake is made when people who come up here hoping to change things, are frustrated and allow their frustrations to create personal animosities. I get along with everyone here; I like everyone. I even get along well with Mendel Rivers; I tease him a lot.

This same freshman's remarks on the House floor on the occasion of Speaker McCormack's announced retirement further illustrate proper, yet dissenting behavior.

> Mr. Speaker, I want especially to join in this tribute to the Speaker today because it is no secret that on some questions we have disagreed, and it is

127

important — if this occasion is to be what it should be — that those of us who have not always agreed with him make it clear that we are no less grateful for having known him than those who have agreed with him.

. . . I will always be grateful that we overlapped here so I could have the opportunity to know this man, generous, considerate, and fair to everyone, never vindictive no matter how great his disagreement or disappointment.

The rules of this body continue to dismay many of us who find them neither democratic nor conducive to efficient procedures. But within these rules, the Speaker has done everything he could to protect the rights of every Member. . . .[9]

Personal Criticism

There were eight freshmen out of twenty-eight who said they would personally criticize a fellow representative. For three of these representatives, this willingness to criticize their colleagues seemed to be rooted in a certain outspokenness of personality and intensity of belief that they realized would surface at some point in their congressional careers, although they did not consciously intend to make personal criticism a regular occurrence. Included among these three is our distrustful ideologue; he said that it was possible he would criticize a fellow representative "if he needed it." None of the five other freshmen had served in the state legislature, so perhaps their earlier experiences had not taught them that personal attacks were normally out of bounds. For one of these five, the lack of state legislative experience was probably less influential than the member's own weak attachment to the House. Two factors that lessened his commitment to the House were his age and his relative financial independence: he perceived himself to be too old to have any lengthy career in the House, and therefore far removed from the worries of career advancement; furthermore, as he mentioned more than once, he had a lucrative business to return to if House service ever became too compromising. Even if he were to criticize, he said that he would do it "with velvet gloves."

Reciprocity/Trading Votes

A striking similarity emerges among the freshman representatives who were not likely to trade votes: All six were Republicans. And the three members of the nonfreshman sample who unqualifiedly refused to trade votes were also Republicans. Four of the freshman responses were resounding "No's," while another was "I hope not," which seemed to imply that vote trading was wrong, but that somehow the Representative might be tempted to participate in it. The only respondent who tried to explain the negative opinion toward vote-trading stated that ten years earlier in the state legislature he had been "burned" because he did not anticipate the consequences of the bill to which he had given his vote. Perhaps what we have here is a tendency by Republicans to view politics more moralistically or ideologically so that trading votes becomes tantamount to catering to unworthy special interests and to abdicating one's own sense of right and wrong.[10]

The Usefulness of Time Spent on the House Floor

The final two norms to be investigated for deviant responses were the ones asked only of freshmen. One inquired whether they thought that senior representatives favored the specialist or the generalist. As mentioned earlier, while eight freshmen did not know the answer to this at t₁, none answered "generalist." The second item was concerned with the value of spending time on the House floor. At t₁, five representatives (four Democrats and one Republican) said that it was not worthwhile because so little was going on. Since we are interested in behavior as well as in attitudes, a crude measure of time spent on the House floor was constructed; it is simply the percentage of the quorum call votes that the member answered in the first session of the 91st Congress. This measure has severe limitations, including our expectation that members from districts relatively close to the Capitol would score low because of the extensive amount of time they would spend in their easily-reached constituencies.[11] And, obviously, members who do answer quorum calls regularly may spend very little time on the floor. Be that as it may, there was a weak, yet consistent relationship between attitudes and behavior. The 22 freshmen who felt floor-time was worthwhile missed 13 percent of the quorum calls; the 3 who were neutral missed 19 percent; and the 5 who felt floor experience was not worthwhile missed 28 percent.[12]

Forces Contributing to Deviant Responses to the Norms

From this discussion of deviant responses, we can winnow out a number of influences that promote compliance and noncompliance to the norms, but we cannot weight these influences in any quantitative fashion because of the very small N involved. Career orientation to the House appeared to be important in furthering adherence to the norms, while aspiration to other office encouraged nonadherence. Also reducing the salience of the House for the newcomer were financial security and age; older freshmen realized that they would be less likely to advance to any great degree up the House hierarchy. Finally, the extremism of the member's ideological views was related to norm compliance: The more ideological members, whether of the left or right, were somewhat more willing to violate the norms, especially those on speaking out in proper fashion. It was significant that only one representative — the distrustful ideologue — gave responses that repeatedly departed from the norms. Personality traits in combination with his view of politics seemed to account quite well for his beliefs. But for most other freshmen, deviant responses were very infrequent, so that it was impossible to talk of types of freshmen who generally did not abide by the norms. In other words, noncompliance to one norm did not predict very well attitudes toward other norms. Probably the most important finding overall is that noncompliance was minimal, implying that by one means or another, freshmen had learned the norms well, the topic to which we now turn.

Freshmen and the Learning of Norms

As already mentioned, and in contradiction to initial expectations, most of the freshmen at t₁ were giving "correct" responses to the norms items. This

129

Table 6-3   Intra-Item Correlations on the Norms Question (t_1 and t_2)

	Tau-B	*N*
Friendly relationships important	1.000	24
Would be likely to trade votes	.721	20
Freshman should serve apprenticeship	.696	24
House rules important	.693	24
Would not personally criticize a fellow representative	.310	22
Worthwhile to spend time on House floor	.169	24

observation has implications for the amount of learning that the panel can uncover. If learning be defined in terms of attitude change, then we would expect little learning from t_1 to t_2 because of the correctness of the t_1 responses. While learning might come in the form of strengthening initial attitudes, the inappropriateness of Likert items for elite populations such as legislators makes it difficult to get a handle on changes in attitudinal intensity. As it was, the responses to the unstructured norms questions were coded to incorporate direction and intensity of attitudes, and changes in both are reflected in the coefficients presented in Table 6-3.

The low incidence of later norm learning may mean that the freshmen knew the norms before entering Congress. If this be true, it is an interesting datum in and of itself. Or perhaps freshmen learned the norms in the short interval between taking office and being interviewed by this investigator, although this possibility appears unlikely (see fn. 4). One way of demonstrating the minimal learning of norms from t_1 to t_2 is to cross-tabulate the t_1 and t_2 responses to each item and examine the intra-item correlations. This is done in Table 6-3 for those norms questions that were coded in an ordinal fashion with at least four valid codes; the measure of association is tau-b.

As one can observe, all of the items except two — personal criticism and spending time on the House floor — were very stable. Of the 22 representatives who responded to the personal criticism question at t_1 and t_2, 13 did not give identical answers at the two time points. Eight of the 13 gave answers at t_2 that made it less likely that they would engage in personal criticism, but the other five indicated a greater willingness to criticize which runs counter to the learning or reinforcement of "proper" behavior. There were no background variables that explained the changes on this item, nor did the freshmen volunteer any information that was helpful in accounting for the shifts. What we may have here is response unreliability elicited by a question whose wording left in doubt just what was meant by personal criticism.

The situation was very different on the other unstable item; here half of the 24 responses were identical from t_1 to t_2. Four of the six Republicans who changed thought it more worthwhile at t_2 to spend time on the House floor, while five of the six Democrats felt just the opposite, and each group was able to justify its own position. The Democrats were all active liberals dismayed by what they considered the scarcity of significant floor work. Republicans, however, generally cited the instructional value of being on the House floor. Thus, a part of the reason for the low intra-correlation on this item was the growing dissatisfaction on the part of some Democrats. As this discontent was basically programmatic, it did not affect the less issue-oriented Republicans, whose changes on this item in the opposite direction were less easily explained.[13]

Subdividing the freshmen according to characteristics such as party and district competitiveness does not change the tau-b's very much. There is, however, some tendency for freshmen with state legislative experience to exhibit greater stability than those without such experience, and this is especially pronounced on vote-trading. While the correlation for this item for all freshmen was .721, it rose to .792 for newcomers who had had state legislative service and plummeted to −.200 for those who had not had such service. Attitudes on vote trading, therefore, appear to be more stable if one has already had the opportunity to confront the situation in reality (as in a state legislature) and not just hypothetically. That is, members who had experienced vote trading first-hand were more consistent in their attitudes toward it, an intuitively appealing result.

Finally, let us examine the percentage agreement with each of the norms at t_1 and t_2, looking only at freshmen interviewed at both t_1 and t_2. This will indicate whether support for the norms increases or decreases (erodes) over time. The appropriate figures are presented in Table 6-4.[14]

The striking point about Table 6-4 is that support for the norms more commonly decreased than increased, although most of the percentage changes were small and probably mean little. The norm that suffered the greatest and most real erosion was apprenticeship; this finding will be analyzed in depth in the next section. Also suffering erosion of more than 10 percent were the items on specialization and the importance of the rules. What may be happening here is that at t_1 freshmen knew the "right" responses and uttered them automatically but that subsequent legislative experience enabled them to take a more sophisticated, knowledgeable, and qualified view of the norms. The norm showing the greatest gain in support was restraint in personal criticism, but no ready explanation comes to mind except that attendance on the House floor would indicate to the freshman, if he did not already know, that personal attacks were very rare, indeed.

The other interesting result in Table 6-4 is that the t_2 freshman responses are somewhat closer to the nonfreshman replies than are the t_1 answers. This does not hold for specialization, committee work, and friendly relationships; here the t_1 answers come closer to the incumbent responses, but the differences involved are small. But for the other norms, the t_2 freshman responses are substantially closer

Table 6-4 Level of Agreement to the Norms at t_1 and t_2

	Freshmen				Nonfreshmen	
	% Agreeing t_1	% Agreeing t_2	Change	N	% Agreeing	N
Freshman should serve apprenticeship	58	42	−16	24	38	65
Congressman should be a specialist	83	70	−13	23	80	40
House rules important	100	88	−12	24	82	40
Important work done in committee	96	87	−9	23	95	40
Friendly relationships important	100	92	−8	24	97	40
Would be likely to trade votes	68	68	0	22	81	21
Worthwhile to spend time on House floor	71	75	4	24		
Senior members favor specialist	70	78	8	23		
Would not personally criticize a fellow representative	69	82	13	22	82	40

than the t₁ responses to the nonfreshman replies. For apprenticeship, the difference between the t₁ and nonfreshman responses was 20 percent, but only four percent when the t₂ replies are used. Eight and 13 percent differences beteeen the t₁ and nonfreshman replies on House rules and personal criticism drop to six percent and zero when the t₂ responses are substituted. Thus, the freshmen were basically similar to their more senior colleagues at t₁, and by t₂ the coincidence of views toward the norms was even closer, suggesting that informal socialization to the norms was still occurring at t₂.

The Norm of Apprenticeship

It is the norm of apprenticeship that is most relevant to freshmen. If the traditional description of the freshman representative as unsure in his actions and ignorant of House rules and procedures is correct, then apprenticeship is obviously the crucial norm for newcomers to follow. The natural expectation is that apprenticeship would be a very commonly accepted norm given the widespread familiarity of the adage about freshmen being seen and not heard. But as Table 6-5 indicates, the very existence of a norm of apprenticeship as defined herein must be called into question.[15] Almost half of the nonfreshman sample flatly denied the necessity of serving an apprenticeship, and if the qualified disagreements are added to this figure, almost two-thirds of the incumbents rejected apprenticeship. And while there was majority agreement to the norm at t₁ on the part of freshmen, a sizable minority of 43 percent deemed it unnecessary. Those freshmen who saw the need for serving an apprenticeship were asked how long they felt it would take in their own particular cases. Four newcomers said that they could not set a specific time limit, two said a year, and only one said the full two years of his first term in office. The remaining ten all indicated that apprenticeships between two and six months would be desirable. Thus, even for freshmen who agreed to apprenticeship, the learning period was usually seen as relatively short, most often under six months. The range of freshman responses to the apprenticeship item is illustrated by the following replies:

> Yes, I'll serve an apprenticeship. Its length depends upon the individual; it will probably take me less time because of my previous legislative experience. A newcomer needs to be informed to be effective.

> Yes. The length depends, probably a few months. You can't lead the army the first day. But you do represent a district that elected you for two years and you can't just sit and do nothing.

> There is no reason for an apprenticeship. You learn best by jumping right in.

> No, you don't have to serve an apprenticeship. But one should not just jump into things. A freshman Congressman is not like a freshman in college; he is a man of some special competence. Senior people will listen to you if you have something to say.

An examination of the apprenticeship replies by party indicates some party differences, as shown in Table 6-6. Seven of the nine freshman Democrats who rejected apprenticeship were urban liberals from districts with heavy constituent

133

Table 6-5 The Norm of Apprenticeship

	t_1 Freshman Responses	Nonfreshman Responses
	%	%
Agreement	40	24
Qualified Agreement	17	12
Qualified Disagreement	17	20
Disagreement	26	44
Total %	100	100
N	(30)	(66)

Table 6-6 Freshman Apprenticeship Responses by Party

	Republicans	Democrats
"Apprenticeship Necessary"	73	40
"No Apprenticeship Necessary"	27	60
Total %	100	100
N	(15)	(15)

demands. These men were generally active and concerned with programs, and, for them, apprenticeship implied a severe restriction on the activities that they deemed most important, particularly speaking up on the floor on such issues as Vietnam, national priorities, and school desegregation. The intention to engage in specific legislative activity, shared by a number of Democratic freshmen, itself runs counter to the image of the bewildered newcomer. For most Republicans, the idea of an apprenticeship or limited participation was not as restrictive, mainly because they were not as concerned with programs and problems. Thus, one's view of the job of the representative appears to influence one's opinions about apprenticeship.

It is reasonable therefore that freshmen who agreed to the importance of apprenticeship would be less active. Table 6-7 presents some evidence on this point using as measures of activity three simple indices constructed from the *Congressional Record.*[16] As expected, Democratic nonapprentices were substantially more active than their apprentice colleagues across all three measures. But this pattern does not hold for Republicans: here the differences between apprentices and nonapprentices are small and inconsistent. Interestingly, Republican and Democratic apprentices had comparable levels of activity, but Democratic nonapprentices were far more active than their GOP counterparts. Thus, Democratic freshmen are less likely to welcome serving an apprenticeship than

Table 6-7 Levels of Activity vs. Apprenticeship by Party

	Republicans		Democrats	
	App.	*No. App.*	*App.*	*No. App.*
Mean Number of House Remarks	22	17	22	39
Mean Number of Extension Remarks	15	19	21	40
Mean Number of Nonprivate Bills and Resolutions Introduced	54	53	56	81
N	11	4	6	9

Republican newcomers, and only for Democrats is the decision to choose or reject an apprenticeship reflected in varying levels of activity.

To help explain this finding one must recall that the Democratic party is the entrenched majority party in the House. The decision to serve an apprenticeship may be more salient for majority party members in general, since it is the majority party that sets the legislative pace, controls the committee, and the like. But more consequential for the freshman Democrat is the domination of his party by senior members, many of them Southerners, who comprise a much larger proportion of his party than senior Republicans do of the GOP.[17] The common perception of the Democratic party is that it is run by its elderly patriarchs. Hence, in making a decision about apprenticeship, the Democratic freshman is choosing a course of action that does have immediate consequences for his legislative career. He is deciding in effect whether "to go along" as Sam Rayburn used to advise freshmen or to strike out on a more hazardous path. And the freshman Democrat is often forced to make this conscious decision about apprenticeship because he may enter Congress with strong intentions to promote a wide range of legislative activities and at the same time realize that his position as a freshman member in a senior-dominated party works against such conduct. The question of an apprenticeship is not nearly as salient for Republican freshmen — members of a relatively junior, minority party, who early in their House careers had the vaguest legislative plans, a condition that would make serving an apprenticeship less onerous.

In addition to one's programmatic intentions, the other variable that was often cited by freshmen as influential in their apprenticeship decision was their perception of their own legislative competence. Three members specifically stated that because of their previous experience in the state legislature, their period of apprenticeship could either be shortened or be totally unnecessary. The relationship between state legislative service and attitudes toward apprenticeship is presented in Table 6-8. For all freshmen, service in the state legislature does not materially affect opinions about apprenticeship. Table 6-8 further indicates that party differences with respect to apprenticeship remain even when previous state legislative experience is considered, thereby suggesting that previous experience is less important than one's own legislative goals in the decision whether or not to serve an apprenticeship. Again, Democratic freshmen were more oriented to legislation than their GOP colleagues.

> Apprenticeship is necessary for a period of time, but I have encouraged them [freshmen] to participate as soon as possible. I suggest that they choose as their area of expertise an area that they've had experience in previously which will let them participate earlier.

The nonfreshman responses to apprenticeship are truly surprising in the extent of their disagreement with the norm. The common political lore has it that nonfreshmen, particularly the more senior among them, would be the strongest advocates of an apprenticeship norm. The nonfreshmen responses to the apprenticeship item were usually brief and to the point, indicating little difficulty in replying to the item. A few of the more detailed, qualified responses are given below:

Table 6-8 Apprenticeship vs. State Legislative Service and Party

	State Service			No State Service		
	R	*D*	*All*	*R*	*D*	*All*
"Apprenticeship Necessary"	70	43	59	80	38	54
"No Apprenticeship Necessary"	30	57	41	20	62	46
Total %	100	100	100	100	100	100
N	(10	(7)	(17)	(5)	(8)	(13)

I don't think freshman congressmen should serve a period of apprenticeship. As a matter of fact, I don't think that term can apply in Congress. Any member has an equal right with any other member. The very nature of the legislative process does require that new members take more time to become acquainted with committee activities than those who have served for many years.

This is a difficult question to answer because of the varying backgrounds of the new members of Congress. . . . Hence, it seems to me that it would be difficult to establish any rule of thumb . . . I am frank to say that I have observed instances of overenthusiastic freshman congressmen who would have done well to have been a bit more observant of the processes and legislative procedure before offering the panacea to a particular problem.

Table 6-9 presents the nonfreshman replies to the apprenticeship item by seniority and party.

The results in this table are somewhat unexpected. Overall, the more senior one is, the less likely he will say that apprenticeship is necessary. For all groups except Republicans with less than six years of service, a sizable majority of respondents were against apprenticeship, and even for this group of Republicans the division was almost even. The reader should have greater confidence in the Republican figures than in the Democratic ones which do not include sufficient senior representation, especially from the South and border states.

Table 6-9 seems surprising because we have been led to believe that it is senior members who keep junior men in their place. But perhaps only a subset of senior members perform this function. The probable candidates would be the senior southern and border (Democratic) members and others who also dominate the committees. After all, it was Texan Sam Rayburn who was credited with the terse description of apprenticeship as "being seen and not heard" and who advised members to go along in order to get along. There are only four southern and border Democrats in the sample with more than ten years of service in the House (in a representative sample, there would be about twice that number), and three of the four said that no apprenticeship was necessary. These figures are too small to be conclusive, especially since it is almost impossible to interview the real patriarchs of the House. We can, however, divide the sample into gross regional categories to see whether apprenticeship is more common in the South, the likely home of a disproportionate number of carriers of the creed. The results of such a division reveal no substantial regional differences; 4 of 12 southern members said that apprenticeship was necessary as compared to 38 percent of the nonsouthern members (N = 54). This conclusion must be hedged a bit because of shortcomings in the southern subsample.

Thus, apprenticeship is far from being a universally accepted norm. Indeed, one wonders why a majority of the freshmen at t₁ still subscribed to the norm, unless it represents a false anticipation. As one newcomer observed, "It may be that freshman classes have been browbeaten before they ever got here by the establishment." The browbeating may very well take place through the widespread circulation of such political lore as Speaker Rayburn's advice cited earlier. Such information about their status may be the only kind available to freshmen at first. Thus, in a sense, freshmen may have to be socialized *out of* the norm of ap-

Table 6-9 Nonfreshman Apprenticeship Responses by Party and Seniority

	6 or fewer years of service			7 to 10 years of service			More than 10 years of service		
	R	D	All	R	D	All	R	D	All
Apprenticeship	53	27	41	43	13	27	36	25	32
No Apprenticeship	47	73	59	57	87	73	64	75	68
Total %	100	100	100	100	100	100	100	100	100
N	(17)	(15)	(32)	(7)	(8)	(15)	(11)	(8)	(19)

prenticeship. Two freshmen at t_1 said that Speaker McCormack himself had urged them to participate fully right from the outset of their service. Yet because of their prior conditioning, they were leery of such advice; they thought the Speaker was "just being nice." As noted earlier, there was erosion in support for apprenticeship from t_1 to t_2 by the 91st class; perhaps this is indicative of learning that is really unlearning. Freshmen may have seen some of their colleagues participate early, observed that no sanctions were levied, and therefore altered their views about apprenticeship. Of course, it is possible that senior members who deny the importance of apprenticeship are saying one thing and believing another. A sophomore Republican argued:

> ... [M]any senior congressmen might say that a freshman should not serve an apprenticeship, but when it came to actual practice, the situation was quite different. I know of numerous instances of senior members grumbling when a freshman member spoke on a subject. Typical comments were: "What's he doing talking, he's a freshman," "What does he know about it, he's only a freshman."

But it seems unreasonable to consider the senior members' responses against apprenticeship as largely misstatements of the members' underlying beliefs.

This argument does not mean that apprenticeship is unnecessary or unexpected. There will be many topics about which the freshman will be uninformed because of his inexperience, and in such areas, his more senior colleagues will expect him to proceed cautiously and to learn gradually. But this type of apprenticeship is a far cry from one in which the newcomer is expected to remain silent in all situations, even when he has a contribution to make. Some years earlier, Charles Clapp came to a similar conclusion, although his evidence was incomplete since his roundtable participants tended to be disproportionately liberal, reformist, and receptive to academicians. At that time, Clapp wrote:

> The old admonition that new members should observe but not participate in debate was swept aside long ago. Apprenticeship may still precede full partnership, but the increased volume and complexity of the problems with which the Congress is compelled to cope dictate more efficient use of the membership. Freshmen are now advised to defer speaking only until the moment arrives when they have something significant to say — indeed, colleagues counsel them not to wait too long — although they are cautioned to be sure they are well informed about their topic.[18]

Finally, it is clear that the House is not alone in its skepticism about apprenticeship; the norm of apprenticeship has fallen into bad times in the United States Senate as well, especially since 1964. The "Inner-Club" has declined in recent years and a new type of Senator, less concerned with internal Senate operations, has become more prominent.[19]

Conclusion

The main finding of this paper is that the amount of norm learning between January and May by the freshman members of the 91st Congress was unexpectedly low. As the concept of norms incorporates the notion of shared expectations, the attitudes of a sample of nonfreshmen were first analyzed to insure that we were studying genuine norms. Apprenticeship was found to be less restrictive on freshmen than originally thought, while other norms were largely adhered to. It appeared that freshmen largely knew the general House norms prior to entering Congress, which made it impossible to talk about the formal agents of socialization involved in transmitting the norms to newcomers. And the extent of change once in office was minimal.

Now this finding may be an artifact of the particular freshman class under investigation, in the sense that the 91st class was unusually well-prepared by prior political experience for House service. Of the six most recent freshman classes, the 91st class had the largest proportion of members with state legislative experience — 51 percent. But an alternative explanation seems more satisfactory, that is that freshman representatives would generally know many of the norms simply because they are rules of behavior appropriate to many institutional settings. Thus, one does not have to be a member of Congress to know that personal criticism and unfriendly relationships may be dysfunctional to one's institution or group or one's own career. This argument asserts that almost any type of prior experience would make the freshman sensitive to the basic rules of behavior. Overall, it was difficult to link compliance and noncompliance to the norms to any particular characteristics because of the small number of deviant responses, but a number of plausible influences were suggested.

These data do not address the learning of committee-specific norms. These norms may not be as salient or as transferable from other contexts as the ones discussed above, and hence they may actually have to be learned anew by freshmen.[20] Unfortunately, the data in this article span only January to May 1969, a time of very little legislative action, both in committee and on the floor. The 91st Congress in its early months was sharply criticized for the slowness of its legislative pace, a slowness that was due in part to the change in partisan complexion of the national administration. And this slowness of legislative pace may have retarded the learning of committee-specific norms. In their California study, Price and Bell found that the norms cited at their later interviews were most often those that concerned committee work and the handling of legislation.[21]

In summary, then, it seems as if the traditional image of the freshman congressman as ignorant and bewildered had mistakenly led us to expect substantial learning of norms on the part of supposedly ill-informed newcomers. This expectation was unwarranted on two counts: the general House norms were not so abstruse as to require formal learning, and the traditional image of the freshman Congressman was found to be out of date, a theme to be developed in a future paper.

Notes

1. The literature on legislative norms is quite extensive. For a discussion of Senate norms, see Donald R. Matthews, *U.S. Senators and Their World* (New York: Random House, 1960) and William S. White, *Citadel: The Story of the U.S. Senate*

(New York: Harper & Brothers, 1957) and two articles by Ralph Huitt, "The Outsider in the Senate: An Alternative Role," *American Political Science Review, 55* (September 1961), pp. 566-575 and "The Morse Committee Assignment Controversy: A Study in Senate Norms," *American Political Science Review,* 51 (June 1957), pp. 313-329. For information on House norms, see Charles L. Clapp, *The Congressman: His Work as He Sees It* (New York: Doubleday & Company, 1963); Donald G. Tacheron and Morris K. Udall, *The Job of the Congressman* (Indianapolis and New York: The Bobbs-Merrill Company, 1966); and Clem Miller, *Member of the House: Letters of a Congressman* (New York: Charles Scribner's Sons, 1962). Also relevant to the House is the growing body of literature on committee integration and the norms that promote it. The foremost articles in this area are Richard F. Fenno, Jr., "The House Appropriations Committee as a Political System: The Problem of Integration," *American Political Science Review,* 56 (June, 1962), pp. 310-324 and John F. Manley, "The House Committee on Ways and Means: Conflict Management in a Congressional Committee," *American Political Science Review, 59* (December, 1965), pp. 927-939. See also the broader studies by these authors: Richard F. Fenno, Jr., *The Power of the Purse: Appropriations Politics in Congress* (Boston: Little, Brown and Company, 1966) and John F. Manley, *The Politics of Finance* (Boston: Little, Brown and Company, 1970). At the state legislative level, the reader can turn to John Wahlke et al., *The Legislative System* (New York: John Wiley & Sons, 1962); Malcolm E. Jewell, *The State Legislature: Politics and Practice* (New York: Random House, 1962); and James D. Barber, *The Lawmakers: Recruitment and Adaptation to Legislative Life* (New Haven: Yale University Press, 1965). Finally, for an example of research in a non-American setting, see Allan Kornberg, "The Rules of the Game in the Canadian House of Commons," *Journal of Politics,* 26 (May, 1964), pp. 358-380.

2. Recently, there has been a greater emphasis on the legislative newcomer and his adaptation to the institution, with one article specifically concerned with the rules of the game, although from a different perspective than employed herein. In a panel study of freshman California assemblymen, Bell and Price found that norm learning did take place. They wrote: "A whole host of 'in-house' norms were cited after legislative experience had been acquired. Rules pertaining to committee decorum and management of bills were frequently cited in the second and third interviews; they were not often cited in the first interview." See Charles M. Price and Charles G. Bell, "The Rules of the Game: Political Fact or Academic Fancy?" *Journal of Politics,* 32 (November, 1970), p. 855. For more general discussions of freshman adaptation, see Charles G. Bell and Charles M. Price, "Pre-Legislative Sources of Representational Roles," *Midwest Journal of Political Science,* 13 (May, 1969), pp. 254-270 and Irwin N. Gertzog, "The Socialization of Freshman Congressmen: Some Agents of Organizational Continuity," Paper prepared for delivery at the 66th annual meeting of the American Political Science Association, Biltmore Hotel, Los Angeles, September 8-12, 1970, pp. 1-26.

3. Herbert B. Asher, "The Freshman Congressman: A Developmental Analysis" (Ph.D. dissertation, University of Michigan, 1970).

4. The selection of the times for the two waves, particularly the first, was no easy matter. Since a prime concern of my research was freshman attitudes to legislative norms, I wished to interview sufficiently early so as to ascertain these attitudes while uninfluenced by House service. But seminars for freshman representatives were held early in the session (January 8 through January 13) and at these meetings a large amount of material, some of it relevant to legislative norms, was presented to the freshmen. Thus, it would have been advantageous to talk to the newcomers before these seminars were held. But in terms of my interest in internal House voting cues,

interviewing in early January would have made little sense as almost no legislative business was underway. In retrospect, the problem was not very serious as evidenced by a question included in the interview schedule designed to measure the impact of the freshman seminars. Freshmen generally indicated that the seminars were interesting and highly informative with respect to parliamentary procedures and the services available to congressmen, but generally attributed little influence to the seminars vis-à-vis House norms. Similar opinions were expressed by freshman participants in the 1959 seminars. My thanks go to Representative Morris Udall for allowing me to rummage through his files on previous freshman seminars.

There remains the possibility that substantial norm learning may have occurred in the postelection period prior to the freshman's formal entry into the House, a "waiting period" during which many freshmen took some action with regard to their future committee assignment or journeyed to Washington to handle personal business. Thus, there was certainly opportunity for norm learning to have occurred in this period, although freshmen indicated little such activity in response to questions about the waiting period. Unfortunately, resource constraints prevented a third wave of interviews shortly after the November elections.

5. The nonfreshman members of the House were stratified according to party, region, and seniority, and proportionate samples were selected randomly within these strata. The interviews obtained were very representative of Republican House membership, while they underrepresented Democrats in general and senior, southern Democrats in particular. The following figures indicate how well the nonfreshman sample matches the overall population in terms of party and seniority where a threefold classification of seniority based on the number of terms served prior to the start of the 91st Congress is used. Low seniority was defined as three or fewer terms, moderate as four and five terms, and high as more than five terms.

	Republicans		Democrats	
	% of population	% of sample	% of population	% of sample
Seniority				
Low	55	49	36	48
Moderate	18	20	22	26
High	27	31	42	26
Total %	100%	100%	100%	100%
N	(174)	(35)	(224)	(31)

Despite the underrepresentation of senior Democrats, there were no significant ideological differences between the samples selected from each stratum and the corresponding parent stratum as measured by CQ conservative coalition support scores and ADA and ACA ratings.

6. The actual question that Wahlke and his colleagues used was: "We've been told that every legislature has its unofficial rules of the game — certain things they must do and things they must not do if they want the respect and cooperation of fellow members. What are some of these things — these 'rules of the game' — that a member must observe to hold the respect and cooperation of his fellow members?" See Wahlke et al., *The Legislative System*, p. 143.

7. The norm of institutional patriotism was also investigated, but its operationalization was so narrow that the responses obtained were not very interesting. Members were asked whether they would ever criticize the House, and, not unexpectedly, most said

that they would which presumably implies that institutional patriotism is not a viable norm. But institutional patriotism is far more complex than merely refraining from criticism so that nothing more will be said about the norm in the remainder of this paper.

8. Some of the nonfreshman interviews were taken at t_1 and the others at t_2. There was very high agreement on some of the norms questions asked at t_1 and these were omitted at t_2 so that more attention could be devoted to other items. This accounts for the various N's on the norms questions. There was no reason to believe that the responses to the norms questions that were omitted at t_2 contained any systematic biases. The actual questions for each of the norms were: Do you think congressmen should specialize in a field or should try to be generalists? Do you think most of the important work of the House is done on the floor or in committees? How important do you think it is to maintain friendly relationships with your fellow congressmen? Do you think that freshman congressmen should serve a period of apprenticeship, that is, be more an observer than an active participant in the legislative process? How important do you think learning the House procedural rule is? Would you ever personally criticize a fellow representative on the floor of the House? Would you vote a certain way on a bill that you cared little about in order to gain the vote of a fellow congressman on a bill that you did care about?

It should be noted here that the question about where the important work of the House is done does not tap a norm in the same sense as the other items, but rather elicits a belief or opinion. Once we have found marked disagreement with certain items thought to be legislative norms, then by definition these items no longer are norms. But for simplicity of presentation, the word norm will be used in the subsequent analysis to apply to those items such as apprenticeship about which there was substantial disagreement.

9. It is very difficult to gather systematic information on the "proper" activist who observes the rules of the game vs. the one who does not, but scattered references to various individuals in the course of interviewing suggested that these two general types were meaningful for some members of Congress. For example, specific comparisons twice were made between the "proper" liberal described above and another liberal Democratic freshman from the same region and with similar issue concerns. These comparisons were unfavorable toward the latter freshman because of his excessive behavior. He was criticized for shooting off his mouth too much and for making too many entries in the *Congressional Record.* An examination of the actual number of entries indicated that the perceptions of his behavior were accurate; he was the most verbose newcomer with nearly twice as many distinct items in the *Record* as his "proper" freshman colleague. It is noteworthy that such behavior is salient to Congressmen and that reputations, whether good or bad, can be created by such activity. In one of the rare attempts to talk in systematic and quantitative terms about the sanctions invoked against nonconformists, Wayne Swanson found that liberals, and especially anti-establishment liberals, lagged behind in advancing up the committee hierarchy in the Senate. See Wayne R. Swanson, "Committee Assignments and the Non-Conformist Legislator: Democrats in the U.S. Senate," *Midwest Journal of Political Science,* 13 (February, 1969), pp. 84-94.

10. There are numerous other plausible sources of party differences toward vote trading; unfortunately, we do not have adequate data to check these out. One explanation concerns the recruitment of candidates by each party. It may be that Republicans in general turn to less political types, often businessmen, who may be naive about politics and therefore not recognize the validity and usefulness of such activities as vote-trading, bargaining, compromise, and the like. While four of the six Republican

freshmen in this group did not serve in the state legislature, it is interesting to note that four of the six also had as their primary occupation a business-related activity rather than the legal profession which was by far the most common occupation of the 91st class. Another explanation of this possible party difference is the position of the Democrats and Republicans as fairly permanent majority and minority parties in the House. This may mean that the responsibility for the passage of legislation is left more to the majority Democrats who must then engage in the vote trading and logrolling necessary to forge a majority coalition. It may be that Republicans tend to see this activity as illegitimate since they so often come out on the losing side, but this is purely speculative.

11. Contrary to my expectation, it turned out that members from districts closer to Washington did not have higher absentee rates. But then one might argue that their scores would have been even higher had their districts been more distant from the Capitol.

12. Overall, Republican freshmen missed 13 percent of the quorum votes and Democrats 17 percent. Southern freshmen in each party had the lowest absentee rates on the quorum votes — 13 percent for Democrats and 8 percent for Republicans. This may be due to the fact that southern freshmen were more oriented toward the House in career terms and were therefore more likely to perform those tasks that promote a legislative career. Although I do not have data on this, there is no reason to believe that southern freshmen returned to their districts less often than their nonsouthern colleagues which then would have accounted for their higher attendance rates. In fact, five of the 11 southern districts were easily within three to five hours of Washington by car. Thus, it appears that there were regional differences in attendance rates which may reflect differing career views of the office of representative.

13. The issue orientation of the freshmen was determined by impressionistically content-analyzing their responses to a series of questions dealing with their legislative goals, the specific pieces of legislation, if any, that they planned to introduce or work for, and the kinds of legislative matters about which their districts were most concerned.

14. The percentages of Table 6-4 are for freshmen in the aggregate. Thus, zero percent change does not necessarily mean that all the freshmen interviewed at t_1 and t_2 remained perfectly stable; shifts in one direction may have balanced out those in the other. As it was, there was general stability in the replies except for the two items discussed in the text (personal criticism and spending time on the House floor) so that the percentage differences in Table 6-4 do not mask much additional shifting.

15. As a reminder to the reader, the actual apprenticeship question was: Do you think that freshman Congressmen should serve a period of apprenticeship, that is, be more an observer than an active participant in the legislative process? In the subsequent discussion, apprenticeship will be treated as a dichotomous variable by collapsing the agreement and qualified agreement categories and by combining the disagreement and qualified disagreement categories.

16. These measures are merely counts of the total number of entries in the Record and the total number of nonrelief bills and resolutions introduced. They could be refined by grouping remarks in the Record according to issue area or by dividing bills according to their scope of impact. But the expenditure of resources in such an endeavor seemed prohibitive. As sponsorship of bills is so prevalent in the House, the number of bills introduced may be a highly misleading measure of legislative activity. A better indicator might be the number of amendments introduced. But since amendments from freshmen are relatively rare (only about one-fourth sponsored any), they cannot provide us with sufficient information.

17. At the start of the 91st Congress, 21 percent of the 243 Democrats had served more

than 20 years (ten terms) in the House as compared to under six percent of the 192 Republicans. Or to restate the figures, the Republicans had only eleven members with more than 20 years of service, while the Democrats had 51 such members. Furthermore, 46.4 percent of the Republicans had served three or fewer terms as opposed to 31.7 percent of the Democrats.

18. Clapp, *The Congressman*, pp. 12-13.
19. See Randall B. Ripley, *Power in the Senate* (New York: St. Martin's Press, 1969), p. 185 and Nelson W. Polsby, "Goodbye to the Inner Club," in *Congressional Behavior,* ed. Nelson W. Polsby (New York: Random House, 1971) pp. 105-110.
20. A good example of such research isn Fenno's treatment of apprenticeship in the context of the House Appropriations Committee. See *The Power of the Purse,* pp. 166-167.
21. Price and Bell, "The Rules of the Game," p. 855.

7. POLITICAL CHANGE AND LEGISLATIVE NORMS IN THE U.S. SENATE, 1957-1974

David W. Rohde, Norman J. Ornstein, and Robert L. Peabody

In the opening sentence of his famous article on Sen. William Proxmire, Ralph Huitt states: "The growing concern of students of politics with the social structure of official bodies and the behavior expected of their members promises to make the Senate of the United States a prime target of research." [1] Unfortunately, this promise has gone largely unfulfilled. Congressional scholars who employ interviews as a primary data base for their research have tended to concentrate almost exclusively on the House of Representatives. [2] One primary reason for the emphasis on the House seems to have been the relatively easier access to representatives as opposed to senators.

The purpose of this chapter — and in a larger study we are undertaking — is to begin to redress this imbalance. Our primary focus is on change: how has the Senate changed since the late 1950s when it was the subject of intensive study by Huitt, Donald Matthews[3] and others? Specifically, in this chapter we are interested in the norms or "folkways" of the Senate described by these earlier researchers.[4] We begin with a brief recounting of the Senate's folkways as described by Matthews. Next we discuss two types or categories of norms, considering how each type of norm might have been affected by certain changes in the distribution

Author's Note: This chapter is part of a general study of political change and the U.S. Senate being conducted by the authors. In the course of any large research project, the investigators incur debts, and this case is no exception. First and foremost, we thank the present and former members of the Senate who generously agreed to grant us interviews. We began interviewing senators in May of 1973, and we are still continuing. At present we have completed 52 interviews, 44 with senators who were serving in the 93rd Congress and 8 with senators who served previously. No attempt was made to draw a random sample of the membership of the Senate to serve as a basis of seeking interviews. Instead we decided to seek interviews with all members. The interviews completed thus far are, however, fairly representative of the membership. The interviews were semistructured in nature, with a prepared list of open-ended questions, and all but one of the interviews were tape-recorded. We particularly want to express our gratitude to the Russell Sage Foundation for a grant to cover the costs of transcription of the interviews. David Rohde and Norman Ornstein wish to thank the American Political Science Association for the opportunity to participate in its Congressional Fellowship Program and thus observe the Senate at close hand. We also express our gratitude to the many other students of the Congress — especially Richard Fenno, Ralph Huitt, Donald Matthews, and Randall Ripley — who shared their advice and views with us. An earlier version of this chapter was presented at the annual meeting of the American Political Science Association, Chicago, Ill., August 29 - September 2, 1974.

of power in the Senate in the years since Matthews and the others did their research. Third, we describe how the distribution of power in the Senate has changed. Finally, we assess the status of the folkways in the Senate today.

The Senate's Folkways in the 1950s

"The Senate of the United States, just as any other group of human beings, has its unwritten rules of the game, its norms of conduct, its approved manner of behavior. Some things are just not done; others are met with widespread approval." [5] The Senate's norms in the 1950s were expectations about how a senator ought to behave and ought not to behave; expectations that were shared by a large number of members. They described what kinds of patterns of behavior were expected of senators by other senators. While the norms were not always followed, the Senate's observers argued that conformity was the rule and deviance was the exception. In his study Matthews cited six folkways, each of which we will now briefly consider.

(1) *Apprenticeship.* "The first rule of Senate behavior, and the one most widely recognized off the Hill, is that new members are expected to serve a proper apprenticeship." [6] Freshman senators were expected to wait a substantial amount of time before fully participating in the work of the Senate. They were expected to put off their first speech — the longer the wait the better — and speak infrequently thereafter. While the expected length of the period of apprenticeship was neither fixed nor clear, it appears to have been rather lengthy. William White stated: "Men who have reached national fame in less than two years in powerful non-Senatorial office . . . have found four years and more not to be long enough to feel free to speak up loudly in the Institution." [7] During this time freshmen were expected to learn about the Senate and to seek the advice of senior members. "The freshman who does not accept his lot as a temporary but very real second-class senator is met with thinly veiled hostility." [8]

(2) *Legislative Work.* This norm expected members to devote a major portion of their time to the legislative tasks that fell to them. Senators were to do their work in committee and on the floor, and not seek publicity at the expense of these obligations.

(3) *Specialization.* According to this folkway, a senator was expected "to specialize, to focus his energy and attention on the relatively few matters that come before his committees or that directly and immediately affect his state." [9] Members were expected to know a great deal about a few things and leave matters outside their expertise largely to other senators.

(4) *Courtesy.* "A cardinal rule of Senate behavior is that political disagreements should not influence personal feelings." [10] Under this norm, and the Senate rules that were structured in accord with it, senators in debate addressed the chair rather than each other and spoke of their colleagues by title rather than by name. Praise of other members was encouraged and personal attacks were to be avoided.

(5) *Reciprocity.* "Every senator, at one time or another, is in a position to help out a colleague. The folkways of the Senate hold that a Senator should provide this assistance and that he be repaid in kind." [11] While this norm applied

to the whole range of senatorial activity, its most important application was to the trading of votes. It also meant that a senator ought not to push his formal powers too far (for example, by systematically objecting to unanimous consent requests). A member was to understand and appreciate the problems of his colleagues and to keep his bargains once they were struck.

(6) *Institutional Patriotism*. As with most human institutions, the Senate demanded loyalty from its members. The Senate was to be esteemed and protected:

> A senator whose emotional commitment to Senate ways appears to be less than total is suspect. One who brings the Senate as an institution or senators as a class into public disrepute invites his own destruction as an effective legislator. One who seems to be using the Senate for the purposes of self-advertisement and advancement obviously does not belong.[12]

Why Did the Folkways Exist?

Norms may exist in social or political institutions for a variety of reasons. They may provide stability to an institution. They may help to give the institution an attractiveness that lures new members and encourages others to remain. Norms may operate to strengthen the power of an institution, facilitating the achievement of the goals of its members, especially in competition with other institutions. Or they may exist to give power to, or perpetuate the power of, certain members within the institution. As we shall see, each of these reasons contributed to the existence of one or more of the Senate's folkways.

For norms or folkways to be operative, the expectations about behavior must be fairly widely shared by senators, at least among those who have the power to impose sanctions for violations of those expectations. For an expectation to be accepted by a member, it must be seen as providing certain benefits to members. This is not to say that all senators who adhere to the norm are benefited by it. As Matthews and Huitt have pointed out, some senators went along with norms only reluctantly, and others violated certain norms because obedience to them would have interfered with the achievement of the member's goals. Some senators may behave in accord with expectations only because deviance would lead to the imposition of sanctions. The senators who must perceive benefit from the norms are those who *hold* the expectations, not necessarily those who adhere to them.

The Senate folkways that Matthews described were of two types: those that provided benefits for most members (which we may term *general benefit norms*) and those that provided benefits primarily for a particular subset of senators (which we call *limited benefit norms*). Specifically, the limited benefit norms primarily served the interests of the group of conservative senators who dominated the positions of power in the Senate of the 1950s — the group that Sen. Joseph Clark labeled "the Senate Establishment." [13]

Before documenting this basically conservative dominance, we will assess Matthews's six folkways in terms of these two broad categories.

149

General Benefit Norms

The norms of legislative work, courtesy, reciprocity, and institutional patriotism can best be described by the term "general benefit norms." This is not to say that in any given situation every member is equally benefited by adherence to these norms, nor that in a particular instance obedience to a folkway may not interfere with the achievement of a senator's goal. But in the long run, adherence to this type of norm benefits all members.

Consider first the general benefit norm of courtesy. Many of the issues with which the Senate deals are controversial. Hard policy choices must be made and there will often be disagreement about which course to follow. While in a given instance of conflict, the proponent of one alternative might gain an advantage by a direct personal attack on the proponent of another alternative, the impact of such a course of action could have a devastating effect on the general pattern of activity in the Senate. Personal attacks would encourage the recipient to retaliate in other situations. Increased acrimony doubtless would slow the pace of activity in a Senate that already finds it difficult to keep pace with legislative demands. Moreover, it would make the compromises that are necessary in passing legislation difficult to achieve. While today's *opponent* may become tomorrow's ally relatively easily, it is far more difficult to make an ally of today's enemy. Courtesy could be almost the prototype of a general benefit norm: little potential benefit to an individual from violating it in a particular instance, and substantial long-term benefits to all members from its general observance.

The norm of legislative work also has its general benefits. Members of the Senate serve on two to four committees and as many as ten to twenty subcommittees. No senator has the time or physical endurance to give detailed consideration to all of his responsibilities. Thus in many areas the task of keeping the Senate's policy making machinery going devolves on one or two members, usually the chairman of a subcommittee and its ranking minority member. If they do not do their work, the Senate becomes institutionally incapable of making coherent policy because these are the only members who will know anything in detail about the policy field. If these members continue to fail to keep up with their legislative work, other senators will have to pick up the slack, forcing them to shortchange their own responsibilities. The division of labor through the committee and subcommittee system in the Senate is, in effect, a tacit bargain that each member will meet the responsibilities that he or she is assigned through the system. If a member fails to keep the bargain, all other members suffer indirectly, and a substantial number of members can suffer directly. While it might be argued that there was a distinct group of members who were disadvantaged because of this norm, we would argue that this was true primarily as it overlapped with the norm of specialization, which we discuss later.

The reciprocity folkway is another norm that benefits nearly everyone if most senators observe it. Many issues with which the Senate deals are of substantial interest only to a small subset of the members. If every senator were to support only legislative initiatives that directly benefited a large proportion of his or her constituents, nothing would pass the Senate in many instances. This would be true not only in the case of a particular public works project that would be constructed in a single state, but also in broad policy areas like agriculture. Thus senators' willingness to support programs that are of little or no direct benefit to their constituents would appear to be a precondition to many senators accomplishing their legislative goals, and there is a general benefit when this willingness is widespread among senators.[14]

Probably no facet of the reciprocity folkway better fits the notion of a general benefit norm than that which might be termed "integrity" — the keeping of agreements. As one of Matthews's interviewees stated, "you don't *have* to make these commitments, ... but if you *do* make them, you had better live up to them." [15] In a legislative body the most practical way to make agreements is verbally, and if members were to fail to keep their commitments, the legislative process would become most unpleasant and much more difficult.[16]

The final folkway that we would characterize as a general benefit norm is institutional patriotism. It is the norm to which Matthews gave the most limited treatment, and thus it is somewhat difficult to categorize clearly. The Senate is the institution through which all members have chosen, at least for the time being, to attempt to accomplish their political goals. Senators who damage the Senate as an institution — either through direct attack or because of their behavior — damage to a degree the ability of themselves and their colleagues to use the Senate as an effective mechanism for goal accomplishment.[17] Thus, in this sense, institutional patriotism is a general benefit norm.

On the other hand, the distribution of power within the Senate at a given time, and the internal institutional arrangements that support that distribution of power, may produce a bias against the achievement of certain policy outcomes. If this is true, then a failure to criticize these institutional arrangements by those senators against whose policy goals the bias exists would make "reform" less likely and therefore the achievement of their goals would be more difficult. In this sense, institutional patriotism could have a limited benefit aspect.

It was precisely his perception of institutional bias that led Sen. Joseph S. Clark and a few other members to launch their attack on the "Senate Establishment" in 1963.[18] Clark's supporters were limited to the old "outsiders" (Sens. Wayne L. Morse, Paul H. Douglas, and William Proxmire), and none of the liberals from the classes of 1958, 1960, and 1962 joined in the debate although many of them supported the reforms that were being advocated. (For example, Clark's proposal to expand the size of the steering committee received 21 of 60 votes in the Democratic caucus.[19]) Perhaps the other liberals thought that a violation of institutional patriotism in this case carried more risks to their own interests than silence.

On balance, institutional patriotism should be classed as a general benefit norm, although it may have a more significant limited benefit aspect than the norm of courtesy, legislative work, and reciprocity.

Limited Benefit Norms

A limited benefit norm gives an advantage primarily or solely to a group of members who occupy certain positions, hold a common set of beliefs, or pursue certain goals. Clearly, since such norms do not benefit everyone, their perpetua-

151

tion depends upon the ability of the group of members who hold these expectations, and benefit from compliance with them, to impose sanctions on members who do not benefit and thus have an incentive to deviate. It is our contention that the folkways that we place in this category — apprenticeship and possibly specialization — primarily benefited the group of conservative senators who controlled most of the positions of power in the Senate at the time Matthews wrote, and it was precisely that control that provided the necessary sanctioning mechanisms.

Consider the norm of apprenticeship. If conservatives dominated the top positions on Senate committees, especially the most important committees, then the bills that emanated from these committees would have been more to the liking of conservatives than of liberals. Freshman senators who were conservative would have been satisfied with such a situation. Freshman senators who were liberal, on the other hand, would have had an incentive to speak against the policies contained in the bills and to attempt to change them. If, however, liberal freshmen adhered to the apprenticeship norm, then senior conservatives had an important advantage. The freshmen liberals would seldom be present on important committees, and even on the committees of which they were members, they would bar themselves from full, vigorous participation. Once a bill came to the floor, their activity in debate would be limited or nonexistent. Moreover, if the participation of liberal freshmen could be held to a minimum in their first term, their opportunities to return for a second term might be damaged.

This bias in the impact of the apprenticeship norm was clearly noted by Matthews:

> A man elected to the Senate as a "liberal" or "progressive" or "reformer" is under considerable pressure to produce legislative results in a hurry. The people who voted for him are not likely to be happy with small favors — dams built, rivers dredged, roads financed — but want major national legislative policy changed. Yet as a freshman or a junior senator, and many never become anything else, the liberal is in no position to do this alone. If he gives in to the pressure for conformity coming from the folkways, he must postpone the achievement of his liberal objectives. If he presses for these objectives regardless of his junior position, he will become tabbed as a nonconformist, lose popularity with his colleagues and, in most cases, his legislative effectiveness as well.

> The conservative does not face this problem. He has committed himself to fewer changes in basic policies; he finds the strategic positions in the Senate occupied by like-minded senators regardless of which party organized them. . . . Conservatives can afford to be quiet and patient. Reformers, by definition, find it difficult to be either.[20]

Thus the conservatives in the Senate benefited considerably from the apprenticeship norm.[21] On the other hand, it is difficult to perceive much *general* benefit from this folkway. Matthews does note that apprenticeship discourages extensive speaking in an institution that has no effective limitation on debate. Such a benefit is, however, distinctly minor when compared with those that flow from the norms we have classified as general benefit. Moreover, Sen. Lyndon B. Johnson, as the Democratic leader in the 1950s, had employed unanimous consent agreements extensively on major bills, which was a separate and far more effective limit on debate.[22]

The situation with regard to the folkway of specialization is not as clear, for the categorization of this norm depends on what one interprets it to demand. We perceive two possible alternative interpretations of specialization, both of which can be supported from Matthews's description.

First, the norm might have demanded that senators develop expertise in the policy areas of their committee assignments, and that they should not speak on matters regarding which they do not have expertise. In this sense, specialization would be a general benefit norm similar to legislative work. Indeed, specialization would largely be an alternative statement of that norm.

On the other hand, specialization might have demanded, in addition to the development of expertise within committee jurisdictions, that a senator should confine his attention almost exclusively to those matters. This is the proper interpretation of the folkway of specialization as Matthews describes it. Indeed, he states that under this norm a senator ought "to focus his attention on the relatively few matters that come before his committee or that directly and immediately affect his state." [23]

In this sense, specialization is a limited benefit norm. As we have already noted, junior liberals were unlikely to receive assignments to the most important, most desired committees — the committees that dealt with the most controversial policy questions before the Senate. Such committees were dominated by conservatives, and the bills coming from them would be shaped in favor of conservative preferences. If, when these bills came to the floor, liberals who were not members of the reporting committee observed the norm of specialization, they would be constrained from making a vigorous attempt to change the bill.

This latter interpretation of the specialization folkway takes no cognizance of independent expertise. A new senator could be an expert in a policy area because of his pre-Senate experience, and this norm would still prevent him from participating in the debate on this policy on the floor. Thus there is not the general benefit that would flow from the first interpretation of the norm. Indeed, one could argue that there would be a general detriment because the Senate would be deprived of available expertise.

To summarize, there are two possible interpretations of the folkway of specialization. If the former interpretation were accepted, we would classify it as a general benefit norm; using the latter interpretation, we would classify it as a limited benefit norm.

This argument concerning apprenticeship and specialization as limited benefit norms is reinforced by considering again Huitt's analysis of Senator Proxmire's choice of the "outsider" role. There is little evidence to indicate that Proxmire had much difficulty with the norms we have termed "general benefit." It was apprenticeship and specialization that he had trouble with, and it was these that he violated in choosing to follow the behavior pattern adopted by Senators Morse and Douglas.

> But almost as if he could not help himself, Proxmire became steadily more active in debate until he was one of the busiest men on the floor. Then came the first

warnings that he was "talking too much." The warnings were characteristic of the operations of the Senate. None of them was direct. They came in friendly tips: someone heard an unnamed person say it; the report was passed on to a Proxmire staff man for what it was worth. Or a very senior senator in the chair would pointedly overlook Proxmire standing at his desk, to recognize other members ahead of him out of turn. . . .

Then the dam broke. In the first week of June, Proxmire offered six amendments to the Mutual Security Act and pressed them to a vote. Inasmuch as Proxmire was not a member of the Foreign Relations Committee, and four of his amendments were first introduced on the floor so the committee had no chance to consider them, the performance was hardly a demonstration of modesty and withdrawal. Criticism was sharp and immediate (though indirect, as always), and it spurred Proxmire to a decision: he would "be a senator like Wayne [Morse] and Paul [Douglas]"; he would talk when he pleased on whatever he chose and would not worry about his influence in the Senate. He had found his role.[24]

The Folkways and Senate Change

There is little reason to expect change in the nature of general benefit norms unless the bases for the benefits they provide are altered. Otherwise, almost all members of the institution have incentives to continue to hold these expectations and to comply with them. On the other hand, what would cause change in, or disappearance of, limited benefit norms? Obviously, if the relative distribution of power between the group of members who benefited from these norms and the group that did not were to change, the incentives for retaining the norms also would change. That is, a major shift in the distribution of power in the Senate should have a profound impact on the limited benefit norms.

Such a major shift in power has taken place in the Senate.[25] Today, important institutional positions are much more equally distributed among liberals and conservatives. Before documenting this shift, however, we will describe our expectations regarding its consequences for each of the Senate's folkways.

First, consider the norm of legislative work. Its benefits depended on the heavy workload of the Senate and the division of labor through the committee system that those burdens made necessary. Since the 1950s, the Senate's collective workload has increased substantially, thus increasing the legislative responsibilities of each individual senator. In 1957, senators averaged 2.8 committee assignments (including standing, special, select, and joint committees) and 6.3 subcommittee assignments each. By 1973, the average number of committee assignments had grown to 3.9 and subcommittee assignments to 11.9.[26] This increase in legislative responsibilities makes it even more necessary that each member carry out the work that the committee system assigns. Therefore we would expect that the norm of legislative work would still be operative in the Senate today.

Similarly, the bases for the norms of courtesy and reciprocity do not appear to have changed. Increased legislative activity also makes the avoidance of bitter interpersonal conflicts more necessary and continues the need for being able to depend on an individual member's word when bargains are struck. Legislation that is of limited interest continues to be considered, and so a willingness on the part of senators to support policies that are not of substantial direct benefit to their constituents is still necessary. Thus we would anticipate that members would maintain their expectations regarding these behavior patterns.

Finally, the general benefit aspects of the norm of institutional patriotism continue. If anything, the recent increase in competition between the Congress and the executive branch for control over policy outcomes in matters like foreign policy and the budget, and the extensive use of the Senate as a base from which members of both parties may launch presidential candidacies, have increased these general benefits. Additionally, as we will see, the limited benefit aspects of the norm have declined. Therefore, institutional patriotism should continue to be an operative folkway in the Senate.

Our expectations are, however, quite different with respect to the limited benefit folkways. The ideological character of the group of senior members who dominate the most important institutional positions in the Senate has changed, particularly among the Democrats. Hence fewer senior senators (who would be most important in transmitting expectations to junior members) would benefit from a continuation of the limited benefit norms. The conservative members who derived the benefit from such norms would be in less of a position to impose sanctions if such norms were not observed. Other changes — especially in the character of Senate leaders and in Senate rules — have significantly increased the relative power of the more junior members of the Senate.

These changes in the Senate lead us to expect a change in the nature of the limited benefit norms. First, we would expect the norm of apprenticeship to have declined in importance or disappeared. Since the group of senior members who dominate the most important positions of institutional power has become much more representative of the Senate as a whole, much of the limited benefit from the apprenticeship of junior liberals is gone. Indeed, as the senior members of both parties become more ideologically similar to their junior colleagues and as the workload steadily increases, it is in the interest of both liberal and conservative senior members to encourage their junior allies to become full participants in Senate business as soon as possible.

Our prediction concerning the specialization folkway is more complex. Insofar as specialization demanded that members develop expertise in their committees and not participate in legislative activity on matters they know nothing about, this folkway would be reinforced, for the same reasons that the norm of legislative work would continue. Clearly, no general benefit is derived if members speak on issues when they have nothing to contribute. Indeed, such behavior could well injure the cause of the side the member supports. However, to the extent that specialization demanded also that members refrain from participating in policy making on matters outside the jurisdiction of their committees, this interpretation or aspect of the norm should no longer be expected by enough members to perpetuate it.

Thus we have certain expectations about how changes in the distribution of power in the Senate should have affected Senate norms. The next step in our analysis is to document those changes.

Changes in the Distribution of Power in the Senate, 1957-1973

In their book on Lyndon Johnson, Rowland Evans and Robert Novak describe the Senate in 1949, when Johnson was a freshman:

> While the two elected Democratic floor leaders were displayed as the *de jure* rulers of the Senate, real power was in the grip of an informal, loosely linked directory of senior Republicans and Southern Democrats. This conservative coalition, born in 1937 in reaction to Franklin D. Roosevelt's Supreme Court-packing plan, by now literally controlled Congress. . . .[27]

By the 1950s this was still a generally accurate picture of the Senate, although the seeds of change already had been laid — in part, as we shall see, by Johnson himself. As Table 7-1 demonstrates, the conservatives had a substantial majority of the Senate membership in 1957.[28] This was partly due to the large number of Republican conservatives, but even among Democrats a majority of senators had conservative coalition scores over 50. Of course, most of the Democratic conservatives were southerners,[29] But more than one-fourth of the northerners (mostly from the West and border states) leaned in a conservative direction.

Moreover, when seniority is taken into account, the position of the conservatives was even stronger. Table 7-2 shows the distribution of conservative coalition scores by party and seniority. (Senior members are those above the median in Senate seniority.) Seventy-three percent of the senior Democrats and 96 percent of the senior Republicans had scores over 50. Indeed, a majority of the senior senators were very conservative, with scores over 80.

This conservative dominance among the senior members of the Senate translated into dominance of Senate committees, especially of the prestige committees: Appropriations, Armed Services, Finance, and Foreign Relations.

Table 7-1 Ideological Distribution in the Senate by Party and Region, 1957-1958 (in percent)

Conservative Coalition Support Scores	Northern Democrats	Southern Democrats	All Democrats	Republicans	All Members
0-20	55.6	4.5	32.7	2.1	17.7
21-50	18.5	9.1	14.3	6.4	10.4
51-80	18.5	36.4	26.5	36.2	31.3
81-100	7.4	50.0	26.5	55.3	40.6
Total	100.0	100.0	100.0	100.0	100.0
(N)	(27)	(22)	(49)	(47)	(96)

Note: As used here, the term "conservative coalition" means a voting alliance of Republicans and Southern Democrats against the Northern Democrats in Congress. A conservative coalition support score is the percentage of conservative coalition votes on which a member votes "yea" or "nay" *in agreement* with the position of the conservative coalition.

Table 7-2   Ideological Distribution in the Senate by Party and Seniority, 1957-1958 (in percent)

Conservative Coalition Support Scores	Senior Democrats	Senior Republicans	All Senior	Junior Democrats	Junior Republicans	All Junior
0-20	23.1	4.2	14.0	43.5	—	21.7
21-50	3.8	—	2.0	26.1	13.0	19.6
51-80	34.6	29.2	32.0	17.4	43.5	30.4
81-100	38.5	66.7	52.0	13.0	43.5	28.3
Total	100.0	100.0*	100.0	100.0	100.0	100.0
(N)	(26)	(24)	(50)	(23)	(23)	(46)

* Rounding Error.

Table 7-3 shows the ideological distribution of senior committee members in the 85th Congress. Among these members, who had the greatest impact on shaping legislation in committees, the representation of liberals was small, and on the prestige committees it was practically nil. And conservative dominance among the senior members of the Senate led, of course, conservative control of the most important positions of all — committee chairmanships and ranking minority memberships. (See Table 7-4.)

Table 7-3   Ideological Distribution of Senior Committee Members in the Senate, 1957-1958 (in percent)

Conservative Coalition Support Scores	Prestige Committees	Other Committees	All Committees
0-20	8.3	21.8	17.5
21-50	2.8	7.7	6.1
51-80	36.1	33.3	34.2
81-100	52.8	37.2	42.1
Total	100.0	100.0	99.9*
(N)	(36)	(78)	(114)

* Rounding Error

Note: The prestige committees are Appropriations, Armed Services, Finance, and Foreign Relations. Senior members are those at or above the median committee seniority in each party on each committee.

157

Table 7-4   Ideological Distribution of Top Committee Positions in the Senate, 1957-1958 (in percent)

Conservative Coalition Support Scores	Committee Chairmanships	Ranking Minority Memberships	Total
0-20	20.0	—	10.0
21-50	6.7	—	3.3
51-80	40.0	40.0	40.0
81-100	33.3	60.0	46.7
Total	100.0	100.0	100.0
(N)	(15)	(15)	(30)

Nor was the power of the conservatives simply due to the many important positions, especially key committee and subcommittee chairmanships, they held; perhaps more importantly, conservatives mutually reinforced each other. As one liberal Democrat told us:

> When I first arrived here in — — —, you had a situation where committee chairmen regularly supported other committee chairmen, ... and members supported the chairmen more regularly — it was pretty much a practice. ... So you had a couple of things going. You had the majority leader [Johnson] supporting all the chairmen, the chairmen supporting the majority leader, and it therefore gave the chairman of each committee more power.

The senior members did not hesitate to use these leadership positions to sanction their opponents. The same Democrat said:

> Now when you had [Robert] Kerr here and Public Works, you may just not end up with any projects going through there, period. And there were a bunch of guys around, old man [Harry F.] Byrd and various old timers, that didn't hesitate at all to stick you.[30]

Thus the conservatives were in control of the Senate in the 1950s, but in the 1970s this is no longer the case. Precisely how, then, has the distribution of power in the Senate change and why did the change occur?

The first seeds of the decline of conservative dominance were planted by a somewhat unlikely source — Lyndon B. Johnson. When he became the Democratic leader in 1953, Johnson began to centralize power in himself as leader.

> Johnson had long since decided that the Senate ... could be mobilized and shaped, depending on the quality of its leaders. Johnson wanted to streamline the Senate's power structure, breaking the power of [Richard] Russell's conservative coalition and making it part of the regular leadership.[31]

We will consider the leadership of Lyndon Johnson in more detail below, when we contrast it with Mike Mansfield's leadership. Here we wish to note only one aspect — the institution of the "Johnson rule." [32] Before Johnson became leader, the Democratic Steering Committee, which makes committee assignments for Democrats, assigned members almost exclusively on the basis of seniority. This was the cause of the dominance of conservative Democrats on the most important committees.

Johnson changed this pattern by instituting the rule that each new Democratic member of the Senate would be guaranteed assignment to at least one major committee — a rule that persists to the present day.[33] Even under Johnson, freshmen liberals were able to get good committee positions earlier than had been true in the past (although Johnson's moderately conservative allies benefited more than the liberals[34]); under Mansfield, the benefit to junior liberals was even greater. As a conservative Southern Democrat who was close to Johnson said:

> When Johnson started putting a freshman guy on a major committee he immediately broke down the strength of the inner club. When the inner club used to meet ——— all the chairmen — and all the young fellows, the fellows who'd been there six years or maybe twelve years and still hadn't got in, that club really ran the Senate. But when Johnson put a freshman on each one of these committees — broadened the base of it — that made everybody a part.[35]

The next step in the transformation of the Senate was the cataclysmic election of 1958. As we have noted, since the election of 1950 the Senate's membership had been divided almost evenly between the two parties. But in 1958, recession, scandal, and Sputnik came together to increase the number of Democrats in the Senate from 49 to 64. Moreover, all of the Democratic freshmen were elected from states outside the South, and most of them were liberals.[36]

The election was the beginning of a period in which the old norms of apprenticeship and specialization would be detrimental to the policy commitments of a large number of junior Democrats. Figure 7-1 shows the number of Northern Democrats who had served less than six years as of the convening of each Congress from 1951 through 1973.[37] From 1951 through 1957, the number of junior Northern Democrats ranged between nine and eleven. The "class of '58" increased this number to 22, and this was supplemented by more northerners who entered between 1959 and 1963. The number sharply decreased with the Republican gains of the late 1960s and the increased seniority of those elected earlier, but by then the impact had already been made.

A related factor in Senate change was the growth of two-party competition in the South. From the end of Reconstruction through 1960, Democrats totally controlled the Senate seats from the South. This control began to break down in 1961, with the election of John Tower (R-Texas) to fill the vacancy caused by Lyndon Johnson's resignation to become vice president, and by 1973 the number of southern Republican senators had grown to seven.

These two patterns — the influx, beginning in 1958, of many Northern Democrats and the decline in the number of Southern Democrats — combined to break the dominance of southerners within the Democratic party in the Senate. Figure 7-2 presents the data on what proportion southerners represented of the Democratic membership of the Senate at the opening of each Congress from 1947

Figure 7-1   Northern Democratic Senators Serving Less Than Six Years, 1951-
1973

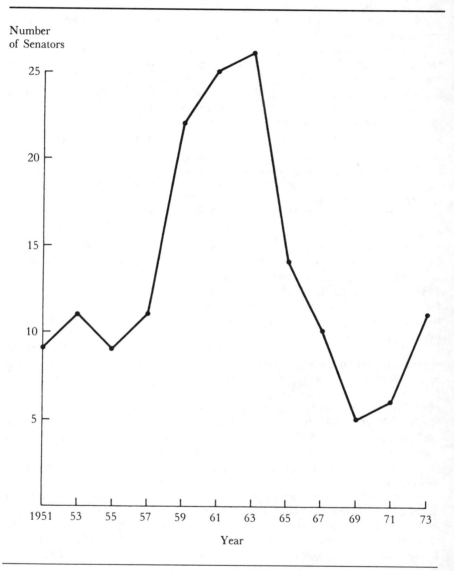

Number
of Senators

Year

to 1973. Their high point was 49 percent in 1947, when, as a result of the 1946
elections, the Democrats lost control of the Senate. Since the 1958 elections, their
proportion has declined almost continuously. In 1973, southerners held barely
one-fourth of the Democratic seats.

Figure 7-2   Southerners as a Percentage of the Democratic Party in the Senate

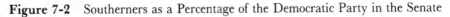

Southerners as
a Percentage of
All Democrats

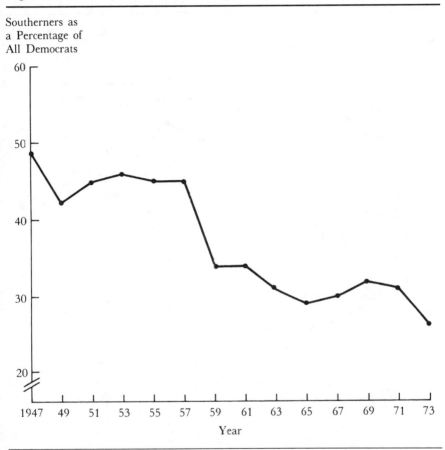

The importance of the "class of '58" in the transformation of the Senate can hardly be overestimated. It turned the already existing ideological gap between junior and senior senators into a gulf. Figure 7-3 graphs the mean conservative coalition scores of senators above and below the median seniority in the Senate from 1957 to 1973. In the 85th Congress the difference between the two groups was 13 points; in the 86th Congress it was 24 points. This difference led a substantial number of the junior Democrats to refuse to follow the wishes of Majority Leader Johnson and the conservatives who dominated the Senate.[38]

More significant than the initial election of the "class of '58" was its survival. The rescinding defeat of Republican presidential nominee Barry Goldwater in 1964 permitted every member of the class who sought reelection to be successful, and most were reelected again in 1970. Their strength, moreover,

161

Figure 7-3   Mean Conservative Coalition Support Scores of Senators Above
and Below Median Senate Seniority

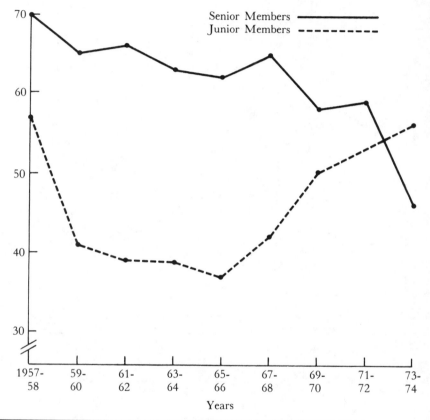

Mean Conservative
Coalition
Support Scores

Senior Members ━━━━━━
Junior Members ━ ━ ━ ━ ━

Years

was buttressed by the survival of the liberals elected in 1960 and 1962. By the
93rd Congress, the senior members of the Senate were on average more liberal
than the junior members (see Figure 7-3).

A fourth factor in Senate change is the transition in the Senate's leadership
from Lyndon Johnson, who served as majority leader from 1955 to 1961, to Mike
Mansfield. Many observers of the Senate have argued that the stark contrast in
the styles of the two leaders has had important implications for the operation of
the body.[39]

Beginning in 1953, Johnson attempted to centralize control over outcomes in
the Senate in himself. As John Stewart has said, Johnson "sought to control the
realistic choices open to senators in such a way that a sufficient majority saw their

immediate political interests better served by supporting the senatorial party program than by opposing it.[40] One liberal Democrat who chafed under Johnson's domination of the Senate described the situation this way:

> When Lyndon Johnson was Majority Leader, the Senate was just like it was an executive agency and he was the head of it, and it was a private corporation which he owned. He made all the decisions.

Mike Mansfield, on the other hand, chose not to attempt to dominate the Senate, but to serve it. The

> word, "coequal," sums up Mike Mansfield's view of his role as leader of the majority Democrats in the Senate: His principal duty was to maintain a system which permitted individual, coequal senators the opportunity to conduct their affairs in whatever way they deemed appropriate.[41]

One Democrat who served with both leaders thus contrasts their leadership styles:

> Johnson was aggressive and Mansfield is more the organizer, manager. I think he sensed his primary duty is to insure the Senate moves in the conduct of its business in the most orderly fashion that we can. The result of our actions, while I'm sure he feels strongly on a lot of issues, he leaves up to each individual. Lyndon Johnson wanted to influence the outcome of every decision — not just insure that we acted, but acted in a certain way.

One of the most important instruments available to Johnson in his attempts to control the Senate was the Democratic Steering Committee. As leader, Johnson appointed members of the Steering Committee and then dominated its deliberations. "Johnson . . . viewed each committee assignment as an opportunity for augmenting his personal resources for bargaining and negotiation on other issues." [42] Senators who went along with Johnson would receive assignments to the committees they coveted, and those who didn't go along wouldn't.[43] And everyone knew that it was Lyndon Johnson who controlled the outcomes. One liberal Democrat on the Steering Committee said, "He [Johnson] would come into the Steering Committee with his list, and that would be it. He'd just tell the Steering Committee who would be on. They had no function at all."

As with other facets of his leadership, Mansfield has approached the Steering Committee differently. He has not attempted to control its decisions, but has permitted it to work its will. Today, most vacancies on committees are filled simply by accommodating the preferences of requesters, and when there is competition for a vacancy, the contest is settled by secret ballot.

This is not to say that Mansfield has had no impact on the Steering Committee, for he has and the impact has been profound. As majority leader, Mansfield has used his power to fill vacancies on the Steering Committee to liberalize the committee's membership and to make it more representative of Senate Democrats. Figure 7-4 presents the mean conservative coalition scores of members of the Steering Committee and other Democratic senators not on the committee from 1957 to 1973. During these years the membership of the committee has become more and more ideologically representative of Senate

163

Figure 7-4   Mean Conservative Coalition Support Scores of Members of the
Democratic Steering Committee and Other Democrats, 1957-1974

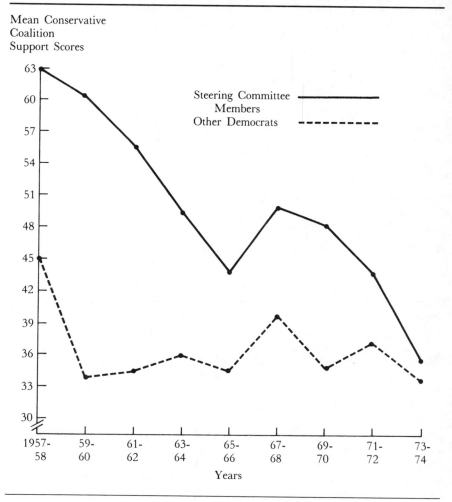

Mean Conservative
Coalition
Support Scores

Steering Committee Members ———

Other Democrats – – – – – – – –

Years

Democrats in general. Indeed, in 1973 the support scores of members on and off
the committee were virtually identical.

As Figure 7-4 shows, the mean conservative coalition score of committee
members began to decline before 1961 when Mansfield became leader and thus
one might suspect that Johnson himself began the deliberate liberalization of the
committee. This, however, is not the case. Each leader was able to choose among
only a subset of the Democratic members; that is, a senator who was already on
the committee could not be chosen again, nor, by tradition, could a senator from

the same state as a committee member be chosen. These constraints left a "pool" of members from which Steering Committee vacancies could be filled. Table 7-5 shows the liberalism of steering committee appointees by Johnson and Mansfield versus the pool of possible appointees. It compares the conservative coalition score of committee appointees to the mean score of all Senate Democrats who were neither committee members nor from the same state as a member during the Congress the appointment was made.[44] Although two of Johnson's three appointments were a bit more liberal than those senators who were already on the committee, all three were more conservative than the average member of the pool. Mansfield, on the other hand, appears (especially in his first six years as leader) to have gone out of his way to appoint liberals. Indeed, the names reveal even more than the scores. Johnson's three appointees were Richard Russell of Georgia, Olin Johnston of South Carolina, and Alan Bible of Nevada. The first was the dean of the "Senate Establishment," and the other two were moderate conservatives like Johnson himself. Mansfield's first four appointments were Thomas Dodd of Connecticut, Harrison Williams of New Jersey, Joseph Clark of Pennsylvania (all in 1961), and Paul Douglas of Illinois (in 1963). All were liberals, and the last two were among the most outspoken opponents of the "Establishment." [45]

Thus, the change in the composition of the Democratic Steering Committee has been both deliberate and extensive. As the data in Table 7-6 show, in 1957 only one-third of the committee's members had conservative coalition scores of 50 or less; by 1973, the proportion was more than two-thirds.[46]

To summarize, during the period between 1957 and 1973 four factors have combined to transform the distribution of power in the Senate. The institution of the "Johnson rule," a substantial influx of liberal Northern Democrats (and their increasing seniority), a decline in the number and relative strength of Southern Democrats, and finally the changing of majority leaders have worked together to redistribute control of the important positions of institutional power in the Senate.

Table 7-5 Liberalism of Steering Committee Appointees vs. the "Pool" of Possible Appointees

| | Appointees | | | | | |
| | More Liberal than "Pool" | | More Conservative than "Pool" | | Total | |
Leader and Years	N	%	N	%	N	%
Johnson: 1957-59	0	—	3	100	3	100
(Mansfield: 1961-66)	(6	86)	(1	14)	(7	100)
(Mansfield: 1967-73)	(8	57)	(6	43)	(14	100)
Mansfield: 1961-73	14	67	7	33	21	100
Total	14	58	10	42	24	100

Table 7-6   Ideological Distribution of Members of the Democratic Steering Committee, 1957 and 1973 (in percent)

Conservative Coalition Support Scores	(1) 1957	(2) 1973	Change (2 - 1)
0-20	26.7	52.6	+25.9
21-50	6.7	15.8	+9.1
51-80	26.7	15.8	-10.9
81-100	40.0	15.8	-24.2
Total	100.1*	100.0	
(N)	(15)	(19)	

* Rounding Error

We already have discussed the change in the membership of the Democratic Steering Committee. Table 7-7 shows the ideological distribution of senior members on all committees in 1957 and 1973, and Table 7-8 presents the same data for the four prestige committees. The data show that the more liberal members gained substantially, among both Democrats and Republicans. Among Democrats, the gain on the prestige committees was enormous. In 1957, only 17 percent of the senior Democratic members of prestige committees had conservative coalition scores of 50 or less; in 1973 more than 60 percent of the members had such scores.

Because of its importance and because of its domination by the conservatives in the 1950s, the Appropriations Committee is due special attention. The committee controlled the money, and thus its members could determine, at lease initially, whose pet programs were funded and whose were not. One index to its importance is that a member had to be quite senior to be assigned to the committee. Matthews's data show that in the 80th through the 84th Congresses, the mean seniority of members appointed to Appropriations was second only to the mean seniority of members appointed to Foreign Relations.[47] And, of course, the appointment of senior members largely meant that appointment of Southern Democrats and conservative Republicans. For example, Paul Douglas, writing about the committee when he first came to the Senate in 1949, said:

> Ten of the thirteen Democrats, including the five top-ranking members, were either Southern or pro-Southern. Moreover, two of the remaining three members were ambivalent in their attitudes and frequently traded with the Southerners.[48]

By 1957 there was little change in the makeup of the committee. The Democratic membership of Appropriations was more conservative than that of any other Senate committee.[49] By 1973, however, the liberal gain was substantial, especially among the more moderate members (See Table 7-9). In 1957, a majority of the members were very conservative (56.5 percent with scores over 80), but in 1973 the liberals and moderate liberals controlled a majority of the seats (57.7 percent with scores under 51). Indeed, liberal-leaning members were close to a majority among Republicans."[50] As a result, the committee was still unrepresentative of the Senate, but in 1973 it was slightly more liberal.[51]

Table 7-10 shows the data on the ideological distribution of subcommittee chairmanships. Although the liberal gains have been less dramatic here than in the other institutional positions we have examined, they are still substantial — especially on the more important committees. Overall, it is the very liberal members who have gained the most (they now have a majority of the subcommittee chairs), and the moderate conservatives who have lost the most.

Finally, we turn to a consideration of the control of the most important positions of institutional power in the Senate: committee chairmanships. As Table 7-11 shows, it is here that the least change has taken place. To be sure, in 1957 the conservative leaning members (scores of 51-100) controlled two-thirds of the chairmanships, and in 1973 the proportion had decreased to less than half, but the shift has been almost exclusively from moderate conservatives to moderate liberals.

As we have seen, the distribution of power in the Senate shifted between 1957 and 1973. Control of the important positions of institutional power passed from a group of conservative (and, in most instances, very conservative) senators to a group of much more liberal senators. But to what extent did the Senate's folkways persist or change?

The Senate's Folkways in the 1970s

General Benefit Norms

As we expected, the general benefit norms have continued to exist largely as Matthews described them. Take courtesy, for example. One cannot observe the Senate today, on the floor or in committee, without noting the continuity of this folkway. One hears the same flowery language, the same deliberate civility, the same praise of colleagues that characterized the Senate of the 1950s.[52] This customary courtesy also was noted in our interviews. One liberal Democrat said:

> There is a feeling of comradeship in the Senate and people never fight against a colleague. Oh, once in a while it happens, but not very often, and that is looked down upon.[53]

The members, moreover, continue to recognize the practical benefits of courteous practices. One moderate Republican said:

> These are little things that at times look highly exaggerated in the Senatorial context and they are; but very frankly, I don't think, if we didn't practice these, that we would have any semblance of order in the Senate. I think it's the catalyst that maintains a semblance of order. If we didn't stand up and go through a lot of this "my distinguished colleague" and on and on, we'd end up probably in trouble at times.[54]

167

Table 7-7 Ideological Distribution of Senior Committee Members in the Senate, 1957 and 1973 (in percent)

Conservative Coalition Support Scores	Democrats			Republicans			Total		
	(1) 1957	(2) 1973	(3) 2-1	(4) 1957	(5) 1973	(6) 5-4	(7) 1957	(8) 1973	(9) 8-7
0-20	28.3	38.2	+ 9.9	5.6	12.7	+ 7.1	17.5	27.5	+10.0
21-50	11.7	30.3	+18.6	—	14.5	+14.5	6.1	23.7	+17.6
51-80	30.0	9.2	−20.8	38.9	18.2	−20.7	34.2	13.0	−21.2
81-100	30.0	22.4	− 7.6	55.6	54.5	− 1.1	42.1	35.9	− 6.2
Total	100.0	100.1*		100.1*	99.9*		99.9*	100.1*	
(N)	(60)	(76)		(54)	(55)		(114)	(131)	

* Rounding Error

Table 7-8 Ideological Distribution of Senior Members of Prestige Committees in the Senate, 1957 and 1973 (in percent)

Conservative Coalition Support Scores	Democrats			Republicans			Total		
	(1) 1957	(2) 1973	(3) 2-1	(4) 1957	(5) 1973	(6) 5-4	(7) 1957	(8) 1973	(9) 8-7
0-20	11.1	26.1	+15.0	5.6	23.5	+17.9	8.3	25.0	+16.7
21-50	5.6	34.8	+29.2	—	—	—	2.8	20.0	+17.2
51-80	38.9	13.0	−25.9	33.3	17.6	−15.7	36.1	15.0	−21.1
81-100	44.4	26.1	−18.3	61.1	58.8	− 2.3	52.8	40.0	−12.8
Total	100.0	100.0		100.0	99.9*		100.0	100.0	
(N)	(18)	(23)		(18)	(17)		(36)	(40)	

Note: The prestige commitees are Appropriations, Armed Services, Finance, and Foreign Relations. Senior committee members are those on each committee at or above the median committee seniority for their party.

Table 7-9 Ideological Distribution of Members of the Senate Appropriations Committee, 1957 and 1973 (in percent)

Conservative Coalition Support Scores	Democrats			Republicans			Total		
	(1) 1957	(2) 1973	(3) 2-1	(4) 1957	(5) 1973	(6) 5-4	(7) 1957	(8) 1973	(9) 8-7
0-20	16.7	33.3	+16.6	—	18.2	+18.2	8.7	26.9	+18.2
21-50	—	33.3	+33.3	—	27.3	+27.3	—	30.8	+30.8
51-80	33.3	20.0	−13.3	36.4	18.2	−18.2	34.8	19.2	−15.6
81-100	50.0	13.3	−36.7	63.6	36.4	−27.2	56.5	23.1	−33.4
Total	100.0	99.9*		100.0	100.1*		100.0	100.0	
(N)	(12)	(15)		(11)	(11)		(23)	(26)	

* Rounding Error

Table 7-10 Ideological Distribution of Subcommittee Chairmanships in the Senate, 1957 and 1973 (in percent)

Conservative Coalition Support Scores	Prestige Committees			Middle Committees			Duty Committees			All Committees		
	(1) *1957*	*(2)* *1973*	*(3)* *2-1*	*(4)* *1957*	*(5)* *1973*	*(6)* *5-4*	*(7)* *1957*	*(8)* *1973*	*(9)* *8-7*	*(10)* *1957*	*(11)* *1973*	*(12)* *11-10*
0-20	23.1	36.6	+13.5	40.4	62.0	+21.6	35.3	47.1	+11.8	34.4	51.9	+17.5
21-50	7.7	29.3	+21.6	19.1	12.7	− 6.4	29.4	11.8	−17.6	17.8	17.8	0.0
51-80	38.5	9.8	−28.7	21.3	9.9	−11.4	23.5	29.4	+ 5.9	26.7	12.4	−14.3
81-100	30.8	24.4	− 6.4	19.1	15.5	− 3.6	11.8	11.8	0.0	21.1	17.8	− 3.3
Total	100.1*	100.1*		99.9*	100.1*		100.0	100.1*		100.0	99.9*	
(N)	(26)	(41)		(47)	(71)		(17)	(17)		(90)	(129)	

* Rounding Error

Note: *Prestige Committees*: Appropriations, Armed Services, Finance, Foreign Relations

Middle Committees: Agriculture, Banking, Commerce, Commerce, Government Operations, Interior, Judiciary, Labor, Public Works

Duty Committees: District of Columbia, Post Office, Rules and (in 1973) Veterans Affairs

Table 7-11 Ideological Distribution of Committee Chairmen in the Senate, 1957 and 1973 (in percent)

Conservation Coalition Support Scores	(1) 1957	(2) 1973	(3) 2-1
0-20	26.7	23.5	− 3.2
21-50	6.7	29.4	+22.7
51-80	33.3	11.8	−21.5
81-100	33.3	35.3	+ 2.0
Total	100.0	100.0	
(N)	(15)	(17)	

And another stated:

> If this group is to function in the sort of informal way that it does in which there is a widespread sharing of information, then there has to be a great deal of mutual confidence. If you are going to share information and get advice from any other senator, you have confidence in him, and this has led to a general abstention from personal criticism within the Senate. Perhaps not because people are not aware of their colleagues' faults, but because talking about them destroys this kind of atmosphere within which the maximum amount of work can be done with the minimum amount of red tape and formality. . . . It is generally a matter of universal reprobation if someone breaches those rules. . . . They are like table manners. They are designed to keep the food off the rug, not to — or not just to — conform to some sort of archaic code.

Similarly, the norm of institutional patriotism continues. Our interviews are replete with references to the high quality of the Senate as an institution and of the individual members who populate it. One freshman southerner said:

> I would say that the standards are very high in the Senate. I have been pleasantly pleased with that. I had a very high opinion of the Senate as it was, but I have been even more impressed with the standards of personal integrity in the Senate. Not that I've seen everybody tested under every circumstance, of course not. But I am exceedingly well impressed with the commitment to the national good and the lack of hypocrisy and the lack of demagoguery, relatively speaking, in the Senate.

Nor is the perception limited to southerners or Democrats. A freshman liberal, asked about the expectations of senior members in regard to freshmen, replied, "they expect you to maintain the dignity of the Senate," and a freshman Republican stated: "One thing members won't tolerate is attacking the Senate or especially attacking the integrity of its members." James Buckley (C/R—N.Y.)

in an article about his first two years in the Senate, described it as "a place where the rules of civility are still observed, and the rights and independence of each individual are still respected." [55]

As we noted earlier, the folkway of institutional patriotism offers special problems for reformers, who, to a degree, still recognize the importance of the institution and respond to it. One liberal who proposed, along with other members, substantial institutional reform told us:

> We were conscious of the problem and we were trying not to be critical. On the contrary, we were trying sympathetically to strengthen the institution. To point, in a sympathetic way, to some of the real difficulties we face. . . . Inevitably criticisms are made and some members may take these criticisms to be criticisms of the institution. I think we were very careful about this.

It is in regard to the existence of the norm of legislative work that the evidence is most overwhelming. Almost all of the senators interviewed made reference to this expectation. A number of senior members were asked what advice they would give to a new member who wanted to be an effective senator. Most of the responses related to this folkway:

> I believe the principle could be stated very simply — that is, keep up your work. (A Southern Democrat.)

> Get to know more about the bills in his committee than any member of the committee. Then when he starts speaking about the legislation he gains the respect of his colleagues and they listen to him and have confidence in what he says. Unfortunately, a great many members don't attend committee meetings except markup, and they know little about what is in the bill. There is no substitute for hard work whatever you do. (Another Southern Democrat.)

> I think that you're accepted by the Senate as a spokesman when they know you've done your homework. And if you haven't done your homework, you soon get a bad reputation. (A moderate Republican.)

> How do you advise a child to be an influential and effective family member? There isn't any big, one-shot, way you do that. It's just year after year of patience, willingness to carry at least your fair share of the work. (A liberal Democrat.)

We found, as did Matthews, a recognition by the members that the degree of observance of this norm of legislative work can produce a disparity between prestige inside and outside the Senate.[56] This recognition is reflected in their advice:

> Members of the Senate appreciate the efforts of the workers in the Senate, and they're not always the people who receive the most notice or the most recognition, or even, for that matter, the most credit on carrying on the work in the Senate. But it's appreciated by their fellow senators. (A Southern Democrat.)

> Establish yourself with those with whom you associate daily or regularly as a person who is competent [and have] a willingness to resist the always available short cut to a spectacular, one-shot news story. (A liberal Northern Democrat.)

As Matthews noted, senators with presidential ambition have special difficulty in conforming to the folkways,[57] and the norm of legislative work provides a serious problem for any member who actually launches a candidacy. A presidential candidacy requires that a great deal of time and attention be devoted to matters outside of a senator's legislative responsibilities, and it also requires frequent absence from the Senate. It was when members were asked about the impact on the Senate of its recent growth as an incubator of presidential candidacies that practically the only criticisms of the behavior of colleagues surfaced. And it was for nonconformity to the legislative work folkway that the criticisms were made. It affects the "willingness [of candidates] to become involved in the day to day operations of the Senate." "It wastes a lot of time. . . . It slows us down." The Senate "can't get a quorum." "It affects the effectiveness of their work and their committees." One liberal Democrat, who served on a committee with a presidential contender, said that, in general, such a candidacy "takes away from their duties," and in regard to his colleague in particular, He said: "he is not a working member at the elementary level of the committee."

Finally we turn to the reciprocity folkway. The norm still existed largely as Matthews described it, although our respondents primarily emphasized the aspect of integrity and keeping one's commitments, rather than the aspect of vote trading emphasized by Matthews's respondents. Like "hard work," integrity often was mentioned by senators as their advice to new members. One southern conservative said that he would tell a freshman:

> On pending legislation you'll have all sorts of urgings by many people to go a particular way, but I'd advise you to be slow in committing yourself — but having committed yourself to go through with your commitment no matter how painful it is.

Indeed, a number of members, when asked why Richard Russell of Georgia was such an effective senator (1933-1971), said that it was primarily his integrity — coupled with seniority and native ability — that led him to have such a great impact on the body. One southerner called Russell "the most respected man in the Senate in his day" and gave that tribute in these times to John Stennis. It was for the same reason in both cases:

> Everybody knows that when John Stennis gets up that John Stennis is going to tell them the truth to the absolute 100 percent of his ability. He's not going to tell them anything that he doesn't believe in and he's as honorable as a man can be.

Although all the senators we interviewed (with a single exception) stated that they had never seen nor taken part in any explicit vote trading, their comments made clear the relevance of votes to reciprocity. The comments, moreover, demonstrate that the relevance is to the spirit of the reciprocity folkway as Matthews described it: the helping of colleagues. The following comments, the first by a conservative Republican and the last two by liberal Democrats, are illustrative:

> A lot of time if a particular project is of great significance to a friend of mine, sure, I'll vote for it just because I like the guy, but not because I want him to support me on something else.

If a Senator wants something for his state, everybody's automatically pretty sympathetic, because we all have states we want to represent and we want to be helpful, whether it's a Republican or Democrat — and you respect a man who's fighting for his state; after all, that's one of your functions.

[It happens] this way — an issue comes up that doesn't mean a damn thing to [my state] and where there's no moral claim at all and [Senator A] sits on one side of me and [Senator B] on the other — or it could be Smith or Brown — and if it's something, by God, the _____ business [in Senator A's state] will just die if we don't get this or [a crop in Senator B's state] are going to evaporate. . . . If everything else is equal you'll vote with [Senator A] or [Senator B] — for them, but not with the idea that two months from now they'll save the _____ business.

As we expected, four of the folkways Matthews described — the four we have termed general benefit norms: Courtesy, institutional patriotism, legislative work, and reciprocity — are "alive and well" in the Senate today. What, then, of the other two?

Limited Benefit Norms

In regard to the apprenticeship folkway, the evidence from our interviews is clear, unequivocal, and overwhelming: the norm is simply gone. We were able to ask more than 40 senators directly whether a period of apprenticeship was expected. Of that number only two (both Republicans) thought that it was. All of the rest — members of both parties and of varying seniority and ideological persuasion — said that such expectations had greatly declined or (in the case of the overwhelming majority) were gone entirely. A senior Republican said:

At the time when I came a man who was very junior . . . served as an apprentice to the senior members. . . . That is all gone now, of course, and the freshmen usually come in as highly vocal young men.

A number of freshmen have spoken or written publicly about this fact. Buckley in his article recounted his experience:

The ancient tradition that stated that freshman senators were to be seen and not heard has disappeared. Somewhat to my surprise, on my initial rounds I was encouraged by the most senior members to speak out when I felt I had learned the ropes and had something to say. . . .[58]

As Buckley's statement indicates, the situation is not one of a large number of junior members deviating from the expectations of their senior colleagues. On the contrary, it is a situation in which the old expectations are gone, and junior members are pressed to participate.

The expectations are not communicated. On the contrary, all the communications suggest "get involved, offer amendments, make speeches. The Senate has changed, we're all equals, you should act accordingly." (A junior Democrat.)

Well that [apprenticeship] doesn't exist at all in the Senate. The senior senators have made that very clear, both Democrats and Republicans. (A junior Republican.)

175

When you are elected to the Senate, the feeling you have immediately is acceptance. You're there, you've made it. This is particularly true on the floor. You're told this in caucus that every Senator is equal, each has one vote. There's no period . . . of apprenticeship. (A middle-seniority Democrat.)

This type of encouragement was affirmed by senior members. One senior conservative Republican said: "We now hope and expect and encourage the younger guys to dive right into the middle of it." Such encouragement, moreover, even comes from outside sources. When he was asked if a period of apprenticeship was expected, a junior Republican described the following occurrence:

No, as a matter of fact, we had a very interesting conversation with the President [Richard Nixon] on that subject matter. After I was elected, those of us who were Republicans elected in _____ were invited down to the White House to talk to the President, immediately after we came. And he said, "I'll only give you one bit of advice." He said, "Speak up early. Don't sit around and just sit in the back and watch. Get up and participate and take part in things." He said, "That's for another day when a senator is supposed to spend the first two years listening to his colleagues. You fellows have been elected because you've got something to contribute, so go ahead and contribute."

The election of the "class of '58," as we have noted, was one important factor in Senate change. This view is buttressed by our interviews. The following quotation — indicative that not everyone was happy with the change — is from a senior, conservative Republican: "It [apprenticeship] was absolutely true when I first came. . . . But then when the class of '58 came in, they landed talking and they never quit, and those that are still there are still talking."

The leadership of Mike Mansfield appears to have been especially important for Democrats and the apprenticeship norm. Mansfield was a firm believer in the equality of senators, regardless of seniority.[59] One freshman told us, "Mansfield, he likes freshmen — period. He likes new blood. He is the first one to say that new members should be seen and heard." And Sen. William Hathaway (D-Maine) said that "one freshman was mildly chastised by Mike Mansfield . . . for not speaking up and making his views known at a Democratic caucus."[60]

Other factors also seem to have played a part in the decline of apprenticeship. One may have been the increased national visibility through the media of certain members. One Southern Democrat who entered the Senate in the mid-1960s said of Republicans Howard Baker, Edward Brooke, Mark Hatfield, and Charles Percy, who all were elected in 1966: "These were people who had been on the front of *Time* magazine, and I think they felt some compulsion to say something almost the day they got to the Senate."

Another factor may have been experience. Although Matthews found that senators who previously had been representatives or state legislators observed the norms more than other members,[61] a number of our interviewees indicated that such experience would be likely to make a member *less* willing to serve an apprenticeship. One Republican, elected from the House, said in regard to apprenticeship: "I don't think that is true in either body anymore. . . . Particularly among people who have had some prior experience in legislation." [62] And a Southern Democrat stated: "There wasn't anything intimidating to me about the U.S. Senate after 12 years of legislative work."

Thus the apprenticeship folkway is, as we expected, no longer operative in the Senate.[63] There remains only the norm of specialization to consider. Earlier we argued that there were two possible interpretations of this norm: first, that members were expected to work hard in their committees and develop expertise in the policy areas that the committees had jurisdiction over, and second, that in addition senators were expected to confine their attention almost exclusively to matters considered by their committees.

Evidence on which of these two interpretations of specialization was the operative one in the Senate of the 1950s is not clear. It is clear, however, that the limited benefit interpretation is not operative in the Senate of the 1970s. All of the senators with whom we discussed the matter said there was no bar to members being active in areas outside their committees if (as many offered the caveat) they know what they're talking about. One junior Republican, when asked whether he felt that other members had the expectation that senators should not introduce floor amendments to bills from committees other than their own, said:

> No, I don't have that feeling at all. I've been encouraged by senior senators to introduce legislation and to speak out on points that I feel it is necessary to vote on. There has been no effort that I have seen, with me or any other freshman, to try to limit you in any way.

And a Southern Democrat said:

> I don't think so. No, I don't think it would have been frowned on. . . . I think that has to be measured by our contribution. If I were a committee chairman, and some senator were popping up and popping off about something he didn't know a great deal about, I might be irritated. But if he could make some contribution to what was before the Senate, then my view is that that has always been welcomed by the Senate.

Finally, another Republican, who previously served in the House, addressed the question:

> No. I was a generalist in the House and I am pretty much of a generalist in the Senate. There are certain areas where I am more inclined to be involved because of my committee duties. I'm involved in all kinds of things. I'm involved with the Special Prosecutor now, which has nothing to do with my committees.

As in the case of apprenticeship, this does not imply that some members do not specialize primarily in their committees. They do, but the members see this as a matter of necessity, not of expectations by others. The senators do recognize, however, that they are expected to do their committee work and develop expertise in those matters, which is the general benefit aspect of the norm. A junior southerner, asked about specialization, said:

> No, in the sense that they're expected to. Yes, in the sense that they inevitably will to some extent. . . . It doesn't mean that another Senator can't work on [a bill from another committee] and can't offer amendments and take part in it. It just is much more difficult for him to do so.

177

And a junior Republican commented on the same point:

> I don't know if you're expected to as much as you're almost forced to because of the wide range of activity that takes place and just the constraints on your time that don't give you the opportunity to delve into other committee areas as much as you might like. I find that it's all I can do just to keep up with my own committee work, let alone get involved in something that's going on in another committee. So you do become dependent on members of other committees whom you learn to respect for their judgment as time goes on.

A senior southern conservative added:

> I don't know. I don't believe it is. I believe that Senators do specialize in their activities as far as their committees. But not entirely. That doesn't mean that they can't learn a lot about other things. If they are interested enough in other things to talk about them. But you are expected to know in greater detail and greater accuracy about the things that your committee has jurisdiction over. That is an obligation.

Some senators indicated that members must expect to be less influential when they speak on bills that do not come from their committees. First a southern committee chairman and then a senior Republican describe the situation:

> Of course it usually develops in the Senate that a senator's influence in that body is somewhat restricted to their own expertise. When I speak on an _____ bill in the Senate a lot of people listen to me. I am chairman of the Committee on _____ and they think I know what I am talking about. Whether I do or not, a lot of them are inclined to follow my leadership. . . . You develop natural leadership in the committees where you have jurisdiction and where you have expertise.

> I think it depends on the individual. He can have interests other than the committee he's on, and if he works on it and shows some ability in it, he has some hearing. But you don't have as much influence speaking outside of the committee.

Senators also indicated that members recently have found themselves less *able* to specialize. In part, this is due to the growth in the workload of the Senate and its individual members, but other influences also have contributed. One has been the growth of visibility of senators through the media, which we noted in considering the apprenticeship norm. One Southern Democrat described this factor:

> Now, the necessity to know something about everything probably comes from the difference in the kind of world we live in today compared to just a quarter of a century ago. You can't go into a major community of your constituency without some television commentator asking you anything he wants to, and most people are reluctant to say "I don't know." I learned to do it. It's a pretty hard thing to learn to do, but I don't know how the public accepts that. I would like to think they're impressed with an honest answer from someone, but the tendency in human nature is that you expound whether you know anything or not; you feel compelled to say something. And so this may, in self defense, compel many senators to know a very little bit about a great many things.

Another factor that members discussed in regard to this matter was the growth of the Senate as a source of presidential candidates, which we also discussed earlier. They said that the potential candidates themselves would be led to be generalists, but also that other members were influenced as well.

On the basis of our analysis of this folkway, we concluded that the limited benefit interpretation of the norm is not operative in the Senate. We also concluded that the general benefit interpretation of specialization does represent senators' expectations.

Summary and Conclusions

We began this chapter by reviewing the folkways which, Donald Matthews argued, described expected behavior in the Senate in the 1950s. We then classified these norms into two categories — general benefit and limited benefit — on the basis of whether, in our view, their observance provided benefits to all members in general or only to a subset of the membership.

The folkways of courtesy, reciprocity, institutional patriotism, legislative work, and (under one interpretation) specialization yielded general benefits, we argued. The folkways of apprenticeship and (under an alternative interpretation) specialization provided only limited benefits, and the beneficiaries were the conservatives of both parties who dominated the positions of institutional power in the Senate in the 1950s. We also stated that the distribution of power in the Senate had been altered greatly in the next two decades with the "conservative coalition" losing their control over most of the important institutional positions.

We then argued that, if our assertions concerning the redistribution of power in the Senate were correct, those norms we classified as general benefit should continue to be operative in the Senate, but the limited benefit norms should have disappeared. The basis for the latter prediction was that much of the basis for the limited benefit was gone and that the conservatives were much less able to impose sanctions on members who did not observe the norms.

Next we documented the change in the distribution of power in the Senate. Four factors that had an important impact on this change were discussed: the institution of the "Johnson rule," the influx of many liberal Democrats, a decline in the relative strength of Southern Democrats, and the change in the majority leadership from Johnson to Mansfield. These developments redistributed control of important institutional positions of power (for example, the Democratic Steering Committee, the Appropriations Committee, and subcommittee chairmanships) from conservative (and, in many instances, very conservative) members to much more liberal members.

Having shown that our predictions about the norms were based on correct factual assertions, we examined the accuracy of the predictions themselves. The information derived from our interviews with senators, supported our expectations. The five general benefit norms still appear to describe behavior that is expected in the Senate, but the folkway of apprenticeship and the limited benefit interpretation of the norm of specialization (if it ever existed) do not.

The Senate has changed in many ways since the 1950s. Yet perhaps the most striking thing about our findings is the continuity in the Senate's folkways.

Only one of the norms that Matthews described has clearly changed. This continuity is strong testimony to the important purposes these folkways serve for members.

Nevertheless, the norms have changed. The apprenticeship folkway is gone, largely because of the redistribution of power in the Senate and the factors that led to that redistribution. Moreover, these variables are interrelated in the contemporary Senate. The absence of an apprenticeship norm has its own independent impact on the distribution of power and on policy outcomes.

First, junior senators — whatever their ideological persuasion — participate more in Senate decisions, both in committees and on the floor. Such participation, if it is to be effective, requires the employment of staff and other resources in support of legislative efforts. Junior members find, however, that their share of such resources is much less than that of the more senior members. As a result, they have begun to press for an expansion of these resources. This has occurred through the Freshman Club. Perhaps the most significant of the handful of informal groups in the Senate, it is an organization of the 40 senators from the classes of '68, '70 and '72. While there have been other class groups in the past, this one is different. As one southern freshman said,

> I think they had some classes before, but I don't think that they leaned on people like we are. I think they were a little more leary of what they would do. They didn't want to rock the boat as much.

The success of the freshmen in expanding their resources means, in turn, further diffusion of power and even greater legislative activism on the part of new members.

Another important consequence of the lack of an apprenticeship norm has been the activism of junior members in internal Senate reform. In December of 1972, two first-term sentors, Charles Mathias (R-Md.) and Adlai Stevenson III (D-Ill.), took it upon themselves to hold ad hoc hearings on congressional reform.[64] These hearings included testimony by other members directed at pressing for and publicizing reform proposals.

Subsequent to these hearings, the freshmen went on to push for enactment of a number of their proposals. Sen. William Roth (R-Del.), elected in 1970, proposed in 1973 an amendment to the Senate rules that would have required Senate committees to hold public meetings unless a majority of the committee members voted to close a particular meeting. The amendment, which was supported by the great majority of other junior members, failed by a narrow 38-47 vote. (A milder open meeting proposal, backed by the Rules Committee, was then approved 91-0).[65]

Another reform proposal backed by junior members related to seniority. In 1973, Sen. Robert Packwood (R-Ore.), elected in 1968, and Sen. Robert Taft (R-Ohio), elected in 1970, proposed that the Republican caucus do away with their seniority method of selecting committee members and create a seven-member committee on committees that would make all assignments, including the choice of the top-ranking Republican on each committee. This proposal narrowly lost by a vote of 16-18, but the caucus did pass a compromise proposal by Sen. Howard Baker (R-Tenn.), elected in 1966, under which the Republican members of each committee would elect their ranking member.[66] In 1975, the Democratic caucus adopted a proposal by Sen. Dick Clark (D-Iowa), elected in 1972, which will permit secret ballot votes by the caucus on any committee chairman if one-fifth of the Democratic members request it.[67] These reforms — and others that have been proposed — further weaken the power of senior members and consolidate the position of junior senators.

Finally, what of the future of Senate norms? The whole basis of our argument leads us to expect that the general benefit norms will continue to be operative and that at least some of them (for example, legislative work) will be reinforced. What if the important positions again become quite unrepresentative of the Senate, this time (as appears possible) with a liberal bias? Will new limited benefit norms develop, or will apprenticeship return? If part of the reason for the disappearance of the apprenticeship norm was the deliberate decisions of Majority Leader Mansfield, could a new leader be successful in recreating the norm? We can foresee no new limited benefit norms, and we think a reinstitution of apprenticeship is most unlikely. Many factors, such as the ongoing redistribution of resources, societal expectations, and different recruitment patterns, make it implausible that these expectations can be revived. The "new" Senate is with us to stay.

POSTSCRIPT 1984

As the title of this chapter indicates, this study dealt with the Senate and its norms in the period from 1957 to 1974. Although it was not feasible to completely re-do the study, incorporating the events of the intervening decade, it is appropriate to provide some discussion of the period from 1974 to 1984.

The Senate

We contended that the change in the distribution of power in the Senate had a significant and predictable impact on Senate norms, so it is appropriate to begin our update with that question. Certainly the major event in the Senate of the last decade was the shift in majority control from the Democrats to the Republicans. During the entire period we considered in this chapter, the Democrats controlled the Senate, usually by a substantial margin. With the election of 1980, the margin shifted from 59-41 Democratic to 53-47 Republican, and the Republicans maintained their majority in 1982. This change in majority control was naturally reflected in the ideological balance of the Senate as a whole and in its committee structure. It will not be surprising that the net gain of a dozen Republicans meant the replacement of a number of liberals with conservatives. This effect was magnified, however, by the fact that, as a group, the Democrats who departed were particularly liberal and the Republicans who replaced them were particularly conservative.[68] These consequences of the 1980 election were coupled with an earlier trend in member replacement by which the ideological character of Northern and Southern Democrats, again as groups, tended to become more similar.[69]

The net effect of these events was to produce a Democratic contingent that was more moderate than that of the mid-1970s and a Republican contingent that was more conservative. Additionally, the Republican party was ideologically divided along seniority lines, with the senior group containing a significant number of moderate to liberal members, while the junior members were disproportionately conservative. The situation when the Republicans took control of the Senate was, to a lesser degree, a mirror image of the situation that existed among the Democrats after 1958. The junior members agitated for policy change in line with their ideological position, but Howard Baker and Ted Stevens of Alaska, both moderate conservatives, were the party leaders, and the major committees of Budget and Finance were chaired respectively by other moderate conservatives, Pete Domenici (N.M.) and Robert Dole (Kan.). Other Senate committees were chaired by even more liberal Republicans such as Mark Hatfield (Ore., Appropriations), Robert Packwood (Ore., Commerce), Robert Stafford (Vt., Environment), Charles Percy (Ill., Foreign Relations), and Charles Mathias (Md., Rules). These "old hands" resisted the more extreme initiatives of the junior conservatives, and this conflict led to friction among the Republicans.

Democrats were less divided along seniority lines. (There were, of course, not that many junior Democrats by the 1980s.) Both the senior and junior groups were divided fairly evenly between moderates and liberals, and the same was true of control of the ranking positions on committees, although here the southern conservatives were somewhat more prominent. Southern Democrats had continued to decline in terms of their share of the total Senate membership and of the Democratic caucus in that body. After the 1982 elections, only 11 of the 22 Senate seats from the South were held by Democrats, and even with the Democrats in the minority, southerners accounted for only 24 percent of the Democratic seats. (Recall that the last time the Democrats were in the minority, in 1953 and 1954, southerners held 47 percent of Democratic seats.) Because of seniority, however, the southerners had power out of proportion to their numbers. Only three of the 22 least senior Democrats were from the South in 1983, while eight of the 24 most senior were, and five of the eight were ranking members of committees.

In terms of party leadership, the situation was not quite as laissez-faire as under Mansfield and Hugh Scott (R-Pa.), but it was still an extremely long way from the dominating style of Lyndon Johnson and Everett Dirksen (R-Ill.). As we noted, Howard Baker was the Republican leader, beginning in 1977. As minority leader under a Democratic president, he sometimes offered Republican alternatives and at other times supplied crucial votes from his party in support of Carter administration policies such as the Panama Canal treaties. As majority leader under Reagan, he marshalled support for the president's economic program and tried to satisfy many of the policy demands of the full range of his colleagues (although the extreme conservatives were least satisfied). Baker did not attempt to dominate his colleagues, and his leadership style was widely admired. One colleague called him "the best leader we've had in the Senate in a half-century." [70]

Robert Byrd (D-W.Va.) also became party leader in 1977. His roles were the reverse of Baker's: first majority leader under a president of his own party, then minority leader under a Republican president. When he became leader, Byrd agreed to submit proposed nominees to fill vacancies on the Steering Committee, which made committee assignments, in advance to the Democratic Caucus. The Steering Committee continues to operate in a democratic and egalitarian fashion as it had under Mansfield. Also a moderate ideologically, Byrd did not try to dominate his colleagues to produce particular policy results, either in the majority or minority.

Senate Norms

The Senate of 1984 is different in many ways from the Senate of 1974. A new majority party is in control, with its senior members ideologically divergent from its junior members. Yet the egalitarian trend that opened up the Senate and shared power more widely among its members still holds sway, and there is no evidence that the norm of apprenticeship is any less dead than we believed it to be a decade ago. To the contrary, events continue to provide evidence that junior members of both parties regard themselves as full and equal participants and are accepted as such. The agreement by Democratic leader Byrd to submit proposed Steering Committee nominees to the party caucus was in response to the demands of junior members. In 1976, the Senate created a Temporary Select Committee to Study the Senate Committee System, which produced a major revision of the Senate's committee structure; the bipartisan panel was chaired by Adlai Stevenson (D-Ill.), who had served in the Senate only six years. The activity and assertiveness of the Republican conservatives elected in 1980 is further evidence of the disappearance of this folkway. There is no apprenticeship norm in the Senate today.

The changes in the Senate have put some strain on the other folkways, and perhaps more than we would have anticipated in 1974. Senators' presidential ambitions continue to interfere with the norm of legislative work. Members are absent from the Senate for extended periods to explore or pursue presidential campaigns. With the ever-increasing Senate workload, this behavior puts a greater pressure on other members. The ideological divisions in the Senate, and the policy initiatives of some "New Right" Republicans such as Jesse Helms (N.C.), have led to more frequent violations of courtesy and reciprocity. Helms has pushed conservative social issues like school prayer and abortion, using tactics that colleagues of both parties believe violate the Senate's unwritten rules. Barry Goldwater (R-Ariz.) said that he didn't think that even "a liberal like Teddy Kennedy" would use tactics like Helms did,[71] and Alan Simpson (R-Wyo.), another mainstream conservative, said of Helms, "Seldom have I seen a more obnoxious and obdurate performance."[72] The important point is that the behavior of Helms is viewed by colleagues as violations of expectations, which tells us that the norms are still intact.

Thus our conclusion is basically the same as it was 10 years ago. The Senate continues to be egalitarian and participatory, although, as a consequence, it finds it ever more difficult to meet its work burdens. Five of the folkways that were identified a quarter of a century ago are still operative, if a bit strained. The one limited benefit norm that disappeared is still gone, and shows no signs of being resurrected. We can conclude again, with more certainty, that the "new" Senate is here to stay.

Notes

1. Ralph K. Huitt, "The Outsider in the Senate: An Alternative Role," in Ralph K. Huitt and Robert L. Peabody, *Congress: Two Decades of Analysis* (New York: Harper and Row, 1969), 159.
2. There have been, of course, exceptions. Randall Ripley's *Power in the Senate* (New York: St. Martin's, 1969) was based in part on a series of round table discussions with senators and Senate staff held at the Brookings Institution. Two studies are Richard Fenno's *Congressmen in Committees* (Boston: Little, Brown; 1973) and David Price's *Who Makes the Laws* (Cambridge: Schenkman, 1972).
3. Donald R. Matthews, *U.S. Senators and Their World* (New York: Vintage Books, 1960).
4. See Ibid., chap. 5, Huitt, "The Outsider," Ralph Huitt, "The Morse Committee Assignment Controversy: A Study in the Senate Norms," in Huitt and Peabody, *Congress*, 113-135. Also relevant are William S. White, *Citadel* (New York: Harper and Row, 1957) and Joseph S. Clark et. al., *The Senate Establishment* (New York: Hill and Wang, 1963).
5. Matthews, *U.S. Senators*, 92.
6. Ibid.
7. White, *Citadel*, 82.
8. Matthews, *U.S. Senators*, 93. Indeed, our own interviews indicate that Matthews described the apprenticeship norm quite accurately. Without exception, all of the senators with whom we talked who were serving at this time agreed that this was expected behavior. One liberal, who deliberately decided to ignore the norm and made his first speech almost immediately, said that when he began the speech a group of senior members got up and walked off the floor to demonstrate their displeasure.
9. Ibid., 95.
10. Ibid., 97.
11. Ibid., 99.
12. Ibid., 102.
13. See Clark et al., *The Senate Establishment*.
14. This assumes that there is no question of principle involved and that no detriment to the *national* interest is perceived to result from such a program.
15. Matthews, *U.S. Senators*, 101; emphasis in original.
16. Our observation of both Houses of Congress leads us to the conclusion that there is no quicker way to become a pariah on the Hill than to become known as a person who doesn't keep his word.
17. According to William White, it would appear that Sen. Joseph McCarthy of Wisconsin was censured for violating the norm. "He was in fact tried not for intellectual crime against the people and the Republic (though this was the charge really debated pro and con among the public) but wholly for his conduct concerning the *Institution*." White, *Citadel*, 126; emphasis in original.
18. See Clark et. al., *The Senate Establishment*.
19. Ibid., 32.

20. Matthews, *U.S. Senators,* 113-114.
21. We do not imply that the apprenticeship norm, or any other limited benefit norm, was devised as a "plot" by conservatives. Clearly, its origins extend far back in the Senate's history. Nor do we imply that it was supported simply because of its policy implications for conservatives. Senators who were policy conservatives were also likely to be institutional conservatives who might expect an apprenticeship by new members quite independent of their policy views. We are simply arguing that a particular group of senators benefited from the existence of this norm in the 1950s and thus had a reason to try to perpetuate it.

    There is some evidence that this norm was not applied to conservatives to the degree that it was purportedly applied to liberals. When Richard Russell of Georgia first entered the Senate in 1933, he was asked by the Democratic leader, Joseph Robinson of Arkansas, what committee assignment he desired. Russell replied that he wanted Appropriations. When he was informed that other, more senior Democrats wanted that assignment, Russell stated that if he could not have this assignment he didn't want to serve on any committee. Robinson worked things out, and Russell got assigned to Appropriations. A strange apprenticeship, indeed, for the man who would become the prototypical "Senate type." See Stephen Horn, *Unused Power* (Washington, D.C.: Brookings Institution, 1970), 17.
22. See Rowland Evans and Robert Novak, *Lyndon B. Johnson: The Exercise of Power* (New York: New American Library, 1966), 114-115.
23. Matthews, *U.S. Senators,* 95; emphasis supplied.
24. Huitt, "The Outsider," 166.
25. Obviously, we are not the first observers of the Senate to notice this. See, for example, Ripley, *Power in the Senate,* chap. 3; Nelson W. Polsby, *Congress and the Presidency* (Englewood Cliffs, N.J.: Prentice-Hall, 1964), chap. 3; and Nelson W. Polsby, "Goodbye to the Inner Club," *Washington Monthly* 1 (August 1969): 30-34.
26. These data on committee assignments, and all others employed in this chapter, are taken from appropriate volumes of the *Congressional Quarterly Almanac.*
27. Evans and Novak, *Johnson,* 30.
28. The basis for all conservative coalition support scores in this chapter, except for those for 1957-1958 and 1973-1974, are from volumes of the *Congressional Quarterly Almanac.* Since Congressional Quarterly's support and opposition scores are both lowered by non-voting, all of these scores were converted by dividing the support score by the sum of the support and opposition scores. Because Congressional Quarterly did not begin compiling these scores until 1959, the scores for the 85th Congress (1957-1958) were computed by the authors from the roll calls in the *Almanacs* for those years. The scores from the 93rd Congress (1973-1974) are taken from *Congressional Quarterly Weekly Report,* Jan. 25, 1975, p. 194. All scores are for the full Congress. If a Senate seat changed hands during a Congress, the score of the member who served the longest time during a Congress is used. The 85th Congress is used as the starting point of our data analysis for two primary reasons. First, Matthews did his interviews during the 85th Congress, and thus provides a continuity between the two studies. Second, it is the Congress before the election of 1958, which was a watershed in Senate change.
29. The South is defined as the 11 states of the Confederacy: Alabama, Arkansas, Florida, Georgia, Louisiana, Mississippi, North Carolina, South Carolina, Tennessee, Texas, and Virginia.

    The prestige committees are Appropriations, Armed Services, Finance and Foreign Relations.

Senior members are those at or above the median committee seniority in each party on each committee.

30. Senator Kerr (D-Okla.) chaired the Public Works Committee's subcommittee on Flood Control, Rivers and Harbors, and Senator Byrd (D-Va.) chaired the Finance Committee.

31. Evans and Novak, *Johnson* 34.

32. See Ibid., 63-64.

33. Republicans, on the other hand, have maintained their practice of that time which was to make committee assignments entirely by seniority. The only exception (recently instituted) is that among newly elected members, every Republican can make one committee choice before any other new member gets a second choice.

34. See Evans and Novak, *Johnson,* 99-102.

35. We agree with Nelson Polsby that the proponents of the inner club "vastly underplayed the extent to which *formal* positions . . . conferred power and status on individual Senators almost regardless of their clubability." Polsby, "Goodbye to the Inner Club," 32; emphasis in original. It is those formal positions that are the primary focus of our analysis.

36. As a result of the election of 1958, the mean conservative coalition score of Senate Democrats dropped 10 points, from 50.2 in the 85th Congress to 40.2 in the 86th. The mean score for the 15 members of the "class of '58" was 18.4.

37. In this instance we have excluded the border states of Kentucky, Maryland, Missouri, Oklahoma, and West Virginia from the group of northern states. We are interested in a rough index of the number of junior Democratic liberals in the Senate, and many of the Democrats elected from the border states in the 1940s and 1950s were of a more conservative bent. The few liberal border staters who are omitted by this procedure would be cancelled, approximately, by the few conservative northerners who were elected.

38. For an account of Johnson's problems with the junior liberals in the 86th Congress, see Evans and Novak, *Johnson,* chap. 10, entitled "Too Many Democrats."

39. One excellent conrast of the two majority leaders is John G. Stewart, "Two Strategies of Leadership: Johnson and Mansfield," in Nelson W. Polsby, ed., *Congressional Behavior* (New York: Random House, 1971), 61-92.

40. Ibid., 61.

41. Ibid., 69.

42. Ibid., 64.

43. For some evidence that those Democratic senators who did not "go along" fared poorly in committee assignments, see Wayne R. Swanson, "Committee Assignments and the Nonconformist Legislator: Democrats in the U.S. Senate," *Midwest Journal of Political Science* 13 (February 1969): 84-94.

44. The data on Steering Committee memberships for 1967 to 1973 were obtained from volumes of the *Congressional Quarterly Almanac.* For 1956 to 1966, membership lists were obtained from Stan Kimmitt, the secretary of the majority, for whose cooperation we are grateful.

45. Mansfield's actions were in accord with the wishes of the Democratic Caucus. In 1961, the caucus passed a resolution endorsing Mansfield's statement that the Steering Committee should reflect the Democratic composition of the Senate both geographically and ideologically. See Clark et. al., *The Senate Establishment,* 31.

46. The larger N in 1973 is due to the increased size of the Steering Committee. Membership was expanded twice during the period: to 17 in 1965 and to 19 in 1973.

47. The mean seniority figures were 8.1 years for appointees to Foreign Relations and 5.8

years for appointees to Appropriations. The committee that ranked next was Finance with a mean of 3.0 years. See Matthews, *U.S. Senators,* 153.

48. Paul Douglas, *In the Fullness of Time* (New York: Harcourt Brace Jovanovich, 1972), 207.

49. The mean conservative coalition support score of Appropriations Committee Democrats was 70.3, while that of all Senate Democrats was 50.2. The corresponding figures for Republicans and all members were committee Republicans 81.7; Senate Republicans 78.4; all committee members, 75.7; all senators 64.1.

50. This was accomplished by the addition of moderate-liberal Republicans between 1971 and 1973: Edward Brooke (Mass.), Mark Hatfield (Ore.), Charles Mathias (Md.), and Richard Schweiker (Pa.). They were able to get on Appropriations because (1) the Republicans make assignments by seniority, (2) they are in the middle of Republican seniority, and (3) the Legislative Reorganization Act of 1970 restricted senators to only one assignment among the four prestige committees, thus preventing the assignments from going to more senior Republicans.

51. The relevant mean conservative coalition scores for 1973 were: committee Democrats, 40.5; Senate Democrats, 34.4; committee Republicans, 53.3; Senate Republicans, 72.2; all committee members, 46.7; all senators, 50.6.

52. This is not to say that there is never a breach. For example, in a meeting of the Senate Judiciary Committee on October 31, 1973, Birch Bayh (D-Ind.) said that Strom Thrumond (R-S.C.) was "browbeating" a witness. Thurmond replied that Bayh was "making a false, malicious statement" and that "If you are impugning my motives, you have gotten below a snake and don't deserve to be a senator." See *Congressional Quarterly Weekly Report,* November 3, 1973, 2881.

53. One senior senator, however, said that while he thought the norm was still strong, it was less strong than it used to be. "I am reminded of the story of a young woman who ran up to Senator Prescott Bush (R-Conn., 1952-1963), who looked every inch a senator, a fine looking man, and said, 'Senator Bush, is it true that members of the Senate treat each other with great courtesy and deference and respect, regardless of their political dispositions.' He said, 'Yes, that is true. Members of the Senate do treat each other with great courtesy and deference and respect, regardless of political dispositions. But if one of us breaks a leg — we eat him.' So it has a terminal capability."

54. The 1975 debate on changing the filibuster rule provides one example of the kind of reaction that occurs when senators think the norms are being violated. Vice President Nelson Rockefeller, who presided over the debate, had favored the reformers in his rulings. At one point he refused to recognize Sen. James Allen of Alabama, the leader of the antireform forces, on a parliamentary inquiry, and ordered the clerk to call the roll on a procedural motion. The reaction of members was immediate and negative. Sen. Russell Long of Louisiana called Rockefeller's action "one of the most improper decisions made by the Chair in the 26 years I have served here." Sen. Barry Goldwater of Arizona inquired whether the chair was required to recognize a senator making a parliamentary inquiry. The vice president informed him that it was not, that such recognition was discretionary. Goldwater responded: "That is what it says, but I never thought I would see the day when the chair would take advantage of it." Then Sen. Ted Stevens of Alaska, who had voted with the reformers, made this statement: "I voted for the first time the other way on this last vote because I believe in a change of these rules to 60 percent. But I also believe in the final analysis, whether it is 50 percent, 60 percent, 67 percent, or whatever it might be, my success in representing the desires and aspirations of the people of Alaska really, in the final analysis, rests upon the courtesy that exists in this body, one Senator to another and one Senator to the

Vice President. . . . I do not believe, really, that the Vice President recognizes how vital it is for senatorial courtesy to be extended to one another, all 101 of us, in order to accomplish the purposes for which we were sent here." *The Congressional Record,* daily ed., February 26, 1975, S 2631-2633.

55. James L. Buckley, "On Becoming A United States Senator," *National Review,* February 2, 1973, 147.
56. Matthews, *U.S. Senators,* 95.
57. See Ibid., 109-110.
58. Buckley, "On Becoming a Senator," 147.
59. In the debate with Sen. Joseph Clark in 1963 concerning the "Senate Establishment," Mansfield said, "So far as new Senators are concerned, I point out — and I have said this many times — that in this body the newest Member is the equal of the oldest Member and is entitled to just as much consideration." See Clark et. al., *The Senate Establishment,* 37.
60. The quotation is from a newspaper article by Sen. Hathaway, reprinted in the *Congressional Record,* daily ed., September 6, 1973, S16001.
61. Matthews, *U.S. Senators,* 103-107.
62. The assertion that apprenticeship is no longer expected in the House by senior members is supported by Herbert Asher, "The Learning of Legislative Norms," *American Political Science Review* 67 (June 1973): 501. Asher finds, however, that freshmen with state legislative experience are not less likely then other freshmen to believe that a period of apprenticeship is necessary, at least not when they first enter the House. See p. 510.
63. We are not saying that no freshmen who have entered the Senate in, say, the last 10 [the last 20?] years have served an apprenticeship. A few members told us that they did so. All of them, however, said that they did not choose to serve an apprenticeship because they felt it was expected, but because they thought it was prudent for them because of their particular circumstances.
64. *Congressional Quarterly Weekly Report,* December 2, 1972, 3094.
65. *Congressional Quarterly Almanac 1973,* vol. 29, 716-718.
66. *Congressional Quarterly Weekly Report,* January 13, 1973, 57-58.
67. See Spencer Rich, "Quiet Revolt Under Way in the Senate," *Washington Post,* January 26, 1975, A-1, A-23.
68. For data on this point, see Paul R. Abramson, John H. Aldrich, and David W. Rohde, *Change and Continuity in the 1980 Elections,* rev. ed., (Washington, D.C.: CQ Press, 1983), 204-205.
69. See Norman J. Ornstein, Robert L. Peabody, and David W. Rohde, "The Senate Through the 1980s: Cycles of Change," in Lawrence C. Dodd and Bruce I. Oppenheimer, eds., *Congress Reconsidered,* 3rd ed. (Washington, D.C.: CQ Press, forthcoming, 1985).
70. Quoted in Ibid.
71. Quoted in Bill Peterson, "Tempers Flare on Prayer Filibuster," *Washington Post,* September 23, 1982, A-5.
72. Quoted in Ornstein, Peabody and Rohde, "The Senate Through the 1980s."

III

CONFLICT AND CONSENSUS
IN CONGRESSIONAL COMMITTEE
DECISION MAKING

The concepts of conflict and consensus are central to the study of Congress and how it makes decisions. Congressional committees are an important ingredient in the process because they are particularly susceptible to external pressures from constituents, interest groups, presidents, administrative agencies, and political parties. Conflicts within congressional committees establish the battle lines among committee factions and structure the types of voting blocks that form and coalesce on the floor of either chamber (Parker and Parker, 1983).

Consensus within committees promotes decision rules that alleviate conflicts among members and enhance the probabilities that the committee's legislation will be approved by the full House or Senate. The more unified the committee, the less likely that damaging amendments to its legislation will be accepted on the floor. In this section we will look at four types of committee conflict: partisan conflict, ideological conflict, executive branch conflict, and constituent and interest group conflict.

Partisan Conflict

The most obvious cleavage within Congress is a consequence of the two-party system that ensures conflict between Democrats and Republicans. Numerous issues historically have divided the parties, and only in the areas of foreign and military affairs have these divisions been somewhat muted. Political parties operate in several ways to affect decisions within the committee, often in ways that create strains.

Not only do party leaders pressure committee members to follow the party's positions on legislation; they also may influence the level of partisanship within a committee through control over committee assignments. For instance, the highly partisan environment of the House Committee on Education and Labor is at least partially a result of the practice of assigning to the committee very liberal Democrats and very conservative Republicans — "members ... come from among those in their respective parties who already are in the widest disagreement" (Fenno, 1963, p. 201). Fenno makes the same observation about the House Committee on Ways and Means:

191

When party leaders make appointments to Ways and Means they make policy orthodoxy a test of membership. Candidates from both parties are checked to make sure they adhere to the party position on such matters as trade and medicare, and to ascertain whether they will follow the party leaders, especially the one in the White House (1973, p. 25).

Parties influence the workings of committees in a less explicit fashion as well. Because members tend to consult exclusively with those of the same party, the communication network that disseminates information among House members contains a partisan bias. "If congressmen turn to informants with whom they agree," John Kingdon (1973, p. 78) observes, "it is only natural that they turn to those within their own party." The party leadership also may supply voting cues by serving as a reference group within Congress (Matthews and Stimson, 1975, p. 97), especially since feelings of compatriotism are a natural product of facing a common electoral opposition.

The particular jurisdiction of a committee also can exacerbate partisanship if its work yields distinct political advantage. For example, the findings of the House Government Operations Committee, whose responsibility is to investigate executive branch agencies, can provide the party in opposition to the president with ammunition to embarrass the administration:

> . . . [W]hen the congressional majority and the President hold different party allegiances, the opportunity for partisan advantage is vastly increased. In such a situation the minority party in Congress is much more likely to be highly sensitive to criticisms of their President. The majority party, on the other hand, is in such circumstances given an ideal opportunity to carry out investigations under the guise of oversight which embarrass the current Administration (Henderson, 1970, p. 42).

In this way, partisan interests may affect the nature of committee activities. The possibility of politically-motivated investigations increases the likelihood of committee conflict. House committees with jurisdictional responsibilities that yield partisan advantages — such as Budget, Government Operations, House Administration, and Rules — tend to divide into partisan factions (Parker and Parker, 1981). The Budget Committee establishes expenditure limits that reflect the policy preferences and priorities of the majority party; the party in control of the House Administration and Rules committees has considerable power over internal House procedures and the perquisites of its members.

Some political issues — such as labor, education, and poverty policy — historically have divided the parties, thereby increasing the level of party conflict within the House Education and Labor Committee that handles them. (Fenno, 1973, p. 31). In a similar manner, opposing party stands on trade, social security, taxation, and medicare produce cleavages among Democrats and Republicans on the House Ways and Means Committee (Fenno, 1973, p. 24). House Public Works Committee members have split along party lines on longstanding issues such as:

> whether private or public power should be supported; whether the federal government or the state governments should assume responsibility for treating

water pollution; how the financial burden of the Interstate and Defense Highway system should be distributed; and finally, whether or not new construction in the District of Columbia should be undertaken (Murphy, 1974, p. 169).

In some cases, the way a committee handles an issue may change it from an obscure, nonpartisan matter to a highly visible, partisan concern. For example, land use policy and surface mining regulations — topics that were not prominent on the national agenda in the 1960s — captured widespread attention in the 1970s, dividing the House Interior and Insular Affairs Committee in significant ways (Parker and Parker, 1981).

Ideological Conflict

The committee system is affected by the same sort of divisions that characterize the composition of Congress in general: those arising from the historic North-South split within the Democratic party and those resulting from differences in ideological outlook between the parties.

Conservative Democrats, particularly those from southern states, tend to vote less frequently with the Democratic majority than their more liberal colleagues. This ideological division has led to the formation of a conservative coalition of Republicans and Southern Democrats who often vote together in committee and on the floor.

The ideological cleavages separating the parties have been intensified by the increased turnover in congressional membership, Norman Ornstein and David Rhode (1977) suggest. They contend that the decreased conservatism of new Southern Democrats and the substantial influx of Northern Democrats have produced a liberal shift in the ideological character of the Democratic party in the House. The result has been a widening of the ideological gulf between the two political parties. This would tend to strengthen ideological-partisan polarization within some congressional committees, especially those dealing with issues that are strongly partisan and ideological. Some examples of congressional committees that face an agenda filled with both unusually ideological and partisan issues are the House Ways and Means, Budget, Commerce and Interior committees.

While committee assignment practices, committee vacancies, and member preferences and personal characteristics may exercise a moderating influence on this ideological conflict, whenever the same conditions that exist on the floor of the House and Senate also arise within a committee (such as a substantial number of Southern Democrats as opposed to few or no Southern Democrats, as in many committees, or sharp partisan differences among committee members on issues that incite ideological feelings), committee cleavages surface.

The level of ideological conflict within committees, or the ideological composition of committees, is dependent upon the types of people leaving and joining the committee. Differences in the types of members who enter and exit the committee can alter its ideological complexion. Parties can exercise some control over the level of ideological conflict by assigning certain types of individuals to specific committees; this accounts for the ideological nature of the House

Education and Labor Committee. But, parties cannot normally make such changes unless there are vacancies on those committees. Furthermore, if there is little member interest in a committee, the parties may have an even more difficult time in trying to fill the vacancies with certain types of members. Therefore, party assignment practices, committee vacancies, and member preferences can operate to mute ideological conflicts. Parties could assign their least ideological members to certain committees, such as Appropriations or Standards, or moderate members may sway the ideological complexion of the committee by requesting assignment to that committee (for example, Southern Democrats on Agriculture).

Executive Branch Conflict

When the executive branch has a strong interest in issues falling within a committee's jurisdiction, differences between administration supporters and adversaries are apt to arise. Those committees with jurisdiction over critical executive functions — such as maintaining the national defense (House and Senate Armed Services), developing foreign policy (House Foreign Affairs and Senate Foreign Relations), and determining the level of government spending and revenue (House and Senate Appropriations, Senate Finance, and House Ways and Means) — are the most likely targets of ongoing executive influence. Foreign policy is particularly sensitive to presidential pressure because the chief executive constitutionally and historically has been viewed as preeminent in the conduct of foreign affairs. At the same time, the Foreign Affairs and Foreign Relations committees have sought to assert a more effective congressional voice in the conduct of foreign policy, resulting in a tug of war between the president and Congress (Fenno, 1973; Parker and Parker, 1979).

In cases where there is disagreement within an administration, divisions within a committee often may reflect differences among executive branch agencies as well as their relative clout within the government. The president may have many powerful allies both inside and outside of a committee, but an obstinate agency may wield equal or greater influence there (Maass, 1951). If there is no intra-agency conflict, however, an executive branch agency is even more likely to garner committee support (Dawson, 1962). The mutual advocacy relationships between agencies and congressional committees ensure that some members are unusually attentive to agency demands:

> Bureaucrats allocate expenditures both in gratitude for past support and in hopes of future congressional support; and congressmen support agencies both because they owe them for past allocations and because they desire future allocations (Arnold, 1979, p. 36).

The influence of the executive branch on committee decision making frequently is a mixture of presidential persuasion and partisanship. Although party loyalty is an appeal that a president invokes in trying to influence members within his own party, administration and congressional party positions may differ. Therefore, not all members of a president's party are courted successfully, nor are all party members susceptible to appeals for loyalty.

The attempts of presidents to gain bipartisan support for their policies exacerbates committee conflict in the sense that it destroys party cohesion. Unless the bipartisanship is consensual, the actions of presidents are apt to create legislative-executive cleavages in addition to partisan divisions. The result is to heighten divisions *within* the parties over support for the president's foreign policies.

Constituent and Group Conflict

Interest groups are ubiquitous features of the legislative landscape and, in the natural pursuit of their legislative objectives, they create an additional source of friction within committees. Normally, an interest group restricts its lobbying efforts to committee members who are sympathetic to or leaning toward its causes, avoiding those in opposition. As a result, committee members who support a group's interest coalesce around its position, and those opposed — either because of attitudes, ideology, or loyalty to other groups — also close ranks.

In addition, the fact that interest groups commonly reward friends and punish enemies at the polls (Fenno, 1973; Magida, 1975; Salaman, 1975) frequently solidifies attachment of groups to members and vice versa. The actions of one group in lining up supporters tends to stimulate other groups to do likewise. The result is a crystallization of group loyalties; furthermore, the existence of a mobilized opposition tends to force members to close ranks. The AFL-CIO, for example, "devotes enormous resources of manpower, money, and organization to help elect liberal Democratic Presidents and Congressmen — including members of the Education and Labor Committee" (Fenno, 1973, p. 34).

Constituency interests also can create conflict within congressional committees. In most cases a member's preference for a committee assignment is influenced by his or her desire to serve constituent needs (Masters, 1961, p. 354; Price, 1975, p. 6). Members with similar constituent interests — for example, House Agriculture Committee members with common interests in specific commodities — may find it strategically beneficial to organize as blocs to ensure that those interests are accommodated within the framework of any policy decision (Jones, 1961). The formation of such voting blocs is evidence of underlying conflicts within the committee over constituency interests; otherwise, there would be little need for such factions to form.

Constituency interests and the influence of organized groups frequently act together to influence committee decision making. An interest group is most effective and influential when it has close ties with members' constituencies. As John Kingdon (1973, pp. 143-146) notes, interest groups have little impact on congressional voting when they lack that constituency connection. Furthermore, members seek to accommodate the demands of their "strongest supporters" in their "reelection constituency" (Fenno, 1978, p. 19) because these supporters — both interest groups and voters — provide the financial aid and campaign assistance that help the incumbent to stave off electoral defeat.

195

Consensus in Committees

Most of what we know about consensus in House committees is based upon Richard Fenno's study (1973) of the "strategic premises" in committee decision making. Strategic premises reflect agreements among committee members on the rules for making substantive decisions. These agreements are designed to implement the goals of committee members:

> Each member of each committee faces this strategic problem: how shall I proceed in the committee to achieve my personal goals, given the environmental context in which my committee operates? It is a problem very difficult to solve on an individualistic, every-man-for-himself basis. For the solution, we can now see, necessitates some fairly complicated accommodations between the desires of the individual committee members on the one hand and the desires of the interested and influential groups that comprise the environment on the other (Fenno, 1973, p. 46).

Despite the uniqueness of each committee's strategic premises, two patterns can be detected, Fenno contends. Some decision rules are oriented toward ensuring the success of the committee's legislation on the House floor, while others seem primarily designed to serve the goals of its members. For instance, the major strategic premises of the House Appropriations Committee involve the reduction of executive budget requests and the provision of adequate funding for presidential programs, both of which appeal to a majority of representatives and thus are likely to be supported (Fenno, 1973, p. 55). Similarly, Budget Committee members "agree" to write legislation that will almost certainly pass the House (LeLoup, 1979, p. 241). These decision rules are designed to enhance the prospects that the House will approve the committee's legislation.

Other committees, however, adopt decision rules that appear to have little relevance for committee success on the floor of the House. In fact the decision rules actually may hinder House approval; at the very least, they diminish prospects for having the legislation accepted by the House without significant amendment. For example, House Education and Labor members have agreed to "prosecute policy partisanship" and to "pursue one's individual policy preferences regardless of party" (Fenno, 1973, pp. 75-76). Such strategic premises have prevented unified action on the Education Committee and often have resulted in challenges to its legislation from both members and nonmembers of the committee on the House floor.

We know relatively little about the role of consensus in Senate committees, but Lawrence Dodd's study of integration in the Senate provides some clues to the forces that promote and minimize committee conflicts. Like Fenno, Dodd (1972, p. 1139) uses the term "integration" to describe "agreement among committee members on very fundamental principles." He identifies two factors that affect committee unity: member seniority and similarities in member constituencies. Committees composed of members representing similar constituencies are more integrated than those composed of members serving dissimilar constituencies, and committees composed of senators with high levels of seniority are less integrated than committees composed of senators with little seniority. In sum, the composition of committees, in terms of the seniority of their members and the similarities in constituencies, appears to influence the degree of conflict among Senate committee members.

Richard Fenno's 1962 study of the House Appropriations Committee is one of the earliest attempts to analyze committee conflict and remains a classic example of the value case studies have for research on committee decision making. The question underlying Fenno's study was how members were able to minimize conflicts within their committee. He identified five characteristics that were instrumental to a committee's capacity to resolve internal conflicts before they spilled onto the floor of the House:

> (1) the existence of a well-articulated and deeply rooted consensus on Committee goals or tasks; (2) the nature of the Committee's subject matter; (3) the legislative orientation of its members; (4) the attractiveness of the Committee for its members; and (5) the stability of Committee membership (Fenno, 1962, p. 311).

These characteristics can promote a committee's harmony and prevent paralyzing conflicts. The fact that the Appropriations Committee deals solely in dollar amounts allocated to specific programs and federal agencies helps keep conflict in check and facilitates compromise because members can easily adjust funding levels for programs and agencies without sacrificing or breaching policy principles. Furthermore, the substantive and procedural repetition of the annual appropriations process promotes familiarity with key problems, provides ample opportunities for testing and confirming the best ways of dealing with them, and creates an environment for the emergence of informal procedural norms.

The relationship between subject matter and the level of committee conflict has implications that go beyond the Appropriations Committee. Conflict may be reduced if the issues under the jurisdiction of a committee permit cooperative solutions.

Barbara Hinckley's study (1976) provides convincing evidence of a linkage between subject matter and conflict. She classifies committees on the basis of "subject matter stakes." Specifically, Hinckley divides committees into two groups: those whose decisions produce only "winners" or "losers" (members only gain at the expense of others), and those with less competitive stakes (one member's gains do not require an equivalent loss on the part of others). The underlying assumption of Hinckley's analysis is that "legislators may find it easier to compromise and to exhibit cohesive behavior on subject matter permitting positive-sum as opposed to zero-sum solutions" (1976, p. 545).

In his 1974 study of the House Public Works Committee, James T. Murphy notes that the relationship between partisanship and the porkbarrel has been a major influence on committee decision making and legislative conflict. Partisanship exercises a considerable influence over the allocation of projects — such as dams, roads, buildings, and waterways — among districts represented by committee members. Contrary to popular lore, most porkbarrel authorizations are not the result of spontaneous and widespread vote trading among committee Democrats and Republicans. Rather, Murphy concludes, partisanship promotes distrust of the motives and behavior of members from the opposition party. Somewhat paradoxically, the electoral benefits of being awarded a project in one's district, combined with the inherent partisan suspicions that committee members harbor, actually leads to a level of cooperation between the parties:

> The threat of partisan allocations has induced the congressional parties to adopt relatively rigid allocation rules such that neither party can make substantial gains at the polls at the expense of the other (Murphy, 1974, p. 170).

Committee factions and coalitions also play a major role in committee harmony or discord, as discussed in the study by Glenn R. Parker and Suzanne L. Parker (1979). Party loyalty is one of the most prevalent pressures and provides a common vehicle for organizing voting blocs within committees. As a result, partisan factions can be identified within most congressional committees. In fact, the only committees without a high-profile partisan tenor to their deliberations (Armed Services, Foreign Affairs, and Standards of Official Conduct) are those dealing with topics that are intended to elicit bipartisan support.

The party, however, is only one of several sources of committee conflict: loyalties to constituencies, groups, ideologies, and the president also divide committees. Like partisanship, these pressures contribute to the formation of committee factions (Parker and Parker, 1979).

8. THE HOUSE APPROPRIATIONS COMMITTEE AS A POLITICAL SYSTEM: THE PROBLEM OF INTEGRATION
Richard F. Fenno, Jr.

Studies of Congress by political scientists have produced a time-tested consensus on the very considerable power and autonomy of Congressional committees. Because of these two related characteristics, it makes empirical and analytical sense to treat the Congressional committee as a discrete unit for analysis. This paper conceives of the committee as a political system (or, more accurately, as a political subsystem) faced with a number of basic problems which it must solve in order to achieve its goals and maintain itself. Generally speaking these functional problems pertain to the environmental and the internal relations of the committee. This study is concerned almost exclusively with the internal problems of the committee and particularly with the problem of self-integration.[1] It describes how one congressional committee—The Committee on Appropriations of the House of Representatives—has dealt with this problem in the period 1947-1961. Its purpose is to add to our understanding of appropriations politics in Congress and to suggest the usefulness of this type of analysis for studying the activities of any congressional committee.

The necessity for integration in any social system arises from the differentiation among its various elements. Most importantly there is a differentiation among subgroups and among individual positions, together with the roles that flow therefrom.[2] A committee faces the problem, how shall these diverse elements be made to mesh together or function in support of one another? No political system (or subsystem) is perfectly integrated; yet no political system can survive without some minimum degree of integration among its differentiated parts. Committee integration is defined as the degree to which there is a working together or a meshing together or mutual support among its roles and subgroups. Conversely, it is also defined as the degree to which a committee is able to

Author's Note: The author wishes to acknowledge his indebtedness to the Committee on Political Behavior of the Social Science Research Council for the research grant which made possible this study, and the larger study of legislative behavior in the area of appropriations of which it is a part. This is a revised version of a paper read at the Annual Meeting of the American Political Science Association at St. Louis, September, 1961.

Source: *American Political Science Review* (June 1962): 310-324. Reprinted with permission from the author.

minimize conflict among its roles and its subgroups, by heading off or resolving the conflicts that arise.[3] A concomitant of integration is the existence of a fairly consistent set of norms, widely agreed upon and widely followed by the members. Another concomitant of integration is the existence of control mechanisms (*i.e.*, socialization and sanctioning mechanisms) capable of maintaining reasonable conformity to norms. In other words, the more highly integrated a committee, the smaller will be the gap between expected and actual behavior.

This study is concerned with integration both as a structural characteristic of, and as a functional problem for, the Appropriations Committee. First, certain basic characteristics of the Committee need description, to help explain the integration of its parts. Second comes a partial description of the degree to which and the ways in which the Committee achieves integration. No attempt is made to state this in quantitative terms, but the object is to examine the meshing together or the minimization of conflict among certain subgroups and among certain key roles. Also, important control mechanisms are described. The study concludes with some comments on the consequences of Committee integration for appropriations politics and on the usefulness of further Congressional committee analysis in terms of functional problems such as this one.

I

Five important characteristics of the Appropriations Committee which help explain Committee integration are (1) the existence of a well-articulated and deeply rooted consensus on Committee goals or tasks; (2) the nature of the Committee's subject matter; (3) the legislative orientation of its members; (4) the attractiveness of the Committee for its members; and (5) the stability of Committee membership.

Consensus. The Appropriations Committee sees its tasks as taking form within the broad guidelines set by its parent body, the House of Representatives. For it is the primary condition of the Committee's existence that it was created by the House for the purpose of assisting the House in the performance of House legislative tasks dealing with appropriations. Committee members agree that their fundamental duty is to serve the House in the manner and with the substantive results that the House prescribes. Given, however, the imprecision of House expectations and the permissiveness of House surveillance, the Committee must elaborate for itself a definition of tasks plus a supporting set of perceptions (of itself and of others) explicit enough to furnish day-to-day guidance.

The Committee's view begins with the preeminence of the House—often mistakenly attributed to the Constitution ("all bills for raising revenue," Art. I, sec. 7) but nevertheless firmly sanctioned by custom—in appropriations affairs. It moves easily to the conviction that, as the efficient part of the House in this matter, the Constitution has endowed it with special obligations and special prerogatives. It ends in the view that the Committee on Appropriations, far from being merely one among many units in a complicated legislative-executive system, is *the* most important, most responsible unit in the whole appropriations process.[4] Hand in hand with the consensus on their primacy goes a consensus that all of their House-prescribed tasks can be fulfilled by superimposing upon them one, single, paramount task—*to guard the Federal Treasury.* Committee members state their goals in the essentially negative terms of guardianship—screening requests for money, checking against ill-advised expenditures, and protecting the taxpayer's dollar. In the language of the Committee's official history, the job of each member is, "constantly and courageously to protect the Federal Treasury against thousands of appeals and imperative demands for unnecessary, unwise, and excessive expenditures." [5]

To buttress its self-image as guardian of public funds the Committee elaborates a set of perceptions about other participants in the appropriations process to which most members hold most of the time. Each executive official, for example, is seen to be interested in the expansion of his own particular program. Each one asks, therefore, for more money than he really needs, in view of the total picture, to run an adequate program. This and other Committee perceptions—of the Budget Bureau, of the Senate, and of their fellow Representatives—help to shape and support the Committee members in their belief that most budget estimates can, should and must be reduced and that, since no one else can be relied upon, the House Committee must do the job. To the consensus on the main task of protecting the Treasury is added, therefore, a consensus on the instrumental task of *cutting whatever budget estimates are submitted.*

As an immediate goal, Committee members agree that they must strike a highly critical, aggressive posture toward budget requests, and that they should, on principle, reduce them. In the words of the Committee's veterans: "There has never been a budget submitted to the Congress that couldn't be cut." "There isn't a budget that can't be cut 10 percent immediately." "I've been on the Committee for 17 years. No subcommittee of which I have been a member has ever reported out a bill without a cut in the budget. I'm proud of that record." The aim of budget-cutting is strongly internalized for the Committee member. "It's a tradition in the Appropriations Committee to cut." "You're grounded in it. . . . It's ingrained in you from the time you get on the Committee." For the purposes of a larger study, the appropriations case histories of 37 executive bureaus have been examined for a 12-year period, 1947-1959.[6] Of 443 separate bureau estimates, the Committee reduced 77.2 percent (342) of them.

It is a mark of the intensity and self-consciousness of the Committee consensus on budget-cutting that it is couched in a distinctive vocabulary. The workaday lingo of the Committee member is replete with negative verbs, undesirable objects of attention, and effective instruments of action. Agency budgets are said to be filled with "fat," "padding," "grease," "pork," "oleaginous substance," "water," "oil," "cushions," "avoirdupois," "waste tissue," and "soft spots." The action verbs most commonly used are "cut," "carve" "slice," "prune," "whittle," "squeeze," "wring," "trim," "lop off," "chop," "slash," "pare," "shave," "fry," and "whack." The tools of the trade are appropriately referred to as "knife," "blade," "meat axe," "scalpel," "meat cleaver," "hatchet," "shears," "wringer," and "fine-tooth comb." Members are hailed by their fellows as being "pretty sharp with the knife." Agencies may "have the meat axe thrown at them." Executives are urged to put their agencies "on a fat boy's diet." Budgets are praised when they are "cut to the bone." And members agree that "You can always get a little more fat out of a piece of pork if you fry it a little longer and a little harder."

To the major task of protecting the Treasury and the instrumental task of cutting budget estimates, each Committee member adds, usually by way of exception, a third task—*serving the constituency to which he owes his election.* This creates no problem for him when, as is sometimes the case, he can serve his district best by cutting the budget requests of a federal agency whose program is in conflict with the demands of his constituency.[7] Normally, however, members find that their most common role-conflict is between a Committee-oriented budget-reducing role and a constituency-oriented budget-increasing role. Committee ideology resolves the conflict by assigning top, long-run priority to the budget-cutting task and making of the constituency service a permissible, short-run exception. No member is expected to commit electoral suicide; but no member is expected to allow his district's desire for federal funds to dominate his Committee behavior.

Subject Matter. Appropriations Committee integration is facilitated by the subject matter with which the group deals. The Committee makes decisions on the same controversial issues as do the committees handling substantive legislation. But a money decision—however vitally it affects national policy — is, or at least seems to be, less directly a policy decision. Since they deal immediately with dollars and cents, it is easy for the members to hold to the idea that they are not dealing with programmatic questions, that theirs is a "business" rather than a "policy" committee. The subject matter, furthermore, keeps Committee members relatively free agents, which promotes intra-Committee maneuvering and, hence, conflict avoidance. Members do not commit themselves to their constituents in terms of precise money amounts, and no dollar sum is sacred — it can always be adjusted without conceding that a principle has been breached. By contrast, members of committees dealing directly with controversial issues are often pressured into taking concrete stands on these issues; consequently, they may come to their committee work with fixed and hardened attitudes. This leads to unavoidable, head-on intra-committee conflict and renders integrative mechanisms relatively ineffective.

The fact of an annual appropriations process means the Committee members repeat the same operations with respect to the same subject matters year after year—and frequently more than once in a given year. Substantive and procedural repetition promotes familiarity with key problems and provides ample opportunity to test and confirm the most satisfactory methods of dealing with them. And the absolute necessity that appropriations bills do ultimately pass gives urgency to the search for such methods. Furthermore, the House rule that no member of the Committee can serve on another standing committee is a deterrent against a fragmentation of Committee member activity which could be a source of difficulty in holding the group together. If a committee has developed (as this one has) a number of norms designed to foster integration, repeated and concentrated exposure to them increases the likelihood that they will be understood, accepted and followed.

Legislative Orientation. The recruitment of members for the Appropriations Committee produces a group of individuals with an orientation especially conducive to Committee integration. Those who make the selection pay special attention to the characteristics which Masters has described as those of the "responsible legislator"—approval of and conformity to the norms of the legislative process and of the House of Representatives.[8]

Key selectors speak of wanting, for the Appropriations Committee, "the kind of man you can deal with" or "a fellow who is well-balanced and won't go off half-cocked on things." A Northern liberal Democrat felt that he had been chosen over eight competitors because, "I had made a lot of friends and was known as a nice guy"—especially, he noted, among Southern Congressmen. Another Democrat explained, "I got the blessing of the Speaker and the leadership. It's personal friendships. I had done a lot of things for them in the past, and when I went to them and asked them, they gave it to me." A Republican chosen for the Committee in his first term recalled,

> The Chairman [Rep. Taber] I guess did some checking around in my area. After all, I was new and he didn't know me. People told me that they were called to see if I was—well, unstable or apt to go off on tangents . . . to see whether or not I had any preconceived notions about things and would not be flexible—whether I would oppose things even though it was obvious.

A key criterion in each of the cases mentioned was a demonstrable record of, or an assumed predisposition toward, legislative give-and-take.

The 106 Appropriations Committee members serving between 1947 and 1961 spent an average of 3.6 years on other House committees before coming to the Committee. Only 17 of the 106 were selected as first term Congressmen. A House apprenticeship (which Appropriations maintains more successfully than all committees save Ways and Means and Rules[9]) provides the time in which legislative reputations can be established by the member and an assessment of that reputation in terms of Appropriations Committee requirements can be made. Moreover, the mere fact that a member survives for a couple of terms is some indication of an electoral situation conducive to his "responsible" legislative behavior. The optimum bet for the Committee is a member from a sufficiently safe district to permit him freedom of maneuver inside the House without fear of reprisal at the polls.[10] The degree of responsiveness to House norms which the Committee selectors value may be the product of a safe district as well as an individual temperament.

Attractiveness. A fourth factor is the extraordinarily high degree of attractiveness which the Committee holds for its members—as measured by the low rate of departure from it. Committee members do not leave it for service on other committees. To the contrary, they are attracted to it from nearly every other committee.[11] Of the 106 members in the 1947-1961 period, only two men left the Committee voluntarily; and neither of them initiated the move.[12] Committee attractiveness is a measure of its capacity to satisfy individual member needs—for power, prestige, recognition, respect, self-esteem, friendship, etc. Such satisfaction in turn increases the likelihood that members will behave in such a way as to hold the group together.

The most frequently mentioned source of Committee attractiveness is its power—based on its control of financial resources. "Where the money is, that's where the power is," sums up the feeling of the members. They prize their ability to reward or punish so many other participants in the political process — executive officials, fellow Congressmen, constituents and other clientele groups. In the eyes of its own members, the Committee is either the most powerful in the House or it is on a par with Ways and Means or, less frequently, on a par with Ways and Means and Rules. The second important ingredient in member satisfaction is the government-wide scope of Committee activity. The ordinary Congressman may feel that he has too little knowledge of and too little control over his environment. Membership on this Committee compensates for this feeling of helplessness by the wider contacts, the greater amount of information, and the sense of being "in the middle of things" which are consequent, if not to subcommittee activity, at least to the full Committee's overview of the federal government.

Thirdly, Committee attractiveness is heightened by the group's recognizable and distinctive political style—one that is, moreover, highly valued in American political culture. The style is that of *hard work;* and the Committee's self-image is that of "the hardest working Committee in Congress." His willingness to work is the Committee member's badge of identification, and it is proudly worn. It colors his perceptions of others and their perceptions of him.[13] It is a cherished axiom of all members that, "This Committee is no place for a man who doesn't work. They have to be hard working. It's a way of life. It isn't just a job; it's a way of life."

The mere existence of some identifiable and valued style or "way of life" is a cohesive force for a group. But the particular style of hard work is one which increases group morale and group identification twice over. Hard work means a long, dull, and tedious application to detail, via the technique of "dig, dig, dig, day after day behind closed doors"—in an estimated 460 subcommittee and full committee meetings a year. And virtually all of these meetings are in executive session. By adopting the style of hard work, the Committee discourages highly individualized forms of legislative behavior, which could be disruptive within the Committee. It rewards its members with power, but it is power based rather on work inside the Committee than on the political glamour of activities carried on in the limelight of the mass media. Prolonged daily work together encourages sentiments of mutual regard, sympathy and solidarity. This *esprit* is, in turn, functional for integration on the Committee. A Republican leader summed up,

> I think it's more closely knit than any other committee. Yet it's the biggest committee, and you'd think it would be the reverse. I know on my subcommittee, you sit together day after day. You get better acquainted. You have sympathy when other fellows go off to play golf. There's a lot of *esprit de corps* in the Committee.

The strong attraction which members have for the Committee increases the influence which the Committee and its norms exercise on all of them. It increases the susceptibility of the newcomer to Committee socialization and of the veteran to Committee sanctions applicable against deviant behavior.[14]

Membership Stability. Members of the Appropriations Committee are strongly attracted to it; they also have, which bears out their selection as "responsible legislators," a strong attraction for a career in the House of Representatives. The 50 members on the Committee in 1961 had served an average of 13.1 years in the House. These twin attractions produce a noteworthy stability of Committee membership. In the period from the 80th to the 87th Congress, 35.7 per cent of the Committee's membership remained constant. That is to say, 15 of the 42 members on the Committee in March, 1947, were still on the Committee in March, 1961.[15] The 50 members of the Committee in 1961 averaged 9.3 years of prior service on that Committee. In no single year during the last fourteen has the Committee had to absorb an influx of new members totalling more than one-quarter of its membership. At all times, in other words, at least three-fourths of the members have had previous Committee experience. This extraordinary stability of personnel extends into the staff as well. As of June 1961, its 15 professionals had served an average of 10.7 years with the Committee.[16]

The opportunity exists, therefore, for the development of a stable leadership group, a set of traditional norms for the regulation of internal Committee behavior, and informal techniques of personal accommodation. Time is provided in which new members can learn and internalize Committee norms before they attain high seniority rankings. The Committee does not suffer from the potentially disruptive consequences of rapid changeovers in its leadership group, nor of sudden impositions of new sets of norms governing internal Committee behavior.

II

If one considers the main activity of a political system to be decision-making, the acid test of its internal integration is its capacity to make collective decisions without flying apart in the process. Analysis of Committee integration should focus directly, therefore, upon its subgroups and the roles of its members. Two kinds of subgroups are of central importance—subcommittees and majority or minority party groups. The roles which are most relevant derive from: (1) positions which each member holds by virtue of his subgroup attachments, *e.g.,* as subcommittee member, majority (or minority) party member; (2) positions which relate to full Committee membership, *e.g.,* Committee member, and the seniority rankings of veteran, man of moderate experience, and newcomer;[17] (3) positions which relate to both subgroup and full, Committee membership, *e.g.,* Chairman of the committee, ranking minority member of the Committee, subcommittee chairman, ranking subcommittee member. Clusters of norms state the expectations about subgroup and role behavior. The description which follows treats the ways in which these norms and their associated behaviors mesh and clash. It treats, also, the internal control mechanisms by which behavior is brought into reasonable conformity with expectations.

Subgroup Integration. The day-to-day work of the Committee is carried on in its subcommittees each of which is given jurisdiction over a number of related governmental units. The number of subcommittees is determined by the Committee Chairman, and has varied recently from a low of 9 in 1949 to a high of 15 in 1959. The present total of 14 reflects, as always, a set of strategic and personal judgments by the Chairman balanced against the limitations placed on him by Committee tradition and member wishes. The Chairman also determines subcommittee jurisdiction, appoints subcommittee chairmen and selects the majority party members of each group. The ranking minority member of the committee exercises similar control over subcommittee assignments on his side of the aisle.

Each subcommittee holds hearings on the budget estimates of the agencies assigned to it, meets in executive session to decide what figures and what language to recommend to the full Committee (to "mark up" the bill), defends its recommendations before the full Committee, writes the Committee's report to the House, dominates the debate on the floor, and bargains for the House in conference committee. Within its jurisdiction, each subcommittee functions independently of the others and guards its autonomy jealously. The Chairman and ranking minority member of the full Committee have, as we shall see, certain opportunities to oversee and dip into the operations of all subcommittees. But their intervention is expected to be minimal. Moreover, they themselves operate importantly within the subcommittee framework by sitting as chairman or ranking minority member of the subcommittee in which they are most interested. Each subcommittee, under the guidance of its chairman, transacts its business in considerable isolation from every other one. One subcommittee chairman exclaimed,

> Why, you'd be branded an imposter if you went into one of those other sub-committee meetings. The only time I go is by appointment, by arrangement with the chairman at a special time. I'm as much a stranger in another subcommittee as I would be in the legislative Committee on Post Office and Civil Service. Each one does its work apart from all others.

All members of all subcommittees are expected to behave in similar fashion in the role of subcommittee member. Three main norms define this role; to the extent that they are observed, they promote harmony and reduce conflict among subcommittees.[18] Subcommittee autonomy gives to the House norm of *specialization* an intensified application on the Appropriations Committee. Each member is expected to play the role of specialist in the activities of one subcommittee. He will sit on from one to four subcommittees, but normally will specialize in the work, or a portion of the work, of only one. Except for the Chairman, ranking minority member and their confidants, a Committee member's time, energy, contacts and experience are devoted to his subcommittees. Specialization is, therefore, among the earliest and most compelling of the Committee norms to which a newcomer is exposed. Within the Committee, respect, deference and power are earned through subcommittee activity and, hence to a degree, through specialization. Specialization is valued further because it is well suited to the task of guarding the Treasury. Only by specializing, Committee members believe, can they unearth the volume of factual information necessary for the intelligent screening of budget requests. Since "the facts" are acquired only through industry an effective specialist will, perforce, adopt and promote the Committee's style of hard work.

Committee-wide acceptance of specialization is an integrative force in decision-making because it helps support a second norm—*reciprocity*. The stage at which a subcommittee makes its recommendations is a potential point of internal friction. Conflict among subcommittees (or between one subcommittee and the rest of the Committee) is minimized by the deference traditionally accorded to the recommendation of the subcommittee which has specialized in the area, has worked hard, and has "the facts." "It's a matter of 'You respect my work and I'll respect yours.' " "It's frowned upon if you offer an amendment in the full Committee if you aren't on the subcommittee. It's considered presumptuous to pose as an expert if you aren't on the subcommittee." Though records of full Committee decisions are not available, members agree that subcommittee recommendations are "very rarely changed," "almost always approved," "changed one time in fifty," "very seldom changed," etc.

No subcommittee is likely to keep the deference of the full Committee for long unless its recommendations have widespread support among its own members. To this end, a third norm—*subcommittee unity*—is expected to be observed by subcommittee members. Unity means a willingness to support (or not to oppose) the recommendations of one's own subcommittee. Reciprocity and unity are closely dependent upon one another. Reciprocity is difficult to maintain when subcommittees themselves are badly divided; and unity has little appeal unless reciprocity will subsequently be observed. The norm of reciprocity functions to minimize inter-subcommittee conflict. The norm of unity functions to minimize intra-subcommittee conflict. Both are deemed essential to subcommittee influence.

One payoff for the original selection of "responsible legislators" is their special willingness to compromise in pursuit of subcommittee unity. The impulse to this end is registered most strongly at the time when the subcommittee meets in executive session to mark up the bill. Two ranking minority members explained this aspect of markup procedure in their subcommittees:

> If there's agreement, we go right along. If there's a lot of controversy we put the item aside and go on. Then, after a day or two, we may have a list of ten controversial items. We give and take and pound them down till we get agreement.

> We have a unanimous agreement on everything. If a fellow enters an objection and we can't talk him out of it—and sometimes we can get him to go along—that's it. We put it in there.

Once the bargain is struck, the subcommittee is expected to "stick together."

It is, of course, easier to achieve unity among the five, seven, or nine members of a subcommittee than among the fifty members of the full Committee. But members are expected wherever possible to observe the norm of unity in the full Committee as well. That is, they should not only defer to the recommendations of the subcommittee involved, but they should support (or not oppose) that recommendation when it reaches the floor in the form of a Committee decision. On the floor, Committee members believe, their power and prestige depend largely on the degree to which the norms of reciprocity and unity continue to be observed. Members warn each other that if they go to the floor in disarray they will be "rolled," "jumped," or "run over' by the membership. It is a cardinal maxim among Committee members that "You can't turn an appropriations bill loose on the floor." Two senior subcommittee chairmen explain,

> We iron out our differences in Committee. We argue it out and usually have a meeting of the minds, a composite view of the Committee. . . . If we went on the floor in wide disagreement, they would say, "If you can't agree after listening to the testimony and discussing it, how can we understand it? We'll just vote on the basis of who we like the best."

> I tell them (the full Committee) we should have a united front. If there are any objections or changes, we ought to hear it now, and not wash our dirty linen out on the floor. If we don't have a bill that we can all agree on and support, we ought not to report it out. To do that is like throwing a piece of meat to a bunch of hungry animals.

One of the most functional Committee practices supporting the norm of unity is the tradition against minority reports in the subcommittee and in the full Committee. It is symptomatic of Committee integration that custom should proscribe the use of the most formal and irrevocable symbol of congressional committee disunity—the minority report. A few have been written—but only 9 out of a possible 141 during the 11 years, 1947-1957. That is to say, 95 percent of all original appropriations bills in this period were reported out without dissent. The technique of "reserving" is the Committee member's equivalent for the registering of dissent. In subcommittee or Committee, when a member reserves, he goes on record informally by informing his colleagues that he reserves the right to disagree on a specified item later on in the proceedings. He may seek a change or support a change in that particular item in full Committee or on the floor. But he does not publicize his dissent. The subcommittee or the full Committee can then make an unopposed recommendation. The individual retains some freedom of maneuver without firm commitment. Often a member reserves on an appropriations item but takes no further action. A member explained how the procedure operates in subcommittee,

> If there's something I feel too strongly about, and just can't go along, I'll say, "Mr. Chairman, we can have a unanimous report, but I reserve the right to bring this up in full Committee. I feel duty bound to make a play for it and see if I can't sell it to the other members." But if I don't say anything, or don't reserve this right, and then I bring it up in full Committee, they'll say, "Who are you trying to embarrass? You're a member of the team, aren't you? That's not the way to get along."

Disagreement cannot, of course, be eliminated from the Committee. But the Committee has accepted a method for ventilating it which produces a minimum of internal disruption. And members believe that the greater their internal unity, the greater the likelihood that their recommendations will pass the House.

The degree to which the role of the subcommittee member can be so played and subcommittee conflict thereby minimized depends upon the minimization of conflict between the majority and minority party subgroups. Nothing would be more disruptive to the Committee's work than bitter and extended partisan controversy. It is, therefore, important to Appropriations Committee integration that a fourth norm—*minimal partisanship*—should be observed by members of both party contingents. Nearly every respondent emphasized, with approval, that "very little" or "not much" partisanship prevailed on the Committee. One subcommittee chairman stated flatly, "My job is to keep down partisanship." A ranking minority member said, "You might think that we Republicans would defend the Administration and the budget, but we don't." Majority and minority party ratios are constant and do not change (*i.e.,* in 1958) to reflect changes in the strength of the controlling party. The Committee operates with a completely non-partisan professional staff, which does not change in tune with shifts in party control. Requests for studies by the Committee's investigating staff must be made by the Chairman and ranking minority member of the full Committee and by the Chairman and ranking minority member of the subcommittee involved. Sub-committees can produce recommendations without dissent and the full Committee can adopt reports without dissent precisely because party conflict is (during the period 1947-1961) the exception rather than the rule.

The Committee is in no sense immune from the temperature of party conflict, but it does have a relatively high specific heat. Intense party strife or a strongly taken presidential position will get reflected in subcommittee and in Committee recommendations. Sharp divisions in party policy were carried, with disruptive impact, into some areas of Committee activity during the 80th Congress and subsequently, by way of reaction, into the 81st Congress.[19] During the Eisenhower years, extraordinary presidential pleas, especially concerning foreign aid, were given special heed by the Republican members of the Committee.[20] Partisanship is normally generated from the environment and not from within the Committee's party groups. Partisanship is, therefore, likely to be least evident in subcommittee activity, strong in the full Committee, and most potent at the floor stage. Studies which have focussed on roll-call analysis have stressed the influence of party in legislative decision-making.[21] In the appropriations process, at any rate, the floor stage probably represents party influence at its maximum. Our examination, by interview, of decision-making at the subcommittee and full Committee level would stress the influence of Committee-oriented norms—the strength of which tends to vary inversely with that of party bonds. In the secrecy and intimacy of the subcommittee and full Committee hearing rooms, the member finds it easy to compromise on questions of more or less, to take money from one program and give it to another and, in general, to avoid yes-or-no type party stands. These decisions, taken in response to the integrative norms of the Committee are the most important ones in the entire appropriations process.

Role Integration. The roles of subcommittee member and party member are common to all.

Other more specific decision-making positions are allocated among the members. Different positions produce different roles, and in an integrated system, these too must fit together. Integration, in other words, must be achieved through the complementarity or reciprocity of roles as well as through the similarity of roles.

This may mean a pattern in which expectations are so different that there is very little contact between individuals; or it may mean a pattern in which contacts require the working out of an involved system of exchange of obligations and rewards.[22] In either case, the desired result is the minimization of conflict among prominent Committee roles. Two crucial instances of role reciprocity on the Committee involve the seniority positions of old-timer and newcomer and the leadership positions of Chairman and ranking minority member, on both the full Committee and on each subcommittee.

The differentiation between senior and junior members is the broadest definition of who shall and who shall not actively participate in Committee decisions. Of a junior member, it will be said, "Oh, he doesn't count—what I mean is, he hasn't been on the Committee long enough." He is not expected to and ordinarily does not have much influence. His role is that of apprentice. He is expected to learn the business and the norms of the Committee by applying himself to its work. He is expected to acquiesce in an arrangement which gives most influence (except in affairs involving him locally) to the veterans of the group. Newcomers will be advised to "follow the chairman until you get your bearings. For the first two years, follow the chairman. He knows." "Work hard, keep quiet and attend the Committee sessions. We don't want to listen to some new person coming in here." And newcomers perceive their role in identical terms: "You have to sit in the back seat and edge up little by little." "You just go to subcommittee meetings and assimilate the routine. The new members are made to feel welcome, but you have a lot of rope-learning to do before you carry much weight."

At every stage of Committee work, this differential prevails. There is remarkable agreement on the radically different sets of expectations involved. During the hearings, the view of the elders is that, "Newcomers . . . don't know what the score is and they don't have enough information to ask intelligent questions." A newcomer described his behavior in typically similar terms: "I attended all the hearings and studied and collected information that I can use next year. I'm just marking time now." During the crucial subcommittee markup, the newcomer will have little opportunity to speak—save in locally important matters. A subcommittee chairman stated the norm from his viewpoint this way: "When we get a compromise, nobody's going to break that up. If someone tries, we sit on him fast. We don't want young people who throw bricks or slow things down." And a newcomer reciprocated, describing his markup conduct: "I'm not provocative. I'm in there for information. They're the experts in the field. I go along." In full Committee, on the floor, and in conference committee, the Committe's senior members take the lead and the junior members are expected to follow. The apprentice role is common to all new members of the House. But it is wrong to assume that each Committee will give it the same emphasis. Some pay it scant heed.[23] The Appropriations Committee makes it a cornerstone of its internal structure.

Among the Committee's veterans, the key roles are those of Committee Chairman and ranking minority member, and their counterparts in every subcommittee. It is a measure of Committee integration and the low degree of partisanship that considerable reciprocity obtains between these roles. Their partisan status nevertheless sets limits to the degree of possible integration. The Chairman is given certain authority which he and only he can exercise. But save in times of extreme party controversy, the expectation is that consultation and cooperation between the chairman-ranking minority member shall lubricate the Committee's entire work. For example, by Committee tradition, its Chairman and ranking minority member are both *ex officio* voting members of each subcommittee and of every conference committee. The two of them thus have joint access at every stage of the internal process. A subcommittee chairman, too, is expected to discuss matters of scheduling and agenda with his opposite minority number. He is expected to work with him during the markup session and to give him (and, normally, only him) an opportunity to read and comment on the subcommittee report.[24] A ranking minority member described his subcommittee markup procedure approvingly:

> Frequently the chairman has a figure which he states. Sometimes he will have no figure, and he'll turn to me and say, "___, what do you think?" Maybe I'll have a figure. It's very flexible. Everyone has a chance to say what he thinks, and we'll move it around. Sometimes it takes a long time.... He's a rapid partisan on the floor, but he is a very fair man in the subcommittee.

Where influence is shared, an important exchange of rewards occurs. The chairman gains support for his leadership and the ranking minority member gains intra-Committee power. The Committee as a whole insures against the possibility of drastic change in its internal structure by giving to its key minority member a stake in its operation. Chairmen and ranking minority members will, in the course of time, exchange positions; and it is expected that such a switch will produce no form of retribution nor any drastic change in the functioning of the Committee. Reciprocity of roles, in this case, promotes continued integration. A ranking minority member testified to one successful arrangement when he took the floor in the 83d Congress to say:

> The gentleman and I have been see sawing back and forth on this committee for some time. He was chairman in the 80th Congress. I had the privilege of serving as chairman in the 81st and 82nd Congresses. Now he is back in the saddle. I can say that he has never failed to give me his utmost cooperation, and I have tried to give him the same cooperation during his service as chairman of this Committee. We seldom disagree, but we have found out that we can disagree without being disagreeable. Consequently, we have unusual harmony on this committee.[25]

Reciprocity between chairmen and ranking minority members on the Appropriations Committee is to some incalculable degree a function of the stability of membership which allows a pair of particular individuals to work out the kind of personal accommodation described above. The close working relationship of Clarence Cannon and John Taber, whose service on the Committee totals 68 years and who have been changing places as Chairman and ranking minority member for 19 years, highlights and sustains a pattern of majority-minority reciprocity throughout the group.

Internal Control Mechanisms. The expectations which apply to subcommittee, to party, to veterans and to newcomers, to chairmen and to ranking minority members prescribe highly integrative behaviors. We have concentrated on these expectations, and have both illustrated and assumed the close correlation between expected and actual behavior. This does not mean that all the norms of the Committee have been canvassed. Nor does it mean that deviation from the integrative norms does not occur. It does. From what can be gathered, however, from piecing together a study of the public record on appropriations from 1947 to 1961 with interview materials, the Committee has been markedly successful in maintaining a stable internal structure over time. As might be expected, therefore, changes and threats of change have been generated more from the environment—when outsiders consider the Committee as unresponsive—than from inside the subsystem itself. One source of internal stability, and an added reason for assuming a correlation between expected and actual behavior, is the existence of what appear to be reasonably effective internal control mechanisms. Two of these are the socialization processes applied to newcomers and the sanctioning mechanisms applicable to all Committee members.

Socialization is in part a training in perception. Before members of a group can be expected to behave in accordance with its norms, they must learn to see and interpret the world around them with reasonable similarity. The socialization of the Committee newcomer during his term or two of apprenticeship serves to bring his perceptions and his attitudes sufficiently into line with those of the other members to serve as a basis for Committee integration. The Committee, as we have seen, is chosen from Congressmen whose political flexibility connotes an aptitude for learning new lessons of power. Furthermore, the high degree of satisfaction of its members with the group increases their susceptibility to its processes of learning and training.

For example, one half of the Committee's Democrats are Northerners and Westerners from urban constituencies, whose voting records are just as "liberal" on behalf of domestic social welfare programs as non-Committee Democrats from like constituencies. They come to the Committee favorably disposed toward the high level of federal spending necessary to support such programs, and with no sense of urgency about the Committee's tasks of guarding the Treasury or reducing budget estimates. Given the criteria governing their selection, however, they come without rigid preconceptions and with a built-in responsiveness to the socialization processes of any legislative group of which they are members. It is crucial to Committee integration that they learn to temper their potentially disruptive welfare-state ideology with a conservative's concern for saving money. They must change their perceptions and attitudes sufficiently to view the Committee's tasks in nearly the same terms as their more conservative Southern Democratic and Republican colleagues. What their elders perceive as reality (*i.e.,* the disposition of executives to ask for more money than is necessary) they, too, must see as reality. A subcommittee chairman explained:

> When you have sat on the committee, you see that these bureaus are always asking for more money—always up, never down. They want to build up their organization. You reach the point—I have—where it sickens you, where you

rebel against it. Year after year, they want more money. They say, "Only $50,000 this year"; but you know the pattern. Next year they'll be back for $100,000, then $200,000. The younger members haven't been on the Committee long enough, haven't had the experience to know this.

The younger men, in this case the younger liberals, do learn from their Committee experience. Within one or two terms, they are differentiating between themselves and the "wild-eyed spenders" or the "free spenders" in the House. "Some of these guys would spend you through the roof," exclaimed one liberal of moderate seniority. Repeated exposure to Committee work and to fellow members has altered their perceptions and their attitudes in money matters. Half a dozen Northern Democrats of low or moderate seniority agreed with one of their number who said: "Yes, it's true. I can see it myself. I suppose I came here a flaming liberal; but as the years go by I get more conservative. You just hate like hell to spend all this money.... You come to the point where you say, 'By God, this is enough jobs.'" These men will remain more inclined toward spending than their Committee colleagues, but their perceptions and hence their attitudes have been brought close enough to the others to support a consensus on tasks. They are responsive to appeals on budget-cutting grounds that would not have registered earlier and which remain meaningless to liberals outside the Committee. In cases, therefore, where Committee selection does not and cannot initially produce individuals with a predisposition toward protecting the Treasury, the same result is achieved by socialization.

Socialization is a training in behavior as well as in perception. For the newcomer, conformity to norms in specific situations is insured through the appropriate application, by the Committee veterans, of rewards and punishments. For the Committee member who serves his apprenticeship creditably, the passage of time holds the promise that he will inherit a position of influence. He may, as an incentive, be given some small reward early in his Committee career. One man, in his second year, had been assigned the task of specializing in one particular program. However narrow the scope of his specialization, it had placed him on the road to influence within the Committee. He explained with evident pleasure:

> The first year, you let things go by. You can't participate. But you learn by watching the others operate. The next year, you know what you're interested in and when to step in.... For instance, I've become an expert on the ____ program. The chairman said to me, "This is something you ought to get interested in." I did; and now I'm the expert on the Committee. Whatever I say on that, the other members listen to me and do what I want.

At some later date, provided he continues to observe Committee norms, he will be granted additional influence, perhaps through a prominent floor role. A model Committee man of moderate seniority who had just attained to this stage of accomplishment, and who had suffered through several political campaigns back home fending off charges that he was a do-nothing Congressman, spoke about the rewards he was beginning to reap.

> When you perform well on the floor when you bring out a bill, and Members
> know that you know the bill, you develop prestige with other Members of
> Congress. They come over and ask you what you think, because they know
> you've studied it. You begin to get a reputation beyond your subcommittee. And
> you get inner satisfaction, too. You don't feel that you're down here doing
> nothing.

The first taste of influence which comes to men on this Committee is
compensation for the frustrations of apprenticeship. Committee integration in
general, and the meshing of roles between elders and newcomers in particular,
rests on the fact that conformity to role expectations over time does guarantee to
the young positive rewards—the very kind of rewards of power, prestige, and
personal satisfaction which led most of them to seek Committee membership in
the first place.

The important function of apprenticeship is that it provides the necessary
time during which socialization can go forward. And teaching proceeds with the
aid of punishments as well as rewards. Should a new member inadvertently or
deliberately run afoul of Committee norms during his apprenticeship, he will find
himself confronted with negative sanctions ranging in subtlety from "jaundiced
eyes" to a changed subcommittee assignment. Several members, for example,
recalled their earliest encounter with the norm of unity and the tradition against
minority reports. One remembered his attempt to file a minority report. "The
Chairman was pretty upset about it. It's just a tradition, I guess, not to have minority reports. I didn't know it was a tradition. When I said I was going to write
a minority report, some eyebrows were raised. The Chairman said it just wasn't
the thing to do. Nothing more was said about it. But it wasn't a very popular
thing to do, I guess." He added that he had not filed one since.

Some younger members have congenital difficulty in observing the norms of
the apprentice's role. In the 86th Congress, these types tended to come from the
Republican minority. The minority newcomers (described by one of the men who
selected them as "eight young, energetic, fighting conservatives") were a group of
economy-minded individuals some of whom chafed against any barrier which
kept them from immediate influence on Committee policy. Their reaction was
quite different from that of the young Democrats, whose difficulty was in
learning to become economy-minded, but who did not actively resent their lack of
influence. One freshman, who felt that "The appropriations system is lousy,
inadequate and old fashioned," recalled that he had spoken out in full Committee
against the recommendations of a subcommittee of which he was not a member.
Having failed, he continued to oppose the recommendation during floor debate.
By speaking up, speaking in relation to the work of another subcommittee and by
opposing a Committee recommendation, he had violated the particular norms of
his apprentice role as well of the generally applicable norms of reciprocity and
unity. He explained what he had learned, but remained only partially socialized:

> They want to wash their dirty linen in the Committee and they want no
> opposition afterward. They let me say my piece in Committee. . . . But I just
> couldn't keep quiet. I said some things on the floor, and I found out that's about
> all they would take. . . . If you don't get along with your Committee and have

their support, you don't get anything accomplished around here. . . . I'm trying to be a loyal, cooperative member of the Committee. You hate to be a stinker; but I'm still picking at the little things because I can't work on the big things. There's nothing for the new men to do, so they have to find places to needle in order to take some part in it.

Another freshman, who had deliberately violated apprenticeship norms by trying to ask "as many questions as the chairman" during subcommittee hearings, reported a story of unremitting counteraction against his deviation:

> In the hearings, I have to wait sometimes nine or ten hours for a chance; and he hopes I'll get tired and stay home. I've had to wait till some pretty unreasonable hours. Once I've gotten the floor, though, I've been able to make a good case. Sometimes I've been the only person there. . . . He's all powerful. He's got all the power. He wouldn't think of taking me on a trip with him when he goes to hold hearings. Last year, he went to ____. He wouldn't give me a nudge there. And in the hearings, when I'm questioning a witness, he'll keep butting in so that my case won't appear to be too rosy.

Carried on over a period of two years, this behavior resulted in considerable personal friction between a Committee elder and the newcomer. Other members of his subcommittee pointedly gave him a great lack of support for his non-conformity. "They tried to slow him down and tone him down a little," not because he and his subcommittee chairman disagreed, but on the grounds that the Committee has developed accepted ways of disagreeing which minimize, rather than exacerbate, interpersonal friction.

One internal threat to Committee integration comes from new members who from untutored perceptions, from ignorance of norms, or from dissatisfaction with the apprentice role may not act in accordance with Committee expectations. The seriousness of this threat is minimized, however, by the fact that the deviant newcomer does not possess sufficient resources to affect adversely the operation of the system. Even if he does not respond immediately to the application of sanctions, he can be held in check and subjected to an extended and (given the frequency of interaction among members) intensive period of socialization. The success of Committee socialization is indicated by the fact that whereas wholesale criticism of Committee operations was frequently voiced among junior members, it had disappeared among the men of moderate experience. And what these middle seniority members now accept as the facts of Committee life, the veterans vigorously assert and defend as the essentials of a smoothly functioning system. Satisfaction with the Committee's internal structure increases with length of Committee service.

An important reason for changing member attitudes is that those who have attained leadership positions have learned, as newcomers characteristically have not, that their conformity to Committee norms is the ultimate source of their influence inside the group. Freshman members do not as readily perceive the degree to which interpersonal influence is rooted in obedience to group norms. They seem to convert their own sense of powerlessness into the view that the Committee's leaders possess, by virtue of their positions, arbitrary, absolute, and awesome power. Typically, they say: "If you're a subcommittee Chairman, it's your Committee." "The Chairman runs the show. He gets what he wants. He decides what he wants and gets it through." Older members of the Committee, however, view the power of the leaders as a highly contingent and revocable grant, tendered by the Committee for so long and only so long as their leaders abide by Committee expectations. In commenting on internal influence, their typical reaction is: "Of course, the Committee wouldn't follow him if it didn't want to. He has a great deal of respect. He's an able man, a hard-working man." "He knows the bill backwards and forwards. He works hard, awfully hard and the members know it." Committee leaders have an imposing set of formal prerogatives. But they can capitalize on them only if they command the respect, confidence and deference of their colleagues.

It is basic to Committee integration that members who have the greatest power to change the system evidence the least disposition to do so. Despite their institutional conservatism, however, Committee elders do occasionally violate the norms applicable to them and hence represent a potential threat to successful integration. Excessive deviation from Committee expectations by some leaders will bring counter-measures by other leaders. Thus, for example, the Chairman and his subcommittee chairmen exercise reciprocal controls over one another's behavior. The Chairman has the authority to appoint the chairman and members of each subcommittee and fix its jurisdiction. "He runs the Committee. He has a lot of power," agrees one subcommittee chairman. "But it's all done on the basis of personal friendship. If he tries to get too big, the members can whack him down by majority vote."

In the 84th Congress, Chairman Cannon attempted an unusually broad reorganization of subcommittee jurisdictions. The subcommittee chairman most adversely affected rallied his senior colleagues against the Chairman's action—on the ground that it was an excessive violation of role expectations and threatening to subcommittee autonomy. Faced with the prospect of a negative Committee vote, the Chairman was forced to act in closer conformity to the expectations of the other leaders. As one participant described the episode.

> Mr. Cannon, for reasons of his own, tried to bust up one of the subcommittees. We didn't like that. . . . He was breaking up the whole Committee. A couple of weeks later, a few of the senior members got together and worked out a compromise. By that time, he had seen a few things, so we went to him and talked to him and worked it out.

On the subcommittees, too, it is the veterans of both parties who will levy sanctions against an offending chairman. It is they who speak of "cutting down to size" and "trimming the whiskers" of leaders who become "too cocky," "too stubborn" or who "do things wrong too often." Committee integration is underwritten by the fact that no member high or low is permanently immune from the operation of its sanctioning mechanisms.

III

Data concerning internal committee activity can be organized and presented in various ways. One way is to use key functional problems like integration as the focal points for descriptive analysis. On the basis of our analysis (and without, for the time being, having devised any precise measure of integration), we are led to the summary observation that the House Appropriations Committee appears to be a well integrated, if not an extremely well integrated, committee. The question arises as to whether anything can be gained from this study other than a description of one property of one political subsystem. If it is reasonable to assume that the internal life of a congressional committee affects all legislative activity involving that committee, and if it is reasonable to assume that the analysis of a committee's internal relationships will produce useful knowledge about legislative behavior, some broader implications for this study are indicated.

In the first place, the success of the House Appropriations Committee in solving the problem of integration probably does have important consequences for the appropriations process. Some of the possible relationships can be stated as hypotheses and tested; others can be suggested as possible guides to understanding. All of them require further research. Of primary interest is the relationship between integration and the power of the Committee. There is little doubt about the fact of Committee power. Of the 443 separate case histories of bureau appropriations examined, the House accepted Committee recommendations in 387, or 87.4 percent of them; and in 159, or 33.6 percent of the cases, the House Committee's original recommendations on money amounts were the exact ones enacted into law. The hypothesis that the greater the degree of Committee unity the greater the probability that its recommendations will be accepted is being tested as part of a larger study.[26] House Committee integration may be a key factor in producing House victories in conference committee. This relationship, too, might be tested. Integration appears to help provide the House conferees with a feeling of confidence and superiority which is one of their important advantages in the mix of psychological factors affecting conference deliberations.

Another suggested consequence of high integration is that party groups have a relatively small influence upon appropriations decisions. It suggests, too, that Committee-oriented behavior should be duly emphasized in any analysis of Congressional oversight of administrative activity by this Committee. Successful integration promotes the achievement of the Committee's goals, and doubtless helps account for the fairly consistent production of budget-cutting decisions. Another consequence will be found in the strategies adopted by people seeking favorable Committee decisions. For example, the characteristic lines of contact from executive officials to the Committee will run to the chairman and the ranking minority member (and to the professional staff man) of the single subcommittee handling their agency's appropriations. The ways in which the Committee achieves integration may even affect the success or failure of a bureau in getting its appropriations. Committee members, for instance, will react more favorably toward an administrator who conforms to their self-image of the hard-working master-of-detail than to one who does not—and Committee response to individual administrators bulks large in their determinations.

Finally, the internal integration of this Committee helps to explain the extraordinary stability, since 1920, of appropriations procedures—in the face of repeated proposals to change them through omnibus appropriations, legislative budgets, new budgetary forms, item veto, Treasury borrowing, etc. Integration is a stabilizing force, and the stability of the House Appropriations Committee has been a force for stabilization throughout the entire process. It was, for example, the disagreement between Cannon and Taber which led to the indecisiveness reflected in the short-lived experiment with a single appropriations bill.[27] One need only examine the conditions most likely to decrease Committee integration to ascertain some of the critical factors for producing changes in the appropriations process. A description of integration is also an excellent base-line from which to analyze changes in internal structure.

All of these are speculative propositions which call for further research. But they suggest, as a second implication, that committee integration does have important consequences for legislative activity and, hence, that it is a key variable in the study of legislative politics. It would seem, therefore, to be a fruitful focal point for the study of other congressional committees.[28] Comparative analysis could usefully be devoted to (1) the factors which tend to increase or decrease integration; (2) the degree to which integration is achieved; and (3) the consequences of varying degrees of integration for committee behavior and influence. If analyses of committee integration are of any value, they should encourage the analysis and the classification of congressional committees along functional lines. And they should lead to the discussion of interrelated problems of committee survival. Functional classifications of committees (i.e., well or poorly integrated) derived from a large number of descriptive analyses of several functional problems, may prove helpful in constructing more general propositions about the legislative process.

Notes

1. On social systems, see: George Homans, *The Human Group* (New York, 1950); Robert K. Merton, *Social Theory and Social Structure* (Glencoe, 1957); Talcott Parsons and Edward Shils, *Toward A General Theory of Action* (Cambridge, 1951), pp. 190-234. Most helpful with reference to the political system has been David Easton, "An Approach to the Analysis of Political Systems," *World Politics* (April, 1957), pp. 383-400.

2. On the idea of subgroups as used here, see Harry M. Johnson, *Sociology* (New York, 1960), ch. 3. On role, see specifically Theodore M. Newcomb, *Social Psychology* (New York, 1951), p. 280; see generally N. Gross, W. Mason and A. McEachern, *Explorations in Role Analysis: Studies of the School Superintendency Role* (New York, 1958). On differentiation and its relation to integration, see Scott Greer, *Social Organization* (New York, 1955).

3. The usage here follows most closely that of Robert Merton, *op. cit.,* pp. 26-29.

4. This and all other generalizations about member attitudes and perceptions depend heavily on extensive interviews with Committee members. Semi-structured interviews, averaging 45 minutes in length were held with 45 of the 50 Committee members during the 86th Congress. Certain key questions, all open-ended, were asked of all respondents. The schedule was kept very flexible, however, in order to permit particular topics to be explored with those individuals best equipped to discuss them. In a few

cases, where respondents encouraged it, notes were taken during the interviews. In most cases notes were not taken, but were transcribed immediately after the interview. Where unattributed quotations occur in the text, therefore, they are as nearly verbatim as the author's power of immediate recall could make them. These techniques were all used so as to improve *rapport* between interviewer and respondent.

5. "History of the Committee on Appropriations," House Doc. 299, 77th Cong., 1st sess., 1941-1942. p. 11.

6. The bureaus being studied are all concerned with domestic policy and are situated in the Agriculture, Interior, Labor, Commerce, Treasury, Justice and Health, Education and Welfare Departments. For a similar pattern of Committee decisions in foreign affairs, see Holbert Carroll, *The House of Representatives and Foreign Affairs* (Pittsburgh, 1958), ch. 9.

7. See, for example, Philip A. Foss, "The Grazing Fee Dilemma," Inter-University Case Program, No. 57 (University, Alabama, 1960).

8. Nicholas A. Masters, "House Committee Assignments," this *Review*, Vol. 55 (June, 1961), pp. 345-357.

9. In the period from 1947 through 1959, (80th to 86th Congress) 79 separate appointments were made to the Appropriations Committee, with 14 going to freshmen. The Committee filled, in other words, 17.7 percent of its vacancies with freshmen. The Rules Committee had 26 vacancies and selected no freshmen at all. The Ways and Means Committee had 36 vacancies and selected 2 freshmen (5.6 percent). All other Committees had a higher percentage of freshmen appointments. Armed Services ranked fourth, with 45 vacancies and 12 freshmen appointed, for a percentage of 26.7. Foreign Affairs figures were 46 and 14, or 30.4 percent; UnAmerican Activities figures were 22 and 7, or 31.8 percent. cf. Masters, *op. cit.*

10. In the 1960 elections, 41 out of the current 50 members received more than 55.1 percent of the vote in their districts. By a common definition, that is, only 9 of the 50 came from marginal districts.

11. The 106 members came to Appropriations from every committee except Ways and Means.

12. One was personally requested by the Speaker to move to Ways and Means. The other was chosen by a caucus of regional Congressmen to be his party's representative on the Rules Committee. Of the 21 members who were forced off the Committee for lack of seniority during a change in party control, or who were defeated for reelection and later returned, 20 sought to regain Committee membership at the earliest opportunity.

13. A sidelight on this attitude is displayed in a current feud between the House and Senate Appropriations Committees over the meeting place for their conference committees. The House Committee is trying to break the century-old custom that conferences to resolve differences on money bills are always held on the Senate side of the Capitol. House Committee members "complain that they often have to trudge back to the House two or three times to answer roll calls during a conference. They say they go over in a body to work, while Senators flit in and out. . . . The House Appropriations Committee feels that it does all the hard work listening to witnesses for months on each bill, only to have the Senate Committee sit as a court of appeals and, with little more than a cursory glance, restore most of the funds cut." *Washington Post*, April 24, 1962, p. 1.

14. This proposition is spelled out at some length in J. Thibaut and H. Kelley, *The Social Psychology of Groups* (New York, 1959), p. 247, and in D. Cartwright and A. Zander, *Group Dynamics: Research and Theory* (Evanston, 1953), p. 420.

15. This figure is 9 percent greater than the next most stable House Committee during

this particular period. The top four, in order, were Appropriations (35.7%), Agriculture (26.7%), Armed Services (25%), Foreign Affairs (20.8%).

16. The Committee's permanent and well integrated professional staff (as distinguished from its temporary investigating staff) might be considered as part of the subsystem though it will not be treated in this paper.

17. "Newcomers" are defined as men who have served no more than two terms on the Committee. "Men of moderate experience" are those with 3-5 terms of service. "Veterans" are those who have 6 or more terms of Committee service.

18. A statement of expected behavior was taken to be a Committee norm when it was expressed by a substantial number of respondents (a dozen or so) who represented both parties, and varying degrees of experience. In nearly every case, moreover, no refutation of them was encountered, and ample confirmation of their existence can be found in the public record. Their articulation came most frequently from the veterans of the group.

19. See, for example, the internal conflict on the subcommittee dealing with the Labor Department. 93 *Cong. Record,* pp. 2465-2562 passim; 94 *Cong. Record,* pp. 7605-7607.

20. See, for example, the unusual minority report of Committee Republicans on the foreign aid appropriations bill in 1960. Their protest against Committee cuts in the budget estimates was the result of strenuous urging by the Eisenhower Administration. House Report No. 1798, *Mutual Security and Related Agency Appropriation Bill,* 1961, 86 Cong. 2d sess. 1960.

21. David Truman, *The Congressional Party* (New York, 1959); Julius Turner, *Party and Constituency: Pressures on Congress* (Baltimore, 1951).

22. The ideas of "reciprocity" and "complementarity," which are used interchangeably here, are discussed in Alvin Gouldner, "The Norm of Reciprocity," *American Sociological Review* (April, 1960). Most helpful in explaining the idea of a role system has been the work of J. Wahlke, H. Eulau, W. Buchanan, L. Ferguson. See their study, *The Legislative System* (New York, 1962), esp. Intro.

23. For example, the Committee on Education and Labor, see footnote 26.

24. See the exchange in 101 *Cong. Rec.* pp. 3832, 3844, 3874.

25. 99 *Cong. Rec.,* p. 4933.

26. *Cf.* Dwaine Marvick, "Congressional Appropriations Politics," unpublished manuscript (Columbia, 1952).

27. See Dalmas Nelson, "The Omnibus Appropriations Act of 1950," *Journal of Politics* (May, 1953).

28. This view has been confirmed by the results of interviews conducted by the author with members of the House Committee on Education and Labor, together with an examination of that Committee's activity in one policy area. They indicate very significant contrasts between the internal structure of that Committee and the Appropriations Committee—contrasts which center around their comparative success in meeting the problem of integration. The House Committee on Education and Labor appears to be a poorly integrated committee. Its internal structure is characterized by a great deal of subgroup conflict, relatively little role reciprocity, and minimally effective internal control mechanisms. External concerns, like those of party, constituency and clientele groups, are probably more effective in determining its decisions than is likely to be the case in a well-integrated committee. An analysis of the internal life of the Committee on Education and Labor, drawn partly from interviews with 19 members of that group, will appear in a forthcoming study, *Federal Aid to Education and National Politics,* by Professor Frank Munger and the author, to be published by Syracuse University Press. See also Nicholas R. Masters, *op. cit.,* note 7

above, pp. 354-555, and Seymour Scher, "Congressional Committee Members as Independent Agency Overseers: A Case Study," *American Political Science Review,* Vol. 54 (December 1960), pp. 911-920.

9. POLICY CONTENT, COMMITTEE MEMBERSHIP, AND BEHAVIOR

Barbara Hinckley

After more than ten years of endeavor, congressional committee research can show considerable accomplishment. Single-committee studies offer richly detailed understanding of the Appropriations, Ways and Means, Labor, and Banking committees, among others (Fenno, 1962; Manley, 1965; Bibby, 1967). Macro-comparative studies can rank order all committees and test propositions concerning their prestige, cohesiveness, and success (Dyson and Soule, 1970; Dodd, 1972). A major work comparing six House committees has been published (Fenno, 1973a). Studies of the selection process have supplied increasing detail on who gets what committee assignment (Masters, 1961; Bullock and Sprague, 1969; Rohde and Shepsle, 1973). So we can rank them and interrank them, recognize them in operation, appreciate their differences, interview their members, analyze their chairmen, and make informed judgments as to their reform (Manley, 1973; Fenno, 1973b). And there's a lot left to do. There are a half dozen House committees, a chance at their Senate counterparts, and the possibility of redoing the earlier studies as members and chairmen change and time goes by.

Nevertheless, little of this cumulates or comes together into more than a set of disparate, and at times contradictory, findings—employing widely different conceptualizations and kinds of data. Having found that "committees vary," we need now the kind of analysis that can order and explain this variation and that can begin to bring some of these very diverse results together.

One such integrative effort may be to organize committees by subject matter or "policy content" of the legislation they consider. It might be expected that policy content profoundly affects the committee assignment process—as to who wants what, who asks for what, and who gets what—and thus shapes the attractiveness of committees, the stability of their membership, and the kind of members selected and self-selected by the process. But it might also be expected that policy content would affect behavior on committees, independently of

Author's Note: My thanks to the "panel" of congressional scholars who contributed to the subject matter in a task far above and beyond usual collegial duty. None, of course, bears responsibility for the resulting analysis. My thanks also to Corey Rosen for research assistance, and to the Meigs Fund of Cornell University for research support.

Source: *American Journal of Political Science*, vol. 19, no. 3 (August 1975): 543-557. Reprinted with permission from author and publisher.

attractiveness or membership. Thus some subject areas permit more cohesiveness among members than others. In other words, attractiveness, membership, and behavioral attributes may all be arrayed and explained within a subject matter classification, and any attempt to interrelate these attributes would first need to isolate the subject matter effect.

For a very well known case in point, Appropriations' "integrated" behavior (defined in part as agreement among members on committee business) is explained by the following variables: the committee's subject matter, its attractiveness as an assignment, the stability of members, the proportion of "responsible" (senior, accommodating, compromising) members, and consensus on goals of members (Fenno, 1962). This has led some to infer, perhaps beyond the author's intention, that committee attributes such as attractiveness and stability should be more generally related to agreement among members: that is, to infer a proposition holding for all committees and not only for Appropriations. Testing the inference has produced results at odds with the Appropriations study (Dyson and Soule, 1970; Dodd, 1972). But at least three of the variables appear closely interrelated. The more attractive a committee, the more its members should wish to stay and the more likely that senior, accommodating congressmen will be accommodated in turn by being assigned to it. And if subject matter shapes (1) attractiveness, (2) membership, and (3) behavior, then most of the variables, including the dependent variable, may be explained by subject matter effects.

This study, then, offers a first exploration of subject matter effects on committee membership and behavior. It selects as its focus those disparities in the literature relating attractiveness and stability of membership to cohesive behavior, and attempts to reconcile and explain them by two selected subject matter effects. These may not be the only two or, ultimately, the most useful two, but should be sufficient for this exploratory purpose. And to the extent that membership and behavioral attributes can be arrayed on these two dimensions, and to the extent that House and Senate committees dealing with the same subject matter exhibit similar membership and behavior, more such integrative efforts may be encouraged.

Two Policy Content Dimensions

As part of the exploratory nature of the inquiry, two policy content dimensions have been selected, of general applicability in that they could be used to classify any political subject matter (e.g., see Froman, 1968; Lowi, 1964), and of particular relevance for their effects on membership and behavior. These dimensions are subject matter *stakes* and *scope:* stakes defined as subject matter permitting positive-sum versus zero-sum solutions; scope defined as subject matter attracting a broad versus restricted number of "interested" actors, in proportion to the total number in whatever political unit is under analysis. If mixed-motive political actors seek influence among their peers, as well as other goods, they may find participation in broad as opposed to restricted subject matter more widely and generally valued by these peers, and esteemed as prestigious. Such participation is more difficult to achieve, and is therefore won by those with more influence to start with. Furthermore, legislators may find it easier to compromise and to exhibit cohesive behavior on subject matter permitting positive-sum as opposed to zero-sum solutions. In other words, we may take Froman's general proposition that "political processes vary in accord with the issues and the stakes of the game" and make it more specific: political processes of membership selection and conflict management may vary across these two subject matter dimensions. Scope and stakes may affect both personnel and procedure—both who does what and how they do it.

More particularly, committees vary in scope, since some raise issues of concern to virtually all congressmen while some raise issues of concern to a more limited number of "interested" congressmen. Committees vary in stakes, since they raise issues that are perceived as tending toward zero-sum (win or lose) versus positive-sum (more or less) congressional allocations. These dimensions are defined by their relevance to congressmen, not in terms of interests outside the Congress or some abstract definition of "intrinsic" scope or stakes, since it is the congressmen's attraction to and behavior on the committee that is to be explained. And needless to say, we are talking of tendencies and not absolute, rigid categories. Most committees' subject matter includes both broadly relevant and narrowly restricted congressional interests and both zero-sum and positive-sum allocations. But the assumption is that they may be classified—by congressional researchers and congressmen—in terms of a predominant character.

If subject matter shapes membership, we would expect that broad-scope committees would be more attractive to members, therefore more stable in membership and possessing more senior members than restricted committees (whether competitive or noncompetitive). The extent of intercorrelation among attractiveness, seniority, and stability variables also needs investigation. If subject matter shapes behavior, we would obviously expect that competitive committees should be less cohesive than noncompetitive committees (whether broad or restricted). Moreover and most critically, if subject matter is important, we would expect strong intercorrelations in the ranking of these attributes for House and Senate committees handling essentially the same jurisdiction.

This argument, of course, does not exclude the possibility of other influences, such as the effect of committees' formal powers on attractiveness or the idiosyncratic effect of members' personality or leadership skills on cohesive behavior. It simply offers one possible organizing scheme.

Design of the Study

These propositions can be examined for sixteen House and Senate committees, matched for subject matter jurisdiction and selected from committees previously studied in some detail. A panel device was employed for the classification, by asking six other congressional scholars to classify the committees for a specific point in time (the 87th through the 90th Congresses) on the two policy content dimensions.[1] Committees as placed in Table 9-1 have received either five or six out of six agreements from the panel on subject matter stakes, and four, five, or six out of six agreements on subject matter scope. Clearly some placements need to be treated more tentatively than others. Nevertheless, the possibility of some agreement among researchers is worth attention. Moreover, the placement accords well with earlier descriptive classifications (Goodwin, 1970; Matthews, 1960). Two additional committees originally offered—Armed Services and Foreign Affairs—received no consensus and were dropped from the analysis. And an alternative dimension of "national" versus "clientele" committees, which has been used in some committee analyses, was also originally offered, but did not produce any evidence of agreement.

The sixteen committees, then, can be classified by subject matter stakes and scope as in Table 9-1.

Very briefly, policy content for the sixteen committees in the 87th through 90th Congresses can be summarized as follows, corroborated by the research from earlier committee studies. Ways and Means and Finance handle issues of great controversy and concern to a large number of congressmen: tax policy, social security, medicare, and so forth. The Judiciary committees are charged with consideration of constitutional questions, controversial "law and order" issues, and others of considerable ideological controversy, visibility, and congressional concern. The Appropriations committees, whose distribution of federal funds may be life or death to the individual congressman, can deal with questions of more or less, with controversy depressed by the nature of money amounts that can be compromised. By contrast, the Labor and Banking committees have dealt with a more restricted set of congressional interests, but one of considerable partisan and ideological controversy: labor legislation, aid to education, housing, big versus small business interests, larger versus smaller federal role. Public Works and Interior committees, while also dealing with a restricted set of congressional interests, were at that point in time perceiving their committees' business as the distribution of federal funding for local and regional purposes. Perception of a restricted, regional set of interests is attested to by the peculiar nature of the committees' membership: overwhelmingly western for Interior, and border-southern and west-of-the-Mississippi for Public Works. Post Office committee members may have less to distribute than Interior members, but have been found similarly concerned with patronage, helping constituents, and serving reelection goals (Fenno, 1973a).

We have, then, a tentative classification on two subject matter dimensions that can receive some agreement from other congressional scholars. It is limited in

Table 9-1 Classification of Committees by Subject Matter Stakes and Scope

	Stakes	
Scope	*Zero-Sum (competitive)*	*Positive-Sum (noncompetitive)*
Broad	Ways & Means/Finance (6,5)* Judiciary/Judiciary (4,6)	Appropriations/Appropriations (6,5)
Restricted	Education & Labor/Labor (4,5) Banking & Currency/Banking & Currency (5,6)	Interior/Interior (6,5) Public Works/Public Works (4,6) Post Office/Post Office (5,6)

* Numbers in parentheses refer to the number of six panelists agreeing to the placement by scope and stakes, respectively.

that it falls short of unanimity, deals with slightly less than half of the congressional committees, and is restricted to one particular time period. While such limits necessarily restrict the generality of the findings, they should serve for this preliminary examination of subject matter effects.

Subject Matter, Committee Attractiveness, and Membership

To what extent do the scope and stakes of subject matter shape such committee attributes as attractiveness, stability of membership, and proportion of senior members? We expect that broad-scope committees will be more attractive, stable, and senior than restricted committees, and expect no difference for zero-sum versus positive-sum stakes.

Table 9-2 reports results employing the traditional index of attractiveness based on transfers to and from the committee from the 81st through 90th Congresses (Goodwin, 1970; Miller and Stokes, unpub. ms.). Stability is measured by mean years' consecutive service of members on the committee, and seniority by mean years' congressional service. (Similar results are obtained if seniority is measured by percent freshman members or percent members with ten or more years' service.) While stability and seniority have only been calculated for the 90th Congress, both measures reflect the formation of committee membership over time, and could easily be shown to hold over a number of Congresses.

A number of observations can immediately be made from the table. First, broad-scope committees are consistently ranked higher in attractiveness, are more stable and composed of more senior members than restricted committees.[2] Second, there is no observable difference between competitive and noncompetitive committees for these attributes within the broad-scope category, and only slight differences between them within the restricted category, with the competitive committees on the average slightly more stable and more senior. In stability, competitive committees average 5.5 years and nonconcompetitive committees 4.4 in the House, and 6.3 and 5.8, respectively, in the Senate. In seniority, competitive committees average 6.4 and noncompetitive committees 6.0 years in the House, and 8.3 and 7.5 years, respectively, in the Senate. Third, there is strikingly strong intercorrelation between the *rankings* of House and Senate committees dealing with the same subject matter. Matching House and Senate committees produced the following rank order coefficients (Kendall's tau), two of which are significant beyond the .05 level:

House and Senate Intercorrelations

Committee attractiveness	tau = .61 (p<.05)
Committee stability	tau = .25 (ns)
Committee seniority	tau = .64 (p<.05)

This House-Senate similarity suggests that subject matter alone is a powerful shaper of committee attractiveness and senior membership. Beyond the ranking, however, the scope distinction alone arrays committees almost perfectly into two categories—of greater or less attractiveness, stability, and seniority.[3] Of the sixteen committees thus arrayed on three dimensions, for a total of 48

Table 9-2 Policy Content, Committee Attractiveness, and Membership

Committees	Attractiveness (rank) House	Attractiveness (rank) Senate	Stability (mean years consecutive committee service) House	(Rank)	Senate	(Rank)	Seniority of Members (mean years congressional service) House	(Rank)	Senate	(Rank)
Broad-Competitive										
Ways and Means/Finance	2	2	6.9	2	9.3	2	12.6	1	12.8	2
Judiciary	3	3	7.0	1	6.5	5	9.0	3	10.6	3
Broad-Noncompetitive										
Appropriations	1	1	6.6	3	10.5	1	10.6	2	17.3	1
Restricted-Competitive										
Banking and Currency	6½	6	5.0	6	5.6	7	6.7	4	8.5	5
Education and Labor/Labor	5	5	6.0	4	6.9	4	6.0	7	8.0	6
Restricted-Noncompetitive										
Interior	6½	4	4.4	7	7.2	3	6.5	6	9.5	4
Public Works	4	8	5.2	5	4.4	8	6.6	5	5.2	8
Post Office	8	7	3.6	8	5.8	6	5.0	8	7.7	7

Committees are ranked from high to low attractiveness, stability, and seniority. The preference ranking for attractiveness is based on transfers to and from the committees in the 81st-90th Congresses. See Goodwin, pp. 114, 115. Stability and seniority are calculated for the 90th Congress, but similarly reflect membership changes over time.

placements, there would be only two errors made: Senate Interior and Senate Judiciary would be misplaced for committee stability.

Subject Matter and Committee Behavior

We can now address the other major possibility concerning the effects of subject matter—that is, its effect on cohesive or noncohesive committee behavior. Cohesive behavior was observed by Fenno in the committee context, and tested by Dodd and by Dyson and Soule using members' roll call voting on the floor. While roll calls permit a convenient and justifiable measure of one important kind of behavior, it is the behavior of individuals outside the committee habitat and not the behavior of the committee-as-group. Moreover, behavior may change as congressmen move from committee to floor. Thus, a member of a cohesive committee may vote with the group in committee, warning members he will have to dissent on the floor. So a closer testing of the proposition inferred from the Appropriations study may be gained from the committee recommendation stage.

One measure of members' cohesive behavior is the percent of nonunanimous recommendations the committee reports. *Congressional Quarterly* records for each bill recommended to the floor whether there was a unanimous recommendation, a minority (party) dissent, or dissent by some individuals, either mentioned by name or by number dissenting.[4] As the subsequent data will show, by far the most frequent committee behavior is a unanimous recommendation. In this sense, then, unanimity may be seen as a kind of empirical "norm." Results also show, however, that committees vary considerably in the percentage of nonunanimous recommendations they report. In other words, some committees deviate from this "norm" of unanimity much more frequently than others. It should further be understood that individual dissent from recommendations is rare. No committees in the study showed more than two cases of individual dissent, and most showed one. So the measure is not reflecting some mavericks' tendency on a few committees to dissent regularly on recommendations. Moreover, nonunanimous recommendations seemed preferred over a measure based on partisanship, since the concept of cohesiveness clearly includes intraparty as well as interparty dissent. Otherwise, committees dominated by a conservative coalition, for example, might appear highly cohesive when actually a number of liberal Democrats would consistently be in dissent. Accordingly, percent nonunanimous recommendations is used as the measure of cohesive behavior.

One caution should be employed in using this measure. Most committees in the study made between 10 and 25 recommendations in the 90th Congress, so the percentages may be taken as fairly comparable indicators within that range. The two Appropriations committees made more (35 and 36 for the Senate and House, respectively). Three commitees made less: House Post Office and Public Works, seven apiece; and Senate Post Office only four. As a reminder in the reporting of results, percentages based on these extremely small numbers are supplied in parentheses.

If subject matter affects the cohesiveness of committee behavior, then what we have called the zero-sum committees will be less cohesive than the positive-sum committees, and there will be no relationship of attractiveness of membership with cohesive behavior.

The results, reported in Table 9-3, show strong support for these expectations. Zero-sum committees, of whichever scope, exhibit less cohesive behavior than positive-sum committees for both the Senate and the House. Of the sixteen committees, at most three would be misplaced by a classification based on subject matter stakes: the two Labor committees and House Public Works. For the House and Senate, the most attractive, stable, and senior committees are found at the most cohesive and least cohesive extremes. If we were to correlate committees ranked from high to low attractiveness and from high to low cohesion, results would show a slight inverse relationship for the House, with tau $= -.18$, and an inverse, still statistically nonsignificant relationship for the Senate of tau $= -.39$ (coefficients based on Kendall's tau). In this case, subject matter stakes, not scope, is the important organizing dimension.[5]

We can note again the strong correlation between House and Senate committees dealing with the same subject matter. The House overall uses more nonunanimous recommendations than the Senate, but correlating the committees' ranked positions within each chamber, a fairly strong correlation coefficient is

Table 9-3 Policy Content and Committee Cohesion in Recommendations

Percent Nonunanimous Recommendations[a]

House:		Stakes	
		Competitive	Noncompetitive
Scope			
Broad		Ways and Means 67%	Appropriations 6%
		Judiciary 56%	
Restricted		Banking and Currency 58%	Interior 36%
		Education and Labor 33%	Public Works (43%)
			Post Office (29%)

Senate:		Stakes	
		Competitive	Noncompetitive
Scope			
Broad		Finance 33%	Appropriations 6%
		Judiciary 47%	
Restricted		Banking and Currency 29%	Interior 18%
		Labor 13%	Public Works 0%
			Post Office (0%)

[a] Percentages based on less than 10 recommendations are reported in parentheses.

produced: tau $= .46$, p $= .07$. Removing the "deviant" House Public Works committee, ranked far below its cohesive Senate counterpart, would of course greatly improve the strength of the correlation. What we are saying, then, for behavior as for the earlier results reported for membership, is that House and Senate committees dealing with the same subject matter exhibit quite similar attributes.

Controlling for subject matter controversy, within the classification as presented in Table 9-3, one can then ask if attractiveness or membership has any independent effect on behavior. For the House, no relationship is observable. Within the competitive category, broad-scope committees (of high attractiveness, seniority, and stability) are on the average less cohesive than clientele committees (of lower attractiveness, stability, and seniority). Within the noncompetitive category, Appropriations is more cohesive. For the Senate, no relationship can be inferred from the noncompetitive category, while for the competitive category, broad-scope committees exhibit less cohesive behavior than restricted committees.

These results may help reconcile some of the very disparate and apparently contradictory findings of the earlier studies. Using interview data, Fenno documented the exceptionally cohesive behavior of the stable, senior, and attractive Appropriations Committee. Using roll call data, Dyson and Soule found no relationship between attractiveness and cohesion in the House. Neither study controlled for subject matter controversy. Also using roll call data, but controlling for subject matter controversy, Dodd found an inverse relationship between attractiveness and cohesion in the Senate. The present study based on committee recommendations indicates, supporting Fenno, that Appropriations is indeed exceptionally cohesive, and supporting Dyson and Soule, that House committees overall show no relationship between attractiveness and cohesion. And controlling for subject matter controversy, the study indicates some support for the inverse relationship for Senate committees that Dodd reported, and no relationship for House committees. The picture that begins to emerge, then, from these very different investigations is that attractiveness and membership attributes appear to be only coincidentally linked with cohesive behavior.

One final summarizing point is necessary. The classification based simply on subject matter stakes and scope can explain a considerable amount of committee variety. In other words, if we arrayed committees by high and low attractiveness (also seniority and stability) and by high and low cohesion, dichotomizing at clear breakpoints in the data, we would produce *almost the same results as if we arrayed them by subject matter scope and stakes* (see Table 9-4). With the exception of placement of the two Labor committees, this is identical to the organization of committees by stakes and scope, presented earlier. In other words, the two subject matter dimensions could place 14 committees and miss 2.

Defining the dichotomy as strongly as possible *against* the proposition while still attempting to keep very similarly cohesive committees together, one could dichotomize cohesion by ranks 1-4 and 5-8, thus calling House Public Works and Senate Interior "low cohesion" committees. It should be clear, of course, that both committees are closer to the next high-cohesion committee than to the next low-cohesion committee, but even if this were done, with maximum possible weighting against the proposition, the scheme would still place 12 committees correctly and miss 4.

Conclusions

In this exploratory study, two findings are of particular importance. First, strong House-Senate intercorrelations of committees dealing with the same jurisdictions argue for some subject matter effect: at least, they suggest an influence beyond the single committee, its group interaction, its chairman, or particular institutional constraints. And second, the two illustrative subject matter dimensions selected for the study are indeed capable of organizing varieties of attractivenss, membership, and cohesive behavior. Perhaps they can help reconcile and explain apparent contradictions between the single committee studies and the macrocomparative studies on the relationship between the attractiveness complex and cohesive behavior. And they indicate that at least some of the bewildering diversity of committees so frequently recorded may be explained by the permutations of attractiveness, membership, and behavior as shaped by subject matter. A provisional summary matrix may then be suggested as in Table 9-5. By identifying major patterns within this diversity, it should be possible to highlight deviant cases requiring more detailed attention. The differences between the two Public Works committees and the curiously cohesive behavior of the Labor committees are cases that would be worth further study for this reason.

Table 9-4 Committee Rankings by Attractiveness and Cohesion

	Cohesion	
Attractiveness	*Low (ranks 6-8)*	*High (ranks 1-5)*
High (ranks 1-3)	Ways & Means/Finance Judiciary/Judiciary	Appropriations/Appropriations
Low (ranks 4-8)	Banking & Currency/Banking & Currency	Interior/Interior Post Office/Post Office Public Works/Public Works Labor/Education & Labor

Table 9-5 Provisional Summary Matrix

Stakes	*Scope*	*Goals (Fenno)*	*Attractiveness*	*Membership*	*Behavior*
Zero-sum	Broad	Prestige	High	More senior, stable	Less cohesive
	Restricted	Policy	Lower	Less senior, stable	Less cohesive
Positive-sum	Broad	Prestige	High	More senior, stable	More cohesive
	Restricted	Reelection	Lower	Less senior, stable	More cohesive

Note, further, that the scheme accords with Fenno's classification of committees by the predominant goals of members (1973a). As committee subject matter varies by scope and stakes, it would be more suited to some members' goals than others. Members seeking congressional influence would desire committees dealing with subject matter of widespread congressional interest: i.e., committees of broad scope, whatever the stakes. Those seeking the making of good public policy may be drawn to those committees handling the most relevant, controversial legislation, which would tend to be the zero-sum committees, whether broad or restricted. And those looking toward a reelection fight may seek the positive-sum, distributive committees, whether broad or restricted.

One final comment may be in order. There are three widely reported ways of "accounting for" congressional behavior—each with its own considerable popular following and academic applications. One emphasizes the desire to be reelected, and cites the distribution of pork, as well as congressional avoidance of controversial issues. A second emphasizes internal social processes: norms and sanctions, socialization, affective leadership, and a Senate Club. A third emphasizes ideology, cites a "Conservative Establishment," and explains assignments or a Rules Committee decision from that point of view. These three, of course, point toward the three separate congressional goals suggested by Fenno's comparative committee study. And the above analysis suggests, corroborating Fenno, that no *one* of these is sufficient for congressional explanation. With congressmen seeking satisfaction for different goals with different kinds of subject matter, some committees will more appropriately fit one explanatory mode than another. Thus Public Works may fit a reelection accounting, Appropriations a sociological accounting, and Judiciary an ideological accounting. So by classifying committees by subject matter, we may not only reduce some of the variety of past committee accounts, but may also point out some of the more fundamental variety that remains.

Notes

1. Six of eight scholars responded to the questionnaire and five gave permission for their names to be used: John Bibby, Charles Bullock, Richard Fenno, David Mayhew, Robert Peabody. The panel was asked to classify the committees according to the dimensions set forth in Table 9-1.
2. The same results are seen measuring "seniority" by percent freshman members. In the House, broad-scope committees average 9 percent freshmen, restricted committees, 20 percent freshmen. In the Senate, broad-scope committees had no freshmen, and restricted committees averaged 14 percent freshmen. The same distinction could be found by measuring the percent of "senior" members (10 years or more congressional service), so the average figure reported in the text is not merely reflecting either freshman or senior extremes.
3. It should also be noted that the attractiveness, seniority, and stability variables are highly intercorrelated in the House and strikingly so in the Senate—so much so that

they may more usefully be treated in future committee analysis as a complex, rather than a number of separate attributes:

	House Intercorrelations	Senate Intercorrelations
Attractiveness & Seniority	tau = .68, p<.05	tau = .93, p<.001
Attractiveness & Stability	tau = .68, p<.05	tau = .79, p<.01
Seniority & Stability	tau = .57, p<.05	tau = .71, p<.01

4. The source is *Congressional Quarterly Almanac,* 1967, 1968, so the measure is limited to the bills reported, as *Congressional Quarterly Almanac* defines them.

5. Seven committees filed some minority party dissents: both Labor committees, both Banking committees, Ways and Means and Finance, House Public Works. These are all what we have called zero-sum committees. Committees highest in nonpartisan dissent (dissent by 3 or more individuals) include House Interior, House and Senate Judiciary, House Banking and Currency and House Post Office. So the measure of nonunanimous roll calls is heavily, though not exclusively, reflecting partisan dissent.

10. POLITICAL PARTIES AND THE PORKBARREL: PARTY CONFLICT AND COOPERATION IN HOUSE PUBLIC WORKS COMMITTEE DECISION MAKING

James T. Murphy

Introduction

In the annals of American political lore, porkbarreling has long been synonymous with domestic legislation having obvious political content. The term "porkbarrel," meaning the distribution of public works expenditures on the basis of political influence, has been applied most frequently and most pejoratively to the legislation processed by the House Public Works committee.[1] And understandably so, for political meaning *does* inhere in public works proposals; public works projects can profoundly alter the living circumstances of citizens within and beyond the areas in which they are built. Thus members of the committee that recommends the construction of roads, dams, public buildings, water pollution treatment plants, the drafting of harbors, the abatement of beach erosion, or any number of economic development projects, are presumed to be in a unique position to alter electoral probabilities in favor of themselves and other members of the House.[2] In the lore of American politics, then, authorizing public works projects is the result of spontaneous, widespread favor trading. One can account for the authorizations by the "simple matter of *quid pro quo* . . . , you scratch my back and I'll scratch yours. . . ."[3]

Such bipartisan favor trading cannot, however, account for the broad patterns of Public Works committee behavior, *party conflict* and *party cooperation*. To account for these patterns of party conflict and party cooperation, one must begin with party affiliation, not with exchange processes. Public Works legislation, as Julius Turner reported more than twenty years ago, is moderately partisan.[4] Since the time of Turner's study, the committee's jurisdiction has

Author's Note: I wish to express my appreciation to the American Political Science Association for a Congressional Fellowship which gave me the opportunity to be a participant-observer with both the Senate and the House Public Works committees during the first session of the 90th Congress, and to the Brookings Institution for a Research Fellowship in Government which facilitated the preparation of this paper. In addition, I am indebted to David W. Adamany, Richard F. Fenno, Jr., Fred I. Greenstein, Russell D. Murphy, James L. Payne, Nelson W. Polsby, and Hubert J. O'Gorman for many helpful suggestions in the revision of earlier drafts.

Source: *American Political Science Review* 68 (March 1974): 169-185. Reprinted with permission of the author.

expanded to include many more issues that are likely to split the parties. Most committee legislation will engender party disputes because committee Democrats and Republicans cannot arive at a consensus either on regional allocation issues (allocations benefiting a minority in each party) or on traditional party issues. The parties have yet to reach a consensus on aid to economically depressed areas. Committee Democrats and Republicans cannot reach agreement on the authority of the federal government or on its position in the economy. The federal government's position in the economy drives the parties apart over issues such as whether private or public power should be supported; whether the federal government or the state governments should assume responsibility for treating water pollution; how the financial burden of the Interstate and Defense Highway System should be distributed; and, finally, whether or not new construction in the District of Columbia should be undertaken. Nor can the parties agree on the authority of the federal government in approving state water quality standards or promulgating federal standards or penalizing the states if they do not comply with highway beautification standards. Very often, then, Public Works Democrats and Republicans are divided when the committee reports legislation to the House. When there is such committee division, it usually means that the committee majority party is attempting to provide leadership for change and must, therefore, depend on the House majority party for success.

But public works legislation is still best characterized as only moderately partisan. Public Works Democrats and Republicans are frequently united when reporting bills to the House. Nonetheless, party affiliation is more important than exchange processes in accounting for this committee party cooperation. Party cooperation is manifest in the national allocation issues (allocations benefiting a majority in each party), such as projects of the Army Corps of Engineers, federally funded highway mileage, federal dollars for waste treatment construction plants, and public buildings *outside* the District of Columbia. This party unity is misleading, however, in that it suggests a consensus between Democrats and Republicans on national allocation issues. Since, however, the distinct possibility of partisan porkbarreling exists, such a consensus is very unlikely. Why, it must be asked, should rational calculating Democrats and Republicans entrust part of their party's fate at the polls to an ad hoc coalition building process such as porkbarreling? The threat of partisan allocations has induced the congressional parties to adopt relatively rigid allocation rules such that neither party can make substantial gains at the polls at the expense of the other. So, while Public Works committee members are, *to some degree,* in a position to push their pet projects and ideas, committee proposals on national allocation issues cannot be explained in terms of bipartisan favor trading. Instead, the committee must use the allocation formulas as the measure of acceptability in the House. The Public Works committee's relationship with the House of Representatives is thus often routine, allowing little or no leeway for change through committee recommendations.

In identifying and accounting for these patterns of party conflict and party cooperation and linkages in them with House decisions, evidence from protocols, congressional documents, and roll calls has been used. During the 1st and 2d sessions of the 90th Congress, all but two of the sitting members of the House Public Works committee were interviewed. Forty-two open-ended structural interviews were conducted with 37 committee members and former committee members. Interviews were conducted on an anonymous basis and averaged 55 minutes in length. Analysis of the internal operations of the committee relies heavily on the interview protocols. Committee reports and House debates on all the major bills from the 84th through the 90th Congresses proved to be essential supplements to the protocol data. Since some of these documentary data can be quantified, they have been used to help establish patterns of internal committee behavior. In addition, documentary evidence, particularly the debates, proved to be indispensable for assessing the relationship between the committee and the House. Finally, the roll-call data proved to be helpful for all aspects of this study. Analysis of the 68 conflict roll calls on Public Works committee bills from the 80th through the 90th Congresses helped establish patterns and account for them. The roll calls also proved helpful in analyzing the relationship between the committee and the House. No one particular kind of evidence for any important aspect of this study was used; all the evidence available from any of the sources used has been brought to bear as seemed appropriate.

The Members and the Issues

Crucial to the relationship between issues and party affiliation on the House Public Works committee is the distribution of membership goals, for they affect committee party conflict. Generally, congressmen find a committee appealing for at least three different reasons: prestige, bringing federal largesse back to the district, and subject-matter interest.[5] Both prestige and constituency goals have a marked tendency to minimize party conflict; subject matter interest is likely to amplify party conflict.[6]

The Members

House members who want a Public Works seat will nearly always be given it. From the data in Table 10-1, which reports some results of interviews with committee members, it is clear that most Public Works members (60 percent) are constituency members—congressmen who see themselves as having come to the committee to accomplish something for their districts. A few (19 percent) are interested in "getting a log rolled" for their state delegation (the delegation members), and about one-fifth (21 percent) are assigned to the committee because preferred seats on other committees are not available (the shuttle members).[7] Constituency members often mentioned, during interviews, a particular problem or geographical characteristic in their district: "My district is bordered on three sides by two big rivers." "My district is bordered on three sides by rivers." "We need industrial development in our district worse than anything else." "Water pollution!" "Beach erosion!" I have over 40 percent of the water projects of [my state] in my district." "We've got to get a road in there [a part of the district]." "We have a real watershed problem." This constituency orientation is really no less important for the few members who take the seat on behalf of their state dele-

Table 10-1   Assignments to Public Works

Congressman's Party	Conditions of Assignment[a]							
	Constituency Members		Delegation Members		Shuttle Members		Total	
	N	(%)	N	(%)	N	(%)	N	(%)
Democrat	16	6	3	14	2	9	21	56
Republican	6	35	4	24	6	41	16	44
	22	60	7	19	8	21	37	(100)

[a] Two members are excluded: a Democrat who was placed on the committee to help vote out the St. Lawrence Seaway legislation and a Republican who wanted a seat because of his occupational background.

gation: "My state has to have someone on the committee because it, in fact the whole area, has real water problems . . ." or, "We have the TVA and we have a lot of Corps work down there." Finally, the constituency aspect of a Public Works seat is evident in a negative way from the perspective of the shuttle member who hopes to move on to a new assignment: "The committee just isn't that important to my constituency. . . " or, "There really isn't anything on the committee that I'm interested in."

Image building in the district is the primary reason for being on Public Works and, as such, it has a direct impact upon transferring from the committee. Since image building is the major reward of a Public Works seat, the shuttle member will leave the committee as soon as possible, *irrespective of his rank.* Since Republicans have a disproportionate share of shuttle members, Republicans have disproportionately more transfers to other committees: if Republicans had transferred at the same rate as Democrats from the 80th through 89th Congresses, they would have had 14 instead of 22 transfers (the Democrats had 20). But not all shuttle members are able to transfer. Inevitably, then, some will become ranking subcommittee minority members—two of the top five Republicans in the 89th, 90th, and 91st Congresses. Because some of the legislation is important to their state or region, delegation members do realize some political return. Nonetheless, these members are as likely as not to transfer from Public Works; if, however, they are unable to transfer during the first four years, they will remain on the committee. Public Works thus has a nucleus of veterans—constituency members who would never leave of their own volition in addition to delegation members who stay. Even more than delegation members, constituency members refer readily to the tangible political consequences of delivering for the district.

Thirteen of these twenty-nine constituency and delegation members were specifically asked if "delivering the goods" brought them votes, and all said yes. "Public Works is a sugar committee," observed a former veteran Republican. "I could always go back to the district and say, 'Look at that road I got for you. See that beach erosion project over there? And those buildings? I got all those; I'm on

James T. Murphy

Public Works.' " "It is the result of being on the committee—what they can see— that helps. They've got to see some brick and mortar," added a Democrat. Another Democrat spoke for many of his colleagues when he said: "If you're going to stay around here, you've got to take care of the folks back home. . . . It's the bread-and-butter issues that count—the dams, the post offices and the other buildings, the highways. . . . You can point to all these things you've done."

Typically, then, Public Works veterans share an interest in bringing construction into their districts. Superficially, this sharing of interest suggests a pattern of favor trading in committee decision making. Party conflict, however, is the committee's dominant decision-making characteristic. Party splits are evident in the committee's internal behavior as well as in its behavior on the floor. Minority reports were filed for 52 percent of the major legislative proposals the committee recommended to the House. As indicated in Table 10-2, from the 84th through the 89th Congress the minority reports were submitted on 43 percent of the road measures, 45 percent of the pollution control measures, one-half of the public buildings and grounds bills, 58 percent of the water and power measures, and all of the economic development bills. Party splits are also evident in the 44 roll-call votes on committee legislation for the same Congresses; a majority of each party stood on the opposite side of the issues on 75 percent of the non-trivial roll calls—those roll calls where the losing vote was at least 10 percent.

The Issues

Three things seem to account for this apparent inconsistency between the shared interest in projects and this pattern of party conflict: (1) the diversity of the committee's jurisdiction, (2) program goals, and (3) party affiliation. The heterogeneity of the issues channeled through Public Works makes it unlikely that any member will have a political stake in each. Not infrequently, then, little or no constituency influence bears on the decisions of many members. Moreover, as noted at the outset, traditional party issues such as power, authority of the federal government, and expenditure levels are referred to the committee. What difference would all of this diversity make in the committee's behavior if members were interested only in the projects? Not much, if Public Works members were not also interested in programs. Committee members are decidedly program-oriented. Moreover, their party affiliation, more than any other single factor, determines their policy preferences.[8]

Constituency and delegation members enjoy the subject matter; they take genuine pleasure in the legislation they handle and great personal satisfaction in their legislative accomplishments. To them Public Works is the "construction committee." Tangible "things that you can see" are, in their view, the products of its decisions. Public Works is the committee that "builds things"; the committee that harnesses the nation's water supply and promotes and protects the "greatest public works program in the history of mankind," the interstate highway system; the committee which, through its flood control and highway construction, preserves property, creates wealth, and, most importantly, saves lives; the committee that brings "comfort" and "reassurance" to flood victims because "it's important for those people to know that somebody, especially the Congress,

238

Table 10-2 Minority Reports on Major Public Works Bills, 84th through 89th Congresses

Reports	Water and Power	Water Pollution	Roads	Economic Development	Public Buildings and Grounds	Total Bills
No Minority Report	12	6	8	0	1	27
Minority Report	11	6	6	5	1	29
	(23)	(12)	(14)	(5)	(2)	(56)
Minority Reports Submitted by:						
Republicans Only	10	5	3	5	1	29
Democrats Only	0	0	0	0	0	0
Both Parties	1	1	3	0	0	5

cares." It's the committee that gets the job done; huge dams, though costlier, are much preferred to a series of small watersheds because "you can't catch one of those damn floods in a bunch of tin cans." Above all, they resent its being labeled "the porkbarrel committee." To these members Public Works authorizes only economically justified projects—"for every dollar that goes out, at least one dollar must come back."

But *what* should be built up, *what* should be authorized, and *how* it should be done are questions which often divide the parties. To begin with, there are the allocation issues; there is a remarkable disparity in the perspectives of uninterested Democrats and Republicans on allocation questions. Consider, for example, the relationship between shared interests and party conflict on the Appalachian regional development legislation. In both 1965 and 1967 the Democratic majority supported the Appalachian Democrats, whereas the Republican majority (charging "favoritism") opposed the legislation and hence the Appalachian Republicans. The uninterested Democrats thus voted for and the uninterested Republicans voted against the new federal program authorizing selective benefits. The lineup on bills such as this suggests that committee party conflict is inversely related to shared constituency interests.

This inverse relationship between the incidence of constituency interest and party conflict varies, itself, from one program area to the next. Extremes in variation between program areas are manifest in the projects of the Army Corps of Engineers projects and the authorizations for construction in the District of Columbia. Authorizations for construction in the District of Columbia are obviously as devoid of constituency influence as any measure can be. It is not then surprising to find on these issues frequent Public Works party conflict, such as the fierce battle in the 89th Congress over the vice-presidential mansion. On the other hand, the widespread constituency interest in the Corps projects provides substantial incentive for cooperation. Virtually every committee member, sooner or later, will have a project somewhere in the Corps's labyrinthine evaluation process. Like the overwhelming bulk of Corps projects, authorizing the annual statutory limit of thirty federal buildings *outside* the federal city engenders little party conflict. Similarly, no noticeable party conflict stems from the authorization of mileage for the interstate highway system. Nor did the parties ever dispute the method of allocating funds for construction of water waste treatment plants; virtually every congressman can claim credit for one. In fact, of the 29 minority reports presented in Table 10-2, just one—occasioned by President Eisenhower's resistance to the 1956 rivers and harbors omnibus bill—was addressed to an allocation question in which a majority of each of the two parties had a long-standing, permanent constituency interest.

For Public Works the relative differences in shared interest from one kind of program to the next are the keys to understanding the two "faces" of the committee: party conflict and party cooperation. But the relative incidence of shared interests does not account for all Public Works party conflicts. In addition, allocation disputes, other party differences respecting finance and the amount of federal government authority contribute to conflict. In both 1955 and 1956 Democrats were adamantly opposed to the so-called "Clay-bond financing plan" to finance the proposed interstate highway system; Republicans, however, gave solid support to the plan which had been endorsed by President Eisenhower. And it has been the Republicans, not the Democrats, who have insisted that the Federal Water Pollution Control Agency share control with state capitals in funding waste treatment construction plans and policing polluters.[9] These instances are but suggestive of the kinds of issues that contribute to committee party conflict and which are, to some degree, similar to those to be found on Education and Labor.[10]

Committee Democrats and Republicans, then, cooperate on national allocation issues but are in conflict on regional allocation and traditional party government issues. The parties cooperate on allocation decisions in which virtually every member has a constituency stake, just as the two parties do on Interior.[11] Conversely, when only a minority in each party shares a constituency stake in an allocation decision, Public Works Democrats and Republicans will disagree just as in the case of Agriculture *but* for a different reason; on Public Works, there is not the coincidence of commodity interest and party affiliation.[12] When only a minority in each party shares a constituency stake on an allocation question, the question becomes a party issue because Democrats prefer to support their minority but Republicans do not.[13] Issues pertaining to the authority of the federal government or its position in the economy consistently divide the parties.

Such are the divisive forces at work on Public Works that committee members emphasize their party affiliations at the expense of committee unity. "There are a number of things," said a veteran Democrat, "that are party matters, and you aren't going to get together on them." "It is," related a Republican newcomer, "the job of the majority to govern; the minority's job is to oppose." A high-ranking veteran Republican clarified the nature of the opposition: "We hear all this talk about developing Republican alternatives. Well, what are our alternatives? What is our position going to be?" "Frankly," added a veteran Democrat, "sometimes we have to let them know what the facts of life are. After all, they are the minority. If they want to write their bill, well, then they can go out and gain the confidence of the people and bring a majority in here and do it." Public Works members clearly value the idea of party government.

The Two Faces of Public Works: Party Conflict and Party Cooperation

The attachment to party affiliation and, further, to the notion of party government at the expense of committee unity can usefully be discussed in terms of Peter M. Blau's idea of particularistic social values—"preferences for attributes like one's own." [14] Such values distinguish non-organized collectivities such as age groups, sex groups, the electorate, or a population in a geographical territory from organized collectivities such as Democrats or Republicans or congressional committees in which the "value standards that govern the orientations and associations" within the collectivity are dependent upon *"the relationship between their status attributes."* [15] Such organized collectivities are distinguished by some collective interest or goal such as power and prestige on the House Ways and Means and Appropriations committees, both of which have the

value of the greatest possible degree of *committee unanimity or consensus.* [16]
Among Public Works members the attachment to party at the expense of
committee affiliation suggests that Democrats and Republicans value the greatest
possible degree of committee *party unity.* Further, as organized collectivities, they
have mutually exclusive goals: for the majority party, the Democrats, the
collective interest is the capacity to determine policy outcomes; for the minority
party, the Republicans, the goal is to devise effective challenges to the majority's
capacity to determine committee recommendations.

What accounts for the remarkable difference between the value of
party unity on Public Works and *committee unity* on Appropriations and
Ways and Means? Further, why is the behavior of Public Works so different
from Interior's characteristic party cooperation when the constituency goal
is the primary reason for wanting a seat on either committee? [17] Finally, why do
the program-oriented Public Works members place such a premium on party
government when the program-oriented Education and Labor members do
not? [18]

The value difference between Appropriations and Ways and Means and
Public Works is, I think, attributable to the relative prestige of these
two top-ranking committees as against the 11th-ranking Public Works. [19] The
prestige goal shared by congressmen on the Ways and Means and Appropriations committees provides a powerful incentive for them to subdue the conflict
ordinarily generated by the numerous party issues brought before these committees. That is to say, these congressmen hold that some degree of committee
unity is essential to committee influence—the predisposition of the House
to accept their proposals. This influence, these members hold further, is necessary for the power and prestige they want from the committees. In Fenno's
words: "The extraordinary effort at internal integration [on Appropriations],
especially at minimizing partisanship, brings success on the floor. Success
on the floor results in committee influence, and committee influence determines
committee member influence." [20] And, in the words of a Ways and Means
Republican: "It's the issues that are partisan, not the members." [21] It is in
this aspect, the modification of conflict to gain influence, that Ways and
Means, Appropriations, and the third-ranking Rules differ from lower-ranking
committees such as Public Works, Education and Labor, Interior, and Agriculture. [22] No matter how unified, no matter how successful these lower-ranking
committees might be, their jurisdictions effectively preclude having as much
influence in the House as the prestigious committees. The top three committees—
the prestigious committees—control, after all, either directly or indirectly,
the fate of nearly all legislation of all other committees—the non-prestigious
committees. [23]

When congressmen, therefore, seek assignment to a non-prestigious committee, they do so for constituency goals and subject-matter interest. Many behavioral
similarities and differences among non-prestigious committees can be traced to
differences in the distribution of these membership goals. For example, the
similarity in the distribution of constituency goals between Public Works and
Interior is paralleled by similarities in party conflict and cooperation, with one

major exception: the constituency stake in the legislation of both provides an apparent incentive for party cooperation, *but* on Public Works the committee is beset with party issues many of which—allocation issues—are directly related to the constituency stake.[24] Likewise, party conflict on both Public Works and Education and Labor can be attributed primarily to the subject-matter interest found on both committees; in each case, the subject-matter interest is, in turn, affected by party affiliation. That Public Works places a higher value on party government than does Education and Labor can be attributed to the differences in the issues between them. Issues processed by the Education and Labor committee are of such a nature that party affiliation does not consistently influence the preference orderings of its members as it does Public Works members. Education and Labor Democrats, for example, will be divided by constituency influence on education bills involving church-state issues; similarly, southern and northern Democrats will disagree on any union or integration issue.[25] Moreover, Education and Labor issues are typically more earthshaking than Public Works issues. Should a Public Works Democrat, for example, be opposed to an amendment for a public power project, he can take a quiet, leisurely walk; the Education and Labor member, however, will be under heavy pressure from his constituents as well as other members to make a lot of noise in openly supporting or opposing almost any issue before the committee.

Does Public Works party cooperation, as is evident in the frequency of committee unanimity in reporting major bills, suggest the committee is an organized collectivity? When interviewed, committee members consistently failed to mention a committee unity value and, further, expressed bewilderment and some irritation when asked questions designed to probe for the existence of a shared committee goal such as success, prestige, power, and others. Such questions produced only some evidence of a fraternal feeling. A veteran Republican noted, for example, that Public Works is a committee with a "great deal of camaraderie"; it is a "good committee." "A lot of that division," cautioned a veteran southern Democrat, "isn't so important or so much as it might look like. . . . They need things, too. . . . I know we helped Bill [Cramer] out on that canal in Florida." Members do expect help from one another on things in which they have a mutual interest (e.g., the Corps projects, the public buildings) or in which questions or party "philosophy" are not at stake (e.g., disaster relief). "All I require," said a veteran Democrat, "is that the project meet the ground rules." But then "that one-to-one ratio [the economic cost-benefit criterion that projects must meet to be authorized], is like putting on a pair of drawers—you stretch them a little once in a while to make them fit." Members of both parties agree that "there is a tendency to help each other out," that "you can bring these projects to fruition because you get support on both sides." This fraternal feeling suggests but a modicum of favor trading; it does not indicate a shared value for the committee suggesting the existence of an organized collectivity.

Thus far, then, the data indicate that committee Democrats and Republicans have a basis for solidarity but do not indicate what governs its degree; for party cooperation, the data indicate neither a basis nor possible determinants of variation in cooperation.

James T. Murphy

Party Conflict and Cooperation

Even though Public Works consists of two organized collectivities, there is no reason to suppose that the party unity value alone will produce a pattern of solidarity. For while it is perhaps true of organized collectivities that shared values "constitute the medium through which its members are bound together . . . [and that] they serve in this way as functional substitutes for the sentiments of personal attraction that integrate the members of a face-to-face group," the values alone are an insufficient guarantee of solidarity.[26] In an organized collectivity, just as in a small group, situations will inevitably arise in which at least one member will have an incentive to promote his interest at the risk of damaging the collective interest.[27] This insufficiency is quite clear in the case of the House Public Works committee.

For any allocation bill not every Democrat is likely to have a constituency stake; moreover, for legislation in general, there is great variability in the policy preferences of committee Democrats. Similarly, there is substantial variability in the policy preferences of committee Republicans; and, conversely, a set of committee Republicans often has a constituency interest in a bill sponsored by the majority but opposed by the minority. The dispersion of policy preferences within the parties and the presence or absence of a constituency stake constitute a direct threat to the goals of each of the two parties. For if a congressman disagrees with his party's position, or if he does not have a constituency stake in a bill, it is a perfect opportunity for him to "hold out" either to change his party's position or to barter for one or more favors in exchange for his vote. The threat of holding out is particularly obvious in the case of a majority party—such as the Democrats for all but two Congresses from the 80th through the 92nd—that is attempting to change the legislative status quo. And it becomes all the more obvious when the ratio of seats between the two parties is very close.

Values of an organized collectivity, then, provide the basis for solidarity, but they do not govern its degree. When incentives contrary to achieving an organized collectivity's goal exist, informal rules of behavior are invariably adopted. These informal rules are generally thought of as norms. Because norms specify legitimate behavior as well as provide rewards and sanctions for conformity to them and deviations from them, they can govern the degree of solidarity within an organized collectivity.[28] Since each party on Public Works is an organized collectivity, and since there exist substantial incentives for contrary behavior in each party, it is reasonable to suppose that one or more norms exist within each party.

Partisanship on the Public Works Committee

Members of each of the two parties are expected to be partisan, to use their party affiliation as the yardstick for what they ought to do. Subcommittee chairmen expect partisan reciprocity from one another and ranking subcommittee minority members are expected "to present the minority position effectively." Partisan behavior is also expected of the other veterans and of junior members as well. This means that the subcommittee chairman or ranking member is not to be "bucked," that questions in hearings and amendments in subcommittee and full committee mark-up are to be "cleared." It obviously means also that Public Works members are expected to vote with their party. Veteran Public Works Democrats are fond of quoting the late Speaker Rayburn's dictum about the rewards and sanctions of legislative life: "If you want to get along, go along." "One thing you notice right away," said a newcomer, "is that you are supposed to vote with your party." "Unless you are really thick," added another, "you pick things like that up right away. It's no problem." "It's assumed" that Democrats will go along with the subcommittee chairman. "A good reason," advised a ranking Republican member, is required to be let off the party hook. For both Republicans and Democrats, "a good reason" means that members are not expected to vote "against their district."

Conformity to this *norm of partisanship* is effected through the myriad of possible rewards and sanctions in the committee's incentive structure. When Chairman Fallon acceded to minority demands to establish an Economic Development Subcommittee to oversee the Economic Development Administration, dependable, interested Representative Ed Edmondson (Oklahoma) got the chairman's nod for the chairmanship over the more senior, interested, but not so dependable Representative Frank Clark (Pennsylvania). The late Chairman Buckley created an entirely new subcommittee in the 87th Congress—Watersheds—for the dependable but politically vulnerable Frank Smith (Mississippi) to help him in a primary battle against Jamie Whitten ("there was a long-standing need for the subcommittee [but] the timing was political"). To veteran Democrats, dependable newcomer Representative James J. Howard (New Jersey) is "just a jewel" who has a large stack of "IOUs"; a not-so-dependable newcomer, whose fiercely independent idealism led him to vote with the committee Republicans against the use of proxies and to "buck" his subcommittee chairman on other occasions is "in hot water" and "hasn't got a prayer." It is in this process of rewarding the conformist and punishing the nonconformist that the newcomer learns what is expected and the veteran is reminded.

That the norm of partisanship can have a profound impact upon committee party solidarity is demonstrated by the data in Table 10-3. In Table 10-3 the voting differences between committee southern and northern Democrats are compared to the differences between House southern and northern Democrats for all major committee bills from 1947 through 1968. From the data in Table 10-3 it is clear that divergences in policy preferences between southern and northern Democrats prevail in the House as a whole but not among Public Works committee members. On 96 percent of the 68 rolls calls, differences between southern and northern committee Democrats are statistically insignificant; differences are statistically significant on just 3 roll calls. House southern and northern Democrats differ significantly on 67.4 percent, or 46, of the 68 roll calls; differences are insignificant on just 22 roll calls. From the standpoint of the norm's effectiveness, those cases in which House differences are significant while committee differences are insignificant are the most interesting. On 66 percent of the roll calls in which committee Democratic differences are insignificant, House Democratic differences are significant. If not for the norm of partisanship, it

Table 10-3   Roll Calls on Major House Public Works Bills, 1947 through 1968: Differences between Northern and Southern Committee and House Democrats[a]

	House Public Works Committee Democrats:			
	Difference between Northern and Southern Democrats Insignificant		Difference between Northern and Southern Democrats Significant	
	N	Proportion	N	Proportion
House Democrats:				
Difference between Northern and Southern Democrats Insignificant	22	.34	0	.00
Difference between Northern and Southern Democrats Significant	43	.66	3	1.00
Totals	65	1.00	3	1.00

[a] Southern Democrats are those representing districts in the Confederate states.
H_0: Proportion Southern Democratic Yeas = Proportion Northern Democratic Yeas
H_a: Proportion Southern Democratic Yeas < Proportion Northern Democratic Yeas
Results are significant at $p \leq .025$.

seems reasonably clear that committee southern and northern Democratic differences would be significant on each of these 43 roll calls. The spirit of this very effective norm is perhaps captured best by the southern Democrat who, during the course of negotiations for the Highway Beautification bill in 1967, said in reference to an identifiable swing group: "We can scuttle the whole thing on ya if we are together but we sure would like to go that extra mile with ya."

It is not always possible, however, to "go that extra mile." Without question, the most obvious limitation of the norm's impact on party solidarity is the influence of constituency. This factor is apparent, for example, in the data on Table 10-4 in which voting differences between committee members who can be thought of as economic development Republicans (10 percent of the population in the congressman's district eligible for benefits) and noneconomic development Republicans are compared with similar groups in the House. For the eight roll calls on economic development legislation from 1965 thorugh 1967, the data in Table 10-4 clearly show that differences between the two groups of Republicans are most likely to be significant. On 75 percent of the eight roll calls, both committee and House economic development Republicans are significantly different from the other Republicans; on just one roll call, the committee economic development Republicans differed significantly from their House counterparts; and again, on just one roll call is there a lack of significance between the groups. Though the data in Table 10-4 are but a slight indication of the influence of con-

Table 10-4 Economic Development Roll Calls, 1965 through 1967: Differences between Economic Development and Other Committee and House Republicans[a]

| | *House Public Works Committee Republicans:* | | | |
| | *Difference between Economic Development and Other Republicans Insignificant* | | *Difference between Economic Development and Other Republicans Significant* | |
	N	*Proportion*	*N*	*Proportion*
House Republicans: Difference between Economic Development and Other Republicans Insignificant	1	.50	0	.00
Difference between Economic Development and Other Republicans Significant	1	.50	6	1.00
Totals	2	1.00	6	1.00

[a] Economic Development Republicans are those representing districts in which at least 10 percent of the population is eligible for benefits.

H_o: Proportion Economic Development Republicans Supporting Party Position = Proportion Other Republicans Supporting Party Position

H_a: Proportion Economic Development Republicans Supporting Party Position < Proportion Other Republicans Supporting Party Position

Results are significant at $p \leq .025$.

stituency on internal party splits, its general significance is apparent in the following remarks of a committee Republican:

A congressman from Poverty Hole, New York, or New Hampshire, or a Duncan from Tennessee, or a Clausen (who has some EDA in that long district of his) sure as hell isn't going to vote against the EDA stuff. And Bill Harsha can't be expected to vote against Appalachia. You know, sometimes we do have to rise above our principles. Someone once said that no one has repealed the law of self-preservation.

Constituency influence does control when constitutency interests are at stake, but, when the parties do disagree, constituency interests are not at stake frequently enough to offset the generally controlling effects of the norm of partisanship. Hence, though constituency influence is important, it is not nearly so significant as the stabilizing effects of the norm of partisanship upon Public Works committee party solidarity.

James T. Murphy

Partisanship and Segregation Between
Committee Democrats and Republicans

Partly solidarity is constantly apparent in the norm of partisanship. Each congressman simultaneously holds that members in his party should be partisan, but that congressmen in the other party should be less partisan, less inclined to ignore the opposite party in preliminary negotiations, and less devoted to the practice of caucusing and party regularity. This paradoxical expectation is clearly manifest in the contradictory observations made by committee Democrats and Republicans about committee party leaders. About the two most recent chairmen, some Democrats made the following remarks: (1) A former subcommittee chairman said, "Charlie Buckley was a great fellow. He was hardly ever around here, but everyone loved him." (2) A veteran Democratic staffer noted that "Mr. Fallon is not quite so much the straight party man that Chairman Buckley was. Fallon is not at all above tripping over the traces on some Administration bills. Buckley never did." (3) A veteran Democrat noted that "Mr. Fallon is certainly not controversial." In contrast, a former veteran Republican sized up the committee under Buckley and Fallon as follows:

> I'll tell you one thing about that committee when I was on it. Buckley was the chairman, and it was a pretty damn lousy committee. He'd appoint somebody acting chairman and those guys would ride roughshod over us. It was straight party-line vote on everything. Now I think it is different since Fallon has taken over. My impression is that it is not quite as partisan as it used to be. I think he is more apt to give a little bit, accept some Republican amendments.

A high-ranking Republican added that Fallon is:

> a very mild-mannered man who doesn't like disagreements—and I say that with special reference to the White House. He is far preferable to Buckley. He was just terrible. He treated the minority like scum! Fallon is very different. He treats us as though we are part of the committee. They just rammed that stuff through when Buckley was chairman.

But not even Fallon received a very high score from the Republicans. At least one veteran observed that Fallon was "not exactly" his "candidate for the fairest chairman in the House." "You know," he added, "some of these chairmen have damn good reputations for being fair, and so forth. Hell, we never have enough time to file a minority report on this committee!"

Similarly, Republicans who are defended by their party colleagues elicit scathing remarks from the Democrats. A subcommittee chairman appraised the ranking minority members during his tenure as follows:

> We've had a number of ranking members since I've been here. Now, let's see, first there was a fellow by the name of Dondero. He was a real fine member, just real great. He had a lot of friends. Then we had this fellow McGregor. He was antagonistic, cantankerous, just obstreperous—he was opposed to almost anything you could bring up. Auchincloss . . . was another Dondero. He was just a prince of a guy. And now—now we've got Bill Cramer. He is another McGregor. He is always opposed.

248

But a veteran non-shuttle Republican noted:

> Cramer is the best; he is the best, by far, of the four. The greatest leader, the most effective one I have served under as a member of the committee. He's a fighter, a pusher. Auchincloss wouldn't fight like Cramer does. Dondero was the kind of guy that everybody loved. You followed him because you loved him. McGregor was a little bit like Cramer. He would fight. He was pugnacious. But he just wasn't as good as Cramer. Cramer is probably the brightest, the most able man on the committee.

In fact, to a man, minority members held Cramer to be a "likeable," "brilliant," member who does his "homework," and who probably is the "most effective ranking member in the House"; and, if perhaps he is somewhat "bullheaded," "adamant," or occasionally "over-zealous," it is just as well because the committee is so "partisan." Minority members note, for example, that Auchincloss was an "awfully nice guy" but that he "didn't push real hard." "Cramer," they note on the other hand, "works with us." "We have," said a veteran, "the majority's respect; they respect me now." "In the past, on this committee as well as a number of others...," explained a high-ranking veteran, "the ranking minority members have worked out things with the majority and just let it go at that. The members weren't in on it, weren't informed, and that's all there was to it." But whereas Republicans praised Cramer for his vigorous leadership, Democrats consistently saw him as unnecessarily partisan—"I don't care what kind of box you put that Cramer in, he'll come out partisan every time." A veteran Democrat best captured the extreme degree of segregation between the two parties when he said: "They have some terrific guys—some that are almost Democrats."

Party Cooperation

Even though the great majority of committee members share constituency goals, they do not articulate a committee goal compatible with them. It thus appears that constituency-related issues alone cannot account for party cooperation. When an allocation decision is before the committee and the House, the truth of the matter seems to be that the two parties *distrust* each other. After all, public works projects are inherently political and, as such, are presumed to have substantial electoral significance. Since each party values majority status, each expects the other to porkbarrel—to authorize and appropriate projects on the basis of political clout or favor—when the other is in the majority. Because they foresee the possibility of partisan allocations and because they take the allocation of public works benefits so seriously, congressmen insist on a fair allocation of the goodies. Hence, they have agreed upon permanent ways to reduce electoral risks when a majority in each party is affected by an allocation. Such agreements are impossible when a minority in each party is affected, because Republicans, as noted previously, consider any such allocation inherently unfair. Moreover, agreements are probably unnecessary because Democrats will vote with their minority as a matter of party allegiance. Only when a majority in each party benefits from an allocation can party cooperation be expected. Since committee Democrats and Republicans are confronted with exactly the same situation as

249

House Democrats and Republicans, the electoral risk-reducing devices explain party cooperation in the committee as well as in the House.

Each member of the House expects public works allocations to be applied across the board without exception. Congressmen expect "fair" treatment for their district, city, state, region, and party. This *expectation of equity* is somewhat parochial, being invoked in debates on public works bills from many different vantage points. The New York delegation, for example, was convinced that New York State should be reimbursed for the interstate highways built in New York prior to the Interstate Defense and Highway Act of 1956. Accordingly, they supported Chairman Buckley's 1959 amendment providing for such a "reimbursement" since it was but "an equitable giving-back of something . . . unfairly taken." [29] But the unmoved delegations from the states who would have to forego the Highway Trust Fund allocations to benefit New York defeated the amendment. Some members of the Pennsylvania delegation opposed the 1957 authorization for the Niagara Power Development Project. The districts these members represented were outside the geographical limits (150 miles for the New York Power Authority) imposed on the distribution of power.[30] Likewise, some members representing districts within the range of the TVA opposed the limitation imposed on TVA power distribution. (The limitation was the asking price for the TVA bond revenue measure which made the TVA self-financing.)[31] Similarly, urban Democrats were less than pleased with the Public Works and Economic Development Act of 1965, because its eligibility criteria effectively sliced out the cities.[32]

Notwithstanding this expectation of equity, Congress has adopted a number of proposals opposed by a minority. Moreover, some of these proposals such as the TVA bond revenue bill, the Niagara power bill, and the Public Works and Economic Development Act of 1965 benefited only a minority in each party, and each bill was opposed by the Republicans. Such majority programs or small bundles of projects, as Turner found, divide the parties.[33] The first several Appalachian regional development bills which consistently split the committee and House are typical of this kind of party division. Though a bill was reported out in 1964, there were not enough votes in the House to call it up. With the influx of 67 Democratic freshmen after the 1964 election, however, the Democrats were able to report out a modest bill which passed by a vote of 257 to 165. The partisan distrust engendered by such majority party behavior is manifest in the remarks of two Republican party leaders during the floor debate on the 1962 Accelerated Public Works Act—the bill did not provide safeguards against partisan porkbarreling but could, conceivably, apply to a majority in each party. Former Minority Leader Charles A. Halleck (Ind.) tagged the measure "a $900 million political slush fund for the President." [34] To this, former Rules veteran William H. Avery (Kan.) added the measure was "a precedent for political boondoggling" and, mixing metaphors, threatened the Democrats by saying: "You are in the majority now. I suppose you want to play games with this. But some day it might be on the other foot. Some day we might be looking the other way." [35] Since neither party can assume it will be the majority party each Congress, there is substantial reason for each party to distrust the other when a majority in each can benefit from an allocation.

Congressmen have, therefore, reduced electoral risks by adopting fixed allocation formulas. Most public works allocations are thus so routine as to suggest automation. A few examples, all of which fly in the face of the image of public works legislation as porkbarreling and of Public Works committee members as dispensers of political goodies, will convey the flavor of the routinization: (1) the Army Corps of Engineers' projects (the most frequent recipient of the porkbarrel label) must have benefits equal to or greater than their costs to qualify for authorization; (2) of the 41,000 miles authorized in the 1956 Interstate and Defense Highway Act, just 1,000 are susceptible to purely political influences, the balance of the mileage being allocated according to the 1947 plan of routes; (3) one-half of the water pollution control dollars are allocated to states in direct proportion to population and the other one-half is allocated in inverse proportion to income.[36] By no stretch of the imagination do these fixed allocation formulas *guarantee* boodle to *any* member of the committee or House; the formulas guarantee *only* fair treatment irrespective of party affiliation.[37] And just as these electoral risk-reducing allocation formulas explain committee party cooperation, membership goals explain the relatively infrequent, mild departures from the fixed rules. Though the committee cannot adopt its own set of rules, the cost-benefit ratio is "stretched," some "political miles" are gained, or an economic development project gets placed on the agenda for a committee member irrespective of party.

Committee Success and Influence

Since Public Works is a mixture of party conflict and cooperation, the committee's behavior presents an unusual opportunity to compare success on the floor of the House under two radically different conditions. Is the House as likely to adopt Public Works proposals when the committee is united as it is when the committee is divided? And, in either case, to what can the success be attributed? For example, should either accurate anticipation of House demands or committee influence be inferred from success? Finally, does the meaning of success for committee-House relations depend upon whether the committee is united or divided?

Committee Success

The House typically adopts Public Works committee recommendations whether the committee is divided or not. From the 84th through the 89th Congresses, Public Works succeeded in having adopted 44 of the 56 major bills reported. For all this legislation from 1955 through 1966, the House was more likely to consider measures having unanimous support of the committee than those having only the support of the majority party. Of 27 bills reported by a united committee, the House considered 25; of 29 bills reported by a divided committee, the House considered 20. For the bills considered during the period in question, the House was about as likely to adopt proposals having bipartisan support as those supported just by the committee majority. All 25 bills having bipartisan support were adopted; and all but one of the 20 bills having only partisan support were adopted. Taking account of all the bills reported, the House adopted 91 percent of the proposals supported only by committee Democrats.[38]

Most committee Democratic defeats—9 out of 10 bills defeated—occurred because bills were not called. Since at least some bills are reported as part of a long-term strategy, committee majority party success is actually higher than 68 percent. And when reported bills are called up, the committee Democrats are just as successful—as measured by the number of amendments adopted—as the Democrats and Republicans are together. From the 84th through the 89th Congresses, when the committee was divided, the House adopted just two of the fifty-nine committee minority (Republican) amendments. All told, the House adopted only eight—five Republican and three Democratic—of a total of seventy-four floor amendments opposed by the committee majority. When the committee was united, just two out of eleven contested floor amendments were adopted. Such has been the committee's success.

What does this success indicate about committee-House relations? There is, first, a remarkably striking relationship between the behavior of committee Democrats and Republicans and House Democrats and Republicans. When Public Works is divided by party, there is a very strong relationship between committee party unity and House party unity as measured by the roll-call votes. On the 68 roll calls on major bills from the 80th through the 90th Congresses, the correlation coefficient, r, between committee and House Democrats is .959, and the coefficient between committee and House Republicans is .881. These unusually strong correlation scores are taken from regression equations used to "explain" House party unity as a function of committee party unity. Squaring these coefficients of correlation, r^2, yields the total amount of variance explained in House party unity by committee party unity. The total amount of variance thus explained is 91.5 percent for Democrats and 77.2 percent for Republicans. Public Works committee party unity is then an unusually reliable predictor of House party unity.

Because Public Works committee party unity is such a good predictor of House party unity and because committee decisions temporally precede House decisions, it is tempting to speculate on whether or not committee party unity *determines* House party unity. Adding to the temptation to speculate about a causal relationship between committee party unity and House party unity are images, often found in the protocol data, of committee members trying to win votes in the House before bills are called. A very high-ranking Democrat said: "If a man delivers his state delegation, he has done a good job." Persuasion is often a necessity. Because of the kinds of issues which occasion committee party conflict, the committee majority cannot use boodle to generate support in the House; committee Democrats must persuade most House Democrats to vote for bills that do not have constituency benefits for them. Obviously, the necessity for partisan persuasion is occasioned by division. Committee division often occurs in the context of legislative discontinuity in the form of new programs or significant new departures in old programs. But much of the committee's legislation has a remarkable continuity. And when this legislative continuity is taken into account, the temptation to infer causality from committee success and the relationship between committee and House party unity is not appealing. Legislative continuity on public works legislation is accompanied by party cooperation. Party cooperation usually means that there are widespread shared interests in the boodle and fixed allocations which make House demands unusually explicit. And these demands temporally precede committee deliberations. It would thus appear that when there is legislative continuity the committee might well be limited to anticipating House demands; when there is legislative discontinuity, however, it might be possible for the committee majority to exercise influence.

Cooperation and Anticipation: The Corps Projects

Of all the Public Works committee's legislation, the Corps projects have the greatest continuity and perhaps best reflect the committee's problem of anticipation. Corps projects are considered by Public Works on a project-by-project basis. A project's life begins with a congressional request for a Corps study. Such requests set in process a series of decisions which, for projects surviving each stage, span an average time of eleven years and eight months. Besides a multitude of Corps decisions up and down the line of authority, the committee and the House each make two decisions vital to the projects' success. Public Works, acting in light of the Corps' recommendation based on a feasibility study, decides whether or not a requested project should be surveyed. If, by committee resolution, a project's survey is authorized, the Corps surveys the project and makes appropriate recommendations to the committee. If the committee decides to recommend the project for authorization, it goes into the large bundle of projects known as the "omnibus rivers and harbors bill." These omnibus bills are usually considered biennially.

At each stage in this authorizing process, a project's worthiness is measured in terms of the cost-benefit ratio. To survive the authorizing process, a project must have benefits equal to or greater than the costs of construction and financing.[39] "The Corps evaluation," in the words of the late Clem Miller, "is a bundle of tangibles and intangibles: 'local interest,' 'cost-benefit ratio,' 'commercial use,' etc."[40] If a project is "economically justified" it will be approved unless its benefits are a matter of dispute. Benefits often become a matter of dispute when either the railroads (calculation of navigation benefits) or the private utilities (calculation of power benefits) question the Corps' calculation. Railroads, for example, opposed Rep. Michael J. Kirwan's (D. O.) Lake Erie and Ohio Canal project ("Mike Kirwan's Ditch"). Since the project offered a competing mode of transportation, the railroads were quick to note that, if benefits were calculated differently, the project would not qualify. Though disputes occasionally arise, there is a long-standing, solid base of support for the ratio in the House. Almost every member of the House, at some point in his career, will have one or more projects in process. "There is nobody, not a member of the House, that is not interested in water. . . . Nobody escapes," explained a subcommittee chairman. The support stems from the idea of a *cost-benefit criterion* for *each* project.

But the support is not just for a cost-benefit ratio. The support is for a specific cost-benefit ratio—namely, unity. Unlike the specifics of benefits and costs, the idea of the ratio and the unity criterion is apparently fixed. Efforts to change the unity criterion have been unsuccessful. Illustrative is the House's response to an amendment offered (85th Congress, 1st session) by a former Appropriations member, Rep. Melvin Laird (R., Wis.) to increase the limit for funding survey studies from 1:1 to 1:2:1.[41] Besides eliminating a number of surveys, the Laird amendment called for a change in the rules of the game. Predictably, the House objected. Floor manager of the bill Rep. Joe L. Evins (D., Tenn.) held the amendment to be "unwise and certainly most unscientific."[42] Rep. Ed Edmondson (D., Okla.) held it to be "an unscientific and unrealistic approach to the problems of flood control" and added that the amendment "would interfere with urgently needed programs in 11 of the 48 states at once.[43] Rep. Glenn W. Andrews (D., Ala.) noted that the amendment would eliminate a project in his district (on the Chattahoochee River) which had a "favorable cost ratio."[44] Rep. Wright Patman (D., Tex.) opposed the amendment because its adoption would eliminate "a very constructive and useful project in the district . . . [he had] . . . the honor to represent—the Cooper Dam and Reservoir."[45] Reps. Everett P. Scrivner (R., Kan.) and D. S. Saund (D., Calif.) observed, respectively, that the proposed change in the unity criterion was "arbitrary" and "unfair on the basis of all that has been done before."[46] It is undoubtedly impossible for Public Works to change the ratio. It was noted by the 1953 Subcommittee to Study Civil Works (the Jones committee) that "a project cannot be expected to create wealth unless the benefits are clearly in excess of the costs."[47] But no bills were reported and no committee resolutions were adopted to implement the Jones committee's recommendation. A veteran Republican exclaimed: "There would be hell to pay if we tried that!" when the author inquired if it was possible to change the ratio from 1:1 to 3:1. Such a change would exclude dozens of projects.

Public Works, as manifest in the Corps legislation, would undoubtedly never be able to change any of the national allocation formulas. And the committee members apparently know this. They thus feel obligated to defend the unity criterion in the cost-benefit ratio and are unwilling and indeed probably too wily to recommend changes in the ratio or any other fixed formula such as the highway allocations. This inability to propose successfully any changes suggests House dominance over the committee—a relationship in which the committee must anticipate House reactions in order to be successful. "If," said a committee staffer, "we ever reported a Corps bill with only about twenty projects in it, every member who didn't have a project in the bill would be jumpin' up and down and hollerin': 'Where's my project?'" The Public Works committee is thus constrained to report bills—omnibus bills—that will receive widespread support. These omnibus bills, which typically have unanimous committee support, are paradigmatic for legislative proposals affected by the fixed allocation formulas. So, then, Public Works committee success on unanimously reported legislation means that the committee is doing what the entire House expects it to do.

Conflict and Influence: Appalachian Regional Development

While the Corps projects are paradigmatic for continuity in public works legislation, the Appalachian Regional Development proposals have been paradigmatic for public works' legislative discontinuity. Proposals for developing the Appalachian region are relatively new and sporadic. And because the Appalachian legislation benefits only a minority in each of the parties, it has generated party conflict. The committee majority party must, therefore, depend on the strength of the House majority party, most of whose members have no constituency stake in the legislation.

Differences in the two Appalachian proposals reported by Public Works in 1965 and in 1967 correlate with the decrease in House Democratic party strength from the 89th to the 90th Congress. The correlations of this decrease in Democratic strength with differences in the legislation do suggest anticipating and eliminating opposition. At the same time, however, reenacting a program that benefits only a minority of congressmen in each party suggests a certain degree of influence.

Democrats, it will be recalled, reported out but could not call up the Appalachian bill. With the influx of 67 freshmen as a result of the 1964 election, however, Democrats passed such a bill in the 89th Congress. But in the 1966 elections Democrats lost a net of 47 seats, mostly outside the South. Committee Democrats suffered a net loss of 34 supporters of the 1965 bill, bringing the majority for a 1967 bill uncomfortably close to the necessary 218 votes for passage—a change from 257 to 223. Significant changes thus had to be made from the 1965 to the 1967 legislation. The anticipation of opposition in these changes is quite striking.

The 1965 bill (S. 3) authorized a total of $1,092,400,000—$840 million for highways and $252.4 million for public works and other federal aid programs. These dollars were for Appalachia as defined in S. 3—all of West Virginia, most of Pennsylvania, and parts of New York, Ohio, Virginia, North and South Carolina, Georgia, Alabama, Tennessee, and Kentucky. As noted above, much of this support for the 1965 bill (89th Congress) was not available when Public Works began consideration of the 1967 bill (S. 602). This bill increased nonhighway authorizations by $185 million and provided for $175 million in additional highway authorizations for the Appalachian region. In addition, the Senate version contained a Title II which increased the monetary authorization for regional commissions authorized by the 1965 Public Works and Economic Development Act. The key to the bill's success, however, was the new definition of the Appalachian region: one new county in New York, two in Alabama, and 18 in Mississippi. Three new counties were added without commensurate increases in nonhighway authorization levels. The increases in nonhighway authorizations were in the bill as originally introduced, and the new highway authorization pertained only to two roads in Pennsylvania and New York.

By effectively holding the authorization level constant while expanding the number of districts eligible for Appalachian dollars, the committee successfully reported the bill. Rather than delete the counties and reduce the basis of support,

James T. Murphy

Public Works Democrats kept the new counties. Retaining these counties provided a number of strategic advantages. For one thing, the committee avoided a tough conference fight. Such a fight would have been a certainty because Senate Public Works Committee Chairman Jennings Randolph (D., W.Va.) was firmly committed to Senator John Stennis of Mississippi to keep the counties in the bill. Keeping the new counties in the bill made it easier for committee Democrats to add still another county in Tennessee. This new definition of the Appalachian region correlates with four votes picked up in the Mississippi delegation. More important than the four votes, however, Mississippians spearheaded the drive among southerners to salvage the bill. And the other provisions unquestionably helped. The change in two Republican votes in New York State, for example, is related to the road allocation for New York and Pennsylvania. With the large majority in the 89th Congress, committee Democrats could get along without the Mississippians and possible Republican support picked up in the new provisions. But in the 90th Congress support of the Mississippi delegation along with new support such as that from New York and Tennessee was crucial.

As is apparent in these Appalachian bills, when the committee Democrats and Republicans are divided, the Democrats often move on their initiative. In such cases, the fate of committee majority party proposals indicates a mixture of House dominance and committee majority party influence. To the extent that adjustments must be made to win support, the House clearly dominates the committee. But there is substantial autonomy in that the committee majority is successfully reporting legislation appealing only to a minority of the House. Obviously, committee Democrats must depend on party loyalty for their success. That committee Democrats can take advantage of party loyalty means they can successfully report legislation without resorting to log-rolling. For the most part, then, majority party success in the Public Works committee means the majority party is generating legislative programs to which *it* is committed, not necessarily to programs to which a majority of the House is committed.

Conclusion

This analysis of the House Public Works committee against a backdrop of the behavior of other congressional committees has assessed the significance of the relationship between the issues and the distribution of membership goals with respect to the degree of party conflict; the significance of the relationship between norms and committee party solidarity on the one hand and the relationships between electoral risk-reduction and party cooperation on the other; and, finally, the response of the House of Representatives to committee party conflict and cooperation.

To a degree unknown in any congressional committee studied to date, the House Public Works committee is a partisan committee. As it is generally considered to be, Public Works is a constituency-oriented committee. But it does not follow that Public Works is an essentially bipartisan, backscratching committee. Far from it, Public Works committee members, besides being constituency oriented, are program oriented. As program-oriented legislators, they are inclined to distinguish good programs from bad programs on the basis of their

256

party affiliation. In addition to this party-influenced program orientation, the constituency-oriented allocation issues are so diverse that Democrats and Republicans often do not share a constituency stake in any particular piece of legislation. Moreover, many issues processed by the committee are not allocation issues at all but are traditional party issues such as the role of the federal government. For all these reasons—program orientation, party affiliation, diversity of the issues— Public Works Democrats and Republicans are driven apart. The parties are thus in conflict, and each party seeks as much internal unity as possible and each thus has a norm of partisanship designed to ensure unity.

Porkbarreling has been challenged as an explanation for Public Works authorization because it cannot possibly account for the fixed allocation formulas. That is to say, the fixed formulas, the safeguard against partisan porkbarreling, guarantee an equitable distribution, a distribution uninfluenced by considerations of power or party. To explain public works outcomes on large national allocation bills, one first notes the party cooperation, then the fixed formulas, and then searches for an explanation of the formulas. The explanation offered here for party cooperation on omnibus public works bills is partisan distrust. Because the broad, national allocation of public works has such enormous electoral significance, neither party can entrust its fate to the other when it is in the minority. Hence, the allocation formulas.

Notwithstanding a general expectation of equity in the House, partisan considerations do influence outcomes on legislation more selective in scope than the national allocation bills. This has been particularly true of the economic development legislation of the 1960s and early 1970s, which benefits a minority of Democrats and a much smaller minority of Republicans. Democrats are apparently willing to be partisan on such legislation because they know that when Republicans are in the majority they will not advance programs designed to benefit a minority of House Republicans.

The committee patterns of conflict and cooperation and the associated House responses demonstrate that committee success is not perfectly correlated with committee unanimity and that it is treacherous to infer committee power or autonomy from success. When the committee is united, the success appears to be attributable to an accurate response to House demands; when the committee is divided, however, its success is attributable to both accurate responses and autonomy. Unfortunately, there is no obvious, feasible method of separating out the effects of the two factors. Nonetheless, this mixture of party division, influence, and success does run counter to previous assertions and conventional wisdom.

Notes

1. Stephen K. Bailey and Howard D. Samuel, *Congress at Work* (New York: Henry Holt & Company, 1952), chap. 7; N.B. pp. 166-168.

2. Angus Campbell, Philip E. Converse, Warren E. Miller, and Donald E. Stokes, *Elections and the Political Order* (New York: John Wiley & Sons, Inc., 1966), chap. 11. Professor Warren E. Miller and Donald E. Stokes discuss the significance of favorable images as against the significance of issues with partisan content in congressional elections.
3. Jack C. Plano and Milton Greenberg, *The American Political Dictionary*, 2nd ed. (New York: Holt, Rinehart & Winston, Inc., 1967), p. 145.
4. Julius Turner, *Party and Constituency* (Baltimore: The Johns Hopkins University Press, 1951), p. 70.
5. Richard F. Fenno, Jr., "Congressional Committees: The Comparative View" (paper presented at the 66th meeting of the American Political Science Association, Los Angeles, California, September 8-12, 1970), pp. 2-11.
6. Ibid., p. 29.
7. It should be noted that the large minority of members assigned to Public Works because other seats were not open contradicts the electoral benefit criterion for committee assignments developed in Nicholas A. Masters, "Committee Assignments," *American Political Science Review* 55 (June, 1961), 345-357. On p. 357, Masters asserts the following: "Although a number of factors enter into committee assignments—geography, group support, professional background, etc.—the most important single consideration—unless it can be taken for granted—is to provide each member with an assignment that will help to insure his reelection." And, on p. 354, Masters writes: "Assignment to Public Works, Interior and Insular Affairs or Merchant Marine and Fisheries are usually based on the ecological make-up of the members' districts, so as to allow them to serve their constituent interests and protect their incumbency." But since such a large proportion of members are apparently assigned to Public Works who do not want to be, it is clear that the party leadership does not systematically attempt "to provide each member with an assignment that will help to insure his re-election" (p. 357). Because of the relative abundance of Public Works seats it is impossible for the leadership to apply an electoral benefit criterion even if they so desired.
8. On the significance of party affiliation in the House of Representatives, see Randall B. Ripley, *Party Leaders in the House of Representatives* (Washington, D.C.: The Brookings Institution, 1967), chap. 6.
9. These results are reported in James T. Murphy, "The House Public Works Committee: Determinants and Consequences of Committee Behavior" (Ph.D. dissertation, University of Rochester, 1969), pp. 317-333.
10. Richard F. Fenno, Jr., "The House of Representatives and Federal Aid to Education," in *New Perspectives on the House,* ed. Robert L. Peabody and Nelson W. Polsby, 2nd ed. (Chicago: Rand McNally and Co., 1969), pp. 286-289; Eugene Eidenburg and Roy D. Morey, *An Act of Congress: The Legislative Process and the Making of Education Policy* (New York: W. W. Norton and Company, Inc., 1969).
11. Fenno, "Congressional Committees," pp. 25-26.
12. Charles O. Jones, "Representation in Congress: The Case of the House Agriculture Committee," *American Political Science Review, 55* (June, 1961) 367.
13. These results are consistent with those on labor, urban, agricultural, and Western issues reported in David R. Mayhew, *Party Loyalty Among Congressmen* (Cambridge: Harvard University Press, 1966). On the general relationship between interdependent interests and reciprocity, see Lewis A. Coser, *The Functions of Social Conflict* (Glencoe: Free Press, 1956), pp. 75-76 and *passim*.
14. Peter M. Blau, *Exchange and Power in Social Life* (New York: John Wiley and Sons, Inc., 1964), p. 266.

15. Blau, p. 266 (italics added).
16. Richard F. Fenno, Jr., *The Power of the Purse* (Boston: Little, Brown and Co., 1966), pp. 82-90; John F. Manley, *The Politics of Finance: The House Committee on Ways and Means* (Boston: Little, Brown and Co., 1970), pp. 53-58.
17. Fenno, "Congressional Committees," p. 6.
18. Fenno, "Federal Aid to Education," pp. 289-293; cf. Eidenberg and Morey, *An Act of Congress*, chaps. 2-3.
19. George Goodwin, Jr., *The Little Legislatures: Committees of Congress* (Amherst: University of Massachusetts Press, 1970), pp. 114-115.
20. Fenno, *Power of the Purse*, pp. 500-501.
21. John F. Manley, "The House Committee on Ways and Means: Conflict Management in a Congressional Committee," *American Political Science Review*, 60 (December, 1961), 927.
22. The standard reference on the House Committee on rules is James R. Robinson, *The House Rules Committee* (New York: Bobbs-Merrill Company, Inc., 1963). For committee rankings, see Goodwin, *The Littᶦ. Legislatures*, pp. 114-115.
23. Richard F. Fenno, Jr., "The Internal Distribution of Influence: The House," in *The Congress and America's Future*, ed. David B. Truman (Englewood Cliffs: Prentice-Hall, Inc., 1965), pp. 52-70.
24. Fenno, "Congressional Committees," pp. 23-28.
25. Fenno, "Federal Aid to Education," pp. 284-300.
26. Blau, *Exchange and Power in Social Life*, p. 267.
27. Blau, pp. 255-263.
28. George C. Homans, *The Human Group* (New York: Harcourt, Brace and World, Inc., 1950), pp. 121-127; John W. Thibaut and Harold H. Kelley, *The Social Psychology of Groups* (John Wiley and Sons, Inc., 1959), pp. 126-142; Theodore H. Newcomb, Ralph H. Turner, and Philip E. Converse, *Social Psychology* (New York: Holt, Rinehart, and Winston, Inc., 1965), chaps. 8, 11, and 12; cf. Charles M. Price and Charles G. Bell, "The Rules of the Game: Political Fact or Academic Fancy?" *The Journal of Politics*, 32 (November, 1970), 839-855.
29. *Congressional Record*, 105, p. 17968.
30. *Congressional Record*, 103, pp. 13196-13211.
31. *Congressional Record*, 105, pp. 7703-7728; N.B. 7703-7705. See the discussion of the Democratic erosion of support in Aaron Wildavsky, "The TVA and Power Politics," *American Political Science Review*, 55 (September, 1961), 576-590.
32. *Congressional Record*, 111, pp. 20240-20244.
33. Turner, *Party and Constituency*, pp. 51-53; p. 70.
34. *Congressional Record*, 108, p. 17333.
35. *Congressional Record*, 108, p. 17927.
36. For the Corps cost-benefit ratio, see Inter-Agency Committee on Water Resources, Subcommittee on Evaluation Standards, *Proposed Practices for Economic Analysis of River Basin Projects*, 2nd ed. (Washington, D.C.: Government Printing Office, 1958); for highway legislation generally, see U.S. Department of Commerce, Bureau of Public Roads, *Federal Laws, Regulations and Other Material Relating to Highways* (Washington, D.C.: U.S. Government Printing Office, 1965); for water pollution control legislation, see U.S. Congress, Senate Committee on Public Works, *A Study of Pollution—Water*, Committee Print, 88th Cong., 1st sess., June, 1963.
37. Since all Bureau of Reclamation projects reported out by the House Interior Committee must go through exactly the same process as the Corps projects, the explanation for party cooperation on Public Works should be just as valid for party cooperation on Interior. And since the Bureau of Reclamation projects—a national

allocation issue—constitutes the overwhelming bulk of Interior's legislative proposals, mutual partisan distrust should account for Interior's party cooperation, the most salient characteristic of its behavior. See Fenno, "Congressional Committees," pp. 36-37; also see Inter-Agency Committee on Water Resources, Subcommittee on Evaluation Standards.

38. Only one of the 12 bills lost was actually called up and defeated.
39. For an extended discussion of the authorization process, see Arthur Maass, *Muddy Waters* (Cambridge: Harvard University Press, 1951), pp. 22-24.
40. Clem Miller, *Member of the House* (New York: Charles Scribner's Sons, 1962), p. 16.
41. *Congressional Record,* 103, p. 9710.
42. *Congressional Record,* 103, p. 9710.
43. *Congressional Record,* 103, p. 9712.
44. *Congressional Record,* 103, p. 9713.
45. *Congressional Record,* 103, p. 9713.
46. *Congressional Record,* 103, p. 9713.
47. House Committee on Public Works, Subcommittee to Study Civil Works, *The Civil Functions Program of the Corps of Engineers, United States Army,* House Committee Print No. 21, 82nd Cong., 2d sess., p. 35.

11. FACTIONS IN COMMITTEES: THE U.S. HOUSE OF REPRESENTATIVES

Glenn R. Parker
and
Suzanne L. Parker

In his classic study, *Congressmen in Committees,* Richard Fenno provides a conceptual schema for analyzing and comparing committee decision making. Although there are several facets to his schema, one important component is the notion of environmental constraints: "Every House committee inhabits an environment in which nonmembers seek to persuade committee members to act in ways the nonmembers deem necessary or desirable" (Fenno, 1973, p. 15). Fenno identifies four prominent influences which exist in the environment of every House committee: the executive branch, the party, clientele groups, and the House itself. These influences do not have the same impact on each committee *or* on each member.

As a result of the differing impact of these environmental influences, cleavages or divisions develop within committees. For instance, partisan differences within the committee are intensified when the influence of the party and/or the administration are salient within the committee's environment. Similarly, clientele groups often cultivate "friends" among committee members to offset the influence of other interest groups or nonsupportive committee members. This leads to the formation of clientele supporters within the committee. Divisions or differences within the House are also likely to appear within committees. Massive membership turnover in the House in the last several years has enhanced the ideological differences *among Democrats* as well as *between the parties:*

Authors' Note: An expanded version of this article was presented at the 1977 annual meeting of the American Political Science Association, Washington, D.C. The authors wish to acknowledge the encouragement and advice of several colleagues: Larry Dodd, Richard Fenno, Leroy Rieselbach, and Herb Weisberg. None of these individuals, however, bears any responsibility for the interpretations presented in this analysis.

Source: *American Political Science Review* (March 1979): 85-102. Reprinted with permission of the authors.

Glenn R. Parker and Suzanne L. Parker

The decrease in conservatism among Southern Democrats, coupled with the substantial increase in the *number* of Northern Democrats has had two important effects on the Democratic party in the House: the ideological character of the party has shifted somewhat to the left, and a significant gap now exists between Democrats who were members in the 91st Congress and members who entered since then. Moreover, at the same time that the Democrats have shifted somewhat to the left, the average conservative coalition score of the Republicans had increased, so that the ideological gap between the parties has also increased (Ornstein and Rhode, 1976, p. 4).

Such membership changes may sharpen the historic cleavages between liberal Democrats and conservative Democrats and Republicans.

The cleavages generated by these environmental influences create factions—pockets of committee support and/or opposition—within the committee. Salient cleavages should be present at important stages in committee decision making. The purpose of this study is to define the factional alignments in committee decision making by analyzing committee roll-call votes, and in the process, illuminate the saliency of particular environmental influences within selected House committees.

Data and Methods

This analysis is based on a subset of roll-call votes in eight congressional committees during the 93rd and 94th Congresses. These committees span the entire range of committee types: exclusive (Ways and Means), semi-exclusive (Agriculture, Education and Labor, International Relations, Interstate and Foreign Commerce, Post Office and Civil Service, Public Works), and non-exclusive (Interior and Insular Affairs).[1] These eight House committees were selected for comparative study because their decision-making processes have been extensively studied.

There are significant differences between our analysis and past studies of these committees. This study is based on recently released committee roll-call votes. In contrast, past studies have placed almost total reliance on interview protocols in interpreting committee decision-making patterns. Since our inquiry uses a different source of data *and* a different period, our conclusions serve to extend and revise present understanding of committee decision making.

Procedural votes have been excluded from the analysis because of their natural partisan complexion,[2] the analysis, therefore, is based on votes on substantive amendments to bills considered by the committee. Roll calls where at least 90 percent of the committee members vote on the same side are removed from the analysis because our measure of vote agreement among committee members—product-moment correlation coefficient—can be severely distorted by skewed distributions. Since the uneven work load across committees results in few roll calls in some committees during the span of this analysis, we have pooled committee votes for both the 93rd and 94th Congresses. Aggregating the votes over the four-year period (1973-1976) insures that the defined factions demonstrate some stability. We have ignored intersession analyses because they tend to be substantively and statistically unreliable. The number of votes in the analysis of factions within each committee is presented in Table 11-1.

In addition to eliminating procedural and near-unanimous roll calls, we have restricted our pool of committee members to those who have: (1) voted on at least 70 percent of the substantive committee roll calls; and (2) served in both Congresses.[3] This requirement does not appear to be overly restrictive. In most cases, our criteria include a substantial proportion of *continuing* committee members: in five of the committees more than 80 percent of the committee members serving in both the 93rd and 94th Congresses satisfy the criteria; in the remaining three committees, 70 percent of the *continuing* members satisfy the conditions (Table 11-2).[4]

Table 11-1   Number of Roll Calls Used in the Analysis of Factions Within Congressional Committees

	Substantive Roll Calls		
Committee	*93rd Congress*	*94th Congress*	*Total Votes*
Agriculture	30	70	100
Education and Labor	60	32	92
Interior and Insular Affairs	40	45	85
International Relations	25	19	44
Interstate and Foreign Commerce	43	91	134
Post Office and Civil Service	13	15	28
Public Works	12	25	37
Ways and Means	68	178	246

Source Recorded votes in eight House Committees (1973-1976).

Table 11-2   Evaluating the Criteria for the Selection of Committee Members in the Analysis

Committee	*Number of Continuing Members*	*Number of Members in the Analysis*
Agriculture	20	18 (90%)
Education and Labor	25	21 (84%)
Interior and Insular Affairs	26	19 (73%)
International Relations	29	20 (69%)
Interstate and Foreign Commerce	27	23 (85%)
Post Office and Civil Service	15	11 (73%)
Public Works	26	25 (96%)
Ways and Means	18	16 (89%)

Source: Committee members who have voted on at least 70 percent of substantive committee roll calls and who have served in both the 93rd and 94th Congresses.

The factional alignments within a committee are analytically defined as the dimensions (factors) derived from a Q-principal component analysis of the substantive roll calls within each committee.[5] A varimax rotation is performed on each committee's factional structure to simplify the interpretation of the alignments.[6] The resulting factor loadings serve as measurements of the attachment of each committee member to the various factions within that committee. The vectors of factor loadings (one vector for each extracted factor) are the dependent variables in the analysis of each committee's voting patterns.

We also subject all substantive amendments voted upon by at least 70 percent of the committee members to an R-component analysis. To simplify and sharpen the interpretation of these dimensions, we have selected only those votes which are strongly correlated with an underlying issue dimension (any vote with a factor loading $>.82$).[7] This restricted pool of issues is subsequently refactored into the same number of extracted issue dimensions, and factor scores which summarize a committee member's position on the various issue dimensions are obtained. These factor scores are referred to as *issue-dimension scores*.[8]

Issue-dimension scores are used as explanatory variables in assessing the independent contributions of political issues to the organization of factions: they measure the extent to which issue dimensions account for unexplained variation in factional alignments. To evaluate the impact of issues on the factional structures, we formulate regression equations representing the three best predictors of each committee faction. The issue-dimension scores are then entered into these equations to explain the residual variance; the impact of issues is evaluated in terms of the increase in explained variation (R^2) resulting from the inclusion of issues in the equations.[9]

In the tables describing the factional alignments, we have included factor loadings less than .50 *only* where we feel they will clarify the interpretation of the factions. Displaying the factor loadings in this manner will illuminate the salient features of the factional structure within a committee. We have also designated with asterisks committee members who were present on the committee when it was previously studied. This information provides some indication of the impact of membership turnover on changes in committee decision making.

We originally used three types of independent variables to identify the nature of factional alignments: constituency demographics (e.g., percent black, median family income), electoral forces (e.g., 1972 and 1974 congressional district vote), and political influences (e.g., group ratings, conservative coalition scores, presidential support scores). Since neither constituency demographics nor electoral forces proved useful in identifying committee factions, these variables have been eliminated from the tables of correlations in this article.

The Q-component analysis delineates the voting blocs within the committee and provides an opportunity for a visual interpretation of the factional structure of the committee. The accuracy and validity of a visual interpretation of a committee's factional structure can be corroborated by examining the correlates of individual committee factions. The product-moment correlations between group ratings,[10] partisanship scores and the individual factions provide a basis for inferences regarding the underlying nature of a committee's factional structure. This procedure also provides additional specification to the visual interpretations. In order to enhance the reliability of the interpretations, we rely upon multiple measures to describe the factions. Our interpretations are based upon the consistency in the patterns of correlations between factional alignments and diverse group ratings. Conceptually similar and strongly intercorrelated variables are treated as measurements of the same underlying dimension. We feel that this strategy is preferable to interpreting individual ratings, which tend to be less reliable than multiple-item measures. We are also reluctant to reduce the variables to a few scales because some of the specificity of a group's interests or concerns is obscured. Our analysis attempts to strike a balance between these two approaches in order to maximize the benefits of each: our interpretation of factions relies upon the patterns which appear in the correlations. At the same time, we display the correlation for each group to allow the reader to examine the different impact of individual group ratings.

One final methodological caveat is in order: we urge caution in interpreting the factional structure of committees where few roll calls have occurred because these factional alignments may be unreliable. Finally, we are painfully aware of the frailties of the data, and the limitations they place on our conclusions. Throughout the analysis, we have taken precautions to insure the robustness of our findings; conclusions and interpretations which are only weakly supported by the data have been ignored.[11]

Analysis

Agriculture Committee

Four factions appear in the Agriculture Committee (Table 11-3). Committee Democrats divide into northern (Faction 1) and southern (Faction 2) Democrats; Republicans form the other major committee faction (Faction 3). The remaining committee members—Melcher (D-Montana) and Jones (D-Tennessee)—form a factional doublet (Faction 4), which tends to vote with the northern Democrats more frequently than with the southern Democrats; Faction 4 has an interfactor correlation of .44 with Faction 1 and .32 with Faction 2. The four committee factions appear to reflect differing levels of liberalism and party support. For instance, we can order the factions in terms of an ideological continuum. Republicans (Faction 3) and southern Democrats (Faction 2) anchor the conservative end, while northern Democrats (Faction 1) form the liberal side of the continuum. Melcher and Jones (Faction 4) fall between these ideological extremes representing a more moderate alignment of committee Democrats. In sum, a visual examination of the factional alignments suggests that partisan and ideological influences structure the voting patterns of committee members.

The correlates of the factional alignments are consistent with our visual interpretation of the committee's voting patterns: ideological (ADA, ACA, COPE, conservative coalition, CCUS, and NFU scores) and partisan measures (party unity and presidential support scores) consistently bear the strongest relationships to the factions (Table 11-3). Unfortunately, ideology and partisan-

Table 11-3 Factions Within the House Agriculture Committee

Committee Members	F_1	F_2	F_3	F_4	h^2
Thomas S. Foley (D-Washington)	.85				.81
Joseph P. Vigorito (D-Pennsylvania)	.80				.72
Bob Bergland (D-Minnesota)	.74				.76
Jerry Litton (D-Missouri)	.86				.85
George E. Brown (D-California)	.54	−.50			.68
**W. R. Poage (D-Texas)		.81			.72
Walter B. Jones (D-North Carolina)		.80			.76
Dawson Mathis (D-Georgia)		.67			.66
David Bowen (D-Mississippi)		.52		(.44)	.66
William C. Wampler (R-Virginia)			.73		.73
Keith G. Sebelius (R-Kansas)		(.45)	.62		.68
Charles Thone (R-Nebraska)			.80		.74
James P. Johnson (R-Colorado)	(−.45)		.61		.59
Edward R. Madigan (R-Illinois)			.75		.72
Steven D. Symms (R-Idaho)	−.54		.55		.80
Ed Jones (D-Tennessee)				.83	.77
John Melcher (D-Montana)	(.47)			.74	.85
Paul Findley (R-Illinois)			(.46)	−.59	.62

Correlates of Factional Alignments

	F_1	F_2	F_3	F_4
ADA Scores	.73*	−.80*	−.71*	.37
COPE Scores	.89*	−.45	−.88*	.64*
NFU Scores	.89*	−.65*	−.84*	.59*
ACA Scores	−.84*	.76*	.73*	−.38
Party Unity (Voting with Democrats) Scores	.88*	−.60*	−.86*	.52*
Conservative Coalition Scores	−.79*	.77*	.75*	−.38
Presidential Support Scores	−.82*	.42	.81*	−.71*
CCUS Scores	−.82*	.69*	.77*	−.49*
Issue-Dimension I Scores	.84*	−.77*	−.83*	.38
Issue-Dimension II Scores	.49	.25	−.45	.66*
Unique Contribution of Issue Dimensions	.13*	.01	.20*	.05

* Statistically significant at the .01 level.
** Committee member during 85th Congress.

Source: U.S. House Committee on Agriculture roll-call votes (1973-1976).

ship are virtually impossible to disentangle; for example, party unity scores are correlated above .9 with the ideological measures which are also highly intercorrelated. We are unable, therefore, to determine which of the two variables, ideology or party, is the most influential in committee decision making. Although issues appear to contribute to the explanation of the alignments of members of Factions 1 and 3, their substantive contribution is modest: 80 percent of the variation in these two factions can be accounted for by other independent variables. Issues related to the Food Stamp Program and the Sugar Act have the strongest factor loadings with the first issue dimension (I), while amendments to the General Farm Bill have a similar relationship to the second issue dimension (II). Since issue dimension I scores are closely associated with party unity ($r = .90$) and measures of liberalism (ADA scores, $r = .94$; conservative coalition scores, $r = -.96$), the first issue dimension appears to reflect the partisan and ideological differences within the committee. Issue dimension II scores fail to reveal a similar pattern of correlations.

The factional structure within the Agriculture Committee reflects the environmental influences of the parties and the House on the committee. The effects of party are evident in the partisan composition of the factional alignments. Ideology creates further fragmentation among the Democrats. The liberal-conservative split among House Democrats appears in the division between committee Democrats (Factions 1 and 2).

Charles Jones' study of the House Agriculture Committee reaches somewhat different conclusions about the decision-making forces within this committee (Jones, 1961, p. 367). He suggests that constituency commodity interests are a primary influence on committee decision making.[12] Further, our analysis reveals a greater degree of ideological voting than Jones observes.

There are several factors which could account for the differences between our findings and those of Jones. For instance, a parallel between commodity interests and partisanship could obscure the impact of commodity interests on decision making. It may also be that commodity interests are more important at earlier stages in the decision-making process. Our data were collected near the final phases of decision making where partisanship becomes a more important factor. As Jones says, "Representatives, whether or not affected by the legislation, tend to support their party's position more as the action moves beyond the basic working level, and most at the final vote" (1961, p. 367). Finally, the dramatic change in committee personnel since Jones' study also may account for some of the differences in the findings: W. R. Poage is the *only* member in our analysis who was also on the committee during the 85th Congress (Table 11-3— asterisks).

Education and Labor Committee

The Education and Labor Committee is divided into three factions (Table 11-4): labor Democrats (Faction 1), liberal Democrats (Faction 3), and Republicans (Faction 2). The importance of party affiliation is evident in the linkages between liberal and labor Democrats—the interfactor correlation (oblique rotation) is .56. In addition to their partisan similarities, Factions 1 and 3 appear to share similar ideological perspectives—support of labor and liberalism. These similarities are evident in the overlap of Democrats Hawkins, Ford, Mink, Brademas, O'Hara, Biaggi, and Lehman in two or more of the factions.

267

Table 11-4 Factions Within the House Education and Labor Committee

Committee Members	F_1	F_2	F_3	h^2
**Carl D. Perkins (D-Kentucky	.73			.60
**Frank Thompson (D-New Jersey)	.82			.85
**John H. Dent (D-Pennsylvania)	.87			.84
**Dominick V. Daniels (D-New Jersey)	.89			.90
**John Brademas (D-Indiana)	.77		(.40)	.79
**James G. O'Hara (D-Michigan)	.60		(.49)	.67
Joseph M. Gaydos (D-Pennsylvania)	.88			.87
Mario Biaggi (D-New York)	.71		(.45)	.70
William Lehman (D-Florida)	.64	.51		.69
**Lloyd Meeds (D-Washington)		.52		.53
**Albert H. Quie (R-Minnesota)		−.84		.85
**Alphonzo Bell (R-California)		−.90		.85
**John N. Erlenborn (R-Illinois)		−.82		.91
Marvin L. Esch (R-Michigan)		−.81		.70
Edwin D. Eshleman (R-Pennsylvania)		−.75	(−.46)	.79
**Augustus F. Hawkins (D-California)	(.49)	.57	.55	.86
**William D. Ford (D-Michigan)	(.45)	(.43)	.52	.66
**Patsy T. Mink (D-Hawaii)	(.43)	(.41)	.74	.90
**Phillip Burton (D-California)			.64	.70
William (Bill) Clay (D-Missouri)			.87	.94
Shirley Chisholm (D-New York)			.77	.80

Correlates of Factional Alignments

	F_1	F_2	F_3
ADA Scores	.64*	.88*	.78*
COPE Scores	.88*	.93*	.79*
NFU Scores	.81*	.88*	.79*
ACA Scores	−.76*	−.91*	−.82*
Party Unity (Voting with Democrats) Scores	.80*	.95*	.81*
Conservative Coalition Scores	−.63*	−.86*	−.88*
Presidential Support Scores	−.74*	−.81*	−.80*
CCUS Scores	−.77*	−.87*	−.86*
Issue-Dimension I Scores	.88*	−.96*	.82*
Unique Contribution of Issue Dimension	.00	.03	.00

* Statistically significant at the .01 level.
** Committee member during 89th Congress.

Source: U.S. House Committee on Education and Labor roll-call votes (1973-1976).

Our visual interpretation of the committee's factional structure is consistent with the correlates of the alignments. The ideological and partisan measures reveal the strongest correlations with the individual factions (Table 11-4— correlates). The pattern of the correlates suggest that Faction 1 is ideological in nature. Furthermore, there is reason to suspect that this faction also reflects the influence of labor on committee decision making: COPE scores have the highest correlation with this factor—.88. This labor orientation is also evident in the fact that the chairpersons of the labor subcommittees (1973-1976) have the strongest attachments to this faction (Thompson, Dent, and Daniels). This information leads us to suspect that labor may be a dominant interest in this faction.

Partisanship and ideology have the strongest correlations with Factions 2 and 3, respectively. The intercorrelations among our independent variables demonstrate the overlap of ideology and partisanship among committee factions. This overlap is evident in the high correlations between ADA scores and party unity scores (.93).

Issues are relatively unimportant in defining the factional alignments. The issue dimension I scores do not contribute significantly to the explanation of the three committee factions (Table 11-4). This is probably due to the strong association of this issue dimension (education related issues) with attributes of the factions—i.e., partisan ($r = .96$), ideology (ACA scores, $r = -.91$) and labor support ($r = .97$).

The Education and Labor Committee's environment is sensitive to partisan and ideological forces. The overlap of party and ideology is evident in the substantial bipolarity of the Republican faction (Faction 2)—conservative Republicans opposing liberal Democrats. When there is a substantial congruence between party and ideology, strong bipolar factors are apt to appear. We can attribute the ideological warfare to the influence of the House within the committee's environment—the ideological polarization between the parties in the House. There is also evidence to suggest that a clientele group (labor) has an impact on decision making.

The existence of ideological and partisan factions within this committee is consistent with Fenno's description of committee decision making: "Partisan-ideological warfare is the normal condition of Education and Labor" (1973, p. 76). Fenno also finds that organized labor is influential in committee decision making. The influence of labor (Faction 1) is also suggested by our findings. Our analysis appears to support Fenno's conclusions that ideology, party, and organized labor are important influences on committee decision making.

Interior and Insular Affairs

The members of this committee divide into two *major* factions (Factions 1 and 2); the remaining two factions (3 and 4) are of minor significance since few members consistently vote with them. The *major* factions appear to reflect ideological and partisan differences among committee members. The partisan-ideological conflict is manifested in the strong bipolarity of Faction 1 where Republican conservatives like Steiger, Young, and Clausen consistently oppose the alignment of Democratic liberals Burton, Mink, and Bingham. Faction 2

269

captures committee partisanship. We observe, for example, that Democrats like Burton, Bingham, Kastenmeier, and Udall align with Faction 2, and are opposed by Republicans like Steiger, Lujan, and Skubitz. As in the Education and Labor Committee, there is considerable overlap in partisanship and ideology within the committee. It is not surprising, therefore, that the *major* factions (1 and 2) are related ($r = .46$).

The ideological and partisan nature of the factional structure is also evident in the correlates of the alignments (Table 11-5). Indicators of partisanship and ideology are consistently the strongest correlates of committee factions. Taken individually, each of these variables explains at least 60 percent of the variation in the attachments of committee members to Factions 1 and 2. The correlates of the two minor Factions 3 and 4 fail to achieve a similar level of importance, but the ideological and partisan patterns in the correlations continue even here.

Although it might be tempting to construe Faction I as reflecting the consumer versus business (or "user versus conservationist") battles that rage elsewhere, such an inference is problematic. Since CCUS scores are strongly correlated with other partisan party unity scores, ($r = -.91$) and ideological (ACA scores, $r = .95$) measures, it is difficult to define Faction 1 solely in terms of its posture toward business interests. It seems more likely that pro- and anti-business orientations are a function of underlying ideological and partisan commitments. Once again, we find that ideological and partisan influences on the committee's factional alignments are difficult to separate. The correlation between party unity and ADA scores is .97 and other ideological and partisan indicators are similarly intercorrelated. These relationships capture the ideological and partisan polarization within the committee.

Issue dimension 1 is of minor substantive importance in the organization of the committee factions. Despite the statistical improvement in explaining the variation in attachments to Faction 1, the substantive contribution of the issue dimension is a mere 6 percent (Table 11-5). This issue dimension reflects votes on land-use policy and surface mining. Such issues seem to incite partisan and ideological sentiment as illustrated by the close association of issue dimension I scores with ideology and party; these scores have a correlation of $-.90$ with ACA scores, and .87 with party unity scores. Thus, issues may fail to exercise an independent impact on the factional alignments because of their close association with the existing ideological and partisan divisions within the committee.

The environment of the Interior Committee appears to be dominated by the influences of the House and the political parties. The congruence between party and ideology, evident in the bipolarity of Faction 1, reflects the ideological polarization of the parties in the House. The factional structure also exhibits clear partisan cleavages (Faction 2) with Republicans consistently opposing alignments of Democratic committee members. Thus, political parties and their ideological polarization within the House are important influences on the committee's decision-making environment.

Fenno's conclusions concerning Interior and Insular Affairs differ from ours. He describes committee divisions more in terms of "East versus West, than Democrats versus Republicans" (Fenno, 1973, p. 59) and this East-West division

Table 11-5 Factions Within the House Interior and Insular Affairs Committee

	Factions				
Committee Members	F_1	F_2	F_3	F_4	h^2
Don H. Clausen (R-California)	−.73		(.43)		.72
**Harold T. Johnson (D-California)	−.70				.55
Keith G. Sebelius (R-Kansas)	−.67		(.42)		.77
Sam Steiger (R-Arizona)	−.88	(−.38)			.94
Donald E. Young (R-Alaska)	−.84				.75
John F. Seiberling (D-Ohio)	.83				.78
**Jonathan B. Bingham (D-New York)	.85	(.46)			.93
**Phillip Burton (D-California)	.84	(.47)			.94
Robert W. Kastenmeier (D-Wisconsin)	.77	.51			.87
Manuel Lujan (R-New Mexico)	−.66	−.53			.79
Patsy T. Mink (D-Hawaii)	.80	(.48)			.87
**Morris K. Udall (D-Arizona)	.73	.53			.84
Joseph P. Vigorito (D-Pennsylvania)	(.38)	.79			.82
**Lloyd Meeds (D-Washington)	(.39)	.82			.84
John Melcher (D-Montana)		.77			.61
**Teno Roncalio (D-Wyoming)		.64		.57	.76
**Joe Skubitz (R-Kansas)	(−.48)	−.55	(.45)		.74
**Roy A. Taylor (D-North Carolina)			.80		.65
Philip E. Ruppe (R-Michigan)				.82	.79

Correlates of Factional Alignments				
	F_1	F_2	F_3	F_4
ADA Scores	.84*	.84*	−.55*	−.35
COPE Scores	.78*	.88*	−.45	−.32
NFU Scores	.87*	.87*	−.53*	−.21
ACA Scores	−.84*	−.88*	.51*	.35
Party Unity (Voting with Democrats) Scores	.81*	.84*	−.43*	−.34
Conservative Coalition Scores	−.86*	−.79*	.65*	.24
Presidential Support Scores	−.76*	−.83*	.62*	.33
CCUS Scores	−.87*	−.80*	.49	.30
Issue-Dimension I Scores	.96*	.92*	−.45	−.23
Unique Contribution of Issue Dimensions	.06	.00	.02	.00

* Statistically significant at the .01 level.
** Committee member during 89th Congress.

Source: U.S. House Committee on Interior and Insular Affairs roll-call votes (1973-1976).

within the committee mirrors the conflict between committee conservationists and commercial users. Fenno also places less emphasis on partisanship in committee decision making: "For a group whose strategic premises involved the close adherence to clientele desires, partisanship is not relevant" (1973, p. 91).

Although unlike us Fenno finds a conservationist-commercial user division in the Interior Committee, it may be that this division can be subsumed under a broader ideological framework. Liberals generally favor conservationist positions, while conservatives support commercial users' interests. In short, ideology may be a more abstract, organizing characteristic of committee factions.

The greater emphasis on partisanship in our study may be owing to the nature of the issues that are *now* considered by the Interior Committee. One committee member interviewed by Fenno attributed the lack of partisanship to the type of issues dealt with by the committee:

> You're more likely to have geographical partisanship or regional partisanship than party partisanship. I have more in common with a Republican from Montana than a Democrat from Florida. . . . You might have one issue a year that's partisan, a real-hot partisan issue—Hells Canyon—but most of them are so noncontroversial. It's not like . . . Education and Labor where you have these great national issues with the parties lined up on either side (1973, p. 59).

Clearly the issues *presently* handled by the committee are different. They are issues that have achieved national saliency and which divide the parties (e.g., surface mining regulations, land-use policy). In addition, there have been some changes in committee membership—only one *Republican* (Skubitz) in our analysis was a member of the committee during Fenno's analysis (Table 11-5— asterisks). This change in Republican membership may result in the greater partisanship we observe within the committee's factional structure. In sum, changes in the nature of issues and in committee membership (among Republicans) may account for the differences between our findings and Fenno's conclusions.

International Relations Committee

The International Relations Committee has the most fragmented factional structure of any of the committees we examine (Table 11-6). It is clear from Table 11-6 that party lines are more permeable in this committee: conservative Republicans and Democrats tend to vote together. For instance, conservative Republicans like Broomfield, Wynn, and Guyer join the conservative Democrats like Fountain and Zablocki (Faction 1) in voting against liberals like Whalen, Bingham, and Rosenthal. Two other factional alignments also appear to be organized along ideological lines. Faction 4 appears to be a small alignment of liberals which is defined by Harrington (D-Massachusetts). The more moderate committee faction (5) is led by Republican duPont. The positive attachments of Republicans to both Factions 1 and 3 suggest that both factions have similar policy interests—i.e., support for administration positions in foreign affairs.

The organizing characteristic of Faction 2 is more difficult to determine. Fenno (1973, p. 284) reports the emergence of a group of activist subcommittee

Table 11-6   Factions Within the House International Relations Committee

Committee Members	F_1	F_2	F_3	F_4	F_5	h^2
Factions						
**Thomas E. Morgan (D-Pennsylvania)	.68					.74
**Clement J. Zablocki (D-Wisconsin)	.87					.85
**L. H. Fountain (D-North Carolina)	.73					.66
**Benjamin S. Rosenthal (D-New York)	−.70	.54		(.41)		.95
**Dante B. Fascell (D-Florida)		.95				.93
**Donald M. Fraser (D-Minnesota)		.81				.84
**Lee H. Hamilton (D-Indiana)		.74				.69
**William S. Broomfield (R-Michigan)	.61		.71			.95
Larry Winn, Jr. (R-Kansas)	.60		.72			.90
John Buchanan (R-Alabama)			.79			.80
Benjamin A. Gilman (R-New York)			.86			.83
Tennyson Guyer (R-Ohio)	.53		.66			.90
**Edward J. Derwinski (R-Illinois)			.74	(−.41)		.93
Jonathan B. Bingham (D-New York)	−.71					.77
Michael Harrington (D-Massachusetts)				.79		.88
Charles W. Whalen, Jr. (R-Ohio)	(−.40)			.48		.48
**Robert N. C. Nix (D-Pennsylvania)				.66	.52	.73
Lester L. Wolff (D-New York)				.60		.73
Pierre S. duPont (R-Delaware)					.87	.77
Edward G. Biester, Jr. (R-Pennsylvania)					.66	.75

Correlates of Factional Alignments

	F_1	F_2	F_3	F_4	F_5
ADA Scores	−.75*	.59*	−.74*	.67*	.19
COPE Scores	−.45	.36	.66*	.58*	.16
NFU Scores	−.58	.51*	−.58*	.63*	.19
ACA Scores	.66*	−.55*	.76*	−.63*	−.39
Party Unity (Voting with Democrats) Scores	−.57*	.53*	−.74*	.56*	.16
Conservative Coalition Scores	.74*	−.51*	.76*	−.67*	−.26
Presidential Support Scores	.56*	−.50*	.82*	−.61*	−.20
CCUS Scores	.64*	−.37	.71*	−.54*	−.30
Issue-Dimension I Scores	.63*	−.03	.50*	−.56*	.29
Issue-Dimension II Scores	−.59*	.85*	−.74*	.64*	.43
Issue-Dimension III Scores	−.29	.34	.37	.02	−.43
Unique Contribution of Issue Dimensions	.03	.24*	.22[a]	.11	.26*[b]

* Statistically significant at the .01 level.
** Committee member during 89th Congress.
  [a] The contribution of issue-dimension I scores is inconsequential and is ignored in the calculation of R^2 for issue dimensions or the test of significance.
  [b] The contribution of issue-dimension II scores is inconsequential and is ignored in the calculation of R^2 for issue dimensions or the test of significance.
Source: U.S. House Committee on International Relations roll-call votes (1973-1975).

leaders as a result of reforms introduced into the 92nd Congress. One of the consequences of these reforms is that Democrats are prevented from chairing more than one subcommittee. This has resulted in a more active subcommittee system. The small cluster of members in the faction (2) appears to fit Fenno's description: Three members of this faction (Fascell, Fraser, and Hamilton) hold subcommittee chairs. The alignment of the four members of Faction 2 may reflect opposition to the control that the executive branch exercises over the committee's environment. The vehicle for this opposition is the rejuvenated subcommittees which could develop sufficient policy expertise to formulate alternatives to administration policies. The significance of issues to the organization of this faction suggests that this bloc of subcommittee leaders may reflect tacit agreement to seek, and support, alternatives to administration policies.

Although we have dismissed partisanship as relatively unimportant to the committee's factional structure, we observe a pattern of significant correlations between the factions and measures of partisanship. In most of the factions (1, 2, and 4) this association can be attributed to the effects of ideology which are strongly related to partisanship: party unity and ACA scores are correlated at $-.94$. Further, our measures of ideology generally have a stronger correlation with these individual factions than do the partisan measures. Finally, the agreement between Democrats and Republicans attached to the same faction, weakens any partisan organization of the factional structure (Table 11-6 — factions).

Issues help to explain the nature of some of the factional alignments within the committee: issue dimension scores are statistically and substantively important in three of the committee factions (2, 3, and 5, Table 11-6). Issue dimensions I and II are identified by foreign aid decisions, but the two dimensions differ in their focus. Issue dimension I deals with the initial question of *supplying* aid to a foreign country, while the second dimension deals with the *level of aid* supplied. The third issue dimension focuses on congressional influence in foreign affairs (e.g., War Powers Resolution, disclosure of executive agreements). The second issue dimension divides the committee factions in predictable directions: pro-administration and conservative members are more apt than their counterparts to support administration-supported aid levels.

The nature of the committee's factions suggest that the administration is a major environmental influence. The effects of the executive branch are reflected in the alignment of Republicans (Faction 3), and the vote agreement between conservative Democrats (Faction 1) and this Republican faction. In addition, the alignment of activist subcommittee leaders (Faction 2) suggests an organized challenge to the primacy of the executive branch in matters of foreign aid and policy. The ideological polarization between and within the parties in the House also finds expression within the committee's factional structure: conservative and liberal Democrats tend to oppose one another. It appears, therefore, that the administration and the House exercise considerable influence within the committee's environment. In short, our analysis reveals that the committee's factional structure is a response to issues, ideology, and the policy initiatives of the executive branch.

Our findings concerning the factional structure of this committee generally follow Fenno's description of committee decision making. The absence of cohesive party alignments supports Fenno's contention about the low level of committee partisanship: "Surely the Committee members' foreign aid policy goals and their environmental pressures are both conducive to a low level of partisanship" (1973, p. 90). In addition, our analysis locates a pro-administration contingent among committee members (Factions 1 and 3) (Fenno, 1973, pp. 71-72). Faction 2 reflects the voting behavior of an activist group of subcommittee members which Fenno describes as supportive of greater committee involvement in foreign policy decisions (1973, p. 72). The one difference between our findings and Fenno's is that our analysis reveals a greater degree of ideology than Fenno suggests.

Interstate and Foreign Commerce Committee

There is little ambiguity about the organization of the factions in the Interstate and Foreign Commerce Committee. Factions 1 and 2 are bipolar with liberal Democrats (Faction 1) opposing conservative Republicans (Table 11-7).[13] There appears to be an ideological and partisan organization to the factional alignments.

The correlates of the committee's alignments are consistent with this interpretation: partisan and ideological measures are strongly related to each of the factions (Table 11-7—correlates). As might be expected, partisanship and ideology are inextricably linked among committee members; for example, ACA and party unity scores are correlated at $-.96$. In fact, both measures of partisanship—party unity and presidential support scores—are correlated above .9 with the several ideological measures.

The major issue dimension within the committee is relatively unimportant in defining factions; issue dimension I reflects differences in the areas of energy policy and consumer protection (e.g., Clean Air Act amendments, consumer product warranties). The lack of influence of issues is probably a result of their partisan and ideological nature: Issue dimension I scores are correlated above .9 with every measure of ideology and partisanship. Therefore, the contribution which issues might make in the interpretation of the committee's factional structure is already captured by our ideological and partisan measures.

The strong bipolar nature of the factional structure reflects the congruence between party and ideology among House members—conservative Republicans oppose liberal Democrats. This suggests that the nature of the House is an important influence on committee decision making. The partisan complexion of the two factions is also clear, indicating that the political parties are also important environmental influences.

Our analysis reaches somewhat different conclusions from those of a recent study of the House Interstate and Foreign Commerce Committee (Price et al., 1975, pp. 50-55). We agree with David Price and his colleagues as to the ideological divergence within the committee, but our findings suggest greater partisanship in committee voting. These partisan alignments may be a function of the data: our roll-call data are collected near the final stages of committee deliberations. It may be, as in the Agriculture Committee, that partisanship

Table 11-7 Factions Within the House Interstate and Foreign Commerce Committee

	Factions		
Committee Members	F_1	F_2	h^2
James T. Broyhill (R-North Carolina)	.75	(−.48)	.79
Tim Lee Carter (R-Kentucky)	.80		.75
Clarence J. Brown (R-Ohio)	.81	(−.45)	.87
Joe Skubitz (R-Kansas)	.77	(−.43)	.78
Louis Frey, Jr. (R-Florida)	.77	(−.44)	.78
John Y. McCollister (R-Nebraska)	.80	(−.40)	.88
Norman F. Lent (R-New York)	.77		.75
H. John Heinz III (R-Pennsylvania)	.64		.43
James M. Collins (R-Texas)	.63	−.66	.84
Samuel L. Devine (R-Ohio)	.70	−.59	.84
David E. Satterfield III (D-Virginia)	.67	−.52	.72
John E. Moss (D-California)	−.65	.56	.73
Brock Adams (D-Washington)	−.54	.60	.65
Bob Eckhardt (D-Texas)	−.64	.62	.79
Ralph H. Metcalfe (D-Illinois)	−.60	.69	.84
John H. Dingell (D-Michigan)	(−.40)	.56	.48
Paul G. Rogers (D-Florida)		.81	.74
Lionel VanDeerlin (D-California)	(−.48)	.58	.56
Fred B. Rooney (D-Pennsylvania)		.83	.70
Richardson Preyer (D-North Carolina)		.77	.61
James W. Symington (D-Missouri)	(−.41)	.70	.66
Charles Carney (D-Ohio)	(−.47)	.72	.74
Harley O. Staggers (D-West Virginia)	(−.44)	.78	.80

Correlates of Factional Alignments

	F_1	F_2
ADA Scores	−.94*	.87*
COPE Scores	−.90*	.91*
NFU Scores	−.92*	.94*
ACA Scores	.89*	−.93*
Party Unity (Voting with Democrats) Scores	−.94*	.96*
Conservative Coalition Scores	.90*	−.88*
Presidential Support Scores	.93*	−.92*
CCUS Scores	.88*	−.93*
Issue-Dimension I Scores	−.98*	.98*
Unique Contribution of Issue Dimension	.00	.02

* Statistically significant at the .01 level.
** All Committee members present during 93rd Congress.

Source: U.S. House Committee on Interstate and Foreign Commerce roll-call votes (1973-1976).

increases as legislative action moves beyond the subcommittee level to the final vote.

Post Office and Civil Service Committee

Partisanship appears to play a major role in the organization of factional alignments within the Post Office and Civil Service Committee. Democrats define Faction 1, while Republicans have similar attachments to Faction 2 (Table 11-8). In addition to partisanship, ideology also structures voting blocs within the committee. For example, conservative Republicans Rousselot and Derwinski tend to oppose Faction 1, and two of the more moderate Democrats (Daniels and Hanley) tend to vote with Faction 3, creating a more moderate voting bloc.

A major exception to this pattern occurs with regard to the voting behavior of Democrats Richard White (Texas) and David Henderson (North Carolina). Both of these Democrats are ideologically conservative, but White votes with the Democrats (Faction 1) and Henderson with the conservative Republicans (Faction 2). It seems that partisan considerations are more important than ideological proximity in White's case, but less relevant to Henderson's voting.

The correlates of the factional alignments are consistent with our interpretations. Ideology and partisanship are strongly correlated with the individual factions (Table 11-8—correlates). These ideological and partisan influences on the factional structure are impossible to disentangle since party unity scores are correlated above .9 with each of our ideological measures.

Issues provide a statistically significant contribution to the explanation of Factions 1 and 2. The issue dimensions deal with Civil Service legislation (I); legislative, executive and judicial salaries (II); and postal rates (III). Issue-dimension III (decisions on postal rates) does more to explain the attachment of members to Faction 1 than the other issue dimensions. Issue dimensions I and II are most relevant to the organization of Faction 2; they are also most likely to have administration positions attached to them. This may account for the significance of presidential support scores in explaining Faction 2.

In sum, partisanship, ideology, and the position of the administration on issues before the committee are the most important influences on the factional structure of the Post Office and Civil Service Committee. We can interpret these relationships as reflecting the saliency of party, the executive branch, and the House within the committee's environment. These environmental influences are not as readily apparent as in other committees because of the relatively few committee members actively involved in committee decision making, and the small number of roll-call votes taken within the committee. Hence, our interpretation of the environmental influences in this committee is more tentative than in other committees where these limitations are not present.

Initially, Fenno characterized the Post Office and Civil Service Committee as a nonpartisan, nonideological committee dominated by postal clientele groups, but this description is modified in his "Epilogue" (1973, pp. 64-69, 281-83). According to Fenno, the 1966 pre-Christmas mail breakdown in Chicago "shattered the monolithic, clientele-dominated environment of the committee" (1973, p. 282). Eventually this, and subsequent events, have served to increase the

Table 11-8 Factions Within the House Post Office and Civil Service Committee

Committee Members	Factions			
	F_1	F_2	F_3	h^2
**Dominick V. Daniels (D-New Jersey)	.78		(.43)	.81
Patricia Schroeder (D-Colorado)	.80			.68
William Lehman (D-Florida)	.84			.76
John H. Rousselot (R-California)	−.72	(.35)	(−.47)	.86
**James M. Hanley (D-New York)	.70		.52	.77
**Richard C. White (D-Texas)	.63	−.50		.67
**David N. Henderson (D-North Carolina)		.78		.67
**Edward J. Derwinski (R-Illinois)	(−.43)	.82		.87
**Albert W. Johnson (R-Pennsylvania)		.81		.66
**Charles H. Wilson (D-California)			.94	.92
William L. Clay (D-Missouri)			.81	.84

Correlates of Factional Alignments

	F_1	F_2	F_3
ADA Scores	.75*	−.64	.74*
COPE Scores	.85*	−.71*	.81*
NFU Scores	.81*	−.62	.83*
ACA Scores	−.81*	.66*	−.81*
Party Unity (Voting with Democrats) Scores	.89*	−.63	.74*
Conservative Coalition Scores	−.67*	.52	−.84*
Presidential Support Scores	−.80*	.71*	−.68*
CCUS Scores	−.78*	.60	−.87*
Issue-Dimension I Scores	.76*	−.90*	.76*
Issue-Dimension II Scores	.28	.41	.46
Issue-Dimension III Scores	.53	−.02	−.42
Unique Contribution of Issue Dimensions	.08*[a]	.46*[b]	.05

* Statistically significant at the .01 level.
** Committee member during 89th Congress.

[a] The contributions of issue-dimension I and II scores are inconsequential and are ignored in the calculation of R^2 for issue dimensions or the test of significance.

[b] The contribution of issue-dimension III scores is inconsequential and is ignored in the calculation of the R^2 for issue dimensions or the test of significance. Aside from the issue-dimensions, the only variable in the equation is presidential support scores.

Source: U.S. House Committee on Post Office and Civil Service roll-call votes (1973-1976).

saliency of postal issues nationally. This has resulted in more administration involvement in these issues, and presidential involvement also introduces partisanship into the committee's deliberations. (Fenno, 1973, pp. 282, 66).

Our conclusion about the partisan nature of committee voting is consistent with Fenno's analysis of changes within the committee—greater presidential involvement producing more partisanship. However, our findings differ in that the linkage between partisanship and ideology in our analysis suggests an ideological component to the partisan alignments.

Public Works Committee

The alignments within this committee are clearly partisan: Republicans (Faction 1) and Democrats (Faction 2) define separate factional alignments (Table 11-9). We also observe a small alignment of more liberal Democrats— Studds, Abzug, and Stanton (Faction 3).

Our description of the committee's factional structure is consistent with the pattern of correlates of the factions: ideology and party are the most important explanatory variables (Table 11-9—correlates) in Factions 1 and 3. The distinguishing characteristic of Faction 2 is party affiliation. As in the other committees, there is a degree of partisan and ideological overlap among the committee members. ACA and party unity scores, for example, are strongly intercorrelated ($r = -.95$) and presidential support and conservative coalition scores are also collinear ($r = .91$). This collinearity prevents us from disentangling the different effects of party and ideological forces on Factions 1 and 3. However, this difficulty does not appear to cloud the interpretation of Faction 2, which contains the largest Democratic voting bloc, and is clearly a partisan faction.

Issue dimensions provide a statistically significant contribution to the explanation of the alignments of Factions 1 and 2 (Table 11-9). The issues underlying the dimensions deal with transportation measures (e.g., Federal Mass Transit Act) and standards to be applied in the funding of transportation projects. Nevertheless, partisan and ideological variables explain a greater proportion of the variation in the alignments. Although the committee's factional alignments may be influenced by the nature of the issues at hand, ideology and party are likely to dominate voting patterns.

It seems clear that party is the *dominant* environmental influence on committee decision making, but the small alignment of liberal Democrats within the committee's factional structure suggests that ideology may be important as well. This split among the Democrats seems consistent with the ideological cleavages within the party in the House. Hence, we suspect that the House is also a significant environmental influence on committee decision making.

This centrality which we attribute to partisanship in the organization of committee factions is consistent with James Murphy's characterization of committee decision making: "Most committee legislation will engender party disputes because committee Democrats and Republicans cannot arrive at a consensus either on regional allocation issues . . . or on traditional party issues" (1974, p. 169). Murphy notes that partisan divisions also occur on ideological

279

Table 11-9 Factions Within the House Public Works Committee

Committee Members	Factions			h^2
	F_1	F_2	F_3	
Gene Taylor (R-Missouri)	.87			.88
James Abdnor (R-South Dakota)	.85			.82
Thad Cochran (R-Mississippi)	.90			.85
William F. Walsh (R-New York)	.59			.40
E. G. (Bud) Shuster (R-Pennsylvania)	.63			.47
John P. Hammerschmidt (R-Arkansas)	.87			.80
M. G. Snyder (R-Kentucky)	.90			.81
**Don H. Clausen (R-California)	.69			.50
**James C. Cleveland (R-New Hampshire)	.81			.68
**William H. Harsha (R-Ohio)	.80			.66
Gerry E. Studds (D-Massachusetts)	−.73		.59	.92
Bella S. Abzug (D-New York)	−.73		.56	.87
**Robert E. Jones (D-Alabama)		.96		.92
**James C. Wright, Jr. (D-Texas)		.71		.50
**Harold T. Johnson (D-California)		.77		.61
**David M. Henderson (D-North Carolina)		.92		.94
**Ray Roberts (D-Texas)		.79		.63
**James J. Howard (D-New Jersey)		.78		.73
Robert A. Roe (D-New Jersey)		.82		.77
Mike McCormack (D-Washington)		.92		.90
John B. Breaux (D-Louisiana)		.87		.78
Bo Ginn (D-Georgia)		.76		.58
Glenn M. Anderson (D-California)		.68	.53	.79
James V. Stanton (D-Ohio)			.78	.80
Dale Milford (D-Texas)			−.84	.81

Correlates of Factional Alignments

	F_1	F_2	F_3
ADA Scores	−.81*	.33	.73*
COPE Scores	−.82*	.61*	.71*
NFU Scores	−.77*	.51*	.72*
ACA Scores	.82*	−.47*	−.76*
Party Unity (Voting with Democrats) Scores	−.88*	.63*	.66*
Conservative Coalition Scores	.84*	−.41	−.74*
Presidential Support Scores	.85*	−.52*	−.75*
CCUS Scores	.75*	−.33	−.62*
Issue-Dimension I Scores	−.80*	.94*	.40
Issue-Dimension II Scores	.53*	.25	−.62*
Unique Contribution of Issue Dimensions	.12*	.14*	.04

* Statistically significant at the .01 level.
** Committee member during 90th Congress.

Source: U.S. House Committee on Public Works roll-call votes (1973-1976).

issues: "Committee Democrats and Republicans cannot reach agreement on the authority of the Federal government or on its position in the economy" (1974, p. 169). Such disagreement may give rise to factions structured by both ideology and party. This may explain the small alignment of liberal Democrats in Faction 3, and the strong correlations between measures of ideology and partisanship among committee members. We therefore agree with Murphy that party is the most important influence on committee decision making, but we also note the influence of ideology on the alignments of committee Democrats.

Ways and Means Committee

Party and ideology define the divisions within the Ways and Means Committee. Faction 1 captures the ideological conflicts within the committee (Table 11-10). The lack of a distinct partisan complexion to this faction (1) and the strong bipolarity exhibited suggests an ideological organization to the faction: liberal Democrats tend to oppose conservative Democrats and Republicans. Partisanship structures the alignments of Factions 2 and 3—Democrats occupy Faction 2 and Republicans identify with Faction 3.

The correlates of the factional alignments are consistent with our definition of committee voting blocs: ideology and partisanship are highly correlated with each of the three factions. Factions 1 and 3 are ideologically conservative and tend to oppose the Democratic majorities. The partisanship reflected by Faction 3 is related to support for the policy positions of the Republican administration. Faction 2 is more liberal and supportive of Democratic policy (Table 11-10—correlates). As in the other committees, the effects of ideology and party are intertwined; party unity scores are correlated above .9 with measures of ideology. Ideology and party, therefore, are important dimensions for the organization of the committee's factional structure.

Issues are relatively unimportant in describing committee factions (Table 11-10). In Faction 1, where issue dimensions significantly improve the explanation of the factional alignment, the contribution is a mere 4 percent. The issue dimensions may lack influence because the major dimension (I) is strongly correlated with partisan and ideological indicators. The impact of issues is probably captured by our measures of partisanship and ideology. The issue dimensions reflect positions on the taxing of oil and gas—Oil and Gas Energy Tax Act (I)—and on tax reform and energy conversion (II).

The ideological polarization within the committee—liberal Democrats voting in opposition to conservatives (Faction 1)—suggests that the nature of the House is an important influence on committee decision making. This is not an unexpected result since ideological cleavages within the House would be especially relevant to commitees like Ways and Means and Education and Labor whose work has liberal-conservative dimensions. In Fenno's words,

Of course, the very make-up of the parent chamber stands as a constraint on the activities of every committee. The changing size, for example, of "the conservative coalition" places outer limits on all committees whose work has liberal-conservative dimensions (1973, p. 22).

Table 11-10 Factions Within the House Ways and Means Committee

Committee Members	Factions			h^2
	F_1	F_2	F_3	
**Phil M. Landrum (D-Georgia)	.87			.77
Omar Burleson (D-Texas)	.88			.84
Joe Waggonner, Jr. (D-Louisiana)	.88			.82
Bill Archer (R-Texas)	.77			.79
Donald D. Clancy (R-Ohio)	.63		(.46)	.63
John J. Duncan (R-Tennessee)	.60		(.45)	.56
**Charles A. Vanik (D-Ohio)	−.76			.78
James C. Corman (D-California)	−.63	(.47)		.61
Sam Gibbons (D-Florida)	−.60			.49
William J. Green (D-Pennsylvania)	−.64	.54		.76
Joseph E. Karth (D-Minnesota)	−.60	.56		.68
**Al Ullman (D-Oregon)		.83		.72
**James A. Burke (D-Massachusetts)		.51	(−.42)	.44
**Dan Rostenkowski (D-Illinois)		.81		.68
**Herman T. Schneebeli (R-Pennsylvania)			.79	.75
Barber B. Conable, Jr. (R-New York)			.87	.77

Correlates of Factional Alignments

	F_1	F_2	F_3
ADA Scores	−.80*	.80*	−.66*
COPE Scores	−.80*	.86*	−.84*
NFU Scores	−.84*	.87*	−.80*
ACA Scores	.89*	−.89*	.72*
Party Unity (Voting with Democrats) Scores	−.82*	.88*	−.81*
Conservative Coalition Scores	.89*	−.85*	.72*
Presidential Support Scores	.77*	−.81*	.87*
CCUS Scores	.90*	−.88*	.76*
Issue-Dimension I Scores	−.79*	.90*	−.87*
Issue-Dimension II Scores	−.61*	.22	.31
Unique Contribution of Issue Dimensions	.04*	.03	.03

* Statistically significant at the .01 level.
** Committee member during 89th Congress.

Source: U.S. House Committee on Ways and Means roll-call votes (1973-1976).

The partisan alignments in the committee's factional structure demonstrate the importance of party within the committee's environment. The impact of the administration on committee decision making may be obscured, however, by ideological and partisan environmental influences.

Our conclusions concerning the ideological and partisan factional structure of the Ways and Means Committee coincides with Fenno's characterization of committee decision making: "Ideological divergence parallels a strong set of partisan predispositions" (1973, p. 56). Thus, party and ideology continue to be important influences on committee decision making.

Summary and Conclusions

The similarity between our findings and those of previous studies may be a consequence of stability in committee membership, in goals of committee members, and in the influences operating on the committee's environment. In those committees where our findings differ from previous studies, we attribute the differences to the following factors: (1) the turnover in committee membership—Agriculture and Interior and Insular Affairs; (2) the change in the nature of the issues considered by the committee—Interior and Insular Affairs; (3) the collinearity between party and ideology—Interstate and Foreign Commerce; and (4) the alteration of environmental influences—Post Office and Civil Service.

We find that ideology is reflected in the factional alignments in the eight House committees. We attribute this to the salience of the House as an environmental influence on committee decision making. Further, this suggests that changes in the composition of the House—for example, greater ideological polarization—may alter committee decision-making practices.

Partisanship is an important explanatory variable in all of the committees except International Relations. This points to the important influence that the parties exert on the environment of House committees. We have suggested that partisanship may be augmented by the stage at which the votes were collected in some committees.

The salience of partisan and ideological elements in the voting patterns of House committees may only be temporary. For instance, clear partisan and ideological differences between Congress and the president during the period of this analysis may have sharpened the partisan and ideological factionalization within committee decision making. As these differences are muted by congressional and presidential elections, partisan and ideological differences between the members may begin to diminish. On the other hand, in light of the increasing complexity of issues, and especially amendments, ideology and party provide simplifying cues for voting on such issues. Increased work loads and less time to become familiar with complex issues may increase the role of such cues in voting.[14]

The effects of the administration are evident in two committees—International Relations and Post Office and Civil Service. This suggests that administration influences are of minor importance in the organization of committee factions; however, some of the effects of the administration may be muted by party, and to some extent, by ideology. As noted earlier, the votes in this analysis were taken during a period of partisan and ideological acrimony between the president and Congress. It may be that this situation augmented the partisan and ideological splits within the committee while concealing the influence of the administration. In fact, in the Post Office and Civil Service Committee, we suggest that increased

283

administration interest in the issues it handled may have increased the amount of partisanship observed. Ways and Means is another example of a committee in which partisanship may be obscuring the effects of administration influences.

In Agriculture, Education and Labor, International Relations, Post Office and Civil Service, and Public Works, variables other than ideology, partisanship, and administration are helpful in explaining factional alignments. In Education and Labor we find an ideological faction that also appears to reflect clientele influence (labor). Although their contribution is generally modest, issues do help to explain two of the factions in the Agriculture Committee and three of the factions in the International Relations Committee. In Post Office and Civil Service, issues reflect administration influences. Finally, issues dealing with mass transportation and the level of funding for such projects are important in explaining two of the factions in Public Works. As with the effects of the administration, some of the influence of issues may be hidden by ideology and partisanship.

In sum, we find that the House and the party, as reflected in ideological and partisan voting patterns, are the two dominant influences in the environment of the eight House committees studied. The dominance of these two factors may obscure some of the effects of administration and clientele influences. While knowledge of a committee's factional structure may not reveal the intricacies of committee decision-making practices, this information provides a baseline for mapping and monitoring changes in committee behavior. Such analyses may clarify voting relationships among committee members. Case studies of individual committees then can provide additional specification of committee decision-making patterns, and further delineate some of the influences which have been obscured by party and ideology. Finally, the type of analysis presented in this article may serve as a guide for other studies of committee decision making where interviews are difficult, if not possible, to obtain.

Notes

1. Since most of the work of the Appropriations Committee is done in subcommittees, there are few substantive roll-call votes in the full committee. Therefore, Appropriations was excluded from the analyses. This classification schema can be found in Tacheron and Udall (1970, pp. 157-60).
2. We have classified the following votes as procedural and have excluded them from analysis: (1) votes of reconsideration; (2) votes about rules (committee); (3) points of order; (4) suspension of rules; (5) referral of bills to subcommittees; (6) recommittal votes; (7) instructions on handling bills on the House floor; (8) discharging a subcommittee from considering a bill; (9) postponing action on a bill; (10) acceptance of subcommittee reports; (11) limitations on committee debate; (12) motions to table legislation; (13) motions to report legislation to the House. What remains, therefore, are the roll calls taken on amendments to legislation considered by a committee.
3. This requirement limits the effects of factoring a product-moment correlation matrix where the correlations themselves are based upon varying numbers of votes.

4. The *total* number of committee members included in this analysis (*new and continuing* members) represents better than 70 percent of the committee membership in seven House committees; the subset of members we analyzed in the International Relations Committee comprise 65 percent of the committee's total membership.

5. For an excellent non-technical treatment of the application of the Q-technique to legislative roll-call analysis, see Grumm (1963, esp. pp. 338-40). Our analysis follows the strategy developed by Grumm for identifying legislative voting blocs from a Q-factor analysis. Generally, we have retained all components with an eigenvalue >1.00.

6. Clearly, a varimax rotation ignores the empirical correlations among factors, and therefore, many obscure important relationships within a committee's factional structure. We have evaluated the effects of ignoring the relationships among factors (factions) by examining the correlations among a committee's factions which appear if we allow the factors to assume a fairly oblique (correlated) solution. The analysis of the interfactor correlations resulting from oblique rotation reveals few correlated factors. The strongest factional relationships are generally moderate in strength. Further, the correlated solutions do not significantly *alter*, or *improve upon*, the simplicity of the factional structure determined by a varimax rotation. Therefore, we have retained the orthogonal rotation—varimax—of the principal component analysis of committee votes for the following reasons: (1) oblique rotations fail to improve upon the "simple structure" identified by the orthogonal rotations; (2) orthogonal rotations are conceptually and mathematically less complex; and (3) very few factors are strongly intercorrelated. Nevertheless, we utilize, when relevant, the interfactor correlations in discussing the substantive nature of the relationships among factions within a committee.

7. In extracting the issue dimensions, we eliminate those factors which fail to account for at least 10 percent of the variation in committee voting. This cut-off point delineates the reliable from the unique factors.

8. The factor scores are computed as a weighted product of the existing data:

Factor Score =

$$\left(\frac{\text{number of committee votes}}{\text{number of non-missing committee votes}} \right)$$

$$\Sigma_i F_i Z_i$$

Where F_i is the factor score coefficient, Z_i is the standardized variable, and the summation occurs over all non-missing votes. We have replaced absences with the mean vote for the issue where a committee member has missed less than one-third of the votes; otherwise, the committee member's issue-dimension score is defined as missing data. These calculations are necessary due to the uneven vote participation of committee members.

9. Issue dimensions are the last variables to enter the equation because they represent the unique contribution which issues make to the organization of committee factions. Therefore, we need to remove that amount of variation which can be explained by the common behavioral influences of party, ideology, and constituency; the residual variation represents the amount of variation in the committee's factional alignments which these common legislative influences cannot explain. Clearly, party, ideology, and constituency may be associated with the substantive aspects of an issue. Still, these variables are conceptually simpler and more reliable than issue dimensions which change from committee to committee and, perhaps, year to year. Descriptions of the regression equations are illustrated in the convention version of this article.

10. In an effort to insure the stability of the committee factions, we have examined the factional alignments among new committee members—those assigned to the committee during the 94th Congress. All of the reported factional structures appear to be stable. New committee members join the same factional alignments that exist among continuing committee members. For a discussion and description of the factional alignments among new committee members, see the extended (convention) version of this article.

11. The group ratings are:

    Americans for Democratic Action (ADA)
    Committee on Political Education (COPE)-AFL-CIO
    National Farmers' Union (NFU)
    Americans for Constitutional Action (ACA)
    U.S. Chamber of Commerce (CCUS)

    These ratings were obtained from *Congressional Quarterly's Weekly Report* (94th Congress).

12. A closer examination of the bloc of southern Democrats reveals that each chairs a subcommittee which deals with a different commodity. These are the same commodities which Jones observes are favored when Democrats control the committee (1961, p. 360). While we suspect that this faction reflects clientele influence (commodity interests) we are reluctant to describe it as a clientele faction in the absence of direct measurement of the attachment of committee members to the individual commodities.

13. The only Democrat which violates this pattern is conservative David Satterfield (D-Virginia).

14. Since committee votes are less "visible" than floor roll calls, ideological voting may have more of an influence on committee roll-call behavior than on House floor votes.

IV

LEADERSHIP INFLUENCE: STRATEGIES, TACTICS, AND CONTEXT

M ajority and minority leaders in Congress are responsible for mobilizing their forces behind party positions. Their job is a difficult one: unlike leaders in parliamentary systems, the congressional leadership cannot count on the overwhelming support of party colleagues. Members of Congress are pushed and pulled in different directions by parties, interest groups, presidents, constituents, ideologies, and executive branch agencies. In addition, members tend to value a sense of individuality that is enhanced by the increasing electoral safety of representatives and the higher public profile of senators. Frequently, these forces create pressures that run contrary to party policy.

The articles included in the following section describe the strategies and tactics leaders employ to mobilize a legislative majority and examine the context in which they operate.

Designing the Rule

In the House of Representatives, the Committee on Rules sets the conditions for considering most major legislation. The rule is extremely useful to the leadership of both parties because it allows them to better anticipate floor actions and develop procedural strategies. At times, a highly restrictive rule may offer the only real hope for ensuring the majority leadership's success. For instance:

> The rule for consideration of the energy program conference report in the 95th Congress was vital to its passage. The rule specified that a vote be taken on the package as a whole; separate votes on less popular components were barred. Passing this rule was difficult; the vote on the previous question on the rule was 207 to 206. Once the rule was approved, however, members were faced with a straight up-or-down vote, and the conference report was adopted by a vote of 231 to 168 (Sinclair, 1983, p. 131).

Carefully designed rules structure the floor choices of members in ways intended to promote the influence and effectiveness of party leaders.

Developing Committee Unanimity

One of the most difficult situations facing the party hierarchy is the need to contend with alternative, and frequently conflicting, pressures from other sources of congressional leadership. Because Congress has developed the committee system to provide it with expertise and advice, the party leaders usually must call on committees to support their aims. When a committee is united behind a bill, acceptance on the floor without extensive modification is more likely. Clearly, it behooves party leaders to promote committee unanimity, at least among the party's contingent, and to ensure that committee members' positions are consistent with those of their party. When committee members are divided, either in debate or voting, party members are more apt to follow the direction of their legislative leaders.

Scheduling Legislation

By controlling the floor agenda and thus determining when legislative battles will occur, the leaders of the majority party in the House have an important means to further party goals. (As discussed below, the Senate environment is much less amenable to such control.) Setting the the agenda, however, does not give the majority power to spring "surprises" in scheduling important bills; in most cases, legislative rules prevent such manipulation. But majority party leaders can delay consideration of legislation until a climate favorable for passage exists. This may mean a short delay of hours or days until enough party members are present to pass a bill, or it may take weeks or months to develop sufficient constituent and interest group pressure to sway the needed votes.

Appeals for Party Support

For most members, the party label stands for a number of common attributes: an emotional attachment, similar perceptions of the world and society and, in many cases, like-minded broad policy orientations. It is also perceived as an asset in gaining or retaining power. Not only do leaders appeal to members' sense of partisan solidarity; they also exploit fears of possible ostracism, which means immediate psychological costs and future loss of tangible benefits:

> Even if a member often votes against his party, he is still concerned with retaining the good will of the leaders and members. His friends are likely to be in his own party, and he knows that he can jeopardize his standing with some of them unless he is willing to stretch a point and occasionally help the party, even though he may feel somewhat differently about the issue. Only a handful act almost independently of party. Their friends are few — usually other mavericks (Ripley, 1967, pp. 158-159).

Personal Contact

Leaders rely heavily upon personal contact with members of Congress in trying to persuade them to support the party's position. Some congressional leaders are more skillful at personal persuasion than others. Lyndon B. Johnson, Senate majority leader from 1955 to 1961, was a master at convincing errant Democrats to vote the party line. Few senators could resist his appeals when he applied "the treatment":

The Treatment could last ten minutes or four hours. It came, enveloping its target, at the LBJ Ranch swimming pool, in one of LBJ's offices, in the Senate cloakroom, on the floor of the Senate itself — wherever Johnson might find a fellow Senator within his reach. Its tone could be supplication, accusation, cajolery, exuberance, scorn, tears, complaint, the hint of threat. It was all of these together. It ran the gamut of human emotions. Its velocity was breathtaking, and it was all in one direction. Interjections from the target were rare. Johnson anticipated them before they could be spoken. He moved in close, his face a scant millimeter from his target, his eyes widening and narrowing, his eyebrows rising and falling. From his pockets poured clippings, memos, statistics. Mimicry, humor, and the genius of analogy made The Treatment an almost hypnotic experience and rendered the target stunned and helpless (Evans and Novak, 1966, 232).

All congressional leaders have sought to influence members through personal contacts, but few have been as successful as Johnson. Much depends upon the personality and style of the leaders themselves as well as their ability to bestow membership "perks," such as the allocation of office space. By doing favors for members individually and providing services to them collectively, leaders accumulate political IOUs and create a reservoir of good will. No matter how routine or mundane the matter may seem, successful leaders view such contacts as opportunities for translating favors into resources that they can draw upon later in managing legislative business.

Leaders also may build credit with their party colleagues by channeling money into their reelection campaigns through the party's congressional and senatorial campaign committees. Given the considerable ability of incumbents to attract other campaign funds, such support may not be essential for reelection. Nonetheless, incumbents are likely to value this relatively small increment of financial aid because it does not require the type of specific commitment that is implicitly or explicitly attached to interest group contributions. Moreover, a party's financial support signifies to constituents and interest groups that a member's reelection is important to the party's ability to fashion a responsive legislative majority. Those signals may generate additional financial support for the member in present and future elections.

Committee Assignments

The allocation of committee slots provides leaders with an opportunity to perform favors for members, repaying past cooperation and making a down payment on future assistance. Committee assignments provide an important base for the goals that representatives and senators seek: reelection, legislative power, and policy leadership. Certain committees, such as Appropriations, have jurisdictions over legislation that affect a wide range of significant national issues. Hence, incumbents desiring to gain and exercise power tend to gravitate to those committees. Other members, primarily concerned with reelection, may prefer a seat on a committee — such as House Interior or Senate Public Works — that allocates projects beneficial to his or her district. Finally, some members who are strongly committed to a particular policy position may seek out a committee assignment that will help them build a reputation for expertise and offer greater contact with like-minded groups. Committees often provide those members with forums (through committee hearings and investigations) that attract national attention.

Although the power to make committee assignments can reinforce the influence of legislative leaders, its impact has diminished for a number of reasons. Irwin Gertzog (1976) has noted that most members are given positions on the committees of their choice early in their legislative careers; thus, using assignments for subsequent bargaining is not available. Moreover, the assignment process has become "routinized"; party leaders less frequently use committee assignments as "rewards" for loyalty. The decline in electoral turnover also has circumscribed the leverage of committee assignments by limiting the number of committee vacancies that arise from one Congress to the next. Westefield (1974) suggests that these circumstances have led House leaders to expand the size of certain committees in an effort to increase the availability and value of assignments as a means of enticing member compliance:

> Why increase the number of positions on committees that are not valued by the members? After all, such committees earn their low prestige standing through their inability to hold current members and attract new members from other committees. Moreover, why dispense more of the most prized positions? Expanding only the very best committees rapidly depletes the values of these leadership resources. In short, the leaders try to buy cheap and sell dear (Westerfield, 1974, pp. 1599-1600).

To expand their resource base and gain as much influence with their colleagues as possible, therefore, party leaders generally "manufacture" slots for less attractive committees. There are, however, notable exceptions to this generalization, as the expansion of the membership of the prestigious House Ways and Means Committee in the 1970s demonstrates.

Position in Information Network

A growing number of informal groups provide members with information about legislation and congressional operations. They include meetings of state delegations, regional groupings, and more policy-oriented organizations such as the Democratic Study Group in the House. Despite such alternative resources, party leaders retain a central place in the network that disseminates information to party members. Regardless of who controls the White House, for example, party leaders generally have greater access to executive branch information than does the average member.

Not surprisingly, leaders have used their unique position to bestow favors on their colleagues by keeping them informed about their pet bills and by providing reliable information. Lyndon Johnson's reign as Senate leader provides a good illustration of how information can be exploited for political ends:

> Johnson believed that simply knowing more than anyone else about all facets of a legislative situation would generally prove to be decisive, first, in identifying the various interests of those senators who held the balance of power on a given

bill, and, second, in designing the precise set of tactics which could capitalize on these interests (Stewart, 1971, p. 66).

Managing the Floor

Although many legislative battles are lost long before a bill comes to a floor vote, leaders can turn some defeats into victories by arranging speakers and influencing voting patterns among members or blocs. Through negotiations and bargains, for example, leaders might be able to persuade a large bloc of voters to defect from their normal voting patterns. We can see this phenomenon in the ways in which Republican presidents have been able to lure Democrats, especially southern ones, into Republican coalitions.

Who speaks for or against a bill is often as important as what is said. The support of well respected, pivotal legislators on an issue makes it easier for others to go along with a policy that may be unpopular with influential interest groups and constituents. It is "easier" to vote the party line when colleagues who normally oppose the leadership relent and actually champion the party's causes. For that reason, Democratic leaders often devote considerable effort to seeking the support of southern conservatives who otherwise might oppose the party's position, while Republican leaders similarly might court northeastern liberals.

On the other hand, leaders may try to dissuade unpopular colleagues from speaking on behalf of a bill supported by the party. And they can ask probable opponents to miss a vote. Finally, leaders can use their parliamentary expertise and powers to orchestrate legislative procedures by calling up particular amendments and motions and by recognizing speakers on the floor.

Before concluding the discussion of strategies and techniques available to leaders, it should be pointed out that majority and minority leaders have different resources at their disposal and that the powers of House and Senate leaders also differ. The resources available to the minority are more restricted in scope and quality than are those available to the party in power. Minority leaders have fewer opportunities to build "credit" with their party colleagues than do majority leaders, who have the means to guarantee a member's involvement in policy decisions through control over the legislative agenda. Furthermore, the minority leadership possesses none of the parliamentary powers wielded by the Speaker of the House.

While Senate leaders may be able to pursue many of the above-mentioned strategies and tactics, the small size and greater independence of individual members make the task of leadership far more difficult than it is in the House. Senate leaders, more than their House counterparts, must weave together "fragments of power" if they are to succeed (Truman, 1959, p. 115):

> The Senate transacts most of its business through unanimous consent; debate is limited, schedules agreed to, rules set aside without objection because leaders respect the rights and interests of individual senators, who in turn go along with reasonable arrangements proposed by their leaders. But nothing is surrendered. One man may object and slow business to a halt. The ultimate expression of a latent institutionalized anarchy in the Senate is, as everyone knows, the filibuster

— the privilege of unlimited talk — which permits a determined minority, and under certain circumstances a single member, to impose a negative on the entire body (Fenno, 1965, pp. 80-81).

Context and Legislative Leadership

No discussion of the strategies and tactics of legislative leaders would be complete without mentioning the context in which they operate. Observing the operations of the House Democratic leadership, Lewis Froman and Randall Ripley noted:

> . . . leadership victories are more likely to occur when (1) leadership activity is high; (2) the issue is more procedural and less substantive; (3) the visibility of the issue is low; (4) the visibility of the action is low; (5) there is little counter pressure from the constituencies; and (6) state delegations are not engaged in collective bargaining for specific demands (Froman and Ripley, 1965, p. 63).

While these conditions are not entirely beyond the control of party leaders, they are, for the most part, "givens" in the congressional political system and help determine a leader's effectiveness. The legislative successes of Speaker Sam Rayburn (who served as Speaker from 1940-47; 1949-53; and 1955-61) frequently are attributed to his exploitation of an informal network of confidants for information and his personal negotiations with key legislative actors. Since Rayburn's time, however, changes in House rules and norms have encouraged junior representatives to become more active in committees and on the floor. The fact that more members participate more directly in the legislative process has reduced the effectiveness of a strategy that emphasizes personal negotiations with a small cadre of key actors.

According to Barbara Sinclair (1983), the House Democratic leadership has responded to this environmental change by relying on positive inducements rather than negative sanctions; by using its formal powers (control over scheduling legislation, recognition of members, and floor management of bills) to influence the voting decisions of members; and by attempting to include as many Democrats as possible in fashioning legislative coalitions.

The four articles included in this section discuss the impact of the political context on the leaders' styles and strategies and describe the kinds of forces that affect their operations.

Randall Ripley has studied how institutional changes in the postwar Senate have affected leadership strategies. He argues that the Senate has transformed itself from an institution where most legislative power rested with committee chairmen into a chamber of shifting leadership groups in which significant legislative power is spread more evenly among senators of both parties and coalitions are organized around specific issues. One result has been the erosion of conservative Southern Democrats' legislative power. A similar dispersion of power also has occurred among Senate Republicans. Ripley concludes that the

Senate environment has so changed that "important institutional positions are being dispersed ever more widely and there are few obstacles to any senator of either party who has the requisite personal skills to develop legislative power and chooses to use those skills" (Ripley, 1969c, p. 492).

Joseph Cooper and David Brady maintain in their 1981 analysis that the institutional context, rather than personal traits, determines the styles congressional leaders adopt in dealing with their party colleagues. They contend that the shift from the previous environment of centralized power and hierarchical control to the present, decentralized bargaining system was necessitated by the decline in party cohesion:

> The higher the degree of party unity or cohesion the more power in both the formal and party systems can be concentrated in the hands of party leaders and the more leadership style will be oriented to command and task or goal attainment. The lower the degree of party unity or cohesion the more power in both the formal and party system will be dispersed and the more leadership style will be oriented to bargaining and the maintenance of good relations. The infrequency of eras of centralized power in the House is thus explicable in terms of the very high levels of party strength required to support it, requirements which have increased as the organization itself has become more elaborate (Cooper and Brady, 1981, p. 424).

The degree of party unity inside Congress and within constituencies is a critical factor in shaping leaders' styles and effectiveness. One reason for the decline in party cohesion is the increased fragmentation of partisan loyalties within members' constituencies; the decrease in party-line voting is a consequence of the disintegration of the constituency bases of the congressional parties. That is, the cohesion in party support among identifiable constituency groups (Blacks, Catholics, labor, farmers) has declined. The result has been the persistence of pressures that run contrary to those of the political parties. Thus, members of Congress frequently represent constituencies that may be atypical of traditional sources of Democratic and Republican support. When constituency characteristics match those of the national party, the cross-pressures on members subside; constituency and party pressures reinforce one another. Under these latter conditions, party support on legislative issues is more likely because the pressures of the party and those of the constituency foster similar actions.

Barbara Sinclair (1981) points to another method House leaders use to exercise control over their members: the formation of ad hoc groups appointed by the leadership (Speaker) and charged with the passage of a specific bill. Sinclair notes that changes in rules, norms, membership, and issues that occurred in the 1970s created an environment that is less predictable than previously. First, rules revisions have diminished the power of committee chairmen and further decentralized power; these changes have made it necessary for leaders to solicit the support of more members than previously. Second, membership turnover has made the development of longstanding personal relationships the exception rather than the rule, even though such personal relationships are central to leaders' persuasive abilities. Third, the weakening of certain norms such as apprenticeship, has undermined the authority of committees and has made it easier to modify committee bills on the House floor. Finally, the kinds of issues confronting Congress in the 1970s and 1980s are extremely divisive of Democratic and Republican party unity.

A strategy based on bargaining among a small group of powerful leaders is doomed to failure, given the growing independence of members and the extensive decentralization of power. Sinclair suggests that these changes have created the need for leaders to develop a strategy that provides greater opportunities for member participation, especially among junior representatives. Congressional leaders could expect to benefit from such a practice:

> If junior Democrats are involved in the vote-mobilization process via task force membership, their very considerable energies are directed towards accomplishing leadership objectives and they are given a stake in the leadership's success (Sinclair, 1981, p. 400).

The strategy of inclusion implies more than just opening the decision-making process to more members; the strategy also demands that those included represent all sections of the party. The participation of a wide spectrum of members on "task forces" allows them to gain a better appreciation of the problems leaders encounter in mobilizing legislative majorities.

Charles Jones (1968) examines the impact of the political environment on the House minority leadership. If favored by auspicious political conditions, the range of available strategies is quite broad: minority leaders may counter the opposition with proposals of their own and may even attempt to build a majority coalition around those policies; they can cooperate with the majority party in the formulation of legislation; or they can try to defeat majority party proposals. When conditions are unfavorable, the range of strategies is more restricted: minority leaders can either go along with the majority party's proposals or can offer only inconsequential opposition. The political conditions that determine the range of strategies available to the minority party are both external and internal to Congress. Jones defines four external conditions that influence minority party strategies: the general tenor of the times, the relative political strength of the minority party outside Congress, the level of presidential power, and the extent to which the national party is unified or divided. The internal conditions that affect minority party strategies are changes in House procedures, the size of the margin enjoyed by the majority party, and the abilities and styles of the leadership corps of both parties.

12. POWER IN THE POST-WORLD WAR II SENATE

Randall B. Ripley

The distribution of legislative power in the United States Senate has changed since the end of World War II. The thesis of this article is that between 1945 and 1968 the Senate has transformed itself from a body in which principal legislative power resided in the chairmen and, to a lesser extent, the ranking minority members of the full standing committees into a body in which significant legislative power is spread among virtually all senators of both parties. This also means that the Senate has changed from a body in which most important legislative decisions were dominated by conservative southern Democrats into a body in which many important legislative decisions are not dominated by conservative southern Democrats.

The literature on the Senate offers a confusing picture of the distribution of legislative power. Commentators who knew well the Senate of the late 1940s and early and middle 1950s concluded that a conservative oligarchy, variously identified as the Club or Establishment, ruled the Senate.[1] They asserted that the role of the oligarchy is perpetuated in part by the continuing emergence of "Senate men" who possess certain personal traits acceptable to the ruling oligarchs. These traits include tolerance for others, courteousness, prudence, and a willingness to help others, to work hard, to compromise, and to keep one's word.[2] The "Senate man" is devoted to certain practices or "folkways" of the Senate: a period of apprenticeship for new members and legislative specialization, for example.[3] Those supporting the Club argument assert that men who do not conform to the model do not wield as much influence or power in the Senate as those who do. The important posts are reserved for members of the Club and the important decisions, legislative and institutional, are made by them.

Author's Note: I am grateful to my colleagues in the Political Science Department at Ohio State for commenting on an earlier version of this paper that I gave at a departmental colloquium. I am also grateful to seventeen senators and thirty Senate staff members for their participation in a series of discussions that helped me form the argument of this article. For a description of these meetings see footnote 20. For a fuller treatment of some of the themes in this article see my *Power in the Senate* (St. Martin's Press) available in the summer of 1969.

Source: *Journal of Politics* vol. 31, no. 2 (May 1969): 465-492. Reprinted with permission of the publisher.

Those who discern a Club or Establishment in the Senate do not necessarily agree on the identity of all of its members. But they do agree that the Club in both parties has both a geographical and an ideological bias: it is dominated by southern Democrats and midwestern Republicans who are dedicated to blocking most liberal legislation, whether sponsored by a Democratic or Republican President.

Those who contest the validity of the Club analysis cite the lack of agreement on its membership.[4] They point out that senators who violate the folkways and do not possess all of the requisite personal traits — men such as Hubert Humphrey, for example — have been identified as members of the Club. They also point out that even the complete, self-acknowledged "outsider" can have substantial power both because of the committee structure of the Senate and because of the great bargaining weight automatically available to each one of the hundred senators. They argue that the members of the so-called Establishment — southern and a few western Democrats — often provide the deciding votes in favor of liberal legislation.

One important factor helping to produce lack of clarity in the literature is that there has been no agreement on how to measure power in the Senate, or even how to conceive of it. Some, for example, have inferred power relationships from roll call votes; others are skeptical of the possibility of doing so.[5]

This article does not propose an exact measure of power to resolve the conflicts sketched above. What it does offer is a two-sided perspective on power in the Senate and some evidence to support the specific view of the post-World War II Senate that is offered.

The Nature of Senatorial Power

Power involves a relationship between at least two individuals. Senator A is powerful (or influential) to the extent that he can induce Senator B to behave in some way in which Senator B would not, of his own volition, ordinarily behave.[6] Occasionally, a senator can appear to wield power unopposed: that is, he defines the desired impact and no one opposes his wishes. But, in reality, he is probably unopposed either because he is stating a position with which everyone agrees, in which case power is not involved, or because silence or lack of opposition is at least an implicit recognition of his power.

A senator's power over other senators comes from two principal sources: the personal skills and expertise of the individual senator and his institutional position or positions.[7]

Personal power may develop because a senator is charming or skillful at personal relations. It may develop because he possesses real expertise on specific subject matter. Senators can and do develop power of this sort regardless of their position or lack of position in the various institutional hierarchies of the Senate.

Institutional power comes from holding institutional positions that are presumed to have some power attached to them and/or place the holder in a strategic position in relation to substantive matters. Party leaders and committee chairmen, for example, almost surely possess some institutional power.[8]

The two types of power complement each other. If a senator possesses personal skills that he can use to achieve the desired impact on legislative results his power is still greatly enhanced when he achieves an important institutional position. And, he is likely to use his personal skills to make the most out of his institutional position. On the other hand, if a person comes to a powerful institutional position before he acquires much personal power, he can still develop it and enhance his total impact on legislative results.[9]

The use of legislative power can either be direct or indirect. A senator can take a position on a specific legislative issue and can work to implement its position. In this case, he acts directly on the issue at hand. Many senators have considerable power on a few specific issue areas but may be relatively powerless on other matters. Thus, in many situations, it is meaningless to say that Senator X is powerful legislatively unless the subject matter on which he exercises power is specified. A few senators, such as active and aggressive party leaders, may develop general legislative power.

Powerful senators may have an impact on internal organizational questions that face the Senate. By having the greatest impact on these decisions, a senator is often indirectly affecting future legislative outcomes. For example, southern senators who, through the years, used their power to maintain the filibuster with only minimal limits, were, at the same time, having an impact on the possibility of civil rights legislation. A senator who uses his power to support a given candidate for a party leadership position is doing so, in part, because he expects that leader to be helpful in the future in supporting substantive positions agreeable to the man making the choice between candidates. If a senator urges changes in the seniority practices of the Senate he is doing so because he expects that the changes will lead to legislative results he desires.

How can changing patterns of institutional power and personal power distribution be ascertained? Institutional positions can easily be identified that are thought to carry power with them. The distribution of these positions can then be analyzed. Personal power presents a more difficult problem. Here it is suggested that there are two major possible ways of finding out about personal power. One is to rely on the reputations for personal power that knowledgeable first-hand observers, often journalists, attribute to various individual senators and groups of senators. A second is to probe the perceptions that senators (and staff members) themselves have both of the power of others and of their own efficacy in achieving the legislative goals they favor. Evidence of all three varieties — on institutional positions, on reputations for power, and on senators' perceptions of their own legislative power and that of others — will be offered in support of the central argument.

The Democrats and Institutional Power

Two critical events in 1946 shaped the post-World War II Senate and gave the southern Democrats a dominant institutional position that only now is beginning to diminish.[10] The first of these events was the passage of the Legislative Reorganization Act, which necessitated a reshuffling of committee assignments when the Eightieth Congress met in early 1947. The second was the election of November 1946. Once these two events had established the southerners in a strong position in the committee hierarchy of the Senate then what they needed to develop dominance was continued re-election and good health and the continued preference of the voters for a Democratic majority.

After the 1946 election the Democrats found themselves with 45 Senate seats instead of 56. The regional composition of the party had swung south:[11]

	Southern Seats	Western Seats	Northern Seats
1946	22	19	15
1947	22	13	10

This change had both immediate and long-run effects on the seniority structure of the party. Immediately, the southerners occupied a stronger position at the highest levels of seniority. For example, in 1946, only two of the nine most senior Democrats in the Senate were from southern states. Five of the nine were loyal supporters of Roosevelt's and Truman's domestic programs. After the 1946 election four of the nine most senior Democrats were from southern states and only three of the nine were loyal supporters of New Deal and Fair Deal legislation.

Death as well as defeat, caused the average seniority of all Democrats from both the south and outside the south to decline for a few years after 1946. But the southerners rapidly began to increase their seniority, again while further electoral misfortunes continued to plague northerners and westerners. Mean seniority figures (in years) by region reflect this situation:

	1945	1949	1953
Southern Democrats	9.7	8.5	9.2
Northern and Western Democrats	8.3	7.6	7.0

The skill of the conservative southerners in perpetuating the strongest possible institutional position for themselves while, at the same time, keeping the chances of revolt by liberals at a minimum, can be suggested by looking at committee reorganization in 1947. During 1945 and 1956 a Joint Committee on the Organization of Congress worked on a number of proposals for modernizing Congress. One of the keys to reform was the standing committee system in both houses. In the Senate, thirty-three standing committees existed in 1946. The Legislative Reorganization Act, signed by the President in August 1946, reduced this number to fifteen and reduced the number of seats on each committee. At the beginning of the next Congress, in January 1947, the Senate put the revised committee structure into operation. Now there were only eighty-six seats on the six most sought after committees (Appropriations, Armed Services, Finance, Foreign Relations, Interstate and Foreign Commerce, and Judiciary) instead of 143.[12] Democrats in the Seventy-ninth Congress had held eighty-six seats on these committees; now they had only thirty-nine. The Republicans were more fortunate: their representation on these committees was reduced from fifty-seven seats to forty-seven seats.

During 1945 and 1946, as the Joint Committee began to work on the specifics of committee consolidation, a great deal of bargaining took place. All thirty-three Democratic chairmen (and the thirty-three ranking Republican members) had an especially heavy stake in reorganization. Even the chairman of an inconsequential committee was entitled to certain perquisites and few chairmen were happy at the prospect of losing the perquisites and becoming just another committee member. Thus a senator who was to lose a chairmanship presumably should get something for it: either assignment to a choice committee on which he had not previously served or retention of a choice committee on which he already had some service.

The Democratic problems were compounded by the election results in November 1946, which decreed that the next Senate would be Republican. Thus the Democrats would have only ranking minority memberships to pass out, not chairmanships, and they would have fewer seats on the choice committees. But the bargains made before the election would still have to be kept. Those Democrats who were slated to be chairmen of the reorganized committees would now have to be content with being number one on the minority side.

The southern Democrats lost more top positions than they retained, but they retained the most important positions. Of the twelve committee chairmen in the Seventy-ninth Congress who returned to the Eightieth Congress and retained their top ranking positions on the Democratic side of the successor Committee, only four were southerners. They were, however, first ranking on three of the most important committees: Appropriations, Finance, and Foreign Relations.

Twelve men who chaired committees in the Seventy-ninth Congress and who returned to the Eightieth Congress lost their top ranking positions on the successor committee. Some left the successor committee altogether. Some also lost assignments on other choice committees, not always because of the new Republican-Democratic ratio after the 1946 elections. Some of these men apparently agreed to give up choice seats to men with less seniority as part of the general reassignment bargain.

Two of the twelve men who lost committee chairmanships and did not retain the ranking minority position were Alben Barkley and Scott Lucas who were, respectively, floor leader and Whip. Obviously, their leadership duties were important and time-consuming and so their changed committee positions cannot be considered a "loss." Of the other ten who "lost" in the committee shuffle, six were southerners. Table 12-1 summarizes what happened to the ten "losers" in the 1946-1947 shuffle.

Several generalizations can be made from this table. First, the committees that these men lost were not very important by themselves: only Civil Service and Education and Labor had much legislative responsibility prior to the Reorganization Act. In both cases, western Democrats lost these places to more senior western Democrats. Only two men with more seniority than their successors as first ranking lost (apparently voluntarily) their committee assignments. These

Table 12-1 Democrats Who Lost First Position on a Committee Because of the Legislative Reorganization Act of 1946

Name, State	Years of Service in 1946	Chairman, 1946	Successor Committee	1947 Committee Assignments	Rank	Also Lost[b]
Downey, Calif.	7	Civil Service	Civil Service	Public Lands Public Works[a]	4 4	Mil. Aff.
Ellender, La.	9	Claims	Judiciary	Agriculture and Forestry Labor and Public Welfare	2 4	
Murray, Mont.	11	Education and Labor	Labor and P.W.	Labor and Public Welfare Public Lands	2 3	For. Rels. Mil. Aff.
Hill, Ala.	8	Expenditures in Executive Depts.	Expend. in Exec. Depts.	Armed Services Labor and Public Welfare	4 5	
Russell, Ga.	13	Immigration	Judiciary	Appropriations Armed Services	5 2	
O'Mahoney, Wyo.	12	Indian Affairs	Public Lands	Appropriations Public Lands	8 2	Mil. Aff.
Stewart, Tenn.	7	Interoceanic Canals	Armed Services	Agriculture and Forestry Interstate and Foreign Commerce	4 2	Mil. Aff.
Pepper, Fla.	9	Patents	Judiciary	Agriculture and Forestry[a] Labor and Public Welfare	6 3	For. Rels.
Green, R.I.	9	Privileges and Elections	Rules	Appropriations Rules	9 2	For. Rels.
Byrd, Va.	13	Rules	Rules	Armed Services Finance	3 4	

[a] New assignment in 1947. All other assignments represent continuations of previous assignments.
[b] These assignments were lost to men of lesser seniority on the committee, not just because of the changed party ratio in the Senate after the 1946 elections.

were both southerners: Lister Hill of Alabama and Richard Russell of Georgia. But they both retained much more important committee assignments: Hill as number four on Armed Services and number five on Labor and Public Welfare and Russell as number five on Appropriations and number two on Armed Services. Hill also lost a place on Foreign Relations, but only because of the changed committee ratio in 1947.

The men who lost the most were the six who not only lost a chairmanship but who also lost a seat on Foreign Relations or Military Affairs (which merged with Naval Affairs to become Armed Services) to a Democrat junior to them on the committee, not just because of the 1946 election results. Of these six, only two were from southern states: Claude Pepper of Florida and Tom Stewart of Tennessee. Pepper was clearly a southern "maverick" — he was one of the most liberal Democrats in the Senate. Stewart was quite junior by southern standards and apparently expendable. The other four "losers" who suffered the most were three liberal westerners and a liberal New Englander. In short, five supporters of President Truman lost most heavily in the committee reorganization, and only one man reasonably loyal to the southern conservative group was among the heaviest losers.

The non-southern "losers" were, however, mollified by the committee assignments they did receive. They lost more than they retained or gained, but they still had enough to prevent serious thoughts of protest. Downey retained Public Lands and got an additional assignment to Public Works — both important committees for California. Murray, perhaps the heaviest single loser in the reorganization, retained high ranking positions on Labor and Public Welfare and Public Lands, the latter of great importance to Montana. O'Mahoney retained a junior position on Appropriations and second position on Public Lands, important for Wyoming. Green retained a junior position on Appropriations.

Thus, those in the strongest positions during reorganization understood both how to perpetuate the interests of their own group and how to reduce the chances of violent objection.

Using their seniority position and their political skills to highest advantage, the southerners, especially the conservatively oriented ones, came, within a few years after World War II, to dominate the standing committees of the Senate. Growing regional overrepresentation in the late 1940s and early 1950s can be documented and some commentators have specifically attempted to document the overrepresentation of the southern Democrats on committees.[13] But these documentations either give no indication of the degree of overrepresentation involved or they lack the time perspective that would facilitate determination of trends.

Table 12-2 presents data that show the pattern of southern Democratic overrepresentation in critical institutional positions. This overrepresentation decreased from a high level before and during World War II for the decade after the war. From the mid-1950s until the mid-1960s it grew in the areas of committee chairmanships, the top three seats on all standing committees, and the top three seats on the four most important committees.[14]

Table 12-2 Southern Democratic Representation on Senate Committees and Subcommittees, 1941-1968[a]
Percent of Southerners Among:

Congress (Year)	All Democratic Senators	Committee Chairmen[b]	Three Highest Ranking Democrats on All Committees[c]	All Democrats on Four Choice Committees[d]	Three Highest Ranking Democrats on Four Choice Committees[d]	Subcommittee Chairmen[e]
77th (1941)	33	62	48	36	67	
79th (1945)	39	50	44	35	50	
81st (1949)	41	40	42	54	67	
83rd (1953)	47	47	56	56	67	
85th (1957)	45	53	44	58	58	45
87th (1961)	34	56	48	46	67	41
89th (1965)	29	62	52	43	83	35
90th (1968)	30	56	46	37	67	31

[a] The South is defined as the eleven states of the Confederacy.

[b] This column applies to ranking minority members in the Eighty-Third Congress, when the Republicans organized the Senate. This column includes the sixteen most important standing committees in the Seventy-Seventh and Seventy-Ninth Congresses (Agriculture and Forestry, Appropriations, Banking and Currency, Commerce, District of Columbia, Education and Labor, Finance, Foreign Relations, Interstate Commerce, Irrigation and Reclamation, Judiciary, Manufactures, Military Affairs, Naval Affairs, Public Lands and Surveys, and Rules), and all standing committees thereafter.

[c] This column includes the sixteen most important standing committees in the Seventy-Seventh and Seventy-Ninth Congresses and all standing committees thereafter.

[d] The four choice committees are Appropriations, Armed Services, Finance, and Foreign Relations. Military Affairs was used instead of Armed Services in the Seventy-Seventh and Seventy-Ninth Congresses.

[e] Data on subcommittees are difficult to obtain before 1955. A few special subcommittees of little importance are omitted from this tabulation.

The two areas in which southern overrepresentation has been decreasing since the mid-1950s are in subcommittee chairmanships and in all seats on the four most important committees. The spread of subcommittee chairmanships and junior seats on choice committees had the effect of keeping dissent and revolt against a southern-dominated committee system at a minimum.

The latest figures, for 1968, show that southern overrepresentation on all of the various measures used is declining. The institutional base of southern power seems to be eroding, although slowly.

Not only have the southerners as a regional grouping been dominant on the most important committees and in the most important positions on all committees, but the *conservative* southerners and their allies and ideological comrades from other regions have dominated most of the six committees on which most senators want to serve: Appropriations, Armed Services, Commerce, Finance, Foreign Relations, and Judiciary.

In order to determine ideological biases in the Democratic contingents on these committees, comparisons were made for all Congresses from 1947 (Eightieth) through 1967 (Ninetieth) between the mean scores of the Democrats on each of the six committees on various *Congressional Quarterly* indices and the mean score for all Democrats in those Congresses. Table 12-3 reports summary findings. Comparative party unity index scores, presidential support scores under Kennedy and Johnson, and federal role support scores were interpreted for evidence of liberal or conservative bias in the composition of the Democratic membership of these six committees. The data support the proposition that during this period the conservative Democrats were dominant on Finance, Appropriations, Judiciary, and Armed Services. The Commerce Committee was not consistently under the control of any ideological group and the liberals tended to control the Foreign Relations Committee.

When these scores are examined individually, there is evidence that a gradual liberalization of the Democratic contingent on these six committees is

Table 12-3 Ideological Bias of Democratic Contingents on Six Senate Committees, 1947-1967

Committee	*Relation of Committee Contingent to all Democrats on Base of 20 Index Scores*[a]	
	More Conservative	*More Liberal*
Appropriations	18	2
Armed Services	16	3
Commerce	10	9
Finance	19	0
Foreign Relations	6	11
Judiciary	18	2

[a] The two figures for each committee do not add to 20 in all cases because some mean committee scores are the same as the mean score for all Democrats.

taking place. For example, Table 12-4 compares the number of Democrats more liberal or more conservative than the average Democratic senator on the six committees in the Eighty-fifth Congress (1957-58) and in the Ninetieth Congress (1967-68). The score used for making judgments in the former case is the Economy Opposition Score and the score used for the latter is the Larger Federal Role Support Score.

Table 12-4 Liberal and Conservative Members on Six Committees, 85th Congress and 90th Congress

| | 85th Congress (1957-58) | | 90th Congress (1967-68) | |
Committee	Liberals	Conservatives	Liberals	Conservatives
Appropriations	5	7	8	9
Armed Services	4	4	7	5
Commerce	3	5	8	4
Finance	3	5	4	7
Foreign Relations	6	2	8	4
Judiciary	2	6	7	4
Total	23 (44%)	29 (56%)	42 (56%)	33 (44%)

[a] The two figures for each committee do not add to 20 in all cases because some mean committee scores are the same as the mean score for all Democrats.

These figures suggest a broader pattern: conservative Democrats are hanging onto their dominance of a few key institutional positions, in this case the Finance Committee, but are seeing their former control of some positions, in this case the Commerce Committee and Judiciary Committee, disappear. In other cases, such as the Appropriations Committee and the Armed Services Committee, the changes are incrementally in the liberal direction. The picture emerges of a slowly dissolving institutional power base for conservative Democrats.

Southern representation on the Democratic Steering Committee (the committee on committees) helps explain southern dominance on the most important committees from 1951 to 1965. Table 12-5 summarizes this representation for twelve congresses. From 1951 to 1965 southern representation on the Steering Committee was consistently just short of half of the committee. This southern strength, coupled with the electoral system in the southern states that has usually returned the same man for term after term, has led naturally to southern dominance of the Democratic side of most of the important committees. Generally, the southerners entered the Senate at a younger age than the other Democrats. This gave them an added advantage in accruing seniority: they could outlive other Democrats more often than not. The figures for 1967, however, suggest that here, too, the institutional base for southern power is dwindling.

The southern Democrats had general, although not universal, success in keeping the formal top leadership offices of the party under their control. Nine men held the position of floor leader or Whip between 1947 and 1968. Two men held the position of secretary of the caucus from 1961 to 1968.[15] These eleven

Table 12-5 Southern Representation on Democratic Steering Committee (Committee on Committees), 1945-1967

Congress *(Year)*	*Number on Committee*	*Number of Southerners on Committee*	*Percent Southerners on Committee*	*Percent all Dem. Senators from South*
79th (1945)	11	3	27	39
80th (1947)	14	4	29	49
81st (1949)	11	3	27	41
82nd (1951)	13	6	46	45
83rd (1953)	15	7	47	47
84th (1955)	14	6	43	46
85th (1957)	15	7	47	45
86th (1959)	15	7	47	34
87th (1961)	15	7	47	34
88th (1963)	15	7	47	31
89th (1965)	17	7	41	29
90th (1967)	17	5	29	30

men constituted the central leadership of the Democratic party in the Senate for these twenty-two years. Three were from southern states, three were from border states, three were from western states, and only two were from the heavily populated states north of the Ohio River and east of the Mississippi River. Only one of the eleven, Hubert Humphrey, had or acquired a national reputation as a leader of the liberal wing of the party. Most of the men were balancers, trying to find a way for the party to stick together, either in inactivity or in activity upon which agreement could be reached. A few were in the conservative wing of the party.

When contests between moderates or conservatives and liberals took place (only three out of a possible fourteen times) the moderate or conservative always won. In 1951 the conference elected Ernest McFarland of Arizona, a moderate dominated by the southerners, as Majority Leader over Joseph O'Mahoney of Wyoming, a staunch Fair Dealer.[16] In 1965, Russell Long of Louisiana won a three-way race for whip over his more consistently liberal opponents, John Pastore of Rhode Island and Mike Monroney of Oklahoma. In 1967, conservative Robert Byrd of West Virginia defeated liberal Joseph Clark of Pennsylvania for the post of Secretary of the Conference. (In early 1969 a contest for whip was decided in favor of the more liberal candidate.)

Part of the reason for the present slow erosion of southern conservative institutional power is numbers: only 19 of a party of 64 in the Ninetieth Congress were southerners and a number of those were liberals. Liberal Democrats who were assigned to junior positions in 1959 and succeeding years are now, through the inexorable process of seniority and the boost given them by the Goldwater candidacy in 1964, succeeding to more important positions.

In addition to changing personnel, several other factors have led to a dispersion of institutional power. The "Johnson rule" for committee assignments — that all Democrats should have one good assignment before any Democrat has more than one — began spreading influential positions to more junior senators soon after its adoption in 1953.[17]

Furthermore, through the late 1950s and early 1960s the number of subcommittees increased. In part, this reflected the skill of the southerners in keeping incipient revolt suppressed. It also reflected a real dispersion of power, occasioned in part by the growing work-load in the Senate. Figures for 1957, 1961, 1965, and 1968 show the number of subcommittees (and thus chairmanships) increasing, but southern representation declining:

Congress (Year)	Number of Subcommittee Chairmen	Number of Southern Chairmen	Percent of Southern Chairmen
85th (1957)	86	39	45
87th (1961)	95	39	41
89th (1965)	98	34	35
90th (1968)	103	32	31

Most northern and western Democrats have subcommittee chairmanships. These bestow both tangible perquisites (including, in some instances, control over staff appointments) and increased influence on legislation on the incumbents. Not all subcommittees are equally powerful, however, and senior southerners can in many cases retain the most important subcommittee chairmanships for themselves and their allies. Thus, again, the erosion of southern institutional power is gradual.

In the Eighty-ninth Congress (1965-66), for example, only sixteen Democrats (out of sixty-eight) failed to attain either committee or subcommittee chairmanships. Table 12-6 lists these men.

Only two of the twenty southern Democrats had no subcommittee chairmanship. One was a freshman and so had no reason to expect a chairmanship and another had a high ranking position on Finance, which has no subcommittees, and a junior position on Foreign Relations. Neither, then, had reason to feel aggrieved.

Of the fourteen northern and western Democrats without chairmanships, four were freshmen. Five of the remaining ten had assignments on Appropriations, Armed Services, or Finance in which they could take consolation. Thus, five non-southern, non-freshman Democrats held neither a subcommittee chairmanship nor a seat on one of the most important four committees in the Senate. These senators — one midwesterner and four from the far west — had some consolation. Three of the far westerners were on Interior and Insular Affairs, which handles matters vital to their region. One of these had been a subcommittee chairman on the Interior Committee in the Eighty-eighth Congress. A senior westerner had waived seniority in order to give him this chairmanship in a year

Table 12-6 Democrats at the Beginning of the Eighty-Ninth Congress (1965) Who Were Neither Committee Nor Subcommittee Chairmen

Name, State	Years of Service in 1965	Committee Assignments	Rank
Bartlett, Alaska	6	Appropriations	16
		Commerce	5
Bass, Tenn.	0	Agriculture and Forestry	9
		Commerce	12
Brewster, Md.	2	Armed Services	12
		Commerce	10
Burdick, N.D.	5	Interior and Insular Affairs	7
		Judiciary	10
		Post Office and Civil Service	8
Harris, Okla.	0	Government Operations	7
		Public Works	12
Hartke, Ind.	6	Commerce	6
		Finance	9
		Post Office and Civil Service	7
Inouye, Hawaii	2	Armed Services	10
		Public Works	9
Kennedy, N.Y.	0	District of Columbia	4
		Government Operations	8
		Labor and Public Welfare	11
McCarthy, Minn.	6	Agriculture and Forestry	7
		Finance	8
McGovern, S.D.	2	Agriculture and Forestry	8
		Interior and Insular Affairs	9
Mondale, Minn.	0	Aeronautical and Space Sciences	10
		Banking and Currency	10
Montoya, N.M.	0	Agriculture and Forestry	10
		Government Operations	10
		Public Works	11
Moss, Utah	6	Interior and Insular Affairs	6
		Public Works	6
Nelson, Wisc.	2	Interior and Insular Affairs	10
		Labor and Public Welfare	10
Neuberger, Ore.	4	Banking and Currency	8
		Commerce	11
Smathers, Fla.	14	Finance	3
		Foreign Relations	11

in which he faced what looked like a close election fight. After he was reelected, the more senior westerner reclaimed the subcommittee. The fourth westerner had made evident her lack of interest in running for another term in the Senate.

The Democrats and Personal Power

The personal skill of the southerners in manipulating the Senate has been widely publicized by those writing about the Senate of the 1940s and 1950s.[18] They seemed to control critical organizational and legislative decisions, but often subtly enough to avoid angering many of those against whom they worked. The graciousness and professional competence of the southerners helped assuage the liberal's pain. They magnified the power that came to them through seniority by their skilled and judicious *use* of seniority. They understood the dynamics of power and their own relation to changing circumstances in the Senate and in the country at large. They accommodated when necessary, for they knew that intransigence rapidly causes the loss of influence. They never were able to win on everything in which they had an interest; but they possessed the most advantageous bargaining positions on matters in which their interests were deepest.

But by the mid-1960s a new situation had emerged in which a number of moderately senior and very junior Democrats, virtually all liberals, had begun to develop significant impact on important legislative matters.[19] They began to make impressive records of their own in their subcommittees. At the same time, several of the senior conservative oligarchs were removed by defeat, death, or retirement. Several more are in bad health or may face electoral problems.

By the mid-1960s virtually all Democrats were content with their lot in the Senate specifically because they perceived that they could be effective legislatively on some matters that were or had become important to them. Their perceptions as articulated by the participants in a series of discussions in 1965 can be summarized as follows:[20]

1. Leadership in the Senate passes from senator to senator, depending on the issue. Few senators are permanently excluded from this shifting leadership group. Personal qualities help determine whether a senator will be effective legislatively. Senators who build credits by being helpful to their colleagues and thoughtful of them can expect them to reciprocate.

2. Committee chairmen do not monopolize power and they are, for the most part, reasonable in their use of the power they do possess, largely because of the general norms of compromise, mutual adjustment, and civility that give form and cohesiveness to Senate life. The committee system as a whole affords the individual senator great satisfaction because of the opportunities it presents for developing personal power.

3. Only a few senators are usually involved in making a committee or subcommittee decision on a substantive matter. Because of the large volume of legislative business, multiple committee assignments, and non-legislative demands on the time of all senators, junior senators necessarily become the decision-makers on a number of matters. Virtually every senator can, if he so desires, become an acknowledged expert on some specific subject matter. In this area his position will almost always be ratified by the entire Senate.

The Republicans and Institutional Power

The principal role of most of the Republicans in the Senate during the post-war years, at least until Everett Dirksen became Minority Leader in 1959, was to support the conservatively-oriented Democrats and their leaders. With the exception of Robert Taft, Republicans were not the leaders in the coalition with the southern Democrats.

Within the Republican party the conservatives (most notably from the midwest) have not consistently controlled the top committee and leadership positions.[21] But, of central importance to understanding the situation in the Senate in the 1950s, the conservatives and midwesterners tended to be overrepresented during that period. At present, liberal Republicans from outside the midwest hold just as many positions of importance as the conservative midwesterners.

Commentators on the Senate who have indicated that the southerners are exceptionally powerful in the Democratic party also usually indicate that the midwesterners are exceptionally powerful in the Republican party.[22]

In order to test this proposition, some of the same kinds of data that were collected on the southern Democrats were also collected on the position of midwestern Republicans within their party. Table 12-7 summarizes the position of midwesterners in relation to the committee assignments open to Republicans.

The Republican pattern is just the reverse of the Democratic pattern. Among the Democrats, the southerners were most overrepresented at the beginning of the 1941-1965 period and again at the end of it. By 1968 their overrepresentation had begun to decline. In the middle of the period the southerners had about the representation that their numbers entitled them to. Among the Republicans, as the table shows, the midwesterners were most overrepresented in the middle of the 1941-1965 period. In 1968 their position was somewhat stronger again.

The Republicans have not kept their contingents on the most important standing committees in the hands of the conservatives. Data on various party and ideological indices for the years between 1947 and 1967 suggest that only the Finance Committee contingent was regularly controlled by conservatives. Appropriations Committee Republicans have tended to be more liberal than most Republicans, especially in the most recent years. The other committees have tended to vacillate between liberal and conservative weighting. Table 12-8 summarizes these data.

The primary reason for the lack of party control by the conservative Republicans, except in the case of the Finance Committee, is that not only committee changes but also initial assignments were made on the basis of seniority. Thus the Republican committee on committees had only very limited opportunities to "stack" committees regionally or ideologically. Occasionally, however, senior Republicans claimed a vacancy for ideological reasons. For example, Taft in 1947 took the Labor and Public Welfare Committee chairmanship, rather than Finance, to prevent a more liberal member from obtaining it. Dirksen in 1963 took a seat on Finance for the same reason.

Table 12-7 Midwestern Republican Representation on Senate Committees and Subcommittees, 1941-1968[a]

			Percent of Midwesterners Among:			
Congress (Year)	All Republican Senators	Ranking Members on Committees[b]	Three Highest Ranking Repub. on All Committees[c]	All Repub. on Four Choice Committees[d]	Three Highest Ranking Repub. on Four Choice Committees[d]	Ranking Members on Subcommittees[e]
77th (1941)	53	56	46	48	58	
79th (1945)	51	50	58	60	58	
81st (1949)	43	47	49	44	58	
83rd (1953)	40	53	53	39	33	
85th (1957)	38	47	44	41	25	51
87th (1961)	34	50	42	39	33	45
89th (1965)	28	31	30	38	42	35
90th (1968)	29	37	33	39	50	39

[a] The Midwest is defined to include Ohio, Indiana, Illinois, Michigan, Wisconsin, Minnesota, Iowa, North Dakota, South Dakota, Nebraska and Kansas.

[b] This column applies to chairmen in the Eighty-Third Congress, when the Republicans organized the Senate. This column includes the sixteen most important standing committees in the Seventy-Seventh and Seventy-Ninth Congresses (Agriculture and Forestry, Appropriations, Banking and Currency, Commerce, District of Columbia, Education and Labor, Finance, Foreign Relations, Interstate Commerce, Irrigation and Reclamation, Judiciary, Manufactures, Military Affairs, Naval Affairs, Public Lands and Surveys, and Rules), and all standing committees thereafter.

[c] This column includes the sixteen most important standing committees in the Seventy-Seventh and Seventy-Ninth Congresses and all standing committees thereafter.

[d] The four choice committees are Appropriations, Armed Services, Finance, and Foreign Relations. Military Affairs was used instead of Armed Services in the Seventy-Seventh and Seventy-Ninth Congresses.

[e] Data on subcommittees are difficult to obtain before 1955. A few special subcommittees of little importance are omitted from this tabulation.

Table 12-8   Ideological Bias of Republican Contingents on Six Senate Committees, 1947-1967

Committee	Relation of Committee Contingent to all Republicans on Base of 20 Index Scores[a]	
	More Conservative	More Liberal
Appropriations	4	13
Armed Services	8	10
Commerce	10	8
Finance	19	1
Foreign Relations	8	12
Judiciary	10	10

[a] The two figures for each committee do not add to 20 in all cases because some mean committee scores are the same as the mean score for all Democrats.

When the Republicans had to make the bargains that led to the reshuffling of committee assignments prompted by the Legislative Reorganization Act of 1946 they had a somewhat easier task than the Democrats. Fewer members were likely to be affected adversely since, in 1946, a few of the most senior Republicans held three or four first-ranking positions each.[23] Presumably they could keep their major ranking positions if the party continued in the minority in 1947; they would not mind giving up the minor ranking positions. If the party became a majority in 1947, each ranking member would become chairman on one committee and the other chairmanships would be available to other Republicans.

When the party actually became the majority in the Senate in 1947 it did not have to deprive many men of chairmanships. The four Republicans who lost the top ranking place on a committee did not have to give up their other choice assignments. All of the four who were displaced retained assignments on either Finance or Appropriations. Table 12-9 lists these men and summarizes their committee positions. Only Senator Reed was senior to the men who became chairmen of two committees on which he had previously served. But he retained high ranking positions on Appropriations and Interstate and Foreign Commerce.[24] Three of the four senators displaced from chairmanships were midwestern Republicans and all were succeeded by midwesterners. Of the ten Republicans who returned to the Eightieth Congress and retained their top ranking committee positions, six were midwesterners.

In short, in 1946-47, the Republicans, both because of the relatively small number of men holding ranking positions before reorganization and because of the electoral victory in 1946, were able to redistribute powerful committee posts without seriously impairing the standing of any Republican who had gained a powerful position before the reorganization.

Since 1947 most Republican leaders have been clearly identified with the conservative element in the party. Three moderately liberal members have also held one of the top positions, but none has become floor leader. Twelve different

Table 12-9 Republicans Who Lost First Position on a Committee Because of the Legislative Reorganization Act of 1946

Name, State	Years of Service in 1946	Ranking Member, 1946	Successor Committee	1947 Committee Assignments	Rank
Bushfield, S.D.	3	Interoceanic Canals	Armed Services	Agriculture and Forestry Finance	3 5
Ball, Minn.	5	Immigration	Judiciary	Appropriations Labor and Public Welfare District of Columbia[a]	5 3 3
Brewster, Maine	5	Library	Rules	Finance Interstate and Foreign Commerce	4 4
Reed, Kans.	7	Mines and Mining Post Office	Public Lands Civil Service	Appropriations Interstate and Foreign Commerce	4 3

[a] New assignment in 1947. All other assignments represent continuations of previous assignments.

senators held the positions of floor leader, Whip, chairman of the conference, and chairman of the Policy Committee between 1947 and 1968. Of these, five were from the midwest, three from the far west, and four from New England. Of the seventeen changes in the top leadership positions between 1947 and 1968 only four were contested. The conservative candidate won three of the four contests in the conference. (In early 1969 the more liberal candidate became Whip.)

These data support the conclusion that institutional power is also widely dispersed in the Republican party at present. For example, by 1965, power was so widespread that no Republican, including freshmen, was without a ranking minority position on at least one committee or subcommittee. This resulted in part from a combination of small numbers of men and large numbers of subcommittees. It had the added effect of making life tolerable in what must seem to Republicans to be perpetual minority status. The midwestern conservative Republicans were not as skillful in retaining power for themselves as the southern Democrats, which suggests that a regional group in a minority party loses the incentive to retain power after a number of years in the minority. Unless ideological purity is important to a number of the minority leaders, shared power makes for a more pleasant existence when most of the power rests in the hand of the majority party anyway.

In addition, the Republicans modified their absolute rules of seniority for committee assignments in 1959 informally and in 1965 formally and gave more chance to junior Republicans to be important legislatively.

The Republicans and Personal Power

When Everett Dirksen became Minority Leader in 1959 he gradually began to disavow ideological purity as a goal of his leadership. His predecessors had, with varying degrees of success, insisted on it. In the pre-Dirksen climate it was difficult for junior Republicans to develop personal power. Dirksen's style fosters the development of such power.

In 1949, for example, when Kenneth Wherry of Nebraska was Minority Leader, the predominantly conservative midwesterners were overrepresented on all of the important committees. Wherry insisted on extremely conservative principles as the only true Republican principles. William Knowland, the floor leader from 1953 through 1958 was torn between being a good soldier for Eisenhower and being a dedicated conservative. Either way he tended to expect the Republicans to follow his lead. Dirksen was not much concerned with ideological purity and, except for the first two years of his regime, did not have a President of his own party. On a few major matters, such as civil rights, a nuclear test ban treaty, and a loan for the United Nations, he was concerned that he produce as much Republican support for his position as possible, in these cases positions also espoused by Democratic Presidents. But in the normal working of the Senate he is usually content to leave every individual Republican free to develop influence by pursuing his own course of action in his own way.[25] In this climate a number of junior Republicans began to exercise their new-found ability to have legislative impact.[26]

315

The Republican participants in the 1965 discussions did not perceive themselves as able to be quite as effective legislatively as Democrats, but this was largely because of their minority status. Their perceptions can be summarized as follows:

1. They agreed with the Democrats that leadership can pass from senator to senator, depending on the issue. They also agreed that the qualities of helpfulness and thoughtfulness were the most useful in allowing an individual senator to develop legislative weight. However, they felt that it is more difficult for a Republican to become important to the whole Senate as an issue leader than for a Democrat because of the special problems of minority status.

2. They, too, were generally happy with the functioning of the committee system. Their ranking minority members had not generally been unfair in their subcommittee appointments, thus giving every Republican an institutional base from which to develop legislative power. They did feel, however, that the lack of activity on the part of ranking Republicans in welding unified Republican positions on pending committee business reduced their effectiveness.

3. They agreed with the Democrats' perception that junior senators can become the leading experts in the Senate on specific areas of substance. It is more difficult for minority party members to do this, but still quite possible.

Conclusion

The shifting patterns of power distribution in the post-World War II Senate are best understood if two types of power are analyzed: institutional power and personal power. If institutional power alone were studied the data would support the conclusion that only now is the hold of the southern Democrats on the Senate beginning to weaken; and it was at its peak during the mid-1960s. Yet this same period of the mid-1960s, especially 1965, was a period of great liberal legislative activity that met with success in many fields. Thus it is suggested that a study of institutional power is necessary, but used alone it cannot logically explain some outcomes. To explain the southern hold on the Senate in the 1950s institutional power is not enough; after all the southerners never did control *all* of the important positions. They needed allies and the techniques they used to identify and win those allies involve personal power. To explain the liberal output of the Senate in the mid-1960s institutional power is not enough either. Liberal non-southern senators of both parties had begun to develop personal power that allowed them to neutralize and even overcome much of the institutional advantage that the conservative southerners still possessed.

In the late 1960s analyses of both types of power point the same way: important institutional positions are being dispersed ever more widely and there are few obstacles to any senator of either party who has the requisite personal skills to develop legislative power and chooses to use those skills. Virtually all senators can acquire substantial legislative influence. Those who do not have it usually have disqualified themselves by violating the Senate's code of acceptable conduct that is understood by most members. The code is not highly restrictive; and only repeated violations bring sanctions. The sometime violator may retain all or most of his power. Only a few senators have ignored the code altogether and thus forfeited most of their legislative impact.[27]

The present Senate is not composed of a few omnipotent and happy senior senators and a great many impotent and unhappy junior senators. Most senators are content with their lot. A central reason for their contentment is that the opportunity to develop both institutional power and personal power is available to all.

Notes

1. The classic Club and Establishment arguments are presented in William S. White, *Citadel* (New York: Harper, 1957), and Joseph S. Clark and Other Senators, *The Senate Establishment* (New York: Hill and Wang, 1963). The idea is still persuasive to some. See Clayton Fritchey, "Who Belongs to the Senate's Inner Club?", *Harper's* (May 1967), pp. 104-10.
2. These two sentences are based on the summary in Ralph K. Huitt, "The Outsider in the Senate," *American Political Science Review,* Vol. 55 (September 1961), pp. 566-67. Huitt, of course, was disputing the validity of some of the argument.
3. See Donald R. Matthews, *U.S. Senators and Their World* (Chapel Hill: University of North Carolina Press, 1960), pp. 92-102. Woodrow Wilson was less specific than Matthews on the content of Senate "folkways," but he described the same phenomenon in general language: "If a new Senator knock about too loosely amidst the free spaces of the rules of that august body, he will assuredly have some of his biggest corners knocked off and his angularities thus made smoother; if he stick fast among the dignified courtesies and punctilious observances of the upper chamber, he will, if he stick long enough, finally wear down to such a size, by jostling, as to attain some motion more or less satisfactory." Woodrow Wilson, *Congressional Government* (New York: Meridian, 1956), pp. 145-46.
4. See Nelson W. Polsby, *Congress and the Presidency* (Englewood Cliffs, N.J.: Prentice-Hall, 1964), Chapter 3. See also the speech by Majority Leader Mike Mansfield in 1963 rebutting the charges of Senator Clark and others that the "establishment" controls committee assignments and legislative results, *Congressional Record,* Vol. 109, Pt. 3, 88 Cong. 1 sess. (1963), pp. 2918-22.
5. For differing positions on this question see David B. Truman, *The Congressional Party* (New York: Wiley, 1959); Robert A. Dahl, "The Concept of Power," *Behavioral Science,* Vol. 2 (July 1957), pp. 201-15; and Duncan MacRae, Jr. and Hugh D. Price, "Scale Positions and 'Power' in the Senate," *Behavioral Science,* Vol. 4 (July 1959), pp. 212-18.
6. There is, of course, an extensive literature that discusses power and influence and, in many cases, distinguishes between them. For present purposes there seemed to be no reason to distinguish between power and influence. The relatively simple conception of power used here resembles the conception of influence in Robert A. Dahl, *Modern Political Analysis* (Englewood Cliffs, N.J.: Prentice-Hall, 1963), pp. 40-41. A similar conception is presented in Barry E. Collins and Harold Guetzkow, *A Social Psychology of Group Processes for Decision-Making* (New York: Wiley, 1964), p. 121: "When the acts of an agent can (actually or potentially) modify the behavior of a person, or group of persons, the agent has power over that person or group of persons." See chapters 6-8 of *A Social Psychology* for a number of propositions that might prove fruitful in a more extended and more formal analysis of power in the Senate.

7. Senators may also wield power outside of the Senate. They may be in a position to influence the public or a segment of it, bureaucrats, interest groups, members of the House, or the President. This power may come from a variety of sources.

8. David Truman, in *The Congressional Party,* argues persuasively that this is the case for both the formal party leaders and the committee leaders ("seniority leaders" is his phrase). For data on the formal party leaders in ten Congresses in this century see Randall B. Ripley, *Majority Party Leadership in Congress* (Boston: Little, Brown, 1969).

9. Despite the links between the two types of power (power based on different sources, to be more precise) it is worthwhile to keep them separate for analytical purposes. Otherwise, as the article seeks to make clear, problems of evidence are unnecessarily complicated.

10. There is no implication here that all southern Democrats think or vote alike. But as a group they were clearly more conservative than other regional groups of Democrats. For material on the complexities of differentiating southern Democrats from other Democrats see H. Douglas Price, "Are Southern Democrats Different? An Application of Scale Analysis to Senate Voting Patterns," in Nelson W. Polsby, Robert A. Dentler, and Paul A. Smith, eds., *Politics and Social Life* (Boston: Houghton Mifflin, 1963), pp. 740-56.

11. For Democratic senators the south is defined as the eleven states of the confederacy. The west includes all states west of the Mississippi River except Arkansas, Louisiana, and Texas. The north includes the rest.

12. These committees were designated as "most sought after" because from 1947 to 1966 they were the only committees that consistently gained more members than they lost. This means that senators were eager to obtain seats on them and were usually not willing to leave them voluntarily. For the figures on 1947-1957 see Matthews, *U.S. Senators,* pp. 148-50. For the figures on 1957-66 see Stephen Horn, *Unused Power: A Study of the Senate Committee on Appropriations* (Washington, D.C.: Brookings Institution, 1970), Chapter 2.

13. See, for example, George Goodwin, "The Seniority System in Congress," *American Political Science Review,* Vol. 53 (June 1959), pp. 412-36, Table 3 and related text; and Clark, *The Senate Establishment,* pp. 105-06.

14. The four most important committees (Appropriations, Armed Services, Finance, and Foreign Relations) are, like the six most sought after committees that have been referred to previously, chosen by the senators themselves. For example, when the Republican senators changed their committee assignment procedure in 1965 they specifically labeled these four as the most important to them.

15. The position of Secretary of the Conference has existed since at least 1907. Until 1961, however, the Secretary had no importance inside the party. George Smathers of Florida, elected in 1961, began to attend White House meetings with the other leaders. His successor, Robert Byrd of West Virginia, became important within the party in a wide variety of ways within a few months after his election as Secretary in January, 1967. See the *Washington Post,* October 4, 1967, for a fine analysis of this development.

16. The same year Lyndon Johnson, then moderately conservative, became Whip. The only other name put forward seriously was John Sparkman of Alabama, who chose not to run. Sparkman was a much more loyal supporter of the Truman program than Johnson. See Rowland Evans and Robert Novak, *Lyndon B. Johnson: The Exercise of Power* (New York: New American Library, 1966), p. 43. Evans and Novak mistakenly assert that McFarland was unopposed. In fact, the contest between McFarland and O'Mahoney was decided by a 30 to 19 vote in the Democratic conference. A few days later the liberal Democrats complained they had been treated

unfairly in committee assignments. See *New York Times,* Jan. 3, 1951, and Jan. 6, 1951.

17. Johnson had a consuming desire to unite the party and prevent intraparty strife such as had occurred during the preceding two years. With the cooperation of Senator Russell he persuaded a number of senior Democrats, including some southerners, that a modification of the use of seniority for committee assignments was for the benefit of all. See Evans and Novak, *Johnson,* pp. 63-64; and *New York Times,* Feb. 15, 1953.

18. See, for example, White, *Citadel;* and Howard E. Shuman, "Senate Rules and the Civil Rights Bill: A Case Study," *American Political Science Review,* Vol. 51 (December 1957), pp. 955-75.

19. For persuasive journalistic accounts of this change in both parties see Dan Cordtz, "The Senate Revolution," *Wall Street Journal,* Aug. 6, 1965; Tom Wicker, "Winds of Change in the Senate," *New York Times Magazine,* Sept. 12, 1965; Meg Greenfield, "Uhuru Comes to the Senate," *Reporter,* Sept. 23, 1965; and Robert C. Albright, "Senate Youngsters Asserting Selves as Never Before," *Washington Post,* January 15, 1968. Nelson Polsby, writing about the Senate in *Congress and the Presidency,* p. 45, concludes, referring to both parties, that "We can think of the internal politics of the Senate not as a small group of powerful men surrounded by everyone else, but as a group which divides labor and power — unequally to be sure, but still significantly — among almost all its members." Even Senator Clark agreed that "the old Senate establishment is gone. Democracy is now pretty much the rule in the Senate." *Congressional Record,* Vol. III, Pt. 17, 89 Cong. 1 sess. (1965), p. 23495.

20. These meetings were held at the Brookings Institution. Each session began with dinner and lasted until about 10 p.m. Usually, about two hours of specific discussion of questions on an agenda prepared by Professor Frederick N. Cleaveland of the University of North Carolina and myself took place at each meeting. Eleven Democratic senators participated in five meetings. Six Republican senators came to another series of five meetings. Fourteen Democratic personal and committee staff members met twice. Sixteen Republican staff members also met twice. The two groups of senators were not perfectly representative of the whole Senate, yet there was a broad geographical, age, seniority, and committee spread among the participants. The Democrats were slightly younger and less senior than the average for all Democrats. Republicans were slightly older and more senior. The participants, especially the Democrats, tended to come from the group of senators that was just coming into substantial power and had expectations of developing a great deal more within the next few years. There were, however, other participants who were either freshmen or committee chairmen or ranking minority members.

21. No suggestion that all midwestern Republicans think and vote conservatively and can be set off clearly from the rest of the party on these grounds is intended. A few mid-westerners have been non-conservatives and some non-midwesterners have been among the conservative leaders. Ideological differences are not as closely related to region in the Republican party as in the Democratic party. But the conservative center of gravity among Republicans is in the midwesterners.

22. See, for example, Goodwin, "The Seniority System," Table 3 and related text. The midwest includes Ohio, Indiana, Michigan, Wisconsin, Illinois, Minnesota, Iowa, North Dakota, South Dakota, Nebraska, and Kansas.

23. Senator Arthur Capper of Kansas was ranking Republican on Agriculture and Forestry, Claims, District of Columbia, and Foreign Relations in 1946. Senator Charles Tobey of New Hampshire was ranking Republican on Audit and Control of Expenses in the Senate, Banking and Currency, and Naval Affairs. Senator Arthur Vandenberg of Michigan was ranking Republican on Commerce, Rules, and

Territories and Insular Affairs. Senator Robert LaFollette, Jr., of Wisconsin, held the top minority party position on Education and Labor, Finance, Indian Affairs, and Manufactures.

24. Reed led an unsuccessful attempt to prevent the holders of party leadership positions from also holding committee chairmanships. His failure to advance in committee standing was punishment for his efforts. See *New York Times,* Dec. 27, 1946, and Jan. 2, 1947. Taft clearly dominated the party during the period of reorganization. See *New York Times,* Dec. 31, 1946, and Jan. 3, 1947.

25. On Wherry see Truman, *The Congressional Party,* pp. 106-108. On Knowland see Ripley, *Majority Party Leadership,* chapter 4. On Dirksen see Meg Greenfield, "Everett Dirksen's Newest Role," *Reporter,* Jan. 16, 1964; and Murray Kempton, "Dirksen Delivers the Souls," *New Republic,* May 2, 1964. Dirksen, of course, may behave differently now that a Republican is President.

26. The material cited in footnote 19, above, gives a number of examples of such impact.

27. For the view that the Senate no longer possesses a meaningful moral code (and for considerable weeping over the loss) see the column by William S. White in the *Washington Post,* December 18, 1967. For the view that a loose code still exists and that its most consistent violators lose influence see the stories on Senator Russell Long by Walter Mears in the *Evening Star* (Washington), December 15, 1967, and by Mary McGrory in the *Sunday Star* (Washington), December 17, 1967.

13. INSTITUTIONAL CONTEXT AND LEADERSHIP STYLE: THE HOUSE FROM CANNON TO RAYBURN

Joseph Cooper

and

David W. Brady

Leadership is an aspect of social life which has been extensively studied in a variety of institutional or organizational settings (Miner, 1980). Yet it remains a topic in which our intellectual grasp falls far short of our pragmatic sense of the impacts leaders have on organizational operations and performance.

This is as true, if not more true, of Congress than of other organizations. Here too analysts are perplexed by the difficulties of conceptualizing key variables, treating highly transient and idiosyncratic personal factors, and identifying relationships amidst a maze of interactive effects. Moreover, the task is rendered even more complex by the highly politicized character of the Congress as compared with most of the organizational contexts in which leadership has been studied.

This is not to say that knowledge and understanding of congressional leadership have remained static. Peabody (1976), Jones (1968), Ripley (1967), Polsby (1969), Manley (1969), Hinckley (1970), and Nelson (1977) have all done instructive and insightful work. Nonetheless, our grip on the topic is as yet not firm; we continue to lack a developed sense of what we should be looking at and how to proceed.

The purpose of this article is to aid in remedying this deficiency. It is premised on two key assumptions. First, the study of leadership requires comparative evidence regarding both behavior and contexts. Hence our use of history as a laboratory and our choice of Cannon and Rayburn as focal points of analysis. Second, the study of leadership requires abstract or analytical concepts to aid in formulating and testing important relationships. Hence our historical analysis relies on several broad concepts and relationships, drawn both from organization theory and from recent work on the operation of the Congress.

Source: *American Political Science Review* (June 1981): 411-425. Reprinted with permission of the authors.

321

In sum, though this article deals with the transition from Cannon to Rayburn, its main objective is not to fill in the historical record. Its primary goals are rather to bring evidence and analysis to bear to improve our understanding of the key determinants and underlying dynamics of congressional leadership, and to suggest a set of propositions or hypotheses that can serve as a basis for more focused and elaborate forms of investigation and theory building.

The House Under Czar Rule

The legacy the House of the nineteenth century left to that of the twentieth was a set of rules which placed the majority firmly in control of the House and centralized power in the hands of the Speaker as the agent of this majority. It was this legacy the House rejected when it revolted against the Speaker in 1910. In so doing it not only stripped the Speaker of many of his important powers, but also paved the way for a metamorphosis in the nature of the House as a political institution.

The Speaker and the House

It was with good reason that Speakers of the House in the years between 1890 and 1910 were often referred to as czars (Galloway, 1961, pp. 134-36). The Speaker appointed the committees. He served as the chairman of and had unchallengeable control over the Rules Committee (Brown, 1922, pp. 87-90). He had great, though not unlimited, discretion over the recognition of members desiring to call business off the calendars, to make motions, or to address the House, and absolute discretion over the recognition of motions for unanimous consent and suspension of the rules (Chiu, 1928, pp. 175-97).

These prerogatives gave the Speaker great power to control outcomes in the House. At the committee stage, those who had received prized assignments from the Speaker naturally felt a sense of gratitude and obligation to him. Those who desired a change in assignment knew full well that their chances of advancement depended on the good graces of the Speaker. Conversely, since in this age seniority was far from as sacrosanct as it is today, members were also aware that to alienate the Speaker was to risk loss of a chairmanship, an assignment, or rank on a committee (Abram and Cooper, 1968; Polsby et al., 1969).

Nor was the appointment power the Speaker's only source of leverage in controlling outcomes at the committee stage. Members of any particular committee were also disposed to cooperate with the Speaker because of the vast array of rewards and sanctions his position in the House bestowed on him. For example, the Speaker could provide access to the floor by granting a rule or recognizing a motion to suspend the rules; he could lend invaluable assistance in getting a project included in a bill or in getting a bill out of committee. Moreover, if all the rewards and sanctions at the disposal of the Speaker still proved to be insufficient, there was yet another factor that discouraged opposition at the committee stage. The plain fact was that to oppose the Speaker would in all probability be fruitless. If a committee refused to report a bill the Speaker wanted reported, the Speaker could pry the bill out of committee either through use of the Rules

Committee or suspension of the rules. Similarly, if a committee reported a bill the Speaker opposed, the bill had little chance of reaching the floor. The power of the Speaker was such that he could obstruct the consideration of any bill he did not want considered. Given the various and potent types of leverage the Speaker possessed, it is not surprising that in this period committee chairmen took their cue from the Speaker regarding which bills they would report and that Speakers referred to the committee chairmen as their "cabinet" (Busby, 1927, p. 219).

As for action on the floor, here too the Speaker's prerogatives under the rules gave him great power. A number of factors combined to give him control over the agenda of the House. Through use of the Rules Committee and other privileged committees, he could interrupt the regular order of business either to give priority to a bill he wanted considered or to block a bill he opposed.[1] He could use unanimous consent and suspension of the rules to give access to the floor to bills he favored and could deny the use of these procedures to bills he opposed. In addition, his discretion in the recognition of motions calling bills up for consideration was a source of leverage.

The Speaker's ability to control the agenda, however, stemmed not merely from his powers of repression, but also from the necessity of relying upon him if the House was to reach the bills it wanted to consider. The volume of legislation before the House made it exceedingly cumbersome to follow the involved order of business set forth in the rules. As a result, the House did not insist on following its regular order. Indeed, the points in the order where committee members could call business off the calendars were usually not reached. Instead, the House relied on the Speaker to bring bills up for its consideration and to determine the time of consideration through the use of privileged reports and special procedures, such as unanimous consent. In short, then, both because of the powers of the Speaker over the agenda and the unwieldiness of proceeding according to the regular order, the House gave the Speaker even more power over the agenda than his power under the rules bestowed on him.[2]

A second aspect of the Speaker's power over floor decisions concerned his ability to control considerations on the floor. Here again, his command of the Rules Committee and his power as presiding officer gave him considerable leverage over floor debate and dilatory tactics. In addition, many of the same rewards and sanctions at the Speaker's disposal for controlling committee decisions could also be used to control floor decisions. Especially for members of the majority party, to oppose the Speaker was to risk the loss of his assistance in matters of vital importance to one's constituency and therefore also to impair one's chances of reelection. Moreover, through bestowing favors over a number of years, the Speaker could build up a substantial fund of credits, credits which could then be expended as needed to secure the cooperation of members in his debt. Thus, the ability of the Speaker to control decisions on the floor and in committee stemmed not only from the immediate impacts the exercise of his formal powers involved, but also from their long-run dividends.

323

Joseph Cooper and David W. Brady

The Speaker as Party Chief

To complement his prerogatives under the rules, the Speaker possessed another source of power that was equally significant. In placing a potent array of rewards and sanctions at his disposal, the rules did of course provide him with considerable leverage. However, the Speaker's ability to command majority support in committee and on the floor was materially aided by another factor: party discipline.

In an age when party regularity is far from an overriding consideration, it is difficult to appreciate how important party was in the House at the turn of the century. In this period the great majority of members in both parties subscribed to the doctrines of party government. Representative government was seen to depend on the existence of a responsible majority which had the power to rule and which, as a result, could be held accountable for performance (Jones, 1968). Only under such conditions, it was believed, could the people effect their wishes. The individual representative was thought to be elected on the basis of a party's platform and was therefore regarded to have an obligation to support party positions, even against personal convictions or desires.

The fact that members in this age thought and spoke in terms of the doctrines of party government had more than rhetorical importance. Party government served as the main justification for vesting great power in the Speaker and permitting him to play the role of Czar. Though the Democrats never fully accepted the proposition and ended by rejecting it, a cardinal tenet of Republican faith was that rule by a responsible majority party required centralizing organizational power in the Speaker.

The Speaker's position as head of his party thus also provided him with an important source of leverage. It is true, of course, that even in this period many issues were not treated as party issues. Nonetheless, most important issues were regarded as matters on which the party as a whole should stand together. In such a context the Speaker derived considerable power from his position as party chief. Initiative in the definition of party policies belonged to him. Moreover, if he could not win the support of all elements in the party, he had at his disposal a powerful mechanism for enforcing adherence to his wishes — the caucus. Through a binding vote in the caucus, he could oblige the opposition to support his policy positions out of party loyalty (Brown, 1922, pp. 92-93, 100, 161-62; and Wilson, 1961, p. 96). In short, the Speaker could rule the House through the force of party discipline. As long as the bonds of party held taut, he had only to command the support of a majority of his party to command a majority in the House.

We may conclude, then, that the House of Reed and Cannon contained a highly centralized power structure with control resting essentially in the hands of the Speaker. The key to the Speaker's power lay not simply in his prerogatives under rules, nor in his position as party chief, but rather in the manner in which these two sources of leverage reinforced each other (Cooper, 1970). The existence of a stable party majority insured the Speaker's ability to implement his formal powers and gave him a degree of maneuverability and control that the rules alone could not give him. Similarly, the rewards and sanctions the rules placed in the Speaker's hands gave party regularity a degree of priority it would not have possessed if it had rested merely on the extent of agreement among party members or their devotion to the doctrines of party government. Speakers could therefore quite appropriately refer to committee chairmen as their "cabinet." During this period the committee and party systems were blended to an extremely high degree. The Speaker was both the party leader and the chairman of the Rules Committee. The majority leader was the chairman of the Ways and Means or Appropriations Committee and, with the start of the whip system in 1897, the whip was chairman of Judiciary or a top member of Ways and Means. Unlike the contemporary House where party leaders and committee chairs are separate, committee and party leaders were one and the same. Tensions between the two systems were accordingly greatly reduced. Whereas in the contemporary House committee chairs often have low party support scores, such was not the case at the turn of the century. It was thus not a mere figure of speech to refer to committee chairs as a "cabinet." Both structurally and behaviorally, committee and party leaders were a cabinet (Brady, 1973).

The Bases of Czar Rule

We have argued that the interaction of the Speaker's formal powers and the strength of party resulted in a centralized form of leadership — Czar rule. This can be shown empirically. Data exist which strongly buttress the argument we have made deductively on the basis of the historical record.

First, if party strength functioned as a key ingredient of Czar rule, then levels of party voting should be markedly higher in congresses with centralized leadership. Table 13-1 presents data on party votes (90 percent of one party versus 90 percent of the other) for congresses from 1881-1921. It thus includes "Czar rule" congresses in which the Speaker possessed the formal powers described above and a ready ability to use the caucus, and congresses in which one or more of these sources of leverage was absent.

Table 13-1 shows a strong connection between centralized leadership power and levels of party voting. In the period from 1881 to 1899 party voting scores attained levels of 25 percent or more only in the three congresses in which centralized leadership power existed. In the period from 1899 to 1921 party voting did not drop below 25 percent until after the 1910 revolt against the Speaker, and then fell to below 10 percent in 1917 for the first time in a quarter-century. To further substantiate our argument, we ran a point bi-serial analysis of the data. This statistic is used when the data are dichotomous and is appropriate for Table 13-1, given a distinction between centralized and non-centralized leadership power. The point bi-serial for this data set was a striking .89, demonstrating the degree to which levels of party voting can be seen as associated with concentrated leadership power.

Second, if an interactive relationship exists between concentrated formal power and party strength, then party strength must have its own sources of determination and impact. Indeed, in our view the causal impact of party strength on the distribution of power in the House is of primary importance. For the Speaker to have the power involved in Czar rule, a majority of the House members had to agree to bestow such power. Since the House is organized on the

Table 13-1   Czar Rule and Levels of Party Voting in the House (1881-1921)

Congress	Year	Percentage Party Votes	Majority Party	Centralized Leadership
47	1881	16.6	Republican	No
48	1883	7.0	Democratic	No
49	1885	15.5	Democratic	No
50	1887	8.7	Democratic	No
51	1889	42.5	Republican	Yes
52	1891	4.2	Democratic	No
53	1893	6.1	Democratic	No
54	1895	24.8	Republican	Yes
55	1897	50.2	Republican	Yes
56	1899	49.8	Republican	Yes
57	1901	38.9	Republican	Yes
58	1903	64.4	Republican	Yes
59	1905	34.6	Republican	Yes
60	1907	26.3	Republican	Yes
61	1909	29.4	Republican	Yes/No
62	1911	23.0	Democratic	No
63	1913	19.9	Democratic	No
64	1915	21.7	Democratic	No
65	1917	9.4	Democratic	No
66	1919	14.9	Republican	No

Source: David Brady and Phillip Althoff, "Party Voting in the U.S. House of Representatives, 1890-1910: Elements of a Responsible Party System," *Journal of Politics* 36 (1974): 753-75.

basis of party and since during this period the Republicans were usually in the majority, it was their potential for group cohesion and loyalty that established the conditions for centralized leadership. In short, the vehicle through which centralized leadership developed was the congressional Republican party (Brown, 1922, pp. 71-126). The rationale underlying this development was that without party government the industrial gains of the late nineteenth century would have been negated by congressional Democrats.

However, to sustain the role and significance we have accorded party strength, we must be able to identify and demonstrate independent sources of determination. In this respect it may be noted that the development of strong party systems in Europe and Britain is associated with the rise of leftist-socialist parties and that in the United States those states where the parties represent polarized constituencies have high levels of party voting. Our argument is therefore that the fundamental bases of party strength at the turn of the century, as in all periods of our history, are largely external, that party strength is rooted in polarized constituency configurations.

In order to ascertain the constituency bases of the congressional parties as well as the differences between them, we calculated the degree to which each congressional party represented agricultural as opposed to industrial districts. For example, in the 55th House (1897-1899), 69 percent of the Democrats and 26 percent of the Republicans represented agricultural districts, that is, districts where the ratio of farms to industrial workers was at least three to one. Thus the difference between the parties was 43 percentage points. This differential was computed for the 47th through the 66th Houses (1881-1921) and serves as a measure of electoral polarization. The specific hypothesis is that there should be a strong relationship between polarization and party voting. Table 13-2 confirms the hypothesis. When polarization was high, so too was party voting. Conversely, in Houses where the differential was less than 20, that is, where the parties were less polarized, the proportion of party votes did not rise above 20 percent and dropped to as low as 4.2 percent. However, perhaps the best overall statistic is Pearson's r, which is .81 for the two variables presented in Table 13-2.

The data also show that during the period from the realignment of 1894-96 to approximately the election of Woodrow Wilson (the 54th through the 61st House), the parties remained polarized and levels of party voting remained high. On the other hand, during the "period of no decision" (47th through the 53rd Houses), the degree of polarization fluctuated, and levels of party voting varied accordingly. Similarly, after 1908 the congressional parties became more competitive in industrial districts, and party voting in the House again declined.

Table 13-2 Polarization of Parties and Party Voting in the House (1887-1921)

Congress	Year	Differential	Party Votes
47	1881	36	16.6
48	1883	15	7.0
49	1885	25	15.5
50	1887	24	8.7
51	1889	41	42.5
52	1891	19	4.2
53	1893	22	6.1
54	1895	36	24.8
55	1897	43	50.2
56	1899	33	49.8
57	1901	35	38.9
58	1903	39	64.4
59	1905	41	34.6
60	1907	36	26.3
61	1909	31	29.4
62	1911	24	23.0
63	1913	12	19.0
64	1915	11	21.7
65	1917	14	9.4
66	1919	18	14.9

Source David Brady and Phillip Althoff, "Party Voting in the U.S. House of Representatives, 1890-1910: Elements of a Responsible Party System," *Journal of Politics* 36 (1974): 753-75.

In sum, then, it is critical to note the correspondence between a polarized electoral system and a highly centralized leadership structure. Though the Speaker's formal powers reinforced party strength, the polarized electoral bases of the party system provided an indispensable platform for Czar rule. Thus, when electoral polarization began to decline, the centralized internal structure also began to come apart (Brady et al., 1979).

The House from Cannon to Rayburn

Despite its power, the system of Czar rule could not maintain itself. It proved to be too rigid a system to accommodate the factional tendencies in the party system. During the early years of the twentieth century, economic and social ferment in the Midwest and West brought to Congress a group of young Republicans passionately devoted to enacting a whole series of reform measures. Cannon used his power as Speaker and party chief to contain and frustrate the desires of these members. In so doing, he soon aroused their enmity not merely for his policies but also for the whole system of power then prevalent in the House (Jones, 1968).

The Revolt against the Speaker

Though the number of Insurgent Republicans in the House was never large, by 1909 their strength in combination with the Democrats was sufficient to bring the revolt to a successful conclusion. The first step came in 1909 with the establishment of a Consent Calendar and a call of the committees every Wednesday to take up business on the House or Union Calendars. At this time more sweeping change was prevented by the defection of a group of conservative Democrats (Hechler, 1940, pp. 42-63). The next year, however, the Insurgent Republican-Democratic coalition gained a decisive victory. On March 19, 1910, after a dramatic two-day fight, the House passed a resolution removing the Speaker from the Rules Committee, enlarging its membership, and providing for election of the committee by the House. This victory was followed two months later by the passage of a resolution which established a procedure through which individual members could initiate the discharge of bills from committees (Brown, 1922, pp. 143-88). Finally, in 1911 the last major objective of the opponents of Czar rule was achieved. The House, now under Democratic control, amended its rules to provide for the election of all standing committees and their chairmen (Hasbrouck, 1927, p. 11).

The immediate results of the revolt against the Speaker did not greatly impair the ability of the party leadership to lead the House on behalf of the party majority. In acting to weaken the Speaker, the Democrats had no intention of weakening the ability of the party majority to pass its program. Most Democrats believed as strongly in party government as most Republicans. Their objection was not to party government and party responsibility but to domination of the majority party and the House by the Speaker. Thus, when the Democrats gained control of the House in 1911, they set up an effective system of rule through the majority party. On the one hand, they made extensive use of the caucus and binding votes in caucus (Haines, 1915, pp. 53-110). On the other hand, they centralized power in the party by making the chairman of the Committee on Ways and Means, Oscar Underwood, both floor leader and chairman of the committee on committees.[3] Under Underwood's leadership, the Democrats controlled the House as tightly as the Republicans had under Cannon. Indeed, it is fair to say that the Insurgent Republicans were no happier in the new "reformed" Democratic House than they had been in the old "tyrannical" Republican one. They had no greater liking for "King Caucus" than for "Czar rule."

The long-run results of the revolt, however, were quite different. If Czar rule was unable to maintain itself in the face of centrifugal pressures in the party system, caucus rule was even less fitted to do so. In the absence of the buttress the formal powers of the Speaker provided for party cohesion, increases in factional discord within the party alignments easily asserted themselves and led both to a disintegration of party control mechanisms and to a dispersion of power within the House (Cooper, 1961, 1970).

The disintegration of party control mechanisms was gradual but extensive. The caucus was the first to go. Once the Democrats achieved the major items in their domestic program, the power of the caucus began to wane. From 1916 on, the divisions within the parties made it difficult to rely on the caucus and usage quickly declined (Luce, 1922, p. 513). This is consistent with the data presented in Table 13-1 that shows party voting at less than 15 percent in the 1917-1921 period — a 22-year low. There were small upsurges in activity in the early 1920s and early 1930s during the initial years of party turnover in the presidency. However, its use for policy purposes soon became rare in the 1920s and simply disappeared in the late 1930s. Thus by the end of the 1930s the caucus was virtually moribund as a mechanism for determining party policy (Kefauver, 1947, pp. 102-03).

When the Republicans regained control of the House in 1919, they set up a steering committee and began to rely on it rather than the caucus (Brown, 1922, pp. 195-224; Chiu, 1928, pp. 329-34). Though this committee from the first was less of a control device than the caucus and more of a coordinating and planning mechanism, during the early 1920s it did serve to augment the leadership's power to direct its partisans. However, the same tendencies toward factionalism and bloc voting that reduced the caucus to marginal significance had a similar effect on the steering committee. By the late 1920s the party leadership had come to see the steering committee as a hindrance to their maneuverability and effectiveness. As a result, they abandoned the mechanism and began to rely instead on informal meetings among themselves, i.e., on an informal board of strategy composed of the Speaker, the floor leader, and a few trusted lieutenants (Chiu, 1928, pp. 334-36). The situation did not change when the Democrats took control of the House in 1931. Though they too established a steering committee, their leadership operated in much the same fashion as the Republican leadership had in the late 1920s (Galloway, 1961, p. 145). In short, then, by the late 1920s reliance on party control mechanisms to coordinate action and enforce cohesion had largely passed from the scene. Instead, the majority party was reduced to operating primarily

329

through a small coterie of men, gathered around the Speaker, who met to plan strategy and whose power of direction was much less than that of the caucus or even the steering committee in their heyday.

Nor were the caucus and the steering committee the only party control mechanisms to lose power and effectiveness in the period after 1916. The power of party mechanisms to control committee personnel also declined. Republican Speakers from 1890 to 1910 respected seniority, but they were quite prepared to violate it in the interests of party policy. The same is true of Underwood. By the 1920s the situation was substantially different. The decline of the caucus and, to a lesser extent, of the steering committee enhanced the power and independence of party factions. Their sheer willingness to stand together and cooperate with the leadership became more important than ever before. In addition, as the power and independence of party factions increased, the appointment mechanisms became more decentralized. Thus, by 1919 the Republicans had taken the power of appointment from the leader of the party and had vested it in a committee on committees, composed of nearly 40 members. Similarly, after 1923 the Democrats no longer combined the posts of floor leader and chairman of the committee on committees. In such a context seniority was transformed from an important consideration to a sovereign principle. It alone provided a standard in terms of which decentralized appointment mechanisms could distribute key committee positions among party factions without provoking disputes that would weaken the party. As a result, in contrast to earlier eras, departures from seniority were rare in the 1920s and even rarer thereafter (Abram and Cooper, 1968; Polsby et al., 1969).

From Hierarchy to Bargaining

Given the reductions in the formal powers of the Speaker between 1909 and 1911, the disintegration of party control mechanisms after 1916 produced a dispersion of power in the House. If in Cannon's day the Speaker's prerogatives as Speaker and as party chief combined to centralize power in the House, now the reduction in the formal powers of the Speaker and the disintegration of party control mechanisms combined to decentralize power in the House.

On the one hand, the rewards and sanctions which the rules placed in the hands of party leaders were reduced. The party leadership no longer had absolute control over committee appointment, the Rules Committee, or the consideration of minor business. On the other hand, the ability of party leaders to consolidate and maintain support in their own ranks was also reduced. If it is true that factionalism in the party system led to the decline of party control mechanisms, it is also true that the decline of these mechanisms had the further effect of allowing party factionalism greater expression. The result of these developments was to heighten the power and independence of the individual member and of key organizational units in the House. Denied the power they possessed over the individual member under Czar rule or caucus rule, party leaders began to function less as the commanders of a stable party majority and more as brokers trying to assemble particular majorities behind particular bills. Denied the power they possessed over the organizational structure under Czar rule or caucus rule, party leaders began to function less as directors of the organizational units and more as bargainers for their support.

These tendencies intensified as time passed. During the 1920s the breakdown of the steering committee and the rise of seniority to predominance cast party leaders more firmly in the roles of brokers and bargainers than had been the case at the start of the decade. (Chiu, 1928, pp. 315-36 and Hasbrouck, 1927, pp. 48-50). Similarly, events during the 1930s confirmed and strengthened these roles. If the level of party cohesion during the 1920s was not high enough to permit reliance on party control mechanisms, it was still of such proportions that in general the holders of key organizational positions were loyal to the leadership and willing to cooperate with it. Nor, despite the increases in factionalism and bloc voting, did party leaders during the 1920s confront any stable and comprehensive basis of division among their fellow partisans, any extensive and consistent split across a whole range of issues. By the late 1930s, however, the situation had changed in both these regards.

After a brief increase in party voting during the initial years of the New Deal, party strength again began to decline in a steady and substantial fashion (Sinclair, 1978). Moreover, this decline gave birth to a new and distinctive feature, the Conservative Coalition (Brady and Bullock, 1980; Manley, 1977). Table 13-3 provides supportive data on both trends.

Thus, as the 1930s came to an end, party politics in the House began to display characteristics and configurations that were to become entrenched in the 1940s and to endure for several decades. These changes, however, made the task of the majority party leadership more, not less arduous. First, party divisions in the majority party now assumed a pronounced bifurcated form. In seeking to build majorities from issue to issue, the leadership accordingly was frequently threatened with the loss of support of a substantial portion of the southern wing of the party, a wing that from the late 1930s to late 1950s was roughly equal in size to the northern wing of the party (Cooper and Bombardier, 1968). Second, the divisions within the majority party now began to be translated into the organizational structure in a manner that far exceeded previous experience. The party leadership's ability to use the machinery of the House to suit its own purposes accordingly declined. It began to encounter difficulty securing the support of particular committees and committee chairmen much more frequently. This was especially true of the one committee in the House on which the leadership was most dependent and which historically had always been regarded as falling within the province of the leadership — the Rules Committee. For the first time in history the leadership found itself confronted with a Rules Committee that regarded itself and acted as an independent agent, rather than as an arm of the leadership (Galloway, 1961, pp. 145-48; Jones, 1968).

These developments further weakened the power and position of the leadership and in so doing further enhanced the independence of individual members and organizational units. Moreover, the impact was long-lasting, not transitory. A divided majority party was less amenable to leadership direction and control than an incohesive one. From the late 1930s on, the leadership was forced

331

Table 13-3   The Decline of Party Voting in the House and the Rise of the Conservative Coalition (1909-1953)

Congress	Year	Percent Party Votes	Percent Coalition Activity	Percent Coalition Victories
61	1909	29.4	—	—
62	1911	23.0	—	—
63	1913	19.9	—	—
64	1915	21.7	—	—
65	1917	9.4	—	—
66	1919	14.9	—	—
67	1921	35.2	—	—
68	1923	13.4	—	—
69	1925	5.3	3.5	63.5
70	1927	5.6	1.4	100.0
71	1929	13.6	5.8	80.0
72	1931	13.8	4.9	62.0
73	1933	18.9	2.1	48.0
74	1935	14.2	4.3	56.0
75	1937	11.8	7.6	67.0
76	1939	17.6	9.3	95.0
77	1941	10.5	12.5	92.0
78	1943	9.6	21.8	96.0
79	1945	12.1	22.1	88.0
80	1947	12.7	19.6	100.0
81	1949	6.5	16.4	83.0
82	1951	4.9	24.9	86.0

Sources: David Brady, Joseph Cooper and Patricia Hurley, "The Decline of Party Voting in the U.S. House of Representatives," *Legislative Studies Quarterly* 4 (1979): 381-407; David Brady and Charles Bullock, "Is There a Conservative Coalition in the House?" *Journal of Politics* 42 (1980): 549-59.

to place even more reliance on brokerage and bargaining than had been necessary in the early 1930s or 1920s (Herring, 1940, pp. 21-45).

The Rayburn House

The period from 1910 to 1940 may therefore be seen as a period of transition in the character of the House as a political institution. By 1940, the year Sam Rayburn assumed the Speakership, a new and distinctive type of House had emerged. It was a House that was destined to endure in most of its essential features until the reform of the Rules Committee in the early 1960s and in many of its essential features until the reemergence of the caucus in the late 1960s (Cooper, 1970; Brady et al., 1979).

The House under Decentralized Rule

The Rayburn House was a far different body from the House of Cannon or Reed. Centralization of power and hierarchical control had given way to a diffusion of power and bargaining.

On the one hand, the majority party leadership could no longer command the organizational units due to the breakdown of party control mechanisms and the elimination of the Speaker's prerogatives over appointment and the Rules Committee. Rather, it had to seek to win their support and do so in a context in which divisions in the majority party had become so pronounced that they had begun to appear at key vantage points in the organizational structure. On the other hand, the majority party leadership could no longer command overwhelming support from the ranks of its partisans on the floor due both to the decline in party strength and the decline in the fund of rewards and sanctions at its disposal. Rather, it had to seek to build majorities from issue to issue and do so in a context in which a deep split existed in the ranks of the majority party and distaste for party discipline was intense and pervasive. Political scientists writing about the House in the 1940s and 1950s accordingly emphasized themes quite different from those emphasized in the initial decades of this century: the primacy and amount of catering to constituency, not party loyalty or discipline; the dispersed and kaleidoscopic character of power in the House, not the authority and responsibilities of party leaders; the role of committee chairmen as autonomous and autocratic chieftains, not their operation as loyal party lieutenants (Young, 1943; Gross, 1953).

However, the fact that power became decentralized in the House does not mean that significant centers of power did not continue to exist. What occurred was a wider dispersal of power, not its fractionalization.

First, the party leadership retained substantial ability to influence and even control outcomes in the House. If party voting decreased, the party bond remained important both because of the degree of agreement still present and because of the interest most members had in establishing some kind of party record. Thus, though the leadership could no longer rule the House on the basis of votes drawn from its own party, it could still usually count on a large and stable reservoir of support from its fellow partisans (Mayhew, 1966). In addition, party leaders continued to derive leverage from other sources. The formal powers remaining to the Speaker aided their ability to control access to the floor and proceedings on the floor. The influence party leaders maintained over the party committee on committees enabled them to alter the political complexion of particular committees through the screening of new appointments. The power party leaders retained, due to their positions in the House and in the party, to dispense favors and build up credits augmented their capacity to secure the cooperation of ordinary members and holders of organizational positions (Ripley, 1967). Finally, the leadership could rely on the president's influence to win the support of reluctant partisans both in committee and on the floor.

Second, committees and committee chairmen emerged as rival power centers of great importance. In a context in which House rules gave the committees immense power over the handling of legislation within their jurisdictions and committee rules and practice gave their chairmen immense power within their committees, the decline in leadership authority and power redounded to the advantage of the committees and their chairmen. Typically, committee opposition to legislation sealed its fate, even when favored by the leadership. Conversely, committees that operated in a unified fashion were accorded great deference on the floor and had high levels of success (Fenno, 1962). Party leaders thus could not treat committees merely as instruments of their will nor chairmen simply as loyal lieutenants. Rather, they had to function largely as petitioners of committee support and floor managers of committee legislation.

In the Rayburn House the committees accordingly reemerged as the feudal baronies they had been in the decades immediately preceding Czar rule. And, indeed, to a significant degree the story of the Rayburn House is a story of conflict among northern majorities in the Democratic party, the majority party leadership, and southern-dominated committees in which northern pressure for action was continuing, leadership efforts sporadic, and committee obstruction very difficult to overcome. Ironically enough, then, the ultimate result of the revolt of 1910 was to redefine the problem of majority rule in the House, not to solve it. A new and equally serious difficulty, i.e., minority obstruction, simply replaced the difficulty that had aroused passions in the preceding era, i.e., autocratic leadership power.

Leadership Style in the Rayburn House

In sum, by 1940 the role and power of the party leadership in the House had been substantially altered. Though the leadership retained responsibility for and continued to provide overall guidance and direction in the conduct of the House's business, it now had to operate within a far harsher set of constraints than in 1910. At the floor stage, the leadership usually had no choice but to engage in the painful process of assembling shifting majorities behind particular bills through bargaining and maneuver. At the committee stage, the leadership was often forced to engage in intricate and prolonged negotiation with committees and committee chairmen. Indeed, the leadership was now placed in a position where inability to accommodate an organizational unit would mean failure to pass party legislation, unless it was able to organize a majority of such strength and intensity that it could force a vote on the floor through the pressure of opinion in the House or the use of a mechanism such as discharge. The result was that by 1940 the personal, political skills of the leadership, rather than its sources of institutional power, had become the critical determinant of the fate of party programs.

All this, in turn, led to the emergence of a leadership style that contrasted markedly with that of Cannon and Reed. The components of this new style emerged gradually in the 1920s and 1930s as power in the House decentralized. It crystalized under Rayburn and was fully applied by him. It represented his experienced and finely tuned sense of what made for effective leadership in a House in which the Speaker lacked the formal powers of a Czar, had to mobilize a majority party fairly evenly balanced between discordant northern and southern elements, confronted a set of committees and committee chairmen with great power and autonomy, and had to deal with individual members who rejected party discipline and prized their independence.

The main facets of the Rayburn style can be analyzed in terms of the following categories: personal friendship and loyalty, permissiveness, restrained partisanship and conflict reduction, informality, and risk avoidance.

Whereas Cannon and Reed relied on their authority and power as Speakers and party chiefs, Rayburn relied on personal friendship and loyalty. If the Speaker could no longer command the House, his vantage points in the formal and party systems as well as his personal prestige provided a variety of opportunities to do favors for members. Rayburn exploited these opportunities in a skillful and imaginative manner. He sought continually to bind members to him as a person on the basis of favors rendered to them as persons, favors which eased their lives in Washington, enhanced their sense of personal worth, and/or advanced their political careers. In contrast to Cannon and Reed, who emphasized policy goals over personal relationships, Rayburn sought to attain policy goals through personal relationships, through nurturing friendships and creating obligations (Bolling, 1965, pp. 65-68; Daniels, 1946, pp. 56-58).

Whereas Cannon and Reed were quite intolerant of party defection and quite amenable to employing punishments as well as rewards as means of inducement, Rayburn was very permissive. He explicitly legitimized party irregularity on the basis of policy disagreement or constituency pressure and was reluctant ever to punish or coerce a member. To be sure, he did withhold rewards or favors from those he felt failed to cooperate with him for light or insubstantial reasons. Nonetheless, his prevailing inclination was not to alienate members whose vote or help he might need on future occasions (Steinberg, 1975, p. 178).

Whereas Cannon and Reed were highly partisan and accepted both intraparty and interparty conflict as necessary aspects of majority party leadership, Rayburn sought to temper partisanship in personal relationships and to restrain conflict generally. He saw party mechanisms, such as the caucus and steering committee, as mechanisms for exacerbating party divisions and studiously ignored them. He established friendly relations with minority party leaders receptive to his overtures and extended advice and favors to rank-and-file minority members. He emphasized reciprocity and compromise as the prime behavioral rules for all members. Thus the guiding motif of his regime was not "serve party policy goals," but rather "to get along, go along," i.e., trade favors (MacNeil, 1963, pp. 84-85).

Whereas Cannon and Reed sought to achieve party programs by mobilizing partisan majorities and working through a stable set of partisan lieutenants, Rayburn's approach was more informal and ad hoc. Bargaining needs and opportunities determined his legislative strategies and personal contact served as his main means of implementing these strategies. Thus, on the whole, he worked through varying sets of trusted friends who were loyal Democrats and whom he had placed in key positions in the committee system. However, he was not averse when pressed at the committee stage to appealing to powerful opponents, who were nonetheless close friends, for help, men such as the southern Democratic stalwart, Gene Cox, or the Republican leader, Joe Martin. Similarly, at the floor stage he customarily asked varying sets of members, who were close friends and/or owed him favors, to insure his majority by standing ready to vote for him if needed, even against their policy preferences and/or constituency interests (Clapp, 1963, pp. 286-87).

Finally, whereas Cannon and Reed were aggressive in the pursuit of party policy goals, Rayburn was cautious. His inclination was to avoid battles when the outcome was uncertain. To be sure, in instances when a Democratic president and/or large number of his fellow partisans pressed him, he would usually wage some sort of fight. But both because he felt that defeat undermined his influence and because he did not like to expend his credits in losing causes, his clear and de- cided preference was to refuse battle, to wait until prospects for victory were favorable. Similarly, he shied away from challenging any of the key facets of decentralized power in the House, despite their restrictive impact on his ability to lead. His inclination was to work with what existed and endure, rather than to seek basic change. Only when extremely provoked did he contest the power of se- nior chairmen or the prerogatives of the Rules Committee and even then only in- directly. Thus he did not discipline Graham Barden but rather took over the Education and Labor Committee by filling vacancies with liberal Democrats. Thus he did not discipline Howard Smith or Bill Colmer or limit the power of the Rules Committee. He rather chose to expand its membership. In short, then, Rayburn was far more inclined to accept the defeat of party programs than to risk his influence and prestige in battles to attain them (Clapp, 1963, pp. 66-69; Wicker, 1968, pp. 43-54).

The Bases of Personalized Leadership

Earlier we argued that Czar rule derived from the interaction of the Speaker's formal powers and his leverage as party chief. We further argued that party strength was the determining factor in this interaction and that it was rooted primarily in the polarized constituency bases of the two parties. The emergence by 1940 of a new type of House and a new leadership style, both of which we may identify with Sam Rayburn, can be explained in terms of the al- tered character and impact of these same variables.

Confining ourselves simply to events in the House, the interaction between formal power and party strength again played a critical, though quite different, role. As we have already suggested, the interaction of these variables now worked to reduce leadership power. Party strength could no longer support or justify high concentrations of formal power in the leadership. Limited formal power, however, allowed party divisions fuller expression and increases in these divisions undermined party control mechanisms. The atrophy of these mechanisms, in turn, augmented the power and independence of party factions and transformed the leadership into bargainers and brokers, into middlemen rather than com- manders (Truman, 1959, pp. 202-27).

Evidence of the continuing decline in party strength, which we interpret as both cause and effect of the decentralization of power in the House, has already been presented in Table 13-3. To reinforce our tabular evidence we regressed party voting against time for the whole period from 1894-1952. The results are presented in Figure 13-1. The slope of the line is negative (B = −1.3) and the correlation between time and party voting −.74. Clearly, changes in party strength and changes in institutional structure covary in a manner that is consistent with our argument.

Nonetheless, if we again would acknowledge the impact of the internal, interactive effect between formal power and party strength and accord party strength the determining role in this interaction, we again would also argue that levels of party strength are subject primarily to external determination. In short, though restricted formal power provided a context in which party divisions could be expressed and extended, the primary engine of increased divisiveness was increased disharmony in the constituency bases underlying the majority party

Figure 13-1   Party Voting in the House of Representatives (1895-1953)

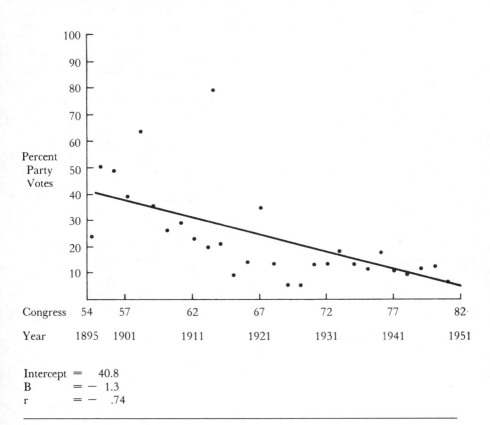

Intercept =   40.8
B   = − 1.3
r   = − .74

Source: David Brady, Joseph Cooper, and Patricia Hurley, "The Decline of Party in the U.S. House of Representatives, 1887-1968," *Legislative Studies Quarterly* 4 (1979): 384-385.

coalition. Thus, as in the case of leadership power and style during the period of Czar rule, the key to the Rayburn House and the Rayburn style lies in electoral alignment patterns.

Table 13-2 shows that from 1881 to 1921 party strength was high when the constituency bases of the parties were highly polarized and that it declined when these bases became less polarized. We have argued that increased factionalization in the party system was the primary source of the increased divisiveness that undermined the use of party control mechanisms in the 1920s. In order to show how constituency alignments are related to the further decline of party and the emergence of the Rayburn House, it is necessary to analyze the New Deal realignment and its aftermath.

The political revolution known as the New Deal was the product of the Great Depression. The voters providing the Democrats their majority came primarily from those groups most affected by the depression, farmers and low-income city dwellers, including blue-collar workers, ethnic groups, and blacks. Thus, the New Deal resulted in an increase in Democratic party allegiance across all constituent characteristics. Rather than recreating polarized congressional parties as in the period of Czar rule, the New Deal created a monolithic majority party which encompassed all types of constituencies. To the Democratic party's traditional base of support, the rural South, it added the urban Northeast and the urban and rural Midwest (Sundquist, 1973, pp. 183-218; Ladd and Hadley, 1975, pp. 31-88).

Table 13-4 illustrates and supports this point. It includes the following data, collected from the 1930 census and mapped onto congressional districts: the number of blue-collar workers, value added by manufactures, and population density. Constituencies are ranked as high or low in relation to these characteris-

Table 13-4 Increases in Congressional Majority Party Composition during 1932 Realignment

District Characteristic	Percent Democratic Congressmen			Absolute Ratio Increase
	70th House (1927-29)	73rd House (1933-35)	Percentage Increase	
Blue-Collar				
Low (Farm)	57	82	25	1.37
High (Labor)	32	64	32	1.97
Value Added				
Low (Non-Industrial)	54	81	27	1.40
High (Industrial)	34	67	33	1.89
Density				
Low (Rural)	53	77	24	1.38
High (Urban)	30	67	37	1.96

Source: Compiled from U.S. Bureau of Census, *Fifteenth Census of the United States* (1930): *Agriculture,* Vol. 2, parts 1, 2 and 3; *Manufactures,* Vol. 3; *Population,* Vol. 3, parts 1 and 2 (Washington, D.C.: U.S. Government Printing Office).

tics in terms of the national mean and the percentage increase as well as the absolute ratio increase calculated for Democratic congressmen.

The monolithic majority party coalition created by the New Deal was formed around the basic issue of government aid to combat the effects of the Depression. Hoover and the Republican party favored voluntarism and nonintervention, whereas the Democrats favored active government involvement. As long as the issue of the role of government in combating the Depression remained the central and defining one, congressional Democrats had a broad basis for unity, despite their increased disparateness. And, indeed, in the 1930s there was a break in the long-term trend toward declining party voting (see Figure 13-1). However, as is now evident, the Roosevelt coalition could not maintain its cohesion across changing issue dimensions (Sinclair, 1978). As a monolithic rather than polarized coalition, it was particularly vulnerable to the emergence of issues that would divide its various components rather than unite them as the Depression had done.

In the late 1930s and early 1940s two factors combined to redefine the political climate and render it far less hospitable to majority party unity. The first was the alteration in the character and thrust of the New Deal, which focused attention and controversy on the federal government's general role as an agent of social welfare rather than its narrower role as an agent of economic recovery. The divisive potential of this development was signaled by the battle over New Deal legislation in the 75th Congress (1937-1939), a battle that in the eyes of many analysts marks the true emergence of the Conservative Coalition (Brady and Bullock, 1980). The second was the worsening international situation, which finally led to the Second World War. This development focused attention and controversy not only on defense and foreign policy, but on the management of a war economy as well. In so doing, it also by-passed or submerged old bases of Democratic unity and reinforced divisions along liberal-conservative lines (Young, 1956).

The emergence and growth of the Conservative Coalition in the late 1930s and early 1940s, documented in Table 13-3, testifies to the impact of these factors in producing a new and enduring split in the congressional Democratic party that was rooted in differences between rural conservative southern constituencies and urban liberal northern ones. Nor is it surprising that as the dimensions of the split increased and finally stabilized, party voting declined. A comparison of the data in Table 13-3 broadly demonstrates the point; but to pin it down we calculated the correlation (Pearson's r) between Conservative Coalition activity and party voting for the period 1931-1953. The result is an impressive $-.67$.

In short, then, external factors are of primary importance in accounting for personalized rule as well as Czar rule. In a context in which the interaction of restricted formal power and declining party strength had already combined to disperse power, the emergence of a basic split in the majority party, rooted in constituency differences, further substantially undermined leadership power. Rayburn's highly personalized style was thus a reaction to his party situation, to the corps of independent and divided partisans he had to work with and lead. Indeed, his style is not only distinguishable in kind from that of Cannon and Reed, but even in degree from that of preceding Democratic Speakers, such as Garner and

Rainey, who did not have to worry continually about southern support on key committees and the floor (MacNeil, 1963, p. 34).

Conclusion

Our historical analysis of the transition from Cannon to Rayburn suggests several broad propositions or hypotheses that explain House leadership roles and behavior and have general import or significance for the analysis of legislative leadership. They are as follows.

First, institutional context rather than personal skill is the primary determinant of leadership power in the House. To be sure, leadership power, like other forms of power, is a combination of the fund of inducements available and the skill with which they are used. Nonetheless, skill cannot fully compensate for deficiencies in the quality or quantity of inducements. Indeed, the very skills required of leaders themselves vary in terms of the parameters and needs imposed by the character of the House as a political institution at particular points in its history. Thus, Rayburn was not and could not be as powerful a Speaker as Cannon or Reed. His sources of leverage in the formal and party systems were simply not comparable. Nor did Reed or Cannon require the same level of skill in building credits or bargaining as Rayburn to maximize their power. Similarly, it is doubtful that O'Neill can be as strong a Speaker as Rayburn whatever the level of skill he possesses, given the increased fractionalization in both the formal and party systems that has occurred in the past two decades.

Second, institutional context rather than personal traits primarily determines leadership style in the House. To be sure, style is affected by personal traits. Nonetheless, style is and must be responsive to and congruent with both the inducements available to leaders and member expectations regarding proper behavior. Indeed, the personal traits of leaders are themselves shaped by the character of the House as a political institution at particular points in time through the impact of socialization and selection processes that enforce prevailing norms. Thus, if Rayburn was a more permissive and consensual leader than Cannon or Reed, this is not because he was inherently a less tough or more affective person, but rather because of his weaker sources of leverage and the heightened individualism of members. If O'Neill's leadership style is far closer to that of Rayburn, McCormack, and Albert than to Cannon or Reed, this is not attributable to basic personality similarities and differences.[4] It is rather attributable to the fact that the House he leads is far more like theirs than the House during the days of Czar rule. Similarly, though leaders remain distinct personalities (note, for example, O'Neill and Albert), range of tolerance for personal traits or predispositions that conflict with prevailing norms is restricted. O'Neill therefore must and does curb the exercise of new sources of leverage gained since the revival of the majority caucus in 1969 to avoid even appearing like a Czar.[5] In contrast, members who cannot eliminate or temper traits that run counter to prevailing norms are disadvantaged in the pursuit of leadership office. Witness Dick Bolling who would have been far more at home in the House of the 1890s.[6] In a basic sense, then, the impact of context on leadership style has something of the character of a self-fulfilling hypothesis.

Third, there is no direct relationship between leadership style and effectiveness in the House. This is true whether effectiveness is interpreted relatively or absolutely. Interpreted relatively, effectiveness is a matter of the skill with which resources are used, not actual results. However, whereas style is primarily determined by the parameters and needs imposed by the political character of the House as an institution at certain points in its history, particular styles can be applied with varying degrees of skill. Note, for example, the differences between Rayburn, McCormack, and Albert. Similarly, if effectiveness is interpreted absolutely, i.e., in terms of actual results of achievements, there is still no direct or simple relationship between style and effectiveness. On the one hand, there is no one best "style"; the relationship between style and effectiveness is rather a highly contingent or situational variable. On the other hand, even when contexts dictate roughly similar styles, they do not necessarily accord them roughly equal chances of success. Thus, given his sources of leverage in the formal and party systems, O'Neill has little choice but to adopt a leadership style that in many key respects is similar to Rayburn's. Yet, the greater degree of fractionalization in both systems in the 1970s, as opposed to the 1940s, reduces his overall prospects for success in passing party programs. O'Neill therefore is likely to have far less success overall than Rayburn, even though he too leads in a highly personal, informal, permissive, and ad hoc manner.

Fourth, and last, the impact of institutional context on leadership power and style is determined primarily by party strength. To be sure, the degree of organizational elaboration substantially affects the intensity of the demands imposed on integrative capacity and is largely a product of factors other than party strength, e.g., size and workload. Nonetheless, integrative capacity derives or flows primarily from party strength (Cooper, 1975). The higher the degree of party unity or cohesion the more power in both the formal and party systems can be concentrated in the hands of party leaders and the more leadership style will be oriented to command and task or goal attainment. The lower the degree of party unity or cohesion the more power in both the formal and party system will be dispersed and the more leadership style will be oriented to bargaining and the maintenance of good relations. The infrequency of eras of centralized power in the House is thus explicable in terms of the very high levels of party strength required to support it, requirements which have increased as the organization itself has become more elaborate. Similarly, the degree of power dispersion now present is explicable in terms of present weaknesses in party unity or coherence both in absolute terms and relative to an organizational structure that has grown far more complex in the past two decades. Given the dependence of internal party strength on appropriate constituency alignments, all this, in turn, means that leadership power and style are ultimately tied to the state of the party system in the electorate, that external or environmental factors have a decisive bearing on the parameters, and needs that institutional context imposes on leadership power and style. In short, then, to be understood Cannon and Reed must be seen in the context of an entire party system, and the same applies to Rayburn in the 1940s and 1950s and to O'Neill today.

Notes

1. Aside from the Rules Committee, nine other committees were privileged to report at any time on certain matters. In addition, the eight committees charged with general appropriation bills also were privileged to report at any time on such bills. *Hinds' Precedents,* Vol. 4, Sec. 4621. It should also be remembered that the unanimous consent procedure at this time consisted simply of motions on the floor to that effect. The rule providing for a Consent Calendar was not adopted until 1909 (Chiu, 1928, pp. 179-88).
2. The total control the Speaker exercised over the consideration of minor legislation thus resulted from the combined impact of the lack of a regular order of business and the need to secure recognition by the Speaker to use either unanimous consent or suspension to bring constituency bills to the floor (Chiu, 1928, pp. 228-30).
3. In changing the rules to provide for election of the standing committees by the House, the Democrats took care to maintain centralized party control. Thus, they blocked the alternative preferred by the Insurgent Republicans, which would have provided for party committees on committees elected by geographic regions. Instead, the Democrats adopted a rule that only provided for election by the House and then made the Democratic members of Ways and Means, led by Underwood, their committee on committees (Brown, 1922, pp. 172-77, and 62 *Congressional Record* 1, pp. 63-64).
4. O'Neill's style is more partisan in personal relationships and more consultative or open than Rayburn's. But it remains highly personal, ad hoc, informal, and permissive. See *National Journal* (1977), pp. 940-46; (1978), pp. 4-9, 1384-88; (1979), pp. 1326-31.
5. Since the mid-1970s the Speaker has had the power to nominate Democratic members of the Rules Committee to the Democratic Caucus and the power to multiply or sequentially refer legislation to committees, to establish time limits for their reports (in effect, Speaker discharge), and to establish special ad hoc committees to receive such reports and report to the House. However, the Speaker has used ad hoc committees and referral with a time limit cautiously. In addition, he has not as yet refused to recommend the reappointment of any sitting Rules Committee member and threatened to do so only rarely and even then only by implication. See *National Journal* (1977), pp. 940-46.
6. Bolling is perhaps more reminiscent of Reed than any recent House leader. Compare Polsby (1969, pp. 343-45), Bolling (1975, pp. 236-44), and *National Journal* (1976), pp. 170-71, with Brown (1922, pp. 84-97) and Robinson (1930, pp. 377-99).

14. THE SPEAKER'S TASK FORCE IN THE POST-REFORM HOUSE OF REPRESENTATIVES

Barbara Sinclair

During the 1970s, changes in rules and norms, high membership turnover, and the rise to prominence of new party-fragmenting issues transformed the environment in which the majority-party leadership operates in the U.S. House of Representatives. The current leaders work in a much less predictable environment than their predecessors did.

Environmental change has not altered the functions which majority-party leaders are expected to perform. The leadership is charged with constructing winning coalitions on major legislation and thereby satisfying the legislative expectations of their membership and of significant actors outside the chamber. "Keeping peace in the family," as the current leaders themselves express it, is an equally important function. Centrally involved in peace-keeping are satisfying expectations of members about their individual roles in the chamber and fostering cooperative patterns of behavior among party members. The two functions are interrelated in a complex fashion. The need to promote harmony places limits upon the coalition-building strategies which can be used. On the other hand, to the extent that leaders are successful at "keeping the peace," their probability of future success in building winning coalitions is increased. The necessity of passing legislation which is controversial within the party inevitably strains party harmony. Yet, to the extent that leaders are successful at building winning coalitions on bills which satisfy their membership's expectations as to legislative results, they contribute to intra-party harmony.

Although the functions of leadership have not changed, successful performance requires strategies different from those appropriate in the pre-reform era.

Author's Note: I would like to thank the American Political Science Association Congressional Fellowship program, which enabled me to do this research. Very special thanks are due to Representative Jim Wright and the staff of the majority leader's office for giving me a home base as well as much help and friendship during my fellowship year. All unattributed quotations are from interviews conducted by the author. I, of course, owe a major debt to the members and staff who talked with me. Finally, several anonymous reviewers and the editor of the Review provided very helpful suggestions.

Source: American Political Science Review 75 (June 1981): 397-410. Reprinted with permission of the author.

Scholars increasingly agree that congressional leadership is best understood from a contextual perspective (Jones, 1980; Cooper and Brady, 1980). The contents or environment shapes and constrains leadership styles and strategies. The highly informal Rayburn style was predicated upon the power of the committee chairmen and the concomitant limited influence of rank-and-file members (Cooper and Brady, 1980; see also Ripley, 1967, 1969; Peabody, 1976; Jones, 1968). A strategy based upon bargaining with a small number of key actors obviously becomes untenable when the number of significant actors expands to include almost the entire House membership. Not only would such a strategy be unsuccessful in the short run, by thwarting members' expectations of full participation in the legislative process, it would also decrease the probability of future success.

In response to the changed environment, Speaker O'Neill has developed the strategy of leadership by inclusion. Effective leadership in the post-reform House, the Speaker believes, requires including as large a proportion of Democrats as possible in the coalition formation process. A central element of the strategy of inclusion is the Speaker's task force, an ad hoc group appointed by the Speaker and charged with passage of a specific bill. The leaders believe task forces have payoffs in terms of both of their central functions. By increasing the number of people working in an organized way to pass the bill at issue, the leaders increase the probability of success on the bill. Work on a task force gives junior members "a piece of the action" and satisfies their expectations of participation. In addition, the leaders believe that task force membership has a positive socializing effect, especially on junior members. Work on a task force gives them an understanding of the problems of the leadership, and, it is hoped, will teach them the value of joint action under the aegis of the leadership.

This study examines the origins of the task force concept, the type of bills on which task forces have been used, task force membership and how task forces operate. One purpose is to describe an as yet little-known leadership tool. A second is to illuminate the relationship between leadership strategies and the environment in which leaders work by analyzing how the leaders see task forces as aiding them in coalition building and as contributing to "keeping peace in the family."

The New Environment

An understanding of why new leadership strategies became necessary requires a brief review of the transformation of the environment in which the leadership works.

Rules Changes

The 1970s saw a constellation of rules changes aimed at curbing the power of committee chairmen and at dispersing positions of influence more widely throughout the House (see Ornstein, 1975; Dodd and Oppenheimer, 1977). Each member was limited to chairing only one subcommittee. Full committee chairmen were stripped of the power to select subcommittee chairmen and that power was vested in the Democratic caucus of the committee. Subcommittees were required to have fixed jurisdiction and adequate budget and staff. Full committee chairmen and the chairmen of Appropriations subcommittees were made subject to approval by secret ballot in the Democratic caucus.

The decade also saw an immense growth in the staff resources available to members of the House. In 1967, personal staff totaled 4,055; in 1979, that figure stood at 7,067. The number of employees of House committees rose from 702 in 1970 to 1,959 in 1979 (Bibby et al., 1980, pp. 69-70). The most junior member is now entitled to hire a staff of at least 18.

The decline in the power of committee chairmen, the dispersal of influence to the subcommittee level, and the augmentation of members' staff resources make wide participation in the legislative process possible. Another set of rules changes which can be summarized under the rubric of "sunshine reforms" further increase the incentives for participation. Except under special circumstances, all committee meetings, mark-up sessions as well as hearings, must be open to the public. Since the advent of the recorded teller vote, voting on amendments in the Committee of the Whole is no longer anonymous. The increased visibility of members' actions in the committee and on the floor encourages the use of these arenas for making a variety of political points and subjects members to a wider range of pressures.

Membership Turnover

Membership turnover in the 1970s has been very high by post-World War II standards. The number of Democratic freshmen and the proportion of Democratic members who were freshmen was unusually high in the 94th, 95th and 96th Congresses. The 75 freshmen elected in 1974 in the wake of the Watergate scandal constituted a little more than a quarter of the Democratic membership during that Congress. The 47-member Democratic freshmen class elected to the 95th Congress and the 42-member class elected to the 96th were larger than any class between 1960 and 1972, except for the 89th Congress class elected in the 1964 landslide. The result of this heavy turnover has been an increasingly junior Democratic membership. In the 94th Congress, 44 percent of Democrats were serving their first, second, or third term; that figure rose to 51 percent in the 95th and to 53 percent in the 96th. In contrast, between 1961 and 1974, the mean percentage of first-, second- and third-termers was only 31 percent; its highest value was 42 percent in the 89th Congress.

For the leadership, the sheer number of newcomers presents a problem, since the rules now make possible full participation by the most junior member. The leaders obviously lack longstanding relationships with these members. Yet for the leadership such relationships are crucial for making informed judgments about the probable behavior of members and provide the basis for effective persuasion.

Changes in Norms

Accompanying the change in rules and membership has been a change in norms. Socialized to politics during the turbulent 1960s, the freshmen of the

1970s entered the House in a period of challenge to the power structure; many of the large '74 Democratic class were elected from previously Republican districts. Both personal inclination and political necessity dictated a high level of activity and immediate participation at the committee and the floor stage. Rules changes which lessened the control of seniority leaders and augmented the staff resources of junior members made such activity possible. Thus norms of apprenticeship and of deference to senior members, already weakened during the 1960s, were given a final blow.

The events of the 1970s have diminished the prestige of the committees and undermined the norm of reciprocity among committees. Previously, there existed a strong presumption in favor of the committee's bill. "Go with the committee on the floor" with the watchword; "the committee has exhaustively examined the matter and has brought its expertise to bear." The reciprocity norm is much weaker now, and there is a much greater tendency to "legislate on the floor." Younger members are simply not willing to defer to committees.

New Issues

The issues at the center of controversy in the 1970s and early 1980s — energy, environmental and consumer issues, and foreign and defense policy questions — split not just North from South in the Democratic party; they also frequently divide northern Democrats (Sinclair, 1981). High inflation has engendered a budget-cutting mood which threatens to destroy the northern Democratic consensus on traditional economic and social welfare policy. Socio-cultural issues such as busing and abortion continue to excite controversy.

Because of the change in floor procedure, many of the divisive issues come to a recorded vote over and over during a Congress. The highly emotional abortion issue is a good example. Anti-abortion members are proposing amendments barring federal funding to more and more bills and are forcing roll-call votes. The frequency with which members are compelled to take public stands on such highly charged issues cannot help but exacerbate the leadership's problems.

Impact upon Party Leadership and the Strategy of Inclusion

The changes of the 1970s have resulted in a much less predictable House environment. According to a top leadership figure, "the democratization of the House has proceeded so far that all kinds of things can come percolating up from below and that can cause problems for the leadership."

The recorded teller vote and the decline of intercommittee reciprocity have severely heightened unpredictability at the floor stage of a bill. Since neither junior status nor party affiliation nor lack of expertise bars members from offering amendments, amendments can come from anywhere; it is impossible to anticipate all that may be offered. The House, according to Morris Udall (D-Ariz.), has become a "fast breeder reactor" for amendments. "Every morning when I come to my office, I find that there are 20 new amendments. We dispose of 20 or 25 amendments and it breeds 20 more amendments" (*Congressional Quarterly*, p. 877). The number of recorded votes grew many-fold during the

1970s. During the 91st Congress, the last before the institution of the recorded teller vote, the House took 443 recorded votes; during the 95th Congress (1977-78), 1540 recorded votes were taken.

As a vote can be recorded upon request by 25 members — 20 until 1979 — almost any member can force a vote. Republicans have become very adept at fashioning amendments with considerable constituency appeal. Votes which a clever opponent back home can represent as favoring reparations to Vietnam, "giving away" the Panama Canal, or supporting federally funded legal aid for homosexuals present a ticklish choice even to the Democrat who would like to support the leadership.

The large number of amendments offered to many major bills strains the leadership's resources and increases the probability of the committee majority and the leadership getting "ambushed" on the floor. "We are in the process of moving from a time in the history of the House when committees had too much power and we are moving to a point where the floor itself becomes a large, unwieldy committee," according to Paul Simon, D-Ill., "We are not doing the job of legislating as we should. We are legislating by whim..." (*Congressional Quarterly*, p. 878).

The heightened level of floor activity is even more of a problem than it might be otherwise, because voting behavior has become less predictable. The leadership cannot count on solid support from northern Democrats as it could on most issues during the 1960s. On the other hand, the southern Democratic contingent in the House became more heterogeneous during the 1970s. As the race issue declined in salience in the South, somewhat more nationally oriented Democrats were elected. Consequently, when the party leadership attempts to build winning coalitions, there are few Democrats who can be written off completely and few who can be counted on to be loyal across the board (Sinclair, 1981).

The Speaker's response to heightened unpredictability is the strategy of inclusion. O'Neill sees effective leadership in the post-reform House as dependent upon including as many Democrats as possible in the coalition formation process. Coping with the decrease in predictability requires more extensive vote gathering. A larger proportion of the Democratic membership must be contacted and persuaded — and this task must be done many times. The task is simply too great to be handled solely by the top leadership. Others must be brought into the process.

The leadership could and, in many cases, does rely upon the whip system for help. During the 1970s, the whip system significantly expanded in size; by 1977, it consisted of the majority whip, a chief deputy whip, three deputy whips, 22 regionally elected whips, and 10 at-large whips. Several factors militate against exclusive reliance on the whip system for aid in coalition building. The whip system is charged with conducting whip polls and, as the number of polls has increased, this has become a time-consuming task. In the 95th Congress, about 80 whip counts were conducted. In addition, because the regional whips are elected by the members of their zones, their loyalty to party and to the leadership is sometimes minimal. The addition of at-large whips, appointed by the leadership, was a response to the problematical loyalty of the regional whips. The zone whips are expected only to do the counting; the appointed whips do act as an arm of the leadership in mobilizing support.

O'Neill's strategy of leadership by inclusion is not predicated only upon the leadership's need for a loyal group of assistants to aid in coalition building. It also encompasses satisfying members' — especially junior members' — desires for participation, for "a piece of the action." If junior Democrats are involved in the vote-mobilization process via task force membership, their very considerable energies are directed towards accomplishing leadership objectives and they are given a stake in the leadership's success. This involvement, it is hoped, will gradually teach junior members the need for "followership" and the value of joint action under the aegis of the leadership.

Origins of the Task Force Concept

The basic notion underlying the task force concept — that of joint organized effort to pass a specific bill — is, of course, not new. As a senior staffer explained: "People have been doing task forces of one kind or another for a hundred years or more. Any time that there's an interested group of people, they're going to get together and work on it in some kind of common front."

Task forces consisting of interest-group representatives have for years worked with the party leadership on legislation of common interest. The leadership has traditionally worked closely with committee leaders in passing major legislation and, during the early 1970s as the number of significant actors increased, the leadership seems to have expanded the number of members included in its vote-mobilization efforts.

The informality of such traditional arrangements distinguishes them from the current Speaker's task force. A senior staffer closely involved in the process explained: "In the sense that it's now defined, which is a pretty structured kind of thing, with a chairman appointed by the Speaker and a list of members, I guess you'd have to say that it started in the 95th Congress." He continued: "We have some tough bills. We had one that we lost and we lost it because we didn't do one or two things we could have done. I remained convinced to this day that we had the votes if we had played our cards right but it would have taken organization to do that."

An early loss which the leadership attributed to lack of organization acted as the catalyst. The loss taught the new leadership team that building winning coalitions in the post-reform House requires more organized and extensive vote-gathering efforts than were needed in the pre-reform era.

The Decision to Establish a Task Force

The decision to appoint a task force is solely the Speaker's, although he may do so upon the advice of other leadership figures or of staff. He will, of course, confer with the prospective floor manager of the legislation.

Asked about the types of bills for which task forces will be formed, a senior staffer explained:

There are significant leadership issues where the Speaker has some prestige on the line, and, much more importantly than that, where the core of the party has to have the bill. Now, that's pretty easy to pick out. You look down the list of bills which came up in the Congress and you'll find the 8 or 10 bills that really had to pass last year — you know, we had to have the budget, we had to have the debt ceiling — some elements of the party had to have Humphrey-Hawkins; CETA comes in the same bag; energy, the Democratic party had to have; a tax bill we had to have of some sort — it isn't the tax bill that we would have liked to have, but we had to have it; and you look down the list of other bills, and I would guess that there aren't any that if they had not passed they would have done as much damage to the party or to the leadership or to the House, the Democratic members of the House, as those bills if they had not gone through, so that's how it's done.

Another staffer made the same point in the imperative voice: "[Task forces] should be used only on significant legislation that is clearly part of the Democratic party program." An important consideration, of course, is "how deep the trouble is." Table 14-1 lists all task forces appointed through the end of 1979. All the bills are ones on which trouble was expected and ones which the Democratic party as a whole or some significant segment thereof "had to have."

President Carter's top domestic priority during the 95th Congress was a comprehensive energy program. His prestige and that of the party and the leadership rode on success in passing energy legislation. Energy policy deeply splits congressional Democrats along consumer versus producer lines; consequently, the leadership knew passage would be difficult. The Energy Organization Act is the first bill on which a full-fledged task force was appointed. It actually consisted of three subgroupings, each charged with defeating or passing a key amendment.

The Senate drastically changed the energy legislation so as to make final House approval more difficult. Liberals were extremely upset by the gas-pricing section and House approval of the conference report rested upon passage of a rule which prevented a separate vote on that section. The expected and actual closeness of that vote made an organized task force effort necessary.

Both the presidential and the party leadership considered legislation to place the social security system on a sound financial footing among the top priority items of the 95th Congress. The steep increase in social security taxes that this entailed resulted in a far from popular bill. The social security task force consisted of subgroups charged with responsibility for specific amendments. The Fisher task force was charged with passing an amendment deleting mandatory coverage of federal workers. The overwhelming passage of the amendment makes that task force something of an anomaly. A staffer who worked with the task force explained:

> The preliminary counts didn't show anything like that. That's part of it, but if you'd asked anyone around here, "Is it going to pass?," we'd have said yes. But the crucial thing is, what if it hadn't? We had no social security bill plain and simple. It had to pass and, while most people would say the chances are 9 out of 10, it was not a situation where one was willing to take that 10-percent risk.

The steep increase in social security taxes, which the social security bill mandated, made it politically advisable to pass a tax reduction bill before the 1978

349

Table 14-1 Speaker's Task Forces, 1977-1979

Task Force	Chair	House Vote	Democratic Vote	Date
Energy Organization Act (HR 8444)				
Natural Gas	Sharp, Ind.	199-227	72-210	8/3/77
Plowback	Gibbons, Fla.	198-223	74-208	8/4/77
User Fees	Mikva, Ill.	221-198	212- 68	8/5/77
Passage	Sharp, Ind.	244-177	231- 50	8/5/77
Social Security (HR 9346)				
Fisher Amendment	Fisher, Va.	386- 38	257- 24	10/26/77
Pickle Amendment	Tucker, Ark.	196-221	74-206	10/26/77
Passage	Gephardt, Mo.-Tucker	275-146	235- 46	10/27/77
Conference Report	Gephardt-Tucker	189-163	174- 54	12/15/77
Humphrey-Hawkins (HR 50)	Rose, N.C.	252-152	233- 41	3/16/78
1st Budget (S. Con. Res. 80)	Derrick, S.C.	201-197	198- 61	5/10/78
Debt Ceiling (HR 13385)	Gephardt, Mo.	205-202	196- 74	7/19/78
2nd Budget (H. Con. Res. 683)	Derrick, S.C.	217-178	215- 42	9/16/78
CETA (HR 12452)	Miller, Calif.			
	Oberstar, Minn.			
	Mineta, Calif.			
Obey Amendment		230-175	114-152	8/9/78
Jeffords Amendment		221-181	101-162	8/9/78
Passage		284- 50	206- 18	9/22/78

Tax (HR 13511)	Gephardt, Mo.			
Kemp Amendment		177-240	37-237	8/10/78
Passage		362- 49	224- 47	8/10/78
Energy (HR 5289, HR 5037, HR 5263, HR 5146, HR 4018)	Sharp, Ind.			
Previous Question on Rule		207-206	199- 79	10/13/78
Adoption of Conference Report		231-168	185- 81	10/15/78
Debt Limit (HR 1894, HR 2534)	Gephardt, Mo.			
Previous Question on Rule		222-197	221- 44	2/28/79
Passage		194-222	191- 73	2/28/79
Previous Question on Rule		201-199	200- 54	3/15/79
Passage		212-195	209- 53	3/15/79
1st Budget (H. Con. Res. 107)	Mineta, Calif.			
Passage		220-184	211- 50	5/14/79
Conference Report		144-260	108-152	5/23/79
Conference Report		202-196	174- 80	5/24/79
2nd Budget (H. Con. Res. 186, S. Con. Res. 36)	Mineta, Calif.			
Passage		192-213	188- 67	9/19/79
Passage		212-206	212- 52	9/27/79
Chrysler Aid (HR 5860)	Blanchard, Mich.	271-136	209- 48	12/18/79

Source: Compiled by the author from task force membership lists.

elections. That some bill would pass was never in doubt; the form of the legislation was at issue. Representative Jack Kemp and Senator William Roth had received a great deal of publicity for their proposal to cut income taxes by 30 percent and the leadership knew Kemp would offer the proposal as an amendment to the tax bill. Its obvious appeal, combined with what the leadership saw as drastic consequences if it should pass, led to the establishment of a task force charged specifically with defeating the Kemp amendment.

The reputation of the House Democratic leadership rests, in part, on its success in gaining passage of presidential priorities. It also depends upon the leadership's ability to uphold the reputation of the House as a functioning legislature on less highly visible matters. Two areas that have been especially problematic for the leadership are the biannual conflicts over the budget resolution and the recurrent fight to raise the federal debt ceiling. In a time of high inflation, building winning coalitions in these areas has become increasingly difficult. Both budget resolutions and debt limit votes offer Congress members nearly irresistible opportunities for "grandstanding." An intensive and well-organized vote-mobilization effort on such legislation has become a prerequisite to success.

The remaining bills on which task forces were established were centrally important to major segments of the Democratic membership. Big city liberals needed the Humphrey-Hawkins Bill and the CETA bill and both seemed to be in deep trouble. Michigan Democrats as well as some others with Chrysler plants in their districts considered the Chrysler bail-out bill "a matter of life or death." Nevertheless this bill, because of its relatively narrow range, fits the criteria least well. The Michigan Democratic delegation, it was reported, "begged" the Speaker to establish a task force.

The technique, then, has generally been restricted to significant legislation which involved the prestige of the leadership and of the party as a collectivity or bills which a major segment of the party badly needed. Restricting the use of task forces to such legislation is vital if the strategy is to contribute to maintaining harmony. Use on a bill perceived by a major segment of the party as threatening its vital interests would undermine the legitimacy of the technique. Instead of teaching members the value of joint action under the aegis of the leadership, it would exacerbate intraparty conflicts.

Task Force Membership

Once the decision to establish a task force has been made, the Speaker appoints the chairman. Leadership staff may suggest one or several names, or he may ask the chairman of the committee, "Who's a bright young guy who would do a good job on this?" As Table 14-1 shows, the chairman is almost invariably a junior member. All task forces but the first were chaired by members first elected in 1972 or later. Dick Gephardt of Missouri chaired several task forces during his first term.

Junior members are chosen, in part, because they have more time to devote to the task than senior members with heavier committee responsibility. In addition, giving junior members an important job to do and drawing them into the leadership's orbit are integral aspects of the strategy of inclusion. One of the leaders said that an effort was made "to pick members who will stay around, who intend to make a career of the House." The chairman is usually, though not invariably, a member of the originating committee. The members chosen to chair task forces are otherwise distinguished from their contemporaries not by objective characteristics such as prior political experience but by the leaders' perception of them as responsible legislators and as leaders among their peers.

The Speaker frequently suggests some of the members of the task force, but also gives the chairman considerable discretion to include "anyone else you feel comfortable working with." In selecting members, the task force chairman works with the Steering and Policy Committee staff, who provide staff work for the task forces. The selection process has become rather elaborate. Prior to meeting with the task force chairman, the staff prepares a list of potential members with information on each. The information includes past support on similar legislation. Commitment to the legislation in question is, of course, a prerequisite to membership. Within that constraint, attention is paid to getting "regional, seniority and ideological balance."

An examination of task force membership will show the extent to which the aims of including a large number and variety of Democrats in the process and especially of getting junior members involved are actually met. The analysis is based upon membership lists of all 95th Congress task forces and the first two task forces established during the 96th.

The strategy of inclusion refers not only to getting a large number of members involved but also to including members from all sections of the party. Overall, the task forces have been fairly representative in terms of region. In both the 95th and 96th Congresses, 74 percent of the Democratic membership was from the North and 26 percent from the South.[1] The average northern membership across the 11 task forces was 76.1 percent; the average southern membership, 23.9 percent. The regional balance varied, but only one task force was clearly unrepresentative: no southerner served on the CETA task force. The unpopularity of the program seems to have made it impossible to find southerners willing to work for the leadership position on the bill.

Table 14-2 presents data on the proportion of northerners and southerners who served on task forces during the 95th Congress. Southerners were less likely to have served than northern Democrats, but the differences are not massive. The leadership has done reasonably well at including southern Democrats in the coalition-building process via task force membership. In fact, a larger proportion of southern than of northern Democrats served on two or more task forces during the 95th Congress. Clearly, those southerners willing to participate get plenty of opportunity to do so.

The requirement that task force members be committed to passing the bill in question prohibits strict ideological balance just as it makes absolute regional balance somewhat difficult. As one would expect, task force members as a group are more loyal to party than non-task force members. Considering each of the 11 task forces separately, one finds that in each case, members have a higher average party unity score than nonmembers and that this pattern holds for both of the re-

353

Table 14-2 Regional Representation on Task Forces, 95th Congress

No. of Task Forces Member Has Served On	All Democrats	Northern	Southern
0	59.7	58.7	62.7
1	19.4	22.1	12.0
2	8.7	6.6	14.7
3 or more	12.2	12.7	10.1
N =	288	213	75

Source: Compiled by the author from task force membership lists.

gional groupings.[2] The differences between members and nonmembers are especially great among southern Democrats.

Table 14-3 shows that Democrats who served on one task force during the 95th Congress are, as a group, appreciably more loyal than those who served on none. Those serving on two or more are slightly more loyal still. The differences are especially marked for southern Democrats. Nevertheless, task force members are relatively heterogeneous ideologically. Southern Democrats who served on two or more task forces are, as a group, significantly less loyal than northern Democrats who served on none. The leadership does find it possible on specific bills to involve members who otherwise frequently defect. A few Democrats who are generally highly disloyal have served on task forces.

An interesting outgrowth of the strategy of inclusion and an indicator of the decline in committee insulation in the House is the committee makeup of the task force membership. Although the chair usually is a member of the originating committee, a majority of the task force membership is not. If the two energy task

Table 14-3 Relationship of Party Unity to Frequency of Task Force Membership and Region, 95th Congress

	Frequency of Task Force Membership		
Group	None	One	Two or More
All Democrats	68.4	78.4	79.6
N =	(171)	(56)	(60)
Northern	77.0	81.2	84.9
N =	(124)	(47)	(41)
Southern	45.6	63.8	68.2
N =	(47)	(9)	(19)

Sources: Compiled by the author from task force membership lists and from *Congressional Quarterly's* party unity scores, *Weekly Report*, December 16, 1978, pp. 3450-51. Scores have been adjusted so that absences do not affect the scores.

forces for which the figures would not be meaningful are excluded,[3] then on the average, only 30.6 percent of task force members are also members of the committee reporting the bill.

The subgroup of members of the Social Security task force charged with passing the Fisher amendment included a number drawn from the Post Office and Civil Service Committee. Since the Fisher amendment dealt with federal workers and thus was related to that committee's jurisdiction, the inclusion of Post Office and Civil Service Committee members on the task force was a way of recognizing their legitimate interest in that aspect of the bill. That case is, however, the exception. On other task forces, members not from the originating committee held positions on a wide variety of committees. They were simply Democrats with an interest in and a willingness to work for the bill in question.

A primary aim of the task force concept is getting junior members involved in the coalition-building process. That objective has clearly been accomplished. During the 95th Congress, 51.7 percent of the Democratic membership had begun its service in 1973 or later; on the average, 69.4 percent of the members of the 9 task forces was drawn from this junior group. Democrats first elected in 1972 through 1976 accounted for 45.8 percent of the party's members in the 96th Congress and for 60.1 percent of the membership of the first two task forces. Freshmen constituted 15.2 percent of the Democratic membership and 18.5 percent of those serving on the two earliest task forces. The first task force of the 96th Congress was set up only a month after Congress convened, yet even in this case freshmen were included; 12.1 percent of the debt limit task force membership consisted of freshmen. On the budget task force established in late spring, freshmen constituted 25 percent of the membership.

Table 14-4 shows that, during the 95th Congress, slightly over half the Democrats first elected in 1972 or later served on at least one task force. Junior members were also more likely than their senior colleagues to be frequent task force participants.

Table 14-4 Relationship Between Seniority and Frequency of Task Force Membership, 95th Congress

No. of Task Forces Member Has Served On	Senior Members	Junior Members*
0	70.5	49.7
1	16.5	22.1
2	5.8	11.4
3 or more	7.2	16.8
N =	139	149

* First elected in 1972 or later.

Source: Compiled by the author from task force membership lists.

The leadership has been successful in getting a large proportion of Democrats generally, and of junior members specifically, involved in task force efforts. Membership has been drawn fairly proportionately from both northern and southern members and, to some extent, from conservatives as well as liberals. From the leadership's point of view, broad inclusion is important because it contributes to the successful performance of both central leadership functions. A broadly representative task force is more likely to be successful in passing the legislation at issue because it includes members with ties to all segments of the party. Giving a large number and a wide variety of Democrats "a piece of the action" but under the aegis of leadership, it is hoped, will foster norms of intraparty cooperation.

The Task Force in Action

The broad strategy to be pursued on a bill often evolves out of what has happened during committee deliberations. On a bill important enough to warrant a task force effort, the party leadership will meet with key committee leaders to discuss strategy. According to a leadership aide. "The chairman of the task force is centrally involved."

Strategy, of course, varies. A participant explained that on the first budget resolution in 1979, "We had made up a careful package in committee. The strategy on the floor was to sell it as a carefully crafted package and beat back all [noncommittee sponsored] amendments." A package amendment adding funds for various social programs, as well as for two destroyers ordered and then canceled by Iran, was brought to the floor by the committee. According to a senior staff member, "Bringing the additions in the Simon amendment to the floor rather than adding them in committee was a conscious strategy. The purpose was to reinforce the notion of a package."

A similar strategy was used on the energy bill. It too was sold as a carefully crafted and balanced package. On Humphrey-Hawkins, it was decided that intense effort should go into defeating amendments because, in the words of a participant: "All you had to do was have one big bad amendment and the bill was finished. Because too many didn't want to vote for it anyway that, if you gave them a chance to say, well, it's got this bad amendment on it now — no bill. You had to win every one." The social security bill reported out of Ways and Means made participation by government workers mandatory, a provision the leadership considered politically untenable. Consequently, the leadership decided that an amendment deleting the provision would be offered on the floor.

Typically, the first task force meeting begins with a "pep talk" by the Speaker. The Speaker, the majority leader and the majority whip are ex officio members of every task force. Their frequency of attendance at meetings depends upon just how much trouble they believe the bill to be in, personal interest, and the absence of conflicting commitments. The Speaker was reported to have attended every meeting of the budget resolution task force in the spring of 1979. When the leaders cannot themselves attend, they send top aides in their stead.

Usually, the task force will begin with a whip count done by the whip system. Because, in the post-reform House, many amendments are offered, the counting process has become much more complicated. The whip system conducts polls on many bills and, consequently, the questions asked by the whips on a given bill must be restricted in number and fairly simple. According to a leadership aide:

> Task forces are especially helpful if the issues involved are very complicated substantively and you really need to run an information campaign to inform members. And where there are lots of possible permutations and you need to really get a feel for the members — that is, what they'll do under a variety of circumstances.

At the first meeting, strategy will be discussed and the task force members will be assigned a list of Democrats "they will be responsible for working [on] throughout" consideration of the bill. A task force chairman explained the process in a case in which no whip poll had been conducted:

> It was just a question of dividing up the states and assigning those members to some specific person. For instance, in the state of California, we had three people on the task force; from New York, I believe we had two. And from Texas, of course, we had Mr. Wright as well _____. Mr. _____ took Pennsylvania and also West Virginia because he's such a good friend of _____ and _____. So we were able to divide among the members of the task force all the Democrats and so then we had to decide what was the critical issue. We knew we were going to have a series of amendments, but I didn't want at the start to have to give 7 or 10 questions to a person to have to ask and so, in our discussion in the task force, we reduced it finally to two.

When the zone whips conduct a whip poll, they are simply counting. For task force members, counting and persuasion are always combined. Consequently, the process differs only slightly if the task force begins with a whip poll. According to a leadership figure:

> We'll kick around arguments — discuss which ones will be good with which members. Then we'll go through the whip poll and assign names. The list of names will be read, and a member will say, "I'll take that one." Or maybe no one will volunteer and someone will say "_____, why don't you take him?" and _____ will say, "I don't want to." But finally all the names will be assigned.

Or, as a senior staffer expressed it, "There will be candid discussion until they pin down where the trigger is."

Region and seniority are the primary bases for assigning names because, according to the participants questioned, they are the primary bases upon which friendships form. The strong belief that members will be more successful at persuading their contemporaries provides an additional reason for the heavily junior membership on the task forces. As in other vote-mobilization efforts, finding the "trigger" may mean going outside the House. According to a staffer, one of the ways of "motivating" members is via outside groups: "To get _____'s vote, you get Kenny Young [of the AFL-CIO] to call him."

The task force will, when possible, work with friendly interest groups. The chairman or the Steering and Policy Committee staffer working with the task force may meet with interest-group representatives to coordinate strategy. Such meetings on the Humphrey-Hawkins Bill involved about 40 interest groups. Information on voting intentions which such groups have gathered allows the task force to double-check its data on Democrats and to get some reading on Republican votes.

Although the results of whip polls are never given out, some trading of information with the Carter administration did occur and Bill Cable, White House liaison with the House, was sometimes invited to task force meetings. But, according to a leadership aide: "[The White House liaison people] will not usually attend the strategy meetings. They will talk to the Speaker separately. They are usually content to leave the details to the House leadership. They will lobby individual members themselves."

The arguments used by task force members as they attempt to persuade their colleagues vary. On the first budget resolution in 1979, the carefully balanced nature of the committee product and party pride were emphasized. A member explained: "Our strategy was that this was basically a majority party document. This was written by the budget committee majority, and we ought not let the minority party dictate what the majority party is going to pass." On debt-limit votes: "You ridicule the opposition arguments, minimize the electoral impact and appeal to their sense of responsibility."

Arguments about the substance of the matter at issue generally play a major role. A budget task force member commented: "There were some of these amendments that were very appealing considering the Prop. 13 mentality. So we had to really explain to them why we ought not to be succumbing to this kind of thing." The most persuasive argument varies from member to member. A participant remarked:

> It's very individualistic — you go by instinct. Members have different motivations. Some you have to puff up. _____: you persuade him he's being patriotic. Others, you persuade them it's the devious thing to do politically. Some you have to convince it's the liberal thing to do; others, that it's conservative.

When a member cannot be persuaded to support the leadership position across the board, the task force will work for partial support. A participant describes this strategy as used on the first budget resolution in 1979:

> Now, part of that frankly was sold on the basis of, "If you're going to vote no on final passage of the budget resolution, help us out at this point by voting no on Holt-Regula or any other Republican substitute." And that argument seemed to hold with a lot of people, that they were willing to help us out by voting no on any Republican substitute, even if they were going to vote no on the resolution. The case of Texas, as an example. Everyone of them voted no on both Latta and Holt-Regula and that really helped us out immensely.

Several days after the first meeting, the task force will meet again and discuss the results. The names of Democrats now committed to voting with the leadership are marked off, and the remaining names may be reshuffled. The task force may go through this process several times. The top leaders always take some names. One of the purposes of setting up a task force, however, is to minimize the number of members whom the top leaders must persuade. They are busy and their personal appeals for votes are most likely to be effective if not made too frequently. Consequently, an attempt is made to save the top leadership, especially the Speaker, for "the tough ones."

The floor manager of the legislation is always invited to task force meetings. His attendance seems to depend primarily upon time pressures. Asked about the relationship among the party leadership, the floor manager and the task force, a top leadership figure said, "The leadership is the general staff, the floor manager, the battlefield general and the task force, the company commanders." The floor manager and the task force chairmen do seem to work together smoothly. Generally, floor managers seem to appreciate the help the task force provides, and the likely working relationship between the task force chairman and the floor manager is probably an important consideration in the choice of the task force chairman. A task force chairman, discussing his working relationship with the committee chairman said:

> Well, of course, Chairman _____ sat in on every one of these sessions. So he saw whatever strategy we were developing within the task force and could say, "Hey, I don't think you ought to be doing that." Whenever I had a chance before going into the meetings, I'd try to check with him on certain things. I'd say, "_____, this is what we're thinking about doing; what do you think?" He'd say yes or no.

Much of the task force's activity takes place during the period of floor consideration. Because numerous amendments are now proposed to most controversial bills, the floor stage has become much less predictable. It is not possible to count every amendment before the bill reaches the floor, both because of the numbers involved and because some will be offered without prior warning. Amendments can be extremely complicated and their actual effects obscure. Consequently, although vote-mobilization efforts in the days before a bill reaches the floor are essential, holding the coalition together during floor consideration and warding off amendments which could seriously damage the bill are equally crucial.

The task force chairman stays on the floor during the entire period of consideration. Members are, at minimum, expected to be on the floor during each roll call. Standing at the doors, task force members hand out information on the amendment pending. They are expected to keep track of the people assigned to them and work on them during a roll call if necessary. The task force chairman and some of the members "cluster around the monitor and look at the vote state by state. If they find someone has voted wrong, they will chase him down and work on him. Even if he comes to the floor, votes and then runs, he's got to be around somewhere and they will find him." Other task force members are charged with keeping pocket votes — those Democrats who have promised to vote with the leadership if they are needed — from leaving the floor. A female task force member was reported to have kept her assignee from leaving the floor by "practically sitting in his lap. He would have had to be a real boor to have gotten up."

The top leadership will also stay on the floor during important votes. This gives the leaders an opportunity to engage in some last minute persuasion and their presence signals the importance they place upon the vote. When the Speaker stands at the monitor examining how members voted, Democrats know "he's really watching this one. He wants it."

The unpredictability of events at the floor stage puts a premium on being able to respond quickly. When things go wrong, remedial action must often be taken immediately to prevent the supportive coalition from disintegrating. Early in the consideration of the budget resolution in May 1979 an amendment cutting $250 million of targeted fiscal assistance passed. If the decision had been allowed to stand, it would have split the coalition supporting the resolution and made the adoption of other major amendments more likely. A participant explained:

> We were using the argument, "Look, this is a very carefully written budget resolution to make sure we're satisfying the agriculturalists, the urban community, the rural, the East, the West, the whole thing, and don't monkey with this very tenuous balance we have." As soon as that $250 million was taken out, you could hear people saying, "Well, the hell with it; I'm not going to vote for this damn thing."

The committee chairman immediately met with a group of his members and with Budget Committee staff to draft a substitute which would restore $200 million. At this point an organized working group was crucial. The task force chair explained:

> Once we had [the Solarz amendment], we got to work. We recalled everybody and said "All right, here's what's happening, we need the votes on this one. Make sure the people you have as your responsibility vote yes on the Solarz amendment." So, within two days we came right back and got that thing reversed and got the $200 million added in.

Because of the number of amendments offered and the availability of recorded votes, an effective method of providing information to members has become necessary. Members simply will not blindly follow the leadership over and over again, especially when their votes are public. Thus the development of the "bullet" — a mimeographed, one-page summary of an amendment. Developed by the Steering and Policy Committee staffer working with the Humphrey-Hawkins task force, bullets have now become a regular part of the process. For anticipated amendments, the committee staff will prepare bullets prior to floor consideration. On amendments offered without warning, bullets will have to be written and duplicated on the spot. The committee and the Steering and Policy staff work together, often using an Appropriations Committee room close to the House floor.

Bullets are widely believed to be effective. A staffer said:

> On bad amendments, you need something to give the members. You've got to give them a rationale for voting against. Otherwise, you can have the "lurch" effect. If they have nothing and they go in, they'll look at the vote totals and may be stampeded.

He explained that many amendments are very complex:

> There may be only three or four or five people in the House — on our side of the House — who understand what some of these amendments really do, and if they don't have a way to reach the whole Democratic caucus, we're in trouble. On the _____ bill, every time we didn't have one we lost.

A task force chairman explained:

> You know these members are coming in through the door and they have essentially 7 to 2 minutes or even a minute to vote on an amendment. They're running in and asking, "What is it?" and you can't explain a four-page amendment, changing aggregates and everything else and subfunctions. So you say, "This is the Grassley of Iowa amendment, vote no," and hand them the sheet. It points out as succinctly as possible what's in it — that it adds $380 million to the deficit — that it cuts out all programs for babies.

If the bill is on the floor for more than one day — an increasingly frequent occurrence — the task force will meet between sessions. Committee staff will brief the members on amendments expected, arguments to be used will be discussed, voting records to that point will be analyzed. The task force may decide that on a given amendment "20 members are targets and everyone will work on them."

Sometimes the current situation will suggest new tactics. Republicans could not agree upon one substitute to the first budget resolution in 1979; consequently, two alternative plans were introduced and brought to a vote. This allowed the leadership and the task force to persuade those Democrats who believed they had to go on record as favoring budget cuts to vote for one or the other, but not both, and to make sure such members divided their votes between the two alternatives evenly so that both would fail. In fact, 33 Democrats did so vote and neither Republican alternative passed.

In addition to orchestrating persuasion efforts, the task force chairman sometimes provides advice on floor strategy. Whether to finish a bill even though it means staying very late or to pull a bill off the floor after one or two amendments have been lost can make a major difference. On important bills, the floor manager and the leadership make such decisions; but the task force chairman can provide another judgment. According to a staffer:

> On _____, we had a bad problem and the task force chairman insisted that we leave the floor and saved us. We went back and we had a day or a day and a half to regroup and, in this case, it was the presence of the task force that pushed us off the floor. The committee sort of wanted to stay. It was the task force chairman who made the difference in getting off the floor. He said, "Hey, look, I know you'd like to stay and finish the bill. Well, I happen to think that if we stay here another five minutes, we're not going to have a bill to manage any more." It wasn't quite that blunt, but it was along these lines, and that got us off the floor. . . . A task force chairman provides another judgment as well as that of the committee members who are often so close they don't see it too well, whereas the task force chairman, though he's pretty close himself, sometimes senses the mood a little better and can determine a little better whether to quit or stay.

By performing tasks the formal leadership group is too small to carry out alone, the task force does increase the probability of floor success. The task force can explain the provisions of a complicated bill on a member-to-member basis; it can get a detailed and precise count of Democrats' voting intentions and engage in face-to-face persuasion efforts with a large proportion of the Democratic membership. It has the organization and the numbers to respond quickly to the unexpected floor developments.

Evaluation of Task Force Success

One of the leadership's objectives in setting up a task force is passing the legislation in question. According to that criterion, all task force efforts have been successful. Because the bills on which task forces worked were highly controversial, winning was seldom easy and victory not always clear-cut. In several cases, success came after an initial defeat and, in some, compromise at the post-committee stage was necessary. In at least one case, the bill reported by the committee was not at all to the Speaker's liking. Nevertheless, all the legislation on which task forces worked was passed without the addition of crippling amendments at the floor stage. The leaders believe the task force device has proven itself as a coalition-building strategy well suited to the post-reform House.

From the beginning, the Speaker saw the task force strategy as having a benefit beyond that of passing a particular bill. "Give me a frustrated guy," the Speaker says, "and I'll give him a job to do and he becomes a 'Tip O'Neill man' " *(New York Times,* June 4, 1979). Rather than attempting to dampen the high rate of rank-and-file participation — an enterprise almost certainly doomed to failure — the leadership seeks to direct it into productive channels. In the process of participating in leadership-directed efforts, it is hoped that Democratic members, particularly the junior ones, will learn the need for "followership" and for some joint action under the aegis of the party.

Participants believe that task forces have been useful in socializing junior members. Working on a task force gives them an understanding of the problems of the leadership and, in some cases, results in an identification with the leadership. One participant explained:

> It's helped the leadership to get to know the new members and the new members to get to know the leadership. And it's certainly helped the new members who I've spoken to — my personal friends — to understand the need for leadership and followership. I think the guys who have served on task forces know a lot more about the need for a party structure with some loyalty than those who haven't.

According to another participant:

> The task force members, particularly the chairmen, got an awareness of the problems of leadership and a feeling of meaningful participation that paid dividends on later legislation, as they felt some obligation to cooperate with other task forces. Many of the task force members, like _____, became emotionally involved with the leadership.

As the socializing effect became clearer, the task force membership selection process changed. There is now a conscious effort to include Democrats specifically for the effect membership may have on their attitudes towards intraparty cooperation. As one observer put it:

Initially — though not necessarily totally consciously — we chose those people who might be most amenable to working in the same philosophical mold as the man who appointed them, the chairman, and the Speaker, and the leadership as a whole. Though not totally — I mean that's not the only reason you choose somebody. But I think what happened was that we realized after a couple of task forces had gone by that we were doing that to any extent greater than we should, and have since then changed the nature of the invitation process a little bit to try and broaden it and bring in people who we're not that used to working with, so to speak. And there's been some discussion about that, and there is a conscious effort currently being made to broaden it, to reach into places we haven't reached into before. You can't always do it because the places you haven't reached into before may be philosophically totally opposed to your bill. But we try, and we're trying pretty hard.

Increased awareness of the socialization benefit of task force membership seems by the 96th Congress to have led to another form of reaching out in making up task force membership lists. Every one of the five new Democratic members of the Ways and Means Committee was included in the debt-limit task force in the spring of 1979. Of the eight new Budget Committee Democrats, six served on the budget-resolution task force; deep policy disagreements precluded the inclusion of the remaining two. This appears to represent a conscious attempt to draw new committee members into the leadership's orbit, to accustom them to working with the leadership on major bills within their committee's jurisdiction.

The transference of techniques learned working on a task force to other situations is still another benefit. A participant explained:

Members who had previously served on task forces undertook to do on the part of their committee that which previously they had done on task forces. In other words, they got some new tools, they saw that they worked, and now they're carrying them back into their work for their committee. I think that's fantastic. You see members of the committee taking sheets of paper [explaining amendments] to the doors. It seems to be becoming more the way you handle things, a more routine kind of thing and I think that's just great.

Conclusion

At the core of successful leadership is satisfying the expectations of followers. Consequently, appropriate strategies change when members' expectations and other aspects of the environment which bear upon the satisfaction of those expectations change. In a House dominated by powerful committee chairmen, one in which junior members did not expect to play a significant legislative role and even senior members largely restricted their activity to their own committees' legislation, a strategy of inclusion was unnecessary and inappropriate. The post-reform House, in which rules allow and member expectations dictate wide participation, requires such a strategy. The use of task forces increases the probability of passing major legislation on the now highly unpredictable House floor. By satisfying members' expectations of significant participation in the process, it contributes to "keeping peace in the family." The leaders believe that service on task forces, in addition, teaches members the value of cooperative behavior.

As the leaders themselves recognize, their success depends not only upon what they do but also upon forces in the environment outside their control. Their ability to satisfy members' expectations about legislative results depends upon some core consensus within the Democratic party. No member expects the leadership to tailor its legislative priority list to his or her individual preferences; all realize the leadership must be responsive to the diversity of interests within the House Democratic membership and to significant actors outside the chamber. The legislative record as a whole must, however, be reasonably satisfactory to a substantial majority of the party membership. The failure to produce legislation that satisfies members' reelection needs and their policy goals cannot be fully compensated for by internal rewards. If, as now seems possible, the Democratic consensus on core elements of social welfare and economic policy totally disintegrates, the leaders will be caught in a conundrum. To the extent that they are successful at building winning coalitions in response to the demands of some set of members, they may so dissatisfy other members that their very success will be extremely expensive in terms of "keeping peace in the family." Each coalition-building effort may exacerbate intraparty conflicts, discourage cooperative behavior, and consequently, make future coalition-building success less likely. The continued adequacy of the strategy of inclusion and its success at fostering norms of intraparty cooperation, thus, depend upon the reestablishment of some consensus within the Democratic party.

Notes

1. Members from Alabama, Arkansas, Florida, Georgia, Louisiana, Mississippi, North Carolina, South Carolina, Texas and Virginia are classified as southern, all other as northern.
2. *Congressional Quarterly* party unity scores are used (*Weekly Report*, December 16, 1978, pp. 3450-51). Scores have been adjusted so that absences do not affect the scores.
3. The energy bill was referred to five standing committees and to the Ad Hoc Energy Committee. Of the members of the first energy task force, 64.3 percent were from Ways and Means or Commerce, the two committees with major jurisdiction, and 44.4 percent from the Ad Hoc Committee. On the second energy task force, 22 percent were from Ways and Means or Commerce and 26.8 percent from the ad hoc panel.

15. THE MINORITY PARTY AND POLICY-MAKING IN THE HOUSE OF REPRESENTATIVES

Charles O. Jones

Considerable attention has recently been focused on political oppositions in democracies. A recent book examines oppositions in various western countries[1] and a journal called *Government and Opposition* was founded in 1965.[2] The significance of the role of an opposition in democracies does not have to be stressed. It is generally accepted.

What of the role of the opposition in the United States? Robert A. Dahl notes that one must use the plural when speaking of opposition in this country since, "a distinctive, persistent, unified structural opposition scarcely exists in the United States ... it is nearly always impossible to refer precisely to 'the' opposition, for the coalition that opposes the government on one matter may fall apart, or even govern, on another." [3]

While it is true that "the" opposition is not institutionalized as a definite cohesive, persistent, distinctive group in American politics, it is also true that there has usually been an identifiable minority party in Congress. Though it does not always oppose the majority, and cannot be expected to be synonymous with "the" opposition very often, it does persist. Despite handsome invitations to disband — in the form of successive defeats at the polls — a sizeable number of congressmen, senators, and congressional candidates continue to call themselves Republicans and to organize as such in Congress.

This study focuses on the range of strategies, including various forms of opposition, available to the minority party in congressional policy-making. Specific attention will be paid to the Republican party as a minority party in the House of Representatives for two reasons: 1) to limit the scope of the article and 2) because the Republican party is the contemporary minority party. The major

Author's Note: This is a much-revised version of a paper presented at the Annual Meeting of the American Political Science Association, Statler-Hilton Hotel, New York City, September 6-10, 1966. Financial support for this study was provided by the Carnegie Corporation in a grant to the American Political Science Association's Study of Congress, Professor Ralph K. Huitt, Director, and the Institute of Government Research, University of Arizona. I wish to acknowledge the comments and criticisms of Samuel C. Patterson, Randall B. Ripley, John Manley, Conrad Joyner, Jorgen Rasmussen, and Phillip Chapman.

Source: *American Political Science Review* (June 1968): 481-493. Reprinted with permission of the author.

questions to receive attention are: What are the principal policy-making strategies of the minority party? What political conditions determine the range of strategies available to it in any one Congress? The major thesis is that there are various types of minority parties when classified by the range of strategies available to them for participating in policy-making. Some minority parties are extremely weak and ineffectual, others have significant sources of power available to them. The role of the minority party in Congress is not a single, consistent role over time. It varies considerably depending on a number of external and internal conditions.

I. Political Setting for the Minority Party in Congress

There are certain relatively stable factors in the American political setting which are of importance in determining the role of the minority party. Notable among these are, of course, federalism, representation, and the separation of powers — all three of which tend to decentralize the political party structure. While distributing power between a central unit and sub-units, federalism also distributes elective offices throughout the land. Parties exist to fill these offices and therefore organize where elections take place. The representation system is based on the land mass of states for the Senate, population for the House, and a combination of the two for the Electoral College. Separation of powers in and of itself allows for only a minimum of coordination at the national level for the majority party and almost none at all for the minority party. Thus, decentralization and lack of cohesion may be taken as "givens" when analyzing American political parties.

The role of the minority party is also determined by the role of Congress in national policy-making. In general, Congress has the primary function of legitimating one course of action, designed to solve a public problem, over another. The legitimation process is ultimately one of some type of majority rule and therefore policy to be legitimate must be traced to a numerical majority. Thus, if a course of action is to be legitimated in Congress, it is necessary for political leaders to consider the majority-building prerequisite. The output of the legitimation process may be called policy and normally it is the result of compromise. Note that reference is made to a legitimation "process." There is considerably more involved in this process than voting on legislation. The final vote is merely the manifestation of success, or lack of it, in building a majority. By legitimation process is meant all those activities to collect a majority which go on in Congress (and specifically in the House for this study).

This process of legitimation is not simply one of ratification of what the executive proposes. The executive is, indeed, a major source of proposed courses of action but there are many other sources too — interest groups, constituents, state and local public officials, members themselves. The process of building a majority involves considerable bargaining. The results of this process may bear only slight resemblance to any one of the courses of action originally proposed — whether from the executive or elsewhere.

There are a number of strategies which may be employed by the minority party in the majority coalition-building process in Congress — depending on the political conditions at the time. A minority party which is severely restricted by political conditions may only be able to *support* the majority party or offer *inconsequential opposition* to the majority-building efforts of the party in power. A minority party which has a President in the White House will have the opportunity of *participating* in majority coalition-building efforts. A minority party which is favored by political conditions may have a range of strategies available — e.g., *consequential partisan opposition,* employed to defeat majority party efforts; *consequential constructive opposition,* where the minority party counters with its own proposals; *innovation,* where the minority party initiates its own proposals and attempts to build a majority in favor; *cooperation,* where the minority works with the majority on a particular problem; *support,* as mentioned above; or *withdrawal,* where the minority party is divided on an issue and can find no basis for agreement.

What are the political conditions which may determine the range of strategies for the minority party? Conditions both inside and outside Congress may be significant. I have identified four "external conditions" and four "internal conditions" which seem to have important effects.

The general temper of the times is the first external condition to consider. Is there a domestic or international crisis which dominates policy-making? Or is there relative calm? To what extent has there been expressed a national mood for action in Congress and the executive? Since there are no simple, scientific measures of this condition, I will have to rely on fairly crude estimates of the temper of the times. The second external condition is the relative political strength of the minority party outside Congress (see Table 15-1). Is the party strong or weak nationally among the voters? in the states? in the White House? The third external condition is national party unity. Obviously a disunified party will be preoccupied with party matters to the exclusion normally of an active role in congressional policy-making as a party.

A fourth external condition is presidential power. A President with a variety of sources of power would normally limit the range of strategies of the minority party whereas a President with only limited sources of power would normally allow more flexibility.[4]

The first of the internal conditions is procedure in the House. Generally speaking procedure is relatively stable but minor changes occur frequently and major changes have occurred in the House in 1910-1911, 1946-1947, and 1961-1965. Such changes may have an important effect on the minority party. A second internal condition is the size of the margin enjoyed by the majority party over the minority party. A third condition is that of majority leadership and organization, and a fourth is minority party leadership and organization. Of particular interest is the ability, style, and sources of strength of both sets of leaders and the nature of the organization relied on.

II. The Minority Party in Four Congresses

I have selected four congresses to illustrate the various political conditions which can set the range of strategies for the minority party. These four — the 63rd (1913-1914), 73rd (1933-1934), 85th (1957-1958), and 87th (1961-1962)

Table 15-1 Various Combinations for the Two Parties Sharing Dominance of the House, Senate, Presidency, and National Voter Preference, 1900-Present

Combination	Democrats Control	Republicans Control	Occurring In
1	NPI, PR, HO, SE	—	1933-47, 1949-53, 1961-67 (24 yrs)
2	NPI, PR, SE	HO	
3	NPI, PR, HO	SE	
4	NPI, PR	HO, SE	1947-49 (2 yrs)
5	NPI	PR, SE, HO	1953-55 (2 yrs)
6	NPI, SE, HO	PR	1955-61 (6 yrs)
7	NPI, HO	PR, SE	
8	NPI, SE	PR, HO	
9	PR, HO	NPI, SE	
10	PR, SE	NPI, HO	
11	PR	NPI, HO, SE	1919-21 (2 yrs)
12	PR, SE, HO	NPI	1913-19 (6 yrs)
13	SE, HO	NPI, PR	
14	SE	NPI, PR, HO	
15	HO	NPI, PR, SE	1911-13, 1931-33 (4 yrs)
16	—	NPI, PR, SE, HO	1900-11, 1921-31 (20 yrs)

Key: NPI—National Party Identification of Voters (Survey Research Center Concept)
PR—Presidency
HO—House of Representatives
SE—Senate

— represent widely differing situations for the Republicans as a minority party in Congress. The first two (63rd and 73rd) illustrate the minority party in its most restricted role, the third (85th) illustrates one of those ambiguous policy-making situations where the minority party has a President in the White House, and the fourth (87th) is an example of greater flexibility for the minority party.

Restricted Minorities — 63rd and 73rd Congresses. As noted in Table 15-2, the differing political conditions in 1913 and 1933 placed serious limitations on the alternative strategies which could be practically employed by the minority party. Of major importance in 1913 was the disunity of the Republican Party. Though the Republican Party was presumably the majority party in terms of voter preference in the nation,[5] the Democrats won control of both houses of Congress and the White House (combination 12, Table 15-1). The result was that Woodrow Wilson had sources of power not ordinarily available to a minority party President. He could capitalize on the disunity of Republicans and the fact that, though there was not a specific domestic or international crisis which dominated politics, there was a mood of dissatisfaction.[6] Arthur S. Link described it as follows:

> The election of 1912 marked the culmination of more than twenty years of popular revolt against a state of affairs that seemed to guarantee perpetual political and economic control to the privileged few in city, state, and nation. The uprising that came so spectacularly to a head in the first years of the twentieth century — the progressive movement — was the natural consummation of historical processes long in the making.[7]

Such sources of strength are formidable but they could be reduced somewhat by internal political conditions favorable to the minority party. This was not the case in 1913, however. As noted in Table 15-2, the internal conditions also favored Wilson and the Democrats. There had been major procedural changes in the House of Representatives in the two preceding congresses which could also be traced to the divisions in the Republican party. As will be noted below, the reduction of the power of the Speaker had the effect of forcing the Democratic party leadership to develop new techniques for building majorities. They proved themselves adept at doing so — without having to rely on minority party support. Further, the Democrats were blessed with a wide margin in the House in 1913 — 290 to 127. To that date, no party had ever had such a comfortable House margin.

Majority party leadership and organization in the House in the 63rd Congress were both strong and effective. With the diminution of the Speaker's power, and the rejection of collegialism and personalism as leadership styles,[8] it was natural that the House would have to go through a period of democratization. Certainly Speaker Champ Clark could not expect to wield power equal to that of his immediate predecessor, Joseph G. Cannon. At the same time, there were 290 Democrats in the House — a great many of them freshmen — who had to be led, and there was a President in the White House who wanted action. The pattern of leadership and organization that the Democrats developed in the

369

Table 15-2 Political Conditions and Range of Minority Party Strategies in Four Selected Congresses

	External Conditions				Internal Conditions				
Congress	Temper	Majority-Minority Combination[a]	Minority Party Unity	President	Procedure	Margin	Majority Party Leadership	Minority Party Leadership	Type of Minority Party by Range of Strategies
63rd (1913-1914)	No Dominant Crisis Mood for Action	12 (Ambiguous)	Weak	Strong (Wilson)	Major Changes	Large	Strong	Weak	Restricted
73rd (1933-1934)	Dominant Crisis Mood for Action	1 (Unambiguous)	Moderate	Strong (Roosevelt)	No Changes	Large	Weak	Weak	Restricted
85th (1957-1958)	No Dominant Crisis Mood Unclear	6 (Ambiguous)	Moderately Strong	Weak (Eisenhower)	No Changes	Small	Strong	Weak	Participating
87th (1961-1962)	No Dominant Crisis Mood Unclear	1 (Unambiguous)	Strong	Moderate Strength (Kennedy)	Minor Changes	Medium	Weak	Strong	Flexible

[a] See Table 15-1 for explanation of combinations.

House as a response to this situation is one of the most fascinating in the history of the modern Congress.

Speaker Clark was almost perfectly suited to the conditions of the moment. An affable, personable, and beloved member, Clark is quoted as saying in the 61st Congress, "Although I am going to be Speaker next time, I am going to sacrifice the Speaker's power to change the rules." [9] He referred to himself as "Dean of the Faculty." Randall B. Ripley classifies him as a "figurehead" Speaker.[10] Clark's majority leader however, was Oscar W. Underwood — the brilliant Congressman, later Senator, from Alabama. Underwood also served as Chairman of the powerful Committee on Ways and Means and therefore of the Democratic Committee on Committees. He became the principal Democratic leader in the House.

Underwood capitalized on the inevitable period of democratization following Cannon's demise by relying on the caucus as a policy-setting group. Though the evidence on Underwood's techniques is still scanty, it is possible to describe the procedure which developed. Following the introduction of major bills, and their assignment to committees, the Democratic caucus would meet to debate the legislation — sometimes for two weeks. A vote would be taken, making the bill a party measure. Unless they rescued themselves, Democrats were bound to vote for the bill and to vote against all amendments except those supported by the party leaders. The bill would then be brought before the appropriate committee, hearings held if the Democratic leadership so desired, and sent to the House floor for debate.[11] The Republicans played a very minor role in these proceedings, and they often expressed their frustrations. For example, Sereno E. Payne (New York), ranking Republican on the Committee on Ways and Means and former majority leader under Speaker Cannon, made the following statement in the minority report on the Underwood Tariff: "In this statement we shall not attempt to analyze this bill or to criticize it in detail. *Our acquaintance with it is too brief to permit this.*" [12] The minority report on the Federal Reserve Act expressed the same frustrations.

> The undersigned regret that when the Committee on Banking and Currency met finally to consider H. R. 7837 they found the majority members of the committee *so bound by their caucus action that they could not consider amendments* to the bill which, if adopted, would have eliminated its unsound and questionable provisions.
>
> Such changes ... are fundamental and vital. The majority members of the committee refused to favorably consider them on the ground that they involved matters of Democratic party policy settled *by the caucus.*[13]

Even with all of these disadvantages, it is conceivable that the minority party's options could be increased simply due to the strength, imagination, and style of its leaders. Unfortunately for the House Republicans in 1913, they could not expect to reply on this source of power either. They were led principally by old-guard leaders — all of whom had supported Cannon in 1910 during the speakership fight. The minority leader was James R. Mann of Illinois — an interesting, rather enigmatic figure in House politics. He was closely identified with

Cannon and won the minority floor leadership post in 1911 because the old-line Republicans still maintained a majority in the House Republican Party. Mann was apparently precise, humorless, and brilliant in his own way — a sort of "thinking man's H. R. Gross." He seemed to be a transitional figure for the House Republicans — not very well liked among his colleagues and charged with the responsibility of holding the party together until they recaptured control of Congress. It is noteworthy that when the party did gain a majority in the House in 1919 Mann was defeated for the Speakership by Frederick H. Gillett of Massachusetts.

This combination of external and internal political conditions effectively neutralized the House Republican Party. Republicans were limited to *inconsequential opposition*. That is, they opposed the principal aspects of Wilson's program but could do little more than try to have amendments accepted, attempt to have the legislation recommitted, and then opppose final passage. Only if the Democrats were seriously split on some issue could the Republicans expect to play a significant role. These instances were extremely rare.[14]

House Republicans were equally impotent during the 73rd Congress but for different reasons (see Table 15-2). The economic collapse of the nation was the dominant condition and it worked to the advantage of the Democrats. In 1928, the Republican Party had firm control of Congress, the White House, and the nation. In 1932, the Democratic Party was unquestionably the majority party (combination 1 in Table 15-1). The 1932 presidential election is classified as a "realigning election" by the Survey Research Center,[15] since major shifts were occurring in voter preference between the two parties. Indeed, even some congressional Republicans failed to support Hoover in 1932. The resulting effect of these external conditions was to provide President Roosevelt with a virtual "blank check" by the public in the 1932 election. He had more impressive sources of power than almost any President in history.

What of the internal political conditions? Did they act to blunt the thrust of presidential leadership sustained by crisis? Several did in later Roosevelt congresses, but in the 73rd Congress there were few roadblocks. There were no major rules changes, but the existing rules were made to serve the President. Major legislation was sometimes processed in a matter of days. The Democratic margin over Republicans was 198 seats — 313 to 117. This was the largest margin for either party in history, though new records would be set in the 74th (219 seats) and the 75th (244 seats) Congresses.

For the most part, of course, majority party leadership in the 73rd Congress was in the White House. It was probably fortunate for the Democrats that there was strong presidential leadership, the margins were large, and the mood was for action. Neither the Speaker, Henry T. Rainey of Illinois, nor the Majority Leader, Joseph W. Byrns of Tennessee, was a strong leader. Randall B. Ripley classifies Rainey as a figurehead who was conservative in his use of power.[16] He classifies Byrns in the same way when Byrns became Speaker in the 74th Congress. The Democratic Whip for the 73rd Congress was Arthur H. Greenwood of Indiana.[17]

If Democratic party leadership in the House was weak, Republican party leadership was weaker. Gone was the strength of Nicholas Longworth of Ohio and John Q. Tilson of Connecticut, who led the House during the Coolidge and Hoover Administrations. The minority floor leader in the 73rd Congress was Bertrand H. Snell. Snell, a staunchly conservative businessman from upstate New York, was never very effective as leader in his eight years as minority leader (though it must be said that he led under extremely difficult circumstances). The Whip was Harry L. Englebright of California.

Given these circumstances, it is not surprising that the minority party in the 73rd Congress varied between the weak strategies of *support* of the majority coalition-building efforts of the President and *inconsequential opposition*. The emergency was there, the President had won an overwhelming mandate to proceed with whatever proposals he thought necessary, and the Republican party had little if any claim to public support. House Republicans could only add a voice to the consensus which served to legitimize unprecedented legislative actions.

The classic instance of Republican support came very early in the first session. The Emergency Banking bill was introduced, debated, and passed in both houses on March 9, the opening day of the 73rd Congress. Majority Leader Byrns asked for and got a unanimous consent agreement to limit debate to 40 minutes *even though members had not seen the bill*. Minority Leader Snell expressed the hope that Republicans would not object to this procedure.

> The house is burning down, and the President of the United States says this is the way to put out the fire. And to me at this time there is only one answer to this question, and that is to give the President what he demands and says is necessary to meet the situation.[18]

The bill passed by a voice vote.

No other legislation in the first session would go through the House with such ease. But the process by no means returned to normal. House Democrats pushed through legislation at a record pace by relying on closed rules which restricted amendments. A total of ten closed rules were employed during the first session, compared to an average of two such rules a session for other Roosevelt Congresses. As Lewis J. Lapham, in his detailed study of the House Committee on Rules, has noted: "Hardly a single important bill having to do with the economic recovery program of the president was considered by the House except under the restrictions imposed by a so-called gag rule." [19] Despite these tactics — so dreaded and heavily criticized by the minority — sizeable numbers of Republicans supported the legislation.

During the second session of the 73rd Congress, House Republicans were considerably less supportive of Roosevelt's efforts. They assumed the slightly more aggressive strategy of *inconsequential opposition*. For example, with the reciprocal trade bill, they issued a minority report which listed 24 separate reasons why Republicans could not support the bill. House Republicans rarely issued minority reports in the first session. When the bill reached the floor Allen T. Treadway (Massachusetts), ranking Republican on the Committee on Ways and Means, served mild notice that Republicans would offer less support in the future.

... in making critical remarks I wish to say that they are in no way reflections on the personality of the President of the United States. I hold the President in the very highest esteem. I have voted with him as far as I could, consistently with my conscience, in his program of recovery; but I claim that when our stern convictions differ from those of the President of the United States, there is but one course for us to pursue....[20]

Treadway's remarks were very circumspect, however, and, it might be added, of no great concern to the President. Roosevelt had a sizeable and dependable majority without Republican support.

The 63rd and 73rd Congresses represent very unusual minority party situations. In both instances, political conditions were such that the minority party could rely on only a very narrow range of strategies in congressional policy-making. House Republicans in both congresses had an immediate, internal party problem — that of survival as a political party.

Yet there are important differences between these two situations for the minority party. As noted in Table 15-2, the Republicans in 1913 had one potential source of power which was not available in 1933 — they were presumably still the majority party nationally. In 1913, the salient condition determining the restriction on the minority party was disunity. Therefore, it was within the power of the minority party to make the adjustments necessary to correct this condition. If successful, the restrictions on the minority party in Congress could well be temporary. If unsuccessful, the party could well disappear as a major party. Thus, there were important stakes in seeking a rapprochement. Given the characteristics of the American party system this reunion might best be accomplished by less aggressive behavior on both sides. That is, the party might accomplish a partial healing by just "holding on" — insuring that the divisiveness not go further and that those disagreements which did exist not be advertised so broadly. For the most part, this is precisely what happened.

In 1933, however, the Republicans did not have it within their power to produce remedies. Events were out of control, as far as the minority party was concerned. The party had to stand aside and hope that, by some miracle, the situation would change. It did not. Of the two situations, that during the 73rd Congress is clearly the most undesirable from the point of view of the minority party since it signals a long period when the minority party can expect to play only the most limited role in policy-making.

A Participating Minority — 85th Congress. As is noted in Table 15-1, the American electoral system makes possible very ambiguous political situations. One such is illustrated by the 85th Congress. President Dwight D. Eisenhower was reelected by a very large margin in 1956 but the Republican Party was unable to capture control of either house of Congress. Thus, the minority party in Congress was faced with conflicting demands and expectations — enacting the President's program while opposing congressional Democratic leadership.

Since the margins in both the House and Senate were narrow (33 seats in the House, 2 in the Senate), there were three conditions — one external, two internal — which could have resulted in a strong role for the minority party in Congress (see Table 15-2 for a summary of conditions). The first of these, the external condition, would be a President with a number of sources of power other than a majority in Congress. President Eisenhower did have one such source of power — his phenomenal popularity among the public. There were several factors which prevented Eisenhower from turning this advantage into success in policy-making, however. First, there was no all-engaging crisis or general mood for action which would rally all legislators to support the President. Second, it was unlikely that a man of Eisenhower's background would have the necessary skills for majority coalition-building in these circumstances (an asset for him at the polls but not in negotiating for majorities in Congress).[21] Third, it seems that the President did not see the need for legislation in many areas and therefore did not press hard for its enactment. Thus, for the very reasons that he did have personal popularity, it was unlikely that he would try to capitalize on this advantage.

The internal conditions which might have strengthened the minority party would be weak majority party leadership combined with strong minority party leadership. If House Democratic leaders had been inept — unable to control their majority — and House Republican leaders had been exceptional negotiators, it is conceivable that the minority party would have been highly successful in building majorities for a Republican program. Unfortunately for the minority, the reverse was the case during the 85th Congress.

In the House, the Democrats were able to rely on Sam Rayburn as Speaker and John W. McCormack as Majority Leader. Rayburn was serving his 22nd term as a member of the House and his seventh full term as Speaker. Though Rayburn apparently lost some of his characteristic alertness in later Congresses, he led his party with strength in the 85th Congress. Rayburn approached the perfect model of the effective Speaker of the House of Representatives. He knew the rules and how to use them, he maintained contact with all of the various wings of the House Democratic party, and he was very protective of his procedural majority — sensing when he may have gone too far with any member. He also retained a fine sense of compromise, and relied on techniques of leadership which emphasized party unity.

McCormack was serving his 15th full term in the House and his ninth term as the second-ranking leader in his party — seven as Majority Leader, two as Minority Whip. Though generally considered to be more partisan than Rayburn, McCormack had proved himself to be a very durable, and generally well-liked, leader.

Rayburn and McCormack did not rely on either the caucus or a steering committee. They maintained a relatively efficient whip system as a formal system of communication (led by Carl Albert, Oklahoma, in the 85th Congress) but both relied more heavily on informal methods of contact than on the formal whip system. Both leaders avoided calling caucuses to set party policy, fearing the effects of such meetings on party unity.

House Republicans were not so fortunate in getting strong leadership. They were led by Joseph W. Martin, Jr., of Massachusetts. Martin certainly was experienced in leading House Republicans — he had done so since the 76th Congress. As contrasted with his longtime friend, Sam Rayburn, however, Martin was losing control over his party. He had lost contact with many of the younger members and his health was failing. Evidence for this appeared in convincing form in the 86th Congress when Martin was defeated for the minority leadership post by Charles A. Halleck of Indiana.

Like Rayburn, Martin relied on "personalism" as a leadership technique. But he was never as successful as Rayburn. It seemed as though conditions in the Republican Party (e.g., less sectional diversity) favored greater use of party caucus and committee action than for the Democrats. Republicans were generally more unified and could gain publicity from such meetings. Martin, however, continued to rely on a coterie of advisers. Halleck was one of these in earlier times but Martin had grown to distrust him. Leslie C. Arends, Illinois, served as his Whip and while performing adequately, Arends took a narrow view of his function as Whip.

Thus, House Republicans had rather uninspired leadership in the 85th Congress. Martin's greatest source of strength was his friendship with Rayburn. But many young members considered this friendship more harmful to the party than helpful. They wanted to establish a more positive image for the party and were frustrated with the leadership of Martin, Arends, and ranking committee members like Clarence Brown (Ohio). These dissatisfied members were to make many changes in the House Republican Party in ensuing years.[22]

The range of strategies for the House Republican Party in the 85th Congress was almost as restricted as that during the 63rd and 73rd Congresses. House Republicans *participated* in majority coalition-building. The President would be expected to count his own party first in building majorities and rely on House Republican leaders to assist him in getting the necessary Democratic votes to enact his policies. Given the weakness both of the President and the House Republican leaders, however, it is reasonable to distinguish between *weak* and *strong* participation. The former, of course, characterized the House Republican Party in the 85th Congress.

The range of strategies for the minority party could be expected to be somewhat broader if a particular proposal became more identified with the House Democrats. Thus, if the Democrats were successful in altering the president's legislation to a considerable extent, then House Republicans would be free to adopt a number of strategies — oppose the legislation, substitute their own proposal, support the Democratic version, etc. Further, if the President compromised with the Democrats without House Republican concurrence, or despite their objections, the range of strategies would be increased. It is obvious that majority coalition building under these conditions requires considerable finesse — particularly if the issue is significant and controversial. The policy-making result in the 85th Congress was often confusion, ambiguity, and stalemate.

There were instances during the 85th Congress when the two parties worked together to pass legislation — with the Republicans forming the principal basis of support. For example, the Civil Rights Act of 1957 was characterized by bipartisanship at every stage of the process. On the other hand, there were cases when a presidential proposal divided House Republicans. Efforts to unify Republicans risked the loss of needed Democratic support. Efforts to gain Democratic support further divided Republicans. The President had a mixed record on such issues. On reciprocal trade and national defense education, he and his party leaders were able to build a coalition sufficiently large for passage. On federal aid to education, he was not only unsuccessful in doing so, but apparently had some doubts about the bill himself.[23] And who can know how many proposals were never even made due to the ambiguity of the congressional situation? The president himself was discouraged following the first session: "I am tremendously disappointed that so many of these bills have not been acted on, and in some cases, not even have held hearings."[24] The editors of the *Congressional Quarterly* summarized the second session: "Adjournment of the 85th Congress . . . brought to a close a second session as remarkable for what it didn't do as for what it did do."[25]

Quite clearly, the external and internal conditions which existed in the 85th Congress resulted in a most confusing policy-making situation. For the most part the House Republican party was limited to a participating strategy in majority coalition-building. Thus, as with the 63rd and 73rd Congresses, the minority party had a restricted range of strategies available. As distinct from those two Congresses, however, the minority party was considerably more involved in congressional policy-making during the 85th Congress.

A Flexible Minority — 87th Congress. The combination of conditions which characterized the 87th Congress provided a greater range of strategies for the minority party than the other three congresses examined here. President Kennedy's view of the presidency was in the tradition of Wilson and Roosevelt, but he did not have their sources of strength. There was no all-pervasive crisis to dominate national politics in 1960, Kennedy's margin over Nixon was extremely narrow, congressional Republicans had increased their numbers in both houses over 1958, Republicans were generally unified, and Democrats were plagued with a measure of disunity (see Table 15-2 for summary of all conditions). Kennedy's greatest sources of power seemed to be his energy in producing new ideas; and renovating old ideas, for solving public problems, and the fact that so little had been accomplished in the 86th Congress. In Neustadt's terms, he was able most to rely on "the expectations of those other men regarding his ability and will to use the various advantages that they think he has."[26] President Kennedy took a very broad view of the presidency:

> Whatever the political affiliation of our next President, whatever his views may be on all the issues and problems that rush in upon us, he must above all be the Chief Executive in every sense of the word. *He must be prepared to exercise the fullest powers of his office — all that are specified and some that are not.*[27]

With the exception of a procedural change in the House, internal conditions also tended to favor the minority party. As noted above, for the first time since 1952, Republicans increased their numbers in the House of Representatives. The Democrats still had a commanding majority — 263 to 174 — but with probable Democratic disunity on some measures, the Republicans could expect some success in building negative majorities so as to defeat the President's proposals. The President was successful in effecting a procedural change of some significance. The House Committee on Rules had become an anti-administration device and could be expected to cause considerable procedural difficulty for the President's program. In a major power struggle between Chairman Howard W. Smith and Speaker Rayburn, Rayburn won (with the critical support of 22 Republicans) and the Committee on Rules was enlarged by three members. Though enlargement did not result in the Committee's loss of power and independence, it did represent a major defeat for those who had relied on it to curb the majority and merely opened the door to other, more drastic reforms.[28]

The House party leadership situation in the 87th Congress was almost the reverse of that during the 85th Congress. The Republicans were much stronger, the Democrats much weaker. Rayburn, McCormack and Albert continued to lead the Democrats but the long-time Speaker was apparently losing his touch. As one senior Democrat put it:

> Rayburn died at a propitious time. During the last three to five years, things were getting out from under his control. And during the last two years people really had no idea, but it was distressing to sit there with his group of about 15, and see him trying to grapple with bills like the foreign aid bill when he had lost his touch.[29]

McCormack was elected Speaker after Rayburn died in November, 1961.

The Republicans changed leadership in 1959. Joe Martin was in poor health and had grown away from many of the party's younger members. The 1958 election, in which House Republicans lost 47 seats, served as a catalyst for change. The new minority leader, Charles A. Halleck of Indiana, was less a friend of Rayburn and was considered more partisan than Martin had been. Though he was not the first choice of many House Republicans who had pressured for a change in leadership, they generally considered him superior to Martin.[30] As it turned out, he was to serve as interim leader only — until the insurgent could muster enough support to get a more preferred candidate elected.[31] At the time that Halleck was elected. House Republicans also reorganized their party. The most significant change was to separate the floor leadership and Policy Committee chairmanship posts. This change was made at the insistence of the insurgents. Though the reorganized Policy Committee by no means satisfied those House Republicans who desired more vigorous and imaginative policy leadership, it did give them somewhat more access to leadership decision-making and served to unify the party.

The first point to establish in analyzing policy-making in the 87th Congress is that a minority party with several sources of power is "consequential" in policy-making. Thus, what the House Republicans did during the 87th Congress, the strategy they adopted on a particular piece of legislation, was often important to the outcome. Further, the very fact that they could mount consequential opposition became important in majority coalition building. Put another way, to the extent that the minority party has flexibility in choosing strategies, the majority party's role in policy-making is limited.

In the 87th Congress, House Republicans had a number of options at different stages of the legislative process. They could simply oppose that which was offered by the majority party (partisan opposition), they could counter with their own proposals (constructive opposition), they could support proposals (support), they could cooperate in developing policy (cooperation), they could initiate proposals of their own (innovation),[32] or they could simply not take a party position (withdrawal). As would be expected, a consequential minority potentially can be involved in policy-making during all stages of the legislative process — and various options may be available at each stage. It must be recognized, however, that there are separate minority party leaders — usually the ranking minority members of the committee or subcommittee — during the early stages of legislation. They may or may not consult the House minority leadership in developing strategies. Thus, it is conceivable that the minority party, through its various leaders, may actually employ different strategies at different stages.[33] By their very nature, one would expect that the cooperative and innovative strategies would be employed during the early stages of the legislative process (notably subcommittee and early committee action); partisan and constructive opposition, withdrawal, and support, during the later stages (final committee action and floor action).

It is not possible in this article to provide illustrations of all of the various combinations mentioned above. Only a few examples of the range of possibilities can be offered. There were many bills in the 87th Congress which illustrated *partisan opposition* by the minority party. In some cases, unified partisan opposition found enough support among Democrats to defeat the legislation. Thus, the federal aid to education bill in 1961, the attempt to establish a Department of Housing and Urban Affairs in 1962, and the first farm bill in 1962, all were defeated by the combination of a cohesive minority and defecting Democrats. The total House Republican vote on these three bills was 20 in favor and 480 against (an overall index of cohesion of 92).[34]

In other cases, House Republicans offered *constructive opposition* on the House floor following unsuccessful efforts in committee to have their proposals adopted.[35] That is, efforts were made on the floor to amend the legislation and/or recommit it with instructions to accept Republican changes. One such effort — on the Area Redevelopment Act of 1961 — was inconsequential. Many House Republicans defected to vote against recommital and for the bill. Other efforts came close to victory. The recommital motion on the Omnibus Housing Act was defeated 215 to 197 and on the Tax Reform Act the recommital motion was defeated 225 to 190. House Republicans were actually successful in substituting their pared-down version of a minimum wage bill on the House floor in 1961 — an important defeat for the Kennedy Administration. The President recovered, however, by a victory in the Senate for his bill. The Conference Committee adopted the Senate bill and their report was approved by the House only because 33 Republicans supported the President.

There were many other patterns of strategy during the 87th Congress. On the important Trade Expansion Act of 1962, there was considerable Republican *cooperation* and *support* during the formative stages of the legislation in the Committee on Ways and Means. The legislation split the House Republican Party, however, and many conservative Republicans opposed the bill. Due to this division, no Republican position was adopted. The minority party "withdrew" on this legislation. The House Republican Policy Committee took no position — allowing members to vote as they wished. The results showed 80 House Republicans in favor, 90 opposed.[36]

The Communications Satellite Act of 1962 is an example of *cooperation* in the formative stages followed by *support* on the House floor. The Manpower Development and Training Act of 1962 is an example of *innovation* followed by *support* on the House floor. The Subcommittee on Special Projects of the House Republican Policy Committee had conducted a general study of employment in the United States. One section of the study dealt with manpower retraining. Many of the recommendations contained in this study eventually found their way into the Manpower Development and Training Act.[37]

There are many other examples which could be given — in this Congress and in the first session of the 88th Congress (where, prior to the assassination, the minority party also had a rather wide range of strategies).[38] The point has been established, however. Conditions were such that the minority party had a range of strategies available in the process of majority coalition-building in the House.

III. Summary and Questions

The principal thesis of this article has been that the minority party's role in the process of majority coalition-building in the House of Representatives is by no means a consistent role over time. External conditions (temper of the times, minority party strength, minority party unity, and presidential power) and internal conditions (procedure, the margin, majority party leadership and organization, and minority party leadership and organization) determine the range of strategies available to the minority in congressional policy-making. As illustrated by four congresses, the range of strategies varies from the limited number available in the most restrictive minority party situations to the large number available in the flexible minority party situations. A number of these strategies are identified and discussed.

There are several important questions raised by this research which require separate analysis. For example, what are the functional consequences for policy formulation and policy administration of these various types of minority parties? It can be hypothesized that if the minority party has available a wide range of strategies, then both policy formulators and policy administrators will take into account minority party interests and views when performing their respective tasks. A consequential minority party may have a definite effect on the policy-making process. If an issue divides the majority, policy formulators may have to court minority party votes; the minority may be developing alternative proposals which become attractive to those affected by a policy problem and thus these proposals may be taken over by the majority party; minority victories in defeating the President may force executive policy formulators to rethink a proposal; minority party research into administration of policy may result in new legislation; and the general expectation that the minority party will oppose with strength and has certain rights, which are protected, to criticize presidential proposals, may induce caution, precision, and careful consideration in policy formulation and administration.

A second major question relates to minority party goal achievement. Do individual strategies in congressional policy-making contribute to the realization of the principal minority party goal of majority party status? If the minority party has a wide range of strategies available, does that result in victory at the polls? On the surface, it appears that the data confirm what every student of Congress knows — electoral success is related to a wide variety of factors, of which the range of policy-making strategies available is relatively minor.[39] In this century the Republicans as a flexible minority have scored impressive gains in the next election (1942, 1946, 1952), scored only slight gains (1962), and lost ground (1944). The greatest victories for Republicans in this century, in terms of net gain of seats, have followed congresses in which the minority party was severely restricted (1914, 1938, and, to a lesser extent, 1966). Republicans as a participating minority in the House have never gained in the next election (1912, 1956, 1958).

If electoral success does not follow from a more active role for the minority party in majority coalition building, a rather anomalous situation results. Minority party leaders are generally expected to rely on strategies which presumably will be rational in terms of the overall party goal of majority party status. Yet the impact of their actions on whether the minority party in fact becomes the majority party may be of very little consequence.

A third major question asks: What of the other combinations of variables not discussed here? Are there other types of minority parties when classified by the strategies available? A cursory examination of the congresses in this century suggests that the categories identified here are generally serviceable. But, as was indicated in the discussion of the differences between the 63rd and 73rd Congresses, a great many refinements can and should be made. Thus, for example, some restricted minorities have little immediate prospect of a greater range of strategies. Clearly, there are degrees of restrictedness and flexibility. Further, it is perfectly conceivable that a participating minority may have a strong, rather than a weak, President in the White House. And what of those rare instances when both parties are in the minority in Congress — one in each house? The two congresses of this type in this century, the 62nd and 72nd, represent highly abnormal policy-making situations wherein the majority party nationally was in the process of being deposed.

This research suggests many other questions as well. Are there differences between the minority parties of the House and Senate in any one Congress? Preliminary analysis indicates that there are. Does the analysis provided here apply to the Democratic party as a minority party? Does it apply to a large number of congresses? What happens to a minority party which fails over a long period of time to achieve majority party status? To what extent are goals of individual members functional or dysfunctional for achieving the party's goal? To what extent is "party" important at all in the formative stages of legislation? These and other important questions must be answered if we are to understand the role of political parties.

Notes

1. Robert A. Dahl (ed.), *Political Oppositions in Western Democracies* (New Haven, Conn.: Yale University Press, 1966).
2. The first issue of *Government and Opposition* was published in November 1965.
3. In Dahl, *op. cit.*, p. 34.
4. I rely to a great extent on Richard E. Neustadt's analysis of presidential power contained in *Presidential Power: The Politics of Leadership* (New York: John Wiley, 1960).
5. Of course, there were no voting behavior surveys for this period. Based on election returns, I am assuming that the Republican Party was the majority party in terms of voter party identification.
6. Woodrow Wilson was not the kind of man to ignore the opportunity. He had expressed himself on the need for a stronger executive in his book, *Congressional Government* (New York: Meridian Books, 1956, first published in 1885). To him, the president had merely been a branch of the legislature (see p. 173).
7. Arthur S. Link, *Woodrow Wilson and the Progressive Era* (New York: Harper, 1954), p. 1.
8. These are terms used by Randall B. Ripley in *Party Leaders in the House of Representatives* (Washington, D.C.: The Brookings Institution, 1967).
9. Quoted in Chang-wei Chiu, *The Speaker of the House of Representatives Since 1896* (New York: Columbia University Press, 1928), p. 303.
10. Ripley, *op. cit.*, Ch. 2. The other categories of leadership style relied on by Ripley are "collegial" and "personal."
11. Various sources may be relied on for a more complete description of this procedure. See Chiu *op. cit.*; George R. Brown, *The Leadership of Congress* (Indianapolis: Bobbs Merrill, 1922); Paul D. Hasbrouck, *Party Government in the House of Representatives* (New York: Macmillan, 1927); Arthur S. Link, *Wilson: The New Freedom* (Princeton: Princeton University Press, 1956); Wilder H. Haines, "The Congressional Caucus of Today," *American Political Science Review*, 9 (November 1915), 696-706.
12. U.S. Congress, House, Committee on Ways and Means, House Report No. 5, 63rd Cong., 1st sess., 1913, p. lv (emphasis added).
13. U.S. Congress, House, Committee on Banking and Currency, House Report No. 69, 63rd Cong., 1st Sess., 1913, p. 133 (emphasis added). It is not suggested that all legislation passed without incident in the House. For example, the Tariff bill and Federal Reserve bill both were controversial within the Democratic Party. Once the principal issues were resolved in the party, and between Democratic congressional leaders and President Wilson, however, major bills passed the House by large margins.
14. One such instance was the legislation to repeal the exemption to American coastwide shipping under the Panama Canal Act of 1912. Speaker Clark and Majority Leader Underwood opposed President Wilson on repeal but, with some Republican support,

Wilson was able to build a majority without their endorsement. See Link, *Wilson: The New Freedom;* and James M. Leake, "Four Years of Congress," *American Political Science Review,* 11 (May, 1917), 252-283.

15. Angus Campbell, et al., *The American Voter* (New York: John Wiley, 1960), Ch. 19: and Philip Converse, et al., "Stability and Change in 1960: A Reinstating Election," *American Political Science Review,* 55 (June 1961), 269-280. See also. V. O. Key, Jr., "A Theory of Critical Elections," *Journal of Politics,* 17 (February, 1955), 3-18.
16. Ripley, *op. cit.,* Ch. 2.
17. The caucus apparently proved useful in canvassing opinion and organizing the great numbers of new Democrats. See E. Pendleton Herring, "First Session of the 73rd Congress," this Review, 28 (February 1934), 65-83. The Democratic caucus minutes for this period are available in the Library of Congress.
18. *Congressional Record,* 73rd Cong., 1st sess., March 9, 1933, p. 76.
19. Lewis J. Lapham, *Party Leadership and the House Committee on Rules* (unpublished Ph.D. dissertation, Harvard University, 1954), p. 52.
20. *Congressional Record,* 73rd Cong., 2nd sess., March 23, 1934, p. 5262.
21. See Neustadt, *op. cit.,* pp. 163-164.
22. For a discussion of the frustrations of House Republicans under Martin's leadership, see Charles O. Jones, *Party and Policy-Making; The House Republican Policy Committee* (New Brunswick, N.J.: Rutgers University Press, 1964), Ch. 2.
23. See Neustadt, *op. cit.,* p. 75.
24. Quoted in *Congressional Quarterly Almanac,* Vol. 13, 1957, p. 87.
25. *Congressional Quarterly Almanac,* Vol. 14, 1958, p. 57.
26. Neustadt, *op. cit.,* p. 179.
27. Quoted in the *New York Times,* January 15, 1960, p. 16 (emphasis added).
28. There are a number of excellent studies of this struggle. See Robert L. Peabody and Nelson W. Polsby (eds.), *New Perspectives on the House of Representatives* (Chicago: Rand-McNally, 1963), Chs. VI and VII; William R. MacKaye, *A New Coalition Takes Control: The House Rules Committee Fight of 1961* (New York: McGraw-Hill, 1963); Neil MacNeil, *Forge of Democracy: The House of Representatives* (New York: McKay, 1963); James A. Robinson, *The House Rules Committee* (Indianapolis: Bobbs-Merrill, 1963). See also my "Joseph G. Cannon and Howard W. Smith — An Essay on the Limits of Leadership in the House of Representatives," *Journal of Politics,* 30 (August, 1968). It should be noted that further changes were made in 1965 to reduce the power of the Committee.
29. Personal interview with a senior House Democrat, June, 1963.
30. For details, see Jones, *op. cit.,* pp. 27-42.
31. See Robert L. Peabody, *The Ford-Halleck Minority Leadership Contest, 1965* (New York: McGraw-Hill, 1966).
32. Theodore Lowi argues that innovation is a principal function of the minority party in Congress. See "Toward Functionalism in Political Science: The Case of Innovation in Party Systems," *American Political Science Review,* 57 (September, 1963), 570-583.
33. This is always true of the minority party; but in more restriced situations, the party's options are limited throughout the legislative process. It also should be pointed out that there is considerable legislative and representative behavior by minority party congressmen which is simply not attributable to party membership.
34. Relying on Stuart Rice's index of cohesion: *Quantitative Methods in Politics* (New York: Knopf, 1928).
35. It should be noted that "constructive" means that the Republicans were offering an alternative. That alternative may well have been "destructive" from the point of view of the President.

36. For details on the Republican dilemma on this legislation, see Jones, *op. cit.*, pp. 126-134.
37. *Ibid.*, pp. 65-66.
38. For evidence on the 89th Congress, see Robert L. Peabody, "House Republican Leadership: Change and Consolidation in a Minority Party," unpublished paper delivered at the 1966 Annual Meeting of the American Political Science Association, Statler-Hilton Hotel, New York City, September 6-10.
39. For a general discussion of the opposition party in governmental decision-making, see Anthony Downs, *An Economic Theory of Democracy* (New York: Harper and Row, 1957), especially Chapter 4.

V

DETERMINANTS OF
FLOOR VOTING

D uring a single Congress, members take about about 1,000 recorded votes. The number of roll calls has been growing rapidly over the last few years. More than 1,500 votes were taken in the House of Representatives in the 95th Congress (1977-78), establishing a postwar record. In 1983 the total for both chambers was 869.

Major legislation usually requires several recorded votes, including those on procedure, amendments, recommital (returning the legislation to the originating committee), and final passage. It is important to note that the final vote may not be the most critical one; moreover, many of the most important decisions on a bill are made in committee before the legislation reaches the floor. And once out of committee, amendments to the bill may alter its thrust considerably.

The value of roll-call votes is that they provide a public record of the voting behavior of representatives and senators. The fact that few controversial or major measures escape a recorded vote means that legislators must make known their positions on what often are highly political issues. Because members usually feel obliged to explain their votes, even when no explanation is asked for (Fenno, 1978), and because those explanations frequently gain media attention, roll-call votes provide considerable data for understanding the forces that influence these "public" decisions. The articles included in this section describe these forces and offer various models or theories to explain Senate and House voting decisions.

Party Influence

The dominant influence on roll-call voting has been a partisan one; Democrats normally are identified with liberal positions, while Republicans are associated with conservative causes. Parties can affect roll-call decisions in a variety of ways. Congressional leaders may make partisanship a major issue in their attempts to mobilize colleagues to support or oppose a measure, or presidents may appeal to party loyalty to rally congressional support. Furthermore, because Democrats and Republicans tend to represent different kinds of constituencies, voting the party line also may satisfy constituent opinion. Finally, members follow the voting cues of colleagues with which they agree, usually fellow partisans. Thus, the influence of party encompasses leadership persuasion,

387

presidential appeals, constituency sentiment, and/or advice from like-minded colleagues.

Despite the importance of party in the voting decisions of representatives and senators, strict party-line voting has been on the decline in the United States. There is no obvious reason for this trend, but it is clear that members who represent constituencies atypical of their political party are the most likely to defect.

Regional Differences

Region also plays a major role in determining congressional voting patterns. Regional factions exist within both parties: Southern Democrats and Eastern Republicans, representing constituencies that are distinct from the national parties, vote as frequently with the opposition as they do with their own party. The decline in Democratic party unity in the Senate is almost entirely due to increased defections among southern senators, and the party loyalty of House Democrats has dropped more precipitously among southerners than among other Democrats. Civil rights is an obvious area for North-South disagreements among Democrats, but the split has increasingly come to include other issues as well.

Compared to the Democrats' divisions, the geographic lines that separate Republicans are not nearly as clear: the more liberal wing of the Republican party tends to represent northeastern and midwestern states and districts, while the party's conservative segment normally is elected from southern and western states. The decline in Republican cohesion in the Senate is largely a result of defections by Eastern Republicans, while the greatest number of House defections occurs among Eastern and Midwestern Republicans. Like the North-South split among Democrats, divisions within the Republican party have spread to more and more issues.

The impact of these factional divisions is particularly apparent in the congressional phenomenon known as the conservative coalition (Brady and Bullock, 1977). The coalition forms when Southern Democrats cross party lines to form an alliance with a majority of Republicans. While it is normally assumed that the coalition emerged in the 1930s as a negative reaction to President Franklin Roosevelt's New Deal programs, Mack Shelley suggests that:

> . . . the data show that the conservative coalition appeared as a major force in congressional decision-making, as measured in terms of relative frequency of roll call vote appearance, during the period of imposition of government social and economic controls in the Second World War and extending through the "decompression" from such controls in the mid-1940s (Shelley, 1978, p. 14).

Both the range of issues on which the coalition forms and the frequency with which the alliance emerges have changed over time. While party-line voting has declined, the percentage of votes on which the conservative coalition appears has increased.

It should be pointed out that the conservative coalition has no formal leadership, staff, or structure. Nevertheless, informal leaders and groups have emerged, among them the cadre of Southern Democrats labeled the Boll Weevils.

Perhaps most important, coalition members have become increasingly aware that they can have a greater impact on legislation by joining forces than by operating as separate factions.

When region is added to the influence of party, the ability to predict the roll-call decisions of senators and representatives is greatly enhanced. Herbert Weisberg (1978) has demonstrated that party and regional divisions among Democrats account for about 85 percent of all of the individual votes cast in the House each Congress between 1957 and 1974.

Presidential Influence

Presidents have several advantages in the influence they wield over senators and representatives. As leader of his party, the president is able to appeal to partisan loyalties to support his policies. On the other hand, when the president sheds his partisan cloak, members of the opposition often can be lured away from their normal partisan predispositions. The legislative success of presidents can be explained by two factors: presidential support levels in both parties and the ratio of Democrats to Republicans in the Senate and House. Party ratios determine the cushion that party leaders of the majority have to work with. The larger the cushion, the greater the number of defections that can be tolerated without losing or disrupting the prevailing majority coalition. Moreover, most presidents are more successful in gaining their party's support on foreign policy than on domestic issues. A study by Aage Clausen (1973) has demonstrated that Democrats more frequently supported the president's foreign, as opposed to domestic, policies under Democratic presidents John F. Kennedy and Lyndon B. Johnson, while Republicans were less supportive of the foreign policies of Kennedy and Johnson than they had been of Eisenhower's foreign policies. Clausen argued that presidents have a greater impact on foreign policy votes because they are better able to sway members of their own party on international matters. On domestic issues, legislators are more likely to adhere tenaciously to established positions of particular interest to their constituencies; while they support the president when his domestic policy coincides with their own interests, legislators are unlikely to shift positions in response to appeals from the president.

In spite of the considerable advantages of the office, presidents never can command the complete support of members of their own party, even in the area of foreign policy. Consequently, they often have found it necessary to cross the aisle to gain the opposition's votes. As with their own party, presidents normally can expect greater support in foreign affairs from the opposition than they might receive on other issues. The authority and prestige of presidents in foreign affairs as well as the continuity of foreign policies from one administration to the next contribute to presidential effectiveness in swaying sentiments within both parties.

Impact of Constituency

The division between Northern and Southern Democrats demonstrates that senators and representatives are influenced by the kinds of constituencies they represent. In fact, constituency characteristics help to explain some of the North-

389

South conflict among congressional Democrats: Southern Democrats represent more rural constituencies than Northern Democrats who are heavily clustered in urban districts. At the very least, these constituency differences exacerbate other ideological and issue splits between the Northern and the Southern wings of the Democratic party. The same is true of Republican party divisions. Republican representatives from lower income, urban areas are less likely to support the party majority than are their colleagues from high income, suburban districts, or rural constituencies.

Three constituency characteristics in particular appear to influence congressional voting and partisanship: the heterogeneity of districts, the similarity between constituency characteristics and party coalitions, and the electoral safety of congressional districts and states.

If a district is relatively homogeneous with respect to the interests and attitudes of its constituents, legislators are less apt to be cross-pressured by conflicting obligations. Furthermore, they can be expected to have a clearer perception of district or state opinion under these circumstances. If, on the other hand, the district or state is composed of mixtures of races, ethnic groups, cities and towns, the heterogeneous nature of constituent demands and interests places the legislator in a precarious position. He or she recognizes that taking one side of an issue is likely to alienate other segments of his or her constituency. Such conditions may lead to partisan defections.

The extent to which the socioeconomic characteristics of a member's district or state match those of the national party also influences his or her voting behavior. Representatives and senators from areas that are typical of those represented by a majority of party members should have little reason to defect from party positions to satisfy their constituents' wishes; constituent and partisan pressures coincide. On the other hand, members from districts and states that are less typical of those represented in the party are more likely to be subjected to the crosscurrents of party and constituent pressure.

There is a simple explanation for expecting a positive relationship between district electoral safety and partisan voting. Legislators who represent marginal districts must be particularly sensitive to constituent opinion and therefore are more prone to defect from the party majority on issues where party and constituency positions conflict. Despite the simplicity of this explanation, there is little evidence of a relationship between electoral safety and partisan voting (Fiorina, 1973).

The influence of constituency on a member's voting record varies according to the issue and its relevance to his or her district or state. If constituents have little interest in, or awareness of, a political issue, legislators may have greater freedom in the way they cast their votes. Senators and representatives can exercise the greatest latitude on issues that are complex and ambiguous; if constituents lack understanding of a subject, they will be less capable of exerting pressure on a member. Issues that have no immediate consequence for the district also allow a member more discretion in voting. Finally, less "visible" or controversial issues also allow representatives and senators more latitude in making legislative decisions.

Voting Cues

There is evidence that some members of Congress rely upon "cues" from others in deciding how to vote (Kingdon, 1973). Cues are taken from those considered particularly knowledgeable about an issue, and especially from those who the legislator feels share his or her views. Donald R. Matthews and James A. Stimson describe the process of cuetaking in the following manner:

> When a member is confronted with the necessity of casting a roll-call vote on a complex issue about which he knows very litle, he searches for cues provided by trusted colleagues who — because of their formal position in the legislature or policy specialization — have more information than he does and with whom he would probably agree if he had the time and information to make an independent decision (Matthews and Stimson, 1975, p. 45).

According to Matthews and Stimson, the cue-taking process follows several stages, as intermediaries pass on advice and suggestions from those who initially provide information and cues, such as leaders of the committees and the parties. Other sources of initial voting cues include presidents, legislative organizations like the Democratic Study Group, subcommittee leaders, and members of state delegations. Cue-givers become persistent sources of advice for many members, regardless of the issue. Committees, of course, cannot function as persistent sources of cues because expertise is likely to vary from committee to committee depending on the issue involved. Informal groups and state delegations, however, can serve as reliable sources of information and guidance on a wide variety of issues.

Policy Dimensions

Aage Clausen (1973) suggests that in order to reduce the time and energy required to make a decision, members respond to issues on the basis of broad policy categories. According to Clausen, the decision rules are quite simple, involving little more than:

> ... (1) sorting specific policy proposals into a limited number of general policy content categories and ... (2) establishing a policy position for each general category of policy content, one that can be used to make decisions on each of the specific proposals assigned to that category. (Clausen, 1973, p. 14)

Clausen goes on to suggest:

> If the legislator's level of support for the policy concept is exceeded by the legislation, he will *reject* it, by either working against it or voting it down. The congressman will *accept* the legislation if the level of support granted by the legislation is equal to, or less than, his ideal level, *providing* that the only perceived alternative is weaker, or no legislation at all; in other words, half a loaf is better than none (Clausen, 1973, p. 17).

Clausen initially described five policy areas that were characterized by stable and consistent voting patterns over time: (1) government management, including fiscal and economic policy, tax, interest rates, regulation of economic and business enterprises, and private versus public development of natural resources; (2) social welfare, including public housing, labor regulation and education; (3) agricultural assistance, such as farm subsidies and production controls; (4) civil liberties and rights; and (5) international involvement.

A more recent analysis of congressional policy categories by Clausen and Carl E. Van Horn added two more dimensions, one involving agricultural subsidies and the other national security commitments. The agricultural subsidy dimension involves efforts to reduce the size of the subsidies paid to individual producers, in contrast to the previously cited agricultural assistance dimension, which deals with the general level of governmental subsidy and not with payments to individual farmers. The reorientation of defense commitments is a response to a number of factors, including "the appropriateness of U.S. commitments abroad . . .; the size and scope of the defense budget; and the responsibilities of Congress and the President in the making of foreign policy" (Clausen and Van Horn, 1977, p. 654). More generally, this dimension deals with such issues as the extent to which the United States should develop its military strength and the degree to which America should support its allies without giving consideration to the internal politics of the country or its attitudes toward political and social change.

These influences — parties, regions, presidents, constituencies, voting cues, and policy dimensions — largely account for the variation in members' voting behavior. The articles included in this section suggest models that incorporate and interrelate these factors in explaining why members vote as they do.

John Kingdon (1977) proposes a model that integrates a number of theoretical postulates. He uses the notions of cue-taking (Matthews and Stimson, 1975), policy dimensions (Clausen, 1973), predispositions and communications networks (Cherryholmes and Shapiro, 1969), consensus (Kingdon, 1973), past behavior (Wildavsky, 1964), and legislative goals (Mayhew, 1974; Fenno, 1973) to create a model of the voting process. The underlying premise of Kingdon's model is that a legislator searches for some sort of agreement among those actors (or influences) that predispose him or her to vote a certain way. In the absence of such agreement, legislators follow additional decision rules:

> Such a process model pictures the legislator as beginning with a very simple decision rule. If that rule can be applied, he does so, and is done with that decision on that particular vote or bill. If he cannot apply that rule, he proceeds to one which is somewhat more complex, which is applied if it can be. Previous steps are seen as controlling subsequent steps in the model, in the sense that if the early decision rule suffices, the congressman uses it and need not proceed further (Kingdon, 1977, pp. 570-571).

For example, if there is conflict among the actors who have influence over a member's voting decisions, the legislator then proceeds to consider his or her own legislative goals. If there is some conflict among these goals, the legislator turns to decision rules that help him or her sort out those conflicts. Kingdon's model correctly predicts 92 percent of the voting decisions made by his sample of representatives and senators.

Herbert Asher and Herbert Weisberg (1978) view congressional voting as an evolutionary process; that is, congressional votes on recurring issues display more constancy than change. In effect, a member's vote on an issue is a "standing decision" based on his or her past performance. Only a major modification in the decision-making context is likely to alter that voting pattern. According to the authors, voting histories are formed on the basis of party affiliation, ideology, and constituency pressures; the normal stability of these forces over time contributes to the continuity of voting behavior. Voting histories are not merely responses to these background factors, however, because a legislator's record also shapes future voting patterns: "as the representative learns that previous votes have not worked to his disadvantage, he realizes that he can safely keep voting that way" (Asher and Weisberg, 1978, p. 394). The only source of deviation from an established voting history arises with the emergence of "new issues" on which voting patterns are less established. As time passes, however, decisions about how to deal with the new issues eventually settle into a regular pattern. Asher and Weisberg conclude that "the forces of continuity predominate in congressional voting" (Asher and Weisberg, 1978, p. 423).

Charles Bullock and David Brady (1983) have devised a model to describe the linkages between constituency, party, and the roll-call voting of senators. Their model relates the similarities and differences in the voting records of senators from the same state to population characteristics, reelection constituency characteristics, party control (of Senate seats), and partisan competitiveness. The authors examine these interrelationships by studying the voting patterns among senators (pairs) with different as well as identical party affiliations. Because Bullock and Brady compare the voting records of two senators from the same state, there are no geographic (state) differences to bias the results. The authors conclude that the policy positions of senators are influenced more by their reelection constituency than by their geographic constituency because the latter includes the senator's opponents as well as his or her supporters. They also find that the party appears to have a greater influence on senators' voting records than either constituency characteristics or electoral competition.

Warren Miller and Donald Stokes (1963) propose a different model to explain the impact of constituency on congressional voting. They suggest that constituent influence can affect the voting behavior of representatives in two ways. First, constituent influence can be heightened if the district selects a legislator who shares its views; hence, in following his or her own convictions, the representative also is expressing the will of the constituents. Under these conditions, district opinion and the representative's actions are connected through the member's own policy attitudes. Second, constituency opinion and the legislator's attitudes are linked through his or her own perceptions of the district's wishes. The authors conclude that "the representative's roll call behavior is strongly influenced by his own policy preferences and by his perception of preferences held by the constituency" (Miller and Stokes, 1963, p. 56).

16. MODELS OF LEGISLATIVE VOTING

John W. Kingdon

In recent years various specialists in legislative behavior have found themselves troubled by what they have considered to be a deficiency in theory-building in the field. After an extended review of the literature on Congress for instance, Robert Peabody argues, "The critical need is for *theory* at several levels for, quite clearly, in congressional research the generation of data has proceeded much more rapidly than the accumulation of theory." [1]

While it is not clear that "the" theory of legislative behavior is on the horizon, scholars have recently developed a number of models of legislative voting which promise substantial theoretical payoff. These models are relevant not only to the specific case of legislative voting itself, but also potentially to legislative decision-making more broadly conceived and to governmental decision-making in general. These models have largely stood in splendid isolation, each supposedly representing a fairly complete accounting of legislative voting, each probably compatible with the others, but none very much related to the others. If we were to be able somehow to arrive at a way to fit important aspects of these models together, our theoretical thinking about behavior might be advanced considerably.

This paper presents one way of furthering this integrative process. First, I briefly describe a few models that have been prominent in the literature. The paper then seeks to provide a framework for fitting them together. We then compare a new integrative model with data on congressmen's voting decisions. We end with some discussion of the broader implications of the work for building theory about decision processes.

The Models

Identifying and describing models of legislative voting is not an easy task, as it turns out. There is actually quite a large number of constructs and arguments

Author's Note: This is a drastically revised version of an earlier paper prepared for delivery at the Conference on Mathematical Models of Congress, Aspen, Colorado, June, 1974. I am indebted to Michael Cohen for his patient counsel and valuable criticism, to Donald Matthews and Herbert Asher for their valuable comments, to Janet Grenzke for comments on an earlier version, to anonymous reviewers, and to various participants at the Aspen Conference for their perspectives. The final responsibility, however, rests with me.

Source: *Journal of Politics* vol. 39, no. 3 (August 1977): 563-595. Reprinted with permission of the publisher.

abroad in the literature which could be considered to be implicit or explicit models of voting. Our first task is to identify a set of models that do purport to be representations of decision processes involved in legislative voting and to summarize their major features. It is impossible in these pages to go into sufficient detail to do full justice to their richness and complexity. Nor is it my purpose to enter into a detailed critique of each model. But I will briefly state the major approach of each model without, I hope, doing violence to its intent.

Cue-Taking. Best exemplified by the Matthews-Stimson model,[2] cue-taking starts with the assumption that legislators must somehow cut their great information costs in order to reach decisions that will further their goals. The dominant strategy for accomplishing this is turning to their colleagues within the legislative body for cues which they follow in voting. These cues may come from individual legislators or from such groups of them as the state party delegation, the party, or even the whole body. Matthews and Stimson operationalize these fundamental tenets through the use of a computer simulation.

Cue-taking is actually a family of models. The genesis of the ideas is to be found far back in the literature, in the notion of specialization among legislators. A well developed committee system is supposed to allow them to specialize in a few areas, and then for the areas in which they are not specialists, to rely on each other's judgments. The notion of cue-taking is also very much a part of communication models and of bloc voting models. Kovenock finds, for instance, that most of the interaction that a congressman has with others takes place with his colleagues in Congress, rather than with people outside the Congress.[3] Truman hypothesizes that the blocs which he discerns in legislative voting, such as regional or state delegation groupings, are the result of regularized communications among the members of the bloc.[4] Jackson's regression models of Senate voting can also be seen as consistent with cue-taking models, although the set of cues he includes is wider than the Senate itself.[5]

Policy Dimensions. Set forth early in the work of MacRae,[6] policy dimensions have been most recently explored by Clausen, who argues that they constitute a theory of voting decisions.[7] According to Clausen, a congressman starts with some notion of the policy content of the issue before him, and thinks of it in terms of a dimension (e.g., more or less government management of the economy). He places himself on that dimension, and compares his position to the position of the legislation, choosing the alternative presented which comes closest to his position. One way in which he may accomplish this matching is by picking the cues on which he will rely according to the degree to which the cue agrees with his own policy position. The cues on which he relies also differ from one policy dimension to another, so that, for instance, constituency is important on civil liberties and party on government management of the economy.

Predisposition-Communication. A predisposition-communication model is presented in the work of Cherryholmes and Shapiro.[8] They argue that a congressman first assesses the strength of his predisposition for or against a bill. He does so by taking account of his own past behavior, the House party position, and the effects the bill would have on his constituency and region. If these factors predispose him strongly one way or the other, he simply votes on the basis of this predisposition. If his predisposition is not sufficiently strong, he enters an elaborate communication process among colleagues and with the President, the outcome of which determines his position. The actual model in this case is a computer simulation.

Consensus. In my own work on congressmen's voting decisions, I have presented a consensus decision model.[9] According to this model, a congressman implicitly asks whether there is any controversy over the issue in the environment. If not, his decision rule is simple: he votes with the consensus in that environment. If there is controversy, he subsets the environment, and asks if there is any controversy in the field of forces that would affect his own decision, and if he finds none, he votes with that field. He can also use this mode of decision if there is a degree of conflict in his field, so long as the conflict is not substantial and so long as a dominant consensus can be discerned. The set of preconsensus processes which affects the degree of consensus present in congressmen's fields is as important as the final consensus rule. These processes include simple contrived consensus among the major reference groups, and the structuring of the fields according to the congressman's personal policy attitudes, his past voting history, or his weighting of potentially intense actors such as constituency.

Past Behavior. In the budgetary process, Wildavsky argues that legislative decisions on agency budgets are structured in large part by past decisions affecting these agencies.[10] The incremental method as an aid to calculation bases this year's budget on last year's budget, with a narrow range of increases or decreases. This concept looms very large in general theories of decision-making, and Asher and Weisberg are working on a study of the impact of voting history on legislators' decisions.[11] In the legislative voting case, one would conceive of a congressman's decisions as being a function of his past behavior on similar issues. If he has always voted for foreign aid, for instance, he will do so again. Changes in past behavior will be made in small and gradual increments.

Goals. Many decision models in other contexts portray decision-makers as being goal-seeking. The first step in such an argument, therefore, is to specify the goals which the decision-makers seek to maximize. Some recent works on congressmen, while not purporting to be complete models of voting decisions, are nevertheless highly relevant. Fiorina constructs a very instructive formal model of constituency-representative relations based on a congressman's goal of re-election.[12] Mayhew argues that re-election structures a congressman's behavior to a considerable degree, and that treating this goal as the congressman's primary preoccupation helps us to understand many features of the legislative process.[13] Fenno's comparative committee study expands the list of goals.[14] In differentiating among congressional committees, he finds it useful to characterize them as primarily serving one of three goals for committee members: re-election, influence within the House, and good public policy. An integrative model of legislative voting decisions might build in this goal-seeking feature and even these particular goals.

Given this array of models, one might be tempted to treat them as alternatives, and to attempt to discriminate among them in some fashion. One would achieve this discrimination, presumably, according to several criteria: the models' ability to account statistically for decision outcomes, the empirical plausibility of the models, their logical features, or some combination of these criteria. One would then choose the best of the models and discard the others as not satisfying these criteria as well as the chosen one does.

Another approach, the one which I take in this paper, is to treat each of these models as having a grasp on an important part of reality. In this view, then, we do not have a case of incompatible, competing models. Instead, there are several compatible models which are in need of a persuasive means of integrating them. Let us turn to a way in which this might be done.

Constructing an Integrative Model

In constructing a model which has a potential for weaving together threads of previous work, we should first keep in mind several features which we would ideally want such a model to exhibit. We would obviously want a persuasive model to be able to account for outcomes statistically. In addition to that conventional consideration, the model should be plausible, in the sense that it should be an accurate representation of legislators' decision-making processes which is intuitively realistic. As such, it should not be too complex or elaborate, picturing a deciding legislator as engaging in an extended search for information or proceeding through an impossibly involved set of steps. It should also be politically sensible, allowing full play for such important political forces as constituency considerations and interaction within the legislative chamber. Finally, it should be comprehensive, including all the relevant forces that might have an important bearing on the decision.

Keeping these considerations in mind, we start the task of developing an integrative model by noticing that most of the previous work on legislative voting begins with similar assumptions about information processing, search behavior, and decision-making capacity. These assumptions, entirely familiar to readers of Herbert Simon and other students of decision-making,[15] posit that legislators, like other decision-makers but perhaps even more than most, must make a large volume of complex decisions, while constrained by limits on time and cognitive capacity to do so without extensive study of each issue. Taking account of this decisional overload, the previous models and our integrative model all largely agree on the need for decision-making procedures that cut legislators' information costs and simplify their choices. They also agree that legislative voting is a repetitive problem-solving situation which calls for standard ways of making voting decisions which can be applied vote after vote. Lest this appear to be an obvious point, one could argue just as plausibly that legislators' simplification of decisions may not be the inexorable result of an impossible set of demands on their time, but rather due to their simple lack of inclination to devote a great deal of time and energy to substantive policy-making, particularly on the floor. In either case, however, from the perspective of describing their behavior, legislators are realistically portrayed as adopting decision rules which drastically simplify their choices, whether or not they have an inescapable need to do so.

In building an integrative model, we also begin with an assumption that is not particularly emphasized in many previous models of legislative voting,[16] namely, that legislators are goal-seekers. Their behavior is purposive, and is not simply reaction to external forces. A natural preliminary step in dealing with that behavior is to identify the goals which seem to affect most legislators most of the time. For the purposes of this paper, I find it useful to work with adaptations of the goals which Fenno specifies. His formulations — the goals of re-election, influence within the House, and good public policy — are restated here so as to make them somewhat more comprehensive. Thus the primary goals of legislators are as follows:

(1) *Satisfying constituents.* It could be that constituency considerations come back ultimately to an interest in re-election. But one observes congressmen taking account of constituency reaction long before and much more frequently than they worry explicitly about gain or loss of votes in the next election.[17] Hence, the more comprehensive formulation here.

(2) *Intra-Washington influence.* Another set of considerations in voting has to do with satisfying a set of actors within Washington, who are not necessarily closely connected to the constituency. These include going along with one's party leadership, favor-trading among fellow legislators, and following the lead of the administration, particularly if the President is of the deciding legislator's party. One takes these into account, presumably, in order to build influence within the government, a set wider than the House itself. The same concept, retitled, could be used for state or foreign capitals.

(3) *Good public policy.* Most legislators have their conception of good public policy, and act partly to carry that conception into being. Their policy attitudes, their ideology (if it can be called that) decidedly affect their behavior. Their previous pattern of behavior, their voting history, enters here as well, since that pattern represents their traditional policy position on the issue currently confronting them.

These appear to be the goals which most legislators seek most of the time. I will shortly present ways of introducing them into an integrative model of legislative voting and of operationalizing and using them empirically.

The Place of Various Previous Models

Building on these assumptions about information processing and goal orientations, we are now in a position to discuss how various previous models of legislative voting might inform the development of a more integrative model.

I have found it useful to portray congressmen's decision-making as a sequential process, for which a version of modelling familiar in this and other contexts seems quite suitable. Such a process model pictures the legislator as beginning with a very simple decision rule. If that rule can be applied, he does so, and is done with that decision on that particular vote or bill. If he cannot apply that rule, he proceeds to one which is somewhat more complex, which is applied if it can be. Previous steps are seen as controlling subsequent steps in the model, in the sense that if the early decision rule suffices, the congressman uses it and need not proceed further. This feature is both plausible as applied to congressmen and congruent with a good bit of more general literature on decision-making.[18]

In terms of the previous models of legislative voting, both the consensus model which I presented earlier and the one developed by Cherryholmes and Shapiro exhibit this kind of general structure. In addition, both of them start by assuming that there is a set of influences on the vote; Cherryholmes and Shapiro call them predispositions, and I call them a set of actors (including the congressman's own policy attitude) which might affect decisions. In my model, if there is no conflict among these actors, the decision is made: the congressman votes with them. If there is conflict, he must search further. The fundamental logic of the Cherryholmes-Shapiro simulation is quite similar. When predisposing factors agree, the die is cast; when they do not, the congressman must consider the issue further, through a communication process. The same thread is found to a degree in the Matthews-Stimson cue-taking model, which works best when the congressman's principal cue-givers agree and is significantly in error when they do not. Several important cue-givers in their model, furthermore, themselves represent an existing consensus in the perceptual fields of congressmen, including heavy majorities of the House, party, or state delegation. Thus the essential driving logic of an integrative model — the legislator's search for some sort of agreement among a set of possible influences on the vote which predisposes him in a certain direction, and some further decisional process in the absence of that agreement — is a thread common to a number of the models of legislative voting previously developed.

As I see it, cue-taking enters the decisional process in two critical ways. First, it is a means to an end. If legislators are goal-oriented, as we have portrayed them as being, then, as Matthews and Stimson rightly argue, taking cues from fellow legislators is a prominent way to translate their goals into votes. If a congressman wants to vote so as to satisfy his goal of bringing about good public policy, for instance, one easy and frequently used way to accomplish this aim is by picking fellow congressmen as cue sources who agree with his own general philosophy. I have developed some evidence elsewhere that this choice of colleagues according to agreement with one's own policy attitude on the issue is in fact what is happening.[19] As Clausen persuasively argues,[20] recognition of this phenomenon implies that a cue-taking model and a policy dimension interpretation of legislative voting, far from being incompatible, are actually quite complimentary. The same general line of thinking applies to goals other than the policy goal. For example, a deciding congressman may follow the guidance of colleagues whom he considers to have "good political judgment," particularly from the same state delegation, in order to vote in a way most likely to satisfy constituents.

The second occasion on which cue-taking enters the decisional process is when such other possible influences on the vote as goals, predispositions, ideology, or constituency considerations do not provide sufficient guidance to make a decision. This situation is particularly exemplified by the many low-visibility, minor issues which come to the floor, about which very few people apart from a few involved colleagues care. Yet these votes must be cast, since a poor attendance record is a considerable liability with constituents in the next campaign. In such a case, the congressman's own policy attitude does not provide guidance, since he does not care about the issue; his constituency may be utterly indifferent; and there may be no intra-Washington consideration which would prompt him to vote one way or the other. This is not the same case as the cue being a means to an end, since here, there appears to be no goal-oriented consideration which would point the legislator in a given direction. Both the literature and practical experience are replete with examples of such votes, in which a deciding congressman is bereft of other guidance and simply follows a trusted colleague, sometimes quite blindly. This view of cue-taking is consistent not only with Matthews' and Stimson's work, but also with the Cherryholmes-Shapiro model, in which it is postulated that a congressman turns to a communication process when predisposing factors do not provide sufficient guidance.

The literature on policy dimensions is relevant in a number of ways. First, policy dimensions can be seen as a major way of describing the final voting behavior. As such, an accounting of the dimensions which one finds in legislative votes may simply be a useful description of the structure of votes, rather than a description of the processes by which legislators arrive at their votes. In addition to this treatment of dimensional analysis as a summary of outcomes, however, there may be ways in which a policy dimension theory can be seen as a part of the decisional processes themselves, as Clausen argues. As I see it, these ways fall generally into two categories. First, policy dimensions enter the process through some attitudinal mechanism. The congressman has a set of attitudes about matters of public policy, obviously closely connected to policy goals, discussed above, which affect his voting quite directly. Thus, a congressman sorts a given issue into a policy dimension, matches his own position on that dimension to the proposal under consideration, and picks the alternative which has the best match to his own position. His policy attitudes also very prominently affect his choice of cues, as stated above. Secondly, as Clausen argues, policy positions taken by the congressman are affected not only by his attitudes but also by such political actors as his constituency and party which he feels are important to him. Thus constituency considerations figure prominently in voting on civil liberties matters, while party affects voting on Clausen's government management dimension. As I have treated these actors above, their importance derives from their clear connection with a congressman's goals: constituency and interest groups with re-election, party and administration with intra-Washington influence, and so forth.

Finally, a legislator's previous voting history is closely aligned with his policy position. If he has a well-established voting history, it is quite likely that he will also have a rather firm policy attitude on the issue, and vice-versa. It would be possible, of course, to have a voting history without a very firm attitude, particularly in the case of rather minor issues to which a congressman has not paid a great deal of attention over the years and has simply taken to voting on by habit. Even in that probably infrequent case, however, the voting history defines the congressman's policy position on the issue, and hence, his position on the policy dimension of which the issue is a part. Thus voting according to voting history and according to policy position is seen in this paper to be closely connected.

An Integrative Model

We are now in a position to present a model which attempts to integrate the various models in a fashion which incorporates the features just discussed. That model is displayed in Figure 16-1.

The first two steps are the same as the first two in the consensus mode of decision, which I have presented elsewhere.[21] If there is no controversy in the environment at all, the congressman's choice is simple: he votes with that environment and is done with it. On many bills, for instance, a unified committee reports the bill and nobody opposes the committee position in any particular. If there is some controversy, he subsets the environment, considering only the actors which are most critical to him — his own constituency, his party leadership, his trusted associates in the House, his own policy attitude, etc. — which I call the "field of forces" which bear on his decision. If there is no conflict among those actors, he votes with his field. I assume, as a legislator does, that if there appears to be no consideration which would prompt him to vote in a way different from that toward which he is impelled by every factor in his field of vision, then there is no reason to think twice. And as I have argued above, this is a beginning to an integrative model which is common to a number of the previous works on legislative voting.

If there is some conflict among the congressman's relevant actors, he then proceeds to consider his goals, which I conceive for the purposes of this paper as being the three discussed above — constituency, intra-Washington influence, and public policy. But a goal is not brought to bear on the decision if it seems unimportant to him on this issue. It must pass what I have labelled a critical threshold of importance in order to be evoked and relevant to the decision. For example, a congressman's constituency may have a vague and largely unarticulated opposition to foreign aid. In that case, he would say that there was a constituency opinion on the issue, but that it was not intense enough to bother taking account of. The same could apply to the other goals. In the next section of this paper, I present some operationalizations of these thresholds and use them to deal with data on voting decisions.

If none of the goals is important enough to the congressman in the given decision to be relevant, he then proceeds to follow trusted colleagues within the House. He chooses colleagues who are on the committee that considered the bill and who agree with him in general philosophical, policy terms.[22] If one or more goals are important enough, he asks if there is conflict among the goals which have been evoked. If there is none, the choice is then clear: to vote with the evoked goal or goals (Step C1). It could be in this case that only one of them is relevant to the decision, or that two or even all three are, but that they all point him in the same direction. For example, it could be that the policy goal on a given issue is the only one which passes its critical threshold, and the other two, while either opposed to, favorable to, or neutral concerning his conception of good public policy, are not in any event important enough to him on that issue to be

Figure 16-1 An Integrative Model of Legislative Voting Decisions

Step

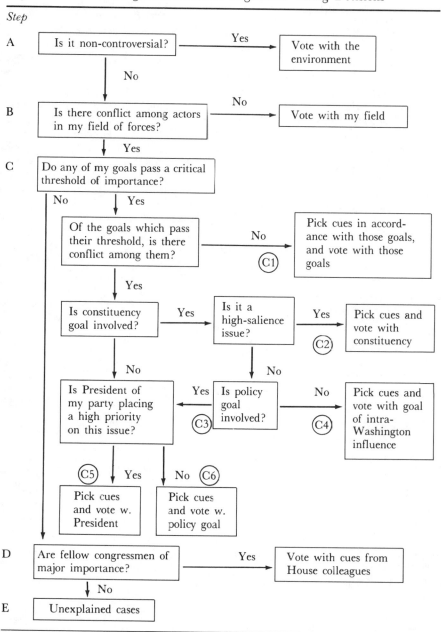

potentially controlling. He votes in that case according to his conception of good public policy. As the model specifies, part of this decision may well be picking cues within the House to reinforce his policy goal, as a means to that end, in the fashion discussed above. Other examples of no conflict among evoked goals could be given, but this one will perhaps suffice.

If there is some conflict among the goals which the legislator considers relevant to his decision, he proceeds implicitly to some decision rules which help him sort out the conflicts and make a satisfactory choice. It might be helpful at this point in the argument to present all the logically possible combinations of conflict among the three goals, which is done in Table 16-1. In the first column, the possible combinations are listed, and the second and third columns contain the

Table 16-1 All Possible Combinations of Conflicts Among Goals, and the Resultant Outcomes

	Outcomes,[a] Expected and Actual		
Combinations	*High-salience Issues*[b]	*Low- or Medium-Salience Issues*[b]	*Totals*
Policy and constituencies *vs* Intra-Washington	Constituency (C2) 1/2[a]	Policy or Pres.[c] (C3) 2/2	3/4
Policy and intra-Wash. *vs* Constituency	Constituency (C2) 0/0	Policy (C3) 3/3	3/3
Constituency and intra-Wash. *vs* Policy	Constituency (C2) 0/0	Policy or Pres.[c] (C3) 0/0	0/0
Policy *vs* Constituency	Constituency (C2) 1/2	Policy (C3) 6/6	7/8
Constituency *vs* Intra-Washington	Constituency (C2) 0/0	Intra-Wash. (C4) 3/4	3/4
Policy *vs* Intra-Washington	President[b] (C5) 3/5	Policy[b] (C6) 3/3	6/8
Totals	5/9	17/18	22/27

[a] The goal stated in each cell is the expected outcome, the goal which the model would predict would dominate the decision. The notation in parentheses refers to the appropriate step in Figure 16-1. The actual performance is captured in the numbers in each cell. The first is the number of cases in which the outcome is as predicted by the model, the second is the total number for that cell. For instance, in the case of a conflict between the constituency and intra-Washington influence goals, on low- or medium-salience issues, the model would predict that the representative would vote according to the intra-Washington consideration. Of the four cases in which there was such a conflict on such an issue, the congressman voted as the model expects in three.
[b] In the case of the conflict between Policy and Intra-Washington, "high-salience" refers to the presidential involvement specified in Figure 16-1, Step C5, low-salience to non-involvement (Step C6). In the others, the salience of the issue refers to the general visibility of the issue in the press, in the public, and among participants. See *Congressmen's Voting Decisions*, 292-293, for the coding particulars.
[c] In these cases, since the congressman cycles through Steps C5 and C6, there is a chance that the President's request may over-turn the policy consideration, and it did in fact happen in one case. Thus that case is coded as accounted for by the model, even though policy did not control, because the model predicted the outcome correctly. In the other case, the President's priority is not involved, so the congressman votes according to his policy position. See the text for further explanation.

outcomes which the model would predict for each of the combinations. The numbers are relevant to the operationalization, which is explained in the next section of the paper.

There is a variety of ways in which the decision rules could be stated in this part of the model. I hypothesize that the congressman considers the constituency interest first. He may not end up voting with the constituency, but he always considers it when it is above the minimal level of importance. Placing this goal first is in keeping with the fact that the congressman owes his tenure in office to his constituency, and as Fiorina and Mayhew argue,[23] re-election is of critical importance to him.

If the constituency is not involved, the only logically possible conflict among the three goals left is between policy and intra-Washington influence. In that case, I hypothesize that the congressman has a disposition to vote with his policy goals, unless he is of the same party as the President and the President places a high priority on the issue. Intra-Washington considerations other than that one, such as party leadership requests or favor-trading, would not, I would argue, be enough to overcome a really strong policy predisposition. But a high-priority request from a president of his party would.[24] The results in Steps C5 and C6 of the model reflect this reasoning.

If the constituency goal is involved, the congressman weighs that consideration against policy and/or intra-Washington influence. I have set forth elsewhere an account of that sort of balancing.[25] The key here is that there is a filter for the salience of the issue — the general visibility of the issue in the press, in the attentive public, and among the participants in the legislative process. If the issue is of high salience, and if constituency is a relevant consideration, the model postulates that in view of the likelihood that important constituents will notice and disapprove of a vote out of keeping with their interests, the constituency consideration will dominate the others (Step C2). If the issue is of lower salience, however, the congressman has more freedom to allow his policy views or intra-Washington considerations to control the choice.

In the case of low- or medium-salience issues, if the policy goal is relevant to the issue, the congressman is disposed once again to favor it. He must check the possibility, however, that the intra-Washington goal would be involved and would center on a priority request from a President of his party which conflicts with his policy goal. He therefore (at Step C3) cycles through the presidential step described above, but in most cases ends up voting in accordance with his policy views (Step C6). If the policy goal is not relevant, the only logically possible conflict (Step C4) is between constituency and intra-Washington influence. Since it involves a low- or medium-salience issue at that point, I hypothesize that the congressman decides in favor of the intra-Washington consideration, in line with the argument presented above.

I have now discussed a framework by which, I would argue, the various models of legislative voting might be persuasively fit together into a general theory of legislative voting decisions which is at once comprehensive, parsimonious, and plausible. I have detailed, both verbally and through the integrative model, the ways in which a set of decision processes may be tied together. It remains now to present ways of operationalizing the key concepts and applying them to a set of data on congressmen's voting decisions.

Another Look at the Data

In this section, I apply the concepts discussed above to my interview data, which are described at length in *Congressmen's Voting Decisions.*[26] Briefly, I repeatedly interviewed a sample of Members of the U.S. House of Representatives in 1969, concerning their sources of information and voting cues, their decision rules, and the importance of various political actors in their decisions. Each of the interviews, in contrast to a survey type of instrument, concentrated on one decision which they had recently made. Generalizations are thus based on my cumulation of these decision histories over the course of the entire session, and the unit of analysis is the decision ($n = 222$).

I should make clear at the outset that, strictly speaking, the theory which I have presented above is not to be completely tested in the pages to follow. The model was generated from the previous literature and from the data set used in my own previous study. Hence, a complete validation would have to rest on a testing against new, independently generated data sets. What follows here is a partial test and an illustration of the ways in which the concepts might be measured and used. That return to the data suggests that the model is plausible, parsimonious, and consistent with what we know about the ways in which representatives actually make their decisions. I obviously consider its validity to be rather strongly indicated, but also obviously, a fully definitive validation would have to be done in a different fashion.

As far as the first two steps in the integrative model are concerned (Figure 16-1), the operationalization is the same as that presented in my earlier model. Since the votes were chosen partly to maximize conflict, there are no cases in these data of non-controversial votes. As far as the second step is concerned, the congressman's field of forces includes his own specific policy attitude toward the issue under consideration, his constituency, fellow congressmen to whom he paid attention, interest groups, his staff, his party leadership, and the administration. There is no conflict among the actors in this field 47 percent of the time, and respondents voted with their fields in all these cases.[27] Given that the votes selected were relatively high-conflict votes, the fact that the first two steps account for nearly half of these cases argues that these steps must have quite a high predictive power for legislative votes in general, since the general case is surely less conflict-ridden than these votes.

Starting with Step C, a major question of operationalization is the critical threshold of importance for each of the three important goals. What indicators would tell that a constituency interest, for instance, is sufficiently important that the congressman considers that constituency goal at Step C, rather than noticing but largely neglecting the constituency position in his decision? There is such an indicator in my data, the "importance" coding for each actor. With this coding, the congressman's comments relative to each actor were coded into four categories: (1) the actor was of no importance in the decision; (2) the actor was of minor importance; that is, the congressman noticed the actor's position, checked it, or the like, but the actor was of no greater importance; (3) the actor was of major importance; that is, whether or not the congressman ended up voting with the actor, he weighed the actor's position carefully and the actor had a major impact on his thinking; (4) the actor determined the decision, to the exclusion of other influences. The inter-coder reliability for this variable was very good.[28]

Building on this coding, the critical thresholds of importance for the goals are operationalized as follows: for the constituency goal, the congressman passes that threshold on the decision at hand if his constituency for that decision is coded as being of major or determinative importance. If it is coded as being of minor or no importance, we consider that the threshold has not been passed, and that the constituency goal is not sufficiently important to the congressman on that decision to be involved in Step C of the model. Substantively, passing this threshold could be due to one or both of two reasons: either the constituency feeling is quite intense on the issue and any congressman would want to take account of it, or the congressman considers catering to constituency interest an important goal regardless of constituency intensity. For present purposes it is not so critical which or what combination of these two reasons is responsible for the constituency being of major importance in the decision. Whatever the reason, the congressman's goal of satisfying constituents is evoked.

The constituency position, it should be noted, may not be the whole constituency, the mass public, or even a majority of the constituency. It could be these, but it could as easily be the position of a fairly narrow subset of the constituency, such as school administrators on education funding. In this connection, interest groups do not appear as a separate force in the model, since, as I have maintained elsewhere, they appear to have little impact on congressmen's voting decisions apart from their constituency connections.[29] Thus interest groups are subsumed under constituency for present purposes, and ignored as being important in their own right.

It might be possible that a coding of "major" or "determinative" importance would be closely associated with the congressman's vote in accordance with the constituency position. If such were the case, the test of the model would not be as good as could be hoped, since passing the critical threshold would by itself imply a constituency-oriented vote, lending an artificial predictive power to the model. It turns out, however, that these apprehensions can be alleviated somewhat. Of the cases in which there is some conflict in the congressman's field, constituency is coded as being of major or determinative importance in 42. Of these 42 cases, the congressman votes with the constituency position 62 percent of the time, a performance somewhat better than chance (which is ½), but not dramatically better. By contrast, the model correctly predicts 93 percent of those cases. Thus, while there is naturally some association between the importance coding and the vote, it is not so strong as to negate the value of defining the critical threshold in the fashion described. The coding does not by itself produce the predictive performance.

The intra-Washington goal is treated in a similar fashion. If either the congressman's party leadership or the administration is coded as being of major or determinative importance, the congressman is considered to have passed the threshold on this decision and the goal is evoked. In addition, fellow congressmen could define the passing of the threshold on this goal, if they are coded as being of major or determinative importance, *and* if some consideration of vote-trading or intra-House power is involved. In other words, fellow congressmen do not trigger this goal, even if coded major or determinative, if the deciding legislator uses his colleagues simply to reinforce ideology, constituency, or party, or if colleagues are used in the absence of other guidance. These uses of fellow congressmen are provided for elsewhere in the model. To be relevant to the goal of intra-Washington influence, colleagues must be important for their own sakes, not because they are convenient surrogates for something else or because they are the only cues left. This supplementary coding was made by a rereading of the interview protocols in the cases involved, to see how colleagues were being used.

The goal of good public policy presents something of a problem in these data. Because the interviewing was done at the time of decision, respondents nearly always held some articulated policy attitude toward the bill or vote at hand, and voted consistent with it. But it would be very difficult, given these data, to determine the intensity or background of that attitude earlier in the process of decision. Therefore, some measure of the importance of the policy goal other than the intensity of the congressman's policy attitude toward the vote at hand is needed. Instead of trying to tap that intensity, I use here two measures of the congressman's policy position. The policy goal is considered to pass the critical threshold of importance if *either* his voting history on similar issues is coded as being of major or determinative importance in his decision, *or* his ideology as measured by Americans for Democratic Action (ADA) and Americans for Constitutional Action (ACA) scores is sufficiently extreme as to be a good guide to his decision. Some congressmen are simply considered extreme "liberals" or "conservatives," by themselves and by everyone associated with the process. If they are, I assume that their ideology is sufficiently strong to give them considerable guidance, and to cause the congressman to pass the threshold on the policy goal. Because of a well-established voting history or a relatively extreme ideological position, in other words, he has a pretty fair notion of what constitutes "good public policy" for him in the current instance. Operationally, the ADA and ACA scores are used to form an index, in which a congressman is considered to be sufficiently extreme if either the ADA or ACA score is 90-100 or 0-10, and if the opposite score is in the opposite three deciles among my respondents. If the ADA score is zero, for instance, and the ACA score is in the upper three deciles, the congressman is considered to be a conservative; if the ADA score is 100 and the ACA score is in the bottom three deciles, for another example, the congressman is defined as liberal. Congressmen who do not meet the criteria described are considered to have a sufficiently "moderate" record that ADA-ACA position is not a guide to votes, and thus do not evoke the policy goal.

An impressionistic scanning of the Members so classified confirms that those labelled the most liberal and conservative by the ADA-ACA criterion would be clearly regarded by most observers of the House as being correctly labelled. The index fails to identify some members for whom certain policy goals are clearly relevant, as, for instance, some very public doves on ABM deployment. In that sense, it may underestimate the importance of policy goals, since it discards some members for whom policy goals may be highly important. That underestimation also lowers the overall predictive performance of the model a bit. But the index does not make the other error: those who are identified as liberal or conservative are not mislabelled.[30] As far as triggering the policy goal is concerned, the ADA-ACA index and the coding for the importance of voting history make a roughly equal contribution. Of the cases which exhibit some conflict in the field of forces in which the policy goal is evoked, the ADA-ACA index alone is responsible for that triggering in 30 cases, voting history alone in 27, and the two together in 25.

Other operationalizations of the model are fairly straightforward. (1) Salience of the issue is a trichotomy (low, medium, high), as defined by the attention the issue appears to be receiving in the press, among congressmen, and among other participants in the legislative system.[31] The model's specification of the cutting point being between high and medium salience is consistent with evidence presented elsewhere,[32] that high-salience issues are distinctively constituency-oriented, whereas low- or medium-salience issues are less so. (2) The priority which the President places on the issue is determined from my knowledge of the administration's position and lobbying activities. In the first year of the Nixon administration, priority items tended to have to do with the budget, and these cases particularly centered on the debt limit and the surtax extension. (3) At Step D, fellow congressman importance is once again the importance coding, major or determinative constituting the criterion of entrance into that step.

The quantitative fruits of the model generation and data analysis are presented in Table 16-2, with a subset for Steps C2 through C6 more fully elaborated in Table 16-1. Overall, the model correctly predicts 92 percent of the voting decisions. Of those, only 10 percent are accounted for by Steps C2-C6, the most elaborate part of the model, which itself is not very elaborate. It seems clear that legislators' voting decisions can be understood as the workings of extremely simple decision rules, rules which are not generated in some arbitrary fashion, but in a way which is consistent with quite a rich body of previous literature on legislative voting. It must be remembered also that this particular sample of votes contains those decisions which should be the hardest to predict. I deliberately selected votes which were among the most conflict-ridden of the session, which makes the high degrees of consensus (at Steps B and C1) really quite striking. One would not have expected these results, given the votes selected. Thus the model should do even better for run-of-the-mill votes. If there is as little conflict among actors and goals with these relatively "big," high-visibility votes, then there should be even less with more routine votes. I would expect, however, that for those votes, the simpler Steps A, B, C1, and D (stressing no conflict and House colleagues) would account for more of the total than these data indicate, and the more elaborate Steps C2-C6 would be resorted to even less frequently than these data indicate.

The model does specify that the congressman *picks cues and* votes in accordance with the specified goal. Thus far, we have only considered the percentage of *votes* predicted, without reference to whether or not the congressman also picked cues to reinforce those votes. I take it that "picking cues" here re-

Table 16-2 Quantitative Performance of the Integrative Model

Step (see Figure 16-1)		Accuracy[a]	Percentage of cases[b]	Cumulative Percentages[c]
A	Non-controversial votes	—	0%	0%
B	No conflict in field	104/104 = 100%	47	47
C1	No conflict among goals	74/79 = 94%	33	80
C2-C6	Conflict among goals (from Table 16-1)	22/27 = 81%	10	90
D	Fellow congressmen	5/5 = 100%	2	92
E	Unexplained cases	n = 7		

[a] Accuracy equals the percentage of the cases in which the congressman votes as the model specifies. For example, at Step C1, there are 79 cases in which there is no conflict among the goals, and the congressman votes in accordance with the evoked goals in 74 of those cases. Thus accuracy = 74/79 = 94%. The number of "mistakes" made by the model at this step is five.
[b] Percentage of cases equals the percentage of the total ($n = 222$) accounted for by that decision step. For example, in Step C1, it is 74/222 = 33%.
[c] The cumulative percentage equals percentage of 222 accounted for by that step plus all previous steps. For example, at
Step C1, it is $\frac{74 + 104}{222} = 80\%$.

fers to choosing fellow congressmen on whom to rely according to their agreement with the goal specified in the model. Thus fellow congressmen at Step C2 should not be opposed to the constituency position, if the model is right; or at Step C6, they should not be opposed to the deciding legislator's policy position. If this factor is taken into account, we lose five cases which would otherwise be correctly predicted. That is to say, there are five cases in which the actor "fellow congressman" is opposed to a decision which was governed by the specified goal. Building this loss into the overall figures, therefore, the overall performance of the model, defined as the congressman's *both* voting as the model specified *and* avoiding colleagues who are opposed to that vote, is 90 percent. The predictive performance, in other words, remains high.

Alternative Formulations

It may be useful to test some alternative formulations of the model, to see if this is the formulation which works best in the sense of correctly accounting for outcomes. Such an analysis would help to evaluate some plausible alternative hypotheses about the structure of the model and the place of several of the variables in it. I present here two types of alternative formulations: (1) changes in the basis structure of the model, and (2) changes in certain parts of the model.

The Basic Structure. There are three changes in the basic structure which have been tried on the data: bypassing the first consensus steps in the model, bypassing the non-consensus part of the model, and substituting one simple decision rule for the non-consensus part.

First, to bypass the first steps, we postulate that the 104 cases correctly accounted for by the consensus step (Step B) can be predicted by subsequent steps in the model (Steps C and D). In other words, we start the model running at Step C. One logical feature of the model becomes immediately clear, namely, that the only way for the goals step (Step C) to fail to predict decisions correctly is for none of the three goals to exceed their critical thresholds. If any do exceed their thresholds, then it is logically impossible in the 104 consensus cases for the goal agreement step (Step C1) not to account correctly for the outcome. If goals pass their thresholds, in other words, there is agreement among them by definition, since the original Step B filtered the cases according to the consensus criterion. Of the 104 cases at issue, then, Step C would correctly account for 82. Of the remaining cases, which then reach Step D, following fellow congressmen of major importance picks up an additional nine cases. Thus Steps C and D account for 91 of the 104 cases, for an 88 percent accuracy rate; the original Step B accounted for all 104, a 100 percent accuracy rate.

Second, to bypass the non-consensus parts of the model, we drop out Steps C2 through C6, and observe what difference it makes. In other words, if there is conflict among the evoked goals (at Step C1), the model proceeds immediately to considering the position of fellow congressmen (Step D), rather than going through the decision rules designed to sort out the goal conflict. The issue then is how many of the 27 cases originally classified as Steps C2-C6 cases are accounted for by Step D, which turns out to be 12 of the 27, or 44 percent. This compares to 22 of the 27 (81 percent) in the original formulation. As with the first reformulation, this one does not improve on the original; in fact, it performs worse.

The third basic structural reformulation, instead of bypassing the non-consensus steps (C2 through C6), substitutes a simple but plausible decision rule for them, namely that in the event of serious conflict among his goals, the legislator votes in accord with his policy position. Of the 27 cases at issue, the policy goal is evoked in 23, and of those 23, the legislator does vote with his policy position in 17. Thus the hypothesized decision rule accounts for 63 percent (17/27) of the cases, compared to 81 percent (22/27) in the original model's steps C2-C6.

Changes in Certain Parts. The last structural reformulation leads directly to some possible reformulations of parts of the model, particularly concentrating on various parts of the goals steps (Step C and substeps thereof). These changes fall into three categories: one concerned with the constituency goal, those concerned with the intra-Washington influence goal, and one which eliminates the threshold requirement at the beginning of Step C.

First, in the steps of the original model which show a conflict between constituency and other goals (C2 through C4), one could state an hypothesis that if constituency is of major importance, given the primacy of re-election to a seasoned politician, the congressman should be expected to vote with the constituency every time. That model, however, would account for only 3 of the 19 cases, whereas the model presented in Figure 16-1 accounts for 16. Thus this reformulation would represent a distinct loss of ability to account for the outcomes quantitatively.

Second, taking up reformulations having to do with the goal of intra-Washington influence, one plausible hypothesis would be that congressmen of the President's party would follow his lead. In the session under study, the hypothesis would state that when Republicans were aware of an administration position and when it played some part in their thinking they would vote with the administration position. It turns out that when the administration was involved in Republican decisions, they voted with the administration position 68 percent of the time. By contrast, the model presented in this paper accounts for 85 percent of the same 59 cases.

Another reformulation involving intra-Washington influence would allow more than simply a president of the legislator's own party to be involved at Steps C5 and C6. Suppose, at that step in the model, that either the President of one's own party, or one's own party leadership, or colleagues within the House engaged in a logrolling exchange, could overturn one's own policy position; in other words, the entire set of evoked intra-Washington considerations could be swung into play, rather than simply a president of one's own party. It turns out that only two cases are affected by that change, and the reformulation fails to predict them correctly, whereas the original model had correctly predicted them.

The final reformulation eliminates the requirement that a goal must pass a critical threshold in order to be evoked (beginning at Step C), and then asks how the 79 cases originally disposed of at the goal consensus stage (C1) fare without that threshold requirement. Operationally, then, the goals are evoked as follows: (1) if either constituency or interest groups are of *any* importance in the congressman's decision (rather than of major or determinative importance), then the constituency goal is evoked; (2) if either administration, party leadership, or fellow congressmen are of any importance, the goal of intra-Washington influence is evoked; (3) the policy goal threshold remains unchanged, since the ADA-ACA index must provide some sort of direction. Then because some conflict among the goals is now introduced into the 79 cases that would previously have been filtered out due to the threshold requirement, we run the 79 cases through the non-consensus steps (C2 through C6) under the new conditions. The result is that Steps C2 through C6 correctly predict 62 of the 79 cases (78 percent), predict a result which does not in fact occur in 13 cases, and fails to provide a decision rule in four cases. If we allow those four cases to proceed to fellow congressmen for resolution (Step D), three of the four are correctly predicted there. Thus, by the combination of the non-consensus and fellow congressmen steps, we have correctly accounted for 65 of the 79 cases (82 percent), whereas the original model at Step C1 accounted for 74 of the 79 (94 percent).

In conclusion, after testing of several alternative formulations, it appears that the original model presented in Figure 16-1 emerges largely intact. None of the reformulations performs better in a quantitative sense, and many of them perform substantially worse. The good quantitative performance, however, does not address all of the questions which one might have about a model's usefulness. We now turn to some further questions.

A Caution about Quantitative Performance

It is appropriate to close with a caution that models of legislative voting should not be accepted solely because of their good ability to account for cases in quantitative terms.[33] In some situations in the social sciences, a good fit to the data is regarded as a sufficient condition to accept a model, since it is difficult to predict outcomes. In other situations, such as the case of legislative voting models, a good quantitative performance is a necessary, but not sufficient condition to accept a model, since outcomes are quite easy to predict. The null hypothesis in the legislative case predicts 50 percent of the cases by itself, since if a congressman were flipping coins between "yes" and "no" in order to decide, and a random model were also flipping coins, the random model and the congressman's behavior would agree half the time. Beyond this "impressive" chance performance, quite a simple model constructed from commonplaces in the literature — e.g., some combination of party, region, constituency, and President position — would probably do quite nicely in a statistical sense. Indeed, a model which simply postulated that all congressmen vote "yea," while not theoretically interesting, would yield a fairly good prediction.[34] As a matter of fact, most of the previous models discussed in this paper do quite nicely on their data sets, and we have become accustomed to models which predict about 85 percent of the cases. This is not to say that all possible models do well in terms of a criterion of ability to predict, as we have seen. Some models can be falsified, but that still leaves a number of models which do well.

In evaluating those remaining models of legislative voting, then, one should add to conventional criteria of statistical fit and quantitative performance, and use more conceptual and theoretical considerations. I outlined above some of these considerations, including plausibility, simplicity, political realism, and comprehensiveness. The advantages of the model presented in this paper have to do with those considerations. Our discussion attempts to use the virtues of various previous models to construct a more integrated view of legislative voting. The resulting model is quite comprehensive, and yet does not achieve this comprehensiveness at the expense of simplicity, plausibility, and realism. There is also a compelling logic to the progression portrayed, as congressmen are seen as moving from the simple to the complex, from a simple judgment about the whole environment, to a subsetting of that environment, to a further subsetting which concentrates explicitly on goals. These sorts of considerations, rather than simply an impressive ability to account for cases quantitatively, commend the model.

An instructive illustration may be the juxtaposition of the model presented here with the analysis found in *Congressmen's Voting Decisions*. I will discuss two of the types of analyses found there: the correlation analysis, which attempts to determine the influence of each of a set of actors on voting decisions, and the consensus model, which presents a process model of the decisions. Taking the correlation analysis first, in *Congressmen's Voting Decisions*, I identify six actors in the legislative system who could conceivably have an influence on a congressman's votes: the congressman's constituency, fellow congressmen, interest groups, the administration and executive branch, his party leadership, and his staff. The position of each on the issue at hand (for, against, neutral) is treated as an independent variable affecting the vote, and agreement scores, bivariate correlations, partial correlations, and stepwise regression are generated from the basic correlation model. The results are presented in great detail in the earlier work,[35] and need not be repeated here. What is relevant to this discussion is that the multiple correlation between the six variables and the vote is .83, and that the residuals exhibit no pattern which would lead one to suspect the adequacy of the equation. Thus the quantitative performance is good, and for some purposes, such as the ability to sort out the influence of various actors on legislative voting decisions, the analysis is quite useful.

As a model of decisional processes, however, the correlation approach does not appear to be entirely satisfying. A major point of a model such as the one discussed in this paper is that most of the time, legislators do not "weight influences" as regression, correlation, or some computer simulations portray them as doing. If legislators were to make decisions in a fashion analagous to regression, they would be required to weight each potential influence and to consider simultaneously the entire set of weighted influences. Given the severe time constraints on decision, and perhaps a general tendency for human beings to avoid thinking in such a simultaneous weighting fashion, this mode would not seem to be a plausible model of decisional processes. Furthermore, such a mode of decision is simply unnecessary on most votes. If the various possible influences agree, or the critical subsets of them agree, as they often do, then there is no need to engage in the weighting procedure that many other types of analysis require. A more minor consideration is that one would come away from the correlation analysis with the impression that fellow congressmen drive the decisions, which for a series of technical and conceptual reasons is probably not a complete model of decision, as I argue both here in this paper and elsewhere.[36] At any rate, it is important to distinguish the objectives of a regression mode of thought from those of a process modelling approach.

The other juxtaposition is between the model presented in this paper and the earlier consensus mode of decision, which is found in *Congressmen's Voting Decisions*.[37] The final steps of that model, unlike this current one, portray a deciding congressman as identifying the actors who were out of line with the dominant consensus in the field, and voting against them. The gain in predictive power of the model discussed here over that earlier model is trivial. What this new model does provide are important theoretical additions to the earlier work. As in the case of most of the models discussed in this paper, this integrative model does not negate or substitute for the earlier work, but rather adds to it in important ways.

To elaborate, the original consensus model in its last steps was not simply a matter of "majority rule" or mechanical counting. Somehow, there are processes at work, conceptualized earlier as "preconsensus" processes,[38] which lead the congressman to the conclusion that these actors against which he votes are isolated, of little consequence, and capable of being safely slighted. The model presented in this paper provides a way to interpret the pattern portrayed in the consensus mode. For example, there are 19 cases in my data in which the constituency is the one actor out of line with the rest of the field and in which the congressman votes against the constituency position. In 15 of those 19, constituency is coded as being of minor importance, meaning, in terms of the model presented in this paper, that the goal of satisfying constituents has not been evoked. The remaining four were all low-salience issues, in which the constituency interest could be overruled. Thus the operation of the model presented in this paper helps us to understand why the deciding congressmen could vote against constituency wishes in these instances. Or to take the other most numerous example, respondents voted against interest groups in 22 cases, of which 18 found constituency to be of minor importance and the remaining four found constituency opposed to the interest group position. Because interest groups are vulnerable without a constituency connection,[39] it seems quite understandable in terms of the integrative model presented here that congressmen should find it possible to vote against an interest group when the constituency consideration either is not evoked or is opposed to the lobby position. Other examples could be discussed.

The point is that deciding congressmen are indeed voting against these actors, as the original consensus model portrays them as doing. This new model adds some further thinking about *why* they are doing so. The same could be said for other models. Thus cue-taking is decidedly taking place, and congressmen are clearly voting in ways that can be interpreted according to policy dimensions. One advantage of the new model rests not in negating previous models but in providing a more comprehensive framework within which they can all be better understood.

Conclusion

This paper has started with a set of models of legislative voting which at first blush have seemed to many scholars to be alternative, contradictory accounts of voting decisions. Instead of treating them as competing models, however, I have chosen to discuss them as entirely compatible with one another, each having a grasp on an important part of the whole reality. Both by a verbal discussion of the models and of their place in legislative voting decisions, and by the generation of an integrative model, I have attempted to weave the various threads of reality together in a way which is satisfying both conceptually and empirically. I have ended by relating the new model to my data on congressmen's voting decisions.

There may be a wider applicability of the key concepts presented here beyond the case of legislative voting, in the sense that wide varieties of decision-makers may use versions of a similar general approach to their decisions. Legislators, bureaucrats, judges, and others may all be thought to search for consensus in their environment, to subset that environment in the event that agreement is lacking and to search for consensus within the most critical subset, to identify their most important goals and ask if there is agreement among them, and to get into more complex decisions if these simpler rules fail them. The well-known use of standard operating procedures in bureaucracies, for example, may be due to consensus among the relevant actors in the bureaucrat's environment — his superiors, the agency clientele, his co-workers, his professional associates outside the agency — that given SOP's are appropriate for a given class of cases.

Or judges deciding on sentencing of convicted defendents, for another example, have been found to impose the sentence recommended by police, prosecutor, and probation departments if the three agree; if they do not agree, the judge must enter a more complex set of decision rules.[40] Mass public voting behavior exhibits similar characteristics: when various important influences agree, the voting decision is made; when they do not, the voter is said to be under "cross-pressure," and the decision becomes more complicated. Space does not permit an extended discussion of the possible applications, but it is worth noting that the model presented here may represent a general decision strategy, an approach to decision-making which is widely used. Thus this work hopefully contributes not only to further understanding of legislative behavior, but also to the general building of theory about decision processes.

Notes

1. In Ralph Huitt and Robert Peabody, *Congress: Two Decades of Analysis* (New York: Harper & Row, 1969), 70. Italics in original.
2. Donald Matthews and James Stimson, "Decision-Making by U.S. Representatives," in *Political Decision-Making,* S. Sidney Ulmer, ed. (New York: Van Nostrand Reinhold, 1970), 14-43. See also their book, *Yeas and Nays* (New York: John Wiley & Sons, 1975).
3. David Kovenock, "Influence in the U.S. House of Representatives," *American Politics Quarterly,* 1 (October, 1973), 407-464.
4. David Truman, *The Congressional Party* (New York: John Wiley & Sons, 1959).
5. John Jackson, "Statistical Models of Senate Roll Call Voting," *American Political Science Review* 65 (June, 1971), 451-470. See also his *Constituencies and Leaders in Congress* (Cambridge, Mass.: Harvard University Press, 1974).
6. Duncan MacRae, *Dimensions of Congressional Voting* (Berkeley, Calif.: University of California Press, 1958).
7. Aage Clausen, *How Congressmen Decide* (New York: St. Martin's Press, 1973), see especially Chapter 2.
8. Cleo Cherryholmes and Michael Shapiro, *Representatives and Roll Calls* (Indianapolis: Bobs-Merrill, 1969).
9. John W. Kingdon, *Congressmen's Voting Decisions* (New York: Harper & Row, 1973); see especially Chapters 10 and 11.
10. Aaron Wildavsky, *The Politics of the Budgetary Process* (Boston: Little-Brown, 1964); and Otto Davis, M. A. H. Dempster, and Aaron Wildavsky, "A Theory of the Budgetary Process," *American Political Science Review* 60 (September, 1966), 529-547.
11. See their paper presented at the Conference on Mathematical Models of Congress, Aspen, Colorado, June, 1974. See also their paper, "A Dynamic Theory of Congressional Victory" (mimeographed, California Institute of Technology, 1975).
12. Morris Fiorina, *Representatives, Roll Calls, and Constituencies* (Lexington, Mass.: D. C. Heath, Lexington Books, 1974).
13. David R. Mayhew, *Congress: The Electoral Connection* (New Haven, Conn.: Yale, 1974).
14. Richard Fenno, *Congressmen in Committees* (Boston: Little-Brown, 1973).

15. See James March and Herbert Simon, *Organizations* (New York: John Wiley & Sons, 1958), Chapter 6; Chester Barnard, *The Functions of the Executive* (Cambridge, Mass.: Harvard University Press, 1966; first published 1938), 189-191; Richard Cyert and James March, *A Behavioral Theory of the Firm* (Englewood Cliffs, N.J.: Prentice-Hall, 1963), 120-122; Raymond Bauer, Ithiel Pool, and Lewis Dexter, *American Business and Public Policy* (New York: Atherton, 1964), Chapter 29.

16. Scholars are increasingly interested in this aspect, however. See John Ferejohn and Morris Fiorina, "Purposive Models of Legislative Behavior," *American Economic Review*, 65 (May, 1975), 407-414.

17. Subsets of constituents, such as constituency elites interested in the content of certain public policy outcomes, are also influentia: without necessarily being directly relevant to re-election chances. On these points see John Kingdon, *Congressmen's Voting Decisions* (New York: Harper & Row, 1973), Chapter 2.

18. For a general discussion of modelling decision processes, see Herbert Simon, *The Sciences of the Artificial* (Cambridge, Mass.: MIT Press, 1969). For an application, see Cyert and March, *A Behavioral Theory of the Firm*.

19. Kingdon, *Congressmen's Voting Decisions*, 72-79.

20. Clausen, *How Congressmen Decide*, 33-35.

21. Kingdon, *Congressmen's Voting Decisions*, Chapter 10.

22. I have presented elsewhere the decision rules used to choose House Colleagues to whom to turn for guidance. See *Ibid.*, Chapter 3.

23. Fiorina, *Representatives, Roll Call, and Constituencies*, and Mayhew, *Congress: The Electoral Connection*.

24. For some evidence on these points, see Kingdon, *Congressmen's Voting Decisions*, Chapters 4 and 6.

25. *Ibid.*, 35-44. The same balancing logic applies to Step C1. If constituency is not sufficiently intense to pass the critical threshold and policy position is sufficiently extreme, for example, policy dominates constituency.

26. For readers who are not familiar with the earlier study, it may be useful to present some details of the research design beyond what is presented in the text. The core of this study, which provides the data base for the quantitative analysis presented in this article, was a set of interviews with congressmen. In contrast to relying on roll call analysis or on standard survey interviewing, each of these interviews concentrated on some specific vote or votes that were currently or very recently under consideration. It sought to develop a kind of life history of that decision, including the steps through which the congressman went, the considerations which he weighed, and the political actors who influenced him.

There are two sampling questions involved: choosing the respondents, and choosing the votes about which to ask. As to the first, the sample of respondents is a probability sample of members of the U.S. House of Representatives in 1969, stratified by party, seniority, and region. I interviewed fifteen congressmen for each vote chosen. Once four draws of 15 congressmen ($n = 60$) had been made, I started to return to the first 15-member sample, and went through the sample in that fashion for the rest of the congressional session, 15 per vote, returning to a given congressman every fourth vote. It should be emphasized that the *decision*, not the congressman, is the unit of analysis. Since each congressman was interviewed about several voting decisions, the resultant number of cases is approximately the number of congressmen interviewed times the number of decisions each was asked about, or precisely, 222 decisions.

As to the selection of votes, given the issue-by-issue design, I had to choose votes weekly, as the issues came up for floor consideration. I therefore could not rely on con-

417

ventional sampling procedures, which require a final population list of votes as a sampling frame. I thus chose votes which were receiving some attention by congressmen, press, lobbyists, and others; votes in which several political actors (e.g., constituency, party, administration, etc.) might have the potential for being involved in decisions; and votes about which there was fairly extensive and intense conflict, upon which people appeared to be expending energy and political resources. The result was a sample of "big" votes of the session: ABM deployment, surtax extension, tax reform, HEW appropriation, state control over the poverty program, cigarette advertising, agriculture payment limitations, electoral college reform, water pollution abatement, foreign aid, campus unrest, elementary and secondary education, the debt limit, HUAC and the seating of Adam Clayton Powell, 15 issues in all. While these were all important votes, they were clearly not uniform in importance or in public salience, with some being considerably more salient than others.

The interview was conducted in a conversational fashion, with no notes taken. After I cited the vote which I wanted to discuss, I asked a general open-ended question: "How did you go about making up your mind? What steps did you go through?" After the question was answered completely and appropriate probes were exhausted, I asked a series of questions about each of several hypothesized influences on the vote, which were designed to pick up any other influence which was not spontaneously mentioned in response to the first question. I asked about the possible involvement of fellow congressmen, party leadership and informal groups within the party, staff, constituents, administration or executive branch, interest groups and reading. Answers to these questions were then coded according to the direction in which each influence would point the congressman and the importance which he appeared to attach to each influence.

For more detail on these procedures and the rationales for them, please consult Kingdon, *Ibid.*, Chapter 1, Appendixes A and B.

27. As I note elsewhere (*Ibid.*, 306) some intra-actor conflict (e.g., among constituents, among colleagues) is ignored here, and properly so. The key question is whether a given *consideration* (constituency, party, etc.) points in one or another direction, and what is the state of conflict among these considerations.

28. On the coding, see *Ibid.*, 16-23, 288-289.

29. *Ibid.*, 143-146.

30. It is also true that ADA and ACA scores relate strongly to other such indexes, lending an additional validity to the measure. See Carol Goss, "House Committee Characteristics and Distributive Politics" (paper prepared for delivery at the 1975 American Political Science Association meeting), 7.

31. See Kingdon, *Congressmen's Voting Decisions,* 292-293, for this coding and for the votes so classified.

32. *Ibid.*, 42-44.

33. For a general discussion, see Herbert Simon, "On Judging the Plausibility of Theories," in *Logic, Methodology, and Philosophy of Sciences,* III, ed. van Rootselaar and Staal, (Amsterdam: North-Holland Publ., 1968), 439-459.

34. For a discussion which makes the same point, see Matthews and Stimson, *Yeas and Nays,* 115. Weisberg has calculated various null models in addition to the 50 percent model, and has concluded that some of them can account for well into the 80 percent range. That fact places all the more importance on such considerations as plausibility, simplicity, and comprehensiveness. See Herbert Weisberg, "The Inherent Predictability of Legislative Votes" (paper prepared for delivery at the Annual Meeting of the Midwest Political Science Association, 1976).

35. Kingdon, *Congressmen's Voting Decisions,* Chapters 1-8, App. E.

36. *Ibid.*, Chapter 3.
37. *Ibid.*, Chapter 10.
38. *Ibid.*, Chapter 11.
39. *Ibid.*, Chapter 5.
40. Bradley Schram, "An Investigation into Disparity in Sentencing in Washtenaw County Circuit Court," (Senior Honors Thesis, Department of Political Science, The University of Michigan, 1972), 73-74. I should mention that Schram's work was done entirely independently of my own, and neither could have influenced the other.

17. VOTING CHANGE IN CONGRESS: SOME DYNAMIC PERSPECTIVES ON AN EVOLUTIONARY PROCESS

Herbert B. Asher

and

Herbert F. Weisberg

The policy decisions of the United States Congress as reflected in voting outcomes exhibit substantial continuity over time. When change does occur, it tends to be evolutionary and incremental as opposed to revolutionary and dramatic. Change is evolutionary because the congressional agenda is largely recurrent, members most often follow their previous votes on an issue, and congressional personnel and procedures are characterized by a high degree of stability. At times dramatic change does occur in Congress; certainly the famous 89th Congress (1965-1966) was characterized by substantial membership replacement as well as congressional approval of an impressive array of new social welfare programs. Yet even here the amount of change can be too easily overstated. Despite the sizable influx of freshman Democrats elected in the 1964 Johnson landslide, total membership turnover in the House was still only about 20 percent. And the numerous social programs finally receiving approval in 1965 had in many cases lengthy legislative histories going back years and even decades. Moreover, while the passage of these measures in 1965 after years of defeat certainly represented a dramatic reversal of past congressional decisions, the predominant voting pattern of members who served in the 89th and previous congresses was one of stability, not change. The point is that voting change in the Congress can best be characterized as an evolutionary process. This assertion

Authors' Note: The authors wish to acknowledge the financial assistance of the College of Social and Behavioral Sciences of the Ohio State University and the Horace H. Rackham School of Graduate Studies of the University of Michigan. Additionally, we are indebted to Fran Featherson, V. Patrick Hornbostel, Sherry Layton, Mary Lee Luskin, Robert Luskin, Richard Murray, Nancy Paulk, Allen Russell, Richard Schottenstein, Walter Stone, and Ron Taylor for their assistance at various stages of the project. The roll-call data were provided by the Inter-University Consortium for Political and Social Research.

Source: *American Journal of Political Science*, vol. 22, no. 2 (May 1978): 391-425. Reprinted with permission of the authors and publisher.

need not imply increasing complexity as does the Darwinian usage of evolution, although the changes observed in congressional voting patterns do often entail a shift from relatively simple to more complex patterns.

Hence, the aim of this paper is to present and test an evolutionary model of congressional voting change. The claim that change is gradual implies the existence of some forces that limit the amount of change. At the level of the individual legislative decision maker, the major force promoting stability to be discussed is the legislator's previous voting history on an issue. The presence of individual voting histories in conjunction with low membership turnover guarantees that the collective decisions of Congress will normally not change much over the short run.

Yet change does occur and is due to a variety of sources. One is membership replacement, particularly when large numbers of seats change partisan hands. But if this were the only source of change, even evolutionary would be too strong an adjective to describe the process. There is, however, one other major source of change, member conversion, in which the legislator switches his stance on an issue for any of a variety of reasons. One such reason is a change in the policy debate surrounding an issue. For example, if an increase in the public debt ceiling is perceived as needed in order to support domestic welfare programs, the liberal Democrat might favor such an increase. But if raising the debt limit is viewed as providing funds for an unpopular war in Southeast Asia, the liberal Democrat may move to oppose debt increases. In short, policy redefinition may result in vote change. Another source of conversion is a change in the external forces impinging on the legislator; foremost among these is a switch in partisan control of the national administration. On many issues, the desire to support the president of one's own party may be sufficient to override previous voting patterns. What makes partisan control of the presidency so important is that it affects entire groupings of legislators simultaneously. Other changes in the external environment are more specific, affecting only a limited number of congressmen. For example, a change in district boundaries or a transfer to a new committee may result in altered voting patterns, but these changes will be idiosyncratic to the specific legislators involved.

The previous paragraphs have laid out in very general and cursory terms some of the key concepts to be used in the paper. The next task is to provide a more systematic justification for positing an evolutionary model and to delineate further the significance of such concepts as *voting history, conversion, policy redefinition,* and others. After that is accomplished, a general model of congressional voting change will be presented followed by a series of case studies that will test the model.

The Evolutionary Hypothesis

Vote History

An evolutionary model assumes that the legislator's votes on recurrent issues exhibit more constancy than change. The congressman's voting history on an issue is, in effect, his "standing decision" on that issue. Once he has decided how to vote on an issue, he can continue to vote that way unless there is a relevant change in the decisional context.

There are numerous reasons to argue that a voting history on an issue would be likely to produce constant behavior on that issue. In interviews with congressmen, Kingdon (1973, pp. 254-257) found that a voting history on an issue simplified the representative's decision-making task; voting on an issue as one has done in the past is an economizing device, particularly when previous votes have not hurt the legislator. Legislators may be forced to fall back on previous votes given the magnitude of their decision-making task. They must cast many votes, often on complex issues, with little opportunity to devote substantial attention to each issue. In such situations, representatives must resort to simplifying strategies. One such strategy may be to rely on cues from various sources; another is to repeat previous votes on an issue unless the situation has changed dramatically since the earlier votes. As one of Kingdon's respondents stated:

> I was precommitted in a way. I had fought that out with myself some time ago — a year or longer — and had decided at that time to support funding for Viet Nam. I'd already been through that, and nothing in my circle of relevant factors had changed since. (Kingdon, 1973, p. 257).

This quote conveys well that the forces impinging upon the legislator are best considered relative to his previous voting history. Departure from previous voting history depends on change in that field of forces.

In addition congressmen do not want to call undue attention to themselves. Explaining one's vote to the constituency is simpler if the member continues to vote as he has always done rather than having to explain a shift in his position. If the electorate has accepted the previous votes, then a continuation of that voting position is deemed a simple and safe decision rule.

Finally, the sources of voting history seem likely to result in constant behavior on an issue over time. Often, voting history is based on party-constituency cues as when a northern, urban, Democratic representative supports certain social welfare programs or when a rural Republican legislator favors certain farm programs. In these cases, voting history is so based in party and constituency interests that a replacement from the same party would undoubtedly continue to vote as his or her predecessor.

How is a voting history formed and how is it maintained? It initially is likely to be a function of certain "background" factors such as party, ideology, and constituency. The stability of these elements over time facilitates continuity in the legislator's vote decisions. Voting history, however, also simultaneously causes and reflects learned behavior. As the representative learns that previous votes have not worked to his disadvantage, he realizes that he can safely keep voting that way. Given the uncertainty as to what issues a potential challenger may raise at the next election, the incumbent may decide to stick with positions that have worked well in the past rather than give his opponent more ammunition — particularly the ammunition that the representative is wishy-washy in his voting on an issue.

New congressmen establish a voting history very quickly; Kingdon (1973, p. 255) found voting history to be of major importance about half the time for votes cast by second term congressmen. A special problem occurs when a "new issue" arises. However, most new issues are actually related to some previous issue, often several. Thus the foreign aid program was not a totally new program when the Mutual Defense Assistance Act of 1949 was passed. It had clear antecedents in terms of aid to European countries after World War II and even to aid to the allies prior to the war. The "newer" an issue, the less settled the voting patterns will be initially, though we would expect vote decisions to settle eventually into a fairly steady pattern in accord with the voting history logic.

The Congressional Agenda

The concept of voting history makes sense only if the congressional agenda is largely recurrent. This point is essential to our argument because an analysis of voting change is possible only if Congress confronts the same issues repeatedly. This does not require that bills be identical over time, only that the general content of legislation be sufficiently similar so as to bring the legislator's previous voting history into play on the current decision. There are instances in which the addition or deletion of a single provision from a bill may radically alter its meaning and make voting history irrelevant or bring an entirely different voting history into play; certainly early aid to education bills that included the Powell antisegregation amendment were very different pieces of legislation for many representatives than the same bill without the Powell amendment. But for most bills, no single provision dominates, the legislator sees substantial continuity between earlier and later versions of legislation, and voting history is brought into play.

The best way of arguing for the recurrence of the legislative agenda is to consider what the business of Congress is in a typical session. First, Congress must fund a large number of governmental programs and departments by passing a set of appropriations and authorization bills. This is explicitly a recurrent agenda, having to provide funding for the same departments and programs year after year. The specific dollar amounts and statutory limitations may certainly change from year to year, but the general content of the legislation exhibits substantial continuity.

Second, many bills have lengthy legislative histories as representatives remain dissatisfied with the existing state of legislation in an area. For example, the initial attempts to introduce new programs often fail so that proponents must introduce them repeatedly before they become public policy. Legislation involving the federal government in aid to education and health care fall into this category. Other areas such as abortion, school prayer, reform of legislative procedures such as cloture, and the like are so controversial that they come up repeatedly for consideration as the losing side tries to reverse the previous outcomes.

Another category of recurrent legislation is that of bills which expire (or effectively expire) and so must be renewed if they are to remain effective. Much

423

legislation such as the Voting Rights Act requires periodic renewal. Other legislation must of necessity be reconsidered due to changing circumstances. For example, the national debt ceiling is fixed "permanently" by legislation at a level sufficiently low so that it must be increased after a few years if the government is to expend money lawfully. Minimum wage and social security legislation falls in a similar situation, having to be increased every few years in response to inflationary trends.

Certainly not all legislation is recurrent; many bills involve topical problems that are inherently nonrepetitive, such as ratification of a particular treaty, confirmation of a particular appointment, admission of a particular territory to statehood, or the authorization of a particular investigation. Such motions are certainly important and often controversial. Nevertheless we would argue that the vast majority of significant congressional business falls in the recurrent category.

Note that our argument pertains more to votes on the passage of bills than to amendments and procedural votes. Some amendments are recurrent (e.g., the Powell amendment and the amendments to end the war in Southeast Asia), but most are not. Moreover, voting history is more likely to be relevant for more visible passage votes than less visible procedural votes. The lesser visibility of the latter to constituents enables party and other pressures to have a greater impact, thereby reducing the impact of voting history on the member's decisions. Our emphasis in this paper will be on passage votes, though some extension to other votes is possible.

Once the congressional agenda is viewed as largely recurrent, this enables us to switch our research focus from the typical enterprise of studying the correlates of legislative voting cross-sectionally (Cherryholmes and Shapiro, 1969; Jackson, 1971; Truman, 1959) to analyzing the patterns of congressional voting change (as in Asher, 1973; Clausen, 1973; Kesselman, 1961, 1965). One reason to switch to a change perspective is to construct a more powerful theory of legislative voting; certainly any theory will be more powerful to the extent that it can account for voting change *as well as* cross-sectional voting outcomes. A focus on change obviously requires a longitudinal design extending over a number of congresses as well as a change in the explanatory model employed. The explanatory variables used in most legislative voting studies — party and constituency characteristics — vary little over time for most congressmen and hence cannot be very helpful in accounting for change. Political and policy variables outside of Congress must be examined in order to account for change; these will be discussed shortly.

In addition, an investigation of voting change departs from the usual emphasis in voting studies of describing or predicting the *collective* decisions of legislators on a *collection* of issues. Such a focus has tended to mask the voting patterns of individual legislators, has usually treated all votes as if similar decisional processes characterized them, and has often ignored the fact that many of the specific issues analyzed are ones that the congressman has made a decision on in previous years. A focus on *individual* decisions of legislators on *specific* and *recurrent* issues overcome these limitations. Thus we would argue that many interesting substantive questions central to a theory of legislative voting can best be studied with a longitudinal design.

Sources of Change

Although continuity best characterizes legislative voting, change does occur and is due to three sources which themselves can be subdivided into systematic and idiosyncratic (see Chart 17-1). The greater payoff for theory development is in initially concentrating on the systematic as opposed to the idiosyncratic sources of change.

Chart 17-1   Sources of Voting Change

Sources of Vote Change	Systematic	Idiosyncratic
Policy Influence	Long-term issue evolution or policy redefinition	Short-term developments (crisis, scandal, etc.)
Membership Effects	Membership evolution	Change in the status or district of an individual legislator
Presidential Influence	Change in partisan control of the White House	Change in presidency without partisan change

The first type of change occurs when the meaning of an issue changes over time in response to new conditions in the external environment. For example, foreign aid programs may initially be viewed in terms of thwarting Soviet aims and hence receive widespread, uncritical congressional support. As the perceived Soviet threat decreases, however, congressmen may bring a different perspective to their decision making about ostensibly similar foreign aid programs. The changes in meaning of an issue are usually gradual, even if a particular external event sometimes accelerates the pace of change. We label this process "issue evolution" to underline its substantial continuity.

As issue evolution occurs, particularly over a lengthy time-span, the content of the initial legislation on a recurrent issue may differ sharply from that in the most recent legislation. Yet for the continuing members of the legislature, the rate of change may be so slow that they will never change their minds enough to pass a program previously defeated or to kill an existing program. Thus, our second source of systematic change —membership replacement — provides an opportunity for policy shifts and policy reversals by the Congress at large even when continuing members never change their votes. Yet the limits on change resulting from the election of new representatives are severe. For one thing, membership replacement in Congress is limited with the overwhelming majority of members reelected at each election. Moreover, newly elected legislators often replace predecessors of the same party, thereby resulting in substantial continuity in policy views. Only those infrequent elections which result in a sharp change in party strength in the legislature provide a large potential for change, and that moreso on partisan issues than on issues related to the district. The most dramatic membership effects would occur as a result of partisan reapportionment, as when a city, formerly divided between two districts which each include sufficient suburban and rural areas to elect a Republican representative, is given its own district and elects a Democrat — an instance where the party *and* district of the new representative differ from those of his predecessor. Yet such changes are the least common. Membership change is a continual process, but the most frequent types of change have such minor effects on voting in Congress that we speak of the process as "membership evolution."

The gradual nature of issue and membership effects is in marked contrast to the sudden and substantial shock that the legislature receives when the voting cue from the White House is altered. Instances in which a president changes his mind on a program are infrequent. But the significance of the White House cue on many issues can change when partisan control of the administration changes, even if the Democratic and Republican presidents take the same stance on an issue. For example, both Republican and Democratic presidents have requested increases in the public debt ceiling so that a switch in partisan control of the executive branch did not result in a change in presidential stance on the issue. However, the meaning of the presidential cue changed markedly for congressmen. Congressional Republicans who opposed debt ceiling increases under a Democratic president suddenly find themselves subjected to strong partisan White House lobbying when their Republican president deems a debt increase needed to carry out the functions of government.

A diagrammatic representation of the forces affecting legislative voting is given in Figure 17-1. Vote history is viewed as the long-term component of the legislator's vote decision and changes in the decisional setting as the short-term elements. The origins of vote history are found in the explanatory variables commonly cited in legislative voting research, namely party affiliation, ideology, and constituency characteristics. A dynamic enters this model because of changing conditions in the real world; vote history is the element of constancy, but it is confronted by continual change in the external environment. Some of these environmental changes may result in substantial departures from past vote history whereas others may have little impact at all. Our aim is to identify departures from vote history and relate these shifts to changes in the decisional setting, particularly policy-related changes and shifts in partisan control of the executive. Overlaid upon these changes are those congressional membership changes which can alter the outcome on a recurrent bill even when continuing members maintain a constant voting pattern.

A further complication is that different sources of change may be prominent in different policy arenas. A massive infusion of freshman Democrats might have tremendous implications for policy in areas noted for partisan battles, such as Clausen's social welfare dimension. But in areas such as international involvement — where Clausen finds very weak party and constituency effects on voting

Figure 17-1   An Overall Model of Congressional Voting

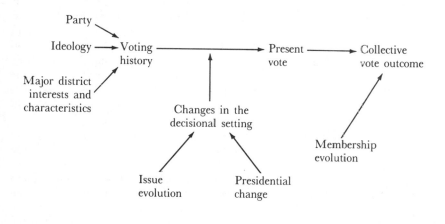

— it may be the case that a change in partisan control of the presidency will be required to alter congressional voting patterns. Likewise, in areas where constituency effects are supreme (such as Clausen's civil liberties dimension), only long-term issue evolution is likely to result in voting change.

Some previous studies of congressional voting have considered evolutionary models of the type employed here. For example, Matthews and Stimson (1975, p. 32) emphasized the role of incrementalism for simplifying vote decisions as well as for maintaining consistency, but decided against an incremental explanation arguing:

> . . . personal precedent is less valuable as a decision strategy than it might seem at first glance. It is a truism to say that nothing ever remains the same, but it is a truism that fits the facts of congressional life. Even if the legislation to be decided upon is identical to past legislation on which the member has a position, circumstances change. Public opinion, party positions, parliamentary and strategic considerations — all these can and do change from year to year, making precedent voting difficult. A bad bill in one session may be the lesser of evils in another, and compromise that had to be accepted before may no longer be necessary.

Notice that we regard what Matthews and Stimson consider the disadvantages of an incremental model to be its very advantages. Once the existence of recurrent votes is admitted, the nature of change, its extent, and its causes can be analyzed in a systematic fashion. In short, a precedent voting or voting history model serves as a useful baseline from which to analyze the voting change that does occur.

In summary, our evolutionary model asserts that stability rather than change characterizes congressional voting and that when change does occur, it tends to be gradual rather than abrupt. Both issue evolution and membership replacement are likely to result in modest voting changes, whereas a switch in partisan control of the Presidency can lead to more substantial voting shifts. In the next section of the paper, we devote considerable attention to delineating the types of vote changes associated with a change in the presidential occupant as well as presenting a model of the individual legislator's decision making.

An Individual Level Model of Congressional Decision Making

Our general model of legislative decision making is presented in Figure 17-2. According to the model, the key elements that the legislator considers in coming to a vote decision are his voting history on the issue, whether his party controls the White House, the position of the president if his party controls the White House (and in special circumstances the position of an opposition president), and whether his own position on the issue has changed. According to Figure 17-2, the

Figure 17-2 A Flow Chart Depicting Legislative Decision Making for Representatives with a Voting History on an Issue

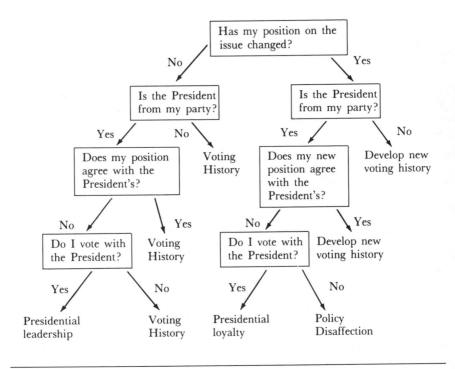

member first asks whether his position on the issue has changed. Such change might arise because of policy redefinition or issue evolution as the issue assumes a new meaning, or because of more idiosyncratic factors, such as alteration in district boundaries or switch in committee assignments. If the member's position has not changed, he can routinely continue voting his voting history unless his old position disagrees with that of the president of his own party, in which case he must decide whether to go along with the president ("presidential leadership") or follow his voting history. If the member's position has changed, we would expect him to change his vote and develop a new voting history unless his new position disagrees with that of the president of his own party, in which case he must decide whether to switch his vote ("policy disaffection") or follow his voting history so as not to embarrass his party's president ("presidential loyalty"). In the case of presidential loyalty, we expect that the member would change his vote as soon as his party loses the White House, adopting a new voting history more in accord with his changed issue position.

While an evolutionary model guides our inquiry, we argued earlier that the most dramatic exception to gradual voting change would occur when partisan control of the White House shifted. An examination of the model presented in Figure 17-2 under a change in control in the national executive helps clarify the different outcomes depicted in Figure 17-2, particularly the difference between presidential leadership and presidential loyalty. To simplify the following discussion, we are assuming that the issues under consideration are ones in which the presidential stance remains constant despite the shift in partisan control of the executive.[1] Studying such issues allows us in effect to control for the president's position while allowing partisanship to vary. Foreign aid, the public debt ceiling, and executive reorganization are examples of issues on which the president's position is likely to be constant regardless of his party affiliation.

Chart 17-2   Types of Individual Voting Change in Congress

	Congressman	*Congressman*
	shifts to support President	shifts to oppose President
Administration changes from opposition party to congressman's party	Presidential leadership	Policy disaffection
Administration changes from congressman's party to opposition party	Idiosyncratic behavior	Presidential loyalty

In comparing the presidential leadership and loyalty outcomes, the greater vote change would occur under the former as each partisan switch in control of the administration would result in substantial vote shifts. Under the leadership model, the presidential cue on certain issues is viewed as partisan rather than policy based, resulting in Democrats supporting their own party's president on an issue, moving into opposition on the issue when Republicans win the White House, and moving back to support when Democrats recapture the presidency. However, the loyalty outcome suggests that once vote shifts have occurred, members will likely retain their new voting histories in spite of subsequent changes in the partisan complexion of the White House. This is because the voting change associated with the loyalty outcome is policy based, even if originally timed so as not to embarrass one's own party's president. These differences will be illustrated in the analysis of foreign aid and public debt votes in the case studies in the next section.

The Case Studies

Introduction

Having developed the evolutionary hypothesis and our general model at some length, we now turn to a series of case studies designed to illuminate the advantages of our evolutionary perspective and to illustrate the methodology of analyzing vote changes in Congress. While a series of case studies cannot conclusively demonstrate the merits of our approach, a careful selection of issues emerging from past research efforts and theoretical perspectives can assure the reader that the deck has not been overly stacked by the choice of specific issues. Clausen (1973) has found five issue domains in postwar Congresses that are marked by continuity and stability: government management, agricultural assistance, social welfare, civil liberties, and international involvement. His analysis of party and constituency effects on voting . . . indicates the following patterns:

Government management	High party effects
Agricultural assistance	High party effects plus some constituency effects
Social welfare	Moderate constituency and party effects
Civil liberties	High constituency effects
International involvement	Moderate constituency effects with much variance unexplained by party or constituency

We would expect that policy areas affected by party would be most susceptible to voting change induced by shifts in White House control and by membership replacement, whereas those areas most affected by constituency would show the greatest vote stability unless long-term policy evolution or redefinition has occurred.[2] We use these expectations to select issues for analysis which minimize or maximize the likelihood of different types of voting change. While Clausen talks of issue domains, our evolutionary approach requires specific issues from broader policy domains. Thus, we will talk about the Mutual Security Program rather than international involvement and the public debt ceiling as opposed to government management.

In general, our data base involves voting in the House of Representatives from 1949 to 1972. This time frame was chosen in order to have three switches in partisan control of the White House — a Democratic administration from 1949 to 1952, Republican control from 1953 to 1960, Democratic control from 1961 to 1968, and a Republican administration from 1969 to 1972. We must occasionally depart from this time frame when the number of votes taken exceeds computer program capacities, when votes were not taken in all years, when there was a long break in the years in which votes were taken, or when new issues arose in the latter part of the time period. We restrict our attention to the House of Representatives to obtain a large number of cases for generalization and to gain comparability with previous studies on one of the issues we will investigate. The analyses we have performed on the Senate, however, do not suggest any contrary conclusions.

Our first two case studies focus on voting change associated with a partisan shift in control of the presidency. We wish to see how much change in individual voting *can* result from a change in partisan control of the executive. Hence we are selecting issues in which we expect voting change to be maximal, implying that if presidential effects are low here than they would be even lower on most other issues. We anticipate maximal presidential effects in policy areas where party effects are greatest — Clausen's government management area — and in areas where much of the variance in voting cannot be explained by either constituency or party and hence the presidential cue might fill the void — Clausen's international involvement domain. We shall test this by examining votes on public debt limit (a government management issue) and foreign aid (the core of international involvement). Both of these issues are characterized by the absence of widespread, effective domestic constituencies for the programs involved, so that presidential appeals for support from his party's congressional contingent could be very important.

The Debt Ceiling: Presidential Leadership Effects

The ceiling on the public debt is set by statute. Whenever the actual debt approaches that ceiling, the government must either decrease its spending or raise the ceiling with the latter being the choice invariably adopted. Fiscal conservatives, primarily Republicans, are most concerned about minimizing or preventing debt ceiling increases, yet Republican presidents have found it necessary to request debt ceiling hikes. Democratic legislators have been somewhat willing to assist Republican presidents with debt ceiling increases, particularly if a reasonable number of Republican representatives join in supporting the bill, while Republican representatives have been much less willing to support a Democratic president's request for a debt ceiling hike. The result is the classic situation leading to presidential leadership effects: members of each party more willing to support debt ceiling bills when their party controls the White House and moving to opposition when they lose the White House. This pattern is more pronounced for Republicans since Democratic liberals tend to support spending programs more than Republicans, and Democratic votes have been necessary to pass debt limit bills in recent Democratic-controlled Congresses, even under a Republican president.

Figure 17-3 shows the partisan support patterns on debt legislation in the House between 1949 and 1972. A majority of Democrats opposed the bill only in 1953, the one case in this period when the Republicans controlled Congress and the White House and could be forced to pass a debt bill with minimal Democratic support, and in 1972 when an authorization for the Republican president to impose a spending limit was a part of the debt ceiling bill. Republican support clearly reflected changes in partisan control of the White House, with majority support forthcoming during Republican administrations only and no Republican votes whatsoever cast in favor of debt increases during many years when the Presidency was controlled by the Democrats.

A stronger test of presidential leadership effects is provided by examining the voting patterns of the same representatives over a change in administration. Table 17-1 summarizes the debt voting patterns of those 225 representatives who were in the House from 1964 through 1971, a period of four Democratic years of presidential control followed by three Republican years. Members are classified according to whether they *always* supported or opposed the debt ceiling during each administration; otherwise members are placed in the residual category. Note the strong presidential leadership effects for Republicans: 45 of 78 Republicans always opposed a debt increase between 1964 and 1968 and then moved to constant support for it between 1969 and 1971 when their own party held the presidency. For the Democrats, movement in the opposite direction is substantially less with only three Democrats actually changing from consistent support to opposition when their party lost the White House. Hence, presidential leadership effects are evident in debt ceiling voting, although they are still smaller than the degree of constancy, especially for Democrats of whom more than half maintained a constant position in support of debt increases throughout 1964-1971.[3]

Another way of demonstrating presidential leadership effects is to conduct a dimensional analysis of debt ceiling votes for each administration. There were 50 votes taken from 1953 to 1972 on debt increases, one of which must be excluded from the analysis because it is virtually unanimous. Cluster analysis and factor analysis of tetrachoric r coefficients were used to determine the cumulative Guttman scale structure, a procedure suggested by Weisberg (1968) and MacRae (1970). Cumulation, i.e., a well-defined Guttman scale structure, was more pronounced for Democratic administrations as evidenced by reproducibilities for the scales for the Democratic administrations of .96, for the Eisenhower years .93, and for the Nixon administration .885. Moreover, the obtained scales were modestly correlated between Democratic and Republican administrations (with coefficients ranging from .18 to .51) and more highly correlated between same-party administrations — .94 for the Kennedy-Johnson administrations and .61 for the Eisenhower and Nixon administrations. When the Democrats control the presidency and Congress, Republican support for higher debt ceilings is unnecessary and practically nonexistent. The actual votes are strongly unidimensional, most Democrats supporting and most Republicans opposing debt increases. But when Republicans control the presidency and Democrats the Congress, both

Figure 17-3 Support for Debt Ceiling Increases by Party, House 1953-1972

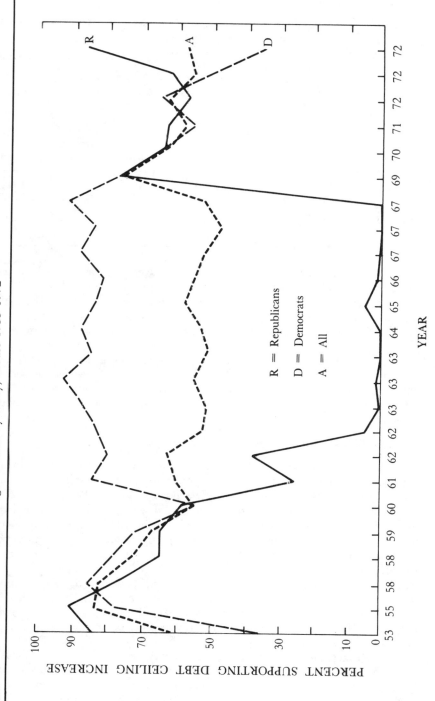

Table 17-1 House Voting Patterns on Public Debt Bills for Members with Continuous Service from 1964 to 1971, by Party

	Debt Voting Patterns					
Party	*Opposition under Democrats, Support under Republicans*	*Support under Democrats, Opposition under Republicans*	*Constant Support*	*Constant Opposition*	*Residual Patterns*	*Total*
Republicans	58% (45)	0% (0)	0% (0)	19% (15)	23% (18)	100% (78)
Democrats	0% (0)	2% (3)	54% (79)	6% (8)	39% (57)	100% (147)

parties are cross-pressured — fiscally conservative Republicans must help their President pass his program by voting for debt increases, while liberal Democrats with a record of supporting spending programs might prefer embarrassing the Republican President by opposing debt increases. These cross-pressures under GOP administrations create shifting coalitions and less partisan voting patterns. To the extent that cumulative scales exist, they include fewer of the votes and have more responses which violate the scale order. Not only does the presidential leadership model result in separate dimensions for Democratic and Republican presidencies, but the overlay of presidential support considerations on ideology results in less dimensional focus under Republican presidents.

Foreign Aid: Presidential Loyalty Effects

Some of the literature on foreign aid voting in Congress would lead one to expect presidential leadership effects similar to those found for debt votes. Particularly relevant here are Mark Kesselman's (1961, 1965) studies of the impact of presidential leadership on foreign aid votes in which he found that members of the president's party move to more internationalist voting records after a change in administration while the new opposition party becomes more isolationist. Kesselman's underlying model is one of presidential leadership; he would predict that not only do proponents of a program continue to support it when their party wins the presidency, but former opponents will shift to support the program. Furthermore, since the issue involves presidential support, the other party will move to opposition. And since presidential support is the basic element, the changes will occur in opposite directions when the next change in national administration takes place.

Another possibility is that foreign aid directly measures the internationalist-isolationist position of the representative or perhaps his fiscal conservatism stance (Jewell, 1962). The representative may take a position on foreign aid and vote accordingly in line with his voting history until changing conditions (such as a change in the economic-military division of the program, a change in the nature of our foreign commitments due to such events as war, or a change in the nation's fiscal situation) result in departures from past voting history. This suggests that presidential leadership in our terms would prevail less than policy dissatisfaction and presidential loyalty considerations.

The regional voting trends on foreign aid shown in Figure 17-4 are quite different from those for debt bills. Northern Democratic support of foreign aid was relatively stable with only the most modest decline in the Eisenhower years and less support (albeit still majority support greater than any other regional party grouping) during the Nixon administration. Southern Democratic support for foreign aid decreased during the Eisenhower years and enjoyed a resurgence during the Kennedy-Johnson years although only back to the support levels of the early Eisenhower years rather than of the Truman era. Republican support increased slightly under Eisenhower, decreased under Kennedy and Johnson, and increased under Nixon, but except for one roll call Republican support levels on foreign aid were always less than that of Northern Democrats. Hence, Figure 17-4 does not indicate sharply increased support for foreign aid when one's party wins the White House; instead, it shows that decline in support for the program occurs mainly when the opposition party controls the presidency. This illustrates very nicely the distinction between presidential leadership and loyalty effects. Loyalty effects dominate with policy disaffection causing decreased support for foreign aid over the years, but that disaffection is reflected in voting only when it would not embarrass the president of one's own party. Increased support of foreign aid when one's party wins the presidency is minimal; decline in support when one's party loses the White House is much more substantial. These initial findings already suggest a tempering of Kesselman's discussion of presidential leadership in foreign policy.

To further explore foreign aid voting change at the individual level, we have checked whether each representative voted for or against foreign aid on a majority of the final passage votes during each period of partisan control of the Presidency — the elected Truman term, the Eisenhower years, the Kennedy-Johnson administrations, and the first Nixon term.[4] The basic unit of analysis is the voting under successive administrations by a given representative. There are 1,071 such comparisons possible in this period, some involving the same representative more than once — as when a legislator serves during a change to a Republican administration and then through a subsequent change to a Democratic one. Table 17-2 shows the patterns of constancy and change associated with change in party control of the presidency.

A constant voting pattern occurred in fully 911 of these 1,071 cases — 592 instances in which the representative voted for the program in two successive administrations and 319 cases in which he opposed it — for an overall stability rate of approximately 85 percent. This latter statistic emphasizes that House voting on foreign aid is not simply a matter of presidential support, that a change in partisan control of the executive does not result in many shifts in final passage voting.[5] Of the change that did occur, the greatest amount involved 85 representatives who stopped supporting the program when their party lost the

Figure 17-4 Support for Foreign Aid by Party and Region, House 1949-1972

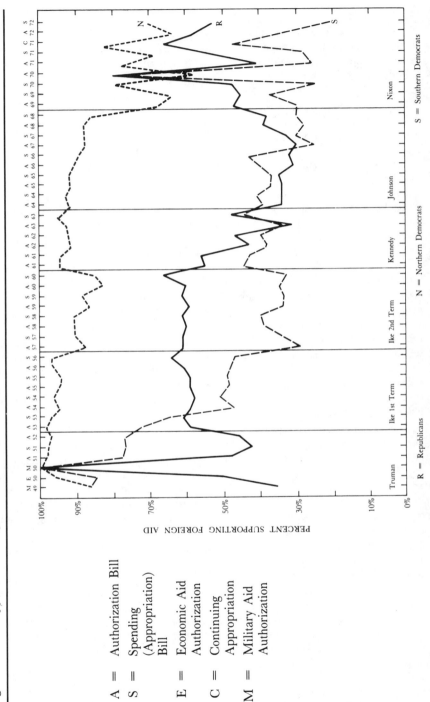

A = Authorization Bill

S = Spending (Appropriation) Bill

E = Economic Aid Authorization

C = Continuing Appropriation

M = Military Aid Authorization

N = Northern Democrats   S = Southern Democrats   R = Republicans

Table 17-2 House Voting Patterns on Foreign Aid Bills for Members Serving in at Least Two Successive Administrations, 1949-1972

Administration Control	*Foreign Aid Voting Patterns*				
	Opposition to Support[a]	*Support to Opposition*	*Constant Support*	*Constant Opposition*	*Total*
Own party takes control of the Presidency	10% (54)	3% (17)	51% (287)	36% (200)	100% (558)
Opposition party takes control of the Presidency	1 % (4)	17% (85)	59% (305)	23% (119)	100% (513)

[a] Opposition and support are defined by how the representative voted a *majority* of the time in an administration.

presidency, mainly Southern Democrats during the Eisenhower years, Republicans during the Kennedy-Johnson administrations, and Northern Democrats during the Nixon presidency. There are 54 cases which fit the presidential leadership model in moving to support foreign aid when their party wins the presidency, but these involve only 21 percent of the 254 representatives who were opposed to foreign aid at the time their party won the White House. The largest number of these shifts was 28 Republicans who moved to support foreign aid under Nixon, though some 82 Republicans still remained in opposition.

One of the best tests between the presidential leadership and loyalty models involves extending the time frame to two successive changes in partisan control of the White House. Presidential leadership would imply that a representative would change back and forth in his voting as his party gains and loses the White House, while the loyalty model would suggest continued opposition once opposition began. There are only eleven cases of complete voting partisanship across two successive partisan changes in control of the executive: five Republicans who moved from opposition under Truman to support under Eisenhower and back to opposition under the ensuing Democratic administrations, three Democrats with the reverse pattern, and three Republicans who switched from support under Eisenhower to opposition under the Democratic presidents and back to support in Nixon's first term. The three Democrats were the only ones in a group of 32 Democrats who favored foreign aid under Truman and opposed it under Eisenhower to move back to support under Kennedy and Johnson. Likewise, the three Republicans were the only ones among 27 GOP members who supported foreign aid under Eisenhower and opposed it under Kennedy-Johnson to move back to support under Nixon. Hence, the great bulk of the cases of change involved a change in voting history which was not reversed when the White House next changed hands.

These results contradict the substantial presidential influence found by previous investigators (Kesselman, 1961, 1965; Clausen, 1973; Tidmarch and Sabatt, 1972). One critical difference seems to be the unit being analyzed. Previous studies have employed Guttman scales of roll calls within Congresses and then measured differences in scale positions between Congresses; we have instead considered only votes on final passage motions. The contrasting results suggest an important difference between final passage votes and the other roll calls which previous studies have included in their scales. Final passage votes are more visible to constituents so that representatives are more likely to follow their established voting history unless external conditions dictate a rethinking of that position. Other votes are less visible, so the member may be more vulnerable to the argument that going along with the White House on them would not be noticed by constituents. The member can explain to his party leader that his district would not accept a change in his vote on foreign aid passage, but finds it harder to justify a vote against his party's President on preliminary motions.[6]

A dimensional analysis of foreign aid votes reinforces our conclusions about weak presidential (especially leadership) effects and also reveals long-term issue evolution in House foreign aid voting. Guttman scales were constructed of the votes taken within each four-year presidential term, omitting only two virtually unanimous votes and a roll call in the Nixon period on which the regional parties were in voting agreement and which was found by factor analysis to tap an independent dimension. The obtained scales all had high reproducibilities, .948 for the Nixon terms and between .976 and .987 for the other administrations. A regional shift in support for foreign aid is evident over time, with greater support for the program among Southerners during the Truman years and among Northerners thereafter. But the most notable trend is seen in the correlations among the scales presented in Table 17-3: higher correlations between adjacent terms and decreasing correlations as the time between terms increases, with the correlation between the Nixon and Truman scales (based on only 73 congressmen) falling to .35.

Table 17-3   Pearson r Correlations between Guttman Scales of Foreign Aid Passage Votes by Administration

Administration		Truman 1949-1952	Eisenhower 1953-1956	Eisenhower 1957-1960	Kennedy-Johnson 1961-1964	Johnson 1965-1968	Nixon 1969-1972
Truman	49-52						
Ike	53-56	.67					
Ike	57-60	.53	.81				
Dems	61-64	.62	.70	.80			
Johnson	65-68	.51	.66	.73	.86		
Nixon	69-72	.35	.53	.62	.66	.73	
Region*		.16	−.18	−.33	−.28	−.33	−.35
Party**		.52	.19	.04	.32	.35	.10

* Positive correlations indicate greater support among Southerners.
** Positive correlations indicate greater support among Democrats.

A similar evolutionary theme is seen in the issue space resulting from factor analysis of the tetrachoric r coefficients. An examination of the space presented in Figure 17-5 shows the Truman years at one point, the Nixon administration about 70 degrees away, and the intervening years along an arc between the two.[7] American relations with the Soviet Union and the nature of the foreign aid program evolved considerably over the years and this evolution is mirrored in the dimensional change. To sum up, we find some evidence of presidential loyalty effects, but little support for leadership effects as uncovered for the debt ceiling votes. And we find issue evolution in the dimension characterizing foreign aid voting.

Figure 17-5   Factor Analysis of Foreign Aid Passage Votes, House 1949-1972

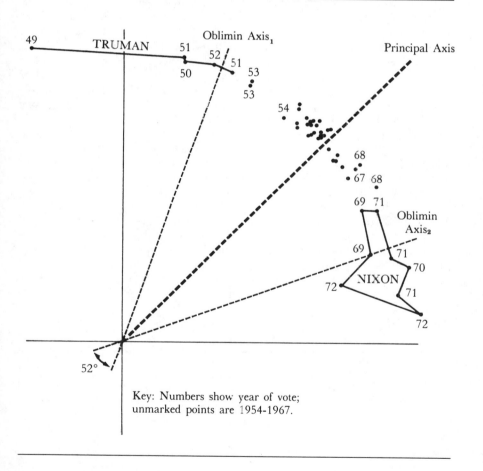

Key: Numbers show year of vote; unmarked points are 1954-1967.

Herbert B. Asher and Herbert F. Weisberg

School Construction: Membership Replacement Effects

The issue of federal aid to education is a good vehicle for demonstrating the effects of membership replacement on vote outcomes. Some of the early efforts to involve the federal government in education revolved around the question of aid for school construction. A school construction bill was defeated in the House in both 1956 (194-224) and 1957 (203-208) and gained ultimate passage in 1960 (206-189). To simplify our discussion we will focus on the first and last of these votes and identify the factors that changed a 194-224 defeat in 1956 into a 206-189 victory in 1960.

Table 17-4 presents the votes cast on school construction for only those representatives who were in the House in both 1956 and 1960. Note that the amount of individual vote change or conversion by the continuing members was minimal, with over 90 percent of the representatives who voted at both time points voting identically, a result in accord with our emphasis on voting history. In fact, among members who took a yea or nay position on school construction in both years, there was a net conversion of ten votes (18-8) or a twenty-vote *loss* over time, even though the bill passed at the latter time. This twenty-vote loss was partially offset by differential abstention rates from 1956 to 1960; eight fewer 1956 supporters than 1956 opponents abstained in 1960. Hence, individual vote changes and abstention patterns made a negative contribution to the ultimate passage of school construction in 1960.

We must turn to other factors facilitating the 1960 passage, focusing in particular on those districts experiencing membership replacement between 1956 and 1960. Table 17-5 presents the frequency of various vote patterns on the 1956 and 1960 school construction bills for those congressional seats which changed hands between 1956 and 1960.

Note that while 78 of the 107 seat changes did not result in vote changes, among the 29 seat changes that did lead to vote changes, there was a net switch in district's supporting school construction of 27 votes — which translates into a 54 vote gain. And most of this 54 vote gain came from the replacement of Republican incumbents with Democratic newcomers elected in the Democratic landslide of 1958. Thus, we have a situation where membership replacement provided the votes needed for a change in the aggregate vote outcome. Individual-level change

Table 17-4   1956 and 1960 School Construction Votes for Representatives in Office at Both Time Points

	1960 Vote			
1956 Vote	*Yes*	*No*	*Did Not Vote*	*Total*
Yes	109	18	11	138
No	8	130	19	157
Did Not Vote	1	4	1	6
Total	118	152	31	301

Table 17-5 Frequency of School Construction Vote Patterns for Districts Which Changed Hands between 1956 and 1960[a]

		Pattern of Seat Occupancy					
1956 Vote	1960 Vote	Always Republican	Always Democratic	Democratic to Republican	Republican to Democratic	Democratic to Republican to Democratic	Total
No	No	16	11	0	3	0	30
Yes	Yes	6	14	3	20	5	48
No	Yes	4	2	0	22	0	28
Yes	No	0	0	1	0	0	1
	Total	26	27	4	45	5	107

[a] To keep this table manageable, only those districts in which the occupant changed and in which the occupants took yea or nay positions in both 1956 and 1960 are included. This excludes 33 districts in which the representative did not vote at at least one time point, but this exclusion does not influence the direction of our results.

was not very consequential, since school construction was one of those domestic welfare programs that was a genuine point of contention between the two parties in the late 1950s. As such, one would expect strong party pressures to keep members in line which would account for the high level of stability observed. The influx of new members was required to bring about a change in the basic vote outcome (Fenno, 1963). Table 17-6 summarizes the components of school construction success; it shows clearly that membership replacement was the most important factor in the passage of school construction in 1960.

We can gain further insight into the nature of the outcome change on school construction by dividing the congressional districts into three groups: those represented by the same person in 1956 and 1960, those represented by different

Table 17-6 Components of School Construction Success

−30	1956 defeat margin

−20	Net vote loss due to conversion
+8	Net gain due to 1956 voters who failed to vote in 1960
−3	Net loss due to 1956 nonvoters who voted in 1960
+54	Net gain due to replacement
	+12 Net gain due to same-party replacement
	+42 Net gain due to partisan replacement
+8	Additional net gain due to replacement, where abstention occurs in either 1956 or 1960

+17	1960 passage margin

representatives from the same party, and those represented by different parties in the two years. The regression equations for predicting the votes of the member in 1960 from the vote of the member from that district in 1956 are as follows for the three groups:

$$V_{60} = 0.058 + 0.800V_{56} \qquad R^2 = .65 \qquad N = 265 \qquad \text{Same person}$$

$$V_{60} = 0.182 + 0.818V_{56} \qquad R^2 = .66 \qquad N = 58 \qquad \text{Same party, different person}$$

$$V_{60} = 0.880 + 0.078V_{56} \qquad R^2 = .02 \qquad N = 49 \qquad \text{Different party}$$

The high regression coefficients for the first two groups reveal considerable stability in voting for the groups with the difference between the constant terms indicating that new members were slightly (.124) more likely to support aid to education than were continuing members.

Clearly we can do a very good job in predicting later votes from earlier votes when the party controlling a district has remained constant, even if the specific occupant of the seat has changed — but not when the district switched parties. This suggests that the observed stability in voting may to a large extent reside in party. But this in no way negates the importance of voting history; instead, it suggests an explanation of the mechanism underlying the importance of voting history. On divisive, partisan issues such as school construction, the development of a voting history is very much rooted in party stances so that the vote outcome could change only if there were considerable partisan replacement.[8]

Civil Rights: Issue Evolution or Policy Redefinition Effects?

In this final case study, we will examine the effects of our third source of voting changes — issue evolution — by focusing on civil rights legislation between 1956 and 1972. This time-span was chosen because it encompasses the major legislative developments in the civil rights movement and because the number of votes taken in this period (100) does not exceed computer program capacity.[9] It is not possible to trace a single civil rights bill through time so we instead have considered all bills directly relating to civil rights. Yet the difficulty in delimiting the area means that some votes have been included in our universe which do not scale with the others.

The analysis yielded two major dimensions in the civil rights area — a traditional and a partisan dimension.[10] Traditionally, civil rights legislation has pitted the South against the North. The civil rights votes through the first half of 1966 exhibit strong cumulation because they all involve a virtually united South against the North.[11] For example, the 1956-1960 scale (with a reproducibility of .99) polarized the regions with 384 of 414 northerners on the liberal third of the scale and 105 of 122 southerners on the conservative third. Within regions, party differences were negligible. This same dimension is visible in some later votes on traditional civil rights issues protecting blacks: votes on the Civil Rights Commission, a 1967 bill to protect civil rights workers, and a 1968 bill prohibiting discrimination in jury selection. A scale based on these votes has a reproducibility of .99 and has very high correlations with the pre-1966 scales (see Table 17-7).

Table 17-7 Correlations (Pearson r's) among Scales on Civil Rights Issues

	Scale				
	1956-1960	*1961-1965*	*1966-1970 Traditional*	*1966-1970 Partisan*	*1971-1972 Partisan*
1956-1960	—				
1961-1965	.88	—			
1966-1970 Traditional	.85	.91	—		
1966-1970 Partisan	.59	.73	.62	—	
1971-1972 Partisan	.34	.48	.41	.73	—
Party*	.36	−.01	.15	−.32	−.29
North/South**	+.89	+.80	+.80	+.53	+.35
Reproducibility	.986	.984	.990	.964	.943
Number of motions	15	15	5	15	15

* Positive correlations show greater support among Republicans.
** Positive correlations show greater support among Northerners.

A new set of civil rights concerns arose as the battle for black rights moved from the South to the North and as issues of busing and open housing became prominent. The changed concerns were related to the occurrence of urban riots beginning in Watts in August 1965, and culminating in the major 1967 riots in Newark and Detroit, to the "white backlash" movement in the late 1960s, and to the Southern strategy of the Nixon administration as reflected in its attempt in 1969 to weaken some provisions in the Voting Rights Act extension. Northern support for the black position had decreased, particularly on the part of Republicans; new legislation aimed at blacks (e.g., antiriot bills) came to the fore.

The second dimension from our analysis corresponds to these changes. Loading high on the dimension are antiriot amendments and bills, the civil rights bills of 1966 and 1968 which involved open housing, and the Voting Rights Act extension votes of 1969 and 1970. In addition, the 1972 votes on Equal Employment Opportunities and the Civil Rights Commission load on this dimension though they are also related to the traditional dimension. It is the busing-related votes from 1968 to 1972, however, that form the core of this dimension.

This new civil rights dimension is characterized by party polarization in the North. On the scale composed of 1966-1970 votes, 164 of 197 northern Democrats are on the liberal third while 94 of 176 northern Republicans are on the conservative third. The 1971-1972 results are similar except that a general conservative trend is evident. Where the traditional civil rights dimension splits the regions, the new civil rights dimension instead splits the central tendencies of the northern parties. The greatest shift is among northern Republicans, but there is a more general change in position from the traditional civil rights dimension to the new partisan one which stops the two sets from cumulating with one another, even though the constant southern opposition on both dimensions and the substantial northern Democratic support on both results in a sizeable correlation between the dimensions — .51 between the factors and .34 to .73 between pairs of Guttman scales.

Civil rights is an issue area where constituency considerations would be expected to predominate. Under such circumstances, voting change would be expected to be slow. Yet the issue has evolved over a long enough time frame so that the original single dimension has split into two: one a clear continuation of traditional civil rights battles and the other a correlated but distinct dimension. The presence of a new dimension was very consequential for the extent of individual vote change on civil rights matters. Staunch opposton characterized the southern stance on both dimensions so that the new dimension did not result in vote change. But for Republicans the new dimension resulted in substantially more opposition to civil rights than is visible on the traditional dimension. And even for northern liberal Democrats with a general record of support for a variety of civil rights measures, the level of support for civil rights measures loading on the second dimension, especially busing-related bills, was lower than their support for more traditional measures. Thus, the voting of individual legislators can and does change in response to evolution of an issue.

Conclusion

There are a number of lessons to be drawn from the preceding analyses. First, the forces of continuity predominate in congressional voting. Stability in individual voting was much more common than change even when the partisan control of the White House was altered and even in issue areas — such as foreign aid and the debt ceiling — where presidential impact was considered substantial. On the school construction votes, where membership replacement best accounted for the ultimate passage of the bill, it nevertheless was the case that the most frequent vote pattern on the issue was one of constancy. And while the dimensional structure of civil rights did change over time, there remained a substantial correlation between the old and new dimension. The point is that the tremendous continuity in congressional voting should be explicitly recognized in attempts to build a theory of legislative voting. Any static theory that ignores this impressive stability is failing to incorporate a central characteristic of legislative decision making.

Second, there are differences in the nature of change between different policy areas. The most substantial changes occurred in the areas with partisan effects (but only after a major election upheaval) and the areas with presidential-partisan effects (but only after the presidency switched partisan control). Change seems to be much slower in areas with constituency influence dominant and in areas with little party or constituency influence (in which case longer-term issue evolution is required if change is to result). Our analysis in this paper does not fully test all these expectations, as a complete test would require a more exhaustive study of a large number of issues than could be reported here. However, the results are sufficient to disprove some prior expectations (the presidential leadership model in foreign aid voting as an example) and to demonstrate that different policy areas will be affected by different types of change.

Third, congressional voting change seems to be primarily evolutionary. There is stability in the process and the change that occurs is slow. More research will be required to determine the extent to which congressional voting fits the evolutionary hypothesis, but the current effort already demonstrates that a focus on patterns of voting change is appropriate. Certainly one path that future research efforts might follow is to examine more systematically several issues with an eye toward comparative patterns of change and stability across these issues. Yet another is to expand the analysis to the Senate so as to facilitate additional institutional comparisons. Additional testing of the evolutionary hypothesis will further increase our understanding of Congress as an ongoing institution influenced by political and societal changes.

Notes

1. Most instances in which the presidential stance changes when a new president takes office involve partisan issues on which most party members will just maintain their partisan vote. For example, conservative Republicans who oppose a social program under a liberal Democratic administration generally continue to do so when a more conservative Republican president also opposes it, and the opposite for liberal northern Democrats. Conservative southern Democrats may pose an exception: they may support a social program to please a Johnson but would oppose it under a Nixon. In such instances changing their voting history is an instance of presidential support.
2. These expectations are similar to Clausen's discussion, pp. 231–236.
3. The residual cases in Table 17-1 generally support this theme with minimal modification, such as the "fair play" Democrats who supported the opposition President in his first years in office before moving to opposition, or the Republicans who supported Johnson's requests for debt increases in his honeymoon period but then moved to opposition until Nixon won office. The major residual pattern which suggests a different theme involves six GOP members who opposed debt increases constantly except for Nixon's first year in office, accepting in 1969 the argument that the new Republican administration merited support in a fiscal situation over which it had no control (see also Kingdon, 1973, p. 247).
4. By using how the representative voted on the *majority* of roll calls during each period, we maximize the possibility of obtaining change in voting associated with the presidential leadership model. Had we examined only those cases where the representative voted constantly for or against the program throughout an administration, we would have much less change than reported here.
5. The Republicans regained control of the White House twice during the time period being studied while the Democrats did so only once, so the top half of Table 17-1

tends to emphasize Republican congressmen while the bottom half tends to emphasize Democrats.

6. This argument implies that there is greater party unity on votes prior to final passage than on final passage votes. As a test, we have examined vote totals on all motions on foreign aid bills from 1949 to 1972 in the House of Representatives. All votes on conference reports are combined with final passage votes, so our comparison will be between votes taken prior to final passage votes on the one hand and final passage votes and beyond on the other. We would expect Republicans to be more supportive on passage than on prior motions during Democratic administrations. During the Truman years on the average motion at the passage stage 60 percent of the Republicans were supportive of aid while at prior stages only 27 percent were; comparable figures for the Kennedy-Johnson years are 37 percent and 22 percent. We would also expect Republicans to be more supportive on prior motions that on passage during Republican administrations. During the Nixon years on the average motion at the passage stage 52 percent of the Republicans were supportive while 68 percent were at prior stages; during the Eisenhower years the comparable figures are 61 percent and 67 percent. Similar trends are apparent for Democrats, though they are considerably muted. Republican support of aid was more variable on prior votes than at the passage stage, though there is little difference among Democrats.

7. The figure shows the most important two factors obtained in varimax rotation of the three factor solution. The vote on a supplemental bill in 1970 which included the Cooper-Church end-the-war amendment is not shown in the figure since it loads nearly exclusively on the third factor.

8. We could have formally included party in the regression equation for continuing members, and we would have found that much of the effect originally attributed to vote history (V_{58}) would now be due to party, although the two predictor variables would have been so highly correlated that it would be impossible to talk about their separate effects. However, if we view party as a cause of voting history, then it makes sense to determine the effect of voting history in summary form while not caring about the extent to which it is itself determined by party.

9. There are three series of civil rights related votes since 1949. The House considered 29 civil rights votes from 1949-1951 but none from 1952-1955, then had 68 votes from 1956-1972 plus 32 votes on busing from 1968-1972. The total of 129 votes is more than our available computer capacity permits, so we have had to drop some votes. Given the absence of votes from 1952-1955, the 1949-1951 votes are those which can most obviously be dropped. Those votes actually cumulate very well with the votes taken in 1956-60, so that dropping them introduces no bias. The busing area is virtually undimensional, but it will be of interest to see whether the busing votes fit in with the other civil rights votes. Therefore the civil rights votes to be analyzed are the civil rights and busing votes from 1956-1972. This analysis owes much to the work of Jeanette Frazer, Anita Pritchard, James Gearhart, and Lyn Halverson.

10. The factor analysis yields two very important factors and possibly two additional factors. The results reported here involve the two most important factors in an oblique rotation of the four factors; scattered votes load on the remaining two factors or load on none of the factors, but the two first factors predominate.

11. The eleven ex-confederate states comprise the South for purposes of this analysis. The lack of complete polarization may be due to inadequacies of this definition.

18. PARTY, CONSTITUENCY, AND ROLL-CALL VOTING IN THE U.S. SENATE

Charles S. Bullock III
and
David W. Brady

After almost 30 years of research on the relationship between constituency and legislators' voting behavior, the results are not definitive. Much of the lingering uncertainty is owing to the tangled interaction of party and constituency and the consequent disagreement among scholars over how to include party in the constituency-voting behavior model. Some have taken what Key (1961) called "the simple constituency pressure model" (Froman, 1963; Flinn, 1964; Markus, 1974). Others have adopted a dual-pressure approach to the problem, arguing that both party and constituency affect voting behavior (Turner, 1951, and Schneier's update, 1970; Mayhew, 1966). In a more sophisticated version of the dual-pressure theory, offered by Clausen (1973) and Stone (1965), party is seen as a shared set of policy concerns which may outweigh constituency preferences. This perspective helps account for such anomalies as George McGovern's liberal voting record while he represented South Dakota.

Our understanding of the nature of constituency has been advanced by scholars who have developed more complex definitions of the concept. Fenno (1977, pp. 1-30) and Fiorina (1974, pp. 103-105) argue that constituencies are not simply the sum of demographic characteristics within a set of geographic boundaries. Fenno identifies four distinct constituencies for each legislator: the geographic, the reelection, the primary, and the personal. The geographic constituency is the largest, encompassing the entire district represented by a legislator; the personal constituency is the most restricted, including only the legislator's closest and earliest supporters. Between these extremes, each representative counts as his reelection constituency those voters who generally vote for him and as his primary constituency only those within his party who are most strongly committed to him. Therefore, simply correlating general district characteristics and representatives' voting behavior may reveal little about the constituent-representative relationship, since the geographic constituency includes both a

Source: *Legislative Studies Quarterly*, vol. 8, no. 1 (February 1983): 29-44. Reprinted with permission of the authors and publisher.

legislator's supporters (whose preferences we might expect to correlate well with the legislator's roll-call voting) and his opponents (with whose attitudes a strong correlation is less likely).

Fiorina (1974) asserts that a heterogeneous constituency is an important case for analyzing representatives' voting behavior. Resurrecting Samuel Huntington's hypothesis (1950), he shows that a representative from a competitive, heterogeneous district will establish a voting record far different from that of a predecessor of the other party, presumably because each represents different parts of the constituency. Since Fiorina studies district heterogeneity and marginality as determinants of voting behavior, he is content to show that the two are related and that heterogeneity is more likely than marginality to be associated with differences in legislators' voting behavior.

Although we rely heavily in this article on the insights of Fiorina and Fenno, our purpose is different. We explore the influences of constituency and party on legislator voting in a new way, by analyzing the voting patterns of pairs of senators from the same state and comparing those pairs who have different party affiliations (whom we refer to as split-party senators) with those pairs who share a party tie. Because we compared the voting records of two senators from the same state, we can be sure that differences in geographic constituencies are not responsible for differences in roll-call voting. Moreover, we can compare their voting behavior on the same set of roll calls; this was not possible for Fiorina (1976), who compared representatives from the same district serving in successive Congresses.

We test a model in which similarities and differences in the roll-call voting of senators from the same state are linked to population characteristics (Fenno's geographic constituency), reelection constituency characteristics, party control, and partisan competitiveness. Our path analysis operates on electoral results from 1968 to 1972 and on two roll-call measures for the 93rd Congress (1973-1974).

Heterogeneity and Representation

Before turning to the path analysis, we will determine whether there has been a relationship between population heterogeneity and party control of Senate seats. Many scholars have argued that heterogeneous districts are more likely to be competitive (Huntington, 1950; Froman, 1963; Kingdon, 1966; and Fiorina, 1974), but here we test whether heterogeneous states are more likely than homogeneous states to be represented by senators of different parties. To determine whether a state is heterogeneous, we use Sullivan's (1973) measure of population diversity. The measure represents the proportion of characteristics upon which a randomly selected pair of individuals will differ. Based on 1960 census data, the scores range from a high of .556 in New York to a low of .330 in Mississippi.[1] These scores can be interpreted to mean that two randomly chosen New Yorkers will differ on 56 percent of the selected educational, social, economic, and religious characteristics, while two Mississippians chosen at random will differ on only 33 percent of these same characteristics.

The dependent variable (incidence of split-party senators) was measured in several ways. The first measure is the number of times from 1947 to 1978 that a state had split-party senators. Since there were sixteen Congresses in this period, the range of value is zero to 16. Massachusetts most often had senators of different parties (in 13 of the 16 Congresses), while a number of states, including Kansas and Alabama, had no instances of split-party representation.

Table 18-1 shows that a heterogeneous population within a state is linked to higher incidences of split-party representation. The five most heterogeneous states had split-party representation over two-thirds of the time, while the five least heterogeneous had split-party senators only 15 percent of the time. The data for the mid and low 20 states corroborated the hypothesis. The raw Sullivan diversity scores are strongly correlated with the number of times a state had split-party senators ($r = .61$), indicating that the relationship shown in Table 18-1 is not a product of the way in which the states were grouped.

Using another measure, we scored a one for a state each time it elected or re-elected a senator whose party affiliation differed from that of his state's other incumbent. This measure was even more strongly related to population heterogeneity ($r = .66$).

This and the measure used in Table 18-1 are affected by incumbents who continue to win reelection. Other measures were devised which excluded instances in which an incumbent was reelected. In the first of these, we scored the number of times that a freshman senator was of the opposite party of the holder of the other seat; in the second, the number of times that a freshman was of the opposite party of his/her predecessor. Eliminating elections in which incumbents won reelection results in smaller correlation coefficients ($r = .41$ and $r = .37$, respectively), although they are in the expected direction. Clearly, constituency heterogeneity and split-party representation have been related over time.

Theory

Having found that state population characteristics have been related to the incidence of split-party Senate representation, we can turn our attention to the ways in which constituency and party characteristics are linked to the voting

Table 18-1 State Heterogeneity and Frequency of Split-Party Representation: 80th to 95th Congresses[a]

States Ranked by Heterogeneity Scores	Number of Instances of Split Party Representation	Total Number of Congresses	Mean Number of Split Party Delegations	% of Split-Party Delegations per Congress
Top 5	50	74[b]	10.0	67.5
Next 20	120	314[c]	6.0	38.2
Next 20	79	320	3.9	24.8
Low 5	12	80	2.4	15.0

[a] Correlation (r) of diversity index and instances of split-party representation = .61.
[b] Hawaii has elected senators only since the 86th Congress.
[c] Alaska has elected senators only since the 86th Congress.

records of pairs of senators representing a single state. We offer a path model to describe the linkages among constituency and party and the degree to which the senators elected from the same state vote together. The dependent variable is the difference in the roll-call votes of a state's pair of senators, not some measure of individual senators' roll-call behavior. The model, for which a theoretical basis will be presented shortly, consists of the following: geographical heterogeneity, reelection constituency, party control of the state's Senate seats, partisan competitiveness, and a measure of the difference in voting behavior of each of the state's pair of senators. It is expected that states which have heterogeneous populations (what we call geographical heterogeneity) will be more likely to elect senators who have different reelection constituencies and therefore will be more likely to have split-party control of their Senate seats. The nature of the reelection constituencies may also be related to the level of partisan competitiveness in a state. Figure 18-1 shows the direct and indirect paths between these variables and the roll-call records of senators from a particular state.

The model has a single exogenous variable, geographical heterogeneity, which (like Fenno's geographic constituency), is a measure of the entire constituency. Geographic constituency should affect the nature of the reelection

Figure 18-1 Model of Constituency Influences, Party, and ADA Support, 93rd Senate[a]

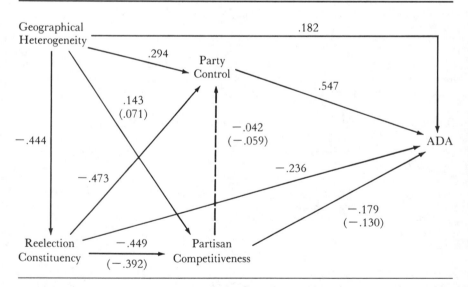

[a] Figures reporting relationships with partisan competitiveness give the beta for the adjusted Pfeiffer measure first, with the beta for the adjusted Ranney measure appearing in parenthesis.

constituency and have a weaker direct influence both on how there is split-party or same-party control of a state's Senate seats. The reelection constituency should have a greater effect than the geographic constituency on these same two variables of partisan competitiveness and of party control of senate seats.

The rationale for our model needs some elaboration. Fenno's (1977) notion of the circles of constituency holds that the geographic constituency is less central to a legislator than the reelection constituency. Since the reelection constituency is a subset of the geographic constituency, the latter will partially determine the nature of the former. Legislators' policy positions should be influenced more by their reelection than their geographic constituency, since the latter includes the legislators' opponents as well as supporters.

Of course, if the geographic constituency is homogeneous, then a legislator's reelection constituency will also be homogeneous. Therefore, to the extent that legislators' voting records reveal their responsiveness to their constituents, greater differences between the records of a state's senators are likely when they attract reelection support from different groups within their common geographic constituency.

It should be recognized that under some circumstances, cleavages in the geographic constituency may not translate into different reelection constituencies. To take what is perhaps an extreme example, until recently the racial and economic cleavage in most southern states did not produce distinct reelection constituencies for senators, since Democratic incumbents had no opposition. We expect that party will have a stronger direct effect on roll-call voting than will the nature of the geographic or the reelection constituencies. Political parties often attract distinct subsets of followers to their banners (cf. Brady and Althoff, 1974). In recent presidential elections, Democratic nominees have fared better among blacks, Republicans among whites. During much of the last half century, Democrats have run stronger in blue-collar precincts and Republicans among white-collar voters. Therefore, when the reelection constituencies of a state's senators are quite dissimilar, it is more likely that the incumbents will represent opposing parties and that partisan competition will be more intense.

Proponents of party government have long deplored the absence of strong party control. Donald Matthews nicely sums up the role of party in Senate roll-call voting: "Party 'discipline' may be weak, but party 'identification' is strong" (1960, p. 123; also see Patterson, 1967, pp. 200-210; Ripley, 1967, p. 143). When other factors have limited salience, legislators will follow the party line (Clausen, 1973, p. 125; Froman and Ripley, 1965). Individual legislators are more likely to vote with their party if the interests of their constituents coincide with the position taken by party leaders (Mayhew, 1966); legislators are less likely to vote with their party if they receive conflicting cues from constituents and party.

Even those legislators — if any exist — who profess total, unwavering commitment to the demands of their constituents are not wholly immune to partisan influences. Dexter (1965) has pointed out a number of difficulties inherent in the role of delegate: legislators are more likely to be contacted by constituents who agree with them and are therefore more likely to hear from constituents who share their party tie (see also Clausen, 1973, pp. 127-132). On many issues, try as they will, legislators get no cues from their constituents because so few in their districts care. In these cases, legislators are most likely to credit their colleagues with influencing them (Kingdon, 1973), and the colleagues from whom they are most likely to get policy guidance are their fellow partisans.

It is expected that both the geographic and the reelection constituency variables will be related to competitiveness (Fiorina, 1974; Froman, 1963). Differences in the geographic constituency make it possible for parties to tap different reelection constituencies, but do not guarantee that this will happen. Therefore, a stronger relationship should exist between the reelection constituency and party competition than between geographic features and competition.

Some studies have observed a relationship between competitiveness and roll-call behavior. Huntington (1950) hypothesized that legislators from marginal districts will be more likely than representatives from safe districts to take extreme positions. Fiorina (1974) has suggested that this happens because legislators from competitive districts are responsive to party activists. It is these whom a legislator will perceive "as having the greatest potential to affect his reelection probability" (Fiorina, 1974, p. 122). Since party activists tend to take more extreme positions on issues than do rank-and-file party adherents, split-party senators (who would be more likely to be responsive to activists in their reelection constituencies), would have more disparate voting records than would same party senators.

To support this reasoning, Fiorina analyzed the roll-call records of legislators from districts in which there were shifts in partisan control during the Johnson years; he found that a change in the party controlling a House seat produced a wide swing in roll-call behavior. Bullock has found similar changes occurring when southern districts have replaced Republican with Democratic representatives (1981, p. 681). Therefore, in more competitive states the two senators may have less similar voting records.

There is an alternative line of reasoning. Deckard (1976), analyzing the relationships between competitiveness and constituency characteristics in the U.S. House, concluded that the nature of the district, but not electoral competitiveness, had an effect on legislators' party loyalty. If this finding is applicable to the Senate, then competition will affect senators' voting records less than will either the geographic or the reelection constituency.

Competition should also affect voting records less than party control does. If both of a state's senators are of the same party, then their voting behavior may be similar even if they were narrowly elected and even if the parties usually compete on equal terms. In contrast, a senator who has become personally invincible may survive, despite being a member of the minority party in a state in which the other party wins most contests. Moreover, legislators from marginal districts have at times been found to be particularly strong partisans (Brady, 1978, p. 96; Froman, 1963). When this happens, competitiveness would add little to the influence of partisanship.

Data

The path model explores the relationship of four variables to two measures of roll-call behavior. Our measure of geographical consistency is based on the Sullivan index, but the variable of race replaces the variable of religion[2] and data from the 1970 census replace Sullivan's data. The 1970 figures are contemporary with the elections (1968-1972) and roll calls (93rd Congress) we analyze.

For our measure of the reelection constituency we estimated the nature of the coalitions which elected the senators of the 93rd Congress.[3] Ideally we would have had sample surveys of voter preferences in each state for the most recent elections of both incumbents. Adjusting hopes to reality, we used ecological regression to estimate the share of the vote received by the Democratic nominee in each election (on ecological regression see Shively, 1969; Jones, 1973; Markus, 1974). The independent variables were the 1970 census figures on education (percentage of the population over 25 years old with at least a high school education), income (percentage of families earning more than $10,000 annually), occupation (percentage of white-collar workers in the labor force), and race (percentage of nonwhites). The regression equations indicated the share of the electorate in a category (e.g., high school graduates) which voted Democratic and the share of the electorate not in that category (e.g., non-high school graduates) which voted Democratic. Counties weighted on the basis of population were the units of analysis in the regressions.

We computed a separate index of likeness across elections using the share of the vote estimated for the Democratic Senate nominees in each of the sociological categories — i.e., white, non-whites, high school graduates, those with less than a high school education, etc. The mean for these comparisons is used to measure the difference in voting coalitions supporting the two senators. High scores indicate the senators' electoral coalitions are very similar; the closer the score to zero, the greater the differences.[4] A score would approach 100 when a category of voters gave each of a state's senators about the same percentage of the vote in the most recent election. To illustrate with only one of the eight categories used, if Senator A received 90 percent of the vote cast by blacks in 1968 and the state's other senator, B, received 85 percent of the black vote in 1970, the index of likeness for black voters in that state would be 95.[5]

The data is drawn from the elections of 1968, 1970, and 1972, during one of which each of the senators serving in the 93rd Congress was elected. Moreover, these elections coincide most closely with the 1970 census.

Two measures of partisan competitiveness within states were tried. In the model for the scale developed by the liberal Americans for Democratic Action, the more successful measure of competitiveness was calculated from that developed by Pfeiffer (1967, p. 464). The other measure is based on Ranney's interparty competition score for 1956-1970 (Ranney, 1971, p. 87).[6]

The Ranney and Pfeiffer competition measures had to be adjusted before they could be used in this analysis; they give high scores to Democratic states and low scores to Republican states, with scores in the intermediate range (.5) indicating high levels of partisan competition. We use the absolute differences between .5 and the scores on the Ranney and Pfeiffer measures; thus, competitive states will have low scores and one-party states (be they Democratic or Republican) high scores. Competitive states should score low on the reelection constituency measure but high in geographic heterogeneity.

The party control measure is a dummy variable; split-party control of a state's Senate seats in the 93rd Congress is coded one and same-party control is coded zero. There are two roll-call measures; one is the scale for items selected by the liberal Americans for Democratic Action, and the other is the score for issues on which the Conservative Coalition was active. For each state's pair of senators, a roll-call score was calculated by taking the absolute difference between the ratings assigned each by the Conservative Coalition; a second roll-call score was calculated as the absolute difference between the ratings assigned each by the ADA. For example, to compute the ADA score for Idaho, James McClure's score of 12.5 was subtracted from Frank Church's 70.5, leaving 58 as the measure of voting difference.

Path Analysis

The results of the path analysis are depicted in Figures 18-1 and 18-2 (on path analysis, see Asher, 1976). They confirm a number of our expectations. The betas indicate that the most important path, particularly for differences in the voting records of pairs of senators on Conservative Coalition roll calls, goes from geographic constituency to reelection constituency to party control to roll-call behavior. Senators are more likely to be elected by different coalitions in states with heterogeneous populations than in states with more homogeneous populations. As hypothesized, the nature of the reelection constituency has a greater direct effect than does geographical heterogeneity on whether there is split-party or same-party control of a state's Senate delegation. For both roll-call measures, the nature of party control has a stronger direct effect than any other variable. The direct effect of party on pairs of senators' ADA support scores is more than twice as great as that of reelection constituency or state partisan competitiveness and three times as great as the direct effect of geographic constituency. The direct effect of party on differences in pairs of senators' Conservative Coalition support scores is one-and-a-half times greater than the direct effect of reelectoral constituency and three times greater than geographic constituency. Electoral competitiveness has no significant effect on pairs of senators' support for the Conservative Coalition, although it is weakly related to senators' ADA votes.

While the nature of party control of a state's Senate seats has the greatest direct effect on pairs of senators' roll-call voting scores, both geographical heterogeneity and reelection constituency have larger total effects when their direct and indirect effects are combined. For ADA support, the total effect of the geographical constituency, as reported in Table 18-2, has the largest total effect; this variable and reelection constituency have almost identical total effects on the variance in Conservative Coalition support scores. The two constituency variables usually have a stronger indirect than direct impact, as had been expected. The nature of the partisan control of a state's Senate seats substantially increases the predictive power of either measure of constituency. The paths through the party

Figure 18-2   Path Model of Constituency Influences, Party, and Conservative
Coalition Support, 93rd Senate[a]

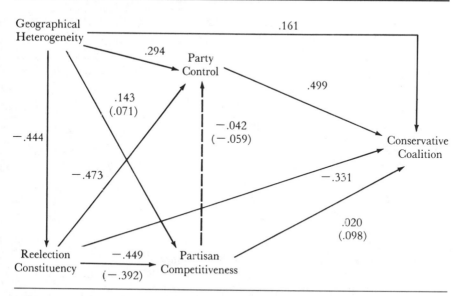

[a] Figures reporting relationships with partisan competitiveness give the beta for the adjusted Pfeiffer measure first,
with the beta for the adjusted Ranney measure appearing in parenthesis.

control variable are stronger than those through the competitiveness measure,
confirming our expectation that the party of the senator is more important than
the level of competition between parties.

The variable of competition has the weakest direct effect on both roll-call
measures. In keeping with Deckard's (1976) findings, we find no relationship
between competitiveness and similarity in senators' support for the Conservative
Coalition. This is in contrast with a beta of −.331 between reelection
constituency and Conservative Coalition support.

Despite strong similarities in the direct paths to ADA and CC, there are
some differences. Notable is the much larger beta between reelection constituency
and CC support than between reelection constituency and ADA support. The
greater direct effect of reelection constituency coincides with a reduced direct
effect for the other variables, most significant being the smaller magnitude for the
Pfeiffer competition measure.

The differences between Figures 18-1 and 18-2 in path coefficient for party
may lie in how the Conservative Coalition and the ADA select the roll calls on
which they compute their ratings. The ADA likes to include procedural votes
(*Congressional Quarterly Weekly Report*, 1974, p. 1751); in the 93rd Congress,
more than one-fifth of the ADA roll calls were on procedural matters, such as

Table 18-2   Effects of Party and Constituency Variables on ADA and Conservative Coalition Scores

Party and Constituency Factors	ADA			Conservative Coalition		
	Direct	Indirect	Total	Direct	Indirect	Total
Geographical Heterogeneity	.182	.443	.625	.161	.399[a]	.560
Reelection Constituency	.236	.339	.575	.331	.236[a]	.567
Party Control	.547	—	.547	.499	—	.499
Partisan Competitiveness						
Pfeiffer	.179	—	.179	.020	—	.020
Ranney	.130	—	.130	.098	—	.098

[a] Compound paths through partisan competitiveness are not included.

motions to table or to invoke cloture. Procedural votes are particularly likely to result in a division along party lines (Turner and Schneier, 1970, pp. 42-44; Froman and Ripley, 1965). In contrast, the CC roll calls, by definition, were ones on which the Democratic party was divided along regional lines. Party differences on these votes were reduced at least to the extent that in the four southern states where there was split-party control, the Democrat and Republican tended to vote together.

Conclusions and Discussion

The results of our analysis largely support the model we are testing and show that the model explains the differences in the roll-call votes of senators elected from the same state. Geographic constituency and reelection constituency are related, but, as Fenno's interviews suggested, the latter, being more central to incumbents, has a stronger direct effect on all other components of the model than does the former. Constituency variables are unrefined, but this drawback can be counteracted to an extent if the reelection rather than the geographic constituency is focused on. Use of the reelection constituency might at times reveal linkages which are obscured in the grosser, all-inclusive, geographic constituency. It is not surprising that legislators are more inclined to vote as their supporters wish than to take often contradictory cues of supporters and opponents (Fiorina, 1974).

The critical role of party is affirmed by this research. Party has a much greater direct effect on roll-call behavior than do the constituency variables or competitiveness. This evidence builds on the work of those who have sought to disentangle constituency and party by analyzing the roll calls of successive representatives from a single district. It improves on the earlier works by analyzing legislators who not only share a constituency tie but who voted on the same roll calls. Our research, then, runs contrary to the simple constituency model. The party variable, while itself being influenced by constituency characteristics, is a stronger direct predictor than constituency operating alone. Whether a state's senators are from the same or opposing parties is influenced by the nature of both the geographical and reelection constituencies, with the latter having a substantially greater direct effect. And there is a significant relationship between different reelection constituencies and split-party control. Thus constituency and party are both related to differences in voting behavior between senators from the same state.

As the dual-pressure perspective suggests, both party and constituency influence roll-call behavior. Constituency has an indirect as well as a direct impact on how senators voted on the two sets of roll calls which were analyzed. Partisan competitiveness is not a strong predictor of roll-call behavior, either directly or indirectly.

Although the model is tested for just one Congress, it seems likely that it has a more general applicability. Under differing conditions, for example in the immediate aftermath of a realigning election, the values of the beta coefficients may vary, but the relative influence of the components should remain.

Notes

This paper is the product of ongoing research; in successive papers we alternate the order of the authors' names to indicate that the studies are in every way joint efforts.

1. We use Sullivan's computations based on 1960 census data for this part of the analysis, since these figures were collected at about the midpoint of the period for which we consider the incidence of split-party senators.
2. In the 1960s, when Sullivan designed this politically sensitive measure of population diversity, it may have been reasonable to exclude race as a variable: black participation was very low then in much of the South. However, this is no longer the case; blacks now participate in politics at about the same levels nationwide (Bullock and Rodgers, 1975, p. 68). We deleted religion from our computations because the estimates religious groups make of their memberships are unreliable.
3. The measure of reelection constituency used here is based on estimates calculated from regression equations. It therefore differs from Fenno's (1977) measure, which relies on legislator perceptions. We created our measure because perceptual data is nonquantitative and was unavailable anyway.
4. This and the remaining analyses in this paper are of data from 47 states. Mississippi and Louisiana were deleted because they did not have partisan competition for both Senate seats during 1968-1972; Alaska was not included in the analysis because no county-level data are available.
5. Note that on the geographical constituency variable a high value indicates heterogeneity, while on the reelection constituency variable a high score indicates homogeneity. A negative relationship between these variables is therefore expected.
6. Measures of competitiveness at the state rather than the individual level were selected because the figures for the states indicate the competitive context in which the senators

Charles S. Bullock III and David W. Brady

must operate. The state-level figures are also generally more stable than figures for a single senator or even pair of senators would be, since a greater number of elections are used to compute the state figure.

19. CONSTITUENCY INFLUENCE IN CONGRESS

Warren E. Miller

and

Donald E. Stokes

Substantial constituency influence over the lower house of Congress is commonly thought to be both a normative principle and a factual truth of American government. From their draft constitution we may assume the Founding Fathers expected it, and many political scientists feel, regretfully, that the Framers' wish has come all too true.[1] Nevertheless, much of the evidence of constituency control rests on inference. The fact that our House of Representatives, especially by comparison with the House of Commons, has irregular party voting does not of itself indicate that Congressmen deviate from party in response to local pressure. And even more, the fact that many Congressmen *feel* pressure from home does not of itself establish that the local constituency is performing any of the acts that a reasonable definition of control would imply.

I. Constituency Control in the Normative Theory of Representation

Control by the local constituency is at one pole of *both* the great normative controversies about representation that have arisen in modern times. It is generally recognized that constituency control is opposite to the conception of representation associated with Edmund Burke. Burke wanted the representative to serve the constituency's *interest* but not its *will,* and the extent to which the representative should be compelled by electoral sanctions to follow the "mandate" of his constituents has been at the heart of the ensuing controversy as it has continued for a century and a half.[2]

Constituency control also is opposite to the conception of government by responsible national parties. This is widely seen, yet the point is rarely connected

Authors' Note: The research reported here was made possible through grants of the Rockefeller Foundation and the Social Science Research Council, whose support is gratefully acknowledged. The authors are indebted also to Ralph Bisco and Gudmund R. Iversen for invaluable assistance.

Source: *American Political Science Review* (March 1963): 45-57. Reprinted with permission of the authors.

with normative discussions of representation. Indeed, it is remarkable how little attention has been given to the model of representation implicit in the doctrine of a "responsible two-party system." When the subject of representation is broached among political scientists the classical argument between Burke and his opponents is likely to come at once to mind. So great is Burke's influence that the antithesis he proposed still provides the categories of thought used in contemporary treatments of representation despite the fact that many students of politics today would advocate a relationship between representative and constituency that fits neither position of the mandate-independence controversy.

The conception of representation implicit in the doctrine of responsible parties shares the idea of popular control with the instructed-delegate model. Both are versions of popular sovereignty. But "the people" of the responsible two-party system are conceived in terms of a national rather than a local constituency. Candidates for legislative office appeal to the electorate in terms of a *national* party program and leadership, to which, if elected, they will be committed. Expressions of policy preference by the local district are reduced to endorsements of one or another of these programs, and the local district retains only the arithmetical significance that whichever party can rally to its program the greater number of supporters in the district will control its legislative seat.

No one tradition of representation has entirely dominated American practice. Elements of the Burkean, instructed-delegate, and responsible party models can all be found in our political life. Yet if the American system has elements of all three, a good deal depends on how they are combined. Especially critical is the question whether different models of representation apply to different public issues. Is the saliency of legislative action to the public so different in quality and degree on different issues that the legislator is subject to very different constraints from his constituency? Does the legislator have a single generalized mode of response to his constituency that is rooted in a normative belief about the representative's role or does the same legislator respond to his constituency differently on different issues? More evidence is needed on matters so fundamental to our system.

II. An Empirical Study of Representation

To extend what we know of representation in the American Congress the Survey Research Center of The University of Michigan interviewed the incumbent Congressman, his nonincumbent opponent (if any), and a sample of constituents in each of 116 congressional districts, which were themselves a probability sample of all districts.[3] These interviews, conducted immediately after the congressional election of 1958, explored a wide range of attitudes and perceptions held by the individuals who play the reciprocal roles of the representative relation in national government. The distinguishing feature of this research is, of course, that it sought direct information from both constituent and legislator (actual and aspiring). To this fund of comparative interview data has been added information about the roll call votes of our sample of Congressmen and the political and social characteristics of the districts they represent.

Many students of politics, with excellent reason, have been sensitive to possible ties between representative and constituent that have little to do with issues of public policy. For example, ethnic identifications may cement a legislator in the affections of his district, whatever (within limits) his stands on issues. And many Congressmen keep their tenure of office secure by skillful provision of district benefits ranging from free literature to major federal projects. In the full study of which this analysis is part we have explored several bases of constituency support that have little to do with policy issues. Nevertheless, the question how the representative should make up his mind on legislative issues is what the classical arguments over representation are all about, and we have given a central place to a comparison of the policy preferences of constituents and Representatives and to a causal analysis of the relation between the two.

In view of the electorate's scanty information about government it was not at all clear in advance that such a comparison could be made. Some of the more buoyant advocates of popular sovereignty have regarded the citizen as a kind of kibitzer who looks over the shoulder of his representative at the legislative game. Kibitzer and player may disagree as to which card should be played, but they were at least thought to share a common understanding of what the alternatives are.

No one familiar with the findings of research on mass electorates could accept this view of the citizen. Far from looking over the shoulder of their Congressmen at the legislative game, most Americans are almost totally uninformed about legislative issues in Washington. At best the average citizen may be said to have some general ideas about how the country should be run, which he is able to use in responding to particular questions about what the government ought to do. For example, survey studies have shown that most people have a general (though differing) conception of how far government should go to achieve social and economic welfare objectives and that these convictions fix their response to various particular questions about actions government might take.[4]

What makes it possible to compare the policy preferences of constituents and Representatives despite the public's low awareness of legislative affairs is the fact that Congressmen themselves respond to many issues in terms of fairly broad evaluative dimensions. Undoubtedly policy alternatives are judged in the executive agencies and the specialized committees of the Congress by criteria that are relatively complex and specific to the policies at issue. But a good deal of evidence goes to show that when proposals come before the House as a whole they are judged on the basis of more general evaluative dimensions.[5] For example, most Congressmen, too, seem to have a general conception of how far government should go in the area of domestic social and economic welfare, and these general positions apparently orient their roll call votes on a number of particular social welfare issues.

It follows that such a broad evaluative dimension can be used to compare the policy preferences of constituents and Representatives despite the low state of the public's information about politics. In this study three such dimensions have been drawn from our voter interviews and from congressional interviews and roll call records. As suggested above, one of these has to do with approval of government

461

action in the social welfare field, the primary domestic issue of the New Deal-Fair Deal (and New Frontier) eras. A second dimension has to do with support for American involvement in foreign affairs, a latter-day version of the isolationist-internationalist continuum. A third dimension has to do with approval of federal action to protect the civil rights of Negroes.[6]

Because our research focused on these three dimensions, our analysis of constituency influence is limited to these areas of policy. No point has been more energetically or usefully made by those who have sought to clarify the concepts of power and influence than the necessity of specifying the acts *with respect to which* one actor has power or influence or control over another.[7] Therefore, the scope or range of influence for our analysis is the collection of legislative issues falling within our three policy domains. We are not able to say how much control the local constituency may or may not have over *all* actions of its Representative, and there may well be pork-barrel issues or other matters of peculiar relevance to the district on which the relation of Congressman to constituency is quite distinctive. However, few observers of contemporary politics would regard the issues of government provision of social and economic welfare, of American involvement in world affairs, and of federal action in behalf of the Negro as constituting a trivial range of action. Indeed, these domains together include most of the great issues that have come before Congress in recent years.

In each policy domain we have used the procedures of cumulative scaling, as developed by Louis Guttman and others, to order our samples of Congressmen, of opposing candidates, and of voters. In each domain Congressmen were ranked once according to their roll call votes in the House and again according to the attitudes they revealed in our confidential interviews. These two orderings are by no means identical, nor are the discrepancies due simply to uncertainties of measurement.[8] Opposing candidates also were ranked in each policy domain according to the attitudes they revealed in our interviews. The nationwide sample of constituents was ordered in each domain, and by averaging the attitude scores of all constituents living in the same districts, whole constituencies were ranked on each dimension so that the views of Congressmen could be compared with those of their constituencies.[9] Finally, by considering only the constituents in each district who share some characteristic (voting for the incumbent, say) we were able to order these fractions of districts so that the opinions of Congressmen could be compared with those, for example, of the dominant electoral elements of their districts.

In each policy domain, crossing the rankings of Congressmen and their constituencies gives an empirical measure of the extent of policy agreement between legislator and district.[10] In the period of our research this procedure reveals very different degrees of policy congruence across the three issue domains. On questions of social and economic welfare there is considerable agreement between Representative and district, expressed by a correlation of approximately 0.3. This coefficient is, of course, very much less than the limiting value of 1.0, indicating that a number of Congressmen are, relatively speaking, more or less "liberal" than their districts. However, on the question of foreign involvement there is no discernible agreement between legislator and district whatever. Indeed, as if to emphasize the point, the coefficient expressing this relation is slightly negative (-0.09), although not significantly so in a statistical sense. It is in the domain of civil rights that the rankings of Congressmen and constituencies most nearly agree. When we took our measurements in the late 1950s the correlation of congressional roll call behavior with constituency opinion on questions affecting the Negro was nearly 0.6.

The description of policy agreement that these three simple correlations give can be a starting-point for a wide range of analyses. For example, the significance of party competition in the district for policy representation can be explored by comparing the agreement between district and Congressman with the agreement between the district and the Congressman's non-incumbent opponent. Alternatively, the significance of choosing Representatives from single-member districts by popular majority can be explored by comparing the agreement between the Congressman and his own supporters with the agreement between the Congressman and the supporters of his opponent. Taking *both* party competition and majority rule into account magnifies rather spectacularly some of the coefficients reported here. This is most true in the domain of social welfare, where attitudes both of candidates and of voters are most polarized along party lines. Whereas the correlation between the constituency majority and congressional roll call votes is nearly $+0.4$ on social welfare policy, the correlation of the district majority with the non-incumbent candidate is -0.4. This difference, amounting to almost 0.8, between these two coefficients is an indicator of what the dominant electoral element of the constituency gets on the average by choosing the Congressman it has and excluding his opponent from office.[11]

These three coefficients are also the starting point for a causal analysis of the relation of constituency to Representative, the main problem of this paper. At least on social welfare and Negro rights a measurable degree of congruence is found between district and legislator. Is this agreement due to constituency influence in Congress, or is it to be attributed to other causes? If this question is to have a satisfactory answer the conditions that are necessary and sufficient to assure constituency control must be stated and compared with the available empirical evidence.

III. The Conditions of Constituency Influence

Broadly speaking, the constituency can control the policy actions of the Representative in two alternative ways. The first of these is for the district to choose a Representative who so shares its views that in following his own convictions he does his constituents' will. In this case district opinion and the Congressman's actions are connected through the Representative's own policy attitudes. The second means of constituency control is for the Congressman to follow his (at least tolerably accurate) perceptions of district attitude in order to win re-election. In this case constituency opinion and the Congressman's actions are connected through his perception of what the district wants.[12]

These two paths of constituency control are presented schematically in Figure 19-1. As the figure suggests, each path has two steps, one connecting the constituency's attitude with an "intervening" attitude or perception, the other connecting this attitude or perception with the Representative's roll call behavior. Out of respect for the processes by which the human actor achieves cognitive congruence we have also drawn arrows between the two intervening factors, since the Congressman probably tends to see his district as having the same opinion as his own and also tends, over time, to bring his own opinion into line with the district's. The inclusion of these arrows calls attention to two other possible influence paths, each consisting of *three* steps, although these additional paths will turn out to be of relatively slight importance empirically.

Figure 19-1   Connections Between a Constituency's Attitude and its Representative's Roll Call Behavior

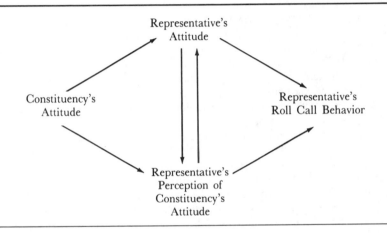

Neither of the main influence paths of Figure 19-1 will connect the final roll call vote to the constituency's views if either of its steps is blocked. From this, two necessary conditions of constituency influence can be stated: *first*, the Representative's votes in the House must agree substantially with his own policy views or his perceptions of the district's views, and not be determined entirely by other influences to which the Congressman is exposed; and, *second*, the attitudes or perceptions governing the Representative's acts must correspond, at least imperfectly, to the district's actual opinions. It would be difficult to describe the relation of constituency to Representative as one of control unless these conditions are met.[13]

Yet these two requirements are not sufficient to assure control. A *third* condition must also be satisfied: the constituency must in some measure take the policy views of candidates into account in choosing a Representative. If it does not, agreement between district and Congressman may arise for reasons that cannot rationally be brought within the idea of control. For example, such agreement may simply reflect the fact that a Representative drawn from a given area is likely, by pure statistical probability, to share its dominant values, without his acceptance or rejection of these ever having been a matter of consequence to his electors.

IV. Evidence of Control: Congressional Attitudes and Perceptions

How well are these conditions met in the relation of American Congressmen to their constituents? There is little question that the first is substantially satisfied; the evidence of our research indicates that members of the House do in fact vote both their own policy views and their perceptions of their constituents' views, at least on issues of social welfare, foreign involvement, and civil rights. If these two intervening factors are used to predict roll call votes, the prediction is quite successful. Their multiple correlation with roll call position is 0.7 for social welfare, 0.6 for foreign involvement, and 0.9 for civil rights; the last figure is especially persuasive. What is more, both the Congressman's own convictions and his perceptions of district opinion make a distinct contribution to his roll call behavior. In each of the three domains the prediction of roll call votes is surer if it is made from both factors rather than from either alone.

Lest the strong influence that the Congressman's views and his perception of district views have on roll call behavior appear somehow foreordained — and, consequently, this finding seem a trivial one — it is worth taking a sidewise glance at the potency of possible other forces on the Representative's vote. In the area of foreign policy, for example, a number of Congressmen are disposed to follow the administration's advice, whatever they or their districts think. For those who are, the multiple correlation of roll call behavior with the Representative's own foreign policy views and his perception of district views is a mere 0.2. Other findings could be cited to support the point that the influence of the Congressman's own preferences and those he attributes to the district is extremely variable. Yet in the House as a whole over the three policy domains the influence of these forces is quite strong.

The connections of congressional attitudes and perceptions with actual constituency opinion are weaker. If policy agreement between district and Representative is moderate and variable across the policy domains, as it is, this is to be explained much more in terms of the second condition of constituency control than the first. The Representative's attitudes and perceptions most nearly match true opinion in his district on the issues of Negro rights. Reflecting the charged and polarized nature of this area, the correlation of actual district opinion with perceived opinion is greater than 0.6, and the correlation of district attitude with the Representative's own attitude is nearly 0.4, as shown by Table 19-1. But the comparable correlations for foreign involvement are much smaller — indeed almost negligible. And the coefficients for social welfare are also smaller, although a detailed presentation of findings in this area would show that the Representative's perceptions and attitudes are more strongly associated with the attitude of his electoral *majority* than they are with the attitudes of the constituency as a whole.

Knowing this much about the various paths that may lead, directly or indirectly, from constituency attitude to roll call vote, we can assess their relative importance. Since the alternative influence chains have links of unequal strength, the full chains will not in general be equally strong, and these differences are of

Table 19-1   Correlations of Constituency Attitudes

Policy Domain	Correlation of Constituency Attitude with	
	Representative's Perception of Constituency Attitude	*Representative's Own Attitude*
Social welfare	.17	.21
Foreign involvement	.19	.06
Civil rights	.63	.39

great importance in the relation of Representative to constituency. For the domain of civil rights Figure 19-2 assembles all the intercorrelations of the variables of our system. As the figure shows, the root correlation of constituency attitude with roll call behavior in this domain is 0.57. How much of this policy congruence can be accounted for by the influence path involving the Representative's attitude? And how much by the path involving his perception of constituency opinion? When the intercorrelations of the system are interpreted in the light of what we assume its causal structure to be, it is influence passing through the Congressman's perception of the district's views that is found to be preeminently important.[14] Under the least favorable assumption as to its importance, this path is found to account for more than twice as much of the variance of roll call behavior as the paths involving the Representative's own attitude.[15] However, when this same procedure is applied to our social welfare data, the results suggest that the direct connection of constituency and roll call through the Congressman's own attitude is the most important of the alternative paths.[16] The reversal of the relative importance of the two paths as we move from civil rights to social welfare is one of the most striking findings of this analysis.

V. Evidence of Control: Electoral Behavior

Of the three conditions of constituency influence, the requirement that the electorate take account of the policy positions of the candidates is the hardest to match with empirical evidence. Indeed, given the limited information the average voter carries to the polls, the public might be thought incompetent to perform any task of appraisal. Of constituents living in congressional districts where there was a contest between a Republican and a Democrat in 1958, less than one in five said they had read or heard something about both candidates, and well over half conceded they had read or heard nothing about either. And these proportions are not much better when they are based only on the part of the sample, not much more than half, that reported voting for Congress in 1958. The extent of awareness of the candidates among voters is indicated in Table 19-2. As the table shows, even of the portion of the public that was sufficiently interested to vote, almost half had read or heard nothing about either candidate.

Figure 19-2 Intercorrelations of variables pertaining to Civil Rights

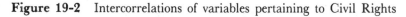

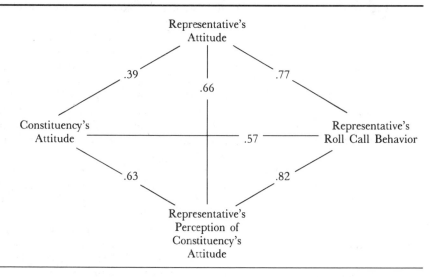

Table 19-2 Awareness of Congressional Candidates Among Voters, 1958

		Read or Heard Something About Incumbent[a]		
		Yes	No	
Read or Heard Something About Non-Incumbent	Yes	24	5	29
	No	25	46	71
		49	51	100%

[a] In order to include all districts where the House seat was contested in 1958 this table retains ten constituencies in which the incumbent Congressman did not seek re-election. Candidates of the retiring incumbent's party in these districts are treated here as if they were incumbents. Were these figures to be calculated only for constituencies in which an incumbent sought re-election, no entry in this four-fold table would differ from that given by more than two percent.

Just how low a hurdle our respondents had to clear in saying they had read or heard something about a candidate is indicated by detailed qualitative analysis of the information constituents *were* able to associate with congressional candidates. Except in rare cases, what the voters "knew" was confined to diffuse evaluative judgments about the candidate: "he's a good man," "he understands the problems," and so forth. Of detailed information about policy stands not more than a chemical trace was found. Among the comments about the candidates given in response to an extended series of free-answer questions, less than two percent had to do with stands in our three policy domains; indeed, only about three comments in every hundred had to do with legislative issues of *any* description.

467

This evidence that the behavior of the electorate is largely unaffected by knowledge of the policy positions of the candidates is complemented by evidence about the forces that *do* shape the voters' choices among congressional candidates. The primary basis of voting in American congressional elections is identification with party. In 1958 only one vote in twenty was cast by persons without any sort of party loyalty. And among those who did have a party identification, only one in ten voted against their party. As a result, something like 84 percent of the vote that year was cast by party identifiers voting their usual party line. What is more, traditional party voting is seldom connected with current legislative issues. As the party loyalists in a nationwide sample of voters told us what they liked and disliked about the parties in 1958, only a small fraction of the comments (about 15 percent) dealt with current issues of public policy.[18]

Yet the idea of reward or punishment at the polls for legislative stands is familiar to members of Congress, who feel that they and their records are quite visible to their constituents. Of our sample of Congressmen who were opposed for reelection in 1958, more than four-fifths said the outcome in their districts had been strongly influenced by the electorate's response to their records and personal standing. Indeed, this belief is clear enough to present a notable contradiction: Congressmen feel that their individual legislative actions may have considerable impact on the electorate, yet some simple facts about the Representative's salience to his constituents imply that this could hardly be true.

In some measure this contradiction is to be explained by the tendency of Congressmen to overestimate their visibility to the local public, a tendency that reflects the difficulties of the Representative in forming a correct judgment of constituent opinion. The communication most Congressmen have with their districts inevitably puts them in touch with organized groups and with individuals who are relatively well informed about politics. The Representative knows his constituents mostly from dealing with people who *do* write letters, who *will* attend meetings, who *have* an interest in his legislative stands. As a result, his sample of contacts with a constituency of several hundred thousand people is heavily biased: even the contacts he apparently makes at random are likely to be with people who grossly over-represent the degree of political information and interest in the constituency as a whole.

But the contradiction is also to be explained by several aspects of the Representative's electoral situation that are of great importance to the question of constituency influence. The first of these is implicit in what has already been said. Because of the pervasive effects of party loyalties, no candidate for Congress starts from scratch in putting together an electoral majority. The Congressman is a dealer in increments and margins. He starts with a stratum of hardened party voters, and if the stratum is broad enough he can have a measurable influence on his chance of survival simply by attracting a small additional element of the electorate — or by not losing a larger one. Therefore, his record may have a very real bearing on his electoral success or failure without most of his constituents ever knowing what that record is.

Second, the relation of Congressman to voter is not a simple bilateral one but is complicated by the presence of all manner of intermediaries: the local party, economic interests, the news media, racial and nationality organization, and so forth. Such is the lore of American politics, as it is known to any political scientist. Very often the Representative reaches the mass public through these mediating agencies, and the information about himself and his record may be considerably transformed as it diffuses out to the electorate in two or more stages. As a result, the public — or parts of it — may get simple positive or negative cues about the Congressman which were provoked by his legislative actions but which no longer have a recognizable issue content.

Third, for most Congressmen most of the time the electorate's sanctions are potential rather than actual. Particularly the Representative from a safe district may feel his proper legislative strategy is to avoid giving opponents in his own party or outside of it material they can use against him. As the Congressman pursues this strategy he may write a legislative record that never becomes very well known to his constituents; if it doesn't win votes, neither will it lose any. This is clearly the situation of most southern Congressmen in dealing with the issue of Negro rights. By voting correctly on this issue they are unlikely to increase their visibility to constituents. Nevertheless, the fact of constituency influence, backed by potential sanctions at the polls, is real enough.

That these potential sanctions are all too real is best illustrated in the election of 1958 by the reprisal against Representative Brooks Hays in Arkansas' Fifth District.[19] Although the perception of Congressman Hays as too moderate on civil rights resulted more from his service as intermediary between the White House and Governor Faubus in the Little Rock school crisis than from his record in the House, the victory of Dale Alford as a write-in candidate was a striking reminder of what can happen to a Congressman who gives his foes a powerful issue to use against him. The extraordinary involvement of the public in this race can be seen by comparing how well the candidates were known in this constituency with the awareness of the candidates shown by Table 19-2 above for the country as a whole. As Table 19-3 indicates, not a single voter in our sample of Arkansas' Fifth District was unaware of either candidate.[20] What is more, these interviews show that Hays was regarded both by his supporters and his opponents as more moderate than Alford on civil rights and that this perception brought his defeat. In some measure, what happened in Little Rock in 1958 can happen anywhere, and our Congressmen ought not to be entirely disbelieved in what they say about their impact at the polls. Indeed, they may be under genuine pressure from the voters even while they are the forgotten men of national elections.[21]

V. Conclusion

Therefore, although the conditions of constituency influence are not equally satisfied, they are met well enough to give the local constituency a measure of control over the actions of its Representatives. Best satisfied is the requirement about motivational influences on the Congressman: our evidence shows that the Representative's roll call behavior is strongly influenced by his own policy preferences and by his perception of preferences held by the constituency. However, the conditions of influence that presuppose effective communication between Congressman and district are much less well met. The Representative

Table 19-3 Awareness of Congressional Candidates Among Voters in Arkansas Fifth District, 1958

		Read or Heard Something About Hays		
		Yes	No	
Read or Heard Something About Alford	Yes	100	0	100
	No	0	0	0
		100	0	100%

has very imperfect information about the issue preferences of his constituency, and the constituency's awareness of the policy stands of the Representative ordinarily is slight.

The findings of this analysis heavily underscore the fact that no single tradition of representation fully accords with the realities of American legislative politics. The American system *is* a mixture, to which the Burkean, instructed-delegate, and responsible-party models all can be said to have contributed elements. Moreover, variations in the representative relation are most likely to occur as we move from one policy domain to another. No single, generalized configuration of attitudes and perceptions links Representative with constituency but rather several distinct patterns, and which of them is invoked depends very much on the issue involved.

The issue domain in which the relation of Congressman to constituency most nearly conforms to the instructed-delegate model is that of civil rights. This conclusion is supported by the importance of the influence-path passing through the Representative's perception of district opinion, although even in this domain the sense in which the constituency may be said to take the position of the candidate into account in reaching its electoral judgment should be carefully qualified.

The representative relation conforms most closely to the responsible-party model in the domain of social welfare. In this issue area, the arena of partisan conflict for a generation, the party symbol helps both constituency and Representative in the difficult process of communication between them. On the one hand, because Republican and Democratic voters tend to differ in what they would have government do, the Representative has some guide to district opinion simply by looking at the partisan division of the vote. On the other hand, because the two parties tend to recruit candidates who differ on the social welfare role of government, the constituency can infer the candidates' position with more than random accuracy from their party affiliation, even though what the constituency has learned directly about these stands is almost nothing. How faithful the representation of social welfare views is to the responsible-party model should not be exaggerated. Even in this policy domain, American practice departs widely from an ideal conception of party government.[22] But in this domain, more than any other, political conflict has become a conflict of national parties in which constituency and Representative are known to each other primarily by their party association.

It would be too pat to say that the domain of foreign involvement conforms to the third model of representation, the conception promoted by Edmund Burke. Clearly it does in the sense that the Congressman looks elsewhere than to his district in making up his mind on foreign issues. However, the reliance he puts on the President and the Administration suggests that the calculation of where the public interest lies is often passed to the Executive on matters of foreign policy. Ironically, legislative initiative in foreign affairs has fallen victim to the very difficulties of gathering and appraising information that led Burke to argue that Parliament rather than the public ought to hold the power of decision. The background information and predictive skills that Burke thought the people lacked are held primarily by the modern Executive. As a result, the present role of the legislature in foreign affairs bears some resemblance to the role that Burke had in mind for the elitist, highly restricted *electorate* of his own day.

Notes

1. To be sure, the work of the Federal Convention has been supplemented in two critical respects. The first of these is the practice, virtually universal since the mid-19th Century, of choosing Representatives from single-member districts of limited geographic area. The second is the practice, which has also become virtually universal in our own century, of selecting party nominees for the House by direct primary election.
2. In the language of Eulau, Wahlke, *et al.,* we speak here of the "style," not the "focus," of representation. See their "The Role of the Representative: Some Empirical Observations on the Theory of Edmund Burke," this Review, Vol. 53 (September, 1959), pp. 742-756. An excellent review of the mandate-independence controversy is given by Hanna Fenichel Pitkin, "The Theory of Representation" (unpublished doctoral dissertation, University of California, Berkeley, 1961). For other contemporary discussions of representation, see Alfred de Grazia, *Public and Republic* (New York, 1951), and John A. Fairlie, "The Nature of Political Representation," this Review, Vol. 34 (April-June 1940), pp. 236-48, 456-66.
3. The sampling aspects of this research were complicated by the fact that the study of representation was a rider midway on a four-year panel study of the electorate whose primary sampling units were not congressional districts (although there is no technical reason why they could not have been if the needs of the representation analysis had been foreseen when the design of the sample was fixed two years before). As a result, the districts in our sample had unequal probabilities of selection and unequal weights in the analysis, making the sample somewhat less efficient than an equal-probability sample of equivalent size.

   It will be apparent in the discussion that follows that we have estimated characteristics of whole constituencies from our samples of constituents living in particular districts. In view of the fact that a sample of less than two thousand constituents has been divided among 116 districts, the reader may wonder about the reliability of these estimates. After considerable investigation we have concluded that their sampling error is not so severe a problem for the analysis as we had thought it would be. Several comments may indicate why it is not.

To begin with, the weighting of our sample of districts has increased the reliability of the constituency estimates. The correct theoretical weight to be assigned each district in the analysis is the inverse of the probability of the district's selection, and it can be shown that this weight is approximately proportional to the number of interviews taken in the district. The result of this is that the greatest weight is assigned the districts with the largest number of interviews and, hence, the most reliable constituency estimates. Indeed, these weights increase by half again the (weighted) mean number of interviews taken per district. To put the matter another way: the introduction of differential weights trades some of our sample of congressional districts for more reliable constituency estimates.

How much of a problem the unreliability of these estimates is depends very much on the analytic uses to which the estimates are put. If our goal were case analyses of particular districts, the constituency samples would have to be much larger. Indeed, for most case analyses we would want several hundred interviews per district (at a cost, over 116 districts, of several small nuclear reactors). However, most of the findings reported here are based not on single districts but on many or all of the districts in our sample. For analyses of this sort the number of interviews per district can be much smaller.

Our investigation of the effect of the sampling variance of the constituency estimates is quite reassuring. When statistics computed from our constituency samples are compared with corresponding parameter values for the constituencies, the agreement of the two sets of figures is quite close. For example, when the proportions voting Democratic in the 116 constituencies in 1958, as computed from our sample data, are compared with the actual proportions voting Democratic, as recorded in official election statistics, a product moment correlation of 0.93 is obtained, and this figure is the more impressive since this test throws away non-voters, almost one-half of our total sample. We interpret the Pearsonian correlation as an appropriate measure of agreement in this case, since the associated regression equations are almost exactly the identity function. The alternative intraclass correlation coefficient has almost as high a value.

Although we believe that this analysis provides a textbook illustration of how misleading intuitive ideas (including our own) about the effects of sampling error can be, these figures ought not to be too beguiling. It is clear that how close such a correlation is to 1.0 for any given variable will depend on the ratio of the between-district variance to the total variance. When this ratio is as high as it is for Republican and Democratic voting, the effect of the unreliability of our constituency estimates is fairly trivial. Although the content of the study is quite different, this sampling problem has much in common with the problem of attenuation of correlation as it has been treated in psychological testing. See, for example, J. P. Guilford; *Fundamental Statistics in Psychology and Education* (New York, 1956), pp. 475-78.

4. See Angus Campbell, Philip E. Converse, Warren E. Miller, and Donald E. Stokes, *The American Voter* (New York, 1960), pp. 194-209.

5. This conclusion, fully supported by our own work for later Congresses, is one of the main findings to be drawn from the work of Duncan MacRae on roll call voting in the House of Representatives. See his *Dimensions of Congressional Voting: A Statistical Study of the House of Representatives in the Eighty-First Congress* (Berkeley and Los Angeles: University of California Press, 1958). For additional evidence of the existence of scale dimensions in legislative behavior, see N. L. Gage and Ben Shimberg, "Measuring Senatorial Progressivism," *Journal of Abnormal and Social Psychology*,

Vol. 44 (January 1949), pp. 112-117; George M. Belknap, "A Study of Senatorial Voting by Scale Analysis" (unpublished doctoral dissertation, University of Chicago, 1951), and "A Method for Analyzing Legislative Behavior," *Midwest Journal of Political Science*, Vol. 2 (1958), pp. 377-402; two other articles by MacRae, "The Role of the State Legislator in Massachusetts," *American Sociological Review*, Vol. 19 (April 1954), pp. 185-194, and "Roll Call Votes and Leadership," *Public Opinion Quarterly*, Vol. 20 (1956), pp. 543-558; Charles D. Farris, "A Method of Determining Ideological Groups in Congress," *Journal of Politics*, Vol. 20 (1958), pp. 308-338; and Leroy N. Rieselbach, "Quantitative Techniques for Studying Voting Behavior in the U.N. General Assembly," *International Organization*, Vol. 14 (1960), pp. 291-306.

6. The content of the three issue domains may be suggested by some of the roll call and interview items used. In the area of social welfare these included the issues of public housing, public power, aid to education, and government's role in maintaining full employment. In the area of foreign involvement the items included the issues of foreign economic aid, military aid, sending troops abroad, and aid to neutrals. In the area of civil rights the items included the issues of school desegregation, fair employment, and the protection of Negro voting rights.

7. Because this point has been so widely discussed it has inevitably attracted a variety of terms. Dahl denotes the acts of *a* whose performance *A* is able to influence as the *scope* of *A*'s power. See Robert A. Dahl, "The Concept of Power," *Behavioral Science*, Vol. 2 (July 1957), pp. 201-215. This usage is similar to that of Harold D. Lasswell and Abraham Kaplan, *Power and Society* (New Haven: Yale University Press, 1950), pp. 71-73. Dorwin Cartwright, however, denotes the behavioral or psychological changes in *P* which *O* is able to induce as the *range* of *O*'s power: "A Field Theoretical Conception of Power," *Studies in Social Power* (Ann Arbor: Research Center for Group Dynamics, Institute for Social Research, The University of Michigan, 1959), pp. 183-220.

8. That the Representative's roll call votes can diverge from his true opinion is borne out by a number of findings of the study (some of which are reported here) as to the conditions under which agreement between the Congressman's roll call position and his private attitude will be high or low. However, a direct confirmation that these two sets of measurements are not simply getting at the same thing is given by differences in attitude-roll call agreement according to the Congressman's sense of how well his roll call votes have expressed his real views. In the domain of foreign involvement, for example, the correlation of our attitudinal and roll call measurements was .75 among Representatives who said that their roll call votes had expressed their real views fairly well. But this correlation was only .04 among those who said that their roll call votes had expressed their views poorly. In the other policy domains, too, attitude-roll call agreement is higher among Congressmen who are well satisfied with their roll call votes than it is among Congressmen who are not.

9. During the analysis we have formed constituency scores out of the scores of constituents living in the same district by several devices other than calculating average constituent scores. In particular, in view of the ordinal character of our scales we have frequently used the *median* constituent score as a central value for the constituency as a whole. However, the ordering of constituencies differs very little according to which of several reasonable alternatives for obtaining constituency scores is chosen. As a result, we have preferred mean scores for the greater number of ranks they give.

10. The meaning of this procedure can be suggested by two percentage tables standing for hypothetical extreme cases, the first that of full agreement, the second that of no agreement whatever. For convenience, these illustrative tables categorize both Con-

gressmen and their districts in terms of only three degrees of favor and assume for both a nearly uniform distribution across the three categories. The terms "pro," "neutral," and "con" indicate a relative rather than an absolute opinion. In Case I, full agreement, all districts relatively favorable to social welfare action have Congressmen who are so too, etc.; whereas in Case II, or that of no agreement, the ordering of constituencies is independent in a statistical sense of the ranking of Congressmen: knowing the policy orientation of a district gives no clue at all to the orientation of its Congressman. Of course, it is possible for the orders of legislators and districts to be *inversely* related, and this possibility is of some importance, as indicated below, when the policy position of non-incumbent candidates as well as incumbents is taken into account. To summarize the degree of congruence between legislators and voters, a measure of correlation is introduced. Although we have used a variety of measures of association in our analysis, the values reported in this article all refer to product moment correlation coefficients. For our hypothetical Case I a measure of correlation would have the value 1.0; for Case II, the value 0.0. When it is applied to actual data this convenient indicator is likely to have a value somewhere in between. The question is where.

Case I: Full Policy Agreement

Congressmen	Constituencies			
	Pro	Neutral	Con	
Pro	33	0	0	33
Neutral	0	34	0	34
Con	0	0	33	33
	33	34	33	100%

Correlation = 1.0

Case II: No Policy Agreement

Congressmen	Constituencies			
	Pro	Neutral	Con	
Pro	11	11	11	33
Neutral	11	12	11	34
Con	11	11	11	33
	33	34	33	100%

Correlation = 0.0

11. A word of caution is in order, lest we compare things that are not strictly comparable. For obvious reasons, most non-incumbent candidates have no roll call record, and we have had to measure their policy agreement with the district entirely in terms of the attitudes they have revealed in interviews. However, the difference of coefficients given here is almost as great when the policy agreement between the incumbent Congressman and his district is also measured in terms of the attitudes conveyed in confidential interviews.

12. A third type of connection, excluded here, might obtain between district and Congressman if the Representative accedes to what he thinks the district wants because he believes that to be what a representative *ought* to do, whether or not it is necessary for re-election. We leave this type of connection out of our account here because we conceive an influence relation as one in which control is not voluntarily accepted or rejected by someone subject to it. Of course, this possible connection between district and Representative is not any the less interesting because it falls outside our definition of influence or control, and we have given a good deal of attention to it in the broader study of which this analysis is part.

13. It scarcely needs to be said that demonstrating *some* constituency influence would not imply that the Representative's behavior is *wholly* determined by constituency pressures. The legislator acts in a complex institutional setting in which he is subject to a wide variety of influences. The constituency can exercise a genuine measure of control without driving all other influences from the Representative's life space.

14. We have done this by a variance-component technique similar to several others proposed for dealing with problems of this type. See especially Herbert A. Simon, "Spurious Correlation: A Causal Interpretation," *Journal of the American Statistical Association*, Vol. 49 (1954), pp. 467-479; Hubert M. Blalock, Jr., "The Relative Importance of Variables," *American Sociological Review*, Vol. 26 (1961), pp. 866-874; and the almost forgotten work of Sewall Wright, "Correlation and Causation," *Journal of Agricultural Research*, Vol. 20 (1920), pp. 557-585. Under this technique a "path coefficient" (to use Wright's terminology, although not his theory) is assigned to each of the causal arrows by solving a set of equations involving the correlations of the variables of the model. The weight assigned to a full path is then the product of its several path coefficients, and this product may be interpreted as the proportion of the variance of the dependent variable (roll call behavior, here) that is explained by a given path.

A special problem arises because influence may flow in either direction between the Congressman's attitude and his perception of district attitude (as noted above, the Representative may tend both to perceive his constituency's view selectively, as consistent with his own, and to change his own view to be consistent with the perceived constituency view). Hence, we have not a single causal model but a whole family of models, varying according to the relative importance of influence from attitude to perception and from perception to attitude. Our solution to this problem has been to calculate influence coefficients for the two extreme models in order to see how much our results could vary according to which model is chosen from our family of models. Since the systems of equations in this analysis are linear it can be shown that the coefficients we seek have their maximum and minimum values under one or the other of the limiting models. Therefore, computing any given coefficient for each of these limiting cases defines an interval in which the true value of the coefficient must lie. In fact these intervals turn out to be fairly small; our findings as to the relative importance of alternative influence paths would change little according to which model is selected.

The two limiting models with their associated systems of equations and the formulas for computing the relative importance of the three possible influence paths under each model are given below.

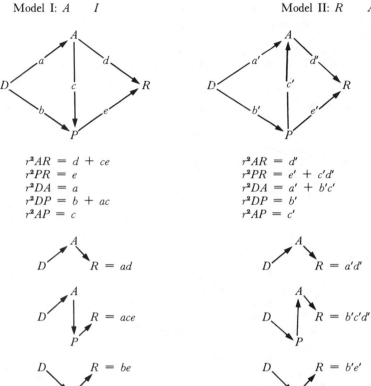

Model I: *A*   *I*   Model II: *R*   *A*

$r^2AR = d + ce$ $r^2AR = d'$
$r^2PR = e$ $r^2PR = e' + c'd'$
$r^2DA = a$ $r^2DA = a' + b'c'$
$r^2DP = b + ac$ $r^2DP = b'$
$r^2AP = c$ $r^2AP = c'$

$D \nearrow A \searrow R = ad$ $D \nearrow A \searrow R = a'd'$

$D \nearrow A \downarrow P \nearrow R = ace$ $D \nearrow A \uparrow P \searrow R = b'c'd'$

$D \searrow P \nearrow R = be$ $D \searrow P \nearrow R = b'e'$

15. By "least favorable" we mean the assumption that influence goes only from the Congressman's attitude to his perception of district attitude (Model I) and not the other way round. Under this assumption, the proportions of the variance of roll call behavior accounted for by the three alternative paths, expressed as proportions of the part of the variance of roll call votes that is explained by district attitude, are these:

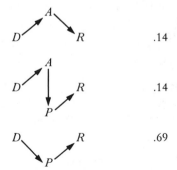

$D \nearrow A \searrow R$ .14

$D \nearrow A \downarrow P \nearrow R$ .14

$D \searrow P \nearrow R$ .69

Inverting the assumed direction of influence between the Congressman's own attitude and district attitude (Model II) eliminates altogether the effect that the Representative's attitude can have had on his votes, independently of his perception of district attitude.

16. Under both Models I and II the proportion of the variance of roll call voting explained by the influence path involving the Representative's own attitude is twice as great as the proportion explained by influence passing through his perception of district attitude.

17. What is more, the electorate's awareness of Congress as a whole appears quite limited. A majority of the public was unable to say in 1958 which of the two parties had controlled the Congress during the preceding two years. Some people were confused by the coexistence of a Republican President and a Democratic Congress. But for most people this was simply an elementary fact about congressional affairs to which they were not privy.

18. For a more extended analysis of forces on the congressional vote, see Donald E. Stokes and Warren E. Miller, "Party Government and the Saliency of Congress," *Public Opinion Quarterly*, Vol. 26 (Winter 1962), pp. 531-546.

19. For an account of this episode see Corinne Silverman, "The Little Rock Story," Inter-University Case Program series, reprinted in Edwin A. Bock and Alan K. Campbell, eds., *Case Studies in American Government* (Englewood Cliffs, 1962), pp. 1-46.

20. The sample of this constituency was limited to twenty-three persons of whom thirteen voted. However, despite the small number of cases the probability that the difference in awareness between this constituency and the country generally as the result only of sampling variations is much less than one in a thousand.

21. In view of the potential nature of the constituency's sanctions, it is relevant to characterize its influence over the Representative in terms of several distinctions drawn by recent theorists of power, especially the difference between actual and potential power, between influence and coercive power, and between influence and purposive control. Observing these distinctions, we might say that the constituency's influence is *actual* and not merely *potential* since it is the sanction behavior rather than the conforming behavior that is infrequent (Dahl). That is, the Congressman is influenced by his calculus of potential sanctions, following the "rule of anticipated reactions" (Friedrich), however oblivious of his behavior the constituency ordinarily may be. We might also say that the constituency has *power* since its influence depends partly on sanctions (Lasswell and Kaplan), although it rarely exercises *control* since its influence is rarely conscious or intended (Cartwright). In the discussion above we have of course used the terms "influence" and "control" interchangeably.

22. The factors in American electoral behavior that encourage such a departure are discussed in Stokes and Miller, *loc cit.*

VI

CONGRESSIONAL CHANGE

Prior to the extensive reforms of the 1970s, it was common to think of the House of Representatives as a relatively stable and to some extent static organization whose operations became increasingly formalized. Nelson Polsby (1968) has described the evolving institutionalization of House procedures that began in the late 1860s and continued into the 1960s. He focused on three factors that are closely related to this phenomenon: "boundedness," "complexity", and "universalism." Boundedness refers to an organization's differentiation from the external environment. As political institutions develop, they establish boundaries that help distinguish them from other institutions and contribute to their autonomy. Turnover is high in institutions lacking such boundaries; but as the demarcation between an organization and the outside world sharpens, the entry of new members becomes more difficult, and the number of voluntary exits decreases. What results is a growth in membership stability as members remain in the institution longer, a trend that Polsby noted in the House from 1867 to 1965.

A second indication of institutionalization is an increase in the organization's internal complexity. In the House, evidence of this trend is found in the growth in the number and importance of committees, the development of specialized structures for party leadership (that is, the development of the role of the Speaker and majority leader, and the formal designation of party whips), and the increase in benefits (such as office space and staff) designed to aid members in performing their legislative tasks. Polsby's final indicator of institutionalization is the decline in the use of particularistic (discretionary) criteria. A prime example of this is the use of an automatic seniority rule as a means of allocating power, a method that replaced the more arbitrary system controlled by the party leadership.

Several important consequences flowed from the House's increasing institutionalization. First, as the process continued, power became more dispersed, flowing away from the party leaders. The adoption of the seniority rule assured members that if they were able to stay in the House long enough, they could share in that power. Decentralization, combined with the adoption of fixed standards for the distribution of power enhanced the attractiveness of a congressional career, thereby providing strong incentives for representatives to stay in the institution.

The result was increased membership stability, greater autonomy for the committees, and the growth of norms that reinforced the established system.

Decline in Electoral Competitiveness

An alternative explanation of the changes that occurred in the House between the 1890s and the 1970s has been provided by H. Douglas Price (1975). He suggests that the impetus for changes in the House was the realignment of 1896; after this date the number of electorally competitive races declined, leading to an increase in membership stability and the lengthening of the congressional career. "Amateurs" were replaced by "professionals" who brought with them a different set of career expectations and perspectives. Lengthening tenure meant that legislators had to wait longer to assume positions of power. The result was increased pressure within the institution to make the time spent waiting for such positions count in attaining them. In contrast to Polsby, who suggests that institutionalization contributed to increased membership stability, Price suggests that the decline in electoral competitiveness led first to members' lengthening service in the House and then to increased pressures for an automatic rule (seniority) that linked power to tenure.

Impact of 1970s Reforms

Whether one supports the Polsby or the Price argument, it is clear that the House underwent several major changes after 1896, and that these changes have helped to shape the present day House. The growing frequency of long tenure and consequent membership stability has been well documented (Witmer, 1964; Bullock, 1972). Reforms instituted in the House of Representatives during the 1970s, however, challenged many of the conclusions suggested by the previous analyses (Cavanaugh, 1982). The changes that took place during this period were designed to strengthen Congress as a whole relative to the presidency, to open the institution to public scrutiny, and to disperse power within the House more widely. Besides accomplishing these goals, the reforms had a significant impact on the institution and on the trends that Polsby (1968) noted.

In the Senate as well, institutional reforms were adopted that made the chamber more open and egalitarian. Organizational and procedural changes enabled less senior members to gain power at the expense of older and more experienced legislators. With more staff, more money and more power, individual senators were able to maintain their independence from party leaders and to pursue more easily their own interests and legislative goals.

Several of the reforms of the period were designed specifically to counter the flow of power away from the legislative branch to the presidency (Sundquist, 1981). The 1973 War Powers Resolution, for example, was designed to limit the president's ability to engage in armed conflict without the explicit consent of both houses of Congress. In the area of economic policy, the 1974 Congressional Budget and Impoundment Control Act was designed to reassert a congressional voice in setting economic priorities and to limit the president's ability to withhold funds that Congress had appropriated. Finally, the period was marked by an increased assertiveness on the part of Congress in setting foreign policy, exemplified by conditions set on military aid.

Committee, Subcommittee Changes

The second major thrust of the reforms was to open to outside scrutiny parts of the legislative process that formerly had been insulated from outside scrutiny. Recorded votes were required on the House floor as well as in committees. The operation of committees was made more public by opening both hearings and mark-up sessions (meetings in which legislation is formulated). The only way a committee could close a session was by a majority vote. Coupled with these reforms were changes designed to disperse power more widely within both chambers. In the Senate, rules governing committee assignments and seniority were revised so that senators could be members of only two major committees and one minor, select or joint committee.

Throughout the early 1970s the House subcommittee system was strengthened by reforms that limited the number of subcommittee chairmanships that could be held by any one person, while at the same time the power committee chairmen wielded over subcommittees was weakened. Prior to the subcommittee reforms, committee chairmen could exercise discretion in the structuring of a committee's subcommittee system by determining the subject matter dealt with by each subcommittee and by handpicking the subcommittee leaders. Chairmen could "stack" the subcommittee to suit their purposes. In this way, some committee chairs effectively stifled points of view that contradicted their own. By limiting the discretion of the committee chairmen in appointing subcommittee leaders, the power of committee chairmen to control the policy outcomes of their committees and subcommittees was diminished. The result was increased autonomy and independence for subcommittees and their members.

A second major change required that committee chairmen be subject to a vote of approval by the Democractic Caucus, when the party was in the majority. This meant that seniority no longer was used as the sole criterion for selection; a Democratic representative could be denied a chairmanship even if that member had the longest tenure on the committee (and held no other chairmanship). In fact, in the 1970s three committee chairmen were denied their positions as a result of a Democratic Caucus vote. It appears that the negative reactions to these chairmen were motivated by criticism of the dictatorial way they conducted committee business (Parker, 1979).

There were several immediate consequences of the reforms. By increasing the importance of subcommittees in the policy process and thereby creating numerous power centers, influence within the House was dispersed more widely than in the pre-reform period. The opening of committee meetings made the actions of individual representatives more visible to their constituents. This reduced the tendency of members simply to go along with the chairman because it was easier for their constituents and groups to hold them accountable for their committee actions.

Increase in Voluntary Retirements

The reforms also had some long-term consequences on House operations that were not so immediately apparent. During the 1970s voluntary retirements replaced electoral defeats as the major source of turnover in the House (Cooper and West, 1981a, b; Hibbing, 1982a, b). Unlike electoral defeats that tended to affect mainly members with low seniority, voluntary retirements affected members with moderate to high levels of seniority. Although the rate of turnover did not increase significantly, the higher departure rate among older members led to a relatively greater number of junior members in the House. A growing trend to voluntary retirements also existed in the Senate, but in that chamber the phenomenon could be explained by traditional factors: the oldest, most electorally vulnerable and most ambitious members were the most likely to retire (Cooper and West, 1981a).

In contrast, the retirements in the House could not be explained by those traditional factors. Instead, the large number of House retirements (centering on mid-level tenured members who were not necessarily vulnerable) appears to indicate the declining attractiveness of a congressional career. Joseph Cooper and William West (1981a, b) note that by the late 1960s and early 1970s the costs of the House career increased (that is, the work load and demands placed on representatives became heavier), while the benefits of holding office declined. The increased work load was matched by decreases in the prestige of the office; moreover, congressional salaries did not keep pace with inflation (Cooper and West, 1981a, b). Additionally, the change in the method of selecting chairmen meant that a member no longer could count on attaining a powerful position in the House by sheer virtue of longevity. When a member did obtain a chairmanship, the position was substantially less powerful than in the pre-reform period. In fact, John Hibbing (1981a) cites the decline of seniority as the major factor in explaining the increasing number of retirements and diminishing membership stability.

The changed organization in the House and the greater influx of junior members eroded adherence to such norms as deference to more senior colleagues, apprenticeship, and, to some extent, the tradition of congressional "courtesy." It became less beneficial to adhere to these norms in the "democratized" House because of the changes instituted by the reforms and the shift toward a larger proportion of junior members. What emerged in the post-reform era was an institution that was markedly different from the previous period:

> What appears to be reemerging is a House that in a number of key respects is like Houses in many periods of the nineteenth century, even though more elaborate or sophisticated in terms of resources, structures and procedures. These Houses too had problems with net level of members' job satisfaction. These Houses too were highly junior, fractious, fragmented and individualistic.... What does seem clear is that as long as the rate of voluntary retirement does diminish and nothing occurs to resuscitate the party as an electoral force, the type of House that has emerged in the 1970s will become further stabilized and entrenched. As this occurs, it is also quite possible that a new type of member will begin to be recruited for service.... This type of member is also likely to be

even more self-oriented and independent than those now in office and thus likely to intensify further the tendencies toward fragmentation, fractiousness, and exploitation of position (Cooper and West, 1981b, p. 299).

Turnover and Voting Behavior

Few analysts see the reforms, however, as leading to far-reaching policy changes. To understand why this is so, it is necessary to examine the factors that provoke comprehensive policy overhauls in Congress as a whole. One major impetus to such change appears to be switched seats — seats where the member of one party is replaced by a member of the opposition (Brady and Lynn, 1973). The reforms of the 1970s led to few switched seats because retiring members usually were replaced with members of the same party (Brady and Lynn, 1981b).

Electoral realignments provide two conditions that promote sweeping rather than incremental policy change: a large number of switched-seat representatives and more polarized and homogeneous parties (Brady and Althoff, 1974). The emphasis on switched seats is important because of the high degree of continuity normally displayed by members of Congress in their voting records. For example, Herbert Asher and Herbert Weisberg (1978) have shown that the major determinate of the future voting behavior of representatives is their past voting pattern. Members entering Congress from switched-seat districts tend to display a higher degree of party loyalty and to provide higher levels of support for policy changes advocated by their party than do their non-switched seat colleagues (Brady and Lynn, 1973). Because solid party cohesiveness generally is necessary to pass packages of comprehensive policy changes, electoral conditions that bring in numerous switched-seat members also are more likely to promote conditions favorable to such innovations.

Certain other conditions within Congress that are favorable to policy change also result from periods of realignment. First, party leadership becomes more centralized and effective when the party displays a high degree of cohesion (Brady and Cooper, 1981). Because realigning elections promote greater party unity in the majority party, they are also more likely to result in the greater effectiveness of the majority party leadership in pushing for comprehensive policy changes. Second, committee decision making, like floor behavior, displays a high degree of stability and continuity. But this may be disrupted by an influx of new members onto the committees, who introduce new conflict into decision making (Parker and Parker, 1981).

The two articles that follow discuss the impact of the 1970s reforms and electoral realignments on policy changes and the allocation of power within the House and between Congress and the executive branch.

The quest for power is offered by Lawrence Dodd (1977) as an explanation of the reforms undertaken in the 1970s. As individual members seek to expand their own influence, they also try to augment the role of Congress relative to the other branches of government, so that the power attained is more meaningful.

Efforts to disperse power more widely within Congress reflect the desire to increase individual influence; attempts to strengthen Congress relative to the executive branch reflect the desire to augment institutional power. An inherent paradox, however, exists in these attempts. There is a basic incompatibility between the wide dispersal of power within Congress and a strong role for the institution in overall government decision making. The result of these tensions is a cyclical trend in reforms that lead first to a diffusion and then to a recentralization of power.

> At the outset, when politicians in a quest for national power first enter Congress, they decentralize power and create committee government. Decentralization is followed by severe problems of congressional decision making, presidential assumption of legislative prerogatives, and an eventual presidential assault on Congress itself. Congress reacts by reforming its internal structure . . . eventually, however, problems of internal congressional leadership and coordination will become so severe that Congress will be forced to take centralizing reforms. . . . As the immediate threat to congressional prerogatives recedes, members of Congress . . . become preoccupied with their immediate careers and press once again for greater power dispersal . . . (Dodd, 1977, p. 283).

If, as Dodd suggests, the changes that occurred in the House have affected the decision-making process, it is important to ascertain whether the reforms have had an impact on policy. One consequence of the changes is that representatives engaged in policy making in the post-reform period are far more inexperienced compared to the older, more senior members they replaced. Second, the dispersal of power has made it more difficult for the majority party leadership to coordinate major legislation; it is no longer possible simply to consult with a few powerful committee chairmen in order to ensure passage of a bill. In the reformed House, far more people hold power and they must be conferred with in order to gain approval of legislation. Further exacerbating this problem is the increased independence of House members. This places an added burden on the leadership and necessitates new mechanisms for coordination.

David Brady (1979) notes that electoral realignments have resulted in a greater congruence between party policies and constituent demands, thus reducing the degree of cross pressures that a representative feels between these two sets of demands. Because a representative will feel greater incentives to support the party when the demands of his or her constituency coincide with the party's policy, there will be a high degree of party voting in realignment periods. Furthermore, the new committee members from switched-seat districts are likely to be more loyal to the party and to increase the level of party voting in the committee. Brady argues that critical elections promote conditions conducive to party government, which in turn increases the likelihood of compehensive policy change.

However, Brady also concludes:

> Elections that bring to the House a substantial number of new members are not sufficient to ensure policy changes for a number of reasons. The most important is that there must exist a program; either party or both must propose major

changes. Another such condition is unified control of Congress and the presidency. . . .

Major shifts in public policy are most likely to occur during periods when the parties and the candidates take divergent issue positions and the electorate sends to Washington a new congressional majority party and a president of the same party (Brady, 1979, p. 99).

20. CONGRESS AND THE QUEST FOR POWER

Lawrence C. Dodd

The postwar years have taught students of Congress a very fundamental lesson: Congress is a dynamic institution. The recent congressional changes picture an institution that is much like a kaleidoscope. At first glance the visual images and structural patterns appear frozen in a simple and comprehensible mosaic. Upon closer and longer inspection the realization dawns that the picture is subject to constant transformations. These transformations seem to flow naturally from the prior observations, yet the resulting mosaic is quite different and is not ordered by the same static principles used to interpret and understand the earlier one. The appreciation and understanding of the moving image requires not only comprehending the role of each colorful geometric object in a specific picture, nor developing a satisfactory interpretation of the principles underlying a specific picture or change in specific aspects of the picture, but grasping the dynamics underlying the structural transformations themselves. So it is with Congress. To understand and appreciate it as an institution we must focus not only on particular aspects of internal congressional structure and process, nor on changes in particular patterns. We must seek to understand the more fundamental dynamics that produce the transformations in the congressional mosaic.

This essay represents an attempt to explain the dynamics of congressional structure.[1] Part I presents a general interpretation of the motives that lead members to organize Congress along particular lines, and attempts to specify the type of institutional structure and behavior that should flow from these motives. The model generated in Part I fits roughly with (and derives from a study of) congressional structure and behavior as represented by scholars of the era from the mid-1950s to the mid-1960s. That time period is treated as one observation point — much like one glance through a kaleidoscope. Part II argues that there is an inherent paradox within the motivational principles uncovered in Part I: to the extent that members of Congress try to maximize their personal goals in the short

Author's Note: For critical assistance at various stages in the writing of the essay, I would like to thank Arnold Fleischmann, Michael N. Green, Bruce I. Oppenheimer, Diana Phillips, Russ Renka, Terry Sullivan, and numerous graduate and undergraduate students who shared with me their questions and insights.

Source: This paper first appeared in *Congress Reconsidered*, 1st ed., ed. by Lawrence C. Dodd and Bruce I. Oppenheimer (New York: Praeger, 1977).

run, they create a congressional structure that undermines their ability to realize the personal goals over the long run. Members of Congress come to realize this fact in periods of institutional crisis and produce the type of structural reforms witnessed in the 1973-75 period. This tension between the short-term and long-term goals maximization generates the basic organizational dynamics of Congress. Part III argues that the pattern of change identified in Part II, a pattern that is cyclical in nature, does in fact characterize congressional organization and American politics generally, particularly in the twentieth century. Part IV argues that this cyclical theory allows us to predict the general fate of current congressional reforms. Part V considers the extent to which the overall cyclical pattern conforms to a Madisonian vision of American politics and the consequent implications for the future of Congress and American politics.

I

As with politicians generally, members of Congress enter politics in a quest for personal power. This quest may derive from any number of deeper motives: a desire for ego gratification or for prestige, a search for personal salvation through good works, a hope to construct a better world or to dominate the present one, or a preoccupation with status and self-love. Whatever the source, most members of Congress seek to attain the power to control policy decisions that impose the authority of the state on the citizenry at large.

The most basic lesson that any member of Congress learns on entering the institution is that the quest for power by service within Congress requires reelection. First, reelection is necessary in order to remain in the struggle within Congress for "power positions." [2] Staying in the struggle is important not only in that it provides the formal status as an elected representative without which an individual's influence on national legislative policy lacks legal authority; the quest for power through election and reelection also signals one's acceptance of the myth of democratic rule and thus one's acceptability as a power seeker who honors the society's traditional values. Second, reelection, particularly by large margins, helps create an aura of personal legitimacy. It indicates that one has a special mandate from the people, that one's position is fairly secure, that one will have to be "reckoned with." Third, long-term electoral success bestows on a member of Congress the opportunity to gain the experience and expertise, and to demonstrate the legislative skill and political prescience, that can serve to justify the exercise of power.

Because reelection is so important, and because it may be so difficult to ensure, its pursuit can become all-consuming. The constitutional system, electoral laws, and social system together have created political parties that are weak coalitions. A candidate for Congress normally must create a personal organization rather than rely on her or his political party. The "electoral connection" that intervenes between the desire for power and the realization of power may lead members to emphasize form over substance, position taking, advertising, and credit claiming rather than problem solving. In an effort to sustain electoral success, members of Congress may fail to take controversial and clear positions, fail to make hard choices, fail to exercise power itself.[3] Yet members of Congress generally are not solely preoccupied with reelection. Most members have relatively secure electoral margins. This security stems partially from the fact that members of Congress *are* independent of political parties and are independent from responsibility for seeking the executive, and thus can be judged more on personal qualities than on partisan or executive affiliations. Electoral security is further reinforced because members of Congress personally control financial and casework resources that can help them build a loyalty from their constituents independent of policy or ideological considerations. The existence of secure electoral margins thus allows members to devote considerable effort toward capturing a "power position" within Congress and generating a mystique of special authority that is necessary to legitimize a select decision-making role for them in the eyes of their nominal peers.

The concern of members of Congress with gaining congressional power, rather than just securing reelection, has had a considerable influence on the structure and life of Congress. Were members solely preoccupied with reelection, we would expect them to spend little time in Washington and devote their personal efforts to constituent speeches and district casework. One would expect Congress to be run by a centralized, efficient staff who, in league with policy-oriented interest groups, would draft legislation, investigate the issues, frame palatable solutions, and present the members with the least controversial bills possible. Members of Congress would give little attention to committee work, and then only to committees that clearly served reelection interests. The primary activity of congresspeople in Congress, rather, would be extended, televised floor debates and symbolic roll call votes, all for show. Such a system would allow the appearance of work while providing ample opportunity for the mending of home fences. Alternatively, were only a few members of Congress concerned about power, with others concerned with reelection, personal finances, or private lives, one might expect a centralized system with a few leader's exercising power and all others spending their time on personal or electoral matters.

Virtually all members of the U.S. Congress are preoccupied with power considerations. They are unwilling — unless forced by external events — to leave the major decisions in either a centralized, autonomous staff system or a central leadership. Each member wants to exercise power — to make the key policy decisions. This motive places every member in a personal conflict with every other member: to the extent that one member realizes her or his goal personally to control all key decisions, all others must lose. Given this widespread power motive, an obvious way to resolve the conflict is to disperse power — or at least power positions — as widely as possible. One logical solution, in other words, is to place basic policy-making responsibility in a series of discrete and relatively autonomous committees and subcommittees, each having control over the decisions in a specified jurisdictional area. Each member can belong to a small number of committees and, within them, have a significant and perhaps dominant influence on policy. Although such a system denies every member the opportunity to control all policy decisions, it ensures that most members, particularly if they stay in Congress long enough to obtain a subcommittee or committee chair, and if they generate the mystique of special authority necessary to allow them to activate the power potential of their select position, can satisfy a portion of their power drive. Within Congress, as one would expect in light of the power motive, the fundamental structure of organization is a committee system. Most members spend most of their time not in their district but in Washington, and most of their Washington time not on the floor in symbolic televised debate but rather in the committee or subcommittee rooms, in caucus meetings, or in office work devoted to legislation.[4] While the staff, particularly the personal staff, may be relegated to casework for constituents, the members of Congress sit through hearing after hearing, debate after debate, vote after vote seeking to shape in subcommittee, committee, and floor votes the contours of legislation. This is not to suggest, of course, that members of Congress do not engage in symbolic action or personal casework and do not spend much time in the home district; they do, in their effort at reelection. Likewise, staff do draft legislation, play a strong role in committee investigations, and influence the direction of public policy; they do this, however, largely because members of Congress just do not have enough time in the day to fulfill their numerous obligations. Seen in this perspective, Congress is not solely, simply, or primarily a stage on which individuals intentionally and exclusively engage in meaningless charades. Whatever the end product of their effort may be, members of Congress have actively sought to design a congressional structure and process that would maximize their ability to exercise personal power within Congress and, through Congress, within the nation at large.

The congressional committee structure reflects rather naturally the various dimensions that characterize the making of public policy. There are *authorization* committees that create policies and programs, specify their duties and powers, and establish absolute funding levels. There are *appropriations* committees that specify the actual funding level for a particular fiscal year. There are *revenue* committees that raise the funds to pay for the appropriations necessary to sustain the authorized programs. In addition, since Congress itself is an elaborate institution that must be serviced, there are *housekeeping* committees — those that provide for the day-to-day operation of Congress. In the House of Representatives there is also an *internal regulation* committee, the House Rules Committee, that schedules debate and specifies the rules for deliberation on specific bills.

These committees vary greatly in the nature and comprehensiveness of their impact on national policy making. The housekeeping committees tend to be *service* committees and carry little national weight except through indirect influence obtained from manipulating office and staff resources that other members may want so desperately as to modify their policy stances on other committees. A second set of committees, authorization committees such as Interior or Post Office, have jurisdictions that limit them to the concerns of fairly narrow constituencies; these are *reelection* committees that allow members to serve their constituencies' parochial interests but offer only limited potential to effect broad-scale public policy. A third group of committees are *policy* committees, such as Education and Labor or International Relations, that consider fairly broad policy questions, though questions that have fairly clear and circumscribed jurisdictional limits. A fourth set of committees are the *"power"* committees, which make decisions on issues such as the scheduling of rules (the House Rules Committee), appropriations (House and Senate Appropriations committees), or revenues (House Ways and Means or Senate Finance) that allow them to affect most or all policy areas.[5] Within a pure system of committee government, power committees are limited in the comprehensiveness of their control over the general policy-making process. No overarching control committee exists to coordinate the authorization, appropriations, or revenue process.

Because an essential type of legislative authority is associated with each congressional committee, members find that service on any committee can offer some satisfaction of their power drive. There are, nevertheless, inherent differences in the power potential associated with committees, differences that are tied to the variation in legislative function and in the comprehensiveness of a committee's decisional jurisdiction. This variation between committees is sufficient to make some committees more attractive as a place to gain power. Because members are in a quest for power, not simply reelection, they generally will seek to serve on committees whose function and policy focus allow the broadest personal impact on policy.

Maneuvering for membership on the more attractive committees is constrained by two fundamental factors. First, there are a limited number of attractive committee slots, and much competition will exist for these vacancies. Most members cannot realize their goal to serve on and gain control of these committees. For this reason, much pressure exists to establish norms by which members "prove" themselves deserving of membership on an attractive committee. Such norms include courtesy to fellow members, specialization in limited areas of public policy, a willingness to work hard on legislation, a commitment to the institution, adherence to the general policy parameters seen as desirable by senior members of Congress who will dominate the committee nominations process, and a willingness to reciprocate favors and abide by the division of policy domains into the set of relatively independent policy-making entities. Members who observe these norms faithfully will advance to the more desirable committees because they will have shown themselves worthy of special privilege, particularly if they also possess sufficient congressional seniority.[6]

Seniority is particularly important because of the second constraint on the process — the fact that service on the more powerful committees may limit one's ability to mend electoral fences. On the more comprehensive committees, issues often can be more complex and difficult to understand, necessitating much time and concentration on committee work; members may not be able to get home as often or as easily. Issues will be more controversial and will face members with difficult and often unpopular policy choices; members will be less able to engage in the politics of form over substance. The national visibility of the members will be greater, transforming them into public figures whose personal lives may receive considerable attention. Indiscretions that normally might go unreported will become open game for the press and can destroy careers. Thus, although it is undoubtedly true that service on the more comprehensive committees may bring with it certain attributes that can help reelection (campaign contributions from interest groups, name identification and status, a reputation for power that may convince constituents that "our member can deliver"), service on the more

493

attractive committees does thrust members into a more unpredictable world. Although members generally will want to serve on the most powerful committees, it will normally be best for them to put off such service until they have a secure electoral base and to approach their quest for power in sequential steps.

Because of the constraints operating within a system of committee government, congressional careers reflect a set of stages. The first stage entails an emphasis on shoring up the electoral base through casework, service on constituent-oriented reelection committees, and gaining favor within Congress by serving on the housekeeping committees. Of course, the first stage is never fully "completed": there is never a time at which a member of Congress is "guaranteed" long-term reelection or total acceptance within Congress, so both constituent and congressional service are a recurring necessity. But a point is normally reached — a point defined by the circumstances of the member's constituency, the opportunities present in Congress, and the personality and competence of the member — when he or she will feel secure enough, or perhaps unhappy enough, to attempt a move to a second stage. In the second stage members broaden their horizons and seek service on key policy committees that draft important legislation regulating such national policy dimensions as interstate commerce, education, or labor. In this stage, representatives begin to be "legislators," to preoccupy themselves with national policy matters. Because of the limited number of positions on power committees, many members will spend most, perhaps the rest, of their career in this stage, moving up by committee seniority to subcommittee and committee chairs on the policy committees. As they gain expertise in the specific policy area, and create a myth of special personal authority, they will gain power in some important but circumscribed area of national policy. For members who persist, however, and/or possess the right attributes of electoral security and personal attributes, a third stage exists: service on a power committee — Rules, Ways and Means, or Finance, Appropriations, and, in the Senate, Foreign Relations. Service on these committees is superseded, if at all, only by involvement in a fourth stage: service in the party leadership as a floor leader or Speaker. Few individuals ever have the opportunity to realize this fourth and climactic step; in a system of committee government, in fact, this step will be less sought and the battles less bitter than one might expect,[7] considering the status associated with them, because power will rest primarily in committees rather than in the party. Although party leadership positions in a system of committee government do carry with them a degree of responsibility, particularly the obligation to mediate conflicts between committees and to influence the success of marginal legislation on the house floor, members will generally be content to stay on a power committee and advance to subcommittee and committee chair positions rather than engage in an all-out effort to attain party leadership positions.

This career path, presented here in an idealized and simplified fashion, is a general "power ladder" that members attempt to climb in their quest for power within Congress. Some members leave the path voluntarily to run for the Senate (if in the House), to run for governor, to serve as a judge, or to serve as president. Some for special reasons bypass one or another stage, choose to stay at a lower rung, are defeated, or retire. Despite exceptions, the set of stages is a very real guide to the long-term career path that members seek to follow. Implicit within this pattern is the very real dilemma discussed earlier: progress up the career ladder brings with it a greater opportunity for significant personal power, but also greater responsibility. As members move up the power ladder, they move away from a secure world in which reelection interest can be their dominant concern and into a world in which concerns with power and public policy predominate. They take their chance and leave the security of the reelection stage because of their personal quest for power, without which reelection is a largely meaningless victory.

The attempt to prove oneself and move up the career ladder requires enormous effort. Even after one succeeds and gains a power position, this attainment is not in itself sufficient to guarantee the personal exercise of power. To utilize fully the power prerogatives that are implicit in specific power positions, a member must maintain the respect, awe, trust, and confidence of committee and house colleagues; he or she must sustain the aura of personal authority that is necessary to legitimize the exercise of power. Although the norm of seniority under a system of pure committee government will protect a member's possession of a power position, seniority is not sufficient to guard personal authority. In order to pass legislation and dominate policy decisions in a committee's jurisdictional area, a committee chair must radiate an appearance of special authority. The member must abide by the norms of the house and the committee, demonstrate legislative competence, and generate policy decisions that appear to stay within the general policy parameters recognized as acceptable by the member's colleagues. Among reelection efforts, efforts to advance in Congress to power positions, efforts to sustain and nurture personal authority, and efforts to exercise power, the members of Congress confront an incredible array of crosscutting pressures and internal dilemmas — decisions about how to balance external reelection interests with the internal institutional career, how to maximize the possibility of power within Congress by service on particular committees, how to gain and nurture authority within committees by specific legislative actions. The world of the congressman or congresswoman is complicated further, however, by a very special irony.

II

As a form of institutional organization, committee government possesses certain attributes that recommend it. By dividing policy concerns among a variety of committees it allows members to specialize in particular policy areas; this division provides a congressional structure through which the members can be their own expert advisers and maintain a degree of independence from lobbyists or outside specialists. Specialization also provides a procedure whereby members can become acquainted with particular programs and agencies and follow their behavior over a period of years, thus allowing informed oversight of the implementation of public policy. The dispersion of power implicit in committee government is important, furthermore, because it brings a greater number of individuals into the policy-making process and thus allows a greater range of policy innovation. In addition, as stressed above, committee government also serves the immediate power motive of congresspeople by creating so many power positions that all members can seek to gain power in particular policy domains.

Despite its assets, committee government does have severe liabilities, flaws that undermine the ability of Congress to fulfill its constitutional responsibilities to make legislative policy and oversee the implementation of that policy. First, committee government by its very nature lacks strong, centralized *leadership*, thereby undermining its internal decision-making capacity and external authority. Internally, Congress needs central leadership because most major questions of public policy (such as economic or energy policy) cut across individual committee jurisdictions. Since each committee and subcommittee may differ in its policy orientation from all others, and since the support of all relevant committees will be essential to an overall program, it is difficult, if not impossible, to enact a coherent general approach to broad policy questions. A central party leader or central congressional steering committee with extensive control over the standing committees could provide the leadership necessary to assist the development and passage of a coherent policy across the various committees, but committee government rejects the existence of strong centralized power. The resulting dispersion of power within Congress, and the refusal to allow strong centralized leadership, ensures that congressional decisions on major policy matters (unless aided and pushed by an outside leader) will be incremental at best, immobilized and incoherent as a norm. And to the extent that a Congress governed by committees can generate public policy, it faces the external problem of leadership, the inability of outside political actors, the press, or the public to identify a legitimate spokesperson for Congress on any general policy question. The wide dispersion of power positions allows numerous members to gain a degree of dominance over specific dimensions of a policy domain; all of these members can speak with some authority on a policy question, presenting conflicting and confusing approaches and interpretations. In cases where Congress does attempt to act, Congress lacks a viable mechanism through which to publicize and justify its position in an authoritative manner. Should Congress be in a conflict with the president, who can more easily present a straightforward and publicized position, Congress almost certainly will lose out in the eyes of public opinion. Lacking a clearly identifiable legislative leader in its midst, Congress is unable to provide the nation with unified, comprehensible, or persuasive policy leadership.

Closely related to the lack of leadership is a lack of *fiscal coordination*. Nowhere within a system of committee government is there a mechanism to ensure that the decisions of authorization, appropriations, and revenue committees have some reasonable relationship to one another. The authorization committees make their decisions about the programs to authorize largely independent of appropriations committee decisions about how much money the government will spend. The appropriations committees decide on spending levels largely independent of revenue committee decisions on taxation. Since it is always easier to promise (or authorize) than to deliver (or spend), program goals invariably exceed the actual financial outlays and thus the actual delivery of services. And since it is easier to spend money than to make or tax money, particularly for politicians, expenditures will exceed the revenues to pay the bills. Moves to coordinate the authorization, appropriations, and revenue processes are inconsistent with committee government, since such an effort would necessarily create a central mechanism with considerable say over all public policy and thus centralize power in a relatively small number of individuals. Committee government thus by its very nature is consigned to frustration: the policies that it does produce will invariably produce higher expectations than they can deliver; its budgets, particularly in periods of liberal, activist Congresses, will produce sizable and unplanned deficits in which expenditures far exceed revenues. The inability of committee government to provide realistic program goals and fiscal discipline will invite the executive to intervene in the budget process in order to provide fiscal responsibility and coordination. The result, of course, will be a concomitant loss of the congressional control over the nation's purse strings.

A third detriment associated with committee government, and one that is exacerbated by the absence of leadership and committee coordination, is the lack of *accountability* and *responsibility*. A fundamental justification of congressional government is that it allows political decision making to be responsive to the will of a national majority. Committee government distributes this decision-making authority among a largely autonomous set of committees. Since seniority protects each committee's membership from removal and determines who will chair each committee, a committee's members can feel free to follow their personal policy predilections and stop any legislation they wish that falls within their committee's jurisdiction, or propose any that they wish. Within a system of committee government, resting as it does on the norm of seniority, no serious way exists to hold a specific committee or committee chair accountable to the majority views of Congress or the American people, should those views differ from the views held within a particular committee. Because of the process whereby members are selected to serve on major committees — a process that emphasizes not their compatibility with the majority's policy sentiment but rather their adherence to congressional norms, general agreement with the policy views of senior congresspeople, and possession of seniority — the top committees (especially at the senior ranks) are quite likely to be out of step with a congressional or national majority. This lack of representativeness is particularly likely if patterns of electoral security nationwide provide safe seats (and thus seniority) to regions or localities that are unrepresentative of the dominant policy perspectives of the country. Responsiveness is further undermined because the absence of strong central leaders, and a widespread desire among members for procedural protection of their personal prerogatives, require reliance on rigid rules and regulations to govern the flow of legislation and debate, rules such as the Senate's cloture rule that allows the existence of filibusters. Under a system of party government, where limiting rules may exist on the books, strong party leaders can mitigate their effects. In a system of committee government, rules become serious hurdles that can block the easy flow of legislation, particularly major, controversial legislation, thereby decreasing the ability of Congress to respond rapidly to national problems. Committee government thus undermines the justification of Congress as an institution that provides responsive, representative government.

Since institutions derive their power not solely from constitutional legalisms but from their own mystique of special authority that comes from their legitimizing myths, committee government undercuts not only Congress's ability to exercise power but also the popular support that is necessary to maintain its power potential.

The lack of accountability and the damage to Congress's popular support are augmented by a fourth characteristic of committee government — a tendency toward *insulation* of congressional decision making. This insulation derives from three factors. First, members of committees naturally try to close committee sessions from public purview, limiting thereby the intrusion of external actors such as interest groups or executive agencies and thus protecting committee members' independent exercise of power within committees. Second, the creation of a multiplicity of committees makes it difficult for the public or the press to follow policy deliberations even if they are open. Third, it is difficult if not impossible to create clear jurisdictional boundaries between committees. The consequent ambiguity that exists between jurisdictional boundaries will often involve committees themselves in extensive disputes over the control of particular policy domains, further confusing observers who are concerned with policy deliberations. By closing its committee doors, creating a multiplicity of committees, and allowing jurisdictional ambiguities, a system of committee government isolates Congress from the nation at large. Out of sight and out of mind, Congress loses the attention, respect, and understanding of the nation and becomes an object of scorn and derision, thus further undermining the authority or legitimacy of its pronouncements and itself as an institution.

Finally, committee government undermines the ability of Congress to perform that one function for which committee government would seem most suited — aggressive oversight of administration. According to the classic argument, the saving grace of committee government is that the dispersion of power and the creation of numerous policy experts ensure congressional surveillance of the bureaucracy. Unfortunately, this argument ignores the fact that the individuals on the committees that pass legislation will be the very people least likely to investigate policy implementation. They will be committed to the program, as its authors or most visible supporters, and will not want to take actions that might lead to a destruction of the program. The impact of publicity and a disclosure of agency or program shortcomings, after all, is very unpredictable and difficult to control and may create a public furor against the program. The better part of discretion is to leave the agency largely to its own devices and rely on informal contacts and special personal arrangements, lest the glare of publicity and the discovery of shortcomings force Congress to deauthorize a pet program, casting aspersions on those who originally drafted the legislation. Members of Congress are unwilling to resolve this problem by creating permanent and powerful oversight committees because such committees, by their ability to focus attention on problems of specific agencies and programs, would threaten the authority of legislative committees to control and direct policy in their allotted policy area. Committee government thus alows a *failure of executive oversight*.

In the light of these five problems, the irony of committee government is that it attempts to satisfy members' individual desires for personal power by dispersing internal congressional authority so widely that the resulting institutional impotence cripples the ability of Congress to perform its constitutional roles, thereby dissipating the value of internal congressional power. Members of Congress thus are not only faced with the daily dilemma of balancing reelection interests with their efforts at upward power mobility within Congress; their lives are also complicated by a cruel paradox, the ultimate incompatibility of widely dispersed power within Congress, on the one hand, and a strong role for Congress in national decision making, on the other. This inherent tension generates an explosive dynamic within Congress as an organization and between Congress and the executive.

In the short run, as members of Congress follow the immediate dictates of the personal power motive, they are unaware of, or at least unconcerned with, the long-term consequences of decentralized power; they support the creation of committee government. The longer committee government operates, the more unhappy political analysts and the people generally become with the inability of Congress to make national policy or ensure policy implementation. With Congress deadlocked by immobilism, political activists within Congress and the nation at large turn to the president (as the one alternative political figure who is popularly elected and thus should be responsive to popular sentiments) and encourage him (or her, if we ever break the sex barrier) to provide policy leadership and fiscal coordination, to open up congressional decision making to national political forces and ensure congressional responsiveness, and to oversee the bureaucracy. Presidents, particularly those committed to activist legislation, welcome the calls for intervention and will see their forthright role as an absolute necessity to the well-being of the Republic. Slowly at first, presidents take over the roles of chief legislator, chief budgetary officer, overseer of the bureaucracy, chief tribune, and protector of the people.[8] Eventually the president's role in these regards becomes so central that he feels free to ignore the wishes of members of Congress, even those who chair very important committees, and impose presidential policy on Congress and the nation at large.

The coming of a strong, domineering, imperial president who ignores Congress mobilizes its members into action. They see that their individual positions of power within Congress are meaningless unless the institution can impose its legislative will on the nation. They search for ways to regain legislative preeminence and constrain the executive. Not being fools, members identify part of the problem as an internal institutional one and seek to reform Congress. Such reform efforts come during or immediately following crises in which presidents clearly and visibly threaten fundamental power prerogatives of Congress. The reforms will include attempts to provide for more centralized congressional leadership, fiscal coordination, congressional openness, better oversight mechanisms, clarification of committee jurisdictions, procedures for policy coordination, and procedures to encourage committee accountability. Because the quest for personal power continues as the underlying motivation of individual members, the reforms are basically attempts to strengthen the value of internal congressional power by increasing the power of Congress vis-à-vis the executive. The reform efforts, however, are constrained by consideration of personal power prerogatives of members of Congress. The attempt to protect personal prerogatives while centralizing power builds structural flaws into the centralization mechanisms, flaws that would not be present were the significance of congressional structure for the national power of Congress itself the only motive. The existence of these flaws provides the openings through which centralization procedures are destroyed when institutional crises pass and members again feel free to emphasize personal power and personal careers. In addition, because policy inaction within Congress often will be identified as the immediate cause of presidential power aggrandizement, and because policy immobilism may become identified with key individuals or committees that have obstructed particular legislation, reform efforts also may be directed toward breaking up the authority of these individuals or committees and dispersing it among individuals and committees who seem more amenable to activist policies. This short-term dispersal of power, designed to break a legislative logjam (and, simultaneously, to give power to additional individuals), will serve to exacerbate immobilism in the long run when the new mechanisms of centralization are destroyed.

Viewed in a broad historical perspective, organizational dynamics within Congress, and external relations of Congress to the president, have a "cyclical" pattern. At the outset, when politicians in a quest for national power first enter Congress, they decentralize power and create committee government. Decentralization is followed by severe problems of congressional decision making, presidential assumption of legislative prerogatives, and an eventual presidential assault on Congress itself. Congress reacts by reforming its internal structure: some reform efforts will involve legislation that attempts to circumscribe presidential action; other reforms will attempt to break specific points of deadlock by further decentralization and dispersal of congressional authority; eventually, however, problems of internal congressional leadership and coordination will become so severe that Congress will be forced to undertake centralizing reforms. As Congress moves to resolve internal structure problems and circumscribe presidential power, presidents begin to cooperate so as to defuse the congressional counterattack; to do otherwise would open a president to serious personal attack as anticongressional and thus antidemocratic, destroying the presidency's legitimizing myth as a democratic institution and identifying presidential motivations as power aggrandizement rather than protection of the Republic. As the immediate threat to congressional prerogatives recedes, members of Congress (many of whom will not have served in Congress during the era of institutional crisis) become preoccupied with their immediate careers and press once again for greater power dispersal within Congress and removal of centralizing mechanisms that inhibit committee and subcommittee autonomy. Decentralization reasserts itself and Congress becomes increasingly leaderless, uncoordinated, insulated, unresponsive, unable to control executive agencies. Tempted by congressional weakness and hounded by cries to "get the country moving," the executive again reasserts itself and a new institutional crisis eventually arises. A review of

American history demonstrates the existence of this cycle rather clearly, particularly during the twentieth century.

III

Throughout the nineteenth century, the national government was not immensely powerful. Most politicians were not drawn to long-term careers in Congress. Those who were drawn to Congress and were concerned with congressional power did struggle for power positions, a struggle that initially served to create a fledgling committee system.[9] The committee system was balanced by and guided by strong central leadership, particularly in the House of Representatives, where the Speakership offered a clear mechanism for legislative leadership. The central leaders were able to maintain considerable authority because they offered services — such as selection of committee members and chairpeople, policy development and guidance, mediation of parliamentary conflicts, scheduling of legislation — that were necessary to avoid the chaos implicit in the high turnover of members throughout most of the nineteenth century. The leaders' authority was challenged occasionally by other members who wanted greater independence and more autonomy for themselves and their committees. These challenges led to a "minicycle" in which forces of decentralization occasionally would assert themselves within Congress and attempt to disperse power.[10] Supporters of decentralization during the nineteenth century were never numerous enough to break the power of central leaders permanently, however, since the number of congresspeople committed to congressional careers of any significant duration was quite low.

Events of the late nineteenth century altered dramatically the nature of national power. The Civil War ended the ambiguities about the supremacy of the national government over the states and clearly established the hegemony of the national government in political affairs. The industrial revolution, whose effects began to multiply in the late nineteenth century, helped create an interdependent economy based on interstate commerce, thus expanding the power potential of the national government by confronting it with social and economic decisions of considerable magnitude that lay within its constitutional mandate. The industrial revolution also provided America (as well as other nations) with the technical means to span the oceans, conquer far-off lands, and gain international markets for American goods. America thus discovered the world, the world rediscovered America, and the national government discovered anew its constitutional responsibility for foreign policy and the regulation of American involvement in foreign commerce.

As these responsibilities served to strengthen the power of the national government over the lives of individual citizens, Congress became a center of national decision making. The Constitution gave to it the delegated powers to regulate interstate and foreign commerce, give advice and consent (on the part of the Senate) to treaties and ambassadorial nominations, control defense authorizations and appropriations, and declare war. Politicians who wanted to exercise these prerogatives had to go to Congress and stay there, which they did in ever-increasing numbers.[11] In the late nineteenth century congressmen attracted to long-term careers found power in the House centralized in the hands of a Speaker and power in the Senate centralized in the majority party leadership and majority caucus.[12] The centralized conduct of congressional operations denied the rank-and-file members the personal congressional power that growing numbers of them sought. Between 1910 and 1915 their numbers were sufficient so that these disaffected members successfully attacked the foundations of party government in both chambers, overthrowing both the Speakership and the party caucus and dispersing congressional power to the standing committees.[13] The system of committee government that emerged was held together by the institutional norms and rules that had been growing up over the preceding decades as congressional turnover had decreased, particularly the norm of seniority. As Congress moved to a system of committee government, the inherent problems began to emerge.[14] The presidency, which had benefited as an institution from the growth of an administrative state that it partially headed, from the visibility given it by the new nationwide system of mass communications, and from the rise of international relations, became increasingly free from congressional constraints and able to assert national dominance.[15]

From around 1910 to 1945 the presidency grew enormously in power, while Congress floundered. In 1921, in an act that recognized the inability of a decentralized Congress to provide policy coordination and a coherent budget, Congress created the Bureau of the Budget (BOB) and placed it in the executive branch. In the 1930s Roosevelt asserted strongly the role of chief legislator, with major laws drafted in the White House or executive agencies. Roosevelt also seized BOB — which was moved directly under his control — as a tool of presidential decision making. In addition, Roosevelt gained more direct control of the bureaucracy. By the early 1940s many congressional committees were overwhelmed by the executive: their staff work was conducted by staffs from the agencies; their legislation came from the president and the agencies; many committees would not consider legislation that was not approved by BOB; and the legislation that did pass Congress provided the executive broad rule-making authority.[16]

The Roosevelt presidency constituted such a direct threat to Congress — to its control over legislative decision making, the budget, and the bureaucracy — that its members moved to put their own houses in order by passing, in modified form, the 1946 Legislative Reorganization Act. In an attempt to resolve the problems of *leadership* and *accountability*, the act proposed the creation of party policy committees for each party in each house.[17] The House defeated this proposal and it was knocked out of the final act. As a means of providing for *fiscal coordination,* the act proposed and Congress approved the creation of a Joint Committee on the Budget to be composed of all members of the House and Senate Appropriations committees, the House Ways and Means Committee, and the Senate Finance Committee. A third provision of the act, passed by Congress, involved the reduction of the number of standing committees from 33 to 15 in the Senate and from 48 to 19 in the House, as well as a reduction in subcommittees. As part of this process, Congress tried to clarify jurisdictional boundaries between committees. These efforts were designed to reduce the degree of committee *insulation,* as well as to make leadership and coordination easier. Fourth, in an attempt to provide for greater *oversight* of the executive, the act directed the standing committees to exercise "continuous watchfulness" over the agencies under each committee's jurisdiction, thereby removing any doubt as to their role in bureaucratic surveillance, and also authorized each standing committee to hire professional staff members, setting a limit of four on all except Appropriations.

The 1946 Legislative Reorganization Act served to bring to a close the first twentieth-century cycle of organizational change within Congress and external struggle between Congress and the presidency. With the passage of the act, Congress was able to assert a greater degree of autonomy from the agencies and the president, particularly because of its increased staff resources. The greater congressional autonomy was assisted, however, by the fact that eight of the fourteen years following the passage of the act witnessed a divided government in which the majority party in Congress failed to control the presidency. The act itself actually did little to resolve the fundamental problems of Congress. In their attempt to protect fundamental personal prerogatives, members of Congress failed to take the really difficult steps that might have helped resolve structural problems within Congress. They left party leadership as weak after the act as before, ensuring that central party leaders would offer no threat to committee autonomy; congressional leadership and accountability remained weak. The members of Congress created a joint budget committee whose size was so large (over 100 members) that it was unworkable, whose membership had vested interests (as members of the appropriations and revenue committees) in protecting the power of outside committees, whose powers were nonexistent, and whose legislative timetable (a budget by the second month of a congressional session) was totally unrealistic. Within four years the new budget process had ceased to operate and the problems of fiscal coordination were free to reign. Third, the act did nothing to open committee meetings, to stop long-run proliferation of subcommittees, or to provide sure-fire centralized mechanisms that could enforce committee jurisdictions; the act did not defuse the problem of insulation. And the primary direct effort toward guaranteeing oversight, a provision encouraging its conduct, was a pathetic attempt at problem avoidance that left responsibility for oversight once again in the hands of those least likely to conduct it.

In the final analysis, the 1946 Reorganization Act did not replace the old order of committee government with a new order of congressional rule; the reorganization refurbished the old order and removed some of its most glaring shortcomings but in the end left committee government intact and strengthened. The new committees, by virtue of broader jurisdictions and increased staff resources, were actually stronger and more potent forces than before. Because the new committees were stronger entities, the committee chairpeople — whose prerogatives had not been reduced — emerged as even more powerful figures. The postwar system of committee government thus possessed all of the fundamental problems of the prior era. The 1946 act, moreover, contributed to the *isolation* of most members from congressional power. In streamlining the committee system the act left a relatively small number of autonomous positions that carried with them real power and status. The reform effort thus provided neither the benefits of decentralization (widespread expertise and policy innovation) nor the benefits of centralization (leadership and coordination).

Throughout the 1950s and 1960s, congressional policy making evidenced considerable deadlock. Part of the deadlock, no doubt, was due to the conservative orientation of its members. But part was clearly due to the nature of the postwar committee government, the most apparent attribute of which was the dominance of conservative committee chairpeople. Liberal Democratic activists, particularly in the House, organized to break this deadlock by breaking up the power of committee chairs and dispersing it to subcommittees and subcommittee chairs, thereby also increasing their potential ability to gain power positions. On a committee-by-committee basis they succeeded until the point that, in the early 1970s, they were strong enough to institutionalize a system of subcommittee government by altering the congressional rules. A similar breakthrough had come more informally and earlier in the Senate, so that by the 1970s power within Congress was far more decentralized than it had ever been in the period before World War II.

As liberal activists within Congress moved to decentralize its internal authority, the presidency again came to the fore as the dominant national institution. In the postwar era, under the rubric of national security, presidents gained control of a "secrecy system" in which they dominated (to the extent that any external institution did) the nation's intelligence community. Congress itself was so pluralistic — and its pluralism was increasing so steadily — that presidents and the agencies could easily "justify" ignoring Congress lest congressional leaks expose national "secrets." In foreign policy, "by the 1960s and 1970s, Presidents began to claim the power to send troops at will around the world as a sacred and exclusive presidential right," a right derived from the greater capacity of the executive branch to respond rapidly to international events and to create a coherent and rational foreign policy.[18] Domestically, Kennedy and Johnson asserted in Rooseveltian tradition the primacy of the president as chief legislator and chief budgetary officer, a role reinforced by the increasing desire of the country for a planned and prosperous economy. By the 1970s the presidency was again ascendant in American politics and undertaking political actions far in excess of its legitimate constitutional role. In Schlesinger's term, "constitutional comity" between Congress and the president had broken down. Vietnam, Cambodia, and Watergate were obvious symbols of this breakdown. But the most serious direct assault on Congress came with the attempts by Richard Nixon to impound duly appropriated funds.

The lack of fiscal coordination within Congress meant that in an age of activist legislators, and without external coordination by the executive branch, Congress would generate huge and unplanned deficits, these deficits being the result of dispersed and incremental decision making. With the coming of the Nixon years, both of these conditions were met: a liberal Congress and a divided government in which the liberal Congress faced a conservative president on whom Congress could not rely to provide a budget geared to liberal priorities. The result was huge budgetary deficits. Nixon's response was not to veto the appropriations, which for a variety of reasons seemed politically untenable and unwise, but to impound specific funds and refuse to spend them. He concentrated his efforts on the social legislation that he opposed, and "from 1969 to 1972 . . . impounded 17 to 20 percent of controllable expenditures. . . ." [19] A final straw in the impoundment controversy was Nixon's assertion that impoundment was a constitutional right of the president. Nixon lost this argument in court battle after battle, but in the process he won his policy goals because his unconstitutional impoundments nevertheless succeeded in destroying or crippling the programs he opposed. And, politically, Congress could not move to impeach Nixon for his unconstitutional acts because he had the political trump card: his unconstitutional acts, so he could argue, were necessary to save the Republic from the economic disaster inherent in the budgetary deficits produced by the fiscal irresponsibility of the decentralized, leaderless, uncoordinated, unresponsive, insulated Congress.

Nixon's impoundment of duly appropriated funds confronted members of Congress with the ultimate dilemma implicit within a system of committee government in the twentieth century. The members of Congress could disperse power internally, play their power game, give half the members of each house a power position. The dispersion of power, however, created policies and budgets that the members of Congress could not defend rationally. The president was free ultimately to ignore congressional decisions if he so wished. He could not be threatened by impeachment because of unconstitutional impoundments, since impeachment is ultimately a political undertaking and the president had the political upper hand as a result of the irresponsible behavior on the part of Congress. Nixon thus presented members of Congress with the clearest message yet that the value of power within Congress depended on its ability to ensure the implementation of the policy results generated by internal congressional decision making. Nixon's actions, however, were "not an aberration but a culmination" [20] of forces at work in twentieth-century society, particularly the internal dynamics of Congress as an institution.

The response of Congress to the external threat that had been growing from the 1960s to the early 1970s, and that materialized most dramatically in the impoundment controversy, was to reform its internal organization and procedures once again. The move toward reform came largely in the Democratic party, which, as the congressional majority party, had the most to lose in a shift of power from Congress to a Republican president. Because the lower national status and visibility of House members made their personal power more dependent on the national power of their institution, and because the size of the House meant that problems of leadership, coordination, insulation, and responsiveness undermined more critically its internal decision-making capacity and consequent external authority, the House of Representatives led the reforms.

These reform efforts — from increased leadership power and fiscal coordination to alterations in oversight procedures — seem to have brought an end to a second cycle of internal organizational change and external congressional struggle with the executive branch. Few calls remain within Congress for further centralization of power. The internal struggle has shifted from planning centralized reforms such as the new budgetary process to an effort to implement and institutionalize them. Externally, the president seems less arrogant and aggrandizing in behavior than did Nixon or Johnson. As a result of these reform efforts, and the Watergate incident, the Congress appears resurgent. Is this true? Will it last?

IV

Congressional history during the era of strong national government can be characterized as cyclical in nature. The cyclical pattern derives from the implicit tension between the quest for power by individuals within Congress and the necessity of maintaining the external authority of the institution. The power motive is a very delicate phenomenon, resting as it does in the psyche of politicians who face incredible obstacles and personal demands in any attempt to realize their power drive. For several reasons, however, it seems unlikely that a significant and permanent decline will occur soon in the interest that politicans demonstrate toward congressional service. First, it seems unlikely that individuals preoccupied with political power can look outside of the nation-state for a realization of their quest. Within the nation-state all tendencies seem to indicate a continuing flow of authority away from local and state levels and toward a national level. Individuals preoccupied with attaining political power have no place to look but at the national level. Second, the recent reforms are the most dramatic alterations of internal congressional power relations since the overthrow of Cannon and have been hailed by James Sundquist as restoring the imbalance between congressional and executive power.[21] Politicans have even more reasons than Sundquist to find these reforms successful, since this conclusion serves to convince them that service is worth it after all, and offers a means to attain their power goal. Third, electoral security of members of Congress has been increasing dramatically over the past decade or so. The demands of reelection should not be so great that members of Congress will feel that their reelection efforts will of necessity deny them the opportunity and time to seek and exercise congressional power. Finally, underneath the centralizing reforms, which might seem to make Congress less attractive for particular individuals, the dispersion of power of the 1947 to 1973 era remains, institutionalized by a Subcommittee Bill of Rights and augmented by further decentralization decisions that occurred as part of the 1973-75 era. Numerous subcommittee chairs and the resources that go with them, as well as an appearance of power and status, all exist to draw members back to Congress.

The thrust of these arguments is that no changes have occurred that alter the power motive underlying the internal congressional cycle. Can we therefore expect the cycle to continue to operate and the centralizing reform efforts to be undercut in the coming years? The answer to this question would seem to depend largely on the extent to which the reforms really did strengthen central policy organs. It could be that the recent institutional crisis was so severe that members did create central mechanisms so strong that those mechanisms cannot be easily undermined. Alternatively, members may have continued their preoccupation with personal prerogatives, even in the midst of external institutional decay. In the latter case, we would expect an examination of the reform attempt to demonstrate failure of action and, in situations in which reforms actually did pass, evidence of built-in structural flaws that will deflate the renewed congressional resurgence and aid the move toward decentralization. As selected illustrations will indicate, this latter interpretation is the more plausible one.

With regard to *leadership*, the Senate made no effort to restructure the institutional authority or roles of its party leaders. In the House, where serious attempts were made, the Democratic party leader's power (that is, the power of the Speaker in periods of majority party status) is still quite problematic. First, the rise of the caucus and the caucus chairperson, and the lack of a central role of the Speaker in the caucus, has served to dichotomize the power of the Democratic party leadership and has created a situation in which the Speaker may be opposed by a strong caucus chairperson, who can maneuver the caucus against the Speaker. The inability of the Speaker to gain central authority in the caucus (for example, as its automatic chair) undercuts severely the authority of the Speaker and his ability to speak for and guide the party. This fragmentation within the leadership ranks continues in the Steering and Policy Committee where the Speaker (who chairs the meeting) and the caucus chairperson both sit, along with 22 other members. While the Speaker has the authority to select 9 of the 22, 12 are chosen by regional caucuses, not by the party caucus as a whole. The emphasis on regional selection of half of the Steering and Policy membership activates not the majority sentiments that might tie the Steering Committee and the party caucus together, but differences that can tear them apart. This is particularly true in light of the *juniority* rule in which Steering and Policy positions within each region must be rotated from Congress to Congress between junior and senior members of the region, even if only one junior member or senior member exists to be chosen. Under such decision rules it is quite possible to generate 12 members who — chosen because of regional affiliations and degree of congressional service rather than policy sentiments — are out of step with the majority of the party and can immobilize the Steering and Policy Committee. The Speaker's authority is also weak because the recent reforms have not given him greater procedural authority on the floor, or personal incentives that the Speaker can use to bargain and cajole with. In addition, in the summer of 1976 the House Democratic caucus defeated the most serious attempt to provide the Speaker with incentives he could use as inducements to party loyalty — the power to select Democratic members of the House Administration Committee and through them control resources such as office space.

The move toward greater *fiscal coordination* — the creation of the new budget committees and a new budget process — has been limited and perhaps crippled fatally by two efforts at protecting the power of existing House committees. First, 10 of the 25 members of the House Budget Committee must come from the House Appropriations and House Ways and Means committees, 5 from each. Second, all members of the House Budget Committee maintain membership on other committees (including Appropriations and Ways and Means) and are limited in service on the Budget Committee (though not on the other committees) to four years out of every ten. These two rules were the price that had to be paid in the House to gain passage of the Budget Act. Together, they help guarantee that the loyalty of House Budget Committee members is not to the Budget Committee, and thus to a centralized coordination of fiscal policy, but to their other committee assignments (particularly to the two committees, Appropriations and Ways and Means, whose fiscal authority and general status is most threatened by the Budget Committee), and thus to the protection of the autonomy and authority of the other committees. It is, after all, the other committees to which they must look for their long-term power, not the Budget Committee (because of the four-year service limit). It would be hard enough to make the new process work even with a united and cohesive Budget Committee; the internal divisions and weakness built into the House committee seem destined to destroy the process altogether.

The moves to increase *accountability* and *responsibility* did produce a mild change in the Senate cloture rule. Unfortunately, the other reforms — those that have focused on the ability of the caucuses (particularly the House Democratic caucus) to discipline committee chairpeople and select chairs more in line with the policy sentiments of the caucus majority — have suffered from a severe irony. Committee power, and to a large extent congressional power, now rests with subcommittees and subcommittee chairs, not committees and committee chairs. The only subcommittee chair nominations that will be reviewed and ratified or rejected by the House Democratic party caucus are those on the Appropriations Committee. Selection of all other subcommittee chairs is left to the party caucus within the parent standing committee. The majority party caucus thus has gained the real power to hold committee chairs accountable at precisely the time that they matter least. The party caucus does not have a direct procedure to hold most subcommittee chairs accountable; there are, in fact, so many subcommittee chairs now that it would be practically impossible for the full caucus, or even the Steering and Policy Committee, to maintain even a cursory knowledge of their behavior. Since it is the committee caucuses that must constrain and guide subcommittee chairs, and ensure that they reflect the dominant sentiments of the House majority, it is increasingly important that committee caucuses be representative of the party at large and reflect its dominant sentiments in their policy jurisdiction. The representativeness of committees, and the accountability that would come from it, will be much harder for the party to ensure and maintain than the discipline of a small number of powerful committee chairs, if only because of the large numbers of members involved. Considering how hard it has been, and how long it has taken, for the party to evolve a system that would allow the disciplining of committee chairs, it may be a much harder and longer process to move to a system that would ensure a representative selection of committee members who could be trusted to reflect dominant party sentiments and discipline subcommittee chairs accordingly. The alternative, to centralize power within committee chairs who would then be held accountable by the new caucus rules, seems politically impossible in the near future, given the power motive that generated — and continues to generate — subcommittee power; such a move seems probable only if a new institutional crisis forces it (or an analogous move) on the members of the House and on Congress generally.

The effort to reduce congressional *insulation* has hardly fared any better. It has produced one victory of sorts — the sunshine rules that have opened virtually all committee meetings. The open hearings, and the widespread publicity of some meetings, may well have increased somewhat the public's respect for Congress, as in the Senate Watergate hearings or the House Judiciary proceeding on impeachment. Even this victory has had its price, in making committees more susceptible to intrusion by powerful external groups, particularly executive agencies, intrusion that may undermine congressional autonomy; but the sunshine has seemed worth it. Elsewhere, unfortunately, the moves against insulation have been far less successful in their initial passage, much less so in their final impact. The plan of the Bolling Committee to provide for clearer and more rational committee jurisdictions had the misfortune to come to the House floor only after years of power dispersion to subcommittees and the institutionalization of the power of subcommittee chairs. The Bolling plan would have undermined many of these new domains and cast uncertainty into the future of others. Most important, the Bolling plan hurt liberals as well as conservatives, throwing the former (who had supported many of the other reforms) into the arms of the latter, thereby producing a majority against the plan. The Bolling plan was defeated miserably. The cause of its defeat lay with the power motive and the desire of members of Congress, even under the greatest assault on the power of Congress in American history, to protect their personal power prerogatives. This concern for personal power prerogatives, and a widespread willingness to create even more power positions, also meant that no reform was proposed successfully to reduce the multiplicity of subcommittees. Instead, the desire to break up the power of committee chairs that had remained strong, particularly Wilbur Mills's power as chair of Ways and Means, led to a rule requiring all committees of more than 15 members to have subcommittees. The move to increase the number of subcommittees also was exacerbated by a provision of the Hansen plan that encouraged the creation of oversight subcommittees. Overall, to the extent that a multiplicity of committees and subcommittees contributes to congressional insulation, that insulation was increased rather than decreased.

Finally, there were the attempts to increase congressional *surveillance* or *oversight* of executive branch behavior. Once again Congress was unable to undertake strong action. This failure was painfully evident in the oversight hearings into intelligence activity of the federal government; Congress, particularly the House, became so bogged down in attempts by each member to assert her or his own policy perspectives that no overarching legislation or powerful oversight mechanism was produced. Less evident, but no less indicative, were congressional mistakes in the War Powers Act. With the War Powers Act, members of Congress wanted a procedure that would leave them each in control of a piece of the congressional decision; at the same time, they wanted a decision procedure that would leave open their option to exercise power, but a procedure that would not force them to do so if that exercise might prove costly in political terms. The desire of each member for a piece of the war power prerogative kept members from establishing a central Congressional Security Council, analogous to the National Security Council, that they could have mandated to exercise congressional prerogatives in a time of imminent emergency. Rather, they left the president free to act for up to sixty days on his own. In so doing, they also left themselves the protection of facing a decision only after public reaction to the president had become established. Although this might seem an astute move on the part of Congress, in effect it gave congressional war-making powers to the president for sixty days *unless* Congress chose to enforce them. Within sixty days, as any student of the modern presidency should know, a president can maneuver the country into a situation in which it is politically impossible for Congress to fail to support the president. And it is simply not the case that international relations are so complex, and events so fast-moving, that Congress had no alternative. If Congress can invest its war-making powers in a president, it can likewise delegate them to a small number of its own members whose advice and consent a president could be required to receive. After all, all modern presidents have had time to consult the National Security Council and key advisers before acting. Short of imminent nuclear attack, an extreme case whose possibility cannot be used to dictate the norm, a Congressional Security Council would be just as feasible as, and far more necessary for government in a democratic society than, the National Security Council. Members of Congress have failed to establish such a council, which could oversee presidential war making and defend congressional prerogatives, because members of Congress do not want to centralize congressional power. The continuing irony, an irony they truly fail to grasp, is that the unwillingness to structure congressional power in a manner that adjusts to the twentieth-century realities of foreign policy ultimately abrogates the war-making authority of Congress.

A concluding illustration of Congress's dilemma is its attempt to encourage oversight of the bureaucracy. The Senate essentially failed to act. The House, in attempting to act, stripped the most meaningful elements out of the Bolling Committee's oversight recommendations. In order to have serious oversight of the bureaucracy, that authority must be taken from the legislative committees and placed in an oversight committee in each house that has real authority and power to investigate and to force Congress to react to the results of its investigation. The Bolling Committee recommended that the House strengthen the ability of the Government Operations Committee to be a real oversight committee by giving it privileged status to offer amendments to authorizing legislation, amendments that would result from its oversight investigations and present the House with the clear opportunity to incorporate the recommendations in the authorizing legislation. This recommendation was the test case of congressional willingness to have oversight activity. The move was defeated; it was a threat to the authority of the other standing committees. Instead, the Government Operations Committee was authorized to make a report on the planned oversight activities of the other committees. The attempt to create independent oversight activity turned to the creation of oversight subcommittees within existing legislative committees. Even this was defeated as a mandatory move and committees were merely told that they had the option of either creating such subcommittees or instructing the existing subcommittees to undertake oversight action. Less than half of the committees have turned to oversight subcommittees. The moral should be clear: Congress fails to conduct oversight of the bureaucracy not because there are no incentives to it (there are, power and publicity for those who conduct it) nor because it fails to help reelection (being a member of a powerful oversight committee would be a sure-fire method of ensuring widespread publicity). Congress fails to conduct oversight because most members of Congress *fear* its impact on the authority of their existing committee assignments and *fear* the power that a strong oversight committee would have in Congress and in national policy making. Because of the underlying power motive, Congress has failed, and continues to fail, to structure itself in a manner conducive to oversight of the bureaucracy.

As this review should demonstrate, Congress in the 1970s has attempted to act on the problems of leadership, coordination, accountability, insulation, and oversight; its actions in each area have been constrained by and ultimately crippled by a preoccupation of its members with personal power prerogatives. In light of this overview, it is quite sensible to expect the reform efforts of the 1973-75 period, the centralizing era, to be slowly but surely undermined as members reassert the exercise of their power prerogatives, thrusting the country into a new cycle. Much depends on the presidency and the willingness of presidents to show a greater sensitivity to Congress. In all probability, given the extensiveness of congressional reaction in the preceding few years, and the impeachment proceedings against Nixon, the high point of presidential aggressiveness during the postwar cycle was reached with Nixon in 1973. In the years immediately ahead, the country should witness a more cooperative presidency as presidents attempt to defuse the congressional resurgence, a phenomenon already witnessed partially in the Ford presidency. The seduction of Congress is most likely, of course, if an era of united government should dawn in which the individual in the White House is an ideological and partisan compatriot of members of Congress. With a less threatening presidency, the internal dynamics within Congress should lead once again to a push toward decentralization, with a maintenance and strengthening of the 1970-73 era reforms. With Congress not being confronted by apparent institutional crisis, the entity that would be the most probable and immediate victim of this move toward decentralization would be the congressional budget system, since it is the entity that can most severely constrain the autonomous decision-making authority of individual committees and subcommittees. The short-term survival of the budget process in its current form, and as an *autonomous* mechanism of congressional decision making, would seem probable only with the election of a president or a series of presidents who continued attacks on Congress analogous to those made by Nixon and would probably be most likely in an era of divided government.

When a period of quiescence does come, and as the personal power motives of congresspeople produce a move within Congress toward decentralized decision making, it is realistic to assume that the problems inherent in congressional decentralization will lead the nation to demand yet another resurgence of presidential power, unleashing again the momentum toward an institutional crisis in which a president or a series of presidents will overstep dramatically the bounds of political and constitutional comity. The resurgence of presidential power may even come through the centralized congressional mechanisms themselves. For example, the internal moves by self-interested members of Congress against centralized policy organs or against the decisions of those organs (such as the new budget process, the Speakership, or the Steering and Policy Committee) would provide a president with the opportunity to intervene forcefully in the congressional process and throw his weight behind the central policy mechanisms. In such a case we should expect Congress to pay a high price for its "salvation," with the president using and altering such mechanisms to meet the policy ends and power advantage of the president. A majority party president with strong policy commitments could begin the manipulation of the central policy mechanisms by use of a strong presidential liaison team to exert executive influence on the budget committees and budget resolution votes, through agency "cooperation" with and "assistance" to the Congressional Budget Office, and by presidential cooptation of congressional party leaders. We would eventually expect formal alterations in the congressional budget process that would institutionalize executive control of it (perhaps through "coordination" of the CBO with the OMB), thus allowing and formalizing an executive branch penetration of the congressional decision-making process far greater than ever before. Alternatively, Congress may overthrow the new centralizing mechanisms in forms as well as reality, leaving in their stead a system totally based on subcommittee government and leaving the executive free to develop other means by which to more strongly coordinate and dominate congressional decision making.

Whatever the precise form of behavior, the logic of the power motive suggests another cycle involving internal moves toward decentralized policy making in Congress, presidential usurpation of congressional authority, and eventual warfare between Congress and presidents over public policy and institutional prerogatives. The immediate question, within the context of this perspective, is not whether a surge toward decentralization and institutional crisis is likely, but rather what such an occurrence will mean when it comes, and what the general cycle tells us about Congress and American politics generally.

V

In order to interpret the significance of the cyclical pattern of internal congressional change for the external struggle between Congress and the executive, we must return to the *Federalist Papers* and James Madison. Madison's analysis of the U.S. Constitution provides us with the most convincing justification of the Constitution and the most prescient projection of the behavioral patterns expected to flow from its institutional structure. The classic summary of his stance is in Federalist No. 51:

> In order to lay a due foundation for that separate and distinct exercise of the different powers of government, which to a certain extent is admitted on all hands to be essential to the preservation of liberty, it is evident that each department should have a will of its own. . . .
>
> [T]he great security against a gradual concentration of the several powers in the same department consists in giving to those who administer each department the necessary constitutional means and personal motives to resist encroachment

of the others. The provision for defense must in this, as in all other cases, be made commensurate to the danger of attack. Ambition must be made to counteract ambition. The interest of the man must be connected with the constitutional rights of the place.[22]

The devices to which Madison refers here are a separation of powers among the legislative, executive, and judicial branches or departments and a system of checks and balances between these branches. Explicit in the Madisonian conception is an assumption that tension will exist between the branches of government, a tension deriving from the natural ambitions of the politicians within each institution. Ambition will naturally lead these politicians to aggrandize power for themselves by asserting a broad political role for their institution. Inherent in this conception of interbranch tension is the expectation of thrust and counterthrust between the institutions, particularly Congress and the presidency, with one branch asserting itself only to be constrained by the other.

From a Madisonian perspective, Congress should have no problem in asserting its "will" and checking executive aggrandizement. This ability will exist, in large part, because a "few of the members, as happens in all such assemblies, will possess superior talents; will, by frequent re-election, become members of long standing; will be thoroughly masters of the public business. . . ." This tendency toward a few involved legislators would be reinforced in the U.S. Congress by the problems of service, "the distances which many of the representatives will be obliged to travel and the arrangements rendered necessary by that service. . . ." [23] In fact, Madison saw the real problem of Congress not in a weakness of will but in a tendency toward too great an internal concentration of authority and too strong a congressional will. For this reason, Madison feared Congress as the primary threat to the Republic and directed the most attention to constitutional constraint on Congress, not on the executive."[24]

In a Madisonian interpretation, the congressional cycle is one additional element that helps the system of separation of powers and checks and balances work. It ensures that the health and vibrancy of the presidency is maintained in the face of the more threatening legislature, and that there will be struggle and compromise between the Congress and the presidency. Because each institution thus can maintain its autonomy and will, and because Congress is sufficiently restrained by both the external checks and its internal dynamics, the power shift between Congress and the presidency revolves around a constant center or balance point, and the parameters of the cycle are relatively constant, with neither institution ever allowing the other to proceed too far in power aggrandizement. When each cycle is complete, the constitutional powers of the two institutions are once again intact and in balance, a balance specified by the Constitution. During each cycle the rise of one institution and the decline of the other is maintained within clearly defined boundaries that are relatively similar from cycle to cycle. No tendency exists for the institutional excesses to increase in extensiveness or severity from cycle to cycle. The cycle thus can last indefinitely and is, in fact, a "good" thing. The current resurgence of Congress demonstrates its resilience as an institution, its ability to rise to the demands of the day. The failure of the centralizing reforms over the coming years will not be a "bad" thing but merely a natural process that is essential to the dynamics of the Madisonian system of government.

Throughout the nineteenth century, American politics probably did conform fairly closely to the Madisonian interpretation, with the minicycles discussed earlier a constraint on internal congressional ambitions and external aggrandizement. Congress probably was the greatest threat (from a Madisonian perspective) to the constitutional system and to property, and the dominant force in American politics. After a review of twentieth-century congressional behavior, there is good reason to suspect that the Madisonian interpretation no longer applies. Madison assumed that each institution would sustain sufficient internal integrity that it could have an "institutional will" and would have the institutional capacity to exert that will and counteract the aggrandizing tendencies of other institutions. That assumption was central to Madison's argument and, in the case of Congress, rested on supporting assumptions of high turnover and unpleasant working conditions that would lead Congress naturally to invest its authority in a few select individuals. The alterations in American society and politics in the late nineteenth century that made Congress a more attractive place in which to serve (owing to the growth of national power) and an easier place in which to serve (owing to greater ease of travel and the existence of professional occupations that would mesh well with congressional service) undermined Madison's supporting assumptions, creating internal problems for Congress as an institution that were of a magnitude Madison never envisioned. These problems — of leadership, coordination, insulation, accountability, oversight — have crippled both the ability of Congress to know its "will" and its ability to assert its will. Simultaneously, the growth in societal complexity and international interdependence put a greater emphasis on the speed and efficiency of national decision making. The standard for congressional performance thus was raised at precisely the time that its capacity to perform was being undercut. Unfortunately for Congress, these same changes that hurt it served to highlight the attributes of the presidency — its ability to act quickly, coherently, and decisively; in fact, the coming of the mass media increased the capacity of the president to publicize his will and project a mystique of special authority that is essential to the exercise of power.

It is unrealistic to expect that this shift to presidential ascendancy can or will be altered by the Supreme Court. The power alterations result from inherent constitutional and institutional problems that the Court largely is unable to address. In addition, the judicial appointive process in the Constitution created an informal alliance between the Court and the presidency,[25] an alliance that should constrain the Court from serious innovative efforts to create conditions and interpretations that might subtly alter the formal Constitution so as to strengthen Congress.[26]

The institutional power struggles of the twentieth century thus are operating by a different set of principles, and toward a different end, than the dynamics of Madisonian government suggest. First, the presidency and the executive branch generally gain more authority or power with each cycle than they are forced to give up. During the cycle from 1910 to 1945, for example, the presidency gained dominance over the bureaucracy (that is, to the degree that any external institution dominates the bureaucracy), gained the legitimate role as the nation's chief legislator, and gained legitimacy as chief budgetary officer. With the resurgence of Congress in the postwar years, the presidency still maintained all of the roles — if not as strongly as in Roosevelt's case, certainly more strongly than before the Roosevelt era. At what appears to be the end of a 1945-73 cycle, the presidency has added to its earlier roles (1) a new and legitimized role as the nation's independent agent in war (as a result of the sixty-day provision of the War Powers Act); (2) a wider range of options with regard to control of the budget and the spending of funds (as a result of the Impoundment Act, which, while trying to limit presidential impoundments, succeeded in giving the president a political weapon, impoundment recommendations, to use against Congress and in legitimizing the president's prerogatives to propose a delay or rescission in spending for reasons other than financial efficiency); and (3) retained central authority over the intelligence community and the bureaucracy generally. At the same time that the balance of power seems to be shifting toward the presidency, a second trend seems also to be occurring: an overall increase with each cycle in the extremity of presidential transgression. Recent presidents' illegal use of the nation's intelligence community, the expanding misuse of presidential war-making powers, and Nixon's unconstitutional impoundments are cases in point.

Existing factors suggest that these trends will continue and worsen. First, the domestic and international problems appear to be increasing in severity, rather than decreasing. The existence of these problems, and the necessity of national action to resolve them, will continue to draw politicians to Congress and sustain the power cycle. The severity of the problems, however, and the existence of congressional immobilism, will justify a continuing and increasing reliance on the executive. This move toward executive power will be reinforced by a second trend: the electoral difficulties of becoming president are so great, and are increasing so significantly with well-intentioned reforms designed to purify presidential politics, that there is an inherent self-selection and weeding process such that the people who rise to that office are, and increasingly will be, immensely power-driven individuals, a phenomenon reinforced by the pressures on and isolation of presidents. In addition, should presidents attempt to forsake proffered power, the structure of American politics and the presidential office probably will offer them no eventual alternative but to accept the expanded authority: with policy immobilism and a resultant economic and social crisis, it would actually be an act of immediate and contextual irresponsibility for presidents not to act in particular and desperate situations.

A final factor which suggests that the momentum toward presidential power will continue and increase is the internal power structure of the current Congress. Underlying the reforms of the 1973-75 era are the reforms of 1970-73. These earlier reforms created a dispersion of power within Congress that is truly unprecedented in American history. As the centralizing mechanisms of the 1973-75 era falter, congressional decision making (as an autonomous process) will depend on an institutionalized system of subcommittee government. Given the greater dispersion of power in that system, the problems of leadership, coordination, insulation, accountability, and oversight that face Congress will be of a magnitude beyond any we have witnessed thus far. The political immobilism implicit in this situation will be intolerable without a strong president. Presidents seeking to assert authority will not face relatively strong committee chairs like Wilbur Mills, who have authority over a moderate range of policy areas, but relatively weak and isolated subcommittee chairs who can at best dominate a small policy domain and thus will have less maneuverability and fewer resources to use in a congressional-executive struggle. Congress increasingly will be a primary justification for a strong presidency and increasingly an ineffective agent in the constraint of presidential imperialism.

The thrust of my argument, then, is that the Madisonian system is self-destructing. An age of strong national government magnifies the power motive underlying politics generally and sets in motion organizational dynamics within Congress that undermine its ability to perform its constitutional roles. These governmental roles are undertaken by a strong presidency whose institutional integrity and external authority are not decreased but actually increased by the complexities and technology of modern society. In light of human nature and the rules of the political struggle specified in the U.S. Constitution, this alteration in the conduct of governmental roles is a natural reaction of the relevant actors and institutions to the growth of the power of the national government. Seen in this context, the ongoing and continuing destruction of the constitutional system does not stem necessarily from evil motives or evil people. Politicians' quest for power within Congress can derive from the most noble of desires to serve humanity. Power aggrandizement on the part of presidents may be forced on them by the very nature of the political immobilism within Congress and the severity of social and economic crises in the country.

The source of constitutional destruction, and the decline of Congress, lies in the Constitution itself and its inappropriateness today as a guide to representative government. The separation-of-power system provides Congress with an autonomy, as is desirable, that allows it an internal organizational life independent of the executive branch. It also properly invests Congress with legislative authority, delegating it in clear and unmistakable terms. Yet legislative authority is a type of responsibility that can be decentralized and thus afflicted by the problems evident in a system of pure committee government. The Constitution provides no function or structure to Congress that would create internal congressional incentives supportive of power centralization, coordination, and institutional integrity. It merely assumes that these will be maintained by the natural operation of political life in a simple, agrarian society. When the latter assumption is no longer valid, when it is no longer true that policy problems will be simple and congressional life will draw only a few legislators committed to long-term congressional careers and power, there is no provision within the constitutional system — no incentive system — that will lead members naturally to sustain mechanisms of institutional centralization.

As a Congress composed of members who are concerned about public policy becomes increasingly and necessarily enmeshed in institutional immobilism — an immobilism that may result from the very genuineness of members' policy concerns — Congress faces the external checks and balances built in the Constitution. Ironically, since the Founding Fathers thought that Congress was the most dangerous branch, the really powerful checks, such as veto and judicial review, were given to the president and the Court to use against Congress. The inability of the legislature to know its will thus is exacerbated by the ability of the president and the Court, separately or in alliance, to debilitate any congressional will that may exist by throwing in front of Congress the requirement that it make legislative policy not by majority vote but by two-thirds vote.

In light of these considerations, a successful end to the debilitating cycles of the twentieth century requires that we direct attention not to internal congressional reform but to fundamental alterations of the constitutional system itself. We must create an incentive system within the Constitution that, while sustaining a degree of congressional decentralization that will allow for innovation and expertise, will lead members of Congress naturally to support centralizing mechanisms that can sustain institutional integrity. We also must reconsider the nature of the checks-and-balances system with the intent of strengthening the position of Congress. Simultaneously, we can redirect the values by which we wish institutional politics to be conducted, shifting from a politics of minority veto and policy inaction toward majority government and social justice.

It may be that changes within the confines of the current Constitution will be sufficient for our ends.[27] Perhaps constitutional specifications of certain electoral laws could ensure a more competitive electoral system at the congressional level which, by generating higher turnover and more internal institutional need for leadership by individual members, would force a greater degree of centralization. Constitutional provisions giving real authority to the Speaker of the House or the president pro tem of the Senate could give them real incentives to use in the creation and long-term maintenance of significant centralized policy organs in each house. The creation at a constitutional level of a Congressional Security Council that could exercise congressional authority under specific emergency conditions might help Congress regain constitutional control of war making. Finally, a revision of the veto provision (making overrides easier or vetoes harder) might help sustain congressional policy making by holding out the hope that congressional decisions eventually could become the law of the land. While some of the above perhaps could be handled legislatively, it is critical that the changes come at the constitutional level, the level most difficult for members of Congress to manipulate and undermine for personal advantage.

Finally, we must realize that the complex and demanding nature of contemporary life raises serious and fundamental questions as to the viability of Congress within a system of separation of powers and checks and balances. We should reconsider, therefore, our constitutional system itself and direct some attention toward assessing the viability of a new constitutional structure less geared to policy immobilism and institutional conflict. As we consider movement toward alternative constitutions we must realize that constitution making is serious and difficult business. It requires realistic and hard-headed assessment of human nature, of the implications of different institutional arrangements, of the social conditions within which politics is to be conducted, and of the consequences that will derive from the interaction of these three elements of political life. In many ways Madison's performance in the *Federalist Papers* is still the best guide to this type of undertaking. A proper respect for his intellect is always advisable. Yet we also must unlock ourselves from the infatuating clarity and logic of Madison's arguments that continue to exert a seductive hold on our imaginations long after the supporting conditions assumed by them have passed. The transformations of our society in the last century undercut the accuracy of his forecasts. The changes in our values, and hopefully the growth of a greater commitment to majoritarian government and popular justice, alter the goals to which a new or modified constitutional arrangement should be committed. The quest for democratic government demands that we throw off the Sisyphean preoccupation with internal congressional reform and reconsider the constitutional structure that today necessarily consigns Congress—our most democratic institution—to an increasingly weakened political role in an ever more powerful national government.

POSTSCRIPT

Since the publication of this essay, several books have documented more extensively the changes discussed here. On the weakening of the seniority system and the long-term historical cycle of change, see James L. Sundquist, *The Decline and Resurgence of Congress* (Washington, D.C.: The Brookings Institution, 1981). Allen Schick discusses the tenuousness of the new budget process in *Congress and Money* (Washington, D.C.: The Urban Institute, 1980). The operation of the new committee and subcommittee system is discussed in Stephen S. Smith and Christopher J. Deering, *Committees in Congress* (Washington, D.C.: CQ Press, 1984). Barbara Sinclair describes the new process of party leadership in *Majority Leadership in the U.S. House* (Baltimore: The Johns Hopkins Press, 1983). Changes in the oversight process are assessed by Lawrence C. Dodd and Richard L. Schott in *Congress and the Administrative State* (New York: John Wiley, 1979). For a subsequent extension of the analysis in this essay, see Lawrence C. Dodd, "Congress, the Constitution and the Crisis of Legitimation" in Lawrence C. Dodd and Bruce I. Oppenheimer, eds., *Congress Reconsidered*, 2d ed. (Washington, D.C.: CQ Press, 1981).

Notes

1. The approach presented here has been influenced particularly by the work of Fenno, Huntington, and Mayhew. See Richard F. Fenno, Jr., *Congressmen in Committees* (Boston: Little, Brown, 1973); Samuel P. Huntington, "Congressional Responses to the Twentieth Century," in David B. Truman, ed., *The Congress and America's Future* (Englewood Cliffs, N.J.: Prentice-Hall, 1965); David Mayhew, *Congress: The Electoral Connection* (New Haven, Conn.: Yale University Press, 1974).
2. By the power positions I mean those formal positions within the congressional institution that carry with them the legal authority over such prerogatives as parliamentary procedure, financial and staff resources, information collection and dispersal, and agenda setting, that are amenable to the control of policy making in a legislative assembly.

3. See Mayhew, op. cit., pp. 32-77.
4. A survey conducted during the 89th Congress under the auspices of the American Political Science Association's Study of Congress found that the average congressperson spent only 5.6 days per month in the home district while Congress was in session (a phenomenon that increasingly covers the calendar year). Although the figure demonstrates that members do take care to return home (a fact that Fenno's research shows is partially related to the location of the family home), members clearly devote *most* of their time to work in Washington. While in Washington, the average member's work week stretches to 59.3 hours per week and has a clear legislative cast to it, with 22.5 hours devoted to work related to legislative research or committee activity, or to party and leadership activities; an additional 15.3 hours are spent on the floor; 7.2 hours are spent answering mail; 5.1 hours handling constituent problems and 4.4 hours visiting with constituents in Washington; 2.7 hours on writing chores, speeches, and magazine articles; 2.3 hours with lobbyists; 2.1 hours on press work, radio and TV appearances. See Donald G. Tacheron and Morris K. Udall, *The Job of the Congressman* (Indianapolis: Bobbs-Merrill, 1970), pp. 303-4; see also Richard F. Fenno, Jr., "U.S. House Members in Their Constituencies," *American Political Science Review,* vol. 71 (September 1977): 883-917.
5. This breakdown of committee types, and the idea of a set of career stages, derive from a very liberal reading of Fenno, *Congressmen in Committees,* together with the literature on committee attractiveness and mobility between committees. For a good summary discussion of this latter literature, see Leroy Rieselbach, *Congressional Politics* (New York: McGraw-Hill, 1973), p. 30.
6. On the existence of congressional norms or folkways, see Donald Matthews, *U.S. Senators and Their World* (New York: Vintage, 1960); and Herbert Asher, "The Learning of Legislative Norms," *APSR* 67 (1967): 501. On the committee selection process, see Nicholas Masters, "Committee Assignments in the House of Representatives," *APSR* (1961): 345-57; and David W. Rohde and Kenneth A. Shepsle, "Democratic Committee Assignments in the U.S. House of Representatives," *APSR* 67 (1973): 889-905.
7. See Robert L. Peabody, *Leadership in Congress* (Boston: Little, Brown, 1976). I am struck in Peabody's discussion by the small number of leadership challenges, the lack of really bitter struggles, and the short amount of time and small amount of resources put into leadership battles.
8. Some of the major academic works that reflect these calls for presidential assertion are Richard Neustadt, *Presidential Power* (New York: Wiley, 1960); Joseph Harris, *Congressional Control of Administration* (Washington, D.C.: Brookings Institution, 1964); James MacGregor Burns, *The Deadlock of Democracy* (Englewood Cliffs, N.J.: Prentice-Hall, 1963). The classic glorification of the twentieth-century presidency is Clinton Rossiter, *The American Presidency* (New York: New American Library, 1956).
9. Joseph Cooper, "The Origins of the Standing Committees and the Development of the Modern House," *Rice University Studies* 56 (1970); Lauros G. McConachie, *Congressional Committees* (New York: Crowell, 1898).
10. The assertion as to a minicycle is based on a reading of George R. Brown, *The Leadership of Congress* (Indianapolis: Bobbs-Merrill, 1922); and Richard Bolling, *Power in the House* (New York: Capricorn, 1968).
11. The literature demonstrating the decline in turnover includes H. Douglas Price, "Congress and the Evolution of Legislative 'Professionalism'," and Morris P. Fiorina, David W. Rohde, and Peter Wissel, "Historical Change in House Turnover," both in Norman J. Ornstein, ed., *Congress in Change* (New York: Praeger, 1975); Nelson

Polsby, "The Institutionalization of the House of Representatives," *APSR* 62 (1968): 144-69.

12. On the House, see Brown, op. cit.; on the Senate, see David J. Rothman, *Politics and Power* (New York: Atheneum, 1969).

13. See Kenneth W. Hechler, *Insurgency: Personalities and Politics of the Taft Era* (New York: Columbia University Press, 1940).

14. Discussions of these problems in the 1920s are contained in Brown, op. cit., and Lindsay Rogers, *The American Senate* (New York: Knopf, 1926).

15. For a more general discussion of the rise of the presidency, see James MacGregor Burns, *Presidential Government* (Boston: Houghton Mifflin, 1965); and Arthur M. Schlesinger, Jr., *The Imperial Presidency* (New York: Popular Library, 1973).

16. See George B. Galloway, *Congress at the Crossroads* (New York: Crowell, 1946), pp. 7-8, 53, 242-54.

17. George B. Galloway, "The Operation of the Legislative Reorganization Act of 1946," *APSR* 45 (1951): 51.

18. Schlesinger, op. cit., p. 298.

19. James P. Pfiffner, "Congressional Budget Reform, 1974: Initiation and Reaction," 1975 APSA convention paper, pp. 4-5; see also Louis Fisher, *Presidential Spending Power* (Princeton, N.J.: Princeton University Press, 1975), pp. 147-201.

20. Schlesinger, op. cit., p. 395.

21. James L. Sundquist, "Congress and the President: Enemies or Partners?" in this volume. Sundquist writes: "Viewed in the perspective of history, the changes in the executive-legislative power balance wrought by a single Congress — the 93rd — are truly momentous. Ever since the era of congressional government at the close of the Civil War ..., the flow of power had been all one-way, in the direction of the president. In just two years, the trend of a hundred years was dramatically reversed. An extraordinary abuse of presidential power triggered a counteraction equally extraordinary, and the ponderous processes of institutional change were expedited." Sundquist seems to reflect an essentially Madisonian conception of the recent changes in congressional structure.

22. James Madison, Federalist No. 51, in Alexander Hamilton, James Madison, and John Jay, *The Federalist Papers,* edited by Clinton Rossiter (New York: New American Library), pp. 321-22.

23. Madison, Federalist No. 53, pp. 334-35.

24. Madison, Federalist No. 48, p. 309.

25. Robert Scigliano, *The Supreme Court and the Presidency* (New York: Free Press, 1971), p. 197.

26. Ibid., pp. 200-201.

27. For an intriguing dialogue on the Constitution and current problems, see Bob Eckhardt and Charles L. Black, Jr., *The Tides of Power: Conversations on the American Constitution* (New Haven, Conn.: Yale University Press, 1976).

21. CRITICAL ELECTIONS, CONGRESSIONAL PARTIES AND CLUSTERS OF POLICY CHANGES

David W. Brady

Profound changes in American public policy have occurred only rarely and have been associated with "critical" or "realigning" elections in which "more or less profound readjustments occur in the relations of power within the community." [1] Since the appearance of V. O. Key's seminal articles on critical elections, an increasing number of political scientists have attributed great importance to such elections. [2] Schattschneider views the structure of politics brought into being by critical elections as systems of action. Thus, during realignments, not only voting behavior but institutional roles and policy outputs undergo substantial change. [3] Burnham, perhaps the most important analyst of realignment patterns, alleges the existence of an intimate relationship between realigning elections and "transformations in large clusters of policy."

> In other words, realignments are themselves constituent acts: they arise from emergent tensions in society which, not adequately controlled by the organization or outputs of party politics as usual, escalate to a flash point; they are issue-oriented phenomena, centrally associated with these tensions and more or less leading to resolution adjustments; they result in significant transformations in the general shape of policy; and they have relatively profound after effects on the roles played by institutional elites. [4]

The importance of the relationship between certain elections and clusters of policy changes is considerable because, if such a relationship in fact exists, then at such times there also exist relatively clear relationships between mass electoral behavior and public-policy changes. This is, of course, contrary to "normal" politics, when there is little if any relationship between elections and public policy. If such a connection between elections and policy changes can be established for realigning periods, then we can better account both for change in the American political system and for the linkages that are responsible for change.

Author's Note: The author wishes to thank James Anderson, Charles Bullock, Joseph Cooper and William Keech for their thoughtful comments on an earlier draft.

Source: *British Journal of Political Science*, no. 8, part 1 (January 1978): 79-99. Reprinted with permission of the publisher.

David W. Brady

A peculiar feature of the discussion of the relationships between critical elections, institutional changes and clusters of policy changes is that, while there are studies available of the effects of critical elections on the "party in the electorate" [5] and on the "party as organization," [6] there are no studies available of the effect of such elections on the vehicle through which policy changes are legitimized: the congressional parties. Whatever connections exist between critical elections and changes in public policy occur in large part within the institutional context of building legitimating congressional majorities. That is, in order for "clusters of policy changes" to become policies a majority of the Congress must vote for them. The relationship between critical elections, changes in congressional parties and clusters of policy changes remains unexplored. This paper examines some of these relationships on the understanding that the theoretical contribution to be made is middle-range, namely a specification only of the major variables and relationships.

The fact that profound changes in public policy have occurred only rarely presents a problem to researchers seeking connections between mass electoral behavior, Congress and policy changes. The limited number of cases available makes it difficult for the researcher to generalize. In this paper the strategy is to compare two realignments, those of 1896 and 1932, in an attempt to determine whether any similarities exist between them and then, in the discussion section, to outline possible connections between types of election and policy changes. The realignment eras of the 1890s and 1930s were chosen because there is universal agreement that both were benchmarks in American political history. The policy changes associated with the election of 1896 were the crystallization of policies favoring industrialization. Expansionism, protective tariffs and the gold standard were the critical issues and each favored industrial interests.[7] After 1896 the industrial future of America was assured. The policy changes associated with the New Deal involved increased governmental action in the hitherto private sphere. Welfare policies, government involvement in the economy and increased regulation of the private sector are prime examples of the major changes associated with the 1930s realignment.[8] These two realignments thus ought to be good examples of eras in which there should exist connections between elections and policies.

It is the thesis of this paper that critical elections have the effect of creating conditions which facilitate the building of partisan majorities in the legislature capable of enacting clusters of policy change. In order to demonstrate this thesis, the effects of the critical elections of 1896 and 1932 on the congressional parties in the United States' House of Representatives will be examined. The analysis will show that the effect of critical elections on the congressional parties is to diminish the two major drawbacks to party government in the House, i.e. party-constituency cross-pressuring and the nature of the committee system.[9] Specifically, critical elections change the constituency bases of the congressional parties along a continuum which reflects the changes that are occurring in the "party in the electorate," thereby helping to diminish party-constituency cross-pressures. Such elections also effectively rearrange the committees of the House so that the party leadership is able to perform its function of organizing coherent majorities for legislative programs. Given these conditions, levels of party voting in the

House rise. Party voting on the programs central to the policy changes is especially high.

Both the 1896 and the 1932 realignments can be said to have begun in the congressional elections prior to the presidential realigning election. The research design therefore includes Houses before the presidential election years of 1896 and 1932 as well as a "normal" House prior to the realigning elections themselves. The study of the 1890s realignment includes the 53rd House (1892) and the 54th and 55th (1894 and 1896 respectively), while the study of the 1932 realignment includes the 70th House (1926) as well as the 71st, 72nd and 73rd (1928 through 1932 respectively). Data analysis occurs at two levels, institutional and individual. At the institutional level, it will be shown that in both realignments the congressional parties are changed along a socio-economic continuum; that there is a drastic turnover in committee membership and leadership, thus disrupting committee continuity; and that these two developments are associated with a rise in the level of both majority-party cohesion and party voting in the realignment Houses. At the individual level, data analysis separates the roll call votes into issue dimensions and then shows that over the realignment period party competition and party identification are highly related to support for the new clusters of policy changes. This combination of institutional and individual data analysis will clearly demonstrate the relevance of party during realignment eras.

Finally, the data analysis includes a section on switched-seat congressmen, i.e., those representatives elected from districts that switched in the direction of the realignment. It will be demonstrated that they are a critical linkage between election results and party voting, which helps to account for the clusters of policy changes. In Clausen's words "the main impetus for changes in the overall policy posture of the Congress comes in the new membership." [10] In sum it will be shown that at both the institutional and the individual level the effect of critical elections is to increase party cohesion and party voting, thus facilitating legislative responsibility and legitimizing the clusters of changes.

The data will be presented as follows: (1) a brief discussion of the cross-cutting issues in the realignment and a sketch of the realignment in the party in the electorate; (2) presentation of the aggregate-level data showing the changes in constituency composition of the parties, the breakdown of committee continuity, and the concomitant rise in majority-party cohesion and party voting; and (3) analysis at the individual level showing the increasing importance of party identification and competition in predicting individual voting behavior.

Proving the thesis outlined above depends upon establishing that party-constituency cross-pressuring and the nature of the commitment system are in fact major drawbacks to party voting. Thus it is necessary first to discuss cross-pressuring and the committee system.

In the American system, congressmen's relationships to their constituencies are paramount, and to the extent that party positions conflict with real or perceived constituency interests cross-pressuring occurs. Cross-pressured representatives will often vote constituency interests, not party position. Constituency interests are so important that both parties' caucuses have formalized the representative's right to vote in accordance with them. Huitt sums it up nicely: "If the member pleases it [the constituency], no party leader can fatally hurt him; if he does not, no national party organ can save him." [11] In the modern House a large number of representatives are cross-pressured; for example, southern Democrats from rural districts have constituency pressures on them not to vote with the Democratic leadership on certain welfare issues. During realignments the freshman members of the new congressional majority are elected from constituencies where the issues of the realignment are causing shifts in party identification; for example, in 1932 the Democratic majority in Congress represented blue-collar and ethnic urbanites who were switching to the Democrats. The number of cross-pressuring districts is thus likely to be substantially reduced.

The committee system is a drawback to party government because committee chairmen, immunized until the 94th Congress by seniority, "are chieftains to be bargained with, not lieutenants to be commanded." [12] And their power to decide is based on the fact that committees have a continuous life of their own. Change in committee membership is "never complete and seldom dramatic." [13] Under these conditions committee norms and decision styles which affect or control public policy can be transmitted to the new members. Committees are normally stable in both membership and norms. Thus public policy decisions are incremental. It will be shown that during realignments committee stability and continuity are affected by a drastic turnover in membership. It follows that, if both cross-pressuring and committee stability are reduced, the level of party voting should increase dramatically—i.e. that the necessary conditions for party government should be fulfilled.

The 1896 and 1932 Realignments

The agrarian revolt that culminated in the critical election of 1896 was the product of the crises of industrialization. Western and southern farmers allied with western silver interests and sought to enlist the "toiling masses" of the industrial East and Midwest, thereby recapturing America from the foreign monied interests responsible for industrialization. The crisis of industrialization squarely placed an agrarian-fundamentalist view of life against an industrial-progressive view of life, and the issue positions taken on this division were polar. [14]

The specific issues that cut across party preferences in the 1890s were the gold-silver question, the protective tariff, and expansionism. These specific issues were subsumed under the more general "crisis of vulnerability" in which urban industrial interests were pitted against rural anti-industrialist forces. The election of McKinley and the Republicans assured America's industrial future. Never again would the agricultural interests capture a major party and come so close to winning control of the government. The crisis of vulnerability was resolvable only by one side or the other winning out. Thus the 1896 realignment resolved the question of whether the northern and eastern industrial interests or the southern and western agricultural and mining interests would be victorious. The effect of the realignment was that it "eventually separated the Southern and Western agrarians and transformed the most industrially advanced region of the country into a bulwark of industrial Republicanism." [15]

Sundquist's analysis of the voters who switched their allegiance to the Republicans during the realignment showed that those who switched were mainly northern, urban and blue-collar, residing in the industrial East and Midwest.[16] In contrast, Bryan did not increase the Democrats' support compared with 1892 in the rural Midwest and East; thus the Democratic party after 1896 was essentially southern and border-state agrarian in its constituency base.

The political revolution that Franklin Roosevelt led was, unlike the 1896 realignment, the product of a single event—the Great Depression. The underlying issue-dimension which separated and distinguished the parties was the question of whether the government would *actively* deal with the problems facing the country. Hoover and the majority of the Republican party came down against greatly increased governmental activity: "Economic depression cannot be cured by legislative action or executive pronouncement. Economic wounds must be healed by . . . the producers and the consumers themselves." [17] The Democrats, while not entirely sure in which direction to move, had formulated activist programs. John Garner, the conservative Speaker of the House, had advocated a $900 million federal public-works program, a billion dollar RFC loan fund and a $100 million mercy-money fund. The Democratic platform in 1932 differed markedly from the Republican on issues regarding the aggregation of wealth, control over the distribution of wealth and the exercise of governmental power. Benjamin Ginsberg's content analysis of party platforms from 1844-1968 showed the above issues to be both salient to parties and divisive across them during the 1932 election.[18] In sum, the parties differed markedly over the role the government was to play in curing the Depression. The Democrats favored active government involvement; the Republicans favored voluntarism and non-intervention.

The voters switching to the Democrats in the 1932 election came primarily from those groups most affected by the Depression: farmers and city dwellers. The farm depression of the 1920s had continued long after industry had recovered. The Republican leadership had done little to deal with the problem and seemed relatively unconcerned; President Coolidge commented: "Well, farmers never have made money [and] I don't believe we can do much about it." [19] This policy resulted in a number of farm protests, such as McNary-Haugenism, and may be viewed as a harbinger of the political revolution precipitated by the Depression. In fact, Sundquist suggests that these farm protests were an integral part of the realignment of the 1930s.[20] We would expect the congressional Democratic party over the 1926-32 period to reflect this change in voter sentiment.

The second and larger group of voters switching to the Democratic party is most readily identifiable by place of residence. The cities, populated by workers, ethnics, and blacks, moved into the Democratic column during this period. In cities formerly Democratic such as New York, the Republicans ceased to be competitive, while in cities such as Boston which had voted for Al Smith in 1928 the Democrats became the dominant party from 1932 onward. Working-class ethnics and northern blacks were hard hit by the Depression and voted for the

David W. Brady

Democrats. We would also expect to see this change reflected in the congressional Democratic party.

Constituency Changes During Realignments

If realignments in the parties in the electorate are reflected in the composition of the congressional parties, then the constituency bases of the congressional parties should show dramatic shifts. Accordingly one would expect that from the 53rd House to the 55th the congressional Republican party would suddenly come to over-represent industrial and eastern constituencies. The shift in the congressional Democratic party during the New Deal should be toward northern industrial urban districts.

In order to test these hypotheses, the following data were collected for the 1896 and 1932 periods. The numbers of farmers and blue-collar workers were collected from the appropriate county sections of the 1890 census and then mapped onto congressional districts. The number of blue-collar workers, the value added by manufacture and the population density were collected from the appropriate county sections of the 1930 census and likewise mapped onto congressional districts. Since in both periods congressional districts varied in size, percentages were used. These percentage data were then arrayed and divided by mean and median and into quartiles. Table 21-1 presents the results of this analysis. The results in both cases show a dramatic shift in the constituency bases of the new majority congressional party. In 1896 the percentage of Republican congressmen from labor districts increased from 44 to 79 percent, while the ratio of increase in absolute numbers of Republicans from such districts was 1.91. In agricultural districts the Republican percentage decreased by 3 percent over the period; the ratio of absolute change was .95. Moreover, the switch in the constituency base of the Republican party was also highly sectional, with over three-fourths of Republicans elected from the East and the North Central region by 1896. Analysis of the same figures for the congressional Democrats showed a shift toward highly agricultural districts located in the southern and border states. In short, the 1896 realignment yielded two relatively homogeneous congressional parties, with distinct centers of gravity on both a sectional and an agricultural-industrial continuum.

During the 1932 realignment Democratic gains were proportionately greater in urban blue-collar industrial districts than in more rural, less industrial districts. During the New Deal realignment the Democrats increased their share of urban seats from 30 to 66 percent; in industrial and labor districts the increase was from 34 and 32 percent respectively to 65 and 64 percent. The ratio of increase, which measures absolute change, shows that in each category the more urban, more industrial, more blue-collar the district, the greater the increase in Democratic strength. The effect of the Roosevelt realignment on the congressional Democratic party was to add a large number of congressmen representing urban blue-collar districts to the solid rural non-industrial southern base that the Democrats had had since 1896. A secondary effect was to increase the Democrats' share of northern farm districts. This, of course, meant a corresponding reduction in the number of Republican congressmen from urban and northern farm

Table 21-1 Shifts in Congressional Majority Party Composition During the 1896 and 1932 Realignments in Percentages and Absolute Ratio of Increase

District composition	1896 Realignment		Percent increase	Absolute ratio
	53rd Congress	*55th Congress*		
Percent Republican Congressmen from:				
Labor				
Low	35	31	−4	.93
High	44	79	+35	1.91
Agricultural				
Low	40	71	+31	1.78
High	36	33	−3	.95
Region				
Dem. from southern and border states	47	64	+17	
Rep. from East and North Central region	62	76	+14	

District composition	1932 Realignment		Percent increase	Absolute ratio
	70th Congress	*73rd Congress*		
Percent Democratic Congressmen from:				
Labor				
Low	57	82	25	1.37
High	32	64	32	1.97
Industry				
Low	54	81	27	1.40
High	34	67	33	1.89
Urban				
Low	53	77	24	1.38
High	30	67	37	1.96

districts. Thus, the "New Deal" coalition so often studied in the party in the electorate was reflected directly in the composition of the congressional Democratic party.

In both realignments the shifts in voter sentiment were reflected in the composition of the majority congressional party. These shifts created relatively homogeneous congressional parties, organized in effect around substantive partisan divisions of policy. Such stable over-time "partisan alignments form the constituent bases for governments committed to the translation of the choices made by the electorate during critical periods into public policy." [21] Under such conditions there is a reduction in party/constituency cross-pressuring because party and constituency are relatively homogeneous. Thus, if our analysis is correct, party voting should rise over the realignment period. However, before we test the party-voting hypothesis it is necessary to determine the effect of realignments on the second obstacle to party government—the committee system.

Realignment and the Stability of the Committee System

In this section it is argued that the effects of this second obstacle are substantially reduced—specifically, that the turnover rates on House committees during the realignments were drastic enough to disturb committee continuity, and that the new members were more partisan than the members they replaced. The result of the realignments was thus the replacement of old committee members with new members more predisposed to partisan voting.

In the modern House of Representatives the committee system has reigned in no small part because of committee continuity. Committee continuity assures gradual changes in leadership and that committee norms can be transmitted easily to new members. The result is incrementalism in policy decisions rather than clusters of policy changes. Professor Fenno observed the importance of personnel turnover for committee decision-making in his study of the congressional appropriations process: "The two occasions on which the greatest amount of open dissatisfaction, threatened rebellion, and actual rebellion occurred coincided with the two greatest personnel turnovers . . . the tendency to rebellion increases as personnel turnover increases, the very stability of committee membership appears, once again, as a vital condition of [the style of decision making]." [22] Huitt and others have also commented on the importance of committee continuity for policy stability. [23]

Demonstrating that committee continuity is drastically affected by realignments and that the change in membership results in more partisanship requires it to be shown:

(1) that turnover on House Committees during the realignments is high;

(2) that a substantial portion of the committee leaders in the 55th (1896) and 73rd (1932) Houses were not prominent immediately prior to the realignment;

(3) and that the new members of the Ways and Means and Appropriations Committees, in particular, were more party-oriented than the members they replaced.

In order to demonstrate the drastic nature of committee turnovers in both realignments, membership lists from thirteen committees were collected for the 53rd through 55th Houses and the 70th through 73rd Houses. A turnover rate for each of these committees was computed both over the whole committee and for the party components of each committee. [24] The turnover rates were computed by taking the number of holdover members on the committee and dividing it by the number of committee members. For example, in the 55th House the Appropriations Committee had seventeen members only six of whom had served on the committee in the 53rd House. The total turnover was thus 64.7 percent; conversely the percentage of carryovers was 35.3 percent. Party turnover rates on these committees were arrived at in the same fashion and are included to demonstrate that the high turnover figures were not solely the result of changes in the relative positions of the majority and minority parties. Table 21-2 shows the results of this analysis for the thirteen committees.

Table 21-2 Committee and Partisan Committee Turnover for Thirteen Selected House Committees in the 1896 (53rd to 55th Houses) and 1932 (70th to 73rd Houses) Realignments in Percentages

Committee	1896 Realignment			1932 Realignment		
	Total turnover	*Dem. turnover*	*Rep. turnover*	*Total turnover*	*Dem. turnover*	*Rep. turnover*
Agriculture	100.0	100.0	100.0	85.2	89.5	75.0
Appropriations	64.7	66.6	50.0	74.3	67.0	85.7
Banking and Currency	76.5	88.9	62.5	79.2	81.2	75.0
Education	100.0	100.0	100.0	85.7	80.0	100.0
Foreign Affairs	86.7	87.5	85.7	80.0	88.2	62.5
Commerce	82.4	100.0	71.4	64.0	85.7	62.5
Judiciary	82.4	100.0	62.5	88.0	88.2	87.5
Labor	76.9	85.7	66.7	85.0	85.7	83.3
Merchant Marine	91.7	100.0	83.3	73.9	82.4	50.0
Mines and Mining	84.6	85.7	100.0	95.5	100.0	83.3
Public Lands	86.7	100.0	71.4	95.7	100.0	83.3
Rules*	80.0	100.0	50.0	67.0	62.5	75.0
Ways and Means	76.5	88.9	62.5	80.0	93.3	60.0

* During the 1890s' realignment the Rules Committee had only five members.

The results are striking. The lowest of any of the rates of turnover was 50 percent. Excluding the Republicans on Rules, Appropriations and Merchant Marine, the lowest turnover rates were 62.5 percent. Thus, during both realignments all thirteen committees found themselves with majorities consisting of new members. Committee continuity was greatly disrupted. Comparing committee turnover during the realignments to turnover in the period immediately preceding them reveals that turnover was much greater during the realignment periods. The average turnover for the thirteen committees from the 52nd House to the 53rd was slightly over 30 percent, while the average turnover from the 53rd to the 55th was over 80 percent. The same pattern holds for the 1930s realignment. Average committee turnover during the pre-realignment Houses was slightly over 20 percent, while during the realignment it was over 80 percent. Comparisons with turnover figures for the modern House of Representatives reveal the same pattern.[25] It seems clear that, no matter how turnover rates are computed, the 1896 and 1932 realignments effected drastic changes in committee composition.

Committee Leaders

Important components of the committee system, facilitating committee continuity and stability, are the seniority and specialization norms. Committee leadership positions come available relatively rarely; leaders are brought along slowly. A committee's leaders serve on the same committee for long periods of time, acquiring expertise and becoming keepers of committee norms and policy.

If in a very short time there are drastic turnovers in membership, one would expect the norms of seniority and specialization to be affected—specifically, that during realignment periods committee turnover would be so drastic that many of the committee leaders in the realignment Houses would not have acquired much seniority. Any committee chairman in the 55th and 73rd Houses who was either not on that committee in the 53rd or 70th Houses or who was below the median rank of seniority in those Houses was considered to have advanced rapidly to committee leadership. Obviously a chairman in the realignment Houses who had not been on the committee two or three terms before could not have acquired either much seniority or much expertise in the intervening period.

During the period of the 1890s realignment, forty-nine House committees with more than five members were continuously in existence. Of these forty-nine committees, in the 55th House, twenty-eight, or 57 percent, had chairmen who were not on the committee in the 53rd House. Another eleven had chairmen who were below the median seniority in the 53rd. Thus thirty-nine of forty-nine committees, or 80 percent of House committees in the 1896 House, had committee chairmen who had not acquired much seniority and were not likely to be subject-matter experts. Of course at this time the Speaker had the power to appoint committees and chairmen. Thus the effect of turnover, which gave the party leadership flexibility in appointments, was further enhanced by the Speaker's power to jump members to committee chairmanships. However, most of these thirty-nine committee chairmen were not the result of the Speaker's appointive powers.[26]

During the period of the 1930s realignment, there were forty-four House committees with more than five members, and analysis of these forty-four committees shows that, within the short period of three elections, eighteen of them acquired chairmen who were either not on the committee at all at the end of the 70th House or were below the median minority rank. Robert Doughton of North Carolina, for example, was the tenth-ranking Democrat, the last, on the Ways and Means Committee in January 1929; he was chairman of Ways and Means in January 1933. Representative Ragon of Arkansas was not a member of Ways and Means in the 70th House; he was the ranking majority member in the 73rd House. Representative Sabath of Illinois was not on the Rules Committee in the 70th House; by the 73rd House he was the fourth-ranking member. The influx of new members plus the high turnover on committees facilitated the kind of rapid committee advancement noted in the above examples. Rather than continue the argument by enumeration, Table 21-3 shows, for both realignments, the committees whose chairmen had risen to power rapidly. The table shows that both important and unimportant committees in both realignment Houses had chairmen who had not acquired long committee seniority and were not the keepers of committee norms. The most obvious effect of the discontinuities in committee leadership was that the committee system became more flexible or pliable in providing party voting cues. Committee leaders and members had not

Table 21-3(A) House Committees in the 55th House Whose Chairman Had Either Not Been on Committee, or Had Been Low Ranking, in 53rd House

Committees	Chairman
# Accounts	Odel (N.Y.)
# Agriculture	Wadsworth (N.Y.)
# Alcohol Liquor Traffic	Brewster (N.Y.)
Appropriations	Cannon (Ill.)
# Claims	Brumm (Penn.)
District of Columbia	Babcock (Wis.)
# Education	Grow (Penn.)
# Election of President	Corliss (Mich.)
# Expenditures in Agriculture	Gillet (N.Y.)
Expenditures in Interior	Curtiss (Kan.)
# Expenditures in Justice	Sullaway (N.H.)
# Expenditures in Navy	Stewart (N.J.)
# Expenditures in Post Office	Wanger (Penn.)
# Expenditures in State	Guigg (N.Y.)
# Expenditures in Treasury	Cousins (Iowa)
# Expenditures in War Department	Grout (Vt.)
# Expenditures on Public Buildings	Colson (Kent.)
# Immigration and Naturalization	Danford (Ohio)
Indian Affairs	Sherman (N.Y.)
Commerce	Hepburn (Iowa)
# Invalid Pensions	Ray (N.Y.)
# Irrigation	Ellis (Ore.)
# Judiciary	Henderson (Iowa)
Labor	Gardner (N.J.)
# Levees on Mississippi	Bartholdt (Mo.)
# Manufactures	Faris (Ind.)
# Merchant Marine	Payne (N.Y.)
# Militia	Marsh (Ill.)
# Mines and Mining	Grosvenar (Ohio)
Pacific Railroads	Powers (Vt.)
Patents	Hicks (Penn.)
# Private Land Claims	Smith (Ill.)
Public Buildings	Mercer (Neb.)
Reform in Civil Service	Brosius (Penn.)
# Revision of Laws	Warner (Ill.)
# Rivers and Harbors	Burton (Ohio)
# Territories	Knox (Mass.)
War Claims	Mahon (Penn.)
Ways and Means	Dingley (Me.)

Chairman had not been on the committee in the 53rd House.

David W. Brady

Table 21-3(B) House Committees in the 73rd House Whose Chairman Had Not Been on Committee, or Had Been Low Ranking, in 70th House

	Committees	Chairman
	Accounts	Warren (N.C.)
	District of Columbia	Norton (N.J.)
	Election of President	Carley (N.Y.)
#	Elections - 1	Gauagan (N.Y.)
#	Elections - 2	Clark (N.C.)
#	Enrolled Bills	Parsons (Ill.)
	Expenditures in Executive	Cochran (Mo.)
	Foreign Affairs	McReynolds (Tenn.)
#	Insular Affairs	McDuffie (Ala.)
#	Irrigation and Reclamation	Chavez (N.M.)
#	Library	Keller (Ill.)
	Military Affairs	McSwain (S.C.)
#	Mines and Mining	Smith (W. Va.)
	Patents	Sirovich (N.Y.)
#	Public Lands	De Roven (La.)
#	Revision of Laws	Harlan (Ohio)
	Territories	Kemp (La.)
	Ways and Means	Doughton (N.C.)

\# Chairman had not been on the committee in the 70th House.

acquired the norms and expertise necessary to provide the committee voting cues so prominent in the modern House of Representatives. The negative effect of committee continuity on party voting was thus diminished.

The final stage of the argument concerning the committee system and party government entails demonstrating the increased partisanship of the new committee members. In order to demonstrate this, party-support scores for majority-party members of the Ways and Means and Appropriations committees were computed for each of the seven Congresses. The score was computed by scoring a 1 each time the member voted with the majority of his party on all roll calls in which a majority of one party opposed a majority of the other. For example, if out of twenty such votes a member voted with the majority of his party on eleven occasions his support score was 55. Only majority-party members were analyzed because of course "clusters of policy changes" are voted through by a cohesive majority party.[27] In the 53rd House the average partisan predispositions of the Republicans on both committees was 65.5, while in the 54th and 55th realignment Houses the equivalent partisan predispositions were 85.0 and 86.0 percent respectively. Thus the influx of new members increased the committees' partisan predispositions. This finding would be strengthened if the new members were found to have higher support scores than the carryovers. The average partisan predisposition of the carryovers was 75.5 in the 55th House, while the same figure for the new members (54th House plus 55th) was 86.7. The average party support score for Democrats on Ways and Means and Appropriations in the 70th House was slightly below 60 percent. In contrast Democratic committee members' support scores in the 72nd and 73rd Houses were over 80 percent. Thus, as in the 1890s, the influx of new members increased the committee's partisan predispositions. However, in contrast to the 1890s, when the new committee members' party scores were compared to the carryover members', the results showed no significant differences. Nevertheless, the results show clearly that during both realignments the majority-party members of both committees became markedly more partisan.

Realignments and Party Voting

The realignments of the 1890s and 1930s resulted in shifts in the constituency bases of the new congressional majority parties, and a drastic turnover in committee membership and leadership. If the thesis of this paper is correct, this combination of factors reduced constituency/party cross-pressuring and disrupted committees' policy continuity, thereby enhancing the ability of the majority party to build partisan majorities.[28] Given these conditions, there should have been a sharp rise in party cohesion and party voting. The hypothesis to be tested in this section is that the elimination of Huitt's two obstacles to responsible parties—constituency/congressmen relationships and the continuity of the committee system—will have resulted in a sharp rise in party voting during both realignment eras.

To test this hypothesis the percentage of roll calls on which a majority of one party opposed a majority of the other party, and the party-unity scores on party-majority versus party-majority roll calls, were calculated for the 52nd through 55th and the 70th through 73rd Houses. Further, for each of the Houses an average Index of Likeness (IPL) was computed by adding the IPL values for each roll call and dividing by the total number of roll calls in the House. The results should show a rise in party unity, a decline in the average Index of Likeness (an increase in party voting) and a sharp rise in the number of party votes. Table 21-4 shows the results of this analysis, using an Index of Likeness of .20 or less, and majority of one party versus a majority of the other party, as measures of party voting.

The results substantiate the hypothesis. The party-unity scores on majority versus majority votes rose from 79.6 to 93.3 for the Republicans during the 1890s while the comparable figures for the Democrats in the 1930s were 76.2 to 89.6— rises of 13.1 and 12.9 respectively. All three measures of party voting show a sharp increase over the realignment period. During the 1890s the percentage of party votes rose from 45.4 to 79.8, while the proportion of party votes with an IPL of ≤ 20 rose from 10.9 to 53.6. The results for the Roosevelt realignment show the same pattern. The proportion of party votes rose from 43.9 to 70.6, while the percentage of IPL ≤ 20 roll calls rose from 10.5 to 33.6. Party cohesion and party voting increased rapidly during both realignments.

Some scholars have suggested that the crucial election in the 'thirties realignment was the 1936 election in which Roosevelt defeated Alf Landon of Kansas. Their argument holds that in this election the party realignment

Table 21-4   The Changing Levels of Party Unity and Party Voting over the Realignments of 1890-96 and 1924-32

Congress	Average index of party likeness	Percent of votes with IPL ≤.20	Percent of votes with Maj. v. Maj.	Party unity average on Maj. vs. Maj. votes Dem.	Rep.
1896 Realignment					
52nd (1890)	61.0	10.9	45.4	76.2	79.6
53rd (1892)	59.6	20.0	44.8	85.1	86.1
54th (1894)	46.1	30.3	68.5	86.9	83.2
55th (1896)	30.8	53.6	79.8	89.3	93.3
% increase or decrease 52nd-55th Congress	−30.2	42.7	34.4	13.1	13.7
1932 Realignment					
69th (1924)	63.7	10.5	43.9	74.7	86.0
70th (1926)	61.8	9.5	48.6	80.5	81.8
71st (1928)	50.9	27.2	58.3	85.1	86.0
72nd (1930)	61.0	19.5	57.7	80.9	78.6
73rd (1932)	42.3	33.6	70.6	87.6	88.5
% increase or decrease 69th-73rd Congress	−21.4	23.1	26.7	12.9	2.5

crystallized and urban ethnics became Democratic identifiers. It may well be the case that among the party in the electorate the realignment was not crystallized until 1936. The linkage between electoral results and the congressional parties, however does not change significantly between 1933 to 1936. That is, the major thrust of change in the congressional parties occurred with the election of the 73rd House in 1932. In the 75th (1936) House the congressional Democratic party represented the same type of constituencies as in the 73rd and committee turnover and committee leadership turnover was not high. The Democratic committee leaders in the 75th House were by and large—almost 90 percent of them—those who had been the leaders of the 73rd House. Levels of party voting and of Democratic party unity were not as high in the 75th House as in the 73rd. For example, the percentage of majority versus majority votes in the 75th House was 62.9 as compared to 70.6 in the 73rd House, and Democratic party unity scores dropped over seven points to a little less than 80.0. Thus, while it may have been the case that the 1936 election crystallized the effects of the realignment on the party in the electorate, the effects of the 1936 election on the congressional party in the House were not of the same magnitude as the changes that occurred between 1928 and 1932.

Party and Issues during Realignments

One of the major points being made in this paper is that during realignments the policy issues central to the realignment are decided in a highly partisan manner. Since our interest is in the changing role of party in connection with the policy dimensions central to the realignment, Clausen's technique for identifying policy dimensions was utilized, and the resulting scores were then correlated with both party affiliation and party competition.[29] Briefly, the technique for determining policy dimensions is, first, to classify roll calls into issue domains on the basis of their substantive content. Secondly, a type of cluster analysis is applied to the role calls within each domain, the result taking the form of several homogeneous issue dimensions. The most comprehensive such dimension is used to represent each domain in the analysis that follows.

This analysis for the 53rd, 54th and 55th Houses yielded three dimensions. The first concerned monetary policy and the question of whether monetary policy should be inflationary—i.e. based on the silver standard or stable—i.e. based on the gold. This issue dimension occurred in all three Houses. The second dimension was tariff policy, the issue being whether or not tariff policy should be protective. The third policy dimension common to all three Houses was foreign policy. This area was dominated by the question of expansionism or isolationism. Each of these policy dimensions was of course central to the 1890s realignment.

During the 1930s realignment the policy dimensions common to the 71st, 72nd and 73rd Houses were social welfare and governmental activism in the economy. The social-welfare dimension included such legislation as providing hardship loans for the unemployed and the relief of hardship in the District of Columbia. The governmental-activism dimension included the National Recovery Act and legislation dealing with bankruptcy proceedings and a uniform coinage. The result of the analysis for both realignments resulted in the homogeneous issue dimensions mentioned above and also a score for each Representative in each House measuring his support for the policies in question.

If the aggregate-level analysis presented earlier in the paper is correct, then the same broad findings should also obtain at the individual level. Namely, during both realignments party affiliation and party competition should become more highly correlated with support for policy changes.

In order to test this hypothesis, the party-affiliation variable was measured by assigning the majority party in each realignment era a one and the minority party a zero (Republicans a one during the 1890s, Democrats a one during the 1930s). The party-competiton variable used was the Hasbrouck-Jones measure of how many times in a five-election period (one census) a congressional seat changes hands.[30] The result was a five-point scale, which is comparable over time because it is not subject to changes in voting percentages patterns as are the Ranney-Kendall and Pfieffer indexes.[31] A district that was Republican four out of five times in the 1890-1900 period is comparable to a district that was Republican four out of five times in the 1920-30 period. The values for the scale are as follows:

1890s	1930s
1 = Democratic 5 times	Republican 5 times
2 = Democratic 4 of 5 times	Republican 4 of 5 times
3 = Democratic or Republican 3 of 5 times	Republican or Democratic 3 of 5 times
4 = Republican 4 of 5 times	Democratic 4 of 5 times
5 = Republican 5 times	Democratic 5 times.

The level of policy support score was operationalized by determining the number of times an individual member voted in the direction of the policy change. For the 1890s this means that on the monetary dimension the higher the score the more the Representative favored non-inflationary or hard-monetary policy; on the tariff and foreign-policy dimensions, the greater the score, the greater the support for protective tariffs and expansionism. In the 1930s higher support scores on the social welfare and government-activism dimensions represents support for welfare programs and support for increased government management of the economy. Table 21-5 presents the correlations between party affiliation, party competition and policy support over the 1890s and 1930s realignments.

The analysis shows clearly the increased strength of the relationship between both party affiliation and party support over the two realignments. Just as party voting over all roll calls increased during both realignments, so does the importance of party increase on the policy dimensions associated with the realignments. Another way to interpret the table is to argue that it shows that over both realignments party improves as a predictor of voting on realignment-related policy dimensions. Our analysis shows that the issues central to the realignment are decided on a highly partisan basis. There is a coming together of party and policy such that many of the elements of a responsible party system are present during realigning eras. Our findings at both the aggregate and individual levels corroborate this thesis.

Switched-Seat Districts

If "the main impetus for change in the overall policy posture of the Congress comes in the new membership," [32] then the new members from districts that changed during the realignment are critical for understanding policy change. It is from these switched-seat districts that new party majorities are formed. The replacement of senior congressmen by freshmen members of the same party does not realign the constituency bases of the parties. Rather, it was districts that switched from Democratic to Republican during the 1892-96 period and from Republican to Democratic during the 1926-32 period that built the "new" congressional parties which supported the respective clusters of policy changes. The congressmen from the switched districts were elected around the issues of the realignment and their high levels of party support provided the majorities necessary to pass the significant policy changes. In this section, after a brief description of their constituencies, the party-support and policy-support scores of switched-district congressmen will be analyzed.

Switched-seat districts in the 55th House are defined as those districts that switched from the Democratic party in the 53rd House to the Republican party

Table 21-5 Simple Correlation (*r*) Between Party Identification, Party Competition and Issue Positions over the Realignments of 1890-96 and 1924-32

1890s
Policy dimensions

Congress	Monetary		Tariff		Foreign policy	
	Party	*Comp.*	*Party*	*Comp.*	*Party*	*Comp.*
53rd (1892)	.62	.51	.69	.57	.64	.50
54th (1894)	.83	.69	.79	.72	.81	.63
55th (1896)	.91	.74	.89	.75	.90	.74

1930s
Policy dimensions

Congress	Social welfare		Government activism	
	Party	*Comp.*	*Party*	*Comp.*
71st (1928)	.56	.42	.49	.41
72nd (1930)	.66	.57	.79	.56
73rd (1932)	.88	.67	.90	.70

David W. Brady

in either the 54th House or 55th Houses and remained Republican through the 56th House. There were forty-nine such districts and they reflected the shift in constituency bases noted in the first section of this paper. Over 85 percent of the switched districts were located in the industrial areas of the East and Midwest. The remaining districts were located in the industrial areas in border states such as Maryland and West Virginia. Switched-seat districts in the 73rd House are defined as those districts that switched from the Republican party to the Democrats in either the 72nd or 73rd Houses and remained Democratic through the 75th House. There were 113 such districts and they also reflected the shift in constituency bases noted above. The largest proportion of these districts was urban and industrial while the next largest proportion was largely rural and agricultural and was located in the Midwest. It is clear that the change in Democratic strength during the 1930s realignment was reflected in the switched-seat districts.

The specific hypothesis is that switched-seat representatives will have higher party-support scores than representatives from districts that have not changed hands. Testing this hypothesis entailed calculating a mean party-support score for the entire majority party and then comparing switched-seat congressmen to the non-switched seat members. The results support the hypothesis (see Table 21-6). Switched-seat congressmen in both realignments were more supportive of the party position than their counterparts. The same analysis was run for each of the policy dimensions discussed above and the results were similar. Congressmen from switched-seat districts in both realignments were highly supportive of the policy changes associated with the respective realignments. The t tests were all significant at the .10 level or below. Congressmen from districts switching their party affiliation thus provided critical support for both clusters of policy changes.

Table 21-6   A Comparison of Party-Support Levels between Switched-Seat and Non-Switched Seat Republicans in the 55th House and Democrats in the 73rd House

	1896		1932	
Party support scores	Switched-seat Republican Congressmen	Non-switched Republican Congressmen	Switched-seat Democratic Congressmen	Non-switched Democratic Congressmen
Percent above party mean*	76	47	65	48
Percent below party mean	24	53	35	52
Total	100	100	100	100
Mean support scores†	77.7	69.9	75.0	67.7

* Mean Republican support score in 55th House is 71.8; mean Democratic support score in 73rd House is 69.8.
† t test significant for both Houses at .05 level.

538

Discussion

This paper has demonstrated that the realigning elections of 1896 and 1932 shifted the constituency bases of the new congressional majority party, thereby reducing constituency/party cross pressuring. In addition, the turnover in membership resulting from the two elections disrupted committee continuity. With these two major obstacles to party government removed, the level of party unity and party voting in the House increased dramatically. The realigning elections of 1896 and 1932 created the conditions for party government, and the clusters of policy changes associated with these realignments were enacted by cohesive, unified majority parties. They were likewise opposed by the minority parties.

While the specific question addressed in this paper concerned the nature of the relationship between these two realigning elections and the House of Representatives' legitimation of the clusters of policy changes associated with them, another broader question was implicit in the analysis: namely, are realigning elections a necessary condition of major policy changes?

In order to answer this question, it is imperative that we analyze the vehicle for the legitimation of policy changes—the congressional majority party. In both the 1896 and the 1932 realignments, it was the newly created, cohesive majority party that voted through the shifts in policy. The cohesiveness of the new majority party was the result of the turnover in membership (switched-seat districts) which reduced cross pressuring and disrupted committee continuity. The new members had high party-support scores and provided the votes that enacted the policy changes. Thus, on this reasoning, any election that generates a substantial turnover in membership can create the conditions necessary for major shifts in policy. The 1912 and 1964 elections resulted in major policy changes, and both were characterized by substantial membership turnover. In the 89th House elected in 1964, members representing switched-seat districts were highly supportive of their party's position and provided the votes necessary to enact the major policy changes that occurred.[33] Committee turnover in that Congress was the highest in over fifteen years, and the level of party voting and party unity rose by over five percentage points in its first session. The 1964 election, which may or may not have been a realigning election, brought in a substantial number of new members, who increased the cohesiveness of the majority party and facilitated the passage of policy changes. Further evidence supporting the assertion that the "impetus for policy changes is the new membership" comes from a recent work which shows that during the period 1886 to 1966 the correlation between the percentage of new members and the level of party voting was .46.[34] That is, the effect of new members is to create the conditions for party government, and over time the larger the percentage of new members the higher the levels of party voting. Thus elections characterized by a high turnover of membership seem to be a necessary if not sufficient condition for significant policy changes. It is interesting to note that the 94th House of Representatives, which had seventy-five new Democratic members, was the most partisan in recent years.

Elections that bring to the House a substantial number of new members are not sufficient to ensure policy changes for a number of reasons. The most important is that there must exist a program; either party or both must propose major changes.[35] Another such condition is unified control of Congress and the presidency. The 1920 election of Warren Harding brought to the House a large number of new members, and the percentage of party votes arose from forty-five in the 66th House to 60 percent in the 67th. However, as Charles O. Jones has shown, the lack of a program prohibited that Congress from distinguishing itself by passing significant policy changes. The most recent Congress, the 94th, might well have passed legislation that might have been considered major, but the threat and the fact of a conservative president's veto prohibited major shifts in policy. Clearly presidential programs and the president's involvement, as well as unified control of the policy-making institutions, are factors affecting the likelihood of policy shifts.

Major shifts in public policy are most likely to occur during periods when the parties and the candidates take divergent issue positions and the electorate sends to Washington a new congressional majority party and a president of the same party. Since 1896 this set of conditions has occurred only four times—in 1896, 1912, 1932-36 and 1964—and in each instance there were major shifts in policy.[36] When these conditions are met, there are relatively strong connections between the electorate, representatives and public policy. During such periods the American system of government exhibits many of the characteristics of responsible party government.

NOTES

1. V. O. Key, Jr., "A Theory of Critical Elections," *Journal of Politics,* XVII (1955), 3-18, p. 5.
2. Key, "A Theory of Critical Elections," and V. O. Key, Jr., "Secular Realignment and the Party System," *Journal of Politics,* XXI (1959), 198-210.
3. E. E. Schattschneider, *The Semi-Sovereign People: A Realist's View of Democracy in America* (New York: Holt, Rinehart and Winston, 1960), pp. 78-96.
4. Walter Dean Burnham, *Critical Elections and the Mainsprings of American Politics* (New York: W. W. Norton, 1970), p. 10. This book is the most comprehensive work but see the exchange between Burnham, Philip Converse and Jerrold Rusk, "Political Change in America," *American Political Science Review,* LXVIII (1974), 1002-58.
5. Burnham, *Critical Elections and the Mainsprings of American Politics;* Key, "A Theory of Critical Elections" and "Secular Realignment and the Party System"; and James L. Sundquist, *Dynamics of the Party System: Alignment and Realignment of Political Parties in the United States* (Washington: The Brookings Institution, 1973).
6. Benjamin Ginsberg, "Critical Elections and the Substance of Party Conflict: 1844-1968," *Midwest Journal of Political Science,* XVI (1972), 603-26.
7. Walter Dean Burnham, "The Changing Shape of the American Political Universe," *American Political Science Review,* LIX (1965), 7-29; and Paul Glad, *McKinley, Bryan and the People* (Philadelphia: Lippincott, 1964).
8. Arthur M. Schlesinger, Jr., *The Coming of the New Deal* (Boston: Houghton-Mifflin, 1958), and *The Politics of Upheaval* (Boston: Houghton-Mifflin, 1960).

9. Ralph Huitt, "Democratic Party Leadership in the Senate," *American Political Science Review*, LV (1961), 333-44.

10. Aage Clausen, *How Congressmen Decide: A Policy Focus* (New York: St. Martin's Press, 1973), pp. 231-2.

11. Huitt, "Democratic Party Leadership in the Senate."

12. Ralph Huitt, "The Congressional Committee: A Case Study," *American Political Science Review*, XLVIII (1954), 340-65, p. 341.

13. Huitt, "The Congressional Committee," p. 341.

14. Burnham, *Critical Elections;* Burnham, "The Changing Shape"; Glad, *McKinley, Bryan and the People;* Stanley L. Jones, *The Presidential Election of 1896* (Madison: University of Wisconsin Press, 1964); V. O. Key, Jr., *Politics, Parties and Pressure Groups* (New York: Thomas Y. Crowell, 1967), pp. 232-6.

15. Burnham, "Changing Shape," p. 18, pp. 7-29.

16. Sundquist, *Dynamics of the Party System*, p. 232-6.

17. Cited in Sundquist, *Dynamics of the Party System,* p. 185.

18. Ginsberg, "Critical Elections and the Substance of Party Conflict," pp. 603-26.

19. William Allen White, *A Puritan in Babylon: The Story of Calvin Coolidge* (New York: Capricorn, 1965), p. 344; also cited in Sundquist, *Dynamics of The Party System,* p. 172.

20. Sundquist, *Dynamics of the Party System,* pp. 181-2.

21. Benjamin Ginsberg, "Elections and Public Policy," *American Political Science Review,* LXX (1976), 41-9, p. 49.

22. Richard Fenno, *The Power of the Purse* (Boston: Little, Brown, 1966), pp. 226-7.

23. Huitt, "Congressional Committee: A Case Study"; and Malcolm E. Jewell and Samuel C. Patterson, *The Legislative Process in the United States* (New York: Random House, 1966), pp. 442-9.

24. While it is certainly true that as an institution the House in the 1890s differed from the House in the 1930s, committees were already well defined and important. In fact Woodrow Wilson called congressional government committee government. Thus turnover on committees was an important component of the system. For an analysis of the House as an institution in the 1890s see David W. Brady, *Congressional Voting in a Partisan Era: A Comparison of the McKinley Houses to the Modern House* (Lawrence: University of Kansas Press, 1973). For the influence of the Speaker on committees see fn. 26.

25. For data on turnover in recent Houses see Richard Fenno, *Congressmen in Committees* (Boston: Little, Brown, 1973).

26. The committee system in the 1890s was centralized under the Speaker who had power to appoint committees. Thus seniority norms were more likely to be violated during this era. However, the Speaker's power to appoint in violation of seniority cannot account for a large portion of either the committee or committee leadership turnover. The two major papers on seniority in the House, Michael Abram and Joseph Cooper, "The Rise of Seniority in the House of Representatives," *Polity*, 1 (1969), 52-85 and Nelson Polsby et al., "The Growth of the Seniority System in the U.S. House of Representatives," *American Political Science Review,* LXIII (1969), 787-807, both show a lower level of seniority violation than could account for the turnover in committee membership. For example, Abram and Cooper say that on major committees only two seniority violations occurred in the 55th House. Polsby et al., show that Speaker Reed followed seniority on thirty-six of fifty-two committee appointments and of the sixteen violations eleven were compensated. Both these figures are far too low to account for the 80 percent turnover.

27. The same analysis was run over the minority party members of the two committees and the partisan predispositions of these members increased.
28. The term "party leadership" is intended to include the President as well as House leaders.
29. Clausen, *How Congressmen Decide,* Chaps. 1 and 2 for the technique to determine issue domains. Product moment correlation was chosen to test the hypotheses because the correlation model assumes strong monotonicity and independence as the null value condition. See Herbert Weisberg, "Models of Statistical Relationships," *American Political Science Review,* LXVIII (1974), 1638-51. Moreover in each case reported below regression analysis was run on the same variables to corroborate whether or not real change had taken place. The unstandardized *B*s in each case changed in the same direction as did the correlation coefficients.
30. Charles O. Jones, "Inter-Party Competition for Congressional Seats," *Western Political Quarterly,* XVII (1964), 461-76; Paul Hasbrouck, *Party Government in the House of Representatives* (New York: Macmillan, 1927), Chap. 9.
31. Austin Ranney and Willmoore Kendall, "The American Party Systems," *American Political Science Review,* XLVIII (1954), 477-85, and David G. Pfeiffer, "The Measurement of Inter-Party Competition and Systemic Stability," *American Political Science Review,* LXI (1967), 457-67. Both measures developed in these articles are based on arrays of data which are time based.
32. Clausen, *How Congressmen Decide,* pp. 231-2.
33. David W. Brady and Naomi Lynn, "Switched-Seat Congressional Districts: Their Effect on Party Voting and Public Policy," *American Journal of Political Science,* LXVII (1973), 528-43; and Jeff Fischel, *Party and Opposition: Congressional Challengers in American Politics* (New York: David McKay, 1973), pp. 162-4.
34. David W. Brady, Joseph Cooper and Pat Hurley, "An Analysis of the Decline of Party Voting in the U.S. House of Representatives: 50th to 90th Houses" (unpublished manuscript, 1976).
35. Ginsberg, "Critical Elections and the Substance of Party Conflict."
36. There have been other instances when new majorities and a new president came to Washington, e.g. Eisenhower in 1953. However, in each of these instances Ginsberg's content analysis of issue differences between parties shows little ideological difference between parties.

REFERENCES

Abrams, Michael, and Joseph Cooper. "The Rise of Seniority in the House of Representatives." *Polity* (Fall 1968): 52-85.

Abramowitz, Alan. "A Comparison of Voting for U.S. Senator and Representative in 1978." *American Political Science Review* (September 1980): 633-640.

Alford, John, and John Hibbing. "Increased Incumbency Advantage in the House." *Journal of Politics* (November 1981): 1042-1061.

Arnold, R. Douglas. *Congress and the Bureaucracy*. New Haven: Yale University Press, 1979.

Arseneau, Robert, and Raymond Wolfinger. "Voting Behavior in Congressional Elections." Paper delivered at the annual meeting of the American Political Science Association, New Orleans, Louisiana, 1973.

Asher, Herbert B. "The Learning of Legislative Norms." *American Political Science Review* (June 1973a): 499-513. (Reprinted in this volume, 119-146.)

_____. *Freshman Representatives and the Learning of Voting Cues*. Beverly Hills: Sage Publications, 1973b.

_____. "The Changing Status of the Freshman Representative." In *Congress in Change*, edited by Norman J. Ornstein, 216-239. New York: Praeger, 1975.

_____. *Causal Modeling*. Beverly Hills: Sage Publications, 1976.

Asher, Herbert B., and Herbert F. Weisberg. "Voting Change in Congress: Some Dynamic Perspectives on an Evolutionary Process." *American Journal of Political Science* (May 1978): 391-425. (Reprinted in this volume, 420-446.)

Bacheller, John M. "Lobbyists and the Legislative Process: The Impact of Environmental Constraints." *American Political Science Review* (March 1977): 252-262.

Bernstein, Robert A., and William W. Anthony. "The ABM Issue and the Senate, 1968-1970: The Importance of Ideology." *American Political Science Review* (September 1974): 1198-1206.

Bibby, John. "The Politics of the Senate Committee on Banking and Currency." In *On Capitol Hill*, edited by John Bibby and Roger Davidson, 170-196. New York: Rinehart and Winston, 1967.

Bibby, John, Thomas E. Mann, and Norman J. Ornstein. *Vital Statistics on Congress*. Washington, D.C.: American Enterprise Institute, 1980.

Bolling, Richard. *House Out of Order*. New York: Dutton, 1965.

Bond, Jon R. "Oiling the Tax Committees in Congress, 1900-1974: Subgovernment Theory, The Overrepresentation Hypothesis, and the Oil

References

Depletion Allowance." *American Journal of Political Science* (November 1979): 651-665.

Born, Richard. "Cue-Taking Within State Party Delegations in the U.S. House of Representatives." *Journal of Politics* (February 1976): 71-94.

_____. "House Incumbents and Inter-Election Vote Change." *Journal of Politics* (November 1977): 1008-1035.

_____. "Generational Replacement and the Growth of Incumbent Reelection Margins in the U.S. House." *American Political Science Review* (September 1979): 811-817.

_____. "Perquisite Employment in the U.S. House of Representatives." *American Politics Quarterly* (July 1982): 347-362.

Bowler, M. Kenneth, "The New Committee on Ways and Means: Policy Implications of Recent Changes in the House Committee." Paper delivered at the annual meeting of the American Political Science Association, Chicago, Illinois, 1976.

Brady, David W. *Congressional Voting in a Partisan Era.* Lawrence: University of Kansas Press, 1973.

_____. "The Conservative Coalition: Origins, Causes, and Consequences." Paper delivered at the annual meeting of the American Political Science Association, Washington, D.C., 1977.

_____. "Critical Elections, Congressional Parties and Clusters of Policy Changes." *British Journal of Political Science* (January 1978): 79-99. (Reprinted in this volume, 521-542.)

_____. "Is There a Conservative Coalition in the House?" *Journal of Politics* (May 1980): 549-559.

Brady, David W., and Phillip Althoff. "Party Voting in the U.S. House of Representatives, 1890-1910: Elements of a Responsible Party System." *Journal of Politics* (August 1974): 753-775.

Brady, David W., Joseph Cooper, and Patricia Hurley. "The Decline of Party in the U.S. House of Representatives, 1887-1968." *Legislative Studies Quarterly* (August 1979): 381-406.

Brady, David W., and Naomi B. Lynn. "Switched Seat Congressional Districts: Their Effect on Party Voting and Public Policy." *American Journal of Political Science* (August 1973): 528-543.

Brown, George R. *The Leadership of Congress.* Indianapolis: Bobbs-Merrill, 1922.

Brunk, Gregory. "Turnover and Voting Stability in the Senate." *American Politics Quarterly* (July 1982): 363-374.

Bullock, Charles S. III. "House Careerists: Changing Patterns of Longevity and Attrition." *American Political Science Review* (December 1972): 1295-1300.

_____. "Redistricting and Congressional Stability, 1962-1972." *Journal of Politics* (May 1975): 569-575.

_____. "Explaining Congressional Elections: Differences in Perceptions of Opposing Candidates." *Legislative Studies Quarterly* (August 1977): 245-308.

_____. "Congressional Voting and the Mobilization of a Black Electorate in the South." *Journal of Politics* (August 1981): 662-682.

Bullock, Charles S. III, and David W. Brady. "Party, Constituency, and Roll-Calling Voting in the U.S. Senate." *Legislative Studies Quarterly* (February 1983): 29-44. (Reprinted in this volume, 447-458.)

Bullock, Charles S. III, and Harrell R. Rodgers, Jr. *Racial Equality in America.* Pacific Palisades, Calif.: Goodyear, 1975.

Bullock, Charles S. III, and Michael J. Scicchitano. "Partisan Defections and Senate Reelections." *American Politics Quarterly* (October 1982): 477-488.

Bullock, Charles S. III, and John Sprague. "A Research Note on the Committee Reassignment of Southern Democratic Congressmen." *Journal of Politics* (November 1972): 493-512.

Busby, L. White. *Uncle Joe Cannon.* New York: Henry Holt, 1927.

Calvert, Randall L., and John A. Ferejohn. "Coattail Voting In Recent Presidential Elections." *American Political Science Review* (June 1983): 407-419.

Campbell, Angus, Phillip E. Converse, Warren E. Miller, and Donald E. Stokes. *Elections and the Political Order.* New York: John Wiley, 1966.

Campbell, James E. "The Return of the Incumbents: The Nature of the Incumbency Advantage." *Western Political Quarterly* (September 1983): 434-443.

Cavanaugh, Thomas E. "Rational Allocation of Congressional Resources: Member Time and Staff Use in the House." In *Public Policy and Public Choice,* edited by Douglas W. Rae and Theodore J. Eismeier, 206-247. Beverly Hills: Sage Publications, 1979.

_____. "The Dispersion of Authority in the House of Representatives." *Political Science Quarterly* (Winter 1982-1983): 623-637.

Cherryholmes, Cleo H., and Michael J. Shapiro. *Representatives and Roll Calls: A Computer Simulation of Voting in the Eighty-Eighth Congress.* Indianapolis: Bobbs-Merrill, 1969.

Chiu, Chang-Wei. *The Speaker of the House of Representatives Since 1896.* New York: Columbia University Press, 1928.

Cimbala, Stephen J. "Foreign Policy as an Issue Area: A Roll Call Analysis." *American Political Science Review* (March 1969): 148-156.

Clapp, Charles. *The Congressman: His Work as He Sees It.* Washington, D.C.: Brookings Institution, 1963.

Clark, Peter, and Susan H. Evans. *Covering Campaigns: Journalism in Congressional Elections.* Palo Alto, Calif.: Stanford University Press, 1983.

Clausen, Aage R. *How Congressmen Decide: A Policy Focus.* New York: St. Martin's Press, 1973.

Clausen, Aage R., and Richard B. Cheney. "A Comparative Analysis of Senate-House Voting on Economic and Welfare Policy, 1953-1964." *American Political Science Review* (March 1970): 138-152.

Clausen, Aage R., and Carl E. Van Horn. "The Congressional Response to a Decade of Change: 1963-1972." *Journal of Politics* (August 1977): 624-666.

Clotfelter, James. "Senate Voting and Constituency Stake in Defense Spending." *Journal of Politics* (November 1970): 979-983.

Commission on Administrative Review. U.S. House of Representatives, *Final Report: Survey Materials.* 95th Congress, 1977, H. Doc. 95-272.

Congressional Quarterly. "The 'Ratings Games': Some Members Object." *Congressional Quarterly Weekly Report,* July 6, 1974, 1748-1754.

_____. "Party Unity and Party Opposition: House." *Congressional Quarterly Weekly Report,* December 16, 1978, 3450-3451.

_____. "House Bogs Down in Budget Amendments." *Congressional Quarterly Weekly Report,* May 12, 1979, 877-878.

Cooper, Joseph. *Congress and Its Committees.* Ph.D. diss., Harvard University, Cambridge, 1961.

_____. *The Origins of Standing Committees and the Development of the Modern House.* Houston: Rice University Publications, 1970.

_____. "Strengthening the Congress: An Organizational Analysis." *Harvard Journal of Legislation* (1975): 307-368.

Cooper, Joseph, and Gary Bombardier. "Presidential Leadership and Party Success." *Journal of Politics* (November 1968): 1012-1027.

Cooper, Joseph, and David W. Brady. "Institutional Context and Leadership Style: The House from Cannon to Rayburn." Paper delivered at the Conference on Understanding Congressional Leadership: The State of the Art, Washington, D.C., 1980.

_____. "Institutional Context and Leadership Style: The House from Cannon to Rayburn." *American Political Science Review* (June 1981): 411-425. (Reprinted in this volume, 321-342.)

_____. "Toward a Diachronic Analysis of Congress." *American Political Science Review* (December 1981): 988-1006.

Cooper, Joseph, David W. Brady, and Patricia Hurley. "The Electoral Basis of Party Voting: Patterns and Trends in the U.S. House of Representatives, 1887-1969." In *The Impact of the Electoral Process,* edited by J. Cooper and L. Maisel, 133-165. Beverly Hills: Sage Electoral Studies Yearbook, 1977.

Cooper, Joseph, and William West. "The Congressional Career in the 1970s." In *Congress Reconsidered,* 2d ed., edited by Lawrence C. Dodd and Bruce I. Oppenheimer, 83-106. Washington, D.C.: CQ Press, 1981.

_____. "Voluntary Retirement, Incumbency and the Modern House." *Political Science Quarterly* (Summer 1981): 279-300.

Cover, Albert D. "One Good Term Deserves Another: The Advantage of Incumbency in Congressional Elections." *American Journal of Political Science* (August 1977): 523-542.

_____. "Contacting Congressional Constituents: Some Patterns of Perquisite Use." *American Journal of Political Science* (February 1980): 125-135.

Cranor, John D., and Joseph W. Westphal. "Congressional District Offices, Federal Programs, and Electoral Benefits: Some Observations on the Passing of the Marginal Representative, 1974-1976." Paper delivered at the annual meeting of the Midwest Political Science Association, Chicago, Illinois, 1978.

Daniels, Jonathan. *Frontier of the Potomac.* New York: Macmillan, 1946.

Davidson, Roger H. *The Role of the Congressman.* New York: Pegasus, 1969.

Davidson, Roger H., and Walter J. Oleszek. *Congress Against Itself.* Bloomington: Indiana University Press, 1977.

———. *Congress and Its Members.* Washington, D.C.: CQ Press, 1981.

Dawson, Raymond. "Congressional Innovation and Intervention in Defense Policy: Legislative Authorization of Weapons Systems." *American Political Science Review* (March 1962): 41-57.

Deckard, Barbara Sinclair. "Political Upheaval and Congressional Voting: The Effects of the 1960s on Voting Patterns in the House of Representatives." *Journal of Politics* (May 1976a): 326-345.

———. "Electoral Marginality and Party Loyalty in House Roll Call Voting." *American Journal of Political Science* (August 1976b): 469-481.

Dexter, Lewis A. "The Representative and His District." *Human Organization* (Spring 1957): 2-13.

———. "The Representative and the District." In *New Perspectives on the House of Representatives.* 1st ed., edited by Robert L. Peabody and Nelson W. Polsby, 3-29. Chicago: Rand McNally, 1963.

Dodd, Lawrence C. "Committee Integration in the Senate: A Comparative Analysis." *Journal of Politics* (November 1972): 1135-1171.

———. "Congress and the Quest for Power." In *Congress Reconsidered.* 1st ed., edited by Lawrence C. Dodd and Bruce I. Oppenheimer, 269-307. New York: Praeger, 1977. (Reprinted in this volume, 489-520.)

Dodd, Lawrence C., and Bruce I. Oppenheimer, eds. *Congress Reconsidered,* 2d ed. Washington, D.C.: CQ Press, 1981.

Downs, Anthony. *An Economic Theory of Democracy.* New York: Harper and Row, 1957.

Dyson, James W., and John W. Soule. "Congressional Committee Behavior on Roll Call Votes: The U.S. House of Representatives, 1955-1964." *Midwest Journal of Political Science* (November 1970): 626-647.

Entin, Kenneth. "The House Armed Services Committee: Patterns of Decision Making During the McNamara Years." *Journal of Political and Military Sociology* (Spring 1974): 73-88.

Epstein, Laurily K., and Frankovic, Kathleen A. "Case Work and Electoral Margins: Insurance is Prudent." *Polity* (Summer 1982): 691-729.

Erikson, Robert S. "The Advantage of Incumbency in Congressional Elections." *Polity* (December 1971): 395-405.

———. "Malapportionment, Gerrymandering, and Party Fortunes in Congressional Elections." *American Political Science Review* (December 1972): 1234-1245.

———. "Is There Such a Thing As A Safe Seat?" *Polity* (Summer 1976): 623-632.

———. "Constituency Opinion and Congressional Behavior: A Reexamination of the Miller-Stokes Representation Data." *American Journal of Political Science* (August 1978): 511-535.

Eubank, Robert B. "Incumbent Effects on Individual-Level Voting Behavior: A Decade of Exaggeration, 1972-1980." Manuscript, 1984.

Eubank, Robert B., and Gow, David J. "The Pro-Incumbent Bias in the 1978

References

and 1980 National Election Studies." *American Journal of Political Science* (February 1983): 122-139.

Evans, Rowland, and Robert Novak. "The Johnson System." In *Readings on Congress,* edited by Raymond E. Wolfinger, 225-241. Englewood Cliffs, N.J.: Prentice-Hall, 1971.

Fenno, Richard F., Jr. "The House Appropriations Committee as a Political System: The Problem of Integration." *American Political Science Review* (June 1962): 310-324. (Reprinted in this volume, 199-221.)

_____. "The House of Representatives and Federal Aid to Education." In *New Perspectives on the House of Representatives.* 1st ed., edited by Robert L. Peabody and Nelson Polsby, 195-236. Chicago: Rand McNally, 1963.

_____. "The Internal Distribution of Influence: The House." In *The Congress and America's Future,* edited by David B. Truman, 52-76. Englewood Cliffs, N.J.: Prentice-Hall, 1965.

_____. *The Power of the Purse: Appropriations Politics in Congress.* Boston: Little, Brown, 1966.

_____. *Congressmen in Committees.* Boston: Little, Brown, 1973a.

_____. "Congressional Committees." Paper delivered at the Study of Congress Conference, Washington, D.C., 1973b.

_____. "If, as Ralph Nader Says, Congress Is 'The Broken Branch,' How Come We Love Our Congressmen So Much?" In *Congress in Change,* edited by Norman J. Ornstein, 277-287. New York: Praeger, 1975.

_____. "U.S. House Members in Their Constituencies: An Exploration." *American Political Science Review* (September 1977): 883-917.

_____. *Home Style: House Members in Their Districts.* Boston: Little, Brown, 1978.

_____. *The United States Senate: A Bicameral Perspective.* Washington, D.C.: American Enterprise Institute, 1982.

Ferejohn, John A. *Pork Barrel Politics: Rivers and Harbors Legislation 1947-1968.* Palo Alto: Stanford University Press, 1974.

_____. "On the Decline of Competition in Congressional Elections." *American Political Science Review* (March 1977): 166-176. (Reprinted in this volume, 44-63.)

Fiellin, Alan. "The Functions of Informal Groups in Legislative Institutions." *Journal of Politics* (February 1962): 72-91.

Fiorina, Morris P. "Electoral Margins, Constituency Influence, and Policy Moderation: A Critical Assessment." *American Politics Quarterly* (October 1973): 479-498.

_____. *Representatives, Roll Calls, and Constituencies.* Lexington, Mass.: D.C. Heath, Lexington Books, 1974.

_____. *Congress: Keystone of the Washington Establishment.* New Haven: Yale University Press, 1977a.

_____. "The Case of the Vanishing Marginals: The Bureaucracy Did It." *American Political Science Review* (March 1977b): 177-181. (Reprinted in this volume, 64-71.)

_____. "Some Problems in Studying the Effects of Resource Allocation in

Congressional Elections." *American Political Science Review* (August 1981): 543-567.

Fiorina, Morris P., and Roger G. Noll. "Majority Rule Models and Legislative Elections." *Journal of Politics* (November 1979): 1081-1104.

Flinn, Thomas. "Party Responsibility in the States: Some Causal Factors." *American Political Science Review* (March 1964): 60-71.

Froman, Lewis A., Jr. *Congressmen and Their Constituencies.* Chicago: Rand McNally, 1963.

———. "The Categorization of Policy Content." In *Political Science and Public Policy*, edited by Austin Ranney, 41-52. Chicago: Markham, 1968.

Froman, Lewis A., Jr., and Randall B. Ripley. "Conditions for Party Leadership." *American Political Science Review* (March 1965): 52-63.

Galloway, George. *History of the House of Representatives.* New York: Thomas Crowell, 1961.

Gertzog, Irwin N. "The Socialization of Freshmen Congressmen: Some Agents of Organizational Continuity." Paper delivered at the annual meeting of the American Political Science Association, Los Angeles, Calif., 1970.

———. "The Routinization of Committee Assignments in the U.S. House of Representatives." *American Political Science Review* (November 1976): 693-712.

Goldenberg, Edie N., and Michael W. Traugott. *Campaigning for Congress.* Washington, D.C.: CQ Press, 1984.

Goodwin, George. *The Little Legislatures.* Amherst: University of Massachusetts Press, 1970.

Gross, Bertram. *The Legislative Structure: A Study in Social Combat.* New York: McGraw-Hill, 1953.

Grumm, John G. "A Factor Analysis of Legislative Behavior." *Midwest Journal of Political Science* (November 1963): 336-356.

Haines, Lynn. *Your Congress.* Washington, D.C.: National Voters' League, 1915.

Harmon, Kathryn Newcomer, and Marsha L. Brauen. "Joint Electoral Outcomes as Cues for Congressional Support for U.S. Presidents." *Legislative Studies Quarterly* (May 1979): 281-300.

Hasbrouck, Paul D. *Party Government in the House of Representatives.* New York: Macmillan, 1927.

Hechler, Kenneth. *Insurgency.* New York: Columbia University Press, 1940.

Henderson, Thomas A. *Congressional Oversight of Executive Agencies: A Study of the House Committee on Government Operations.* Gainesville: University of Florida Press, 1970.

Herring, Pendleton. *Presidential Leadership.* New York: Farrar and Rinehart, 1940.

Hibbing, John R. "Voluntary Retirements in the House in the Twentieth Century." *Journal of Politics* (November 1982): 1020-1034.

———. Voluntary Retirements from the U.S. House of Representatives: Who Quits?" *American Journal of Political Science* (August 1982): 467-484.

References

Hinckley, Barbara. "Congressional Leadership Selection and Support: A Comparative Analysis." *Journal of Politics* (May 1970a,b): 268-287.

_____. "Incumbency and the Presidential Vote in Senate Elections." *American Political Science Review* (September 1970): 836-842.

_____. "Coalitions in Congress: Size and Ideological Distance." *Midwest Journal of Political Science* (May 1972): 197-207.

_____. "Policy Content, Committee Membership, and Behavior." *American Journal of Political Science* (August 1976): 543-558. (Reprinted in this volume, 222-233.)

_____. "The American Voter in Congressional Elections." *American Political Science Review* (September 1980a): 641-650.

_____. "House Reelections and Senate Defeats: The Role of the Challenger." *British Journal of Political Science* (October 1980b): 441-460.

_____. *Stability and Change in Congress.* New York: Harper and Row, 1983.

Hinds, Asher C. *Hinds Precedents of the House of Representatives of the United States.* vol. 4. Washington, D.C.: Government Printing Office, 1907.

Huitt, Ralph K. "The Morse Committee Assignment Controversy: A Study in Senate Norms." *American Political Science Review* (June 1957): 313-329.

_____. "Democratic Party Leadership in the Senate." *American Political Science Review* (June 1961a,b): 333-344.

_____. "The Outsider in the Senate." *American Political Science Review* (September 1961): 566-575.

_____. "The Internal Distribution of Influence: The Senate." In *The Congress and America's Future,* edited by David B. Truman, 77-101. Englewood Cliffs, N.J.: Prentice-Hall, 1965.

Huitt, Robert K., and Robert L. Peabody. *Congress: Two Decades of Analysis.* New York: Harper and Row, 1969.

Huntington, Samuel. "A Revised Theory of American Party Politics." *American Political Science Review* (September 1950): 669-677.

Jackson, John E. "Statistical Models of Senate Roll Call Voting." *American Political Science Review* (June 1971): 451-470.

_____. *Constituencies and Leaders in Congress.* Cambridge, Mass.: Harvard University Press, 1974.

Jacobson, Gary C. "The Effects of Campaign Spending in Congressional Elections." *American Political Science Review* (June 1978): 469-491.

_____. *Money in Congressional Elections.* New Haven: Yale University Press, 1980.

_____. "Incumbents' Advantages in the 1978 Congressional Elections." *Legislative Studies Quarterly* (May 1981): 183-210.

_____. *The Politics of Congressional Elections.* Boston: Little, Brown, 1983.

Jacobson, Gary C., and Samuel Kernell. *Strategy and Choice in Congressional Elections.* New Haven: Yale University Press, 1981.

Jahnige, Thomas P. "The Congressional Committee System and the Oversight Process: Congress and NASA." *Western Political Quarterly* (March 1968): 227-239.

Jewell, Malcolm E. *Senatorial Politics and Foreign Policy*. Lexington, Ky.: University of Kentucky Press, 1962.

Johannes, John R. "Casework as a Technique of U.S. Congressional Oversight of the Executive." *Legislative Studies Quarterly* (May 1979): 325-351.

_____. "The Distribution of Casework in the U.S. Congress: An Uneven Burden." *Legislative Studies Quarterly* (November 1980): 517-544.

Johannes, John R., and John C. McAdams. "The Congressional Incumbency Effect: Is it Casework, Policy Compatibility, or Something Else?" *American Journal of Political Science* (August 1981): 581-604.

_____. "Congressmen and Constituents: A Panel Study, 1977-82." Paper delivered at annual meeting of the American Political Science Association, Chicago, Illinois, 1983.

Jones, Charles O. "Representation in Congress: The Case of the House Agriculture Committee." *American Political Science Review* (June 1961): 358-367.

_____. "Inter-party Competition for Congressional Seats." *Western Political Quarterly* (September 1964): 461-476.

_____. "The Role of the Campaign in Congressional Politics." In *The Electoral Process*, edited by Harmon Zeigler and Kent Jennings, 21-41. Englewood Cliffs: Prentice-Hall, 1966.

_____. "The Minority Party and Policy-Making in the House of Representatives." *American Political Science Review* (June 1968a): 481-493. (Reprinted in this volume, 365-384.)

_____. "Joseph G. Cannon and Howard K. Smith: An Essay on the Limits of Leadership in the House of Representatives." *Journal of Politics* (August 1968b): 617-646.

_____. *The Minority Party in Congress*. Boston: Little, Brown, 1970.

_____. "Senate Party Leadership in Public Policy." In *Policymaking Role of Leadership in the Senate*. U.S. Senate Commission on the Operation of the Senate. 94th Cong., 2d sess., 1976.

_____. "House Leadership in an Age of Reform." Paper delivered at the Conference on Understanding Congressional Leadership: The State of the Art, Washington, D.C., 1980.

Jones, E. Terrence. "Ecological Inference and Electoral Analysis." *Journal of Interdisciplinary History* (Spring 1979): 593-596.

Kazee, Thomas A. "The Deterrent Effect of Incumbency on Recruiting Challengers in U.S. House Elections." *Legislative Studies Quarterly* (August 1983): 469-480.

Kefauver, Estes. *A Twentieth Century Congress*. New York: Duell, Sloan, and Pearce, 1947.

Keiser, K. Robert, and Woodrow Jones, Jr. "Congressional Cohorts and Voting Patterns." *American Politics Quarterly* (July 1982): 375-384.

Kesselman, Mark. "Presidential Leadership in Congress on Foreign Policy." *Midwest Journal of Political Science* (August 1961): 284-289.

References

――――. "Presidential Leadership in Congress on Foreign Policy: A Replication of a Hypothesis." *Midwest Journal of Political Science* (November 1965): 401-406.

Key, V. O., Jr. *Public Opinion and American Democracy*. New York: Alfred A. Knopf, 1961.

Kingdon, John. *Candidates For Office: Beliefs and Strategies*. New York: Random House, 1966.

――――. *Congressmen's Voting Decisions*. New York: Harper and Row, 1973.

――――. "Models of Legislative Voting." *Journal of Politics* (August 1977): 563-595. (Reprinted in this volume, 395-419.)

Kofmehl, Kenneth. "The Institutionalization of a Voting Bloc." *Western Political Quarterly* (June 1964): 256-272.

Kostroski, Warren. "Party and Incumbency in Post War Senate Elections: Trends, Patterns, and Models." *American Political Science Review* (December 1973): 1213-1234.

――――. "The Effect of Number of Terms on the Re-election of Senators, 1920-1970." *Journal of Politics* (May 1978): 488-497.

Krehbiel, Keith, and John Wright. "The Incumbency Effect in Congressional Elections: A Test of Two Explanations." *American Journal of Political Science* (February 1983): 140-157.

Kritzer, Herbert M., and Robert B. Eubank. "Presidential Coattails Revisited: Partisanship and Incumbency Effects." *American Journal of Political Science* (August 1979): 615-626.

Kuklinski, James H. "Representatives and Elections: A Policy Analysis." *American Political Science Review* (March 1978): 165-177.

Ladd, E. C., and C. P. Hadley. *Transformations of the American Party System*. New York: William Norton, 1975.

LeLoup, Lance T. "Process Versus Policy: The U.S. House Budget Committee." *Legislative Studies Quarterly* (May 1979): 227-254.

Light, Larry. "Pressing the Flesh: For Many Incumbents, Running for Re-election is Now a Full-Time Job." *Congressional Quarterly Weekly Report*, July 7, 1979, 1350-1357.

Loomis, Burdett A., and Jeff Fishel. "New Members in a Changing Congress: Norms, Actions, and Satisfaction." *Congressional Studies* (Spring 1981): 81-84.

Lowi, Theodore. "American Business, Public Policy, Case Studies, and Political Theory." *World Politics* (July 1964): 677-715.

Luce, Robert. *Legislative Procedure*. Boston: Houghton-Mifflin, 1922.

Maass, Arthur. *Muddy Waters*. Cambridge, Mass.: Harvard University Press, 1951.

MacNeil, Neil. *Forge of Democracy*. New York: David McKay, 1963.

MacRae, Duncan. *Issues and Parties in Legislative Voting*. New York: Harper and Row, 1970.

Magida, Arthur. *The Environmental Committees: A Study of the House and Senate Interior, Agriculture and Science Committees*. New York: Grossman Publishers, 1975.

Manley, John F. "The House Committee on Ways and Means: Conflict Management in a Congressional Committee." *American Political Science Review* (December 1965): 927-939.

_____. "Wilbur D. Mills: A Study of Congressional Influence." *American Political Science Review* (June 1969): 442-464.

_____. *The Politics of Finance: The House Committee on Ways and Means.* Boston: Little, Brown, 1970.

_____. "The Conservative Coalition in Congress." *American Behavioral Scientist* (1973): 223-247.

_____. "Congressional Control of the Budget." Paper delivered at the Study of Congress Conference, Washington, D.C., 1973.

_____. "Wilbur D. Mills: A Study in Congressional Leadership." In *Congress Reconsidered.* 1st ed., edited by Lawrence C. Dodd and Bruce I. Oppenheimer, 75-95. New York: Praeger, 1977.

Mann, Thomas, and Norman J. Ornstein, eds. *The New Congress.* Washington, D.C.: American Enterprise Institute, 1981.

Mann, Thomas, and Raymond Wolfinger. "Candidates and Parties in Congressional Elections." *American Political Science Review* (September 1980): 617-632.

Markus, Gregory. "Electoral Coalitions and Senate Roll Call Behavior: An Ecological Analysis." *American Political Science Review* (August 1974): 595-607.

Master, Nicholas. "Committee Assignments in the House of Representatives." *American Political Science Review* (June 1961): 345-357.

Matsunaga, Spark M., and Ping Chen. *Rulemakers of the House.* Urbana: University of Illinois Press, 1976.

Matthews, Donald R. *U.S. Senators and Their World.* New York: W. W. Norton, 1973.

Matthews, Donald R., and James A. Stimson. *Yeas and Nays.* New York: John Wiley, 1975.

Mayhew, David R. *Party Loyalty Among Congressmen.* Cambridge, Mass.: Harvard University Press, 1966.

_____. *Congress: The Electoral Connection.* New Haven: Yale University Press, 1974a.

_____. "Congressional Elections: The Case of the Vanishing Marginals." *Polity* (Spring 1974b): 295-317. (Reprinted in this volume, 15-34.)

McAdams, John C., and Johannes, John R. "The 1980 House Elections: Reexamining Some Headlines in a Republican Year." *Journal of Politics* (February 1983): 143-162.

Miller, Arthur H. "Political Issues and Trust in Government: 1964-1970." *American Political Science Review* (September 1974): 951-972.

Miller, Warren E., and Donald E. Stokes. "Constituency Influence in Congress." *American Political Science Review* (March 1963): 45-57. (Reprinted in this volume, 459-477.)

_____. "Representation and the American Congress." Manuscript, n.d.

References

Miner, John B. *Theories of Organizational Behavior*. Hinsdale, Ill.: Dryden Press, 1980.

Murphy, James T. "Political Parties and the Porkbarrel: Party Conflict and Cooperation in House Public Works Committee Decision Making." *American Political Science Review* (March 1974): 169-185. (Reprinted in this volume, 234-260.)

Nelson, Garrison. "Partisan Patterns of House Leadership Change, 1789-1977." *American Political Science Review* (September 1977): 918-939.

New York Times, June 4, 1979, D-10.

Norpoth, Helmut. "Explaining Party Cohesion in Congress: The Case of Shared Policy Attitudes." *American Political Science Review* (December 1976): 1156-1171.

Ornstein, Norman J., ed. *Congress in Change*. New York: Praeger, 1975.

Ornstein, Norman J., and David W. Rohde. "Shifting Force, Changing Rules, and Political Outcomes: The Impact of Congressional Changes on Four House Committees." In *New Perspectives on the House of Representatives.* 3d ed., edited by Robert L. Peabody and Nelson W. Polsby, 186-269. Chicago: Rand McNally, 1977.

Parker, Glenn R. "The Selection of Committee Leaders in the House of Representatives." *American Politics Quarterly* (January 1979): 71-93.

_____. "The Advantage of Incumbency in House Elections." *American Politics Quarterly* (October 1980a): 449-464.

_____. "Sources of Change in Congressional District Attention." *American Journal of Political Science* (February 1980b): 115-124.

_____. "Cycles in Congressional District Attention." *Journal of Politics* (May 1980c): 540-548.

_____. "Incumbent Popularity and Electoral Success." In *Congressional Elections,* edited by Joseph Cooper and L. Maisel, 249-279. Beverly Hills: Sage Publications, 1981a.

_____. "Interpreting Candidate Awareness in Congressional Elections." *Legislative Studies Quarterly* (May 1981b): 219-234.

Parker, Glenn R., and Roger H. Davidson. "Why Do Americans Love Their Congressmen So Much More Than Their Congress?" *Legislative Studies Quarterly* (February 1979): 52-61.

Parker, Glenn R., and Suzanne L. Parker. "Factions in Committees: The U.S. House of Representatives." *American Political Science Review* (March 1979): 85-102. (Reprinted in this volume, 261-286.)

_____. "The Comparative Study of Factions in the House Committee System." Paper delivered at the annual meeting of the Midwest Political Science Association, Cincinnati, Ohio, 1981.

_____. "Stability and Change in House Committee Cleavages." Paper delivered at the annual meeting of the American Political Science Association, New York, New York, 1981.

_____. "The Size of Successful Coalitions in Congressional Committee Decision

Making." Paper delivered at the annual meeting of the American Political Science Association, Chicago, Illinois, 1983.

———. "The Causes and Consequences of Congressional District Attention." *Legislative Studies Quarterly* (February 1985).

———. *Factions in Committees*. Knoxville: University of Tennessee Press, 1985.

Patterson, James T. *Congressional Conservatism and the New Deal*. Lexington, Ky.: University of Kentucky Press, 1967.

Payne, James C. "Show Horses and Work Horses in the United States House of Representatives." *Polity* (Spring 1980): 428-456.

Peabody, Robert L. "The Enlarged Rules Committee." In *Perspectives on the House of Representatives*. 1st ed., edited by Robert L. Peabody and Nelson W. Polsby, 129-164. Chicago: Rand McNally, 1963.

———. *Leadership in Congress*. Boston: Little, Brown, 1976.

Perkins, Lynette P. "Influences of Members' Goals on Their Committee Behavior: The U.S. House Judiciary Committee." *Legislative Studies Quarterly* (August 1980): 373-392.

Polsby, Nelson W. "The Institutionalization of the U.S. House of Representatives." *American Political Science Review* (March 1968): 144-168. (Reprinted in this volume, 81-118.)

———. "Goodbye to the Inner Club." *Washington Monthly* (August 1969a): 30-34.

———. "Two Strategies of Influence: Choosing a Majority Leader, 1962." In *New Perspectives on the House of Representatives*. 2d ed., edited by Nelson W. Polsby and Robert L. Peabody, 237-270. Chicago: Rand McNally, 1969b.

Polsby, Nelson W., Miriam Gallagher, and Barry S. Rundquist. "The Growth of the Seniority System in the U.S. House of Representatives." *American Political Science Review* (September 1969): 787-807.

Pressman, Jeffrey L. *House vs. Senate: Conflict in the Appropriations Process*. New Haven: Yale University Press, 1966.

Price, David E. *The Commerce Committees: A Study of the House and Senate Commerce Committees*. New York: Grossman Publishers, 1975.

———. "Policy Making in Congressional Committees: The Impact of 'Environmental Factors." *American Political Science Review* (June 1978): 548-574.

Price, H. Douglass. "Congress and the Evolution of Legislative 'Professionalism.'" In *Congress in Change*, edited by Norman J. Ornstein, 2-23. New York: Praeger, 1975.

Ranney, Austin. "Parties in State Politics." In *Politics in the American States*. 2d ed., edited by Herbert Jacob and Kenneth N. Vines, 82-121. Boston: Little, Brown, 1971.

Rieselback, Leroy N. "The Demography of the Congressional Vote on Foreign Aid, 1939-1958." *American Political Science Review* (September 1964): 577-588.

———, ed. *Legislative Reform: The Policy Impact*. Lexington, Mass.: Lexington Books, 1978.

Ripley, Randall B. *Party Leaders in the House of Representatives*. Washington, D.C.: Brookings Institution, 1967.

References

———. *Power in the Senate.* New York: St. Martin's Press, 1969a.

———. *Majority Party Leadership in Congress.* Boston: Little, Brown, 1969b.

———. "Power in the Post-World War II Senate." *Journal of Politics* (May 1969c): 465-492. (Reprinted in this volume, 297-320.)

Robinson, James A. *Congress and Foreign Policy Making.* Homewood, Ill.: Dorsey Press, 1961.

Robinson, William A. *Thomas B. Reed: Parliamentarian.* New York: Dodd, Mead, 1930.

Rohde, David W., Norman J. Ornstein, and Robert L. Peabody. "Political Change and Legislative Norms in the United States Senate." Paper delivered at the annual meeting of the American Political Science Association, Chicago, Illinois, 1974. (Reprinted in this volume, 147-188.)

Rohde, David W., and Kenneth Shepsle. "Democratic Committee Assignments in the House of Representatives." *American Political Science Review* (September 1973): 898-905.

Rummel, R. J. *Applied Factor Analysis.* Evanston, Ill.: Northwestern University Press, 1970.

Rundquist, Barry S., and Lyman A. Kellstadt. "Congressional Interaction with Constituents: A Career Perspective." Paper delivered at the annual meeting of the American Political Science Association, Denver, Colorado, 1982.

Salaman, Lester. *The Money Committees: A Study of the House Banking and Currency Committee and the Senate Banking, Housing and Urban Affairs Committee.* New York: Grossman Publishers, 1975.

Salisbury, Robert H., and Kenneth A. Shepsle. "U.S. Congressman as Enterprise." *Legislative Studies Quarterly* (November 1981): 559-576.

Schick, Allen. *Congress and Money.* Washington, D.C.: Urban Institute, 1980.

Schuck, Peter H. *A Study of the House and Senate Judiciary Committees.* New York: Grossman Publishers, 1975.

Shannon, W. Wayne. *Party, Constituency and Congressional Voting.* Baton Rouge: Louisiana State University Press, 1968.

Shelley, Mack C., II. "A Time Series Analysis of the Appearance and Success of the Conservative Coalition, 1933-1976." Paper delivered at annual meeting of the Midwest Political Science Association, Chicago, Illinois, 1978.

Shively, W. Phillips. "Ecological Inference: The Use of Aggregate Data to Study Individuals." *American Political Science Review* (December 1969): 1182-1196.

Sinclair, Barbara. "Party Realignment and the Transformation of the Political Agenda: The House of Representatives, 1925-1938." *American Political Science Review* (September 1977): 940-953.

———. "From Party Voting to Regional Fragmentation: The House of Representatives, 1933-1956." *American Politics Quarterly* (April 1978): 125-147.

———. "The Speaker's Task Force in the Post-Reform House of Representatives." *American Political Science Review* (June 1981a): 397-410. (Reprinted in this volume, 343-364.)

———. "Coping with Uncertainty: Building Coalitions in the House and Senate."

In *The New Congress,* edited by Thomas Mann and Norman Ornstein, 178-220. Washington, D.C.: American Enterprise Institute, 1981b.

_____. *Congressional Realignment, 1925-1978.* Austin: University of Texas Press, 1982.

_____. *Majority Leadership in the House.* Baltimore: Johns Hopkins University Press, 1983.

Spohn, Richard. *The Revenue Committees: A Study of the House Ways and Means and Senate Finance Committees and the House and Senate Appropriations Committees.* New York: Grossman Publishers, 1975.

Steinberg, Alfred. *Sam Rayburn.* New York: Hawthorn Books, 1975.

Stewart, John G. "Two Strategies of Leadership: Johnson and Mansfield." In *Congressional Behavior,* edited by Nelson W. Polsby, 61-92. New York: Random House, 1971.

Stokes, Donald, and Warren Miller. "Party Government and the Saliency of Congress." In *Elections and the Political Order,* by Angus Campbell et al., 194-211. New York: John Wiley, 1966.

Stolarek, John S., Robert M. Roof, and Marcia Whicker Taylor. "Measuring Constituency Opinion in the U.S. House: Mail Versus Random Surveys." *Legislative Studies Quarterly* (November 1981): 589-596.

Stone, Clarence. "Issue Cleavage Between Democrats and Republicans in the United States House of Representatives." *Journal of Public Law* (1965): 343-358.

Sullivan, John. "Political Correlates of Social, Economic and Religious Diversity in the American States." *Journal of Politics* (February 1973): 70-84.

Sundquist, James. *Dynamics of the Party System.* Washington, D.C.: Brookings Institution, 1973.

_____. *The Decline and Resurgence of Congress.* Washington, D.C.: Brookings Institution, 1981.

Swanson, Wayne R. "Committee Assignments and the Non-Conformist Legislator: Democrats in the U.S. Senate." *Midwest Journal of Political Science* (February 1969): 84-94.

Tacheron, Donald G., and Morris K. Udall. *The Job of the Congressman.* Indianapolis: Bobbs-Merrill, 1970.

Tedin, Kent, and Richard Murray. "Public Awareness of Congressional Representatives: Recall versus Recognition." *American Politics Quarterly* (October 1979): 509-517.

Tidmarch, Charles M., and Charles M. Sabatt. "Presidential Leadership Changes and Foreign Policy Roll-Call Voting in the U.S. Senate." *Western Political Quarterly* (December 1972): 613-625.

Toscom, Jean E. "Leadership: The Role and Style of Everett Dirksen." In *To Be A Congressman,* edited by Sven Groennings and Jonathan P. Hawley, 185-223. Washington, D.C.: Acropolis Books, 1973.

Truman, David B. "The State Delegation and the Structure of Party Voting in the United States House of Representatives." *American Political Science Review* (December 1956): 1023-1045.

References

_____. *The Congressional Party.* New York: John Wiley, 1959.

Tufte, Edward R. "The Relationship Between Seats and Votes in Two-Party Systems." *American Political Science Review* (June 1973): 540-554.

Turner, Julius. *Party and Constituency: Pressures on Congress.* Baltimore: Johns Hopkins Press, 1951.

Turner, Julius, and Edward Schneier. *Party and Constituency: Pressures on Congress.* rev. ed. Baltimore: Johns Hopkins Press, 1970.

U.S. House of Representatives. *Toward the Endless Frontier: History of the Committee on Science and Technology, 1959-1974.* Washington, D.C.: U.S. Government Printing Office, 1980.

Waldman, Loren K. "Liberalism of Congressmen and the Presidential Vote in Their Districts." *Midwest Journal of Political Science* (February 1967): 73-85.

Waldman, Sidney. "Majority Leadership in the House of Representatives." *Political Science Quarterly* (Fall 1980): 373-393.

Weingast, Barry R. "A Rational Choice Perspective on Congressional Norms." *American Journal of Political Science* (May 1979): 245-262.

Weisberg, Herbert F. *Dimensional Analysis of Legislative Roll Calls.* Ph.D. diss., University of Michigan, Ann Arbor, 1968.

_____. "Evaluating Theories of Congressional Roll-Call Voting." *American Journal of Political Science* (August 1978): 554-577.

Westefield, Lewis P. "Majority Party Leadership and the Committee System in the House of Representatives." *American Political Science Review* (December 1974): 1593-1604.

Westyle, Mark C. "Competitiveness of Senate Seats and Voting Behavior in Senate Elections." *American Journal of Political Science* (May 1983): 253-283.

White, William S. *Citadel: The Story of the U.S. Senate.* New York: Harper and Row, 1957.

Wicker, Tom. *JFK and LBJ.* New York: William Marrow, 1968.

Wildavsky, Aaron. *The Politics of the Budgetary Process.* 2d ed. Boston: Little, Brown, 1974.

Wilson, Woodrow. *Constitutional Government in the United States.* New York: Columbia University Press, 1961.

Witmer, T. Richard. "The Aging of the House." *Political Science Quarterly* (December 1964): 526-541.

Yarwood, Dean L. "Norm Observance and Legislative Integration: The U.S. Senate in 1850 and 1860." *Social Science Quarterly* (June 1970): 57-69.

Yiannakis, Diane. "The Grateful Electorate: Casework and Congressional Elections." *American Journal of Political Science* (August 1981): 568-580.

Young, Roland. *This Is Congress.* New York: Alfred A. Knopf, 1943.

INDEX